THE UNITY OF PUBLIC LAW?

This major collection contains selected papers from the second Public Law Conference, an international conference hosted by the University of Cambridge in September 2016. The collection includes contributions by leading academics and judges from across the common law world, including senior judges from Australia, Canada, New Zealand and the UK. The contributions engage with the theme of unity (and disunity) from a number of perspectives, offering a rich panoply of insights into public law which significantly carry forward public law thinking across common law jurisdictions, setting the agenda for future research and legal development. Part 1 of the volume contains chapters which offer doctrinal and theoretical perspectives. Some chapters seek to articulate a unifying framework for understanding public law, while others seek to demonstrate the plurality of public law through the method of legal taxonomy. A number of chapters analyse whether different fields such as human rights and administrative law are merging, with others considering specific unifying themes or concepts in public law. The chapters in Part 2 offer comparative perspectives, charting and analysing convergence and divergence across common law systems. Specific topics include standing, proportionality, human rights, remedies, use of foreign precedents, legal transplants, and disunity and unity among subnational jurisdictions. The collection will be of great interest to those working in public law.

The Unity of Public Law?

Doctrinal, Theoretical and Comparative Perspectives

Edited by
Mark Elliott
Jason NE Varuhas
Shona Wilson Stark

•HART•
OXFORD • LONDON • NEW YORK • NEW DELHI • SYDNEY

HART PUBLISHING
Bloomsbury Publishing Plc
Kemp House, Chawley Park, Cumnor Hill, Oxford, OX2 9PH, UK

HART PUBLISHING, the Hart/Stag logo, BLOOMSBURY and the Diana logo are trademarks of Bloomsbury Publishing Plc

First published in Great Britain 2018

A catalogue record for this book is available from the British Library.

Library of Congress Cataloging-in-Publication data

Names: Public Law Conference (2nd : 2016 : Cambridge, England) | Elliott, Mark, 1975- editor. | Varuhas, Jason, editor. | Stark, Shona Wilson, editor.

Title: The unity of public law? : doctrinal, theoretical, and comparative perspectives / edited by Mark Elliott, Jason N.E. Varuhas, Shona Wilson Stark.

Description: Oxford [UK] ; Portland, Oregon : Hart Publishing, 2018. | Includes bibliographical references and index. | "This major collection contains selected papers from the second Public Law Conference, an international conference hosted by the University of Cambridge in September 2016"—ECIP data view.

Identifiers: LCCN 2017053833 (print) | LCCN 2017055290 (ebook) | ISBN 9781509915200 (Epub) | ISBN 9781509915187 (hardback : alk. paper)

Subjects: LCSH: Public law—Congresses. | Law and globalization—Congresses.

Classification: LCC K3150.A6 (ebook) | LCC K3150.A6 P83 2016 (print) | DDC 342—dc23

LC record available at https://lccn.loc.gov/2017053833

ISBN: HB: 978-1-50991-518-7
ePDF: 978-1-50991-519-4
ePub: 978-1-50991-520-0

Typeset by Compuscript Ltd, Shannon

Foreword

JOHN BELL

In founding the journal *Public Law* 60 years ago, John Griffith wrote that '[t]he problems of constitutional and administrative law are the oldest and the most fundamental in any society ... The problems are those of power, of individual rights and of the nature of the social organisation under which we live; and the paradox is that public law is so often spoken of as a new subject'.[1] Although the problems may be ancient, in organisational terms, common law public lawyers have spent much of the subsequent years playing catch-up with private law colleagues. Compared to the substantial growth in public law writing and teaching in Germany and France, especially since the last quarter of the nineteenth century, the common law has had to wait almost until the last quarter of the twentieth century for public law to achieve equal prominence. But that is very much a problem of the past. The Second Biennial Public Law Conference held in Cambridge in 2016, from which this book arises, brought together over 200 scholars, judges and practitioners from over 20 jurisdictions, to examine *The Unity of Public Law?*. The vibrancy of the gathering, enhanced by the presence of so many younger scholars from across the common law world, demonstrated that public law scholarship is recognised as central to dealing with the most fundamental problems of our societies.

In 1956, Griffith eschewed a definition of 'public' law. For him, 'Public law is both part of the administration of affairs and of the ways in which that administration is controlled.'[2] That statement neatly avoids a distinction familiar to continental jurists between 'public law' (the rules governing the competence and exercise of power: *Öffentliches Recht*, *droit public*) and 'public law litigation' (*Öffentliche Gerichtsbarkeit*, *contentieux public*). But, despite Griffith, much scholarship has tended to focus on the prioritisation of the latter over the former; within the latter, to a concentration on courts at the expense of other forms of complaint mechanism. The Public Law Conference retains the broader vision that Griffith set out. As David Feldman put it: 'public law is treated as including both the rules governing the allocation of power and responsibility between different tiers and agencies of government and those controlling the relationship between the institutions of government and private citizens'.[3]

The theme of unity was approached in the conference from a number of perspectives. Unlike many continental European legal systems, common law systems do not

[1] [1956] *PL* 1.
[2] ibid, at 2.
[3] D Feldman, *English Public Law* (Oxford, Oxford University Press, 2004) ix.

tend to differentiate public law from private law by having different courts in which such matters are litigated. Typically, common law courts handle both public law and private law matters, at least in the higher courts. Procedure is one of the less-helpful criteria for differentiation. Much more significant is the preoccupation with the control of the power of government. Public law finds its unity not in procedure (eg different rules on standing to bring an action) nor in techniques (eg the use of proportionality as a test for the exercise of powers) but in fundamental values about how government should be conducted. Lawyers naturally pay attention to the rule of law as a core value, both in the narrow sense of government according to law and in the wider sense of government conducted with respect for the fundamental rights of the governed and for their human dignity. But there are other features within the portfolio of values which underpin all public law. Public service requires decisions to be taken for the common good. It is not simply a matter of ensuring that officials are not corrupt or furthering personal interests. Public service has a higher ambition—that decisions are taken in the long-term interest that will enable all the governed to flourish, even those of whose lifestyles the governors do not necessarily approve. Process matters in public law as much as outcomes. Participation in decision-making is a way of respecting the value of individuals in society. People don't just vote every few years and then leave representatives to get on with the job of governing. Participation reflects the importance of allowing individuals to have a say in decisions which affect them. Even if people have views and interests which are in the minority, they have to be allowed the opportunity to express their point of view in a meaningful way. The law is one mechanism for ensuring this happens. Accountability for decisions is also important. Those who govern do not simply have to have authority for the decisions they make. They need to explain them and be open to questioning and criticism both from supporters and from opponents of their actions. In this way, power is controlled and the value of those who are governed is respected. These values of legality, respect for fundamental rights, public service, participation and accountability pervade the different branches of public law. That is not to suggest that these values are not also respected in other branches of the law, but the nature of the relationship of the governors and the governed in a democratic society makes the control of power distinctive from that within contractual or family relationships.

For a comparative lawyer, one of the interesting features of both the presentations at the conference and the papers collected in this volume is the breadth of knowledge of other common law jurisdictions that is on display. Often for linguistic reasons, European public lawyers tend only to know their own system and the laws of the European Union and the European Convention on Human Rights. By contrast, it is not unusual to listen to a New Zealander discussing recent Canadian or South African developments or for an Irish lawyer to refer to Australia and the United States, as well as to England. There is a significant unity of the common law which cannot be mirrored in Europe, despite the efforts of authors like Jürgen Schwarze.[4]

[4] See his *Zukunftsaussichten für das Europäische Öffentliche Recht* (Nomos Verlag, Baden-Baden, 2010).

If the European influence on public law within the UK is likely to diminish in future (whether due to Brexit or simply to the decline in the study of modern languages) then the debate amongst common lawyers is likely to be of increasing significance in the future. A shared language and shared legal traditions are the basis for a fruitful cross-fertilisation of ideas. The location of Melbourne for the third Public Law Conference should ensure that Asian countries are significantly represented within these debates. That Conference will reflect the continuing growth, vibrancy and strength of public law scholarship across the whole of the common law world.

Contents

Contributors

John Bell is Professor of Law at the University of Cambridge and a Fellow of Pembroke College, Cambridge.

Janina Boughey is Senior Lecturer at the University of New South Wales.

Anne Carter is a PhD candidate at the University of Melbourne.

Johannes Chan is Professor of Law at the University of Hong Kong.

Lisa Burton Crawford is Senior Lecturer at the University of New South Wales.

Paul Daly is Senior Lecturer in Public Law at the University of Cambridge and a Fellow of Queens' College, Cambridge.

Dame Sian Elias is the Chief Justice of New Zealand.

Mark Elliott is Professor of Public Law at the University of Cambridge and a Fellow of St Catharine's College, Cambridge.

Robert French is a former Chief Justice of Australia.

Claudia Geiringer holds the Chair in Public Law at Victoria University of Wellington Faculty of Law and is the Co-director of the New Zealand Centre for Public Law.

Cora Hoexter is a Professor in the School of Law at the University of the Witwatersrand, Johannesburg.

Audrey Macklin is Professor of Law, Chair in Human Rights, and Director of the Centre for Criminology and Sociolegal Studies at the University of Toronto.

Roger Masterman is Professor of Law at Durham University.

Aileen McHarg is Professor of Public Law at the University of Strathclyde.

Elizabeth O'Loughlin is a PhD candidate at the University of Manchester School of Law, and a Teaching Assistant at the University of Leeds School of Law.

Robert Reed (Lord Reed) is a Justice of the Supreme Court of the United Kingdom.

Ellen Rock is a PhD candidate at the Australian National University and a Lecturer at the University of Technology Sydney.

Cheryl Saunders is Laureate Professor Emeritus at the University of Melbourne.

Shona Wilson Stark is College Lecturer in Law at Girton College and an Affiliated Lecturer at the Faculty of Law, both at the University of Cambridge.

David Stratas is a Justice of the Federal Court of Appeal of Canada.

Jason NE Varuhas is Associate Professor at the University of Melbourne.

Se-shauna Wheatle is Assistant Professor of Law at Durham University.

Hanna Wilberg is Associate Professor of Law at the University of Auckland.

Table of Cases

Australia

Botswana

Canada

European Court of Human Rights

European Union

Fiji

Hong Kong

India

Ireland

Kenya

Nepal

New Zealand

South Africa

Tanzania

Trinidad and Tobago

Uganda

United Kingdom

United States

Zimbabwe

Table of Legislation

Australia

Germany

India

International

Kenya

Nepal

New Zealand

South Africa

Switzerland

Tanzania

Trinidad and Tobago

Uganda

United Kingdom

United States

1

Introduction

MARK ELLIOTT, JASON NE VARUHAS AND SHONA WILSON STARK

THIS COLLECTION ORIGINATES from the second biennial Public Law Conference, a major international conference held at the University of Cambridge Faculty of Law in September 2016. The theme of the conference, from which this volume derives its title, was 'The Unity of Public Law?'.

The 2016 conference was the second in an ongoing series of major international conferences on public law, the first of which was also held in Cambridge in September 2014. This volume follows on from that derived from the first conference, John Bell, Mark Elliott, Jason NE Varuhas and Philip Murray (eds), *Public Law Adjudication in Common Law Systems: Process and Substance* (Oxford, Hart Publishing Ltd 2016). As recorded in the editors' introduction to that collection, the motivation for founding the Public Law series was to provide a leading forum for common lawyers from a broad range of jurisdictions to discuss and debate the most important public law issues of the day. While the bedrock of commonality among common law systems offers a basis and framework for meaningful engagement—a 'consensus ad idem' of sorts—the shared problems faced by common law systems of public law and the inevitable variations across systems offer a basis for comparison, discussion and debate.

Since its inception the Public Law series has fulfilled this vision, emerging as the pre-eminent forum for the scholarly discussion of public law issues in the common law world. The 2014 conference and the volume deriving from it were very well received. The 2016 conference built upon the foundations laid by the first conference, cementing the importance of the series in facilitating cross-jurisdictional dialogue and debate at the highest level. The 2016 conference brought together over 200 participants drawn from over 20 jurisdictions including Australia, Bangladesh, Barbados, Canada, Egypt, France, Germany, Hong Kong, Ireland, Japan, Kuwait, Mexico, Nepal, New Zealand, Nigeria, Poland, Portugal, Singapore, South Africa, Switzerland, The Netherlands, the United Kingdom and the United States of America. The conference opened with a panel comprised of Robert French, the then Chief Justice of Australia, and Lord Reed, Justice of the UK Supreme Court, who discussed the uses of comparative law by apex courts; the keynote address was delivered by Dame Sian Elias, the Chief Justice of New Zealand. Approximately 60 papers were delivered by leading scholars, practitioners and judges drawn from across the common law world.

Consonant with the intellectual case for the conference series, it was always the intention of the convenors that following the first two conferences held in Cambridge, the third would be held outside the United Kingdom, in another common law jurisdiction. This would enable those in different parts of the world to more easily participate in the conference and focus attention on public law issues pertinent to different regions of the common law world. In this regard we are very pleased that the third biennial Public Law Conference will be held in Australia in July 2018 at Melbourne Law School, to be co-organised by the University of Melbourne and the University of Cambridge.

In common with the previous collection, this volume brings together leading scholars from across the common law world, drawn from the academy and the Bench, to discuss and debate cutting-edge issues in public law. The outstanding essays collected herein provide an invaluable reference point for public lawyers in common law jurisdictions (and civilian lawyers) seeking the views and perspectives of leading scholars and judges on the most important issues facing common law public law systems today. Importantly the essays will also serve to frame and prompt further debate and discussion across common law systems. More generally, the chapters in this book, and the papers presented at the 2016 conference, affirm the strength and vibrancy of public law scholarship in the common law world today and the appetite for, and rich insights to be gained from, scholarly engagement across jurisdictional boundaries.

I. THEME AND BOOK STRUCTURE

The theme of this collection is 'The Unity of Public Law?'. The question mark is quite deliberate, inviting inquiry into the various ways in which public law—itself a term which calls for inquiry—may evince unity or disunity, with the aim that such inquiries will precipitate fresh and insightful perspectives on the nature of public law and emerging issues and recurrent themes in public law.

The spurs for this theme are multifarious. At the level of doctrine certain norms, concepts, values, or methods have increasingly been appealed to and at times claimed to provide a common basis for public law adjudication. These have included, for example, appeals to the rule of law, rights, rationality, deference, proportionality, and balancing. These moves towards unifying concepts, methods etc in turn have prompted responses which seek to emphasise and reinforce the plurality of public law fields, and the normative attractiveness of such plurality.

At a higher level of abstraction, on the plane of theory, scholars have increasingly searched for One Big Idea which might explain public law as a whole or provide a normative vision of a unified public law. These accounts have often sought to identify the distinctiveness of public law as a field, for example by appealing to a distinctive set of functions or a distinctive method or mode of reasoning which gives public law unity. Similarly private lawyers are increasingly engaged in the search for what makes private law, as a whole, distinctive from public law. Arguably this increased search for distinguishing features, and attempts at reassertion of the 'autonomy' of public law and private law, is a response to the reality that any distinction between the two fields is increasingly difficult to locate, as the public and private spheres of life—and as a consequence, law—become increasingly intermingled.

A further spur for the 'Unity?' theme is comparative. In this regard, questions arise about convergence and divergence among common law systems. To what extent do common law systems of public law share common features, and to what extent are they diverging? To the extent that patterns of convergence or divergence are evident, what are the drivers of change or maintenance of the status quo? Allied to these questions are debates over the limits of comparativism: is it desirable and/or feasible to search for common solutions across different jurisdictions and for one jurisdiction to transplant legal phenomena, ideas, doctrines etc, from another jurisdiction, and if so, in what circumstances? In this regard, do distinctive considerations arise in the context of public law, compared to other fields of law? These issues are of acute importance, not least because of increasing tendencies, spurred in part by the phenomena of 'global administrative law' and 'global constitutional law', to seek to distil common values or principles from across different jurisdictions or develop general explanations or theories of public law or fields of public law, which are claimed to hold across jurisdictions.

The multiple spurs for interrogating the 'Unity?' theme are in turn reflected in the variety of perspectives which the chapters herein bring to bear on the unity question: doctrinal, theoretical and comparative. The chapters are arranged along these lines: Part 1 is comprised of chapters which offer doctrinal and theoretical perspectives, and Part 2 is comprised of chapters which offer comparative perspectives. Dame Sian Elias's chapter, the first substantive chapter, offers a critical introduction to both strands of inquiry.

Those chapters in Part 1 focus on specific doctrinal issues that arise in particular jurisdictions and/or specific theoretical questions. Albeit these chapters are not explicitly comparative in their orientation, they do often engage with case law from different jurisdictions and address issues which find their analogues in other jurisdictions. As such the chapters will be of relevance and importance across jurisdictions. Varuhas's chapter examines the plurality of public law through the method of legal taxonomy. Chapters by Daly and Rock consider core values that are said to underpin public law. A number of chapters consider the theme of unity in the context of particular doctrines or trends. Hoexter examines difficulties faced by courts in distinguishing public from private power for the purposes of delineating the scope of review. Wilberg identifies plurality in the types of interpretive presumptions utilised by courts in public law. Masterman and Wheatle explore the themes of unity and disunity in the context of contemporary common law constitutionalist trends in the UK. Macklin's chapter explores the intersection of administrative and human rights law, focusing on judicial method in substantive review. Stratas's chapter serves as a concluding chapter for Part 1. He focuses on the decline of doctrine in judicial review, offering a critique of trends towards a more 'intuitive' judicial approach to public law adjudication.

Those chapters in Part 2 are more explicitly comparative in orientation. The first three chapters by French, Reed and Saunders consider issues in comparative common law in more general terms, the chapters by French and Reed examining the use of foreign legal material by common law courts and inter-jurisdictional dialogue while Saunders considers the phenomenon of legal transplants in public law. The remaining chapters consider particular topics from a comparative perspective. These include divergence among the jurisdictions of the UK (McHarg); consideration of the Commonwealth model of rights-protection (Geiringer); damages for breaches of constitutional rights (Chan); standing rules in new constitutional orders (O'Loughlin); the courts' approach to fact-finding in the context of proportionality analysis (Carter); and jurisdictional error (Boughey and Crawford).

While this division between Parts 1 and 2 was adopted for organisational purposes, the boundary between the Parts is not impermeable nor is it intended to be. Indeed there are significant, sometimes surprising, synergies between chapters in each Part. For example Saunders' chapter on transplants in public law raises similar methodological questions, albeit in a different context, to Varuhas's chapter on taxonomy and public law, each exploring issues that arise when legal phenomena are extracted from their original 'home' context and imported into a new 'destination' context. Boughey and Crawford's chapter offering comparative perspectives on jurisdictional error, and Carter's chapter offering a comparative analysis of the judicial approach to fact-finding in proportionality analysis have natural synergies with a number of those chapters in Part 1 which address core issues in judicial review within single systems. Similarly both Chan's chapter in Part 2 and Rock's chapter in Part 1 address issues in public authority liability, the former from a comparative perspective and the latter from a doctrinal and theoretical perspective. Chapters in Part 1 which seek to offer a unifying account of the values underlying administrative law, such as Daly's, have points of contact with those chapters in Part 2 which address the extent of variation in the nature of administrative law systems and doctrines across jurisdictions. More generally an interesting and perhaps unexpected recurring theme among the chapters in Part 1 is exploration of the legitimacy of judicial methods in contemporary public law, and concerns over intuitive or subjective judicial decision-making. Given that the chapters examine a range of different issues in the context of different common law jurisdictions, the emergence of this recurring theme may be suggestive of a certain unity across the public law systems of different jurisdictions in that they face a common set of emergent issues related to judicial decision-making and method in public law adjudication. There are many further interconnections to be explored.

II. THE CHAPTERS

The chapter by Dame Sian Elias derives from her keynote address at the Conference. It offers an important analysis of the different dimensions of the question with which this volume is concerned: the extent to which public law evinces unity. In so doing the chapter serves as a critical introduction to core issues and themes addressed by the chapters in this volume. The chapter considers a number of important issues in public law today from a comparative perspective. In a stimulating survey Elias examines convergence and divergence in the ways that different common law jurisdictions have approached and resolved key issues such as the role of judicial review in the context of other administrative justice mechanisms. The Chief Justice considers the nature of administrative law today, reiterating the discretionary nature of the field, and questioning the role of rigid legal classification and binary distinctions or labels such as law and merits and jurisdictional and non-jurisdictional error. The chapter then examines judicial supervision of discretion, observing the intimate connection between judicial review and constitutional values and traditions, which in turn helps to explain why common law systems may diverge in their approaches to controlling discretion, a theme also interrogated in the context of deference on questions of law and reasonableness review. The Chief Justice's chapter ends with a provocative question: despite the illumination provided by good scholarship in this area, is the search for better doctrine ultimately doomed? Scholarly work keeps everyone up to the mark, but perhaps too much is expected of overarching theories: 'Public law has unity and disparity and much of it is untidy and tentative'.

These questions posed by the Chief Justice's chapter offer the ideal prompt for the chapters in Part 1 which engage with the 'Unity' theme from doctrinal and theoretical perspectives.

Jason NE Varuhas's chapter takes the first steps towards developing a legal taxonomy of public law fields, systematically identifying, mapping and explaining different categories of law that are typically identified with English public law. Varuhas argues that legal categorisation is fundamental to full understanding of the law, rigorous and complete legal analysis and coherent and rational legal development. Yet legal taxonomy and debates over legal categorisation have not been a significant feature of public law scholarship, in contrast to contemporary private law scholarship. Varuhas's chapter begins by exploring the reasons for this general absence of work in legal categorisation in public law. It proceeds to make the case for why legal categorisation is of fundamental importance in public law, and explains that such work is of peculiar significance today in the light of trends towards open-ended balancing in public law adjudication which threaten to radically undermine the rational ordering of the legal system and render coherent legal development impossible. The chapter begins the mapping process. The chapter rejects the division between public law and private law as a starting point for legal categorisation, placing no normative weight on that putative divide. Rather it seeks to simply categorise different fields of law, often associated with the label 'public law', according to their primary functions. The chapter identifies and explains two distinct categories: (1) the law relating to regulation of public power in the public interest; (2) the law relating to protection and vindication of basic individual rights. Having taken the first steps towards legal categorisation the chapter proceeds to demonstrate how identification of discrete fields has a bearing on analysis of contemporary legal issues, examining the question of whether the proportionality method developed in human rights law ought to be read across to the common law of judicial review.

Writing on substantive review, Audrey Macklin engages critically with Supreme Court of Canada decisions which have imported the strong notion of judicial deference found in ordinary Canadian administrative law into decisions concerning the Canadian Charter of Rights and Freedoms. Such deference is arguably inappropriate for cases where constitutionally protected interests are at stake and has resulted in the erosion of Charter rights. Where fundamental rights are concerned, Macklin calls for less fixation on labels such as reasonableness and proportionality—a 'proxy war between administrative law and human rights law'—and more transparent reasoning focusing on the context of each particular case. She therefore proposes certain considerations which should be borne in mind by courts when evaluating exercises of administrative discretion which engage fundamental rights. These include: giving appropriate weight to Charter rights as compared to other interests; giving more consideration to the nature of the decision-maker (specifically considering closeness to the political world as a potential reason for being less, rather than more, deferential); and the court not supplying its own reasons for a decision-maker's actions. Such considerations seem eminently suitable for adoption or adaption beyond Canada and her chapter reads as a 'cautionary tale' to other jurisdictions.

The impetus for Paul Daly's chapter is the very substantial growth in the scope and intensity of judicial review in English law in recent decades. As Daly observes, the question arises whether such developments amount to 'an illegitimate power grab'. Answering that question in the negative, Daly draws upon, and develops, some of his earlier work in which he argues that modern administrative law is structured and animated by four interacting values, namely: the rule of law, good administration, democracy and separation of powers. Using that earlier, interpretive work as a foundation, Daly seeks to demonstrate the relevance of his four values to the broader question of administrative law's legitimacy. In particular, he argues that the legitimacy—in its democratic and normative, as distinct from its sociological and procedural, senses—of contemporary expansions of judicial review can be established by reference to those four values. This follows, he suggests, because the four values lend administrative law—including in its modern, extended form—coherence, and because the values are legal in nature. Critically, argues Daly, these characteristics of the values that drive administrative law's development serve to shield judges from (what are on this view) unwarranted charges of improper activism.

In their chapter, Roger Masterman and Se-shauna Wheatle examine contemporary trends in UK public law from the particular perspective of the common law. They observe that in recent decades, the common law has acquired new prominence as a legal-constitutional medium in the UK, thanks to (among other things) the development of the notion of common law constitutional rights, the identification—by the common law—of 'constitutional statutes', judicial deployment of the principle of legality, and curial invocation of the common law as a potential constraint upon Parliament's legislative authority. Masterman and Wheatle argue that while such developments have the potential to destabilise the domestic constitution—and the common law's place within it—such risks may be obviated provided that judges proceed with sufficient sensitivity to relevant aspects of the common law tradition. Among other things, they argue, this requires: adherence to the incrementalism that is characteristic of the common law's developmental trajectory; transparent judicial articulation and curation of the body of constitutional principle to which effect is increasingly given at common law, such that the relationship between principle and its application in particular cases is more carefully and clearly drawn; and an openness to inter-jurisdictional dialogue that might serve to make up for UK judges' relative inexperience when it comes to more fully fledged forms of constitutional adjudication. Masterman and Wheatle conclude that proceeding in this way is not merely desirable: it may be essential if judges are to avoid charges of subjectivity and overreach.

Cora Hoexter's chapter examines the vexed distinction (and relationship) between the notions of public and private power. Hoexter observes that the need to make such a distinction—so as to determine amenability to judicial review—arises in many common law jurisdictions, and that the drawing of the line is rarely unproblematic. Hoexter's focus, however, is on the issues to which the demarcation of public powers has given rise in the particular context of South Africa, where the carrying out of public functions is critical to the availability of judicial review. A key difficulty, observes Hoexter, is that attempts to characterise activities as public or private in any inherent or abstract sense are generally doomed to failure, while senses of where the boundary ought to be placed are liable to shift over time. As a result, the identification of that boundary risks collapsing into an intuitive, instinctive exercise. Hoexter explores these issues through detailed examination of the South African case law in a number of relevant contexts, including the amenability to judicial review of sports regulatory bodies and public actors' exercises of contractual power. She concludes that the approach of South African courts—like that of courts in some other parts of the common law world—is unsatisfactory, and that judicial identification of public functions too often reduces to little more than a question of 'feel'.

Accountability is often taken for granted as a 'core public law value'. But Ellen Rock's chapter reveals that some deeper thought is needed as to what accountability actually means in this context and, consequently, what its functions are and whether it fulfils them. Rock identifies four functions accountability may serve: (1) to ensure transparent decision making; (2) to control the legality of exercises of public power; (3) to punish abuse of power; and (4) to provide restoration to those who suffer such abuses. Accountability currently, however, only performs the first two of those four functions in public law, thus undermining its supposed centrality to the area. Rock focuses on the current deficiencies of public law remedies to punish and to restore. Specifically, Rock's inquiry relates to the relevance of a decision-maker's state of mind to her accountability. She argues that we need to move away from the fallacy that public law exhibits a strict liability attitude to fault, and towards accepting that certain public law principles already recognise that a decision-maker's motives, knowledge or intention may be relevant to her consequent fault. As such, her chapter should provoke a discussion as to whether remedies could be adapted to serve all four functions of accountability without radically altering public law's underlying foundations.

Hanna Wilberg's chapter focuses on the role of 'interpretive presumptions' as means of giving effect to such things as fundamental rights, constitutional principles and international obligations. Into this interpretive category Wilberg places not only presumptions as to legislative intent *per se*, such as the principle of legality and rules of strict construction, but also interpretive instructions contained in statutory bills of rights, whereby courts are directed to favour constructions that are consistent with human rights. Against this background, Wilberg distinguishes 'weak' and 'moderate' from 'assertive' uses of such presumptions, evidence of the latter being discernible, she argues, in the case law of Australia, New Zealand and the UK. Wilberg takes as her guiding criterion a default requirement, rooted in democracy, that those who interpret legislation should, in doing so, respect the intention of the enacting institution. It is this normative point of departure that leads Wilberg to single out 'assertive' uses of interpretive presumptions for special treatment, the defining characteristic of such uses, within Wilberg's taxonomy, being that they involve assigning constructions to statutory provisions that fail to respect legislators' likely understanding of their meaning. Wilberg does not say that such constructions are inevitably improper, but does contend that departure from the underlying normative requirement to respect legislators' understanding means that assertive uses of interpretive presumptions call for special justification. She goes on to argue that in identifying the assertive-use category, established approaches—which focus upon such matters as whether the provision is ambiguous or whether express words have been used to override the protected right or value—are unsatisfactory, and cannot adequately substitute for more direct judicial engagement with questions about legislators' likely understandings.

David Stratas's chapter stems from his remarks offered during the closing plenary session of the conference, and serves as a concluding chapter for Part 1 of the book. His chapter reflects on the unity theme in the light of the doctrinal and theoretical perspectives advanced by the chapters in Part 1, and the themes that emerge from those chapters and which emerged from the conference more generally. His chapter issues a clarion call for the reassertion of doctrine in judicial review, and a rejection of approaches which eschew a framework of principle in favour of an approach which rests on case-by-case analysis of whether judicial intervention is warranted according to all the circumstances of the case. He takes as his focus the administrative law jurisprudence of the Supreme Court of Canada but his analysis and the arguments he advances have wider implications for the administrative law systems of all common law jurisdictions. He observes that an approach that eschews a framework of principle, and rests more on individual judges' exercises of discretion, has led to a fraught and unsatisfactory administrative law jurisprudence in Canada. This raises a host of issues. For instance, Stratas argues that public confidence in the judiciary can be diminished if it is perceived that decisions rest on the individual judge's sense of right and wrong, that it will be difficult to maintain equal treatment under the law, and that predictability may be compromised. Such concerns lead him to call for greater articulation of the principles that underpin judicial decisions. In this regard he sees the chapters in Part 1 as offering key insights into the path forward.

The chapters in Part 2 offer comparative perspectives on the unity of public law. The focus of Robert French's chapter is cross-jurisdictional, or inter-jurisdictional, dialogue. He argues that while such dialogue can be beneficial, it is necessary to be alive to its limits. Far from being a mechanism for delivering uniformity across different jurisdictions, dialogue is instead a technique that enables 'learning by comparison'. It follows, argues French, that we should not necessarily expect unity—either in the full sense of that term, or in the more diffuse form of 'convergence'—to be dialogue's product. It is also the case, he points out, that dialogue in the public law sphere is complicated (and limited) by constitutional diversity—and that for all that a given country's written constitution may borrow or take inspiration from other such documents, each constitution is inevitably shaped by local conditions, both in initial design and subsequent operation. In the light of this, French draws upon the metaphor of a 'quilt of legalities'—a phrase coined by Boaventura de Sousa Santos to describe legal pluralism in Brazil—as a means of capturing both the potential and the limits of dialogue. On this view, while such dialogue may be valuable, proper attention to jurisdictional (including constitutional) diversity necessarily constrains its practical application. 'Unity', argues French, 'is a mirage', and inter-institutional dialogue should not be entered upon in the expectation of arriving at such a mythical destination.

An invaluable first-hand account of the use of foreign jurisprudence in public law cases is provided by Robert Reed's chapter. As one of the two Scottish Justices on the UK Supreme Court, Lord Reed recalls some resistance towards comparativism during his own legal education—at least when English law was the comparator. Pockets of resistance can also be seen, for example, in the United States, fuelled by the late Justice Scalia. Reed's own view is very different. Our increasingly globalised society has caused a shift in the issues the Supreme Court hears, with more cases concerning, for example, national security, data sharing, immigration and human rights. As judges increasingly 'face problems which transcend national boundaries' looking to other countries for guidance can promote harmony and avoid conflict of law issues. Even where no such issues necessarily arise, Reed positively endorses looking at foreign jurisprudence as part of a constant comparative process to ensure that UK laws are fit for purpose. He notes, however, that looking to other common law countries for inspiration is less prevalent in public law cases due to the increasing European influence on UK public law. Reed nevertheless argues that British judges should not limit themselves to European sources—an argument which will have even more force now that the European influence may be waning.

Cheryl Saunders examines the increasingly common and important phenomenon of transplants, that is the movement of relatively structured legal phenomena across jurisdictional boundaries. Saunders considers issues raised by transplants specifically in relation to public law in common law systems, though her analysis has broader implications. She articulates an important and valuable analytical framework for considering transplants, identifying and considering issues in relation to three phases of any decision about a transplant. First, identification of a possible transplant, utilising the case study of proposals for establishing a Constitutional Court for the United Kingdom. Second, evaluation of whether the transplant should proceed, taking as an illustrative example the introduction of statutory bills of rights into Australian jurisdictions. Third, any adaptation to the transplant in its original form that is deemed appropriate, focusing on the historic adoption of the referendum procedure to govern constitutional change in Australia. Through this analysis Saunders emphasises and illustrates the importance of taking context into account in making decisions about transplants—the context of both the 'donor' jurisdiction and the 'recipient' jurisdiction. In turn she raises important questions about practices and theories that encourage transplants divorced from considerations of relevant contexts. Saunders concludes with a series of valuable observations on the implications of transplants for the unity of public law across common law systems.

Issues of unity and disunity have not only been evident internationally but, increasingly, within the UK itself. Aileen McHarg's chapter on the UK's territorial constitution is, therefore, extremely timely. She notes that the UK has always had greater diversity in its governance than the average unitary state. Developments (such as increasing devolution, English Votes for English Laws, the 2014 Scottish independence referendum and, perhaps above all else, sharply differing attitudes to Brexit across the UK's constituent territories) reflect such diversity, but have also increased it. Despite the UK constitution having always accommodated a certain amount of divergence between its constituent parts, recent developments beg the question of how much divergence a constitution can endure. To combat such constitutional drift, calls have been heard for a unifying framework 'to bind the UK state together'. Such a framework would render the UK a federal state, or at least give it a more federal character. After examining the need for greater unity in the territorial constitution from four different perspectives—empirical, conceptual, normative and political—McHarg is pessimistic about the future of the UK. The most likely eventual way out of the current fractured territorial constitution is, she suspects, a clean break rather than a repair.

Comparative human rights law is the focus of Claudia Geiringer's chapter, specifically the so-called new 'Commonwealth model' of human rights protection found in Canada, New Zealand, the UK, Victoria and the Australian Capital Territory. Geiringer finds the existing scholarship on the new Commonwealth model 'radically incomplete'. Gaps have been caused by Commonwealth model scholars' preoccupation with the distinctiveness of the new Commonwealth model as compared to the American model of constitutionalised human rights protection. That, in turn, has caused those scholars to unduly fixate on the tension between parliamentary sovereignty and the judicial role in upholding rights. This chapter starts the process of filling those gaps, the most glaring of which is the lack of consideration as to the Commonwealth model's role in controlling the functions of the executive, caused by the hitherto fixation on the parliamentary sovereignty/judicial supremacy dichotomy. Geiringer also gives further thought to the important variations between the various Commonwealth instruments (including issues as fundamental as which rights are protected) and the reasons for those variations. In so doing, a more complete picture of the Commonwealth model begins to emerge.

In his chapter, Johannes Chan addresses the topic of remedies for violation of constitutional rights. He observes that in the public law sphere, the focus tends to be upon questions of validity, meaning that, at the remedial level, there is a corresponding emphasis upon devices—such as declarations and quashing orders—that serve to clarify or determine the legal status of impugned measures. In contrast, argues Chan, damages in this context is (or at least has, until recently, been) a relatively neglected area. He goes on to argue that greater attention should be paid to questions of damages for public law wrongs, and, in particular, that there are compelling arguments in favour of making available 'vindicatory' or 'constitutional' damages when constitutional rights are violated. Breaches of such rights, Chan contends, should be treated as independent wrongs. Chan's approach to these questions is comparative, Canada, New Zealand, South Africa and the United Kingdom being his chosen comparator jurisdictions. Chan argues that, in empirical terms, a degree of convergence towards the approach favoured in Canada can be discerned (the UK being an outlier) and that, in normative terms, this is to be welcomed, not least because the 'composite approach' preferred in Canada brings together the public and private law dimensions of damages for human rights violations. Chan does not, however, consider the Canadian model to be a panacea, arguing that there are several respects in which it could—and should—be improved upon.

In English administrative law, the liberalisation of public interest standing has allowed for the vindication of the rule of law in cases where an illegality might otherwise have been allowed to go unchallenged for want of another claimant. In her chapter, Elizabeth O'Loughlin highlights a similar—but even more judicially creative—trend in post-colonial settings. Using Kenya as her main case study (but also discussing, for example, Tanzania and Uganda), O'Loughlin argues that a generous approach to standing is all the more important in developing countries. Public interest standing allows for the 'maturation and diffusion' of new constitutional orders in line with indigenous rights in a way that a stricter standing test would prohibit, given that high levels of poverty and illiteracy in the general population hinder access to the courts. A trend for such a liberal approach to standing started in India and spread throughout South and East Africa. Such 'transnational judicial dialogue' has in turn allowed an individualised approach for each jurisdiction to mould its own constitution to its own values, and to respond to each nation's specific challenges. Without an ability to bring cases in the public interest, courts in developing countries would be deprived of the steady stream of case law necessary to flesh out new constitutions.

In her chapter, Anne Carter compares proportionality reasoning in the UK and Australia. Carter argues that although the proportionality test might be more firmly and clearly established in the UK, issues raised by the factual nature of the court's proportionality inquiry are comparatively unresolved in both countries. She therefore suggests that, despite certain important differences in the reception to, and methodology of, proportionality itself, the countries might profitably learn from each other with regard to the court's fact-finding role. A dialogue in three particular areas is recommended: (1) in terms of defining more clearly different types of 'fact'; (2) in ascertaining what types of material the courts should look at in making proportionality assessments; and (3) in terms of the meaning and role of deference. In these three areas the two countries have much to learn from each other, and the relationship is a symbiotic one since neither country has the perfect solution across all three areas. For example, different types of fact are more clearly distinguished in Australia, whereas the concept of deference is more developed in the UK after a 'lively' debate there. Greater communication may help to clarify matters in both countries, even if the eventual solution may not be precisely the same.

Janina Boughey and Lisa Burton Crawford examine the extent to which the centrality of jurisdictional error in Australian administrative law renders Australia exceptional among common law systems of public law. At first blush the centrality of jurisdictional error as the organising principle of Australian administrative law does mark Australia out as distinct compared to other common law jurisdictions such as Canada and the United Kingdom. However, Boughey and Crawford demonstrate that this surface-level divergence distracts attention from important points of unity between Australia and these other common law jurisdictions. They examine and reject those rationales propounded by the High Court of Australia for maintenance of jurisdictional error as an organising concept. However, they argue the concept can nonetheless be justified and that it performs the important constitutional role of distinguishing those errors of law Parliament has authorised from those it has not. This distinction is necessitated by the concept of parliamentary supremacy: it is open to Parliament to insulate decisions vitiated by certain legal errors from invalidity. In turn this reveals an important point of commonality between Australia, Canada and the United Kingdom. Although there are marked differences in terminology and approach, each system provides for some mechanism to distinguish legal errors which lead to invalidity from those that do not. Such mechanisms follow from the principle of legislative supremacy, which is common to all three systems, albeit there may be variations across jurisdictions as to the scope Parliament has, constitutionally, to prescribe that unlawful administrative acts shall not be invalid.

III. ACKNOWLEDGEMENTS

In organising the conference on which this collection is based, and in preparing this volume for publication, we have received assistance and support from a number of sources.

We are particularly grateful to John Bell. He was a co-convenor of the 2016 conference, and of the inaugural conference in 2014, during this time also serving as Director of the Centre for Public Law at Cambridge. We, and the conference series, have greatly benefited from his involvement in, and contributions to, the organisation of the conferences and the setting up of the conference series. In particular we have greatly benefited from his insights as one of the leading comparative lawyers in the common law world, and he has consistently been a source of wisdom in respect of the practical aspects of conference organisation, in the light of his significant experience in this regard. It is therefore fitting that John has written the preface to this collection.

We are grateful to the group of students at the Faculty of Law in Cambridge who served as assistants at the conference: Jason Allen, Darragh Coffey, Trina Malone, Alex Schäfer and Barry Solaiman. We have also appreciated the support and advice of the members of the Conference Advisory Board in our planning of the conference. The members of the Board for the 2016 conference were: Professor Mark Aronson (UNSW), Professor David Feldman (Cambridge), Professor Carol Harlow (LSE), Mr Richard Hart (Founder, Hart Publishing Ltd), Professor Cora Hoexter (Witwatersrand), Professor Janet McLean (Auckland), Lord Reed (UK Supreme Court), Professor Cheryl Saunders (Melbourne) and Professor Robert Thomas (Manchester).

We are grateful to Hart Publishing Ltd, the exclusive sponsor of the Public Law Conference, for their ongoing commitment to, and support of, the conference series. Hart has been heavily involved in the conference series from its inception, having played a significant role in the founding of the series. We have also greatly benefited from the more general support and advice of those at Hart, specifically Sinead Moloney and Bill Asquith, in respect of the planning of the conference and preparation of this volume.

The 2016 conference marked a number of innovations designed to further encourage the involvement of early career scholars. These innovations included the introduction of dedicated panels for doctoral students to present their work, which were a tremendous success and a highlight of the 2016 conference. These panels will be maintained for the 2018 conference in Melbourne. The 2016 conference also marked the establishment of the Richard Hart Prize for the best paper delivered by an early career scholar. We are very grateful to Richard Hart, the founder of Hart Publishing Ltd, who had a significant role in the establishment of the conference series, for kindly donating the prize. The inaugural winner of the prize was Jennifer Raso, a doctoral student at the University of Toronto, for her paper entitled, 'Unity in the Eye of the Beholder? Reasons for Decision in Theory and Practice'. Two papers were highly commended by the judging panel: Anne Carter's paper, 'Constitutional Convergence? Some Lessons from Proportionality' (chapter eighteen in this collection) and Janina Boughey and Lisa Burton Crawford's paper, 'Jurisdictional Error: Do We Really Need It?' (chapter nineteen in this collection). We are very grateful to the members of the judging panel: Professor David Feldman (Cambridge), Professor Carol Harlow (LSE) and Lord Reed (UK Supreme Court). The Prize will be offered again at the 2018 conference.

More information on the Public Law Conference series, including video-recordings of the plenary sessions at the 2016 Conference, can be found at the conference website: www.publiclawconference.law.cam.ac.uk.

2

The Unity of Public Law?

DAME SIAN ELIAS

I. INTRODUCTION

THE THEMES OF this book, and the conference from which it stems, revolve around familiar questions in public law arising out of the pull of unity and the push of pluralism set up by the diffusion of public power in the modern state. In my chapter I have attempted a judicial perspective on the forces that impact on convergence and divergence across common law jurisdictions. That was perhaps over-ambitious. The law concerned with public power and its control is a subject of uncertain boundaries and in constant change. As the chapters by Chief Justice French and Lord Reed make clear, the differences across jurisdictions are more than label deep. It does not help that I come from a jurisdiction which, although long in scholarly tradition in public law, has a judicial tradition which has generally taken the simple path of optimistic contextualism and is thought to be short in doctrine. So you will have to make some allowances.

In this chapter I do not address one of the principal sources of convergence in public law: the role of public international law. New Zealand being a small jurisdiction, we have long been used to looking for ideas wherever we can find them and the principles and values obtained from international law are drawn on unselfconsciously and without suspicion in our courts. I concentrate here on some of the domestic public law matters we have in common with other common law jurisdictions and some where we diverge. I want to reflect a little on public power and the role of judicial review in its control today, before discussing the challenges of law and discretion and the way they are being addressed in constitutional traditions which share common roots but have differences which impact upon public law.

In his inaugural lecture at the London School of Economics and Political Science, Professor SA De Smith said that constitutional law and administrative law, the two domestic branches of public law, occupied 'distinct provinces, but also a substantial area of common ground'.[1] The latest edition of *De Smith's Judicial Review* suggests that the distinct provinces have become less clear.[2]

[1] SA De Smith, 'The Lawyers and the Constitution: an Inaugural Lecture' (speech at the London School of Economics and Political Science, London, 1960), as cited in M Taggart, 'The Province of Administrative Law Determined?' in M Taggart (ed) *The Province of Administrative Law* (Hart, Oxford, 1997) 1, 1.

[2] Lord Woolf and others (eds), *De Smith's Judicial Review*, 7th edn (Sweet and Maxwell, London, 2013) [1-013]. The shift is attributed to dissatisfaction with ultra vires as the basis of judicial review and increasing recognition that judicial review protects the rights of the individual against abuse of power.

We have been here before. In 1940, the then Chief Justice of New Zealand announced that the Council of Legal Education had agreed to include in the curriculum for the law degree what he said the 'the law professors are pleased to call "Administrative Law"'.[3] It was clearly not a move welcomed by the Chief Justice, even though it had been a long time coming.[4] The Chief Justice followed Dicey in this. He said that the view taken by the judges and the practising profession was that there was 'really no such special branch of the law' because administrative law was 'properly included in and is part of what is generally called Constitutional law'.[5] A compromise was, however, reached. The prescription of the constitutional law course was expanded to include the requirement of 'a general knowledge of the principles of Administrative Law', copying the elements used by Professor Frankfurter, indicating the pull of unity exerted by American legal thinking in public law.[6] It was Frankfurter who had dismissed Dicey's rejection of a separate system of administrative law as 'brilliant obfuscation', saying that it illustrated the truth of the view that 'many a theory survives long after its brains are knocked out'.[7]

For much of the past 50 years the development of administrative law has meant that public law has been less court-centred, less-lawyer-led than formerly. During that period the methods of government and its controls, internal as well as external, have been transformed. Better bureaucratic checks, new institutional checks, and the development of specialist systems of administrative adjudication have prompted a reassessment of the role played by the general courts.

These reassessments have taken place in all common law jurisdictions but against constitutional backgrounds and traditions which vary. So, although a comparative law perspective comes naturally to those who share the common law tradition, we need to be particularly careful with borrowings in public law. Adding to the complexity of the topic is the contestability of many of the concepts that mark out this area of law from others, if indeed it can properly be separated.

The problems of power and its abuse are not confined to public law.[8] What we call public law is itself not isolated from the general body of common law from which it developed.[9] Many of the principles of administrative law were developed

[3] M Myers, 'The Law and the Administration' (1940) 3 *NZ J Pub Admin* 38 at 44.

[4] The inclusion of administrative law in the curriculum in the United Kingdom had been urged by academics from the middle of the nineteenth century. By 1888, as Maitland pointed out in a speech published in FW Maitland, *The Constitutional History of England* (Cambridge University Press, Cambridge, 1908) 505–506, the law reports were full of cases about administrative law, although they were not indexed as such. Even so, it was a daring move for New Zealand legal education. Only five years before, in England, Lord Hewart, writing under the long shadow cast by Albert Venn Dicey, had dismissed the term 'administrative law' as 'Continental jargon', when writing in the *News of the World*: as we are told by SA de Smith, *Constitutional and Administrative Law* (Harmondsworth (UK), Penguin, 1971) 509.

[5] M Myers, 'The Law and the Administration' (1940) 3 *NZ J Publ Admin* 38 at 44.

[6] See F Frankfurter, 'The Task of Administrative Law' (1927) 75 *U Pa L Rev* 614 at 615.

[7] Citing Huxley in F Frankfurter, 'Foreword' (1938) 47 *Yale LJ* 515 at 517. The issue had as its topic: 'Discussion of Current Developments in Administrative Law'.

[8] In *Ridge v Baldwin* [1964] AC 40 (HL), for example, Lord Reid drew on private law cases concerned with control of power.

[9] As scholars such as Dawn Oliver and Peter Cane have been at the forefront in pointing out: see D Oliver, *Common Values and the Public-Private Divide* (London, Butterworths, 1999); P Cane, 'Accountability and the Public-Private Divide' in N Bamforth and P Leyland (eds), *Public Law in a Multi-Layered Constitution* (Oxford, Hart Publishing, 2003).

in tort, contract, company law, labour law, criminal law, and equity.[10] Sir Anthony Mason has written of the extent to which modern administrative law is founded on equitable principles and 'has its roots in private law'.[11] Those roots suggest caution in seeing public law as an island.

That is not to say that better development of a theory of public law is not valuable or that it is not important to cultivate a sense of what is public power. Such power is necessarily limited because unfettered government discretion in a constitutional order based on the rule of law is, as Sir William Wade said, a contradiction in terms.[12] Public power must always be 'public-regarding'.[13] It cannot be exercised at whim. The exercise of public power must be reasonable, as *Associated Picture Houses v Wednesbury* affirmed.[14]

In addition, because government is uniquely powerful, governmental power requires special attention.[15] Sir David Williams once said that 'where big government moves there is no such thing as "ordinary powers", for those powers are exercised in a context of financial dominance and control of information and access to political channels to which no natural person could aspire'.[16] The same thinking was expressed by Justice McLachlin in the Supreme Court of Canada in a 1994 case concerning contracts of procurement by municipal government, when rejecting the argument that the municipality should be treated like any private sector contractor.[17]

In the modern state, finding where public power resides is not always easy. In all jurisdictions there have been huge changes in how government is delivered and corresponding movement in the scope of judicial review to extend to bodies private in form which operate through contract.[18] The 'contracting state' may throw up special challenges, but it is the responsibility of the courts, as Lord Diplock said,

[10] A point made in 1987 by DGT Williams, 'Criminal Law and Administrative Law: Problems of Procedure and Reasonableness' in P Smith (ed), *Criminal Law: Essays in Honour of JC Smith* (London, Butterworths, 1987) 171.

[11] A Mason, 'The Place of Equity and Equitable Remedies in the Contemporary Common Law World' (1994) 110 *LQR* 238 at 238.

[12] HWR Wade and CF Forsyth, *Administrative Law*, 11th edn (Oxford, Oxford University Press, 2014) 296.

[13] As Michael Taggart liked to describe it, contrasting it with 'the primacy of self-regarding behaviour' which was the starting point of private law: M Taggart, 'The Province of Administrative Law Determined?' in M Taggart (ed), *The Province of Administrative Law* (Oxford, Hart, 1997) 5.

[14] *Associated Provincial Picture Houses Ltd v Wednesbury Corporation* [1948] 1 KB 223 (CA).

[15] M Elliott, 'Judicial Review's Scope, Foundations and Purposes: Joining the Dots' [2012] *NZ L Rev* 75 at 79.

[16] DGT Williams, 'Statute Law and Administrative Law' (1984) 5 *Statute L Rev* 157 at 168.

[17] *Shell Canada Products Limited v Vancouver City* [1994] 1 SCR 231 at 240–41, a case concerning City Council resolutions not to buy Shell products while it continued to do business with South Africa; Shell challenged the decision on public law principles. McLachlin J said that the Council members, undertaking commercial and contractual activities with public funds and with wider consequences than for the parties to the contract, and under statutory powers which were limited, could not act in pursuit of their own private interests, but must exercise their contractual power in the public interest.

[18] See *Mercury Energy Ltd v Energy Corporation of New Zealand Ltd* [1994] 2 NZLR 385 (PC) (where the scope for judicial review was suggested to be limited). In New Zealand, however, see *Ririnui v Landcorp Farming Ltd* [2016] NZSC 62. In Canada, in *Alberta v Elder Advocates of Alberta Society* 2011 SCC 24, [2011] 2 SCR 261 at [83]–[91], the Supreme Court accepted that liability may attach to public actors in equity even if in limited and special circumstances which did not undermine their public law responsibilities.

to adapt 'to preserve the integrity of the rule of law' despite changes in 'methods of government'[19] and to supervise for legality new bodies possessing the 'essential characteristics' upon which the supervisory jurisdiction of the High Court has been based.[20] The scope of judicial review has been extended by procedural reforms which have described amenability to judicial review in expansive terms.[21] In many jurisdictions, judicial review now operates with wide definitions of public function and public power adopted in statements of rights.[22]

II. JUDICIAL REVIEW TODAY

Judicial review is supervisory jurisdiction. It checks the boundaries of power conferred on others. It is not original decision making and it is therefore inevitably deferential to the primary decision-maker, to a greater or lesser extent. Space for proper choice, what we call discretion, is at the heart of judicial review.

The direct impact of judicial review in administrative justice is slight. If it was 'inevitably sporadic and peripheral' when the first edition of *De Smith* was published in 1959,[23] it is even more so today. Discretion is now systemised by policy statements, manuals, and other forms of 'soft' law which protect against arbitrariness and provide fair processes. Checks within government provide supervision and may be accessed for review of decisions by those affected. More or less elaborate systems for the review of decisions are provided by adjudicators or officials who observe principles of natural justice, an obligation now imposed on all who exercise public functions which affect rights. Ombudsmen provide independent scrutiny and assistance for those affected by administrative decision making. Improved access to official information and reasons for decisions[24] have not only changed the culture and method of government but have revolutionised administrative law by laying bare

[19] *Inland Revenue Commissioners v National Federation of Self-employed and Small Businesses Ltd* [1982] AC 617 at 639–40 (HL).

[20] *R v Criminal Injuries Compensation Board, ex parte Lain* [1967] 2 QB 864 at 884 (CA); *R v Panel on Take-overs and Mergers, Ex parte Datafin plc* [1987] QB 815 (CA) was an early harbinger of movement in the scope of judicial review to extend to private bodies which operate through contract. *Finnigan v New Zealand Rugby Football Union* [1985] 2 NZLR 159 (CA) (a private law case in which principles of public law were applied) remains an outlier. *Datafin* and *R v Panel on Take-overs and Mergers, ex p Guinness plc* [1990] 1 QB 146 (CA) have prevailed in New Zealand: see, for example, *Electoral Commission v Cameron* [1997] 2 NZLR 421 at 429 (CA); *Royal Australasian College of Surgeons v Phipps* [1999] 3 NZLR 1 at 11–12 (CA); followed by the Court of Appeal in *Wilson v White* [2005] 1 NZLR 189 at [21] (CA); itself adopted by the Supreme Court in *Ririnui v Landcorp Farming Ltd* [2016] NZSC 62 at [89].

[21] Such as New Zealand's Judicature Amendment Act 1972, as discussed in *Electoral Commission v Cameron* [1997] 2 NZLR 421 at 429 (CA).

[22] Such as s 3 of the New Zealand Bill of Rights Act 1990; and s 6(1) of the Human Rights Act 1998 (UK), discussed in *YL v Birmingham City Council* [2007] UKHL 27, [2008] 1 AC 95, where the compelling dissenting judgments by Lord Bingham and Baroness Hale seem likely to point in the direction most of us will follow.

[23] SA De Smith, *Judicial Review of Administrative Action*, 1st edn (London, Stevens, 1959) 1.

[24] In New Zealand, s 23 of the Official Information Act 1982 requires reasons to be provided on request by those whose interests are affected.

the justification for actions taken. Effective redress for administrative error for most people does not entail access to a court possessing general supervisory jurisdiction.[25] This climate has implications for judicial review's scope and methods.

Local conditions have also prompted reconsideration of adjudicative correction in a number of jurisdictions which also impact on judicial review and on public law more generally. Under the Tribunals, Courts and Enforcement Act 2007, the adjudicative appellate administrative tribunals in the United Kingdom are positioned in the judicial branch. The reform seems to represent a unified rather than a pluralistic aspiration for public law. It was prompted by the need in the United Kingdom to take the strain off the courts in judicial review. In Australia, by contrast, the Commonwealth Administrative Appeal Tribunal (AAT), although presided over by a senior judge, has been held by the High Court to be part of the Executive.[26] The different locations of adjudicative administrative power (in the judiciary or in the administration) may have implications for the scope and method of judicial review by the courts.

There are some suggestions that greater deference may be accorded to decisions of inferior courts or administrative appeal tribunals comprising members of the judiciary. That does not seem to me a sound distinction. First the difference between the functions being fulfilled by and the methods and expertise of an appellate administrative panel and a court of limited jurisdiction may be largely indistinguishable. Whether appeal is to a tribunal within the courts system or within the administration is a matter of institutional design which is as likely to turn on considerations such as volume of work or questions of cost as on any real difference in function.

Secondly, I doubt whether judicial review of courts of limited jurisdiction is appropriately more tolerant of error than judicial review of specialist administrative bodies. The reasoning and interpretative functions being fulfilled by a court or a judicialised tribunal may often be of wider application in the legal order because such a body will usually deal in legal principles of general application, will observe judicial methodology and its decisions may have the sort of consequences (as precedents or in application of *stare decisis*) which might be thought to prompt close judicial supervision.

Development of more elaborate review or adjudication as part of a system of administrative justice may not seem justified in every jurisdiction. It is possible that any increased judicialisation of administrative review processes could come at the expense of desirable plurality in administration (as some administrative lawyers have feared).[27]

The development of administrative adjudication may also affect the unity of law maintained through the courts of general jurisdiction. It is at first sight startling to those brought up in a tradition influenced by Dicey to see in recent decisions of the UK Supreme Court[28] the protection of decisions of the Upper Tribunal from judicial

[25] See PA Keane, 'Democracy, Participation and Administrative Law' (2011) 68 *AIAL Forum* 1 at 14.

[26] *Bushell v Repatriation Commission* (1992) 175 CLR 408 at 425.

[27] HW Arthurs, 'Rethinking Administrative Law: A Slightly Dicey Business' (1979) 17 *Osgoode Hall LJ* 1.

[28] *R (Cart) v Upper Tribunal* [2011] UKSC 28, [2011] 3 WLR 107; and *Eba v Advocate General for Scotland* [2011] UKSC 29, [2011] 3 WLR 149.

review unless they would qualify for second-tier appeal (and with the indication of at least one senior Judge that intervention might be further restricted once there is more experience of 'how the new tribunal system is working in practice').[29] It is even more startling to see this deference provided for reasons of proportionality in dispute resolution.[30]

As Sir John Laws pointed out in an article about reasonableness in public law some years ago, it is one thing to say that reasonableness means different things in context.[31] It is quite another to say that there are circumstances in which unreasonable exercise of power is not amenable to judicial review at all. It is more appealing for some of us to think that the basis of review remains constant for all bodies amenable to judicial review.

I am not sure that it is a complete answer that *Cart* preserved the formal power of judicial review of the Upper Tribunal, so that refusal to intervene did not entail relinquishment of jurisdiction. It is true that on this approach the Supreme Court can intervene if the Upper Tribunal seems to be developing 'local law' in a way that injures the coherence of the legal order. But if the Supreme Court is prepared to allow that a statutory tribunal with many of the attributes of a superior court will be judicially reviewed for error only if the effort is proportionate measured against the resources available to the legal system, why should the legislature not act to restrict judicial review where it finds it too expensive or inconvenient?

The new systems of administrative adjudication may well be better placed to promote the interests of good administration as well as the reasonableness, fairness and observance of law which are the concerns of judicial review and which are the constitutional responsibility of the superior courts. I am not entirely convinced that it is a function of judicial review to secure good governance, although some thoughtful commentators think it is.[32] Good governance may well be a central purpose of a mature system of administrative justice, such as I think we can see developing in some common law jurisdictions, shaking off the legacy of Dicey. But I question whether it is the function of the supervisory system of judicial review through the ordinary courts. It seems to me that the function of judicial review is securing the rule of law in relation to public power.

III. THE NATURE OF ADMINISTRATIVE LAW

Frankfurter said of administrative law that it is an area of law where standards, not rules, have to be applied to 'the unlimited versatility of circumstance'.[33]

[29] *R (Cart) v Upper Tribunal* ibid at [92] (Lord Phillips).

[30] See criticisms made in M Elliott and R Thomas, 'Tribunal Justice and Proportionate Dispute Resolution' (2012) 71 *CLJ* 297.

[31] J Laws, '*Wednesbury*' in C Forsyth and I Hare (eds), *The Golden Metwand and the Crooked Cord: Essays on Public Law in Honour of Sir William Wade QC* (Oxford, Clarendon Press, 1998) 196.

[32] C Forsyth and others (eds), *Effective Judicial Review: A Cornerstone of Good Governance* (Oxford, Oxford University Press, 2010).

[33] F Frankfurter, 'The Task of Administrative Law' (1926) 75 *U Pa L Rev* 614 at 619.

Administrative law is concerned, he thought, 'pre-eminently with law in the making; with fluid tendencies and tentative traditions' and in which it is necessary to be wary of 'premature synthesis' and fixed rules.[34] A similar warning was repeated by Lord Hailsham half a century later in 1979 about the use of 'rigid legal classifications' in exercising the supervisory jurisdiction in the field of administrative law.[35] The jurisdiction is, he said, 'inherently discretionary, and the court is frequently in the presence of differences of degree which merge almost imperceptibly into differences of kind'.

Is this a lesson we are fated never to learn? To the dangers of 'premature synthesis' highlighted by Frankfurter perhaps we should add 'premature antithesis' of the kind that seems particularly appealing in administrative law (law and merits, private and public, jurisdictional error and non-jurisdictional error, interpretation and discretion, judicial and non-judicial, policy and fact, and so on) and big theories such as *ultra vires* and the rule of law.

I do not suggest that these ideas are not valuable. Indeed, they are inescapable. But they are not themselves tests or standards for judicial review.

Questions of vires and jurisdiction account for a great part of judicial review of administrative action because a principal function of the supervisory jurisdiction is to ensure that decision-makers have the power they purport to exercise and keep within any limits imposed on it. Especially in a jurisdiction where the constitutional balances are fragile, there may be good sense in structuring intervention in terms of vires and parliamentary intent wherever it provides an answer.[36]

Such tactical considerations should not obscure the fact that ultra vires has to be stretched to fit the scope of judicial review as it has been developed to meet the needs of our societies in securing administrative justice. It requires emphasis on a constructed and artificial legislative intent for decisions not concerned with the exercise of statutory powers. It obscures the overlap between legality and reasonableness by suggesting judicial review can be reduced to an exercise in statutory construction alone.[37]

The acceptance that the distinction between jurisdictional and non-jurisdictional error of law is not a useful test for the effect of ouster clauses was reached in the United Kingdom following *Anisminic*[38] although it is probably fair to say that the implications of that Delphic decision were appreciated earlier and more enthusiastically in New Zealand, under the influence of Sir Robin Cooke in *Bulk Gas Users Group v Attorney General*.[39] Nevertheless, as Cooke J pointed out, the shift was

[34] See also DGT Williams, 'Justiciability and the Control of Discretionary Power' in M Taggart (ed), *Judicial Review of Administrative Action in the 1980s: Problems and Prospects* (Auckland, Oxford University Press, 1986) 122.

[35] *London & Clydeside Estates Ltd v Aberdeen District Council* [1980] 1 WLR 182 at 190 (HL).

[36] Although, as Paul Craig points out, a search for legitimacy in this way is not the manner in which the common law has developed in general. The ultra vires doctrine is, he thinks 'predicated on highly contestable assumptions about the correct normative relationship between common law and statutory power in a constitutional democracy': P Craig, 'The Nature of Reasonableness Review' (2013) 66 *CLP* 131 at 159.

[37] Compare the reasoning in *Padfield v Minister of Agriculture, Fisheries and Food* [1968] AC 997 (HL).

[38] *Anisminic Ltd v Foreign Compensation Commission* [1969] 2 AC 147 (HL).

[39] *Bulk Gas Users Group v Attorney General* [1983] NZLR 129 (CA).

not out of a blue sky and represented a decision in favour of one of two bodies of existing doctrine.[40]

Justice Scalia described the label 'jurisdictional' as 'an empty distraction because every new application of a broad statutory term can be reframed as a questionable extension of the agency's jurisdiction'.[41] This is the same sort of thinking used by Lord Diplock in *O'Reilly v Mackman*, to explain that, if a tribunal of limited jurisdiction mistook the law applicable, 'it must have asked itself the wrong question, ie, one into which it was not empowered to inquire and so had no jurisdiction to determine'.[42] Justice Scalia thought 'judges should not waste their time' on such 'mental acrobatics'.[43]

Yet, the pull of 'jurisdiction' as a touchstone remains.[44] That is for the very good reason that, although not a test, it is an idea that underlies much of the supervisory jurisdiction. As Mark Aronson has observed it 'expresses a conclusion that judicial intervention is appropriate'.[45] If so, 'jurisdiction' is perhaps best seen as a 'mediating' concept for judicial review, as Harry Arthurs described it many years ago.[46] Even in Australia (where a search for jurisdictional error is still required to preserve the decencies of strict division between merits review and judicial review), post-*Kirk*[47] and post the relaxation of *Wednesbury* unreasonableness by the majority in *Li*,[48] the different basis for intervention for error of law (jurisdictional or not) may not yield very different in results in the end.

IV. LAW AND DISCRETION

What, then, of supervision of discretion? In the same year that Lord Hailsham was expressing concern about 'rigid legal classifications',[49] Harry Arthurs suggested 'Rethinking Administrative Law'.[50] He argued for recognition that law and discretion

[40] The triumph of *Anisminic* was completed in the United Kingdom in *O'Reilly v Mackman* [1983] 2 AC 237 (HL); *R v Hull University Visitor (ex parte Page)* [1993] AC 682 (HL); and *Boddington v British Transport Police* [1999] 2 AC 143 at 154 (HL). In *O'Reilly v Mackman* at 278, Lord Diplock spoke of the liberation of English public law from court-imposed fetters based on 'esoteric distinctions between errors of law committed by such tribunals that went to their jurisdiction, and errors of law committed by them within their jurisdiction'.

[41] *City of Arlington, Texas v Federal Communications Commission* 569 US (2013) at 9.

[42] *O'Reilly v Mackman* [1983] 2 AC 237 at 278 (HL).

[43] *City of Arlington, Texas v Federal Communications Commission* 569 US (2013) at 9.

[44] As can be seen in the Court of Appeal decision in *Regina (Cart) v Upper Tribunal* [2010] EWCA Civ 859, [2011] QB 120.

[45] M Aronson, B Dyer and M Goves, *Judicial Review of Administrative Action*, 5th edn (Sydney, Thomson Reuters, 2013) [1.140].

[46] HW Arthurs, *'Without the Law': Administrative Justice and Legal Pluralism in Nineteenth Century England* (Toronto, University of Toronto Press, 1985) 208–09, as cited in M Taggart, 'The Contribution of Lord Cooke to Scope of Review Doctrine in Administrative Law: A Comparative Common Law Perspective' in P Rishworth (ed), *The Struggle for Simplicity in the Law: Essays for Lord Cooke of Thorndon* (Wellington, Butterworths, 1997) 212–13.

[47] *Kirk v Industrial Court of NSW* [2010] HCA 1, (2010) 239 CLR 531.

[48] *Minister for Immigration and Citizenship v Li* [2013] HCA 18, (2013) 249 CLR 332 at 364 [68].

[49] *London & Clydeside Estates Ltd v Aberdeen District Council* [1980] 1 WLR 182 at 190 (HL).

[50] HW Arthurs, 'Rethinking Administrative law: A Slightly Dicey Business' (1979) 17 *Osgoode Hall LJ* 1.

are not distinct and that generalist judges are not best-placed to interpret public law legislation knowledgeably. We have been worrying away at this bone ever since.

Arthurs did not support the development of an entirely distinct system of public law under 'unifying principles of public law'.[51] He thought such repositioning would depend too much on lawyers, including as decision-makers. He questioned whether common approaches to procedural fairness were really useful. He asked whether any higher-order principles which might be adopted to provide coherence would be at such general level of abstraction as to be 'hardly legal rules'. Arthurs suggested that useful rules for administrative justice were likely to emerge 'only in the specific and varied contexts of administrative activity'.[52]

The approach Harry Arthurs argued for in 1979 was a 'functionalist' one. Under it, there would be a move away from the 'slippery slope' of supervision by way of judicial review under terms such as 'reasonable', 'fair' and '*bona fide*'.[53] A more rigorously 'functionalist' approach would be shaped by inquiring into whether there are elements of the decision relative to which generalist judges might have special competence. If so, judicial review would be appropriate. Such element might be found in the need to have authoritative resolution of constitutional questions or the interpretation of statutes of general application. 'Presumptive deference' available to an administrative body acting within its area of specialist expertise might be displaced by its failure to provide a credible explanation for adoption of a particular procedure. Arthurs suggested it was 'functional' to defer to those possessing specialist knowledge where they have, in fact, considered the matter.

This thinking has been highly influential in the jurisprudence of the Supreme Court of Canada and its development of deferential standards of judicial review. Despite the efforts in development of doctrine over the past three decades, it is, however, sobering to read the views of Chief Justice McLachlin of Canada in a recent paper that 'administrative law arguably is beset by more difficulty than any other branch of the law'.[54] She says it is a 'barbed and occluded thicket'. In support of that verdict, the Chief Justice traced the twists and turns of Supreme Court doctrine on review of discretion. From this experience, she makes the suggestion that we should give away what she calls 'linguistic games' such as qualifiers or spectrums of reasonableness. Courts, she says, should recognise that 'most questions don't admit to a single right answer and ask, in all humility, whether interference is necessary in the interests of fairness and preservation of the rule of law'.[55]

Disagreements and expressions of doubt have been expressed in a number of recent judgments of final courts concerning administrative law. In the United Kingdom, Trevor Allan has suggested that the different approaches adopted by members of the United Kingdom Supreme Court in *Evans v Attorney General*[56]

[51] ibid, at 30.
[52] ibid, at 31.
[53] ibid, at 32–33.
[54] B McLachlin, 'Administrative Law is Not for Sissies: Finding a Path through the Thicket' (2016) 29 *CJALP* 127 (Paper delivered to CLEBC Administrative Law Conference, 16 November 2015, Vancouver, BC).
[55] ibid, at 133–34.
[56] *Evans v Attorney General* [2015] UKSC 21, [2015] 2 WLR 813.

indicate deep disagreements about the nature and function of law.[57] Similar differences in approach can be seen in the decision in *Bank Mellat v HM Treasury (No 2)* where Lord Neuberger and Lord Dyson, although agreeing with the analysis of Lord Reed, expressly declined to join him in endorsing the views earlier expressed in *Huang*[58] and *Denbigh High School*[59] that compliance with rights was to be objectively determined by the court.[60] In Canada the recent decision of the Supreme Court of Canada, *Wilson v Atomic Energy of Canada*, indicates divisions over deference. Three judges in that case disagreed with the presumption of deferential review of a home statute observed by the majority, citing rule of law concerns and indicating the view that the decision of the majority 'would abandon rule of law values in favour of indiscriminate deference to the administrative state'.[61]

These disagreements indicate the extent to which judicial review engages with constitutional values and other values fundamental to the particular legal order. The connection between administrative law and constitutional law explains why jurisdictions with much in common may diverge in the manner of controlling administrative discretion.

V. CONSTITUTIONAL TRADITIONS

If 'behind every theory of administrative law there lies a theory of the state' as Carol Harlow and Richard Rawlings say,[62] close attention to constitutional law and traditions is necessary in administrative law. Constitutional traditions provide coherence within a legal order but may limit convergence across jurisdictions.

In the United States, the development of the modern administrative state was characterised by dispersal of executive power under wide discretion both as to rule making and in application of power, conferred in broad terms, to particular cases. While this dispersal of power and the discretion which was an indispensible part of it responded to the needs of modern government, it is also explained by the constitutional tradition of the United States. As Peter Cane has explained, in the United States, the three institutions of government are co-ordinate and share power including in relation to policy development.[63] It is a tradition in which development of

[57] TRS Allan, 'Law, Democracy, and Constitutionalism: Reflections on *Evans v Attorney General*' (2016) 75 *CLJ* 38 at 39. Among other comments, Allan points to difficulties in the distinction drawn by members of the Supreme Court that the Attorney General was bound by the view expressed by the Upper Tribunal of the law but not by its assessment of the public interest in disclosure (at least where the Attorney General had confronted the reasons of the Tribunal, as the majority considered to be necessary).

[58] *Huang v Secretary of State for the Home Department* [2007] UKHL 11, [2007] 2 AC 167.

[59] *R (SB) v Governors of Denbigh High School* [2006] UKHL 15, [2007] 1 AC 100.

[60] *Bank Mellatt v Her Majesty's Treasury (No 2)* [2013] UKSC 39, [2014] AC 700 at [123]–[124] (Lord Reed) at [175] (Lord Neuberger) at [197] (Lord Dyson).

[61] *Wilson v Atomic Energy of Canada* 2016 SCC 29 at [79] (Moldaver, Côté and Brown JJ).

[62] C Harlow and R Rawlings, *Law and Administration*, 3rd edn (Cambridge, Cambridge University Press, 2009) 1.

[63] P Cane, 'Judicial Control of Administrative Interpretation in Australia and the United States' in H Wilberg and M Elliott (eds), *The Scope and Intensity of Substantive Review: Traversing Taggart's Rainbow* (Oxford, Hart, 2015) 227–28.

institutional deference is congruent with the constitutional values of the state. It is understood that, as Justice Scalia put it: 'Congress knows to speak in plain terms when it wishes to circumscribe, and in capacious terms when it wishes to enlarge, agency discretion.'[64]

The deference extended to to an administrator in interpretation of its home statute extends to the provisions conferring jurisdiction as well as to other provisions. It applies to rule making. Adjudicatory decisions under the Administrative Procedure Act of 1946[65] are subject to *Skidmore* deference by which the court decides on matters of interpretation but takes account of the agency's view and looks to whether it is preferable.[66] Interpretation of regulations that the agency itself has made are deferred to unless plainly erroneous.

The constitutional conditions which led to the development of the *Chevron* doctrine are not encountered in other common law jurisdictions. In Australia, Canada, the United Kingdom, and New Zealand the parliamentary tradition and what Bagehot called the 'efficient secret' of Cabinet government means that the Executive is subject to less control by institutional balances and divided power.[67] In such contexts, judicial review is a principal constitutional check. It is one the courts cannot avoid without affecting the constitutional balance.

In Australia, the separation of powers provided by the Constitution has been used by the High Court to protect its constitutional responsibility to say what the law is.[68] That has had implications for the development of Australian administrative law. It has been taken to emphasise a distinction between legality and merits which in other jurisdictions is less sharp. In Australia, the strict line observed between legality and merits means it is difficult to develop standards for judicial intervention from values obtained from the common law, international conventions or the statutory Bills of Rights found in Victoria and the Australian Capital Territory.[69] Reference to such values is seen to give rise to 'merits review', a line the courts will not pass.[70]

[64] *City of Arlington, Texas v Federal Communications Commission* 569 US (2013) at 5, referring to the *Chevron* doctrine: *Chevron USA Inc v Natural Resources Defense Council Inc* 467 US 837 (1984). *Chevron* applies to cases in which an agency interprets its own constitutive statute or a statute it administers. If the intent of the legislature is clear, that prevails. Cane says that the standard reading of *Chevron* is that deciding whether more than one meaning is available is a question of law. If it is, the second step involves exercising discretion: Cane, ibid at 221.

[65] Administrative Procedure Act of 1946 Pub L No 79–404, 60 Stat 237.

[66] *Skidmore v Swift and Co* 323 US 134 (1944).

[67] Although the Australian constitution is modelled on that of the United States in large measure, its adoption of a parliamentary system produces a tension, see Stephen Gageler, 'Foundations of Australian Federalism and the Role of Judicial Review' (1987) 17 *Fed L Rev* 162 at 164.

[68] In Australia, judicial review by the High Court of the exercise of power by officers of the Commonwealth is entrenched in s 75(v) of the Constitution. The High Court has held that Chapter III of the Constitution protects by implication the supervisory jurisdiction of the State Supreme Courts: *Kable v DPP for New South Wales* [1996] HCA 24, (1996) 189 CLR 51; *Kirk v Industrial Court of NSW* [2010] HCA 1, (2010) 239 CLR 531.

[69] As illustrated by the Court's decision in *R v Momcilovic* [2011] HCA 34, (2011) 245 CLR 1.

[70] In *Craig v South Australia* (1995) 184 CLR 163 and *Corporation of the City of Enfield v Development Assessment Commission* (1999) 199 CLR 135, the High Court has made it clear that judicial review is concerned with legality, not merits. Cane notes that while in the US that is reason to give weight to administrative decisions, in the High Court it is a reason not to review them on grounds of reasonableness or for error of fact or mixed fact and law. Constitutional rights protective of freedom of speech were recognised in *Australian Capital Television Pty v The Commonwealth* (1992) 177 CLR 106 and *Lange*

Chief Justice Gleeson in a 2008 lecture identified both the constitutional balances and the federal administrative law reforms of the 1970s as an explanation why Australian law had not taken up either the North American jurisprudence of judicial deference or the English attraction for abuse of power as a touchstone.[71] Rather, he said, in Australia the focus has been on jurisdiction and legality.

In the United Kingdom and New Zealand, where executive dominance of Parliament and parliamentary sovereignty is untrammelled by a constitutional text which distributes powers, judicial review is less secure. That institutional insecurity has, I think, shaped judicial development of administrative law. It may, as I have suggested, account for the attraction of ultra vires as the underpinning justification for judicial review, because it is seen to have constitutional validity. In both the United Kingdom and New Zealand there are signs of constitutional repositioning around values derived from the common law, ancient statutes and charters and modern statements of human rights.[72]

In Australia, if the High Court continues to move away from the common law constitutional foundation earlier recognised by Sir Owen Dixon,[73] public law may develop more distinctly from other branches of law. It may achieve greater unity within itself. The elaboration of the original executive power under the Constitution touched on in recent decisions of the High Court may also provide a point of further difference.[74] Peter Cane considers that the power of conclusive statutory interpretation developed by the High Court is here to stay in part because of the concentration

v Australian Broadcasting Corporation (1997) 189 CLR 520 to be implicit in the Constitution and have been confirmed in *Unions NSW v New South Wales* [2013] HCA 58, (2013) 252 CLR 530. There seems to be resistance to extending such rights beyond protection of political participation, as can be seen in the cases in which the High Court has declined to infer a freedom of association: *Mulholland v Australian Electoral Commission* [2004] HCA 41, (2004) 220 CLR 181 at [148] (Gummow and Hayne JJ), [364] (Heydon J); *Wainohu v New South Wales* [2011] HCA 24, (2011) 243 CLR 181 at [72] (French CJ and Kiefel J) at [112] (Gummow, Hayne, Crennan and Bell JJ) at [186] (Heydon J); cited by Hayne J in *Tajjour v New South Wales* [2014] HCA 35, (2014) 254 CLR 508 at [95].

71 M Gleeson, 'The Role of a Judge in a Representative Democracy' (speech to the Judiciary of the Commonwealth of the Bahamas, 4 January 2008).

72 Most notably in the decision of the UK Supreme Court in *AXA General Insurance Ltd v HM Advocate* [2011] UKSC 46, [2012] 1 AC 868 where members of the Court went out of their way to emphasise fundamental values of the common law. See also *R (HS2 Action Alliance Ltd) v Secretary of State for Transport* [2014] UKSC 3, [2014] All ER 109 at [207] where Lord Neuberger and Lord Mance referred to fundamental common law principles in addition to constitutional instruments like Magna Carta and the Petition of Right 1628. The New Zealand Supreme Court recently invoked the 'principle of equality' (the need to treat like cases alike): *Ririnui v Landcorp Farming Ltd* [2016] NZSC 62 at [94]–[95], citing acceptance of such a principle as 'a general axiom of rational behaviour' by the Privy Council in *Matadeen v Pointu* [1999] 1 AC 98 at 109 (PC) per Lord Hoffmann, referring, in turn, to Professor Jowell's article 'Is Equality a Constitutional Principle?' (1994) *CLP* 1 at 12–14. The Supreme Court in *Ririnui* pointed to the explanation for the omission of a statement of equality in the New Zealand Bill of Rights Act given in the White Paper that preceded it that such a statement was unnecessary because the principle of equal treatment is part of the rule of law.

73 O Dixon, 'The Common Law as an Ultimate Constitutional Foundation' (speech to the Tenth Convention of the Law Council of Australia, Melbourne, 16 July 1957), printed in O Dixon, *Jesting Pilate and Other Papers and Addresses* (Sydney, Law Book Company, 1965) 203–213.

74 See *Pape v Commissioner of Taxation of the Commonwealth of Australia* [2009] HCA 23, (2009) 238 CLR 1 and *Williams v The Commonwealth of Australia* [2012] HCA 23, (2012) 248 CLR 155.

of power in the executive under the Australian constitution.[75] The High Court is not likely to do anything to undermine its work in protecting the judicial power of the Commonwealth and, under it, a single common law of Australia.[76] So the constitutional pull to unity is strong. The marked version of the separation of powers under which the judicial power is protected also, however, marks out a separate sphere for the executive power towards which traditionally there has been much deference to administrative choice. If the line between legality and merits cannot be maintained (and cases like *Li* will make it difficult to maintain) I do not think movement towards greater tolerance of administrative choice in interpretation and in application could be ruled out. This is, of course, highly speculative. However, it is not inconsistent with the strong sense of separation of powers in Australia and with the positioning of the administrative adjudication system within the executive.

In New Zealand and the United Kingdom, administrative law remains grounded in common law doctrine under the supervisory jurisdiction. Deference in matters of interpretation has not been the general tradition, although it is not unknown. Lord Denning thought that tribunals dealing with statutes such as the Supplementary Benefits Act 1966 should be given latitude to interpret the legislation in a 'broad reasonable way, according to the spirit and not to the letter'.[77] Such latitude has been expanded for decisions of the tribunals organised under the Tribunals, Courts and Enforcement Act 2007.[78] Any errors otherwise reviewable will be reviewed only if they fall within the criteria for second tier appeal. The legislation and its interpretation in this way is a point of divergence between UK and New Zealand law. Writing in 2009, the first chair of the Upper Tribunal, Lord Justice Carnwath, now a member of the Supreme Court, looked to the establishment of the new UK Supreme Court as an opportunity to 'develop the relationship' between administrative justice and general law.[79] He took the view that the over-riding concern of the court in any case not involving fundamental human rights is not to become involved in policy choices but to confine itself to ensuring that the decision complies with fairly undemanding standards of irrationality. Some recent decisions of the UK Supreme Court may move in that direction.[80] Whether, in the long run, however the development of a

[75] P Cane, 'Judicial Control of Administrative Interpretation in Australia and the United States' in H Wilberg and M Elliott (eds), *The Scope and Intensity of Substantive Review: Traversing Taggart's Rainbow* (Oxford, Hart, 2015) 224–33.

[76] The High Court is said by Cane to be 'gradually re-writing history by, for instance, renaming the prerogative writs as 'constitutional writs': Cane, ibid, at 234; referring to *Re Refugee Tribunal, ex parte Aala* [2000] HCA 57, (2004) 204 CLR 82 at [21] (Gaudron and Gummow JJ) at [138]–[139] (Kirby J).

[77] *In R v Preston Supplementary Benefits Appeal Tribunal, ex parte Moore* [1975] 1 WLR 624 at 631 (CA). See also *Cooke v Secretary of State for Social Security* [2001] EWCA Civ 734, [2002] 3 All ER 279 at [15]–[17], adopted in *R (Wiles) v Social Security Commissioners* [2010] EWCA Civ 258 at [53]–[55].

[78] The Upper Tribunal is the superior court of record presided over by the senior president, first of all Carnwath LJ. Members of the Court of Appeal are *ex officio* members who sit when a request has been made by the President. High Court judges are *ex officio* members. The Upper Tribunal has powers of judicial review in cases transferred (either by category or case by case) from the High Court.

[79] Lord Carnwath, 'Tribunal Justice—A New Start' [2009] *PL* 48 at 68.

[80] *R (Cart) v Upper Tribunal* [2011] UKSC 28, [2011] 3 WLR 107 and *R (Jones) v First-tier Tribunal (Social Entitlement Chamber)* [2013] UKSC 19, [2013] 2 WLR 1012. Compare *R (Keyu) v Secretary of State for Foreign and Commonwealth Affairs* [2015] UKSC 69, [2016] AC 1355.

mature distinct system of administrative law is helped or hindered by being positioned in the judicial branch remains to be seen.[81] It is not the vision Harry Arthurs urged for administrative law.

In Canada, my impression is that there is less anxiety about constitutional fundamentals. If so, that may go some way to explain the preparedness of the Supreme Court of Canada to countenance a marked degree of deference to administrative decision-makers, even in cases affecting Charter rights.[82] The other reason for the Canadian approach may be the example across the border. It would, however, be unwise to think that positions may not move around on this question of deference according to the subject matter and even the personnel on the Court, as some of the recent divisions in the Supreme Court may indicate.

The pull of legality is strong for courts. That can be seen even in the United States where from time to time the Supreme Court has been obliged to rein in appellate court preferences for interpretation being a judicial responsibility, especially when the jurisdiction of the decision-maker is in issue.[83] Most of us do not feel very deferential when it comes to interpretation.[84] The *Chevron* doctrine has an appeal in North America that Australia and New Zealand have largely resisted to date, although in Australia some more latitude seems to be accorded to inferior courts (at least on the basis that errors made by inferior courts will not normally constitute jurisdictional error).[85]

One of the problems with questions of interpretation is that they are judicial meat and drink. Although Justice Abella of Canada has said that she thinks very few questions of interpretation have only one right answer,[86] I am not sure many judges would agree. Once the exercise is completed and conviction is reached, anyone who has worked through to a conclusion is unlikely to believe there is a range of reasonable interpretations, even if—or perhaps especially if—their judicial colleagues take a different view.

I would have said until recently that it seems unlikely that in common law traditions, where authoritative interpretation of law is highly valued, the courts will cede the responsibility to say what the law is, except in very limited circumstances. But I am less certain today. It has become clear that the line between interpretation and application is not so much blurred as impossible in much administrative decision-making. There are questions of meaning which can be decided very narrowly by

[81] Although in general there seems to have been more deference accorded to judicial adjudication, I wonder whether that will prevail in the long run. I wonder whether it is by judicial adjudicators that we can expect a developed system of administrative law to develop which has space for values of administration or decision making which are different from those used by the courts.

[82] Discussed below at text to n 103 onwards.

[83] See, eg, *Commodity Futures Trading Commission v Schor* 478 US 833, 844–45 (1986).

[84] Generally, the courts cannot defer to the views of the Executive in matters of interpretation because to do so would be to abdicate their responsibility when adjudicating between the state and the private individual. Lord Denning, who was firmly of this view, thought that if the Executive was not happy with an interpretation, it should go to Parliament to have the law amended: *Royal College of Nursing v Department of Health and Social Security* [1981] AC 800, 806–07 (CA).

[85] *Craig v South Australia* (1995) 184 CLR 163.

[86] *Wilson v Atomic Energy of Canada Ltd* 2016 SCC 29 at [35].

reference to language and the context in which it is used. However, the dispersal of executive power under statutes which employ broad concepts means that much application of discretionary power entails interpretation. The effect of words very often cannot be ascertained except in relation to known or supposed facts (Stephen Sedley instances 'speech' in relation to 'flag-burning').[87] In such circumstances, meaning is always evaluative. And evaluation entails choice and therefore discretion.

Where the evaluation may properly be influenced by expertise possessed by an independent decision-maker then there is room for the courts to accept the interpretation preferred by the decision-maker, as long as it is reasonable.

VI. BASIS OF REVIEW FOR REASONABLENESS OF INTERPRETATION AND APPLICATION

Once it is accepted that interpretation and application are not able to be separated and that each entails evaluation, it is then difficult to maintain a strict separation between review for legality and merits. A conclusion that a decision is unreasonable is a conclusion about its merits. It is inevitably concerned with matters of weight and balancing, often of values that are not directly comparable.

The concept of reasonableness takes its colour from context. Supervisory jurisdiction accords respect to the primary decision-maker and observes any separation of powers between the judiciary and the Executive where a range of options is reasonably available. Where there are no such options, the courts insist on the correct outcome, as acknowledged in *Dunsmuir v New Brunswick* in Canada.[88] In others, where there is a range of reasonable options, the choice is left to the administrative decision-maker. But Lord Cooke was surely right to say in *Daly* that 'it may well be … that the law can never be satisfied in any administrative field merely by a finding that the decision under review is not capricious or absurd'.[89] That seems to me to be where the majority of the High Court of Australia have ended up in *Minister for Immigration and Citizenship v Li*.[90]

What is unreasonable or erroneous has to be explained by the supervising court. Since that cannot be done by assertion, the supervisory jurisdiction necessarily entails close attention to the decision and to the principles of law against which it

[87] S Sedley, 'Construct or Construe' [2012] 34(16) *Lond Rev Books* 19.

[88] *Dunsmuir v New Brunswick* 2008 SCC 9, [2008] 1 SCR 190 at [58]–[61]; see *Wilson v Atomic Energy of Canada* 2016 SCC 29 at [23] (Abella J).

[89] *R v Secretary of State for the Home Department, ex parte Daly* [2001] UKHL 26, [2001] 2 AC 532 at [32].

[90] *Minister for Immigration and Citizenship v Li* [2013] HCA 18, (2013) 249 CLR 332. Hayne, Kiefel and Bell JJ concluded at [68] that the standard of unreasonableness is not limited to 'an irrational, if not bizarre, decision—which is to say one that is so unreasonable that no reasonable person could have arrived at it'. French CJ at [30] preferred to stay with 'rationality', to avoid any connotation of merits review or opening for proportionality. Gageler J was at the more stringent end of the spectrum ('so unreasonable that no reasonable repository of the power could have so exercised [it]') but considered, at [108]–[110], that the standard for intervention was comparable to that for appellate correction of a discretionary decision.

is assessed (including values recognised by the legal order). Where rights or fundamental values of the legal system are affected, proportionality methodology is preferable because it provides a structured approach which confronts the need to avoid unnecessary infringement of rights (a duty imposed on the courts under the Human Rights Act 1998 and the New Zealand Bill of Rights Act 1990) and unnecessary infringement of important values of the common law (equality of treatment, avoidance of arbitrariness in use of public power, presumptions of freedom among them). Proportionality is superior methodology for supervising for reasonableness in cases where fundamental values are affected, rather than a standalone basis for judicial review applicable in human rights cases.

Because the jurisdiction is supervisory, it is necessarily deferential, to an extent inevitably determined by the context. That insight has been used in Canada to set standards for intervention by way of judicial review. Since adoption of an openly deferential approach[91] instead of the former categories justifying review for the merits according to a 'pragmatic and functional' test,[92] recalibration has been necessary on two occasions.

A recent decision of the Canadian Supreme Court indicates that, while there is not yet a majority for further change, further adjustment may be down the track. It was the shifts in standard of review that Chief Justice McLachlin used to illustrate her view that administrative law is 'a barbed and occluded thicket'.[93] The twists and turns have been well described by others[94] and do not need to be repeated by me at any length.

In 1979 the Supreme Court had allowed deference to a tribunal's interpretation of its home statute as long as there was no single correct interpretation and the interpretation adopted was not 'patently unreasonable'.[95] In *Baker* the Supreme Court endorsed a 'pragmatic and functional' approach to determine the standard of review, recognising three standards of review: patent unreasonableness, reasonableness *simpliciter*, and correctness.[96] In *Dunsmuir*, Justice Binnie criticised the former 'pragmatic and functional' analysis used to identify whether administrative action fell within one of the categories of review.[97] The majority in that case considered the phrase may have been misleading and preferred to describe the inquiry as 'standard of review analysis'.[98] Standard of review followed the level of deference accorded. The three standards were contracted to two: 'reasonableness' and 'correctness'.[99] It was envisaged that it would be unnecessary to consider standard of review first in cases where it was established by previous case law for the decision making in issue.

[91] In *Dunsmuir v New Brunswick* 2008 SCC 9, [2008] 1 SCR 190.
[92] Adopted in *Baker v Canada (Minister of Citizenship and Immigration)* [1999] 2 SCR 817.
[93] See above at n 55.
[94] See L Sossin, 'The Complexity of Coherence: Justice LeBel's Administrative Law' (2015) 70 *SCLR* (2d) 145.
[95] *CUPE Local 963 v New Brunswick Liquor Corporation* [1979] 2 SCR 227 at 237.
[96] *Baker v Canada (Minister of Citizenship and Immigration)* (1999) 2 SCR 817 at [55].
[97] *Dunsmuir v New Brunswick* 2008 SCC 9, [2008] 1 SCR 190.
[98] ibid, at [63].
[99] ibid, at [34].

In *Dunsmuir*, the Court explained its concept of deference as moving from a 'court centric conception of the rule of law' by acknowledging that 'courts do not have a monopoly on deciding all questions of law'.[100] The purpose of judicial review was said to be to ensure that decision-makers do not exercise authority they do not have. That required 'correctness' to be applied to 'true questions of jurisdiction or *vires*', questions of general law outside the adjudicator's specialised area of expertise and of 'central importance to the legal system as a whole', constitutional questions concerning division of powers, and questions concerning the respective jurisdiction of two or more tribunals.[101]

In *Doré v Barreau du Québec*,[102] the Court applied *Dunsmuir* and held reasonableness to be the correct standard of review even though the case concerned adjudication affecting human rights.[103] Such reasonableness inquiry would, in cases of human rights, entail consideration of whether the primary decision-maker had appropriately weighed the human rights by application of proportionality analysis. It may be noted that this approach departs from the direct human rights analysis applied by the courts in the United Kingdom where human rights are in issue.[104]

In Canada, there is now a presumption of deference which attaches both to application and interpretation, at least when tribunals are interpreting their own or related statutes. The extent of the Court's preparedness to defer in matters of interpretation is illustrated by the approach in *McLean v British Columbia (Securities Commission)* where a standard of reasonableness was applied to interpretation of a time limit instead of the standard of correctness usually applied to questions of jurisdiction.[105]

There may, however, be more ambivalence about Charter rights in application. In *Loyola High School v Quebec*,[106] a case concerning freedom of religion, three of the Judges did not join Justice Abella and the other Judges in the majority in applying *Doré's* administrative review approach (although with the expectation that the primary decision-maker would adopt a 'robust proportionality' assessment of reasonableness appropriate for rights)[107] but applied a standard of correctness as on

[100] ibid, at [30].

[101] ibid, at [58]–[61]. See P Daly, 'Dunsmuir's Flaws Exposed' (2012) 58 *McGill Law Journal* 483. *Dunsmuir* led to further refinements and some outcomes which may well have gone different ways: see *Alberta (Information and Privacy Commissioner) v Alberta Teachers' Association* 2011 SCC 61, [2011] 3 SCR 654 at [34]–[39].

[102] *Doré v Barreau du Québec* 2012 SCC 12, [2013] 1 SCR 395.

[103] In *Multani v Commission Scolaire Marguerite-Bourgeoys* 2006 SCC 6, [2006] 1 SCR 256 the Supreme Court, by majority, had itself applied *Oakes* proportionality analysis to a decision concerning *Charter* rights on the basis that the application of administrative law standards of review would diminish the fundamental rights and freedoms recognised by the *Charter*. In a concurrence, Abella and Deschamps JJ took the view that the case was one for application of administrative law principles on reasonableness review rather than the justificatory review of proportionality analysis. The minority view prevailed in the later case of *Doré*.

[104] As discussed below at n 112.

[105] *McLean v British Columbia (Securities Commission)* 2013 SCC 67, [2013] 3 SCR 895. David Mullan has commented of this case that the scope for jurisdictional error in any practical sense seems effectively eliminated: DJ Mullan, *Unresolved Issues on Standard of Review—An Update* (Canadian Institute for the Administration of Justice, 19 May 2014) 1–2.

[106] *Loyola High School v Quebec (Attorney General)* 2015 SCC 12, [2015] 1 SCR 613.

[107] ibid, at [3].

constitutional review,[108] perhaps because the case, unlike *Doré*, was not concerned with an adjudicative determination.[109]

In *Doré*, a case concerning a disciplinary professional body, the Court's supervision was directed at ensuring that the adjudicative body had given appropriate consideration to the rights in issue, applying proportionality analysis. The conclusion reached, however, was one that the Court treated as for the tribunal if within the range of what was reasonable. That can be contrasted with the approach taken in the United Kingdom in *Denbigh High School*[110] and *Miss Behavin'*[111] where the House of Lords held that it was for the reviewing Court to assess whether there had been breach of rights.[112]

If a balance affecting rights must be struck in application to individual circumstances by the decision-maker, it is hard not to feel a little uneasy about limitation of rights according to standards that have not been prescribed by law and by specialist bodies which may not have a sense of the whole. In such cases the prescription is in the application. The supervising court, itself bound to observe the rights and freedoms in what it does, may not properly avoid making its own determination of whether the objective is a proper one and the limitation is rationally connected with it and no more than is necessary to achieve the objective. It is not sufficient that the balance is within a range that could be said to be reasonable. The courts will consider the reasons given for the decision. Supervising the reasoning process is, however, an insufficient description of the function the courts fulfil in supervising for objective compliance with rights.[113] This is to express agreement with the approach taken by Lord Reed in *Bank Mellat* rather than that suggested by Lord Neuberger and Lord Dyson and the approach adopted by the Canadian Supreme Court in *Doré*.

Doré involved adjudication, the decision of a disciplinary tribunal reviewing the conduct of a lawyer; *Loyola* considered a Minister's exercise of discretion. It is not clear whether the Judges who preferred to make the *Charter* assessment directly in *Loyola* were drawing a distinction between adjudication and administrative discretion.

Where authority is conferred in broad terms, the court is more likely to take the view that there is a range of reasonable interpretative options in identifying the

[108] ibid, at [88].

[109] Walters sees the minority judgment as the Judges having 'retreated back across the frontier into the field of constitutional law in cases dealing with administrative discretion and fundamental rights, for reasons that they have, so far, kept to themselves': M Walters, 'Respecting Deference as Respect: Rights, Reasonableness and Proportionality in Canadian Administrative Law' in H Wilberg and M Elliott (eds), *The Scope and Intensity of Substantive Review: Traversing Taggart's Rainbow* (Oxford, Hart, 2015) 422.

[110] *R (Begum) v Denbigh High School Governors* [2006] UKHL 15, [2007] 1 AC 100.

[111] *Belfast City Council v Miss Behavin' Ltd* [2007] UKHL 19, [2007] 1 WLR 1420.

[112] But see *Regina (Lord Carlile of Berriew and others) v Secretary of State for the Home Department* [2014] UKSC 60, [2015] AC 945. Although the Supreme Court continued to take the view that in cases where human rights are affected a court must undertake a proportionality assessment, it was careful to point out that an administrator's decision which is neither irrational nor displays errors of fact or principle must be given due weight. See at [49] (Lord Sumption), [67]–[68] and [80] (Lord Neuberger); and at [98] (Baroness Hale); and compare with the reasons of Lord Clarke at [115] and Lord Kerr at [158].

[113] See P Craig, 'The Nature of Reasonableness Review' (2013) 66 *CLP* 131.

factors to take into account when making a broadly evaluative decision.[114] The matter is then treated in Canada less as one of interpretation and more as one of discretion. *Katz Group Canada Inc v Ontario (Health and Long-Term Care)* concerned whether regulations were within the scope of the empowering legislation.[115] Justice Abella held that if the regulations were consistent with the purposes of the legislation, it was not for the Court to consider whether they would meet their objectives or whether they were over or under-inclusive or 'necessary, wise or effective in practice'.[116] Only where objectives were 'irrelevant' or 'completely unrelated' to the statutory purpose would judicial review lie for wrongful purpose.[117]

In the latest twist, *Wilson v Atomic Energy of Canada*,[118] Justice Abella, who wrote the decisive opinion in *Doré*,[119] indicated that further change was necessary. She took the opportunity, in obiter, to spell out her vision of judicial review of administrative determinations, including interpretation. Four Judges who concurred in the result that judicial review was not warranted on the accepted standard of reasonableness preferred not to express agreement with the suggestions made by Justice Abella for further change 'at this time'.[120] The fourth concurring Judge, Justice Cromwell, said that there was no occasion for 'yet another overhaul' of the standard of judicial review and that while *Dunsmuir* might continue to be further refined, the 'basic *Dunsmuir* framework' was sound.[121] While accepting the reasonableness 'takes its colour from context', Justice Cromwell expressed concern, however, about the approach taken by the Federal Court of Appeal in developing 'new and apparently unlimited numbers of gradations of reasonableness review'. That, he thought, was not 'an appropriate development of the standard of review jurisprudence'.[122]

The Judges in the minority, Moldaver, Côté, and Brown JJ, would have applied a correctness review to what they thought to be a 'narrow and distilled legal issue'.[123] In their opinion, the case exposed the risks for the rule of law in 'presumptively

[114] In *Agraira v Canada (Public Safety and Emergency Preparedness)* 2013 SCC 36, [2013] 2 SCR 559 it was held that the Minister had considerable latitude in interpreting a statutory provision requiring decisions to be made in the 'national interest'.

[115] *Katz Group Canada Inc v Ontario (Health and Long-term Care)* 2013 SCC 64, [2013] 3 SCR 810.

[116] ibid, at [27]–[28].

[117] As David Mullan notes, effectively regulations have a presumption of validity: DJ Mullan, *Unresolved Issues on Standard of Review—An Update* (Canadian Institute for the Administration of Justice, 19 May 2014) 4.

[118] *Wilson v Atomic Energy of Canada* 2016 SCC 29. In *Wilson*, a labour adjudicator interpreted the Labour Code as preventing dismissal of an employee without cause, even though generous severance pay was provided. The adjudicator upheld the complaint that the dismissal was without cause and thereby was unjust. On appeal, the Judge found the decision to be unreasonable because he interpreted the Code as providing no impediment to dismissal without cause. The Federal Court of Appeal dismissed an appeal, but on the basis that the interpretation was wrong, applying a correctness standard to the question of interpretation, rather than assessing the interpretation adopted by the adjudicator for reasonableness.

[119] And had earlier joined the view in *Multani v Commission scolaire Marguerite-Bourgeoys* 2006 SCC 6, [2006] 1 SCR 256 that administrative law principles rather than constitutional review should be used.

[120] *Wilson v Atomic Energy of Canada* 2016 SCC 29 at [70] (McLachlin CJ, Karakatsanis, Wagner and Gascon JJ).

[121] *Wilson v Atomic Energy of Canada* 2016 SCC 29 at [72]–[73].

[122] ibid, at [73].

[123] ibid, at [76].

deferential review of a decision-maker's interpretation of its home statute'.[124] They pointed out that the lower courts had taken opposite views of reasonableness. 'Rule of law values' should not, they thought, be abandoned 'in favour of indiscriminate deference to the administrative state'. They were concerned, too, at the possibility of different interpretations in the law which 'go to the heart of the federal employment law regime'.

It would be rash to think that this latest word is the last word. The ideas that Justice Abella floated, to start a 'conversation',[125] revert to some of the basics about administrative law raised in the piece by Arthurs.[126] Justice Abella thought that cases where only one reasonable outcome was available were likely to be 'rare' and largely confined to the categories identified in *Dunsmuir* as attracting a correctness standard.[127] She considered the standard of review adopted in *Dunsmuir* should be further refined by accepting that unreasonableness review is a single standard which, in context, may admit only one correct answer.

Justice Abella thought that the extent to which lower courts were grappling with standard of review was 'insupportable' and that the hoped-for simplicity of the *Dunsmuir* two standards (collapsing 'patent unreasonableness' with 'reasonableness simpliciter') had 'not proven to be the runway to simplicity'.[128] It was incumbent on the court to consider 'whether this obstacle course is necessary or whether there is a principled way to simplify the path to reviewing the merits'. She suggested that much of the confusion had arisen over 'what to call the category of review in a particular case' and questioned whether it was necessary to engage in such 'rhetorical debates about what to call our conclusions at the end of the review':[129]

> Are we not saying essentially the same thing when we conclude that there is only a single 'reasonable' answer available and when we say it is 'correct'? This leads to whether we need two different names for our approaches to judicial review or whether both approaches can live comfortably under a more broadly conceived understanding of reasonableness.

It is possible to see in Canada a more pluralist approach which steers by the 'functionalist' view of the competence of the reviewing court. It is now shorn of a 'categorical' testing to establish the degree of deference to be accorded. It is simplified into two standards of review, although with a presumption of deference. The presumption is displaced where deference is not appropriate because the case involves fundamental values of the legal order or principles of general application throughout the legal system or where there is only one correct answer. Such assessment is inevitably highly contextual.

There may be something in the criticism that the New Zealand courts have tended to be light on doctrine and that our administrative law jurisprudence is

[124] ibid, at [79]–[91].
[125] ibid, at [19].
[126] HW Arthurs, 'Rethinking Administrative Law: A Slightly Dicey Business' (1979) 17 *Osgoode Hall LJ* 1.
[127] *Wilson v Atomic Energy of Canada* 2016 SCC 29 at [35]–[36].
[128] ibid, at [20]–[24].
[129] ibid, at [24].

underdeveloped.[130] But I wonder whether the inescapably contextual assessment of when to intervene by way of judicial review is greatly assisted by attempting to articulate standards of review. Reasonableness may be 'a single standard', as the Supreme Court of Canada now says, but if it 'takes its colour from context' as the Court also accepts[131] how useful is it to strain to identify standards of review?

VII. CONCLUSION

Ambivalence about the relationship between constitutional law and administrative law, shown by Sir Michael Myers in New Zealand in 1940, has never been entirely shaken off by judges and legal practitioners. Although a number of thoughtful administrative lawyers resist the pull to 'constitutionalisation' of administrative law,[132] judicial review strikes me as inevitably located in that space. It is concerned with the rule of law values which underpin the constitution in any law-state and which provide coherence to the legal order which it is for the superior courts to supervise, whether they operate under a constitutional instrument which shares power or under an unmodified Westminster system. Where rule of law concerns end, the supervisory jurisdiction ends too. That may well not satisfy good government values which are a proper end of administrative justice. Their promotion is best served by institutions with freedom to act without further court supervision than the requirements that they act lawfully, reasonably and fairly.

Perhaps we have loaded too much into the supervisory jurisdiction which could be better addressed in a distinct (but supervised) administrative justice system. The challenge for administrative law remains to develop within the scope left for it by constitutional law. In a developed system of administrative law perhaps more respect for administrative choices in interpretation and application of enacted rules is better policy for supervising courts. But we have to be careful not to throw the baby out with the bathwater. It is surely time to move on from always beating up courts about their constitutional obligation to ensure that constitutional balances and values, including rights, are observed and not sacrificed to expediency.

We have had enough experience to know that we can expect successive waves in which growth of discretion gives rise to anxiety about the rule of law. So we cannot expect this area of law to stand still. And although I acknowledge with gratitude the illumination provided by good scholarship in this area, of which there is much, is

[130] C Geiringer, 'Process and Outcome in Judicial Review of Public Authority Compatibility with Human Rights: A Comparative Perspective' in H Wilberg and M Elliott (eds), *The Scope and Intensity of Substantive Review: Traversing Taggart's Rainbow* (Oxford, Hart, 2015) 357–58.

[131] *Canada (Citizenship and Immigration) v Khosa* 2009 SCC 12, [2009] 1 SCR 339 at [59]; *Catalyst Paper Corp v North Cowichan (District)* 2012 SCC 2, [2012] 1 SCR 5 at [18]; as cited by Abella J at [22] and Cromwell J at [73] in *Wilson v Atomic Energy of Canada* 2016 SCC 29.

[132] See I Hare, 'The Separation of Powers and Judicial Review for Error of Law' in C Forsyth and I Hare (eds), *The Golden Metwand and the Crooked Cord: Essays on Public Law in Honour of Sir William Wade QC* (Oxford, Clarendon Press, 1998) and JNE Varuhas, 'Against Unification' in H Wilberg and M Elliott (eds), *The Scope and Intensity of Substantive Review: Traversing Taggart's Rainbow* (Oxford, Hart, 2015) 91.

the search for better doctrine ultimately doomed? I do not suggest that the effort is not worthwhile. It keeps everyone up to the mark. But I wonder how much can be expected of overarching theories. Public law has unity and disparity and much of it is untidy and tentative.

Let me end with some views expressed by Sir David Williams, which are on point. Sir David said that the principles of administrative law 'can sensibly be considered only with proper regard for the statutory, institutional and broader social or policy context of a particular case'.[133] And he thought that, in the long term, the courts 'would help in the development of a more ordered legal system if they insisted on clear authority where clear authority is needed ... and if they intervened where intervention is constitutionally desirable'.[134]

[133] DGT Williams, 'Criminal Law and Administrative Law: Problems of Procedure and Reasonableness' in P Smith (ed), *Criminal Law: Essays in Honour of JC Smith* (London, Butterworths, 1987) 171.
[134] ibid, at 168.

Part 1

Doctrinal and Theoretical Perspectives

3

Taxonomy and Public Law

JASON NE VARUHAS[1]

Without good taxonomy and a vigorous taxonomic debate the law loses its rational integrity ... some forms of thought and language ... make legal taxonomy almost impossible and thus undermine the law's rationality. All forms of appeal to very broad ideas tend to allow intuition to operate unrestrained by an analysis anchored in authority. Every fundamentalist believes his values make for the public good, and the more zealous he is the less he will be able to bear in mind the possibility that he may be mistaken ... It is essential to come to the law armed with a belief in the fallibility of intuition and a consequent aversion to all forms of thought and expression which are no more than vehicles of the gut reaction. Interpreters must consent to be prisoners of their own expertise.

P Birks, 'Equity in the Modern Law: An Exercise in Taxonomy' (1996) 26 *University of Western Australia Law Review* 1, 22.

I. INTRODUCTION

THIS CHAPTER TAKES the first steps towards developing a legal taxonomy of public law fields, systematically identifying, mapping and explaining different categories of law that are typically identified with English public law. Legal categorisation is fundamental to full understanding of the law, rigorous and complete legal analysis and coherent and rational legal development. Yet legal taxonomy and debates over legal categorisation have not been a significant feature of public law scholarship, in contrast to contemporary private law scholarship. This chapter begins by exploring the reasons for this general absence of work in legal categorisation including that the very notion of public law was long unknown to English law and is steeped in theoretical disagreement, that modern legal taxonomers have followed their Roman forebears in focusing on private law, and contemporary trends in legal scholarship away from doctrinal work, and particularly doctrinal scholarship that looks across different fields of law. The chapter goes on to argue that legal categorisation is of fundamental importance, especially

[1] I am grateful to Mark Aronson, Nick McBride, Donal Nolan, Andrew Robertson, and Julian Sempill for comments. Earlier drafts were presented at the second biennial Public Law Conference, 'The Unity of Public Law?', 12–14 September 2016, University of Cambridge, and at a meeting of the Legal Theory Workshop at Melbourne Law School in April 2017. I am grateful to participants at both events for stimulating discussions. The usual disclaimer applies.

in the light of emergent trends towards open-ended balancing in public law adjudication. Legal categorisation enhances our understanding of the law, and facilitates right answers to legal questions, maintenance of a rationally ordered system of law and coherent legal development. Legal taxonomy promotes formal rule of law principles whereas approaches that eschew categorisation, such as open-ended case-by-case balancing, are likely to radically undermine those principles and imperil the coherence and stability of the legal system. Legal scholars are uniquely well-placed to undertake analytical doctrinal work, including legal taxonomy, and such work therefore offers an important avenue for legal scholars to make a distinctive contribution to knowledge, and the legal system.

The chapter takes the first steps towards developing a map of different fields. The taxonomy does not take the division between public law and private law as its starting point, placing no normative weight on that putative divide. Rather, it seeks to simply categorise different fields of law, often associated with the label 'public law', according to their primary functions. In order to illustrate the taxonomic method, and to begin the process of legal categorisation, the chapter identifies and explains two distinct categories: (1) the law relating to the regulation of public power in the public interest; (2) the law relating to protection and vindication of basic individual rights. These different fields each perform discrete and distinctly valuable functions. Different rules, principles, concepts and methods characterise each field, these differences being explicable and normatively justified by reference to the different functions that each performs. Having taken the first steps towards legal categorisation the chapter proceeds to demonstrate how identification of discrete fields has a bearing on analysis of contemporary legal issues, examining the question of whether the proportionality method developed in human rights law ought to be read across to the common law of judicial review. The chapter concludes that without good legal taxonomy and vigorous taxonomic debate, rigorous legal analysis and coherent legal development may be impossible.

II. REASONS FOR THE GENERAL ABSENCE OF LEGAL TAXONOMY IN PUBLIC LAW SCHOLARSHIP

While much important work in taxonomy has been done in English private law over the last 30 or so years, in significant part due to the pioneering efforts of the late Professor Peter Birks, little fine-grained work in doctrinal categorisation has been undertaken in English public law. My claim here is not that public lawyers do not engage in legal classification. Public lawyers, in common with lawyers in general (and all human beings), constantly are and must necessarily be engaged in reasoning and thinking that is classificatory in nature. Such categorisations invariably form core but often unarticulated premises of claims and arguments made about public law.[2]

[2] As Jolowicz and Fairest observe, 'problems of classification [are] continually present, even though often unrecognised as such, at all stages of legal research and law reform' (JA Jolowicz and PB Fairest, 'Summary of Discussion' in JA Jolowicz (ed), *The Division and Classification of the Law* (London, Butterworths, 1970) 90.

My contention is that public lawyers have in general not, in the way that private lawyers have, self-consciously and deliberately engaged in systematic scholarly inquiry into and debate over the proper classification of public law fields. Why might this be? I suggest several reasons which may go some way towards explaining the general absence of public law scholarship on legal categorisation.

A. Absence of, and Debates Over, Public Law

The first is the comparatively recent development and recognition of major fields of English public law, and indeed of public law as a discrete subject for scholarly inquiry.

For most of English legal history a recognised field of 'public law' was unknown, as was a recognised field of 'private law'. Rather than being ordered around such concepts the legal system was historically organised around disparate writs or forms of action, with remedies issuing in response to a given pattern of facts. However, one important difference between the development of public law and private law is that fields of law that are today associated with the label of private law, such as contract and tort, came to be recognised as discrete categories of law during the eighteenth and nineteenth centuries. This followed from the break-down of the boundaries of the forms of action, the increasing need for judges (as opposed to juries) to decide matters for themselves, and importantly the emergence of scholarly treatises on contract and torts which identified and sought to systemise these bodies of doctrine.[3] As broad outlines of discrete categories of law emerged, their anatomies could be interrogated, as could the boundaries of and interconnections between these fields.[4] In contrast, major fields of what we now describe as public law such as the law under the HRA simply did not exist. Recognition of a field of administrative law was very late in coming. Whereas tort and contract emerged as recognised categories from the eighteenth century, administrative law only found acceptance as a recognised field in the second half of the twentieth century.[5] Even in this later time period the inclusion of administrative law as a standalone subject in law degrees and professional courses was slow in coming.[6] While scholarship on administrative law emerged during the first half of the twentieth century, the principal focus was on debating whether such a field existed and/or ought to be recognised, while there was no practitioner treatise

[3] See, eg, DJ Ibbetson, *An Historical Introduction to the Law of Obligations* (Oxford, Oxford University Press, 1999) Part Three; M Lobban, 'Contract' and 'Tort' in W Cornish et al, *The Oxford History of the Laws of England, Volume XII: 1820–1914 Private Law* (Oxford, Oxford University Press, 2010).

[4] For example, of the recognition of the law of contract as a discrete field of law from the end of the late eighteenth century, Waddams observes: 'The demarcation of contract law from other bases of obligation had far-reaching implications, including a division between property and obligation, and divisions among different classes of obligation. It also implied that the contract law of a particular legal system was a manifestation of a universal order, with which, therefore, it might be critically contrasted and compared' (S Waddams, *Dimensions of Private Law: Categories and Concepts in Anglo-American Legal Reasoning* (Cambridge, Cambridge University Press, 2003) 7).

[5] HWR Wade, 'Crossroads in Administrative Law' (1968) 76 *CLP* 75 at 78, 85–86.

[6] SA De Smith, *The Lawyers and the Constitution* (London, G Bell and Sons, 1960) 18–19.

on 'administrative law' or 'public law'.[7] If the field was not recognised it could not be mapped, its internal structure interrogated etc. Not only was administrative law not recognised, but there was deep-seated normative opposition towards the idea of a special field of rules to regulate government action, especially among judges and practitioners: 'Our English law does not allow a public officer to shelter behind a droit administratif'.[8] From the late nineteenth century onwards this resistance to the idea of a separate body of administrative law or public law rules owed much to the strong and lasting influence of Dicey's rule-of-law principle of equality, which held that officials should be subject to the same ordinary law as everyone else, administered by the ordinary courts. Administrative law and public law more generally were viewed as foreign concepts, associated with continental jurisdictions, which would lead to special exemptions for public authorities, imperiling liberty. Administrative law was 'an exotic brand of un-English anti-law'[9] or alternatively, 'an almost unqualified evil'.[10]

That English law did not recognise a field or fields of public law does not mean that officials were free from legal regulation. For example, actions in tort have long performed an important role in constraining the power of public officials, vindicating rule-of-law principles of equality and government under law, defining our most basic rights, defining the position of the Crown and public officials and providing remedies for those who suffered damage or loss through official abuses of power. But that the law of torts, a field of private law which (in principle) applies equally to individuals, performs these functions, and was—and remains—one of the most significant fields of law to regulate official action, in itself illustrates the serious difficulties in identifying a discrete field of public law, separate from private law. In an important sense private law was public law.

One might point to the prerogative writs as representing a discrete field of administrative or public law. But while the writs operated as a control on public power they were not generally recognised, collectively, as comprising a discrete field of public or administrative law until at least the middle of the twentieth century. Rather things might be seen the other way around: 'the absence in the common-law systems of a distinct body of public law, whereby proceedings against public authorities are instituted only before special administrative courts and are governed by a special

[7] See Wade (n 5) at 86 (noting that the second and last edition of Short and Mellor—notably not a treatise on 'administrative law' or 'public law'—had been published in 1908: FH Short and FM Mellor, *The Practice on the Crown Side of the King's Bench Division* 2nd edn (London, Stevens and Haynes, 1908)).

[8] *Ministry of Housing and Local Government v Sharp* [1970] 2 QB 223 at 266; *Re Grosvenor Hotel Ltd (No 2)* [1965] Ch 1210 at 1261; Wade (n 5) 79, 84–86 ('One feels that the profession still cherishes the fallacy—derived chiefly from Oxford, I regret to say—that administrative law is fundamentally inconsistent with classical constitutional doctrine'). For an example of deep-seated judicial scepticism see Lord Hewart, *The New Despotism* (London, Benn, 1929). Robson suggests that Hewart's hostility 'represented 99 per cent of the opinion then held by the bench, the bar, and the solicitor's branch of the profession' (WA Robson, *Justice and Administrative Law* 2nd edn (London, Stevens, 1947) 316). For a more nuanced practitioner perspective see: CT Carr, *Concerning English Administrative Law* (New York, Columbia University Press, 1941).

[9] See De Smith, *The Lawyers and the Constitution* (n 6) at 23.

[10] PHW, 'Review of CT Carr, *Concerning English Administrative Law*' (1943) 8 *CLJ* 220 at 220.

body of rules, is directly traceable to the extensive use of the prerogative writs by the Court of King's Bench'.[11] Further, as Oliver has argued, the prerogative writs were not historically specifically conceptualised as a means of controlling government or public administration.[12] Rather, as De Smith put it, the writs were adapted to this purpose.[13] A writ such as certiorari traditionally ran to control decisions of courts or court-like bodies, and did not extend to purely 'ministerial' or administrative decisions (albeit a broad conception of 'judicial' functions was adopted over time). This focus on judicial functions and associated concepts such as jurisdiction inhibited the writ's efficacy in controlling administrative action into the twentieth century.[14] Mandamus had a distinctly 'private' character in that it principally issued to compel performance of a duty to which the applicant had a specific legal right (though broader applications can be found), early on operating as a 'writ of restitution' to restore an office-holder to an office of which they had been wrongly deprived. Indeed a centralised government administration was late in developing in England, which in turn was one reason for the non-admission of the idea of a distinct body of rules dedicated to regulating 'government'.

Moreover, while there was presumed to be a relationship between the writs—thus the collective label 'prerogative writs'—the nature of the relationship 'was not defined'.[15] The prerogative remedies were spread across disparate procedures, each developing 'piecemeal', so that it was 'virtually impossible' to find a definition that would meaningfully link them.[16] In this regard it is worth recalling that the prerogative writs survived abolition of the forms of action in the nineteenth century, being governed by discrete procedures up until the late 1970s.[17] Further, what we would now describe as judicial review cases were not analysed as if they formed a corpus of doctrine, a single field of law concerning control of government, but rather streams of cases were identified and analysed on the basis of the subject matter they addressed, such as railways or corporations.[18] This lack of 'joined-up' thinking about the control of public power continued into the twentieth century, as recorded by Wade and De Smith, among others.[19] This varied legal development militated against the emergence of a unifying idea of public law and a recognised field or system of public or administrative law, based in a common set of normative concerns.

Thus, the combination of an historical absence of recognised fields of public law and non-admittance of an organising idea of public law, Dicey's influence and the fragmented nature of the prerogative writs, among other factors, meant that up until at least the Second World War 'the subject [of administrative law] could barely be

[11] SA De Smith, 'The Prerogative Writs' (1951) 11 *CLJ* 40 at 48.

[12] D Oliver, 'Public Law Procedures and Remedies—Do We Need Them?' [2002] *PL* 91 at 100–105.

[13] SA De Smith, 'Wrongs and Remedies in Administrative Law' (1952) 15 *MLR* 189 at 206.

[14] ibid, at 206–07.

[15] See De Smith, 'Prerogative Writs' (n 11) at 56.

[16] ibid.

[17] Note, however, that the procedures were simplified by the Administration of Justice (Miscellaneous Provisions) Act 1938.

[18] S Anderson, 'Judicial Review' in W Cornish et al, *The Oxford History of the Laws of England, Volume XI: 1820–1914 English Legal System* (Oxford, Oxford University Press, 2010) 486.

[19] De Smith, 'Wrongs and Remedies' (n 13) at 189; Wade (n 5) at 78, 85–86.

said to exist, except as a raw mass of cases'.[20] Indeed, through the 1960s and 1970s, courts and commentators were still observing the absence of a fully fledged system of English administrative or public law.[21]

With the establishment of a unified procedure for seeking the prerogative orders in the late 1970s, judges began to reason by reference to an idea of public law and to seek to construct a system of public law, that is an integrated body of procedural and substantive law rendered coherent by a set of unifying normative concerns.[22] The increased focus on the idea of public law, however, did not necessarily serve to clarify the nature and bounds of public law. Exploration of the idea threw up both competing accounts of public law and its boundaries and competing views on whether a distinctive field of public law even existed. In part, this reflected the Diceyan 'baggage' that went with the idea of a separate body of law to govern officials, as well as the difficulty in identifying a discrete field of public law in a system in which private law applied equally to citizens and officials alike. Thus, if the impediment to mapping public law in earlier times had been that there was no recognised field to map, from the 1980s 'public law' could not form the starting point for an exercise in categorisation because the nature and scope of 'public law' were steeped in theoretical disagreement and uncertainty.[23] Further, emergent scholarship militated against an inquiry into distinct sub-fields in another way. These accounts generally sought to identify monistic explanations or models of public law, which in turn prompted debates among protagonists of different monistic models. The terms of the debate thus excluded—or at least did not encourage—inquiry into the possibility that public law was not a monolith but a loose collection of different fields each characterised by discrete functions. We also see these modes of thinking in judicial decision making. For example, in the early 1980s, senior judges began to refer to 'public law' as though that label denoted a field unified by common characteristics. This, in turn, discouraged thinking in terms of discrete categories and encouraged debate over this unitary idea.[24]

Importantly, just as judges and scholars began to explore the idea of public law in more detail, the brave new world of privatisation, contracting-out and marketised public services was emerging, which posed and continues to pose difficult questions, in particular over the bounds or scope of the field of public law. Thus, Milsom, in considering whether it would be possible to produce a modern equivalent of Blackstone's organisational scheme,[25] considered 'the most intractable difficulty

[20] P Birks, *An Introduction to the Law of Restitution* (Oxford, Clarendon Press, 1985) 2–3.

[21] See, for example, *Ridge v Baldwin* [1964] AC 40 at 72; JDB Mitchell, 'The Causes and Effects of the Absence of a System of Public Law in the United Kingdom' [1965] *PL* 95; Lord Diplock, 'Administrative Law: Judicial Review Reviewed' [1974] *CLJ* 233 at 245.

[22] See JNE Varuhas, 'The Public Interest Conception of Public Law: Its Procedural Origins and Substantive Implications' in J Bell et al (eds), *Public Law Adjudication in Common Law Systems* (Oxford, Hart, 2016).

[23] Offering similar reasons to explain why the history of administrative law has not been written see: M Loughlin, 'Why the History of English Administrative Law is Not Written' in D Dyzenhaus et al (eds), *A Simple Common Lawyer* (Oxford, Hart, 2008).

[24] See Varuhas, 'Public Interest Conception' (n 22).

[25] SFC Milsom, 'The Nature of Blackstone's Achievement' (1981) 1 *OJLS* 1 at 3. It is worth noting that Blackstone's scheme included a division between public and private *wrongs* but did not include a division between public and private *law*.

would be that a mixed economy has generated two intersecting systems'. If the two systems—to the extent there ever were two distinct systems—are increasingly intermingled, it is difficult to take 'public law' as a starting point for an exercise in legal categorisation.

B. Romans

Second, the focus on private law in prominent modern taxonomies is unsurprising as they are rooted in and draw heavily upon the Institutes of Gaius and Justinian, which focused squarely on private law. Similarly the nineteenth century German 'legal scientists', who produced systematic treatises which have been influential within the civil law world, focused principally on private law, specifically that part equivalent to the Roman civil law, which they saw as being the 'heart' of the legal system.[26] However, it is important to note that, as will be discussed further below, the convincingness of drawing heavily upon the Roman schemes in a common law jurisdiction is questionable given the starting point within those taxonomies is the division between public law (*ius publicum*) and private law (*ius privatum*), yet there is no such clear division in common law systems.

C. Flight from Doctrine and Other Trends in Legal Scholarship

Third, more generally there has arguably been flight from doctrinal and associated analytical legal methods in public law scholarship. This helps to explain the absence of taxonomic scholarship as doctrinal scholars, particularly those with a deep understanding of the full scope of public law doctrine are those best equipped and most likely to be interested in developing a taxonomy of public law fields.

An important reason for the decline in analytical doctrinal work is that doctrinal methods must compete for attention with an increasing range of other methods. In public law there is an increasing focus on empirical methods, and 'law in context' approaches, which seek to understand the law in the light of the administrative and political context in which it operates. Public lawyers have expanded their remit, investigating the work of bodies other than courts, such as the Ombudsman, public inquiries, tribunals and government agencies, while in respect of courts there has been an institutional turn, with academics increasingly studying courts as an institution as opposed to studying legal doctrine. Of course many of these phenomena link into but also mark an expansion of a longstanding functionalist tradition in English public law characterised by empiricist and contextual methods.[27]

[26] JH Merryman and R Perez-Perdomo, *The Civil Law Tradition* 3rd edn (Stanford CA, Stanford University Press, 2007) 62, 65.

[27] C Harlow and R Rawlings, *Law and Administration* 2nd edn (Cambridge, Cambridge University Press, 1997) ch 3; M Loughlin, 'The Functionalist Style in Public Law' (2005) 55 *UTLJ* 361; *Public Law and Political Theory* (Oxford, Oxford University Press, 1992).

There has also been a flight to high theory and the search for One Big Idea in public law. Such theoretical work does not generally involve detailed analysis of doctrine nor typically offer (or indeed purport to offer) answers to concrete doctrinal questions.

This flight to other methods contrasts with scholarly trends in private law. As Burrows has observed, in general English private law scholarship remains focused on doctrine.[28] Albeit the association of private law with doctrinal scholarship has, in Burrows' opinion, led to fewer academics being attracted to private law, as alternative methods associated with other fields, including public law, are seen as more attractive.[29] So perhaps private law has maintained its doctrinal focus in part because those attracted to other methods self-select out of private law scholarship. But there are further factors, not present in the public law domain, which may shed greater light on the reasons why private law scholarship continues to focus on doctrine. One reason why the doctrinal focus remains may be because leading English private lawyers, having glimpsed the move to 'law and' methods in the United States and high Kantian philosophy in Canada, made a concerted effort to invigorate and demonstrate the value of methods which engage with doctrine on its own terms. Taxonomy was at the core of this response. Birks, who engaged in a programme of work on legal taxonomy which had a powerful and lasting influence on private law scholarship, explicitly argued for the reassertion of 'legal science' to counter the rise of the 'realists and the fundamentalists of the school of critical legal studies', whose influence on legal coherence Birks did not view favourably.[30] More recently Burrows has engaged in a programme of work to produce restatements of fields of private law, in part driven by a concern to stimulate interest in and reinforce the merits of doctrinal private law scholarship.[31]

Another important reason why the doctrinal tradition continues to dominate in English private law is because there is a healthy market demand for doctrinal scholars and scholarship in practice areas such as commercial equity and contract, insurance and product liability. In contrast there are comparatively fewer opportunities for academics for paid consultancy in public law practice areas such as prison or welfare law, and what opportunities there are will invariably be less well paid than offering advice on multi-million pound litigation between big corporate players. These market dynamics operate to keep private law scholarship grounded in legal practice.

Perhaps the most important reason for the lack of serious doctrinal scholarship in public law relative to private law, however, is the view that public law is in some way exceptional. In particular that it is simply an extension of politics, not being a

[28] A Burrows, 'Challenges for Private Law in the Twenty-First Century' in K Barker et al (eds), *Private Law in the 21st Century* (Oxford, Hart, 2017) 32ff.

[29] ibid, at 34–35. Of course, as Burrows also observes, in the last half-century we have seen a proliferation of new fields of law, including fields of public law and fields based in statute, so that private law must compete for attention with an array of newer fields, notwithstanding the methods that characterise these fields.

[30] P Birks, 'Equity in the Modern Law: An Exercise in Taxonomy' (1996) 26 *University of Western Australia Law Review* 1 at 3–4.

[31] See Burrows (n 28) at 45. See A Burrows, *A Restatement of the English Law of Contract* (Oxford, Oxford University Press, 2016); *A Restatement of the English Law of Unjust Enrichment* (Oxford, Oxford University Press, 2012).

field sensibly analysed or capable of analysis through orthodox doctrinal analytical methods and techniques. But unless one adopts the radical view that public law is not law at all—which would throw up a host of issues (eg why should courts hear claims based in public law norms and grant coercive remedies for breach if these are not legal norms?)—then it is hard to see how one could sustain the argument that analytical legal methods are not applicable or important in public law. It is particularly difficult to sustain this argument for exceptionalism in a jurisdiction that has not known a distinctive idea or recognised field of public law, and in which the same *ordinary* law, administered by *ordinary* courts, applies equally, in principle, to citizens and officials alike. Attempts to demonstrate and explain the exceptionalism of public law are tied up in longstanding disagreement, and as far as such theories purport to explain English public law as it in fact exists, they have largely failed.[32]

Other trends in public law scholarship do not necessarily militate against doctrinal work but rather against a particular type of doctrinal work, that is doctrinal work that seeks to look across the entire field of public law (or at least fields of public law). Academics increasingly focus their attentions on blogging, tweeting or otherwise commenting on current affairs, and this is especially so in public law. This may have important impacts on doctrinal work. It may leave less time for more traditional forms of scholarship. These phenomena may have the effect of encouraging 'event-based' thinking and commentary, the focus being on particular developments, such as a recent important case or political event, rather than systematic consideration of an entire field or fields of doctrine. Of course, this is not invariable. For example, analysis of a particular event may serve as a prompt for further reflection and refinement of one's wider understanding of fields of law.

More generally, there has been an increasing tendency to focus on particular fields, such as human rights law, the law of the ombudsman, immigration law or the law of public procurement or particular topics such as legitimate expectations, deference, proportionality, dialogue, rights-consistent interpretation, so on and so forth. This increasing specialisation arguably has been encouraged by, but is by no means a necessary consequence of, legal academics increasingly having completed in-depth doctoral research on specific topics, this focus then shaping their future research agenda. Specialisation has also been encouraged by the incredible expansion of public law itself coupled with a concomitant increase in the amount and type of commentary, which in turn may make it more difficult to keep abreast of developments across the entire field. Linked to this are changes in the sources of law considered by public lawyers; for example if one wishes to be expert in human rights law one must not only follow the decisions of domestic courts but also be familiar with the supranational human rights system and decisions of the ECtHR and ECJ, and also possibly the jurisprudence of other international bodies and domestic apex courts. The specialisation of the public law academy and public law scholarship is important for present purposes as it helps to explain the general absence of taxonomic work: increased specialisation militates against scholarly doctrinal work that transcends different public law fields. In a similar vein, the way law is taught in

[32] See JNE Varuhas, *Damages and Human Rights* (Oxford, Hart, 2016) ch 4.

law schools, which fundamentally shapes legal thinking, does not generally encourage thinking across fields or teach students the ability to move nimbly between fields. As Birks observed, it is not the existence of categories which leads to a 'stove-pipe mentality', it is a failure to consciously think and talk about the categories and their inter-relationships.[33]

It is important to note that it is not my intention to argue that doctrinal work that looks across the terrain of public law is inherently any more or less 'valuable' than scholarship based in other methods, such as empirical or contextual work. Each is capable of enriching our understanding of the law and carrying forward knowledge more generally. Rather my concern has simply been to postulate some of the reasons for the relative scarcity of doctrinal work, particularly that which looks across fields of public law.

III. WHY LEGAL CATEGORISATION MATTERS

This section explains why legal categorisation is of fundamental importance in public law and ought to be undertaken. Given its importance, the relative paucity of such scholarly work should concern us a great deal, and problems arising from a lack of serious taxonomic thinking are beginning to manifest.

A. Deeper Understanding of the Law

The first and most important reason for engaging in legal taxonomy is that it will provide us with a deeper understanding of the law as we find it. Lack of awareness or understanding of doctrinal boundaries and the distinct normative concerns of particular fields of doctrine can result in confused doctrinal development. However, awareness of the distinctiveness of different fields helps to facilitate coherent legal development, and right answers to legal questions. When we seek to answer legal questions we do not do so against the backdrop of a blank canvas, but rather against the background of a rich tapestry of pre-existing rules and principles. Our answer to any particular legal question has to be comprehensible and make sense as against that background.

Consider an example from private law. When we ask what the rules of causation ought to be for money awards for misapplication of trust funds versus damages in negligence versus damages in contract, we need to take heed of the distinctive nature of each field to give an answer which 'fits' with the pre-existing rules and principles within the particular doctrinal context in which the question arises and which is consonant with and does not work at cross-purposes to the basic normative concerns of each field. We might expect quite different answers as to what the causal rules ought to be given the normative concerns of equity, negligence and contract are rather different. However, if we were to look across different fields and find that

[33] P Birks, 'Preface' in P Birks (ed), *The Classification of Obligations* (Oxford, Clarendon Press, 1997) v.

the normative concerns of each field were the same or analogous we might question variations in rules between those fields. Awareness of doctrinal categories is no less important in public law in ensuring full understanding of particular fields and rational and coherent legal development.

Thus, awareness and understanding of distinct doctrinal contexts is important, but it is of acute importance within public law today. As public law expands and becomes more varied, important issues will inevitably arise as to how fields ought to interact. Similarly, a key trigger for greater focusing on questions of taxonomy in private law was the emergence of new fields, specifically restitution, which in turn raised new questions over classification and field interaction. In public law, the Supreme Court has, in the last few years, been presented with arguments and explored the possibility that norms, concepts, methods or general approaches developed within one doctrinal context could be read across to other doctrinal contexts. We shall lack the analytical legal tools to resolve such matters rigorously and coherently if we have not thought deeply about issues of legal classification. In deciding, for example, whether a concept developed in human rights law ought to be read across to the common law of review, we need to inquire into the normative foundations of that concept as it has developed in human rights law so as to fully understand why the concept has been recognised and developed as it has in that field. We must also inquire into the nature of common law review, so as to ensure that any read across would be consonant with the basic functions of the 'destination' field and would 'fit' or cohere with the pre-existing matrix of rules and principles in that field. To decide whether to read across the concept without undertaking this analysis raises a serious risk that any read-across will create incoherence in the 'destination' field and either undermine or impede the distinctive functions of that field. These are important matters which ought to at least be taken into account in making such decisions.[34]

There are many examples of interactions between fields where the insights and analytical tools afforded by legal categorisation would be of use. The most high-profile is the question of whether the method of proportionality balancing developed in human rights law and EU law ought to be read across to the common law of judicial review, along with the allied question of whether common law review ought to recognise fundamental 'rights' or 'values'.[35] So far, much of the debate over these changes has revolved around the benefits and burdens of the proportionality method as well as institutional considerations. But the issue does not arise in a vacuum. Rather, it arises within a particular field of doctrine and the conclusion reached as to whether proportionality ought to be adopted at common law must be—if the law is to be coherent—one intelligible against the background concerns of *that field*, and

[34] Interestingly, in another chapter in this collection which explores the 'unity' theme from a comparative perspective, Saunders makes an argument not dissimilar to that advanced herein in relation to comparative law method. She argues that context ought to be taken seriously in deciding on whether and how to read across doctrines and ideas developed within one jurisdiction to other jurisdictions: C Saunders, ch 13 in this volume.

[35] For general discussion and a range of views see the essays collected in H Wilberg and M Elliott (eds), *The Scope and Intensity of Substantive Review* (Oxford, Hart, 2015).

consonant with the surrounding rules and principles *at common law*.[36] On the other hand, some judges wish to subordinate proportionality balancing in human rights law to traditional common law methods, such as *Wednesbury* unreasonableness and irrelevant considerations.[37] These moves equally implicate questions of legal categorisation, specifically questions over whether such an approach would be consonant with the nature of human rights law.

Many other examples of field-interaction can be identified which, similarly, cannot be analysed rigorously without an awareness of the nature of the particular fields in play:

— Courts have drawn upon core aspects of the remedial approach in common law review, which is discretionary, focused on specific-type and declaratory relief, and subject to public interest calculations, to fashion the remedial approach in human rights law and review on EU grounds.[38]
— The Law Commission argued that a damages principle akin to that which applies in EU law ought to be adopted in the common law of review.[39]
— The courts have examined whether the approach developed in human rights law to ultra vires official representations or promises should be read across to the common law of legitimate expectations.[40]
— In *SG*, Lord Kerr, albeit in minority, arguably drew upon the principle of direct effect, developed in EU law, in holding that certain provisions of UNCROC create enforceable rights at common law.[41]
— The ECtHR has developed requirements that soft law governing the exercise of administrative discretion that may interfere with Convention rights must be sufficiently clear and publicly stated so as to meet rule-of-law demands. This jurisprudence has arguably inspired aspects of the emergent 'law of policy' or 'law of fettering' at common law.[42]
— There are signs that changes in the operation of the judicial review procedure precipitated by the fact-sensitive nature of many human rights claims, such as a greater judicial willingness to order cross-examination and disclosure, are now filtering through to alter the operation of the procedure as it applies to common law claims.[43]
— In *Osborn*, the Supreme Court, heavily influenced by human rights law, articulated an individualist dignitarian rationale for common law duties of procedural

[36] See the discussion below: text to n 137 onwards.

[37] See, eg, Lord Sumption's judgment in *R (Lord Carlile of Berriew QC) v Secretary of State for the Home Department* [2014] UKSC 60; *Kennedy v The Charity Commission* [2014] UKSC 20 at [54]; and see the approach taken in the joint judgment of Lord Neuberger and Lord Dyson in *Beghal v Director of Public Prosecutions* [2015] UKSC 49.

[38] See Varuhas, 'Public Interest Conception' (n 22) at 70–84.

[39] Law Com Consultation Paper No 187, *Administrative Redress: Public Bodies and the Citizen* (London, 2008); Law Com No 322, *Administrative Redress: Public Bodies and the Citizen* (London, 2010).

[40] *Rainbow Insurance Company Ltd v The Financial Services Commission (Mauritius)* [2015] UKPC 15 at [52]–[53]; *Rowland v Environment Agency* [2005] Ch 1.

[41] *R (SG) v Secretary of State for Work and Pensions* [2015] UKSC 16 at [257].

[42] M Elliott and JNE Varuhas, *Administrative Law* 5th edn (Oxford, Oxford University Press, 2017) [5.3.3].

[43] ibid, at [13.2.3]; *R (Bourgass) v Secretary of State for Justice* [2015] UKSC 54 at [126].

fairness, and held duties of fairness at common law to be co-extensive with those in human rights law on the facts of that case.[44] This conception of procedural fairness has had knock-on effects, as discussed further below.
— It has been suggested that devolution arrangements ought to influence the judicial approach to proportionality analysis in human rights adjudication, so as to allow scope for variations in policy choice across the devolved nations.[45]

One could add to this selection many examples of issues that arise at the intersection of fields often classified as public law and fields often classified as private law, rigorous analysis of which requires an understanding of relevant legal categories. Examples include the interrelationship between certain torts and human rights law;[46] between common law judicial review and those principles governing exercise of decision-making powers under contracts;[47] between common law review principles and principles governing the administration of trust assets;[48] and the influence of proportionality balancing method from human rights law on various doctrines including the penalties doctrine in contract[49] and the illegality defence.[50]

B. Rule of Law and Associated Concerns

Taxonomy and rigorous doctrinal analysis more generally is of particular importance in public law now because we are beginning to see the Supreme Court—and other common law apex courts (with the possible exception of the High Court of Australia)—slide towards an open-ended, 'contextual' balancing approach to judicial review, particularly in the field of substantive review. This method has demonstrated an imperialist quality, increasingly being spread beyond public law to other fields, including those of private law.[51] According to such an approach every case turns on

[44] *Osborn v Parole Board* [2013] UKSC 61. See further text to n 153 below.

[45] *Bank Mellat v Her Majesty's Treasury (No 2)* [2013] UKSC 39 at [75].

[46] See Varuhas, *Damages and Human Rights* (n 32) chs 2–3.

[47] See *Braganza v BP Shipping* [2015] 4 All ER 639; JNE Varuhas, 'Judicial Review beyond Administrative Law: *Braganza v BP Shipping Ltd* and Review of Contractual Discretions', UK Const L Blog (31 May 2017) <https://ukconstitutionallaw.org/>.

[48] PG Turner (ed), *Equity and Administration* (Cambridge, Cambridge University Press, 2016).

[49] See *Cavendish Square Holding BV v Talal El Makdessi* [2015] UKSC 6, the Supreme Court applying a proportionality-like test to determine whether contractual clauses that provide for the payment of money sums constitute penalty clauses. The influence of proportionality analysis is most evident in the application of the test in the joint judgment of Lord Neuberger and Lord Sumption: see in particular [98]–[100].

[50] See *Patel v Mirza* [2016] UKSC 42, a majority of the Supreme Court favouring a proportionality-style multi-factor balancing approach to adjudicating the illegality defence.

[51] See the examples in nn 49–50 above, and the more 'flexible' approach to determining whether damages ought to be awarded in lieu of an injunction suggested by *Coventry v Lawrence* [2014] UKSC 13. See also, eg, Lord Neuberger's recent speech favouring an all-things-considered case-by-case 'policy-based' approach to decision-making in tort, and suggesting scepticism of an approach based in concrete legal rules and principles: 'Implications of Tort Law Decisions', Address to the Northern Ireland Personal Injury Bar's Inaugural Conference, County Down (13 May 2017) <www.supremecourt.uk/docs/speech-170513.pdf>. The problems with such approach are clear and reflect the concerns discussed herein; as Waddams says, 'if every question were to collapse into unstructured policy, private law would lose all appearance of coherence and stability' ((n 4) at 19). Contrast the High Court of Australia's scepticism

a balancing of disparate factors on the facts of that case. Judicial decisions in judicial review increasingly rest on judges identifying a set of values, freedoms, principles, interests or rights (individual, third party and/or public) which they consider important and relevant to the case at hand, according each such value, right etc a particular weight, weighing these variables according to a methodology (typically an open-ended balancing method) they consider apt for the case before them, and deciding, according to a further open-ended menu of open-ended variables, what degree of 'deference' they consider it is right to afford the primary decision-maker on the facts of the case. I note that this account is a rose-tinted reconstruction of emergent methods, given the judicial 'approach' adopted is not commonly so structured.[52] The courts have been encouraged in this approach by trends in academic commentary which favour a flexible, 'context-sensitive' approach to review, and which elevate to the level of ideology Lord Steyn's dictum in *Daly*, which his Lordship is unlikely to have intended to be taken literally: 'In law context is everything.'[53]

This emergent mode of decision-making, characterised by open-ended criteria and a sea of potentially relevant considerations is, in many ways, the opposite of the approach I explore in this chapter because, on these emergent trends, there are no doctrinal categories. Rather, all depends on whatever factors the courts consider arise in the light of the background factual circumstances. Decisions are simply responses to given facts. Juxtaposing these new trends with an approach to adjudication grounded in and disciplined by legal taxonomy helps to draw out how the latter promotes important rule of law and other principles, whereas current trends risk completely undermining rule of law principles and rendering rigorous analytical legal reasoning impossible.

The new trends raise serious rule of law concerns. There are concerns over coherence. Above we saw that legal taxonomy promotes coherence. A rationally and clearly ordered legal system helps to ensure that given types of legal issues are identified with the field dedicated to govern such issues, and that judgments in respect of such issues cohere with the given rules and principles associated with the identified field, and the normative goals the field is constituted to fulfil. However, on an open-ended balancing approach there is no set framework of rules and principles, only a sea of potentially relevant considerations. While there is no set goal that the law performs. Rather what goals should be prioritised will vary depending on which goals a judge considers ought to take precedence on the facts before them. Instead of judges working on a common understanding of the normative concerns of a field, the field is reinvented with each new case. Public law adjudication risks aimlessness as it loses any clear sense of mission. The resulting decisions will be akin to a series of random

towards policy-based reasoning in tort, and view that 'the law of tort develops by reference to principles, which must be capable of general application, not discretionary decision-making in individual cases' (*Sullivan v Moody* (2001) 207 CLR 562 at [49]).

[52] Though there are some examples of a more rigorously structured approach being adopted. See, eg, Lord Reed's judgment in *Bank Mellat* (n 45).

[53] *R (Daly) v Secretary of State for the Home Department* [2001] 2 AC 532 at [28]. The literature is voluminous. For a selection of essays for and against adoption of a context-sensitive balancing approach within substantive review see Wilberg and Elliott (n 35), and the special edition of the *New Zealand Law Review*: [2010] 2 *NZ L Rev* 229ff.

points on a graph, rather than a series of points clustered around a line of best fit. This, in turn, raises concerns over arbitrariness and inconsistency. Where the law is rationally ordered, it is more likely that like issues will be dealt with consistently, and that courts can maintain the appearance of consistent treatment. For example in private law issues arising in the context of duties based in consent will be adjudicated according to a particular, defined set of norms which have been formulated specifically to govern such obligations, whereas issues arising in the context of duties imposed by the law so as to protect basic rights will be adjudicated according to a different set of norms in the law of torts, formulated specifically to govern such cases.

Rational ordering promotes predictability and stability. These qualities are important because, inter alia, law seeks to guide action, there may be serious consequences of breaching legal norms, and prospective litigants need to be able to evaluate their chances of success, otherwise good claims will be abandoned, leading to injustice, and bad claims pursued, leading to wasted resources, unnecessary disruption of administration etc. Where the law is clearly ordered and categorised we will have a good chance of predicting outcomes, even absent a prior decision on a given legal question or set of facts. Within an ordered system we will be able to identify the 'penumbra' of relevant rules and principles and the relevant underlying normative goals, and extrapolate out from those resources what action the law is likely to require. We can understand the 'gist' of the given field. Furthermore we will be reassured in our approach by the fact courts committed to a system of rationally ordered law will approach the legal question in the same spirit, striving to reach an outcome intelligible against background norms, and given normative goals. In contrast, under interest-balancing the law is fluid—there is no set backdrop against which adjudication occurs. Rather, decisions are individualised responses to facts: 'The nature of judicial review in every case depends on the context';[54] 'Every case turns on its own facts, and analogies with other decided cases can be misleading.'[55] It will be very difficult for an administrator trying to comply with the law, or a citizen assessing their prospects of success, to predict all of the variables a court will consider relevant, what weight each will be accorded, the method of balancing, the degree of deference adopted, and the normative goals that will take precedence, while past decisions will be unsafe guides.[56] Administrator and citizen alike shall be 'mid-ocean, bereft of the equipment necessary for navigation'.[57]

[54] *Kennedy* (n 37) at [51]. This approach was subsequently reiterated in *Pham v Secretary of State for the Home Department* [2015] UKSC 19 at [60], [94], [105]ff.

[55] *Bank Mellat* (n 45) at [26]. In some contexts it has even been indicated that lower tier judicial bodies conducting balancing should not in general find it necessary to refer to prior authorities: *Ali v Secretary of State for the Home Department* [2016] UKSC 60 at [82].

[56] Such concerns have been raised by Supreme Court Justices in connection with case-by-case decision-making in public law albeit the Justices have not as yet recognised these concerns in connection with current trends in substantive review: *Bank Mellat* (n 45) at [60] (the problem with case-by-case judicial decision-making 'is that it can make it difficult in practice for decision-makers (and individuals affected by decisions) to predict what is required ... In a context in which vital national interests are engaged ... it is of great importance that the Treasury should be in no doubt as to what is required').

[57] See Birks, 'Preface' (n 33) at vi. And see T Poole, 'Between the Devil and the Deep Blue Sea: Administrative Law in an Age of Rights' in L Pearson et al (eds), *Administrative Law in a Changing State* (Oxford, Hart, 2008) 39, 42, using the same metaphor to describe unstructured balancing in judicial review.

Commentators who favour moves towards a more 'flexible' approach to review seek to meet the foregoing concerns by articulating various models or schemes of how the new flexible approach will operate, and/or structures which may operate to constrain balancing. The aims are admirable. But these fine schemes have had little influence in practice and are unlikely to have any. Even if these schemes and structures were to have some influence they would not operate to constrain judicial decision-making in such a way as to adequately meet the concerns discussed. The thing about balancing approaches is that they are not intended to be bridled or to settle down, but are rather meant to be kept fresh for the next exercise and ready to meet the specific demands of the next set of facts. Furthermore even if some structure is imposed, the general approach is such that it would be all too easy for courts to effect departures from the relevant structure based on the facts of the case before them, while a structure would not remove the inherently open-ended, highly fact-sensitive nature of concepts such as deference and balance between ends and means. Moreover, the experience in jurisdictions where appellate courts have experimented with such schemes and structures has not been positive; ironically the result has been incoherence and inconsistency and a peripatetic, labyrinthine body of jurisprudence.[58]

These concerns lead onto a further concern: judicial accountability. On an open-ended balancing approach it becomes nearly impossible to hold judges to account for their decisions, because there are no determinate legal standards against which their decisions can be judged and there is no clear idea of the goals which the law is seeking to fulfil. If one disagrees with a court's decision, the obvious retort will be that the court simply took a different view from you given its assessment of the facts, the weight it accorded relevant factors etc. Further it will be difficult to assess whether decisions are consistent or not. Any differences in result between cases could be explained away on the basis of differences in facts, factors, weight of factors, degree of deference, or that the law was simply prioritising different functions on different facts.

The absence of a stable framework of rationally-ordered rules and principles and any clear sense of the guiding goals that fields exist to serve, will lead to another casualty: judges shall be freed 'from the shackles of traditional legal rationality'.[59] Judges traditionally justify their decisions according to generally applicable legal norms identified with the particular legal field implicated by the case. However, under a discretionary, interest-balancing approach there are no such generally applicable legal norms, but rather a sea of potentially relevant factors and any generally applicable concepts—such as deference or balance—are so open-ended they could be applied in any number of ways on a given set of facts, and impose minimal burdens of justification. As Poole observes, such concepts are a 'principled patina';[60] labels to be attached to preferred conclusions to add an air of legal respectability. This open-ended approach will free judges from the traditional discipline and

[58] D Stratas, 'The Canadian Law of Judicial Review: A Plea for Doctrinal Coherence and Consistency' (2016) 42 *Queen's LJ* 27; D Stratas, ch 10 in this volume; *Wilson v Atomic Energy of Canada Ltd* [2016] 1 SCR 770, [19]ff, [78].

[59] P Birks, 'Three Types of Objection to Discretionary Remedialism' (2000) 29 *UWALR* 1 at 17.

[60] See Poole (n 57) at 40.

constraint imposed by a pre-existing framework of rules and principles and lead to decision-making based on instinct and subjective preference;[61] in other words, such approaches leave judges free to—and indeed encourage if not require—judges to decide cases by appealing to their individual sense of right and wrong.[62] Judges are no longer recognisably engaged in decision making *according to law*, or it becomes increasingly difficult to claim that they are. Similarly, judges, confronted by a novel issue or ambiguity in a field of law, have generally resolved such matters so as to ensure coherence with surrounding rules and principles, which provide a guide as to how the ambiguity should be resolved and, importantly, a check or constraint on possible solutions, as do the field's overarching normative goals. However, there is no such guidance or constraint on an open-ended contextual approach, or the guidance is thin and constraints weak.

So far, we have discussed concerns over coherence, consistency, predictability, accountability and decision making according to law. There is a deeper point still. These are not just desiderata which we hope courts will emulate, a type of best practice guide. Adherence to these prescriptions is fundamental to the legitimate exercise of judicial power. While public lawyers are often preoccupied with the legitimacy of and legal constraints on the exercise of public power by government officials, we must not forget that judges are also public officials and that they exercise the coercive power of the state. It goes to the foundation of the legitimacy of judicial power that judges exercise that great power with a commitment to principled consistency and non-arbitrariness, and are capable of being held to account for their exercises of coercive power. Importantly it will be difficult for the courts to command the moral authority to hold other officials, such as administrators, to rule-of-law standards, if judges themselves do not adhere to them. There may be many further knock-on effects that flow from non-adherence to rule-of-law principles. They cannot all be broached here. But, to give one example, the more judicial decision-making is perceived to be based in subjective preference, the more difficult it will be to maintain the appearance of judicial independence from ordinary politics.

Appeal to notions of flexibility, context-sensitivity, fine calibration, not letting form or technicalities get in the way of substance, so on and so forth, all sounds very appealing, modern, progressive, and maybe even inspiring for some—a 'noble dream' of sorts.[63] But the appeal is surface-deep. As has been argued, approaches based in these ideas generally work better in theory than practice, and on closer inspection they are highly questionable at the level of theory. The rule of law concerns discussed herein ought to cause great concern for public lawyers and judges

[61] See, eg, Forsyth's critical analysis of the Supreme Court's reasoning in a series of recent decisions: CF Forsyth, '"Blasphemy Against Basics": Doctrine, Conceptual Reasoning and Certain Decisions of the UK Supreme Court' in J Bell et al (eds), *Public Law Adjudication in Common Law Systems: Process and Substance* (Oxford, Hart, 2016).

[62] As judges have acknowledged in other contexts: open-ended balancing tests reveal 'no principle whatever to guide the evaluation other than the judge's gut instinct … An evaluative test dependent on the perceived relevance and relative weight to be accorded in each individual case to a large number of incommensurable factors leaves a great deal to a judge's visceral reaction to particular facts' (*Patel* (n 50) at [263] per Lord Sumption (dissenting), in the context of the illegality defence).

[63] Poole (n 57) 37.

given it is often said—and increasingly asserted with ever greater fervour by courts and commentators—that the whole rationale for judicial review is the rule of law. It would be a catastrophic failure of the field if it were to actively undermine the very precept it was constituted to uphold.

The open-ended discretionary judicial methodology is on the rise. But it has not yet effected a complete takeover. Rather, recent decisions of the Supreme Court, particularly those which evince increased enthusiasm for balancing and a 'contextual' approach within substantive review, have moved public law closer to an embrace of that method.[64] That Court may, over the coming years, take the great leap towards an essentially discretionary approach to public law adjudication, or it may, having glimpsed what lies down such a path, think again and turn away.[65] The concern of this chapter is to present an alternative vision and basis for legal development which resists reducing public law adjudication to case-by-case subjective analysis of an ocean of disparate considerations. The vision is future-looking, but it is informed by the historical development of English administrative law. It was painstaking doctrinal work by scholars such as SA De Smith and HWR Wade from the 1950s onwards coupled with concerted judicial efforts, by Lord Diplock among others, which transformed the law governing the prerogative writs from a Tennysonian wilderness of single instances into a recognisable field of judicial review, characterised by an identifiable internal anatomy of general rules and principles, and underpinned by a clear sense of 'mission' which rendered the field coherent. We must be careful now not to return to a situation where public law exists only as a raw mass of cases.

One last point should be made. Above I considered reasons why public lawyers have not engaged in taxonomic scholarship. One further reason, at least in the last few years, may be judicial moves towards a more open-ended approach to public law adjudication. The more public law is characterised by subjective analysis of an open-ended menu of considerations the less that analytical legal thinking can usefully contribute to the development of the law—the law shall have no rational structure or ordering by reference to which one may engage in analytical reasoning.

C. The Role of the Legal Academy

Detailed analytical doctrinal work is the sort of work that legal scholars are distinctly well placed to undertake. The legal academy ought not to pass up the opportunity to make a significant and distinctive contribution to knowledge and the legal system by undertaking such work—a contribution which may be well complemented by other methods, but which cannot be replaced by other methods.

In this regard the distinctive contributions legal scholars can make include doctrinal exegesis of streams of case law, so as to distill and systematise relevant rules and

[64] In particular: *Kennedy* (n 37) [46]–[56], especially [54], this approach being approved and reiterated subsequently in *Pham* (n 54).

[65] There may be some possible signs of retreat, at least outside cases of 'fundamental rights': *R (Keyu) v Secretary of State for Foreign and Commonwealth Affairs* [2016] AC 13; *Poshteh v Royal Borough of Kensington and Chelsea* [2017] UKSC 36 at [42].

principles that emerge from that case law, so as to enhance our understanding of the law, promote access to the law, and facilitate more coherent thinking about a particular field within and without universities. Such systematic analysis may also reveal incoherence, inconsistency and ambiguity in the law which legal academics may then critique, and in respect of which they may seek to offer solutions. Such close doctrinal work may not only facilitate better judicial decision-making, but it also serves to hold the judiciary to account for its decisions.

These sorts of tasks, which legal scholars are best placed to undertake, are the very essence of legal taxonomy; classification is a 'fundamental activity of lawyers and law reformers'.[66] Such method therefore offers an important avenue for legal scholars to make a distinctive contribution to knowledge and the legal system. On the other hand, as Feldman observes, recourse to tools or approaches which make analytical work harder or impossible make it less likely that legal academics will be able to make distinctly valuable contributions:[67]

> If public law has, and public lawyers have, anything to offer the management of state institutions, it is their distinctive talent for deploying analytical rigour and principled consistency to find resolutions for intractable disputes, both in dealing with individual cases and in designing systems. When we try to use tools which make analytical rigour and principled consistency more difficult, we make it less likely that our talents and labours will produce anything which non-lawyers consider to be useful.

One must also bear in mind, in this regard, that if analytical doctrinal work is difficult or impossible this may make it difficult or impossible to apply other methods which are dependent on such analytical work.

IV. MAPPING PUBLIC LAW

Thus, there are good reasons why public lawyers ought to engage in legal categorisation and debates over legal categorisation, especially given contemporary trends in judicial decision making and commentary. In this section I offer the beginnings of a map of public law. The section articulates a basis for identifying legal categories and applies this criterion to identify two major categories of law. It goes on to demonstrate how taxonomic analysis can help us to rigorously analyse contemporary legal issues.

The categories I identify herein by no means constitute an entire map of public law fields, though those identified are significant fields of law. Production of a complete map is beyond the scope of this section. But it is safe to say that there are more categories to be identified and explained. In the end, I hope to convince the reader of the merits of my general approach and the categories I identify and explain. However, others may well have different views as to the best way of categorising fields, and

[66] W Twining et al, 'Ernie and the Centipede' in JA Jolowicz (ed), *The Division and Classification of the Law* (London, Butterworths, 1970) 29.

[67] D Feldman, 'Comparison, Realism and Theory in Public Law' in J Bell et al (eds), *Public Law Adjudication in Common Law Systems: Process and Substance* (Oxford, Hart, 2016) 370.

different accounts of the relevant categories. In a crucial respect this is the very point. A core aim of this chapter is to stimulate new thinking and vigorous taxonomic debate.[68]

A. The Public Law-Private Law Distinction as a Starting Point?

An important preliminary point must be made. Although the title of this chapter includes 'public law' I place no normative weight on public law as a doctrinal category. Elsewhere I have argued in detail why nothing of legal significance should rest on a general normative distinction between public law and private law.[69] It is unnecessary to repeat the analysis here. However, it is important to observe that the public law-private law division has been a common starting point for those concerned to map legal fields. That division was the starting point in Roman taxonomies. It has also long been the starting point for civil law scholars, following the Romans. It was the starting point for Birks's taxonomy of private law, which adopted the division from Roman law, and is the starting point for those who have continued his work. However, even in the Roman schemes the division is not without problems. For example, as Samuel has observed, within the respective Institutes of Gaius and Justinian the law concerning the status of persons as slaves, freeborn or freemen was catalogued under The Law of Persons, an aspect of *ius privatum*: the law concerned with the wellbeing of individuals (as defined in Justinian's Institutes). However, the status of individuals within the polity surely also must be an aspect of *ius publicum*: the law governing the organisation of the state (as defined in Justinian's Institutes).[70] Even if this field was properly categorised as private law in the Roman schemes, today the right to be free of slavery and forced labour is encapsulated in Article 4 of the Convention, and thus forms a part of human rights law—a field concerned with the wellbeing of individuals, but which is commonly associated with public law.

Moving to modern times, even in civil law jurisdictions, in which the division has been entrenched in legal thought, the law and legal institutions, the distinction is said to be in 'crisis', though it continues to be of practical significance.[71] Merryman and Pérez-Perdomo conclude that 'a rather drastic reshaping of the traditional conceptions of private and public law is under way in the civil law world' and that while the distinction retains some force, 'at the frontier [between public law and private law] there is great flux, and few sophisticated civil lawyers today would attempt any functional definition of private law or public law'.[72] Many of the reasons why the distinction is under pressure in civil law jurisdictions are the same reasons which I have propounded for why we ought not to place normative weight on the divide in common law systems.[73] The argument for not placing weight on a

[68] See Birks, 'Equity in the Modern Law' (n 30) at 7 (making a similar point).

[69] See Varuhas, *Damages and Human Rights* (n 32) ch 4.

[70] G Samuel, 'English Private Law: Old and New Thinking in the Taxonomy Debate' (2004) 24 *OJLS* 335 at 345.

[71] Merryman and Perez-Perdomo (n 26) at 95.

[72] ibid, at 98.

[73] ibid, at 95–98; Varuhas, *Damages and Human Rights* (n 32) ch 4.

grand division between public and private law carries all the more force in common law systems, particularly England, in which the public law-private law division has been unknown; we lack the institutional and other machinery which are premised on and give effect to such a divide, such as separate administrative courts,[74] and we lack core concepts crucial to drawing the distinction, such as a concept of the state.[75] And indeed, one reason why civilian lawyers have grown more critical of the division is exposure to common law systems, which demonstrate the dichotomy 'is not a necessary part of every developed legal order'.[76] Given the distinction is under increasing pressure in systems in which it has been a defining feature, in part because of learning derived from common law jurisdictions, it is somewhat ironic and also misguided that there is increasing recourse to the division in common law systems.

Problems become apparent when any attempt is made to draw the distinction. For example, Birks considered that the idea of 'realisable rights' formed the common basis of those fields of law he categorised as private law.[77] But there are also fields characterised by realisable rights beyond those Birks classified as making up private law, such as human rights law. This also serves to demonstrate that, notwithstanding the legal genius of the Roman schemes, they may not serve us well in navigating contemporary law. As Collins argued, in response to Birks, a single, binary division cannot possibly serve as the starting point for explaining the contemporary legal system because, over time, the law tends towards greater complexity; in turn, this will cause the breakdown of broad categorisations. In part, this is driven by the subject matter regulated by law (ie society, economy, government) itself becoming more complex over time: 'In order to comprehend and analyse events, [the law] must develop increasingly variegated systems of classification in order to cope with the complexity of social life.'[78] Particularly relevant here is the ever-greater intermingling of the public and private spheres of life in modern society. This will invariably lead and has increasingly led to the modification or breakdown of legal norms premised on strict separation.

Thus, the division should not form the starting point of any legal taxonomy. Does this conclusion cast doubt on the exercise of legal categorisation, given established and influential legal taxonomies have rested on the division between public law and private law? No, such grand division is unnecessary. Indeed we saw above that difficulties in identifying and delineating the bounds of 'public law' have been a

[74] See further JWF Allison, *A Continental Distinction in the Common Law* (Oxford, Oxford University Press, 1996).

[75] Alternatively, one might say that the lack of a concept of the state is a distinctive state tradition of the English common law system: J McLean, *Searching for the State in British Legal Thought* (Cambridge, Cambridge University Press, 2012).

[76] Merryman and Perez-Perdomo (n 26) 95.

[77] P Birks, 'Introduction' in P Birks (ed), *English Private Law* (Oxford, Oxford University Press, 2001) xxxvi; P Birks, 'Definition and Division: A Meditation on *Institutes* 3.13' in P Birks (ed), *The Classification of Obligations* (Oxford, Clarendon Press, 1997) 9.

[78] H Collins, 'Legal Classification as the Production of Knowledge Systems' in P Birks (ed), *The Classification of Obligations* (Oxford, Clarendon Press, 1997) 66. See also: S Deakin, 'Private Law, Economic Rationality and the Regulatory State' in P Birks (ed), *The Classification of Obligations* (Oxford, Clarendon Press, 1997); Samuel (n 70) 355ff.

major barrier to taxonomic work. Instead we can cast off the yoke of the public law–private law divide and simply proceed to identify and map discrete fields of law, such as those concerned with regulating public power in the public interest and those concerned with fulfilment of expectations generated by promise. Indeed what the exercise in mapping shows is that those fields we commonly associate with the umbrella category of public law lack any meaningful unity, each performing radically different functions, and being characterised by distinct types of legal norms, concepts and methods—a point obscured by much debate in public law which, as discussed above, has tended to pit one monistic theory against another. Furthermore, some of these fields have close affinities to and could even be placed in the same categories as certain fields we commonly associate with the umbrella category of private law.

Thus my project is concerned to map public law only in the sense of mapping fields of law that are sometimes referred to as fields of public law. Within my taxonomy I place no normative weight on the category of public law itself.

B. Criterion of Categorisation

In formulating a taxonomy one must settle on a basis for sorting doctrine into categories. There is a range of criteria that we could possibly use.

We might sort doctrines alphabetically. This would produce a catalogue of doctrines: proportionality (from human rights law), the no-profit rule (from fiduciary law), the defence of lawful excuse (from false imprisonment), so on and so forth. This might produce a neat categorisation, which may make the law very accessible, but it would not enhance our understanding of the law. Furthermore the apparently simple task of listing phenomena alphabetically requires important choices over what precisely is to be listed, which in turn, implicates deeper questions of categorisation.

We might categorise the law according to the subject-matter it regulates. This produces categories such as administrative law, being the law governing public administration, or media law, being the law governing the media. However, that certain doctrines govern a particular phenomenon does not necessarily tell us anything of significance about those doctrines. The administration is subject to human rights law, the common law of review, the law of torts, the law of unjust enrichment, the law of contract, so on and so forth. It is clear that there is far more that divides these areas of law than unifies them. It has been common to examine common law judicial review as it applies to certain subject-matters, such as housing, welfare, immigration etc. For example De Smith, invoking these subject-matter categories, observed 'judicial review in each individual branch of administrative law has tended to develop in a distinctive manner'.[79] It is true that the way particular principles are concretised through application may differ as between judicial review as it applies

[79] See De Smith, 'Wrongs and Remedies' (n 13) at 189.

to tribunal decisions versus executive determinations concerning refugees; without knowledge of these variations one would have an incomplete understanding of common law judicial review. However, one would not be in a position to observe these differences, and to compare the different fields of application, if one did not first know that one was in the province of common law judicial review. One would not be able to explain *Wednesbury*, standing rules, the approach to cross-examination and disclosure, and remedial discretion simply on the basis that the case concerned an executive decision on refugees. Thus one cannot have complete knowledge of the law without understanding that review might be applied differently in the context of decisions concerned with different subject-matters. But one could not understand legal decisions at all if one did not understand the category of common law judicial review, its doctrines and terminology, suggesting common law review is the category of most significance.[80]

We could sort the law according to consequences that follow non-compliance with legal requirements. This would give rise to categories of norms sorted according to responses to breach: damages, imprisonment, fines, mandatory orders, specific performance etc. But it seems odd to pick out only one doctrinal feature and focus on it. Consequences may well tell us something important about the body of law to which they relate. But so might rules of standing for enforcement of the relevant primary norms, the nature of primary norms, and substantive doctrines. Indeed only focusing on consequences could lead us to a distorted view of the law by lumping together norms and doctrines which manifestly have little in common. For example, damages are available in tort and for non-compliance with EU norms, but the rationale for damages in each context is rather different.[81] Similarly, declarations and injunctions are available in the common law of review, for breach of equitable obligations, and for breach of contract. Yet it is manifest that these are fundamentally different fields. Another way to put this is: the fact one can be granted a declaration for breach of a particular norm does not tell us a great deal about that norm.

My own method is to identify and sort fields of doctrine according to function.[82] I settle on functions because I consider that out of all possible criteria this criterion has the greatest explanatory force. Further, it does not suffer significant weaknesses of, and has advantages over, other approaches. The method proceeds by identifying significant doctrinal features of a field and demonstrating how these features are explicable by reference to a given primary function. This approach thus necessitates deep and systematic engagement with doctrine. The discipline of having to explain and justify categorisations by systematic analysis of core features of doctrine guards against ideological capture of the process and is transparent. Analysis in terms of functions, according to my approach, is pitched at such a level of generality that it does not collapse into mere description of the law, in which case there would be no

[80] See also Birks, 'Definition and Division' (n 77) at 33–34.

[81] See Varuhas, *Damages and Human Rights* (n 32) at ch 7.II.

[82] It is necessary to distinguish intrinsic and extrinsic functions. Intrinsic functions are those normative goals of a field of law which are revealed by or are immanent in its significant doctrinal features. Extrinsic functions are the effects or consequences that legal norms actually have through their practical operation. Herein I am concerned with intrinsic functions.

real point to undertaking the taxonomy, yet is not pitched at such a high level of abstraction that we would be unable to derive anything of practical utility from the resulting classification. Importantly, the functional approach is capable of explaining newer, significant fields which are heavily based in statute, such as financial regulation or labour law, which other prominent taxonomies have struggled to account for.[83] Indeed leading private law taxonomies have largely ignored statute;[84] though, interestingly, earlier efforts to spark taxonomic debate, though they did not ultimately take off, fully engaged with and seem in large part to have been spurred by emergence of these newer fields.[85] Within a functionalist framework these newer fields can be understood as fields which regulate certain types of activity, such as provision of financial services or employment, to secure certain economic or social public ends, such as competitive markets or maintenance of labour standards.

One potential criticism of or problem with a functionalist approach is that it may be unreliable to assume that doctrines can be identified with a single function: fields may 'straddle several policy dimensions'.[86] I accept that fields often do perform a range of functions. But, as I demonstrate below, one function typically dominates and can be identified clearly as the primary function; my classification is based on these primary functions. Nonetheless inevitably there will be fields which belie such compartmentalisation, and fall between other categories, sharing features with each. Some consider overlapping categories or categories that are not mutually exclusive to be problematic. One view is that where a taxonomy produces overlaps this is a sign that the taxonomy could be rendered more parsimonious.[87] Another view, forcefully put by Birks, is that overlapping categories will cause chaos and injustice.[88] My view is that to start a process of legal taxonomy believing that one can create a perfectly neat taxonomy is not only unrealistic but will invariably lead one to distort doctrine to fit a preordained taxonomic scheme.[89] This undermines what I consider to be the principal purpose of taxonomy, which is to enhance understanding of the law; a commitment to exclusive categories will thus be 'self-defeating'.[90] Law is a complex normative system based in multiple sources and shaped by many hands over many years. The idea that a map of the law would not make provision for overlaps or exceptions, or acknowledge that certain doctrines fit more comfortably than others within a given category, is to deny the law's complexity and ultimately to obscure our understanding of the law; as Sir Robert Goff observed, one must resist 'the temptation of elegance'.[91] If one considers overlapping categories liable to

[83] See Deakin (n 78).

[84] J Dietrich, 'What is "Lawyering"? The Challenge of Taxonomy' [2006] *CLJ* 549 at 572–73.

[85] JA Jolowicz (ed), *The Division and Classification of the Law* (London, Butterworths, 1970).

[86] Collins (n 78) at 65.

[87] NJ McBride, 'The Classification of Obligations and Legal Education' in P Birks (ed), *The Classification of Obligations* (Oxford, Clarendon Press, 1997).

[88] See Birks, 'Definition and Division' (n 77) at 23. Though the point cannot be analysed in detail here Birks's commitment to exclusive categories arguably rests on an unsafe analogy between taxonomy in the natural sciences and legal taxonomy. See further G Samuel, 'Can Gaius Really Be Compared to Darwin?' (2000) 49 *ICLQ* 297; Waddams (n 4) at 226ff.

[89] See also Dietrich (n 84) at 556–60.

[90] Waddams (n 4) at 2.

[91] R Goff, 'The Search for Principle' (1983) 69 *Proceedings of the British Academy* 169 at 174.

cause injustice and chaos then it is preferable to acknowledge the existence of such phenomena and seek to address the source of injustice than to airbrush the overlap away. Failure to endogenise overlaps can alternatively lead taxonomers to adopt a normatively meaningless 'miscellaneous' category into which is lumped all doctrines which do not fit perfectly into the other mutually exclusive categories.[92] Of course if we look inside this category we are very likely to find doctrines which, while they do not fit perfectly within the 'neat' categories, may well overlap those categories.[93] Put another way, the miscellaneous category is another way of hiding those doctrines which could jeopardise one's otherwise perfect taxonomic scheme. This is again to obscure understanding of the law.

Thus, far from being a weakness it is a great strength of a functional approach that such method is capable of comprehending and endogenising into the taxonomy that certain fields will not fit neatly in one category or the other. This is preferable to distorting doctrines so that they conform to given categories, and is a more transparent approach than hiding inconvenient doctrines. Not having the option of hiding away doctrines also guards against an ideological approach to taxonomy—one is forced to confront and explain those doctrines that challenge what may be one's preferred taxonomic scheme. In turn such doctrines provide a prompt for continual refinement and improvement of one's taxonomy. Furthermore, examining a given field in the context of the categories it overlaps can produce fascinating insights into that field, and also the categories which are overlapped and the relationship between those categories. One often learns the most about categories at their fringes. A further benefit of being open to blurring at the margins is that this militates against a common criticism of taxonomic work: overly rigid boundaries can cut off insights that can be garnered from looking across categories.

Ultimately, the test of the strength of any criterion of categorisation, and thus the categorisation it produces, must lie in how well it meets the purposes for which categorisation is being undertaken.[94] My principal concern in undertaking this enterprise is, consonant with those reasons for engaging in legal categorisation stated in section III, to enhance our understanding of the law, and by so doing, to facilitate rational and coherent legal analysis and legal development. The proof is ultimately in the pudding.

C. Mapping Public Law: Beginnings

The remainder of the chapter focuses on identifying and distinguishing two major fields in order to illustrate my taxonomic approach and also the value of engaging in the enterprise. The categories, which I define according to their primary functions,

[92] The famous example being Birks's taxonomy of the law of obligations: 'every obligation arises from a contract, a wrong, from an unjust enrichment, *or from some other kind of event*' (Birks, 'Definition and Division' (n 77) at 19 (emphasis added)).

[93] See Dietrich (n 84) at 557; Waddams (n 4) at 11–12.

[94] See Twining et al (n 66) at 18–19.

are (1) the law relating to regulation of public power in the public interest; and (2) the law relating to protection and vindication of basic personal rights. I argue that the bulk of common law judicial review falls within (1) and that the bulk of the law under the HRA falls within (2).

It is important to emphasise that each of these categories may not be fully occupied by the doctrines just mentioned. For example many torts, the law under the EU Charter of Rights, and aspects of EU and domestic anti-discrimination law may also fall within (2). Also, the entirety of the bodies of doctrine mentioned may not fall within the relevant category with which they are associated. For example, certain common law review doctrines, such as legitimate expectations, may fall outside category (1), or they may straddle category (1) and another category comprised of fields concerned with the enforcement of promises, for example. Furthermore, the categories are unlikely to be mutually exclusive. There is likely to be blurring at the margins, overlaps and exceptions, and some fields will fit more neatly in particular categories than others. For example, pursuant to section 149 of the Equality Act 2010 public authorities must, in performing their functions, have due regard to certain considerations including the need to eliminate discrimination and foster good relations between people who share a 'protected characteristic' and people who do not. On the one hand, one could view this duty as concerned with protection of basic equality rights. On the other hand, the formulation of the factors suggests they are broader public goals that transcend the rights of any one individual (albeit fulfilment of the goals will operate to benefit individuals), while their status as relevant considerations, suggests that the aim is to integrate these considerations into decision-making as an aspect of good public administration.

It is equally important to observe that these two categories do not occupy the full province of those fields that might be associated with the label 'public law'. For example, another major field is that body of law which creates public institutions and confers public powers, ie that field concerned to establish the framework of government. There are also fields of law concerned to facilitate political accountability and, as mentioned above, many fields, created by statute, which regulate various activities in accordance with public goals, including social and economic goals, such as competition law and environmental regulation.

Thus there is much work in legal categorisation to be done. For now let us return to the two categories that are our focus. In outline the categories are as follows. The common law of review is a field of law concerned to ensure public power is exercised properly in pursuit of the public goals for which the powers have been conferred by Parliament. Put simply the law's concern is to keep decision-makers broadly on track, and to ensure they do not stray from their legislative mandate. Consider duties on decision-makers such as the duty to take into account relevant considerations and ignore irrelevant considerations, act for statutory purposes, not act out of personal bias, not act wholly irrationally, and listen to interested parties. These are all concerned to ensure powers are exercised in genuine pursuit of public goals, and also that exercise of power accords with very basic expectations of good decision-making practice, on the basis that this produces better decisions which better serve the public good. The basic norms in this field are public duties; in other words duties such as legality and rationality are not duties owed to any one individual but are free-standing duties, or duties owed to the public as a whole for the benefit of the public as a collectivity.

In contrast to the public-regarding nature of common law review, human rights law is an individual-regarding field. The law's concern is not with ensuring public powers are broadly exercised properly in accordance with public goals set by a parent statute. Rather, its principal function is protection and vindication of fundamental individual interests in the face of public power otherwise properly exercised. Many features of human rights law reflect the field's strong protective and vindicatory nature, including that claims are in general actionable per se, liability is generally strict, the primary rights are construed generously and defences are construed narrowly.[95] The focus in human rights claims is not, as in common law review, on the qualities of the exercise of the power itself,[96] but rather on protecting basic individual interests impacted by such exercises of power. The basic norms are personal, individual rights possessed by specific individuals, such as the right that authorities not interfere with one's liberty or freedom of expression. Thus, whereas common law review concerns itself with 'general duties' which 'do not confer enforceable rights' or 'individual or specific dut[ies]', the focus being upon 'arguable abuse[s] of power', in contrast HRA rights are 'clearly' 'civil or private law rights'.[97]

These functional differences are most starkly illustrated by considering significant doctrinal features of the fields side-by-side, albeit not all features can be examined here.[98]

(i) Standing

The standing rules in common law review are exceptionally liberal. In general a public interest group or public-spirited citizen will have standing to bring a judicial review challenge on common law grounds if they have an arguable case of administrative unlawfulness, regardless of whether their own rights or interests are directly affected by the challenged measure.[99] In contrast standing rules in human rights law are narrow: subject to a few exceptions only an individual whose protected interests have been directly affected by the defendant's actions will have standing.[100]

95 See Varuhas, *Damages and Human Rights* (n 32) at ch 3.I.B.

96 Common law review challenges do not turn on rights but rather 'the propriety of the acts and omissions which have brought about the interference with [individual] interests and rights' (*R (Maftah) v Secretary of State for Foreign and Commonwealth Affairs* [2012] 2 WLR 251 at [28]–[29]).

97 *R (R) v Children and Family Court Advisory Support Service* [2012] 1 WLR 811 at [91], [94]; [2013] 1 WLR 163 at [73], [83].

98 See further Varuhas, *Damages and Human Rights* (n 32) chs 2–3; JNE Varuhas, 'Against Unification' in H Wilberg and M Elliott (eds), *The Scope and Intensity of Substantive Review* (Oxford, Hart, 2015).

99 *R v Inland Revenue Commissioners, ex parte National Federation of Self-Employed and Small Businesses Ltd* [1982] AC 617; *R v Secretary of State for Foreign and Commonwealth Affairs, ex parte World Development Movement Ltd* [1995] 1 WLR 386; *AXA General Insurance Ltd v The Lord Advocate* [2012] 1 AC 868; *Walton v Scottish Ministers* [2013] PTSR 51; Elliott and Varuhas (n 42) at 549–68.

100 HRA, s 7(7). For examples of standing being denied to non-victims see, eg: *R (Children's Rights Alliance for England) v Secretary of State for Justice* [2013] 1 WLR 3667; *Application for Judicial Review by the Northern Ireland Commissioner for Children and Young People* [2007] NIQB 115.

This marked difference of approach across the categories is not arbitrary. The variation is explicable by reference to the different nature of the two fields. Standing rules are wide at common law because what is at stake in such claims is something in which all citizens and groups have a legitimate concern—the proper exercise of public power in pursuit of public goals—while many abuses would go unchecked, to the ultimate detriment of the common good, if standing were dependent on the applicant showing they were personally aggrieved.[101] In contrast wide standing rules would be out of place in human rights law. The basic norms are personal rights. It is a core aspect of the holding of a right that one has the liberty to make decisions over the subject-matter of the right, including whether the right should be enforced, or a potential claim waived. If a third party or interest group could make these decisions this would undermine the right-holder's autonomy. There are certain confined exceptions to the narrow victim test in human rights law; these are justified on the basis that they are required to ensure the law's ultimate goals of protecting and vindicating individual rights is achieved.[102] For example, where the victim was killed in violation of their right to life, their claim may be brought by a family member.[103] Such exception is necessary to ensure the deceased's rights are ultimately vindicated. Consonant with the individualistic, rights-based nature of human rights law, HRA claims may not be assigned as they are inherently personal to the rights-holder.[104]

(ii) Remedies

Remedies in common law review are limited to declaratory, quashing and specific-type relief. This remedial focus reflects the law's basic concern: to regulate public power so that it is actually exercised as it ought to be in the public interest. This goal can best be achieved by quashing decisions not taken in proper pursuit of public goals, prohibiting improper decision making and/or mandating that decisions be properly taken. Decisions whether to grant a remedy and which remedy lie in the wide discretion of the court.[105] This enables the court to modulate grant of remedies according to the demands of the public interest.[106] For example, a court may refuse a quashing order where its grant would undermine interests in effective, certain and final public administration, such as where quashing a decision would cause significant administrative disruption and lead to reopening of hundreds of decisions. Such public interest concerns raised by quashing orders explain why the declaration has arguably become the dominant remedy in common law review proceedings: it marks

[101] See, eg, *Inland Revenue Commissioners* (n 99) at 644; *AXA* (n 99) at [58], [62]–[63], [159]–[175]; *Walton* (n 99) at [90]–[95]; *R v Somerset County Council, ex parte Dixon* [1998] *Env LR* 11 at 121.

[102] Elliott and Varuhas (n 42) at [14.7.7].

[103] *Rabone v Pennine Care NHS Foundation Trust* [2012] UKSC 2.

[104] *Nassau Verzekering Maatschappij NV v Netherlands* (4 October 2011) App no 57602/09 (ECtHR Third Section).

[105] *Inland Revenue Commissioners* (n 99) 647; *R v Panel on Take-overs and Mergers, ex parte Datafin Plc* [1987] QB 815, 840–41. See also those recent Supreme Court decisions cited at n 150 below, reasserting the remedial discretion.

[106] See, eg, the authoritative statement of principle in *R v Monopolies and Mergers Commission, ex parte Argyll* [1986] 1 WLR 763 at 774–75.

an illegality, educates the authority as to what the authority must do to act lawfully into the future, but does not necessarily disrupt past decisions and can thus preserve public interests in administrative certainty and finality.[107] There are numerous other aspects of remedies that reflect the distinctive nature of common law review. For example, in rights-based fields such as tort an injunction would only be granted upon application by an individual right-holder, in respect of the subject-matter of their right. However, in common law review, the courts have recognised a novel 'group' or 'class' interim injunction which may apply to preserve the position of a group of similarly placed individuals, including those who have not yet initiated review proceedings and who are not parties to the application.[108] This wider application is possible because the concern is not with individual rights, but with ensuring the powers to be applied to this group are exercised properly in pursuit of the common good. Damages are not available for breach of common law duties. They would be out of place. As traditionally conceptualised, damages redress setbacks personal to individuals, whereas the principal focus of common law review is not individual rights and interests, but ensuring public power is exercised properly for the common good.[109]

In human rights law a wider range of remedies is available. The same relief available in common law review is available in human rights law, such as injunctions, the prerogative orders and declarations. In addition, damages may be recovered for personal losses.[110] In turn, this reflects the individual-regarding nature of the field: it is concerned to preserve personal interests. The panoply of remedies also reflects the field's basic concerns to ensure strong protection of fundamental rights. The remedies allow courts to prevent violations, bring ongoing violations to an end and compensate for losses suffered through past violations. It is true that all of these remedies are discretionary.[111] However, the discretion to deny remedies altogether is narrower than at common law given that the ECHR prescribes a right to an effective remedy (Article 13), and it is the object of the remedial provisions of the HRA 'to provide in English law the very remedy Article 13 declares is the entitlement of everyone whose rights are violated'.[112] More generally where rights are in play the longstanding domestic principle of *ubi ius, ibi remedium* has application and mandates some remedy ought generally to be given for breach. To the remedies already mentioned we may add the unique remedy of a declaration of incompatibility.[113] Provision for this remedy reflects the fundamental nature of the rights under the HRA: they are so important that the courts are bestowed with power to draw the attention of Parliament and the polity to any statute incompatible with enjoyment of those rights.

[107] See, eg, *Datafin* (n 105) 842; Elliott and Varuhas (n 42) at [12.3.1].

[108] *R (HN (Afghanistan)) v Secretary of State for the Home Department* [2015] EWCA Civ 1043.

[109] See, eg, the discussion in *Bourgoin SA v Ministry of Agriculture, Fisheries and Food* [1986] QB 716 at 761, 763.

[110] HRA, s 8.

[111] Though the reasons for a discretionary approach differ from those at common law, albeit there may be some overlap, being less to do with protecting the public interest and more with enabling the court to do individual justice on the facts of the case: Varuhas, *Damages and Human Rights* (n 32) at 154.

[112] *Re S* [2002] 2 AC 291 at [61].

[113] HRA, s 4.

(iii) Nature of the Court's Role

Albeit an otherwise clear legal position has been blurred by recent Supreme Court decisions, the orthodox position is that in human rights law courts exercise a primary or original jurisdiction whereas within common law review the courts exercise a secondary, supervisory jurisdiction. This difference in the court's role reflects the different nature of each field.

In human rights law, it is well-established that courts exercise a primary or original jurisdiction, determining for themselves substantive issues raised by human rights claims, such as questions over whether a right is engaged, the scope of rights, and justifications for interferences, and the courts may find the facts of the case as they would in ordinary proceedings.[114] These matters are for the courts because human rights claims are claims of individual legal rights; matters of individual rights and duties are quintessentially matters for courts within the separation of powers. That such matters ought to be for the courts is reinforced by the strong protective and vindicatory policy underpinning human rights law; if decisions over rights were first and foremost for the public authority then it would be judge in its own case and protection of basic rights could be undermined. Thus, it is well established that it is for the courts, in a claim for breach of the operational duty under Article 2, to determine objectively whether there was a real and immediate risk to life from a third party that was known or should have been known to the defendant authority.[115] If so, a positive duty to protect life arises, and it is for the court to determine whether the authority took reasonable steps to protect life in light of the threat. No margin of appreciation or deference is applied in determining what steps it was reasonable for the authority to take.[116] In an Article 8 claim it is for the court to determine the scope and content of the right to privacy, whether the right was engaged and whether any interference with the right could be justified as proportionate.[117] In adjudicating the proportionality defence, the courts will accord weight to the informed view of the decision-maker, to the extent they possess greater expertise in the matter than the court.[118] But the ultimate question of whether the wrong is justified is for the court to determine objectively for itself; the court must make its own value judgment.[119]

In contrast the longstanding, orthodox conception of judicial review on common law grounds is that it is a secondary, supervisory jurisdiction. The court's role must necessarily be secondary and supervisory because the primary power of decision

[114] *Belfast City Council v Miss Behavin' Ltd* [2007] 1 WLR 1420 at [12]–[15], [30]–[31], [37], [44]; *R (Begum) v Governors of Denbigh High School* [2007] 1 AC 100 at [29]–[31], [68]; *Huang v Secretary of State for the Home Department* [2007] 2 AC 167; *Tweed v Parades Commission* [2007] 1 AC 650 at [55]; *R (Quila) v Secretary of State for the Home Department* [2012] 1 AC 621 at [46], [61], [91]; *E v Chief Constable of the Royal Ulster Constabulary* [2009] 1 AC 536 at [13], [52]ff; *Bank Mellat* (n 45) at [124]; *Carlile* (n 37) at [57], [105], [115], [137], [152]. In regard to fact-finding specifically see: *Manchester City Council v Pinnock (Nos 1 and 2)* [2011] 2 AC 104 at [74]; *R (Kiarie) v Secretary of State for the Home Department* [2017] UKSC 42 at [46]–[47].

[115] *Van Colle v UK* (2013) 56 EHRR 23 at [95]; *In Re Officer L* [2007] 1 WLR 2135 at [20].

[116] See *Rabone* (n 103) at [43].

[117] See *Quila* (n 114).

[118] See *Huang* (n 114) at [16]; *Bank Mellat* (n 45) at [129].

[119] See references in n 114.

has been bestowed by Parliament on the executive decision-maker. If the courts exercised a primary jurisdiction they would supplant the role of the executive decision-maker and contravene Parliament's sovereign will. It is for the repository of the power to make the principal decision over how the power ought to be exercised, with the court's role limited to ensuring that the decision-maker does not go off track in exercise of their power. As noted above, duties to exercise powers for proper purposes, to consider relevant considerations and exclude irrelevant considerations and to take into account representations by those with a stake in the decision are duties concerned to keep a decision-maker on course, genuinely pursuing public goals set by Parliament, and to facilitate the best possible decision in the public interest by upholding basic standards of good decision-making practice. Not only would it be contrary to Parliament's will for the court to exercise primary jurisdiction but the courts, if they intervene too readily, may end up impeding the exercise of public power in pursuit of the common good or distorting such exercises of power. More generally, each executive decision is in essence a determination as to what decision would best serve the public interest, whether it be the public interest in border control, education, defence, fisheries management, or provision of welfare. The courts are simply neither equipped nor possessed of the requisite constitutional legitimacy to make such determinations. These are the reasons why, when it comes to the substance of the executive decision, the courts have, pursuant to the *Wednesbury* standard, traditionally reserved their interventions for cases where it is plain and obvious that the decision reached cannot plausibly be defended as one taken in genuine pursuit of the public goals set by Parliament.

It is important to reiterate that within the common law of review courts are not adjudicating or enforcing legal rights which are impacted by the exercise of the public power, but rather controlling the exercise of the power itself. As I have discussed elsewhere,[120] it may be that a primary decision-maker ought to take into account the interests of a particular individual and consider the implications of their decision for that individual, on the basis that consideration of how a decision may impact an individual's interests is an aspect of good public decision-making.[121] But this does not involve courts enforcing rights. Rather this is one manifestation of the relevant considerations doctrine.[122] As Lord Carnwath has observed, at common law, even in cases where important individual interests are implicated 'the role of the court is often more about process than merits'.[123] If an individual's basic interests, which are protected by a genuine legal right, are impacted by an executive act that individual can simply bring an action via ordinary procedure. There would be no need to have recourse to the court's residual supervisory jurisdiction. For example if one's right to physical integrity or liberty were breached one could bring a claim in battery or false imprisonment or under the HRA, and the court would exercise original jurisdiction.

[120] See Varuhas, 'Against Unification' (n 98) at 108–14.

[121] See, eg, *R v Ministry of Defence, ex parte Smith* [1996] QB 517.

[122] *Secretary of State for the Home Department v MN and KY* [2014] UKSC 30 at [31].

[123] See *Kennedy* (n 37) at [245]. Other cases have similarly distinguished the treatment of 'rights' in common law review and under the HRA: eg *Miss Behavin'* (n 114) at [31]; *Kiarie* (n 114) at [47]; *Smith* (n 121) at 541.

(iv) Procedure

Significant differences in the procedural treatment of human rights and common law claims have emerged, which reflect the different nature of the two fields. Common law claims are generally streamed via the judicial review procedure.[124] This procedure provides for many safeguards for the protection of various public interests, particularly the public interests in effective and certain public administration and preservation of court and public authority resources. For example, there are severe restrictions on potentially costly and time-consuming processes of disclosure and cross-examination[125] and a very short limitation period applies (which is even shorter in contexts where third party and economic public interests are implicated).[126] The permission stage is used to filter out certain types of claims, in particular those that are tardy and unmeritorious, in the interests of ensuring that authorities are protected from challenges which could unduly undermine administrative certainty and finality and cause unnecessary disruption, thus jeopardising effective administrative pursuit of public goals. More generally the courts have taken it upon themselves to cut down access to judicial review where they consider the public interest warrants this.[127] These protections reflect the overarching concern of common law review with preservation of the public interest; the courts are particularly concerned not to allow the operation of judicial review to unnecessarily and unduly undermine administrative pursuit of public goals.

In contrast human rights claims may be brought concurrently with other rights-based claims, such as claims in tort, via ordinary procedure, and the courts have gone so far as to prescribe that certain types of HRA claim ought to be brought via ordinary procedure, whether pleaded concurrently with claims in tort or not.[128] Where human rights claims are brought via review procedure, that procedure may be substantially modified so that it more closely matches ordinary procedure. For example, disclosure and cross-examination are more freely available in human rights claims than common law claims.[129] The time limit for human rights claims is one year (when not brought via judicial review)[130] which matches that for certain vindicatory

124 Pursuant to *O'Reilly v Mackman* [1983] 2 AC 237.

125 CPR Practice Direction 54A, para 12.1; *O'Reilly,* ibid, at 257, 263, 282, 284; *Inland Revenue Commissioners* (n 99) at 638, 654; *Tweed* (n 114) at [2], [29]; *R (CC) v Commissioner of Police for the Metropolis* [2012] 1 WLR 1913 at [28]; *R (Z) v Croydon LBC* [2011] PTSR 748 at [24]. More generally, courts traditionally emphasise review procedure is inappropriate for determining factual questions: *Roy v Kensington and Chelsea and Westminster FPC* [1992] 1 AC 624 at 650, 654; *R v East Berkshire HA, ex parte Walsh* [1985] QB 152 at 173.

126 CPR 54.5(1), (5)–(6).

127 *R (Cart) v The Upper Tribunal* [2012] 1 AC 663.

128 *ID v Home Office* [2006] 1 WLR 1003 at [105]; *R (Wilkinson) v Broadmoor Hospital* [2002] 1 WLR 419 at [61]–[62]; *Ruddy v Chief Constable Strathclyde Police* [2012] UKSC 57.

129 *Tweed* (n 114) at [32], [53]–[54], [56]–[57]; *Wilkinson,* ibid, at [24]–[26], [56]–[59], [62]; *R (Al-Sweady) v Secretary of State for Defence* [2010] HRLR 2 at [26]–[27]; *R (A) v Chief Constable of Kent Constabulary* [2013] EWCA Civ 1706 at [58]; *Kiarie* (n 114) at [47]. On damages claims specifically see: *R (Faulkner) v Secretary of State for Justice* [2013] 2 AC 254 at [13](5), [39]; *Ruddy*, ibid.

130 HRA, s 7(5).

torts such as defamation, while the courts have been willing to extend the limitation period to match that for torts for which the limitation period is longer.[131]

There are several reasons for these procedural differences. First, claims grounded in basic rights are quintessentially the province of the courts; the courts would be in dereliction of their constitutional responsibility for adjudication and protection of legal rights if they were to turn away claims of breach of basic rights simply to protect the defendant authority.[132] This is why other types of claims based in basic rights, such as claims in tort, are streamed via ordinary procedure, which is not characterised by the special protections for public authorities that characterise judicial review procedure.[133]

Second, several features of human rights claims require the courts to engage closely with the facts of the case and to act as a primary fact-finder, thus necessitating greater provision for disclosure and cross-examination.[134] The courts exercise a primary jurisdiction in human rights law, and primary fact-finding is an aspect of such a jurisdiction; if the court is to properly determine issues such as reasonableness-simpliciter or proportionality for itself then it must have a full understanding of the facts of the case. Further, proportionality and reasonableness-simpliciter are highly fact-sensitive concepts. Human rights claims are individualised claims[135] which require the court to have a full understanding of the specific circumstances of the individual case before them; a court does not inquire into questions of proportionality in the abstract, but asks whether a particular exercise of government power, which interfered with a particular claimant's rights, was proportionate on the facts of the individual case. Damages may be claimed for breach of human rights, and assessment of personal loss requires close attention to the factual circumstances of the individual case, including the subjective effects of the violation on the claimant.[136]

Thus, from the foregoing one can clearly see that there are fundamental doctrinal differences between human rights law and common law review, which reflect that the two fields perform distinct functions. In turn, this fundamental functional difference justifies placing common law review and the law under the HRA in different legal categories.

D. Using the Map to Navigate Contemporary Legal Issues

Thus we have the beginnings of our map. Let us then move on to consider briefly how this exercise in legal categorisation can help us to better understand the nuances

131 *Dobson v Thames Water Utilities Ltd* [2011] EWHC 3253 at [1072]–[1074]. See also *Rabone* (n 103) at [108].

132 See, eg, *R v Board of Visitors of Hull Prison, ex parte St Germain* [1979] QB 425 at 455; *Wandsworth LBC v Winder* [1985] AC 461 at 510.

133 See *Roy* (n 125) at 654.

134 The courts have emphasised the fact-sensitive nature of the proportionality inquiry in particular: eg *Tweed* (n 114) at [32]–[39], [53]–[57]; *Bank Mellat* (n 45) at [20]. On fact-finding in HRA claims more generally see: *Pinnock* (n 114) at [74]; *Kiarie* (n 114) at [46]–[47].

135 See, eg, *Quila* (n 114) at [59], [80].

136 *R (Faulkner) v Secretary of State for Justice* [2011] HRLR 23 at [19]; *Faulkner* (n 129) at [13](5), [39].

of contemporary legal issues. I focus here on the question whether a structured proportionality method of the type applied to certain qualified rights in human rights law ought to be read across to common law review, as a test of substantive review.[137] Elsewhere I have argued against this development.[138] However, for present purposes my concern is to demonstrate how legal categorisation can shed light on important aspects of the legal issue which might otherwise be missed.

A core argument given by the Supreme Court in favour of the read-across is the 'no reason why not' argument.[139] That is, there is no reason not to read across the proportionality method to common law review. Allied to this is the consistency argument.[140] That is, it would be wrong to treat two similarly placed claimants differently depending on the type of claim they choose to make.

These arguments are highly problematic. One problem, brought clearly into focus by legal categorisation, is that the 'no reason why not' argument passes over the distinctiveness of different doctrinal contexts. To illustrate this point, let us draw on an example from private law. One might argue there is no reason why common law damages principles should not be read across to govern the remedy of equitable compensation. The obvious response is that damages principles developed within contract law or the law of torts respond to, and are fundamentally shaped by, the normative concerns that underpin those fields and may not, therefore, be apt for importation into equity—which is a distinct doctrinal context, characterised by distinct normative concerns. For example, to apply a compensatory approach derived from contract to money awards in equity for unauthorised disbursements of trust funds would be to fundamentally mistake the nature of the award, which is an award in satisfaction of a debt.[141]

A further example drawn from private law helps to illustrate the problem with the consistency argument. One set of facts may give rise to a claim for damages in contract and deceit. Different primary measures of loss will however be applied—in contract, an expectation measure; in deceit, a reliance measure. One could argue this is inconsistent: a claimant who brings a claim in contract will recover damages assessed differently from a claimant who brings their claim in tort. But there are good reasons why different measures are applied. An expectation measure is applied in contract because the law's concern is that expectations generated by promises ought to be fulfilled. It would make no sense and create incoherence to apply such a measure in the law of deceit, where the primary duty is a negative one

137 See, eg, *Kennedy* (n 37); *Pham* (n 54); *Keyu* (n 65); *Youseff v Secretary of State for Foreign and Commonwealth Affairs* [2016] UKSC 3. My focus here is on substantive review cases, but it is worth noting that the Supreme Court has recently explicitly applied proportionality as an aspect of the principle of legality, ie as an aspect of a vires inquiry: *R (UNISON) v Lord Chancellor* [2017] UKSC 51. Why some 'fundamental common law rights' cases are analysed through substantive review, and others via the principle of legality is neither clear nor explained.

138 See Varuhas, 'Against Unification' (n 98).

139 See *Kennedy* (n 37) at [54]; *Pham* (n 54) at [95].

140 See *Pham*, ibid, at [104].

141 See J Edelman, 'An English Misturning with Equitable Compensation' in S Degeling and JNE Varuhas (eds), *Equitable Compensation and Disgorgement of Profit* (Oxford, Hart, 2017); cf *AIB Group Plc v Mark Redler & Co Solicitors* [2014] 3 WLR 1367.

requiring individuals not to make fraudulent misrepresentations—not a duty, generated by consent, to secure a promised outcome. Where a fraudulent representation is made the remedial concern is to place the claimant back in the position as if the representation had never been relied upon, that is the situation the claimant would have been in if the defendant had never breached their negative duty. This mode of reasoning is commonplace in private law, and the reason for this is likely that there is a strong tradition of recognising and thinking in terms of legal categories in private law fields.

The very same mode of analysis can help us to understand why the question of whether proportionality should be read across to common law review is more complex than the 'no reason why not' and consistency arguments suggest. Fundamental features of the proportionality doctrine, as developed in human rights law, can only be understood by reference to the nature of human rights law. First, the burden of proving proportionality lies with the defendant, because in human rights law proportionality is a defence to breach of a right. When the proportionality stage of the analysis has been reached the claimant will already have established a legal wrong (ie that the defendant breached their rights). It is because the defendant has perpetrated a wrong that it must justify itself, otherwise it shall be liable. Requiring the defendant to justify any interference with basic rights is also consonant with the basic concern of human rights law, which is to afford maximal protection to basic rights, and reflects the law's starting point that basic rights ought to be maintained inviolate—as such every interference calls for explanation. Second, the court is justified in objectively determining for itself the question of proportionality, along with other matters such as the scope of the primary right, because the claim is a claim of legal right, and claims of legal right are quintessentially for the courts to determine. Third, as the courts have recognised time and again, even accounting for questions of weight,[142] the proportionality analysis involves far deeper scrutiny of administrative action than application of the free-standing *Wednesbury* standard. This is in part because proportionality is a defence to a breach of a legal right, and breaches of legal rights, and especially the most fundamental legal rights, require strong justification if the defendant is to escape legal liability. This is reinforced by the basic concerns of human rights law, to afford strong protection to basic human interests—that rights are to be interpreted liberally, and defences cast a heavy burden and are to be construed narrowly reflects these basic concerns.

So fundamental features of proportionality as developed in human rights law can only be understood properly in the light of the rights-based nature of the field, and its basic normative concern to afford strong protection to and vindicate fundamental individual, personal legal rights. Obviously common law review, in this case the 'destination' field, has radically different primary functions and is not a rights-based field. In turn, this raises a number of questions which are missed or passed over by 'no reason why not' and consistency arguments. For example, say the method is

[142] See *Daly* (n 53) at [27]–[28] and see the judgments of all Justices in *Carlile* (n 37) save Lord Sumption, arguing that adoption of a relevant considerations or *Wednesbury* style of review under the HRA would prevent the judges from performing their constitutional duty of rights-adjudication.

read across, but without the rights-driver. This raises a number of questions including how to justify features of the method which, in human rights law, are justified by reference to the presence of legal rights. The read-across also raises questions of legitimacy. Without the rights-driver a judicial approach which involves objectively determining the balance between competing considerations, factors and interests is suspect in terms of legitimacy. Remember the basic judicial task in common law review is to supervise the exercise of public power itself. If the courts interfere with such exercises of power on the basis they would have weighed and balanced variables differently to the executive decision-maker, this raises a clear concern over courts supplanting the primary decision-maker's role. Put another way, if the courts assert that they can make their own value-judgment over how the factors should be balanced, in scrutinising an exercise of power in itself, it becomes difficult to maintain that judicial review is a secondary, supervisory jurisdiction; courts will be exercising the equivalent of a primary or original power of decision. These types of concern arguably underpin Lord Reed's judgment in *Pham* in which he was careful to state that even if heightened scrutiny *Wednesbury* and structured rights-based proportionality might lead to the same result in some cases, they are not the same test—the approach at common law involves a lighter-touch review. That Lord Reed took this view is unsurprising given that of all judgments delivered in *Pham* his was particularly sensitive to the importance of doctrinal context: he specifically distinguished application of proportionality in assessing a justification for a breach of a *legal right*, from balancing that might be involved in application of general grounds of *review* at common law.[143] We see similar sensitivity to doctrinal context in Lord Carnwath's judgment in *Kennedy*.[144] Lord Carnwath observed that even where basic interests are implicated in common law review the concern is generally more with decision-making process—reflecting that the primary decision over how power should be exercised is for the executive decision-maker. In contrast he said the court's task in HRA claims is more akin to merits review.

Of course, the courts might avoid some of these issues if they start to recognise actionable rights within the common law of review, to which the proportionality method could then be attached. Thus, for example, members of the Supreme Court in *Pham* reached back to Blackstone to locate a right to reside in one's own country at common law, and considered proportionality analysis could be applied to determine whether any interference was justified. There are serious questions as to whether this is a genuine legal right, given breach of it cannot found an action independently of the common law of review in the way that the right to liberty (false imprisonment, habeas corpus) or the right to physical integrity (battery) can, for example. In this case we end up with all of the problems discussed in the previous paragraph.

But maybe the Supreme Court Justices, through their judgments, have transmuted this 'right' into a genuine legal right, which in turn helps to justify the adoption and then application of the proportionality method in relation to that right. But if the Supreme Court is now in the business of creating new legal rights where and when

[143] *Pham* (n 54) at [113]ff.
[144] *Kennedy* (n 37) at [245].

they wish, this raises a question over the legitimacy of this new practice. In the law of torts it is generally accepted that the courts will not create new rights which found new causes of action, or at least they will be very slow to do so. This is because the creation and allocation of legal entitlements involves bare questions of distributive justice, such matters properly being for the political branches, not courts. This legitimacy concern is even greater where the courts are claiming to create *fundamental* rights, given one would expect the representatives of the polity to be those best placed to determine which rights are constitutive of British society.

One might counter that to the extent that the rights recognised at common law mirror those under the HRA then the courts are not out of step with Parliament's view of which rights are fundamental. First, the right to reside, recognised in *Pham*, is not a right recognised by the HRA (even if certain distinct rights such as the right to private life might through their operation serve to protect interests in residence). Further the common law rights might differ in scope from those under the HRA, as explicitly contemplated in *Kennedy*[145]—which in turn undermines the very consistency argument on which the new rights-developments at common law are premised. In addition the Court has only shown willingness to replicate certain HRA rights at common law. For example when cases concerning freedom of expression have reached the Court, the Court has been very keen to emphasise that the right is recognised at common law and also that these common law rights should be the analytical starting-point, rather than rights under the HRA. But in cases concerning liberty or privacy,[146] there has been no discussion of equivalent rights at common law at all, with the cases being determined solely on the basis of the HRA. This again undermines the consistency argument. Importantly it also begs the question—so far unanswered—as to why certain rights are being replicated at common law but not others; in turn this squarely brings into focus that these decisions raise complex issues of distributive justice: why are some entitlements recognised and allocated but not others?

Second, insofar as the common law is simply replicating the HRA then what is the point? Indeed, not only is it difficult to see the point, but moreover this move to rights at common law could have negative consequences. We have seen through the foregoing mapping exercise that each of common law review and HRA law perform distinctly valuable functions. This brings into focus what may be lost if common law review comes to be dominated by rights-thinking. A more general turn to rights may over time transmute a field concerned with securing the public interest into yet another rights-based field, to add to torts, human rights law, anti-discrimination law etc. The result will be the loss or stymieing of an axiomatic public law function: ensuring public power is exercised properly in accordance with the basis of its grant, for the common good. There are further possible outcomes of the intermingling of rights-based and public interest fields including that rights-based fields may be

[145] See *Kennedy* (n 37) at [101], Lord Mance, holding that Kennedy would succeed on the basis of the common law freedom of expression claim, regardless of whether he would succeed on the basis of the Article 10 claim.

[146] Liberty: *R (Hicks) v Commissioner of Police of the Metropolis* [2017] AC 256. Privacy: *SXH v Crown Prosecution Service* [2017] UKSC 30.

watered down; courts may begin to apply an approach to review under the HRA akin to review under *Wednesbury* or relevant considerations grounds.[147]

The map developed above helps us to further see that the move to introduce a rights-dimension into common law review will have ramifications for the coherence of common law review and/or could lead to significant knock-on effects within the common law of review. These matters are pertinent to assessing the wisdom of any move to rights at common law. For example, the more rights are recognised at common law, and the more courts engage in proportionality analysis, the harder it will be to justify the special protections within the judicial review procedure. In turn, this will have implications for the public interests safeguarded by those protections including those in effective, certain and final public administration and preservation of court resources. It will be harder to refuse permission for claims framed as claims of right. Despite real judicial concern over and resistance to allowing the proliferation of cross-examination and disclosure in judicial review proceedings,[148] it seems all but inevitable that the effect of adopting proportionality at common law will be that courts will be required to more frequently order cross-examination and disclosure given the highly fact-sensitive nature of proportionality. Indeed, the beginnings of these knock-on effects are now manifesting.[149] It may also be more difficult to sustain the short three-month time limit on claims, given there will now be an analogy with rights-based claims, such as those in tort for which limitation periods are longer.

There will be pressure to narrow the discretion to refuse relief in common law review. It might be possible to justify refusal of relief in the public interest where the nature of the duty breached is a public duty. But it will be more difficult to do so where the breach is of a fundamental right, given the traditionally close bond between right and remedy in English law. This is something one would imagine the courts ought to take into account in considering the wisdom of a move to rights, not least as the higher courts have recently sought to positively reassert the discretion to refuse relief on review.[150] There will also be greater pressure for recognition of a damages remedy. If the basis of the claim is breach of a personal right, and a fundamental right at that, it will be harder for the courts to continue to refuse to develop a damages remedy within common law judicial review—if the very gist of the law is protection of individual personal interests, then surely the law ought to

[147] See the material cited above at n 37.

[148] For example, Lord Neuberger MR observed that in the 'overwhelming majority of judicial review cases' oral evidence should be out of the question. It should be contemplated only in 'the most exceptional case'. This followed from 'reasons of both principle and practice' including that (i) 'if judges regularly allow witnesses and cross-examination in judicial review cases, the court time and legal costs involved in such cases will spiral'; and (ii) 'judicial review involves a judge reviewing a decision, not making it; if the judge receives evidence so as to make fresh findings of fact for himself, he is likely to make his own decision rather than to review the original decision' (*Bubb v Wandsworth LBC* [2012] PTSR 1011 at [24]–[25]). See further those authorities cited in n 125 above.

[149] *Bourgass* (n 43) at [126].

[150] *Walton* (n 99) per Lord Carnwath; *R (Champion) v North Norfolk DC* [2015] UKSC 52 at [54] ff; *Youseff* (n 137) at [61]. Contrast earlier moves to narrow the discretion to refuse relief: *Berkeley v Secretary of State for the Environment* [2001] 2 AC 603.

cure setbacks to those interests.[151] Further, the analogy with claims under the HRA, for which damages are available, will be patent, so that the absence of such remedy at common law will be viewed as increasingly anomalous. While the duties at common law continue to be conceptualised as public duties it will be much easier to sustain an argument against damages for individual loss, given the duties are not imposed for the benefit of individuals but for the benefit of the collectivity.

If common law review claims are rights based, this will create an obvious incongruity with prevailing standing rules. If the basis of the claim is a personal right, then granting standing to an interest group is objectionable on the basis that this involves an interference with the right-holder's autonomy to make choices in regard to the subject matter of the right. In turn, increasing recognition of rights at common law may have the knock-on effect of narrowing standing rules. This is a consequence that must be taken seriously given expansion of public interest standing at common law has generally been seen as a good thing—especially by the judges responsible for so expanding those rules, including current members of the Supreme Court—because wider standing enables the courts to more effectively police illegality.[152] Linked to this, it is not difficult to see how reorientation of common law review towards rights may operate to narrow the scope of substantive review doctrines. For example, in *Osborn*, Lord Reed, giving the lead judgment, held, heavily drawing on human rights law, that common law procedural fairness is underpinned, at least in part, by a dignitarian rationale.[153] In the subsequent case of *Moseley*, concerning the law of consultation, we can observe a knock-on effect of this individualist conception of procedural fairness.[154] In that case Lord Reed held that the law of consultation, being an aspect of procedural fairness, does not 'bite' outside of cases where the decision consulted on would have a particularised impact on specific individuals (unless statute dictates otherwise). The result of this individualist, human-rights-inspired conception of procedural fairness is thus to potentially radically cut down the scope of application of the law of consultation. For example, in previous case law, it had been held that the law of consultation applied to a policy proposal regarding the future of nuclear power, the requirements of procedural fairness operating to ensure meaningful public participation in the formulation of an important public policy.[155] But on the individualist view of procedural fairness the doctrine would not apply in such circumstances given a decision over future plans for nuclear energy is not a decision with individualised impact—rather it is a general policy decision. The individualist conception thus scuppers the potential for the law of consultation to promote wider interests in public engagement and citizen participation in public life.

[151] Especially if, as Lord Sumption did in *Pham*, the Supreme Court analogises these new fundamental rights to other longstanding personal rights in private law, for which damages are a standard remedy: (n 54) at [106] (invoking 'the rights of persons' analysed in Blackstone's *Commentaries*).

[152] See those cases cited at n 99 and n 101.

[153] See above (n 44).

[154] *R (Moseley) v Haringey LBC* [2014] UKSC 56; JNE Varuhas, 'Judicial Review at the Crossroads' [2015] *CLJ* 215. See also *Bank Mellat* (n 45) at [44], emphasising individual rights cases as the 'core' of procedural fairness.

[155] *R (Greenpeace) v Secretary of State for Trade and Industry* [2007] EWHC 311.

It is not possible here to reach firm conclusions on all of the matters raised in this section. But what this section has shown is that insights of great importance can be gained through analysis in terms of legal categories, and indeed that complete and rigorous legal analysis may elude us without legal taxonomy.

V. CONCLUSION

This chapter has explored the application of methods of legal categorisation within fields of public law. It propounded reasons for the general absence of work in legal categorisation within public law, and reasons why such work is important and necessary, especially given contemporary trends in legal development and academic commentary. The chapter took the first steps towards developing a taxonomy, adopting a functionalist method. Two legal categories were identified: the law relating to regulation of public powers in the public interest and the law relating to protection and vindication of basic individual rights. Application of these categories to analyse a contemporary legal issue demonstrated that deeper thinking about legal categories in public law would greatly enrich legal analysis, and that complete, nuanced and rigorous legal analysis may be impossible absent good legal taxonomy and vigorous taxonomic debate.

4

On Being Reasonably Proportionate

AUDREY MACKLIN*

I. INTRODUCTION

THE UK DEBATE about judicial review methodology shows no signs of abating. To this outside observer, it plays like a proxy war between administrative law and human rights law waged by their respective doctrinal combatants, reasonableness and proportionality. The former is engaged in a defensive action, seeking to protect its own juridical turf, while the latter—depending on one's perspective—seeks either unification or takeover. Of course, the normative stakes go deeper than doctrinal technique, and implicate the rule of law, separation of powers, and the nature and scope of the judicial role. I do not have a dog in this British fight, but my acquaintance with the Canadian variation on this theme may offer some comparative insight—or at least a cautionary tale.

I begin by setting out salient features of the Canadian legal landscape that are important to understanding the intersection of administrative law and the Canadian Charter of Rights and Freedoms (the Charter). I will next describe the state of Supreme Court of Canada jurisprudence on the doctrinal method for evaluating exercises of administrative discretion that engage constitutionally protected interests. The lesson I draw is that it may be reductive and unhelpful to cast the choice as administrative law vs constitutional law, reasonableness vs proportionality, or even deference vs intervention. Instead, I suggest that it is crucial to pry open the blackbox called 'context', which is said to explain how doctrinal tools are deployed, and begin the process of delineating precisely what contextual factors matter, how they matter and what implications flow from that recognition. The aspiration is not to simply to choose between two off-the-shelf doctrinal products, but to encourage courts to explicitly ask the pertinent questions when deciding whether and how to evaluate exercises of discretion that affect fundamental rights. Too many years of reading and teaching administrative law jurisprudence have made me wary of expecting more from doctrine.

* The author thanks Riaz Sayani Mulji for his excellent editorial assistance and the participants at the Cambridge Public Law Conference for insightful questions and comments.

II. SUBSTANTIVE JUDICIAL REVIEW, CANADIAN STYLE

About four decades ago, in *CUPE v New Brunswick Liquor Corporation*[1] the Canadian Supreme Court announced that it had reconciled itself to the legitimacy of the modern administrative state. Privative clauses that sought to oust meddling courts had to mean something, and administrative actors deserved respect. After all, the legislator had allocated a certain set of tasks to administrative decision-makers, not to the courts. Across a wide range of legal, factual, policy and discretionary decisions, there was not one correct answer anyway. Courts should resist using formalist tricks to subvert the legislator's intention to confer certain functions on administrative actors. The courts' new posture was deference; the measure of its restraint would be this: simple disagreement with the decision-maker's result would not suffice to justify intervention. A decision warranting deference would have to be some kind of unreasonable to warrant a remedy, whereas simple disagreement was enough where no deference was owed.

Matthew Lewans encapsulates the broad sweep of the change:

> The pre-*CUPE* model assumed that the purpose of judicial review was to preserve constitutional hierarchy anchored by Parliamentary sovereignty over law-making and judicial supremacy over legal interpretation; the post-*CUPE* model is premised on a more complex, democratic conception of Canadian constitutionalism, in which the line between legislative, adjudicative, and executive functions is blurred and institutions traditionally regarded as 'inferior courts' now play a significant role both in interpreting enabling legislation and fundamental values across a broad range of government policy.[2]

Despite the salutary goals of *CUPE* and its progeny, the task of selecting the standard of review (whether and how much to defer) and applying the relevant standard to the case at bar, generated recurring problems of indeterminacy. The Supreme Court has struggled ever since to devise a coherent and practicable mechanism for operationalising its vision. Every few years, it hits the reset button and tries again.[3]

The current iteration commenced with the 2008 *Dunsmuir* decision,[4] in which the Supreme Court described deference as 'both an attitude of the court and a requirement of the law of judicial review'.[5] Courts now presumptively defer to virtually all administrative actors because, and only because, the legislature has created a specialised administrative scheme that confers authority to act on those administrative decision-maker. Relative expertise in performing the statutorily mandated

[1] *CUPE v New Brunswick Liquor Corporation* [1979] 2 SCR 227.

[2] M Lewans, 'Administrative Law, Judicial Deference and the *Charter*' (2014) 23(2) *Constitutional Forum/Forum Constitutionnel* 19 at 21.

[3] After *CUPE*, the Court's attention focused on whether, in the presence of a privative clause, the disputed issue was 'jurisdictional', in which case the standard of review was correctness, or whether it was not a question of jurisdiction, in which case a court should only intervene if the decision was 'patently unreasonable'. Two standards (correctness/patent unreasonableness) were supplemented by a third (reasonableness simpliciter), as the Court's formal interest in the presence of a private clause declined. The test for standard of review became a multi-factorial balancing test largely orientated around the decision-maker's relative expertise compared to the court.

[4] *Dunsmuir v New Brunswick* [2008] 1 SCR 190.

[5] ibid, at [48].

tasks—previously the most important determinant of deference—is either deemed to exist by virtue of statutory delegation or matters only in specific circumstances. Contrary to US judge Richard Posner's rebuke to immigration decision-makers that '[d]eference is earned; it is not a birthright',[6] *Dunsmuir* (as interpreted in subsequent case law) actually does make deference a birthright of Canadian administrative decision-makers.[7]

Since *Dunsmuir*, there is only one standard of review applicable to all cases where deference is owed, and that is reasonableness. In principle, no deference is owed to cases involving 'true questions of jurisdiction', the constitutionality of a statutory provision, questions of 'central importance to the legal system as a whole and outside the expertise of the decision-maker' or matters of procedural fairness.[8] The standard of review applicable to these questions is 'correctness'. In practice, in the nine years since *Dunsmuir* was decided, the Supreme Court has declared the category of jurisdictional questions virtually extinct,[9] has identified a single question of central importance,[10] and in recent jurisprudence, has mooted the possibility of eliminating correctness review in favour of all deference, all the time.[11]

How does a reviewing court assess the reasonableness of a decision? According to *Dunsmuir*, it does the following:

> A court conducting a review for reasonableness inquires into the qualities that make a decision reasonable, referring both to the process of articulating the reasons and to outcomes. In judicial review, reasonableness is concerned mostly with the existence of justification, transparency and intelligibility within the decision-making process. But it is also concerned with whether the decision falls within a range of possible, acceptable outcomes which are defensible in respect of the facts and law.[12]

A decade earlier, the *Baker* decision recognised a general common law duty to give reasons. Though not universally required, the availability of reasons furnishes the evidence from which the justification, transparency and intelligibility of the reasoning process can be evaluated. With or without reasons, a court can also assess outcome.

The extraordinary diversity of administrative actors, subject areas, types of activities, and grounds of review might seem to test the viability of a single deferential standard of 'reasonableness'. Nevertheless, a majority of the Supreme Court resists calibration and insists that reasonableness is a single, invariant standard; there is no 'spectrum' of reasonableness.

6 *Kadia v Gonzales* 501 F3d 817 at 821 (7th Cir 2007).

7 For example, in *Canada (Public Safety and Emergency Preparedness) v Tran* 2015 FCA 237, appeal heard by Supreme Court of Canada, 13 January 2017 (judgment reserved), the Federal Court of Appeal deferred to a decision by an immigration enforcement officer that applied a particular interpretation of criminal law after expressly refusing to consider arguments on statutory interpretation raised by counsel. The decision contained no reasons about the contested issue. The Federal Court of Appeal retrofitted the enforcement officer's decision with an interpretation that would generate an outcome consistent with the officer's decision, and then concluded that the decision was reasonable.

8 See *Dunsmuir* (n 4) at [58]–[61]; *Mission Institution v Khela* [2014] 1 SCR 502 at [79].

9 *Alberta (Information and Privacy Commissioner) v Alberta Teachers' Association* [2011] 3 SCR 654. The question concerned the scope of solicitor-client privilege.

10 *Alberta (Information and Privacy Commissioner) v University of Calgary* [2016] 2 SCR 555.

11 *Wilson v Atomic Energy of Canada Ltd* [2016] 1 SCR 770.

12 See *Dunsmuir* (n 4) at [47].

To date, lower courts have tried unsuccessfully to persuade the Supreme Court that one need not endorse a sliding scale of reasonableness to recognise that what may be required to demonstrate reasonableness will vary according to the specificities of the case. The Court has gone so far as to acknowledge that the application of reasonableness 'takes its colour from the context'.[13] Unfortunately, it has applied reasonableness for close to a decade without identifying the contextual crayons that do the colouring. Sometimes, reasonableness looks a lot like close scrutiny,[14] sometimes it looks like a casual glance in the direction of the administrative decision,[15] and sometimes it looks like something in between.

Where does the Charter fit into this? First, and most obviously, the mechanism for testing the reasonableness of a decision differs from the proportionality analysis used to justify a breach of a Charter right under section 1. Section 1 of the Charter provides that:

> The Canadian Charter of Rights and Freedoms guarantees the rights and freedoms set out in it subject only to such reasonable limits prescribed by law as can be demonstrably justified in a free and democratic society.

The so-called *Oakes* test stipulates the following analytical framework for determining whether a rights limitation prescribed by law is demonstrably justified:[16]

1. There must a pressing and substantial objective for the law or government action.
2. The means chosen to achieve the objective must be proportional to the burden on the rights of the claimant:
   (a) The objective must be rationally connected to the limit on the Charter right.
   (b) The limit must minimally impair the Charter right, within a margin of appreciation.
   (c) There should be an overall balance or proportionality between the benefits of the limit and its deleterious effects.

Clearly, the *Oakes* test is not reducible to a general inquiry into the intelligibility or rationality of the chain of reasoning or the defensibility of the outcome.

Secondly, in the 2003 *Martin*[17] decision, the Court unanimously ruled that administrative decision-makers who decide questions of law are competent to rule on Charter challenges to their constitutive statute. In so doing, the Court adopted the views expressed a few years earlier in the dissenting judgment of Justice McLachlin (as she then was) in *Cooper*.[18] Apart from the practical contribution that administrative decision-makers could make in marshaling valuable empirical data and

[13] *Canada (Citizenship and Immigration) v Khosa* [2009] 1 SCR 339 at [59].

[14] *Canada (Canadian Human Rights Commission) v Canada (Attorney General)* [2011] 3 SCR 471; see *Alberta (Information and Privacy Commissioner)* (n 9).

[15] *Newfoundland and Labrador Nurses' Union v Newfoundland and Labrador (Treasury Board)* [2011] 3 SCR 708.

[16] *R v Oakes* [1986] 1 SCR 103.

[17] *Nova Scotia (Workers' Compensation Board) v Martin* [2003] 2 SCR 504.

[18] *Cooper v Canada (Human Rights Commission)* [1996] 3 SCR 854.

field expertise, McLachlin J evoked an ethos of democratic constitutionalism, in which all branches of government (legislative, executive, judicial) are partners in a co-ordinated project of realising the Charter as the apex of Canada's legal order:

> The *Charter* is not some holy grail which only judicial initiates of the superior courts may touch. The *Charter* belongs to the people. All law and law-makers that touch the people must conform to it. Tribunals and commissions charged with deciding legal issues are no exception. Many more citizens have their rights determined by these tribunals than by the courts. If the *Charter* is to be meaningful to ordinary people, then it must find its expression in the decisions of these tribunals. If Parliament makes it clear that a particular tribunal can decide facts and facts alone, so be it. But if Parliament confers on the tribunal the power to decide questions of law, that power must, in the absence of counter-indications, be taken to extend to the *Charter*, and to the question of whether the *Charter* renders portions of its enabling statute unconstitutional.[19]

As noted earlier, administrative determinations of constitutionality attract no curial deference.

Thirdly, the landmark *Baker* decision in 1998 cast the net of deference over judicial review of discretion.[20] Deference did not insulate decisions entirely, however, because 'discretion must be exercised in accordance with the boundaries imposed in the statute, the principles of the rule of law, the principles of administrative law, the fundamental values of Canadian society, and the *principles of the Charter*'.[21] In so stating, the Court swept the Charter into the ambit of potentially relevant considerations that circumscribe the exercise of discretion. The Court did not explain whether a principle of the Charter is the same as, or different from, a Charter right. But since the Court in *Baker* did not consider it necessary to address the Charter on the facts of the case, the question was neither asked nor answered.

III. DISCRETIONARY DECISIONS THAT ENGAGE THE CHARTER

A. The *Oakes* Test vs Administrative Law Proportionality

The Supreme Court of Canada has vacillated in its guidance about how to review discretion that engages the Charter. *Multani*[22] concerned a Sikh schoolboy in Quebec who sought to carry a ceremonial dagger as part of his religious observance. The district school board had a 'no weapons in the school' policy, but the local school board negotiated an arrangement with the boy's parents that would neutralise the safety risk by requiring that the dagger be kept in a pouch sewn into the boy's clothes. The district school board refused to accept the accommodation. The case was litigated to the Supreme Court of Canada. Multani argued that the discretionary decision to not accommodate the student violated his constitutionally protected freedom of religion.

[19] ibid, at [70].
[20] *Baker v Canada (Minister of Citizenship & Immigration)* [1999] 2 SCR 817.
[21] ibid, at [56], emphasis added.
[22] *Multani v Commission Scolaire Marguerite-Bourgeoys* [2006] 1 SCR 256.

The infringement of Multani's religious freedom was obvious. A majority of the Court approached the decision through the lens of section 1 of the Charter, and found that the failure to accommodate Multani could not be justified according to the *Oakes* test. A minority led by Abella J insisted that the better lens was administrative law reasonableness and found the decision unreasonable. In *Doré*,[23] Abella J's position unanimously prevailed.

At issue in *Doré* was a decision by the Barreau du Quebec's disciplinary body to reprimand a lawyer for writing an intemperate personal letter to a judge complaining about that judge's hostile and uncivil conduct in the courtroom. The lawyer objected that the reprimand breached his freedom of expression under section 2(b) of the Charter.

The disciplinary panel concluded that Doré breached article 2.03 of the Code of Ethics of Advocates, which states that 'The conduct of an advocate must bear the stamp of objectivity, moderation and dignity.' By the time the case reached the Supreme Court, Doré's argument was that the unconstitutionality did not reside in the provision of the Code of Ethics, but rather in its discretionary application to his specific case in a manner that breached his freedom of expression.

Something else happened to freedom of expression on its way to Ottawa. It departed the Quebec Court of Appeal as a Charter *right*, but arrived at the Supreme Court of Canada as a Charter *value*. At the outset of the Court's analysis, Abella J describes the appellant's position as a violation of 'the expressive *rights* protected by s. 2(b) of the *Charter*'.[24] Two paragraphs later, she reformulates the issue as follows: 'It goes without saying that administrative decision-makers must act consistently with the values underlying the grant of discretion, including *Charter values*.'[25] For the remainder of the judgment, Abella J conspicuously and repeatedly refers to Charter values, not Charter rights.

The choice of language seems deliberate. Freedom of expression is indisputably a protected Charter right, and sanctioning Doré for his letter undeniably limited his freedom of expression. The use of 'value' rather than 'right' can only signify that freedom of expression is protected differently when it is limited by the exercise of discretion than when it is limited by statute or regulation. But how? Two possibilities spring to mind. First, the scope or depth of the protection afforded to freedom of expression is diminished where it is limited through discretion. Alternatively, the quantum of protection does not vary, but the analytical framework by which the limitation is assessed is different where it arises in the context of discretion.

Doré purports to convey the latter meaning. Abella J explains that 'while a formulaic application of the *Oakes* test may not be workable in the context of an adjudicated decision, distilling its essence works the same justificatory muscles: balance and proportionality'.[26] The goal, then, is to subject the exercise of Charter-infringing discretion to a proportionality test that is tailored to the specificity and individualised nature of discretion. The essence of proportionality is that a decision

[23] *Doré v Barreau du Québec* [2012] 1 SCR 395.
[24] ibid, at [22], emphasis added.
[25] ibid, at [24], emphasis added.
[26] ibid, at [5].

should 'interfere[...] with the relevant *Charter* guarantee no more than is necessary given the statutory objectives'.[27] Later in the judgment, Abella J provides the roadmap:

> [The administrative decision-maker] balances the *Charter* values with the statutory objectives. In effecting this balancing, the decision-maker should first consider the statutory objectives ... Then the decision-maker should ask how the *Charter* value at issue will best be protected in view of the statutory objectives. This is at the core of the proportionality exercise, and requires the decision-maker to balance the severity of the interference of the *Charter* protection with the statutory objective.[28]

The Court's abbreviated account of proportionality analysis for administrative actors amounts to instructing them to name the relevant Charter 'value', identify the statutory objectives, and then balance them. One wonders whether this description is adequate to guide decision-makers about what they are expected to do. The concern is made more acute by the fact that jurisdiction to determine the constitutionality of a statutory provision is limited to decision-makers with authority to interpret law, but the Court has not imposed similar qualifications on administrative decision-makers exercising discretion that may infringe the Charter.

The task of integrating the Charter into the exercise of discretion is distinct from determining the standard of review applicable on judicial review of the discretionary decision. While *Martin* and then *Dunsmuir* stated that constitutional questions would be reviewed on a correctness standard, *Doré* further shrinks the ambit of correctness review by preferring a deferential reasonableness standard for questions of constitutionality where they arise in the individual exercise of discretion.

According to the Court, deference to discretionary decisions that engage the Charter is warranted because of the administrative decision-maker's relative expertise:

> Deference is still justified on the basis of the decision-maker's expertise and its proximity to the facts of the case. Even where *Charter* values are involved, the administrative decision-maker will generally be in the best position to consider the impact of the relevant *Charter* values *on the specific facts of the case*.[29]

At this point, the Court turns to explicating why deferring to an administrative actor's application of the administrative proportionality test will not dilute the level of protection that individuals would receive via the *Oakes* test. The key claim is that judicial deference in administrative law is not so different from the element of judicial deference built into the *Oakes* test. According to the Court:

> [T]he role of judicial review for reasonableness aligns with the one applied in the Oakes context. As this Court recognized in *RJR-MacDonald Inc. v. Canada (Attorney General)*, [1995] 3 S.C.R. 199, at para. 160, 'courts must accord some leeway to the legislator' in the Charter balancing exercise, and the proportionality test will be satisfied if the measure 'falls within a range of reasonable alternatives'. The same is true in the context of a review of an administrative decision for reasonableness, where decision-makers are entitled to a measure of deference so long as the decision, in the words of Dunsmuir, 'falls within a range

[27] ibid, at [7].
[28] ibid, at [55]–[56].
[29] ibid, at [54], emphasis in original.

> of possible, acceptable outcomes' … Though this judicial review is conducted within the administrative framework, there is nonetheless conceptual harmony between a reasonableness review and the Oakes framework, since both contemplate giving a 'margin of appreciation', or deference, to administrative and legislative bodies in balancing Charter values against broader objectives.[30]

I dispute the Court's depiction of 'conceptual harmony' for several reasons. First, the replacement of Charter 'right' or 'freedom' with Charter 'value' obscures the recognition of rights and freedoms in play. Secondly, the administrative law proportionality analysis that the Court endorses in *Doré* does not respect the primacy or priority of Charter rights. Finally, curial deference toward the outcomes it produces exacerbates the dilution of rights protection. More insidiously, it creates negative incentives for governance according to the rule of law by making the executive less accountable for Charter breaches committed via discretion than by operation of a legal norm.

B. What is a Charter Value?

Before proceeding further, let me emphasise that my critique of 'Charter values' applies only to the use of 'Charter value' as a proxy for 'Charter right' when applied to a discretionary decision. Unfortunately, the term 'Charter values' has multiple meanings, depending on where it is deployed. Sometimes, Charter values refer to the ideals that underlie and animate Charter rights. In *Oakes*, Dickson CJ described them as follows:

> The Court must be guided by the values and principles essential to a free and democratic society which I believe embody, to name but a few, respect for the inherent dignity of the human person, commitment to social justice and equality, accommodation of a wide variety of beliefs, respect for cultural and group identity, and faith in social and political institutions which enhance the participation of individuals and groups in society.[31]

These Charter values *qua* values-underlying-Charter-rights are invoked as tools for interpreting the meaning and scope of Charter rights themselves. The same Charter values may play a role in statutory interpretation in circumstances of 'genuine ambiguity … where a statutory provision is subject to differing, but equally plausible, interpretations'.[32] Ruth Sullivan explains that constitutions, including the Charter:

> [S]et out the norms that are most highly valued in our culture. For this reason, quite apart from questions of validity or showing deference to the legislature, it is appropriate for courts to prefer [statutory] interpretations that tend to promote those norms over interpretations that do not.[33]

[30] ibid, at [56]–[57].
[31] See *Oakes* (n 16) at [64].
[32] *Bell ExpressVu Limited Partnership v Rex* [2002] 2 SCR 559 at [62].
[33] R Sullivan, *Sullivan on the Construction of Statutes*, 6th edn (Markham, LexisNexis, 2014) section 16.12.

What counts as a Charter value and the meaning ascribed to it may be contestable, but whatever Charter values are in *Oakes* or in statutory interpretation, they are not synonymous with Charter rights.[34]

Elsewhere, when a common law rule is challenged for non-compliance with the Charter, Charter value is more or less synonymous with Charter right. The use of the term 'value' rather than 'right' seems intended to signal the different context in which the Charter is deployed. Here, a Charter value means a Charter-right-impacted-by-a-common-law-rule. As Matthew Horner explains,[35] section 32 confines the Charter's application to emanations of the legislature and executive (including the administration); it does not encompass judicially produced common law. Moreover, a common law does not qualify as a 'limit prescribed by law', to the extent that 'law' is understood as primary or subordinate legislation.

Subjecting common law rules—whether in private law, evidence or procedure—to the discipline of Charter 'values' retains the content of Charter rights, but adapts the method of constitutional analysis to the specificity of the common law. The concept of a Charter 'value' was invoked in *Dolphin Delivery*[36] and the associated analytical structure developed in *Hill v Church of Scientology*.[37] The purpose of the exercise was to enable courts *qua* neutral arbiters to review and revise potential Charter-infringing common law rules applicable as between private litigants, without unfairly imposing the section 1 justificatory burden on private parties. These considerations are not germane to evaluating Charter compliance of discretionary decisions by a government actor.

Back to Charter values in discretion: the Court has yet to offer a precise definition of Charter values or principles in the context of discretion. Indeed, even before one arrives at the question of proportionality, one must figure out if a Charter 'value' is engaged on the facts of the case. Sometimes, the answer seems easy, as in *Multani* and *Doré*. Yet, in *Divito*,[38] judges of the Federal Court, the Court of Appeal and the Supreme Court of Canada disagreed about whether the exercise of discretion to withhold consent to the transfer of a Canadian prisoner from the US to Canada engaged a citizen's right under section 6(1) of the Charter to enter Canada.[39] The majority of the Supreme Court rejected the argument that refusing a prisoner's transfer request prima facie infringed the appellant's section 6 Charter right to enter Canada, yet went on to comment that the individual discretionary decision to consent to a prisoner transfer request must comply with Charter 'values'. The Court did not explain what the Charter 'value' would be, and how it would differ from the

[34] Indeed, courts must walk a fine line when interpreting statutes in light of the Charter; if they read a provision 'down' to achieve conformity with a Charter right (as distinct from an underlying norm or value), rather than submitting the provision to a full constitutional challenge, they risk depriving the government of the opportunity to justify a non-conforming interpretation under s 1 of the Charter.

[35] M Horner, 'Charter Values: The Uncanny Valley of Canadian Constitutionalism' (2014) 67 *The Supreme Court Law Review: Osgoode's Annual Constitutional Cases Conference* 361.

[36] *RWDSU v Dolphin Delivery Ltd* [1986] 2 SCR 573.

[37] *Hill v Church of Scientology* [1995] 2 SCR 1130.

[38] *Divito v Canada (Public Safety and Emergency Preparedness)* [2013] 3 SCR 157.

[39] ibid, at [10]–[12], [18]–[48].

section 6 Charter right to enter one's country of citizenship, which the Court had just ruled was not engaged.

Administrative decision-makers must make a preliminary assessment of whether a given exercise of discretion engages a Charter value, bringing whatever insight their field expertise and proximity to the facts of the case offers in aid of this determination. As the *Doré* case illustrates, even determining whether a Charter 'value' is at stake in the first place demands a certain level of legal sophistication. It is worth recalling that the decision-makers in *Doré* happened to be lawyers acting as a disciplinary body for the Barreau du Québec. Most administrative decision-makers who exercise discretion are not trained lawyers performing a formal adjudicative role.

C. Normative Primacy and Priority

I commend the Court's democratic impulse to 'bring the Charter to the people' by enabling administrative decision-makers to consider the Charter in the course of executing their functions. But if the aspiration is that the Charter should permeate the legal order from the bottom to the top, the project is imperiled by an analytical method that purports to marry a simplified proportionality analysis with *Dunsmuir*'s deferential reasonableness review.[40] In my view, this jurisprudential mash-up respects neither the primacy nor priority of Charter rights and produces instead a Charter-lite approach to discretion.

The Court asserts that an administrative decision-maker 'exercising a discretionary power … has, by virtue of expertise and specialization, particular familiarity with the competing considerations at play in weighing *Charter* values'.[41] If this is true, then this expertise would presumably be equally pertinent and advantageous in a constitutional challenge to the administrative body's constitutive statute or legislative provisions granting discretion. After all, virtually all constitutional issues before an administrative decision-maker will arise in a concrete and specific factual context that engages the decision-maker's expertise and specialisation.

Returning to *Doré*, there is no reason to think that the Barreau's disciplinary body's expertise and specialisation would be any less salient had the Code of Ethics for advocates explicitly proscribed oral or written communication that failed to display moderation or dignity. Yet, had the disciplinary body been called upon to determine the constitutionality of the discretion-conferring provision itself, that decision would have attracted no deference *per Dunsmuir*, and would have been assessed against a standard of review of correctness. What the Court does in *Doré* is take valid reasons for permitting an administrative decision-maker to consider the Charter and repackage them into reasons for deferring to the result of that consideration. This either contradicts the logic of *Dunsmuir*'s retention of correctness for constitutional matters or portends the demise of correctness review for constitutionality.

Any competent administrative decision-maker who exercises discretion should be acquainted with the objectives of the statute he or she administers, and will

[40] See *Dunsmuir* (n 4).
[41] See *Doré* (n 23) at [47].

have acquired experience in determining facts, drawing inferences and balancing competing factors. If all that proportionality analysis demanded of decision-makers is that they add 'Charter value' into the mix of costs and benefits to be weighed en route to a decision, and then ask whether it is necessary to limit the Charter protection to advance the statutory objectives, one might indeed suppose that administrative decision-makers' expertise will serve them well enough.

But that is not how proportionality operates under section 1 of the Charter. The normative primacy of Charter rights structures a more demanding inquiry. A proportionality analysis in the context of rights adjudication is not neutral as between rights and freedoms protected by the Charter and other interests, entitlements or 'values'. To denominate an interest as a right is to recognise its normative primacy. A Charter right intrinsically 'weighs' more (by virtue of being a right) than something called an interest, value or entitlement.[42]

One might reply that a court on judicial review would notice the administrative decision-maker's failure to assign sufficient weight to a Charter value, and set aside the decision as unreasonable. However, the Court's standard of review jurisprudence emphatically insists that deferential review of discretion precludes reweighing the factors relevant to the exercise of discretion. When the Court in *Baker* appeared to fault an immigration officer for failing to give appropriate weight to the best interests of children affected by deportation of their mother, the Supreme Court in *Suresh* was anxious to correct that impression. It denied that *Baker* endorsed re-weighing of discretionary factors in the course of a reasonableness review:

> It follows that the weighing of relevant factors is not the function of a court reviewing the exercise of ministerial discretion ... The Court's recent decision in *Baker* ... did not depart from this view ... *Baker* does not authorize courts reviewing decisions on the discretionary end of the spectrum to engage in a new weighing process, but draws on an established line of cases concerning the failure of ministerial delegates to consider and weigh implied limitations and/or patently relevant factors.[43]

The Court's concern with reweighing the elements in a discretionary decision is that it will erode curial deference by opening up discretionary decisions to excessive judicial intervention. The Court has subsequently reiterated its opposition to reweighing evidence, inferences or factors when engaging in a reasonableness review of discretion.[44]

Doré does not depart from this admonition against re-weighing. After describing the technique of incorporating Charter values into the reasonableness inquiry, Abella J states that '[i]f in exercising its statutory discretion, the decision-maker has properly balanced the relevant *Charter* value with the statutory objectives, the decision will be found to be reasonable'.[45] Perhaps the modifier 'properly' in front

[42] Lord Bingham recognised this in the UK context: *R (Daly) v Secretary of State for the Home Department* [2001] 2 AC 532.

[43] *Suresh v Canada (Minister of Citizenship and Immigration)* [2002] 1 SCR 3 at [34]–[37].

[44] See, eg, *Khosa v Canada (Minister of Citizenship and Immigration)* [2009] 1 SCR 339.

[45] See *Doré* (n 23) at [58].

of 'balanced' is intended to introduce the possibility of judicial re-weighing when Charter values are involved, but this would represent such a significant departure from the Court's resistance to re-weighing that it seems unsafe to infer it from an adverb.

A Charter right, once established, also asserts normative priority. A rights-bearing individual need not justify the exercise of a Charter right; rather, the state must justify infringing it, and the state's burden is a heavy one. Both of these requirements flow from the intrinsic heftiness of rights. The stages of the test are designed to ensure that limiting a right serves important objectives, actually advances those objectives, and limits the right no more than is required to achieve the objective. Only after clearing each of those hurdles does one arrive at the ultimate balancing of the last step, in which the failure to accord sufficient weight to the Charter right may yet yield the conclusion that the government has not discharged its burden.

The priority of Charter rights exemplifies what David Dyzenhaus describes as a rule of law culture of justification, as opposed to a 'managerial culture':

> [The culture of justification] is shaped by the assumption that *the public authority bears the onus of justifying the limit on the right asserted*, and it requires that the authority regard persons as bearer of rights, not as individuals who may or may not be accorded a privilege.[46]

The confounding feature of discretion, of course, is that it presupposes that the person has no right to a particular outcome (indeed, the outcome may, in this technical sense, be a 'privilege') but insofar as the Charter is implicated in the decision, the individual should be regarded as a rights bearer.

While *Doré* does instruct decision-makers to assess the necessity of limiting the Charter protection to achieve statutory objectives, the Court provides no practical advice about how to do that. On its face, it encourages a mere balancing of the Charter as one factor among others. Perhaps the Court in *Doré* intends to convey the normative primacy and priority of the Charter and all that is entailed when it enjoins decision-makers to 'remain conscious of the fundamental importance of *Charter* values in the analysis'.[47] If so, it should have said more.

D. Democratic Legitimacy vs Independence

Another incongruity that runs through *Doré* proportionality concerns the value attached to political versus judicial accountability. Some Supreme Court jurisprudence suggests that the proximity of a decision-maker to the political branch of government is relevant to deference. As Binnie J commented in *Dunsmuir*, 'different administrative decisions command different degrees of deference, depending on who is deciding what'.[48] Sometimes, judges show deference to administrative

[46] D Dyzenhaus, 'Proportionality and Deference in a Culture of Justification' in G Huscroft, BW Miller and G Webber (eds), *Proportionality and the Rule of Law: Rights, Justification, Reasoning* (Cambridge, Cambridge University Press, 2014) 234, 251, emphasis added.

[47] See *Doré* (n 23) at [54].

[48] See *Dunsmuir* (n 4) at [135].

decision-makers located at or near the top of what Binnie J, in *Dunsmuir*, dubbed the administrative food chain:

> A minister making decisions under the *Extradition Act* ... to surrender a fugitive, for example, is said to be 'at the extreme legislative end of the *continuum* of administrative decision-making' ... On the other hand, a ministerial delegate making a deportation decision according to ministerial guidelines was accorded considerably less deference in *Baker* (where the 'reasonableness *simpliciter*' standard was applied). The difference does not lie only in the judge's view of the perceived immediacy of the defect in the administrative decision. In *Suresh v. Canada (Minister of Citizenship and Immigration)* ... a unanimous Court adopted the caution in the context of counter-terrorism measures that '[i]f the people are to accept the consequences of such decisions, they must be made by persons whom the people have elected and whom they can remove' (para. 33) ... Then there are the Cabinet and Ministers of the Crown who make broad decisions of public policy such as testing cruise missiles, *Operation Dismantle Inc. v. The Queen*, [1985] 1 S.C.R. 441, or policy decisions arising out of decisions of major administrative tribunals, as in *Attorney General of Canada v. Inuit Tapirisat of Canada*, [1980] 2 S.C.R. 735, at p. 753, where the Court said: 'The very nature of the body must be taken into account in assessing the technique of review which has been adopted by the Governor in Council.'[49]

Similarly, in *CUPE v Ontario (Minister of Labour)*,[50] Bastarache J (dissenting) remarked that a statutory grant of discretion to a Minister 'as opposed to an apolitical figure'[51] signaled legislative preference for political accountability over legal accountability, and supported a posture of curial deference.[52] In a Westminster system, ministers tend to attract higher deference precisely because of their proximity to the legislative branch—if the legislator has delegated decision-making authority to a member of the executive who is also a legislator, perhaps it is because the decision calls upon those skills, perceptions and knowledge that a political actor possesses and courts should defer accordingly. Although sometimes elided with expertise, the stature of an elected decision-maker furnishes a slightly different rationale for deference.

The judicial posture toward ministers exposes a fundamental tension between the democratic impulse that underwrites deference and the counter-majoritarian dimension of constitutional rights adjudication. Judges are entrusted with adjudicating the Charter not only because of their legal expertise, but also because of their independence from government. Some Charter cases engage questions of redistribution that resist straightforward classification as state infringement of individual right, but many Charter challenges do conform to type. The judiciary's real and perceived insulation from political pressure matters to the legitimacy of rights adjudication when government actors are alleged to have breached the constitutional rights of individuals subject to their authority. Yet, standard of review jurisprudence currently justifies deference by reference to democratic delegation. Quasi-judicial tribunals

[49] ibid, at [136].
[50] *CUPE v Ontario (Minister of Labour)* [2003] 1 SCR 539.
[51] ibid, at [18].
[52] See also *Mount Sinai Hospital Center v Quebec (Minister of Health and Social Services)* [2001] 2 SCR 281 at [58] (Binnie J).

who enjoy a measure of relative independence enjoy no more or less deference than front-line bureaucrats and possibly less than ministers of the crown. The independence of the administrative decision-maker from government does not matter to deference.

But in Charter litigation, proximity to the political branch of government pulls in the opposite direction—decisions by elected officials (legislators) are distrusted precisely because they might be inclined to trade off individual rights for political gain through appealing to majoritarian interests. In other words, democratic legitimacy, political acumen and access to expert staff may incline courts to display particular deference to ministers in judicial review of discretion, but this translates awkwardly into a rationale for deference where the Charter is at issue. The fact that an administrative decision-maker is also a high-ranking elected official is not a reason to defer to the balance he or she strikes between protection of individual rights and advancement of other public objectives (statutory or otherwise). It may even be a reason *not* to defer.

It must be acknowledged, however, that the Supreme Court of Canada in *Lake* was not troubled by this tension. It counseled deference to the minister's determination of whether the minister's own decision to extradite would infringe a fugitive's Charter rights.[53] This comes close to allowing, as Tom Hickman describes, ministers confronting the constitutionality of their actions to be judges in their own cause.[54] When a court refrains from scrutinising a minister's Charter calculus on account of that minister's political status, it is not engaging in deference-as-respect, but rather deference-as-abdication. It is not the same careful and circumscribed exercise restraint that a court might exhibit in assessing alternative options under the minimal impairment branch of the *Oakes* test; it is, rather, a casual and tacit declaration that courts ought not to interfere with ministerial power in certain politicised contexts, even where constitutionally protected human rights are at stake. Some might defend this posture on some account of justiciability or institutional legitimacy, but that does not alter the character of the act. In the interests of transparency, it would be preferable if the Court were to provide a normative justification for deeming certain rights violations non-justiciable, rather than disguising it behind a timid 'reasonableness' review.

In *Doré,* the discretion was exercised by the Barreau du Québec, an independent, quasi-judicial tribunal composed of lawyers. Administrative decision-makers situated elsewhere on the executive spectrum between legislator and judiciary should not be presumed to possess comparable expertise or neutral disposition toward rights protection. As Ruth Sullivan notes of many 'non-judicial' administrative actors:

> Their focus tends to be narrow and coloured by the concerns and possibly by the biases of their own professional culture. They may have particular interests to promote on behalf of their department or agency or they may have strong views respecting the groups or

[53] *Lake v Canada (Minister of Justice)* [2008] 1 SCR 761 at [34], quoted in *Doré* (n 23) at [50].

[54] T Hickman, 'Adjudicating Constitutional Rights in Administrative Law' (2016) 66 *University of Toronto Law Journal* 121 at 128.

> problems regulated by their legislation. This may put them into an adversarial position with other interested parties.[55]

This does not suggest that decision-makers with authority to interpret law should not consider the Charter when exercising discretion. Their valuable 'field expertise' may enhance the fact-finding process, the elaboration of the statutory scheme and the richness of the evidentiary foundation. Some individual decision-makers may also produce legally sophisticated and cogent Charter analyses. Many will not, either for lack of ability, time, resources or independence, or some combination thereof. There is simply no basis for a presumption that a decision-maker's 'field expertise', which may contribute constructively to some aspects of a Charter analysis, equips the decision-maker to manage all aspects of a Charter analysis. On judicial review, judges should certainly pay respectful attention to the reasons given by decision-makers exercising Charter-impacting discretion. Sometimes the reasons may be persuasive, and a judge should be as open to benefitting from a rigorous and compelling set of reasons in the same way he or she is open to persuasion from high quality submissions by counsel, analyses by law clerks, or opinions of fellow judges.

In other words, the arguments in favour of Charter jurisdiction do not explain why deference is owed to their Charter outcomes. Nor do arguments about why courts should defer to the exercise of discretion on non-Charter matters automatically extend to those aspects of discretion that implicate the Charter. Yet *Doré* commits both of these errors. The slippage is exacerbated by the fact that Court in *Doré* equips administrative decision-makers with a Charter-lite methodology that is approximate, vague and incomplete. The problems begin with the Court's imprecise invocation of Charter values and continue to its breezy account of proportionality.

The Court in *Doré* might plausibly have taken the view that the constraints facing administrative decision-makers generally make it unrealistic to expect a sophisticated and thorough Charter analysis (even if, in practice, some administrative decision-makers do it very well). Fair enough. The Court might also have adapted its Charter methodology to the context of discretion without sacrificing the priority and primacy of rights, just as the Court did for common law rules. But if the Charter-lite approach to discretion lacks the rigour of a proper Charter analysis, it is not apparent why the outcomes it generates should merit a deferential posture on review.

An obvious objection to curial deference is that it insulates the violation of fundamental rights and freedoms from judicial scrutiny and remedy. The words 'I may have come to a different conclusion, but I cannot say that the tribunal was unreasonable in its decision' plays like an appropriate expression of judicial modesty in the twenty-first century administrative state. The statement 'I may have concluded that the applicant's Charter rights were violated, but I cannot say the Minister was unreasonable in concluding that they were not' sounds a more discordant note. Perhaps the Court wished to deflect this concern with its account of how elements of curial deference are already built into the *Oakes* test. This would invite an inference that judicial review of the reasonableness of a discretionary decision and judicial

[55] R Sullivan, *Sullivan on the Construction of Statutes*, 6th edn (Markham, LexisNexis, 2014) section 23.114.

review of a direct application of the *Oakes* test, will produce comparable Charter protection. The routes might be different, but the destination is the same.

So, for example, the Court finds purported symmetry in the reasonableness standard of judicial review and the 'minimal impairment' inquiry in the *Oakes* test:

> This is where the role of judicial review for reasonableness aligns with the one applied in the *Oakes* context. As this Court recognized in *RJR-MacDonald Inc. v. Canada (Attorney General)*, [1995] 3 S.C.R. 199, at para. 160, 'courts must accord some leeway to the legislator' in the *Charter* balancing exercise, and the proportionality test will be satisfied if the measure 'falls within a range of reasonable alternatives'. The same is true in the context of a review of an administrative decision for reasonableness, where decision-makers are entitled to a measure of deference so long as the decision, in the words of *Dunsmuir*, 'falls within a range of possible, acceptable outcomes'.[56]

In the next paragraph, Abella J reiterates her view of 'conceptual harmony' between reasonableness review and the *Oakes* test:

> As LeBel J. noted in *Multani*, when a court is faced with reviewing an administrative decision that implicates *Charter* rights, '[t]he issue becomes one of proportionality' (para. 155), and calls for integrating the spirit of s. 1 into judicial review. Though this judicial review is conducted within the administrative framework, there is nonetheless conceptual harmony between a reasonableness review and the *Oakes* framework, since both contemplate giving a 'margin of appreciation', or deference, to administrative and legislative bodies in balancing *Charter* values against broader objectives.[57]

The scope, meaning and application of deference by the Supreme Court in the context of 'minimal impairment' are matters of considerable complexity and nuance.[58] In any event, I concur with David Mullan's scepticism that administrative law deference and 'margin of appreciation' in the context of minimal impairment share as much in common as Abella J implies. As Mullan comments:

> [E]ven when translated to the world of judicial review of administrative action, that limited concession [in the *Oakes* test] to a margin of appreciation in the context of a justification of a *prima facie* violation of a protected right or freedom seems far removed from the respect for agency choice found in the normal application of an unreasonableness standard of review.[59]

Mullan correctly observes that the deference contemplated by judicial review on a standard of reasonableness is qualitatively different and quantitatively broader than that which is contemplated under the narrower and more confined 'leeway' accorded to the legislator under the minimal impairment stage of the *Oakes* test. After all, deference is currently predicated on the claim that the choice of the legislator to confer authority on the executive (rather than directly on the courts) signals a preference

[56] See *Doré* (n 23) at [56].
[57] ibid, at [57].
[58] See R Moon, 'Justified Limits on Expression: The Collapse of the General Approach to Limits on *Charter* Rights' (2002) 40 *Osgoode Hall Law Journal* 337 at 358–65.
[59] D Mullan, 'Unresolved Issues on Standard of Review in Canadian Judicial Review of Administrative Action—The Top Fifteen!' (2013) 42 *Advocates' Quarterly* 1 at 53.

for the state actor's view of how best to fulfil the legislator's mandate. The Charter tilts in the opposite direction. The adjudication of rights and the judicial authority to invalidate legislation or otherwise remedy Charter-infringing government action are predicated on the relative institutional competence, expertise and independence that courts enjoy over the legislator and the executive. The limited space allocated to a 'margin of appreciation' for legislative choice does not make deference a defining feature of the Charter's analytical framework.

Paul Daly also conducts an extended, incisive, comparative analysis of each step of the *Oakes* test and the elements of reasonableness review in administrative law. He tests the hypothesis that proportionality (using *Oakes* as the paradigm) is broadly reconcilable with reasonableness review in administrative law. He concludes that it is not: *Oakes*' proportionality test is a more intrusive standard of review.[60]

It is difficult to resist the conclusion that *Doré*'s breezy methodology may sometimes but not always or necessarily deliver the same level of Charter protection as would a more meticulous Charter analysis. Cracks at several points expose its structural weakness: From the outset, the term Charter 'value' rather than 'right' obfuscates the crucial questions that should lie at the core of the inquiry, which are first, whether the decision engages a constitutionally protected right or freedom; and second whether that right or freedom is infringed, whether by the exercise of discretion or by application of a legal rule. Next, the proportionality analysis that the Court commends to administrative decision-makers does not acknowledge or respect the primacy or the priority of constitutionally protected rights. As such, administrative decision-makers are not instructed to treat a Charter right or freedom (if that is what a 'value' is) as intrinsically weightier than other types of interests or considerations.

This Charter-lite methodology would not be fatal, if courts on judicial review were authorised to measure the outcomes reached by the administrative decision-maker against a substantive metric that did value Charter rights and freedoms appropriately. But according to *Doré*, a reviewing court must assess the result of the proportionality analysis on a standard of reasonableness, and must not re-evaluate the weight accorded to the Charter value as against competing interests or objectives. To re-weigh would undermine fidelity to the principle of curial deference in administrative law. Despite *Doré*'s promise, it seems beyond peradventure that an administrative actor exercising discretion will form the view that the Charter value is less important than the objectives sought by its infringement, and a reviewing court will not intervene because it is not supposed to reweigh the factors, even if it might have given greater weight to the harm inflicted by the Charter violation.

Not all Charter violations are equal; some rights infringements are graver than others. Sanctioning a lawyer for an impudent letter and deporting a person to torture may both infringe the Charter, but are orders of magnitude apart in harmful impact. Yet, *Doré* discloses no sensitivity to this variability and its implications for

[60] P Daly, *A Theory of Deference in Administrative Law: Basis, Application and Scope* (Cambridge, Cambridge University Press, 2012) ch 5.

judicial review. When administrative law's logic of curial deference collides with the Charter's logic of rights protection, *Doré* sides with deference.

What is at stake if *Doré*'s Charter-lite does not convey individuals seeking rights protection to the same destination as a more exacting Charter analysis? To fulfill the promise of bringing the Charter to the people by requiring administrative decision-makers to apply it, it matters not only that administrative decision-makers consider the Charter; it matters how they consider it and how carefully a reviewing court supervises their decision. Instructing administrative decision-makers to apply *Doré*'s Charter-lite proportionality test creates the appearance that, as McLachlin J states, 'The Charter belongs to the people. All law and law-makers that touch the people must conform to it'.[61] But if judicial review applies a deferential standard that does not inquire into weight, it disables itself from distinguishing superficial appearance from genuine conformity. One should question whether 'the people' benefit from enabling administrative actors to incorporate the Charter into discretionary decision making if, in effect, the methodology tilts toward under-enforcing the Charter and the results are insulated from meaningful scrutiny.

From a governance perspective, the divergence between the *Doré* model and a more conventional Charter analysis raises important questions. Governments select from a range of options about how to effectuate policy choices through law. *Doré* embodies the salutary aspiration that all branches and institutions of government share a primary commitment to the rule of law (including the Constitution) and manifest that fidelity in the performance of their assigned mandates. But a government who regards the strictures of legality as an impediment to the achievement of its ends might derive another lesson from *Doré* about its governance options in fields that may touch on Charter rights: for instance, it may choose to govern by articulating rules that explicitly or by necessary implication breach a Charter right. Or, it could grant an administrative actor discretion, and then structure and confine potentially Charter-infringing discretion by stipulating the purpose of the discretion and relevant factors to guide the decision. In either case, the government must be prepared to defend the constitutionality of those rights-limiting provisions under the *Oakes* test.

However, a government reading *Doré* might rationally conclude that conferring broad, open-ended and non-specific discretion (especially on a minister) will maximise the latitude available to limit Charter rights and minimise the likelihood and intensity of judicial oversight. In these instances, a reviewing court will restrict itself to asking whether the decision-maker balanced the relevant Charter 'value' against competing factors. Following *Doré*, a reviewing court will eschew second-guessing the quality of the balancing exercise. The upshot is that the more the state governs through discretion, the less accountable it will be for Charter violations that happen within that zone of discretion.

Reading *Doré* as a lesson about governance is disquieting. The rule of law is better served if law-makers communicate through transparent and defined grants of legal authority, even when governing through discretion, and it is undermined

[61] *Cooper v Canada (Human Rights Commission)* [1996] 3 SCR 854 at [70].

when they do not. This is particularly the case for powers that carry the potential to infringe constitutionally protected rights. A doctrine that creates incentives to govern opaquely in order to minimise legal accountability for Charter violations deflates the aspirations of the rule of law.

IV. CONCLUSION: TAKING RIGHTS SERIOUSLY IN ADMINISTRATIVE LAW

Although *Doré* was a unanimous decision of a seven-member Court, at least one subsequent decision suggests that its grip on the jurisprudence is tentative. In the 2015 *Loyola* decision,[62] a private Catholic school appealed the refusal of the Quebec Minister of Education to exercise discretion to exempt a private Catholic boys' school from elements of an ethics and religious culture curriculum mandated across the province. Loyola argued that the neutrality of the curriculum toward different belief and ethical systems infringed its freedom of religion. Although the Court was unanimous in allowing the appeal, only four of seven judges applied the *Doré* framework. Three concurring judges reverted to section 1 of the Charter (the *Oakes* test) as the framework, and did not even cite *Doré*.[63] The minority gave no explanation for its departure from *Doré*, but the answer may lie in the remedy: the majority provided detailed reasons about the failings of the original decision and itemised with precision what kind of exemption the Minister should have granted. Operating from within the supervisory logic of judicial review, it then 'set aside the Minister's decision, and remit[ted] the matter to the Minister for reconsideration in light of these reasons'.[64] The minority approached the case as a Charter challenge. Having decided that the Minister breached the Charter in a manner that could not be justified under section 1, the Court declared that 'The Court is empowered by s. 24(1) of the *Charter* to craft an appropriate remedy in light of all of the circumstances'.[65] It proceeded to make an order of mandamus compelling the Minister to 'grant an exemption to Loyola ... to offer an equivalent course to the [ethics and religious culture] Program in line with Loyola's proposal and the guidelines we have outlined'.[66]

If my speculation is correct, the split in the Court—ironically—illustrates the enduring influence of common law on constitutional method. For here we see the tail (of remedies) wagging the dog (of doctrine). The common law of prerogative writs precludes an order of mandamus that expressly dictates the outcome; section 24 of the Charter permits it. Whatever the motivation of the concurring judges, the split suggests that the methodology for evaluating discretionary decisions that intersect with the Charter has not yet stabilised around *Doré*'s administrative proportionality approach.

[62] *Loyola High School v Quebec (Attorney General)* [2015] 1 SCR 613.

[63] 'We ... evaluate the Minister's decision in light of Loyola's constitutional right to religious freedom—first, determining whether Loyola's freedom of religion was breached, and second, determining whether that breach was minimally impairing and therefore justified under s. 1 of the *Canadian Charter of Rights and Freedoms*': ibid at [88].

[64] ibid, at [81].

[65] ibid, at [163].

[66] ibid, at [165].

The contest between the traditional *Oakes* test and administrative proportionality maps onto two endemic pathologies of judicial review of the administrative state: One is the disregard or undervaluing of vulnerable individuals' interests, rights and entitlements by inept, under-resourced or politicised bureaucrats. The other is a retrograde or inexpert judiciary thwarting administrative actors in fulfilling the mandate given to them by a democratically elected legislator. Over-judicialisation of the administration may paralyse it. Inadequate attention to legality may produce injustice.

David Mullan captures an important intuition about the risks of overweening judicial scrutiny. In a passage quoted with approval by Abella J in *Doré*, he states:

> If correctness review becomes the order of the day in all *Charter* contexts, including the determination of factual issues and the application of the law to those facts, then *what in effect can occur is that the courts will perforce assume the role of a de novo appellate body from all tribunals the task of which is to make decisions that of necessity have an impact on Charter rights and freedoms*: Review Boards, Parole Boards, prison disciplinary tribunals, child welfare authorities, and the like. Whether that kind of judicial micro-managing of aspects of the administrative process should take place is a highly problematic question.[67]

Yet Mullan is also alert to the dangers of judicial abdication. In a passage *not* quoted by Abella J in *Doré*, Mullan qualifies his earlier caution against judicial micro-management by referencing the discretionary power of the Minister of Immigration, Refugees and Citizenship to deport a designated security threat to face a substantial risk of torture:

> It may also be the case that there are situations where the institutional framework that forms the context for the judicial review application is one where there can be no reasonable assurance that the decision-maker can or will give the *Charter* rights and freedoms at stake their appropriate weighting. In those instances, the Court may be completely justified in correctness review. Thus, for example, in the context of *Suresh* and *Ahani*, where the decision-maker's primary concerns are the security interests of Canada, the expectation that *Charter* rights and freedoms will be evaluated properly may simply not he justified at least in the absence of some internal, independent check. If so, then correctness review may be necessary if, indeed, *Charter* rights and freedoms are not to be devalued.[68]

Mullan's two examples usefully orient one toward the ingredients of a more refined and transparent account of how courts on judicial review ought to assess the legality of discretionary decisions that affect Charter rights. Recall that the logic of deference animating standard of review analysis derives from the legislator's choice to confer authority on emanations of the executive (agencies, boards, tribunals and bureaucrats) rather than on the judiciary. Unlike administrative law doctrine concerning the requirements of procedural fairness, standard of review jurisprudence is formally indifferent to the interests at stake in the decision. Nor does standard of review

[67] See *Doré* (n 23) at [51], quoting D Mullan, 'Administrative Tribunals and Judicial Review of Charter Issues after *Multani*' (2006) 21 *National Journal of Constitutional Law* 127 at 145, emphasis added by the Court.

[68] See Mullan, ibid, at 148, n 75.

analysis attend to the independence of the decision-maker. But interests (or impact) and independence must matter when fundamental rights are issue, because they are key motivators animating a judicially enforceable human rights instrument.

One might agree that *Doré* fails to take Charter rights seriously (or seriously enough) in the context of discretion, but also maintain that the approach to Charter adjudication (including the *Oakes* test) is poorly suited to the exercise of discretion. Perhaps a tailored proportionality test is as necessary for discretion as it is for common law rules.

I concur with Mark Elliott's claim that 'calibration which exposes and harnesses the relationship between underlying normative factors and administrative law's doctrinal superstructure'[69] is a vital prelude to the deployment of new, old or modified doctrinal tools. The foregoing critique of *Doré* has identified the normative fault lines that expose the defects of its hybrid administrative proportionality test. But instead of trying to solve the problem by devising yet another test (or a return to *Oakes*), I conclude by proposing that judicial review of rights-impacting discretion should explicitly take account of the decision, the decision-maker and the signaling function of judicial review. In brief, here is a list of desiderata.

First, a Charter right is a Charter right, regardless of whether it is infringed by operation of law or discretion; labeling it as a 'value' is conclusory and obscures rather than clarifies.

Secondly, a Charter right weighs more than other interests, and the graver the impact of the violation, the more it weighs.

Thirdly, the independence of the decision-maker from political influence matters. Proximity between the decision-maker and the legislator provides no reason to defer to a balancing of individual Charter rights against majoritarian interests.

Fourthly, where no or inadequate reasons are provided for the exercise of discretion that infringes a Charter right, curial deference neither requires nor authorises retrofitting reasons to support the result reached by the administrative decision-maker.

Finally, it matters whether discretion is structured and guided through constitutionally valid legislation, regulation or 'soft law'. Where the exercise of discretion will routinely and predictably limit Charter rights (eg in civil or criminal commitment, parole, immigration detention, child apprehension, extradition, etc), legislators can and should stipulate the purposes for which the discretion is granted, and identify the factors relevant to the exercise of discretion. If these provisions withstand an ordinary Charter challenge (including the *Oakes* test), then the individual exercise of discretion within those demarcated constitutional boundaries should benefit from greater deference than exercises of broad, general and unstructured discretion. Legislators and administrative agencies should be encouraged to structure discretion. It advances the rule of law goal of publicity and predictability. But if the legislator declines to structure the discretion, courts should not reward opacity by undertaking

[69] M Elliott, 'From Bifurcation to Calibration: Twin-Track Deference and the Culture of Justification' in H Wilberg and M Elliott (eds), *The Scope and Intensity of Substantive Judicial Review: Traversing Taggart's Rainbow* (Oxford, Hart Publishing, 2015) 61, 76.

to generate the optimal justification for the outcome, just as they should not reward the absence of (adequate) reasons by generating better ones.[70]

Whether these considerations travel under the rubric of reasonableness, correctness, proportionality or *Oakes*, or some other label matters less than that they receive proper and explicit attention. After *Multani*, David Mullan correctly (and reasonably) concluded that there is 'room for deference to the discretionary judgments of statutory authorities exercising powers that have the potential to affect *Charter* rights and freedoms', but in order to prevent devaluation of those rights and freedoms 'there should he recognition that the framework within which deference operates will often, perhaps invariably need to be different than in the case of judicial review of administrative action that docs not affect *Charter* rights and freedoms'.[71] Justice McLachlin (as she then was) observed that many more people have their rights determined by administrative decision-makers than by courts. The quality of Charter protection they receive should not depend on who makes the determination.

What lessons can other common law jurisdictions glean from the Canadian experience? The particularities of doctrine may be unique to each jurisdiction but the underlying tensions that both animate and distort jurisprudence are common across jurisdictions. Ultimately, I make a plea for greater transparency by judges in order to create the conditions for contestation, deliberation, and expression of what ought to matter when courts review the exercise of administrative discretion that touches on human rights. My proposed list of desiderata is almost certainly incomplete, and may not attract unanimous support, although I believe they are apposite to both the UK and to Canada. At this stage, I aim to simply launch the discussion, with the hope that it will be enriched by conversation across borders.

[70] Ideally, this should incentivise legislators to be more transparent in structuring and defining the scope of discretion in legislation. For a thoughtful elaboration of this idea, see P Daly, 'Prescribing Greater Protection for Rights: Administrative Law and Section 1 of the Canadian Charter of Rights and Freedoms' (2014) 65 *Supreme Court Law Review* (2d) 247 at 282.

[71] See Mullan (n 67) at 149.

5

Administrative Law: Characteristics, Legitimacy, Unity

PAUL DALY

THE BREADTH AND depth of judicial review of administrative action have increased dramatically in recent decades. No longer can it plausibly said that reviewing judges simply confine administrative decision-makers within the 'four corners' provided by the relevant empowering statute. A dramatic shift in the law has occurred, at the behest of the judges. Such a shift invites close assessment, with a view to determining whether it represents an appropriate exercise of the judicial function, or an illegitimate judicial power grab. I will offer a defence of the legitimacy of modern administrative law.[1]

In brief, the defence is that judicial review of administrative action is inevitably a values-based enterprise; that the structure of administrative law is provided by the interaction of four values—the rule of law, good administration, democracy and separation of powers; that these values generally complement each other and, where they appear to come into conflict, can be reconciled so as to guide doctrinal development and the decision of cases; that the values lend coherence and provide conceptual unity to modern administrative law; that the values are legal in nature, drawn from the decided cases, such that judicial reliance upon them cannot be dismissed as legislating from the bench; and that the values are in themselves and through their interaction normatively attractive. Hence, I argue, the modern law of judicial review of administrative action is legitimate. Although my defence is mounted primarily to protect English judges from accusations of illegitimacy, it should also prove effective against charges that may be levelled in other Commonwealth jurisdictions.

[1] I use the terms administrative law and judicial review of administrative action interchangeably, solely for the purposes of readability. This chapter is about judicial review (ie, the doctrines that determine *how* courts are to exercise their reviewing function and *what* sorts of decisions are subject to judicial review). This hardly exhausts the broad field of administrative law. Notably, I have little to say about the structure of the administrative state, not because I find it uninteresting (*cf* A Cameron and P Daly, 'Furthering Substantive Equality Through Administrative Law: *Charter* Values and Education' (2013) 63 *Supreme Court LR* (2d) 169; P Daly, 'Les appels administratifs au Canada' (2015) 93 *Canadian Bar Review* 69; P Daly, 'Best Practices in Administrative Decision-Making: Viewing the Copyright Board of Canada in a Comparative Light' (2017) *Journal of Intellectual Property* (forthcoming)) but because judicial review cries out for detailed theoretical discussion for the reasons given in Part I of this chapter.

My posture here is somewhat awkward. My argument in favour of the legitimacy of modern administrative law (by which I mean the body of law currently applied by the common law courts) has a theoretical spine two components of which have already been put into place by my earlier work. The purpose of this chapter is to slot in the first and fourth components on either side, saying enough about the other components to permit the reader to understand the argument without repeating at length that which I have already written elsewhere. Accordingly, a brief overview will assist the reader in grasping the objectives of this chapter.

First, there is a descriptive component which aims to set out the key characteristics of judicial review of administrative action. This includes describing the rapid development of the breadth and depth of judicial review of administrative action and the academic debates that the rapid development has provoked.

Second, there is an interpretive component, in which I lay out my values-based approach to judicial review of administrative action.[2] This is the core component of the theoretical spine. I argue that modern administrative law is structured by the four values set out above, which shape the doctrinal rules that judges apply and the decisions that judges reach. For the purpose of tracing the contours of the four values, reference can usefully be made to political and legal philosophy, but as far as administrative law is concerned, the values have quite specific meanings that can be observed in the decided cases.

Third, there is a prescriptive component, which addresses how judges should respond to situations of potential conflict between the values. I advocate a pluralist approach (though the meaning of pluralism here is circumscribed and drawn from a particular application in private law)[3] pursuant to which judges ought to reconcile the values; I also demonstrate the feasibility of this approach.[4]

Fourth, there is an evaluative component, in which I set out to assess whether the modern law of judicial review of administrative action is legitimate. This assessment is based on the descriptive analysis that highlights the open texture of administrative law; the interpretive analysis that explores the values holding administrative law together; and the prescriptive analysis that guides the resolution of potential conflicts between the values. These components do not slot neatly into one another; there are overlaps between them, as one would expect: 'in practice, nearly all interpretive theories include historical, prescriptive, and descriptive elements'.[5] Only when these other components have been put in place and can be properly appreciated does it become possible to move to evaluation and engage the important

[2] P Daly, 'Administrative Law: a Values-based Approach' in J Bell, M Elliott, JNE Varuhas and P Murray (eds), *Public Law Adjudication in Common Law Systems: Process and Substance* (Oxford, Hart Publishing, 2016). See also S Nason, *Reconstructing Judicial Review* (Oxford, Hart Publishing, 2016), for a values-based approach that is informed by empirical evidence.

[3] SR Munzer, *A Theory of Property* (Cambridge, Cambridge University Press, 1990).

[4] P Daly, 'A Pluralist Account of Deference and Legitimate Expectations' in M Groves and G Weeks (eds), *Legitimate Expectations in the Common Law World* (Oxford, Hart Publishing, 2017).

[5] S Smith, *Contract Theory* (Oxford, Oxford University Press, 2004) 5.

question with which I began: is the increased breadth and depth of judicial review of administrative action legitimate?

In Part I of this chapter, I introduce the descriptive component by setting out in summary form the rapid development of administrative law in recent decades. A longer Part II follows, in which the key characteristics of judicial review of administrative action are described. Integrated into this description of the *openness*, *contestability* and *dynamism* of administrative law are the values-based framework—the interpretive component—and the pluralist approach—the prescriptive component—introduced above and developed in detail elsewhere.

In Part III, I answer the legitimacy question. There are many different approaches that one could take to assessing legitimacy. When accusations of illegitimacy are levelled at judges, they are typically based on normative theories of what judges ought to be doing (ie, where the judges deviate from a normative theory of legitimacy, they act illegitimately). As a counter to such accusations, I offer a defence of the legitimacy of judicial review of administrative action that builds on the characteristics of administrative law outlined in Part I and the important role of values as explained in Part II. Modern administrative law is a unified whole—its structure provided by the rule of law, good administration, democracy and separation of powers—and it is legitimate.

I. THE GROWTH OF JUDICIAL REVIEW OF ADMINISTRATIVE ACTION

Where once administrative decision-makers could gaily err 'within jurisdiction'[6] (especially when sheltered by a privative clause), now they must accord significant participatory rights to individuals whose legal position may be modified by their decisions,[7] which, in turn, are subject to searching review for the robustness of the legal analysis,[8] the evidentiary basis of the underlying findings[9] and the reasons given (sometimes as a matter of legal obligation)[10] in support of the conclusions.[11] Even in jurisdictions that have a doctrine of 'deference', judicial review is more intense than the word 'deference', with 'its overtones of cringing abstention to superior status',[12] suggests. In Canada, although administrative decision-makers are permitted now to 'choose' between competing possible interpretations of statutory terms, their choice

[6] *R v Nat Bell Liquors* [1922] 2 AC 128. See further DM Gordon, 'The Relation of Fact to Jurisdiction' (1929) 45 *LQR* 459; DM Gordon, 'The Observance of Law as a Condition of Jurisdiction' (1931) 47 *LQR* 386 and 557.

[7] See, eg, *Re Pergamon Press Ltd* [1971] Ch 405; *Dellway Investments v National Asset Management Agency* [2011] IESC 4.

[8] See, eg, *Anisminic Ltd v Foreign Compensation Commission* [1969] 2 AC 147.

[9] See, eg, *Bugdaycay v Home Secretary* [1987] AC 514; P Craig, 'Judicial Review and Anxious Scrutiny: Foundations, Evolution and Application' [2015] *PL* 60.

[10] See, eg, *Baker v Canada (Minister for Citizenship and Immigration)* [1999] 2 SCR 817.

[11] See, eg, *Re JR55* [2016] 4 All ER 779 at [30].

[12] *R (Lord Carlile of Berriew QC) v Home Secretary* [2015] AC 945 at [22] (Lord Sumption).

is subject to judicial oversight,[13] and in the United States, changes made to policy positions must be justified in terms that will satisfy a reviewing court.[14] These are enormous changes that have altered the balance of power between the executive and judicial branches. For that reason alone, asking whether these developments can be justified is an important endeavour.

To be sure, the individual parts of this vast judicial construction project have been carefully scrutinised. Review of factual error,[15] close control of errors of law,[16] enforcement of substantive legitimate expectations[17] and an ever-wider right to reasons[18] have, for instance, attracted sustained academic attention, as has the extension of judicial review to non-statutory bodies.[19]

However, the whole has come in for less scrutiny.[20] This may simply reflect a belief that these developments are salutary, or that they can only be studied in isolation because they are products of a common-law system in which the law moves forward (or back) only incrementally.[21] Yet, with or without cries of a 'legitimacy crisis' [22] and whether or not one thinks that modern judicial review is the product of underlying principles or values,[23] the sweeping changes to judicial review of administrative

[13] *McLean v British Columbia (Securities Commission)* [2013] 3 SCR 895.

[14] *Encino Motorcars v Navarro* 579 US _____ (2016); *Federal Communications Commission v Fox Television Stations* 556 US 502 (2009).

[15] See, eg, P Craig, 'Judicial Review, Appeal and Factual Error' [2004] *PL* 788; P Daly, 'Judicial Review of Factual Error in Ireland' (2008) 30 *Dublin University LJ* 187; C Forsyth and E Dring, 'The Final Frontier: The Emergence of Material Error of Fact as a Ground for Judicial Review' in C Forsyth et al (eds), *Effective Judicial Review: A Cornerstone of Good Governance* (Oxford, Oxford University Press, 2010) 245.

[16] Compare BC Gould, '*Anisminic* and Jurisdictional Error' [1970] *PL* 358 with P Daly, 'Deference on Questions of Law' (2011) 74 *MLR* 694.

[17] See, eg, F Ahmed and A Perry, 'The Coherence of the Doctrine of Legitimate Expectations' [2014] *CLJ* 61; M Elliott, 'Legitimate Expectations and the Search for Principle: Reflections on *Abdi & Nadarajah*' (2006) 11 *Judicial Review* 281; I Steele, 'Substantive Legitimate Expectations: Striking the Right Balance?' (2005) 121 *LQR* 300.

[18] See, eg, M Elliott, 'Has the Common Law Duty to Give Reasons Come of Age Yet?' [2011] *PL* 56.

[19] M Elliott, 'Judicial Review's Scope, Foundations and Purposes: Joining the Dots' [2012] *New Zealand LR* 75; D Oliver, 'Is the Ultra Vires Rule the Basis of Judicial Review?' [1987] *PL* 543.

[20] *cf* T Poole, 'The Reformation of English Administrative Law' [2009] *CLJ* 142. For an elaborate attempt to develop a general theory of public law adjudication based on the rule of law, see TRS Allan, *Constitutional Justice: A Liberal Theory of the Rule of Law* (Oxford, Oxford University Press, 2001); for an institutionalist approach to some aspects of judicial review of administrative action, see A Vermeule, *Judging Under Uncertainty: An Institutional Theory of Legal Interpretation* (Cambridge MA, Harvard University Press, 2006); for an approach to administrative law that emphasises the importance of the democratic principle, see D Dyzenhaus, 'The Politics of Deference: Judicial Review and Democracy' in M Taggart (ed), *The Province of Administrative Law* (Oxford, Hart Publishing, 1997) 279 and 'Form and Substance in the Rule of Law: A Democratic Justification for Judicial Review?' in C Forsyth (ed), *Judicial Review and the Constitution* (Oxford, Hart Publishing, 2000) 141; and for the potential utility of a reinvigorated conception of the separation of powers, see E Carolan, *The New Separation of Powers* (Oxford, Oxford University Press, 2009).

[21] See, eg, S Waddams, *Dimensions of Private Law: Categories and Concepts in Anglo-American Legal Reasoning* (Cambridge, Cambridge University Press, 2003).

[22] JNE Varuhas, *Judicial Capture of Political Accountability* (Policy Exchange, London, 2016) 50–51; R Ekins, 'A Legitimacy Crisis in Judicial Review', *ConservativeHome* (8 June 2016), though see below for a closer look at whether a 'legitimacy crisis' has indeed been claimed.

[23] See, eg, D Oliver, *Common Values and the Public-Private Divide* (London, Butterworths, 1999).

action have been so far-reaching as to require, or at the very least invite, an evaluation of the whole, not just the individual parts, to determine whether 'an open-ended lawmaking power' has been conferred 'on unelected judges'.[24]

Moreover, those who are generally content with the current state of judicial review of administrative action should be on their guard. Already there have been important political reactions against the expanding powers of the courts[25] and academic talk of legitimacy crises will doubtless increase public awareness of the extent to which, on the whole, courts control an ever-wider swathe of public administration and to a much greater extent than they did in the past.

Finally, there is an important theoretical and methodological point about the role of public law scholars. If the various components of judicial review doctrine are treated as discrete developments, scholars will be tempted to analyse them in silos. However, treating these important developments on a case-by-case basis—justifying them, perhaps, on the basis that they are internally consistent or rational when viewed in light of the purposes of a particular doctrine—risks causing incoherence. If the same principles or values are not uniformly relied upon in developing administrative law, doctrinal rules may shoot off in different directions. Not only might scholars risk missing the wood for the trees, but the wood may come to resemble clumpy outgrowths of shrub with no discernible pattern, making it an irresistible target for those who would like to reduce the breadth and depth of judicial review of administrative action.

II. THE CHARACTERISTICS OF JUDICIAL REVIEW OF ADMINISTRATIVE ACTION

Administrative law is characterised by three features: openness, contestability and dynamism.

A. Openness

It has been said, especially since the English courts began to reformulate administrative law in the latter half of the twentieth century,[26] that the purpose of judicial review is to combat 'abuse of power'[27] or to subject government to legal constraints: through judicial review judges seek to prevent public officers from using their powers

[24] J Jowell, 'Of *Vires* and Vacuums: the Constitutional Context of Judicial Review' [1999] *PL* 448 at 449.

[25] See, eg, on Australia, M Aronson, 'The Growth of Substantive Review: The Changes, their Causes and their Consequences' and on England, C Harlow & R Rawlings, '"Striking Back" and "Clamping Down": An Alternative Perspective on Judicial Review' in Bell, Elliott, Varuhas and Murray (n 2).

[26] JNE Varuhas, 'The Public Interest Conception of Public Law: Its Procedural Origins and Substantive Implications' in Bell, Elliott, Varuhas and Murray (n 2).

[27] See, eg, *In re Preston* [1985] 1 AC 835, 851 (Lord Scarman), 864 (Lord Templeman); *R v North and East Devon Health Authority, ex parte Coughlan* [2001] QB 213 at [71]. For an early usage see A Denning, *Freedom under the Law* (London, Stevens & Sons, 1949) 99–126.

in legally inappropriate ways.[28] However, identifying the sort of 'abuse' and the types of 'power' with which judicial review ought to be concerned is a difficult task.

Abuse of power 'goes no distance to tell you, case by case, what is lawful and what is not'; rather, '[l]egal principle lies between the overarching rubric of abuse of power and the concrete imperatives of a rule-book'.[29] Abuse of power is an abstract concept that needs to be operationalised. Those of a more cynical bent might even describe it as a 'motherhood statement',[30] something to which all concerned could subscribe, safe in the knowledge that they would not be committing themselves to any concrete outcomes. Nonetheless, the idea that the role of the courts is to ensure that administrative decisions are made in legally appropriate ways provides general, high-level guidance to those engaged in shaping judicial review doctrine by prompting the questions they ask of doctrinal rules and administrative decisions.

Guidance is necessary because legislation rarely, if ever, specifies how judges are to go about the task of reviewing administrative decisions. Even when the courts are required by legislation to ensure that decision-makers acted in accordance with 'the law', the key term must be interpreted—it is not self-applying, as ample North American experience demonstrates.[31] In general, judicial review is concerned with legality, rationality and procedural fairness.[32] However, the 'application' of these heads of review 'to the facts of any particular case—and hence their concrete meaning—is largely dependent on the specific context under review';[33] they must somehow be translated into 'hard clear law'.[34] Various doctrinal rules are typically grouped under the broad heads of legality, rationality and fairness. To take one example from each head: a decision-maker must take into account all relevant factors identified by its governing statute;[35] a court may quash a decision that is one that no reasonable decision-maker would take;[36] and a decision-maker must give reasons for a decision of great importance to an individual.[37] Applications of these doctrinal rules to factual situations result in decisions in judicial review cases.

[28] For the sake of convenience, in what follows I will generally refer to abuse of power, but the reader should remain mindful of these various ways in which the raison d'être of judicial review of administrative action can be expressed.

[29] *R (Nadarajah) v Secretary of State for the Home Department* [2005] EWCA Civ 1363 at [67] (Laws LJ).

[30] See, eg, M Groves, 'The Surrogacy Principle and Motherhood Statements in Administrative Law' in L Pearson, C Harlow and M Taggart (eds), *Administrative Law in a Changing State: Essays in Honour of Mark Aronson* (Oxford, Hart Publishing, 2008) 71.

[31] See, eg, *Canada (Citizenship and Immigration) v Khosa* [2009] 1 SCR 339, discussed in P Daly, 'Canada's Bi-Polar Administrative Law: Time for Fusion' (2014) 40 *Queen's LJ* 213 at 219–223. The American literature on 'administrative common law' is voluminous. For a useful introduction, see GE Metzger, 'Foreword: Embracing Administrative Common Law' (2012) 80 *George Washington LR* 1293.

[32] *Council of Civil Service Unions v Minister for Civil Service* [1985] AC 374; *Canada (Attorney General) v TeleZone Inc* [2010] 3 SCR 585.

[33] TRS Allan, 'Doctrine and Theory in Administrative Law: An Elusive Quest for the Limits of Jurisdiction' [2003] *PL* 429 at 431.

[34] *R v Department of Education and Employment, ex parte Begbie* [2000] 1 WLR 1115 at [77] (Laws LJ).

[35] See, eg, *Tesco Stores v Secretary of State for the Environment* [1995] 2 All ER 636.

[36] *Associated Provincial Picture Houses Ltd v Wednesbury Corporation* [1948] 1 KB 223.

[37] *R v Secretary of State for the Home Department, ex parte Doody* [1994] 1 AC 531.

The resulting picture can be portrayed as follows:

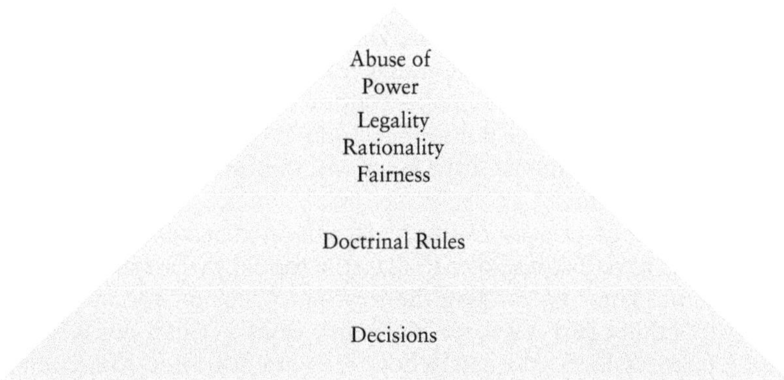

Given the absence of concrete guidance from 'abuse of power' or the broad heads of legality, rationality and procedural fairness, the conclusion that substantive values must shape doctrinal rules and decisions in individual cases is irresistible. Because judges have insufficient guidance from abuse of power and the broad heads of review they must, of necessity, have resort to values. These values could be political[38] or based on the personal preferences of judges about the constraints that ought to be placed on public administration and whether particular decisions should stand or be struck down. But they could also be legal, drawn from primary sources of law. Indeed, I have previously argued that the modern law of judicial review is shaped by four values immanent in the law—the rule of law, good administration, democracy and separation of powers[39]—that draw together individual strands of doctrine to form a coherent tapestry.

These values can be understood against a theoretical background. Political and legal philosophers, political scientists, economists and others have produced reams of interesting material on the rule of law, good administration, democracy and separation of powers. Reference to this material is useful in tracing the contours of these values. However, in administrative law, these values have quite particular meanings, which are derived from the cases.[40]

From the rule of law comes judicial concern for the protection of substantive and procedural interests that promote individual dignity and autonomy, on an equal basis. In the area of legitimate expectation, this concern is manifested by strong judicial protection of interests generated by reliance on official promises.[41]

Good administration sharpens the judicial focus on the efficient and effective achievement of statutory goals by administrative decision-makers. For instance, the

[38] D Feldman, 'Public Law Values in the House of Lords' (1990) 106 *LQR* 246.

[39] See Daly (n 2).

[40] The subsequent paragraphs draw on 'Procedure, Values and the Conceptual Unity of Administrative Law' in M Elliott and R Thomas, *Public Law*, 3rd edn (Oxford, Oxford University Press, 2017) 586–88.

[41] See the discussion in *R (Bibi) v London Borough of Newham* [2002] 1 WLR 237. See also *Glenkerrin Homes Ltd v Dun Laoghaire-Rathdown Corporation* [2007] IEHC 298.

procedural requirements imposed by courts should not be so onerous as to compromise the smooth functioning of administrative machinery.[42]

Democracy requires careful judicial attention to legislative intention as expressed in statute—such that where decision-making authority has been granted by the legislature to an administrative decision-maker it would be inappropriate for a court to step into the other body's shoes and substitute its preferred decision[43]—but also to the broader functioning of the political decision-making process—such that where elected officials exercise administrative functions, they are subject to a more relaxed requirement of impartiality.[44]

Finally, separation of powers captures the notion that administrative decision-makers and courts have distinct roles to play, the former by carrying out their statutory mandates, the latter by holding the former to account for the lawfulness of their acts. So it is that courts impose a right to reasons in situations where it would otherwise be impossible to adequately hold the administration to account, in law, for its decisions.[45]

It bears re-emphasising that my values-based approach is interpretive rather than descriptive. The values are immanent in the cases. It is not necessarily the case that judges have been relying upon them explicitly: 'What an interpreter is trying to understand—to interpret—is the law, not what motivated the judges who made the law.'[46] The goal is to reveal 'an *intelligible order* in the law, so far as such an order exists'.[47] On an interpretive approach the claim is that the judges have, like Molière's bourgeois gentleman, been adjudicating in terms of values all along, without necessarily knowing it.[48] Indeed, my practice in identifying and formulating the values has been reflective, starting with understanding of the values drawn from legal and political theory but revising those understandings to bring them into line with those manifest in the case law.[49]

Finally, these values are not directly enforceable. It would be asking too much of the values to give them 'immediate normative operation'.[50] A litigant could not ask a court to intervene simply because a public body violated 'the rule of law' or acted contrary to the principles of good administration. Rather, the values play a mediating role. Courts have relied on these values to guide their design of doctrinal rules and the exercise of judicial discretion.

[42] See, eg, *Lloyd v McMahon* [1987] 1 AC 625.

[43] *Associated Provincial Picture Houses Ltd v Wednesbury Corporation* [1948] 1 KB 223.

[44] See, eg, *R (Lewis) v Persimmon Homes* [2008] EWCA Civ 746.

[45] See, eg, *Mallak v Minister for Justice, Equality and Law Reform* [2012] IESC 59.

[46] See Smith (n 5) at 6.

[47] ibid, at 5 (emphasis in original).

[48] See also A Beever and C Rickett, 'Interpretive Legal Theory and the Academic Lawyer' (2005) 68 *MLR* 320 at 324: 'Ex post facto rationalisation in private law is problematic only if the theorist claims that her rationalisation of a case necessarily reflects the intentions of the judges who decided that case. That is not the endeavour of the interpretive legal theorist. The interpretive legal theorist does not try to interpret the judges' actual intentions, but to determine what their intentions should have been.'

[49] See the discussion of reflective equilibrium in J Rawls, *A Theory of Justice* (Cambridge MA, Belknap Press, 1971) and the application to administrative law in A Vermeule, *Law's Abnegation* (Cambridge MA, Harvard University Press, 2016).

[50] *Minister for Immigration and Multicultural Affairs, ex parte Lam* (2003) 195 ALR 502 at 519 (Gummow J).

The role of values alters the picture introduced above slightly:

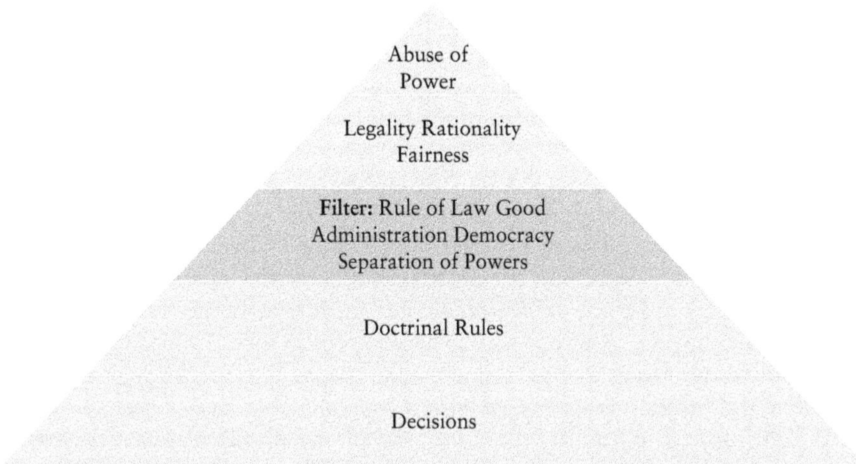

B. Contestability

How these values will influence the design of administrative law doctrine cannot be described in advance with scientific precision. In easier cases, the values will be cohesive, perhaps even complementary and supplementary, each guiding a court towards the same conclusion. In other cases, however, the values may appear to come into conflict. In all cases, other considerations will influence the design of the rules of judicial review of administrative action; administrative law is not solely a values-based enterprise.

On occasion, the values might all point in the same direction. Consider procedural legitimate expectations, the doctrine whereby an individual who has been promised a *procedure* pursuant to which her substantive interests will be determined is entitled to insist that a public body abide by its promise.[51] The rule of law, with its concern for personal autonomy and dignity, is respected by enforcing a promise that an individual could reasonably have relied upon; good administration is respected by ensuring that the individual actively participates in the process, thereby enhancing the probability that an accurate decision will be reached; democracy is respected because the final decision will be taken by the public body; separation of powers is also respected because the court need not trespass outside the bounds of the judicial domain (of providing oversight of the administrative process) and venture any opinion on the forbidden merits of the decision. Inasmuch as the values all point in the same direction—and there are many areas of administrative law doctrine where this is so—the characteristic of contestability does not require any adjustment to the interpretive approach discussed above.

On other occasions, however, the values might need to be reconciled. Review for error of law is a useful example. Democracy and separation of powers might point

[51] *Attorney General of Hong Kong v Ng Yuen Shiu* [1983] 2 AC 629.

in the direction of an exclusive role for the judiciary in interpreting the law (with the result that any decision based on an erroneous interpretation of statutory provisions is *ultra vires*):[52] democracy because the judiciary can claim simply to be carrying out the will of the legislature as expressed in the statute in question; and separation of powers because the judicial role has long been—in the common law tradition—to provide authoritative determinations of the law. Yet good administration might well be furthered by giving expert public bodies some interpretive power.[53] Democracy might, in fact, be better respected by considering the whole of the statute (with, perhaps, an evident intention to grant interpretive authority to a body other than a court) rather than the isolated provision in question.[54] In this situation, it will be necessary to make a choice as to the appropriate doctrinal rule in light of the competing values. They are contestable and a court must resolve the contest.

I have argued that the best approach in these circumstances is for judges to accommodate each of the values as much as possible, reconciling them where necessary.[55] Of course, if the values prove to be genuinely irreconcilable, one of them would have to yield and, more importantly, the attraction of the pluralist approach would be significantly diminished.[56] However, what seems on first glance to be an irreconcilable difference may disappear on closer inspection, perhaps due to consideration of empirical evidence or due to reconsideration of values which, once applied to a concrete problem, turn out to have been too broadly conceived in the abstract.[57] Declarations of irreconcilability should only be a last resort. This pluralist approach is different in a subtle but important way from the interpretive approach described above. Whereas the interpretive approach seeks to construct a values-based framework for administrative law, the pluralist approach addresses what judges *ought* to do in situations where the values appear to come into conflict. It is prescriptive rather than interpretive. It is nonetheless a necessary adjunct to the values-based framework, because in the absence of the pluralist account, judges and jurists might reasonably ask what guidance the values-based framework is capable of providing in difficult cases.

In resolving contests and in shaping administrative law doctrine generally, courts may refer to things other than values. It would be naïve to claim that these values *alone* are responsible for the shape of administrative law doctrine. Other considerations may be important. *Institutional considerations* matter: in the common law world at least, judges are limited in the sources they can legitimately look to, the consultation they can engage in, and how widely they can range in deciding cases.[58]

[52] See, eg, *Re Racal Communications* [1981] AC 374.

[53] See, eg, *National Corn Growers Association v Canada (Import Tribunal)* [1990] 2 SCR 1324.

[54] See generally P Daly, *A Theory of Deference in Administrative Law: Basis, Application and Scope* (Cambridge, Cambridge University Press, 2012).

[55] See Daly (n 4) This approach relies heavily on Munzer (n 3).

[56] Developing priority rules would be one way of ensuring that the theory would remain coherent even if the values were to prove irreconcilable in some circumstances. However, I do not propose to develop priority rules. First, I am happy to argue that in situations of perceived conflict closer analysis will reveal that the conflict is apparent rather than real. Second, priority rules which do not take account of the weight of the clashing values are unattractive. Just because three values are ranged against one does not mean that the value in the minority should yield, if it is engaged to a greater extent than the others.

[57] This links back to the reflective stance described in the text to n 49.

[58] See, eg, *Watkins v Olafson* [1989] 2 SCR 750; *Woolwich Building Society v Commissioners of Inland Revenue* (1992) 65 *Tax Cases* 265.

In addition, different jurisdictions might have different *constitutional rules*; to take a well-known example, Australian judges are constitutionally prohibited from exercising non-judicial power, something that imposes limits on the doctrinal rules that courts can develop in the area of judicial review of administrative action.[59] Similarly, the law in a particular jurisdiction might have developed by way of *precedent and tradition* so as to rule out a particular doctrinal innovation; in Australia and Canada, for example, judges have repeatedly—and strongly—insisted that substantive enforcement of legitimate expectations by courts cannot be countenanced, which greatly reduces the scope for creative judicial innovation in this area.[60] Finally, *analytical arguments* might be made, perhaps on the basis of incoherence in the application of concepts (eg jurisdictional error) or perhaps on the basis of consistency with other areas of domestic law (eg if there is no reliance requirement for, say, estoppel, it is inappropriate to have one for legitimate expectations). These will have greater or lesser force depending on the historical development of the law in a particular jurisdiction.[61] In sum, by giving effect to these values in the context of particular factual situations, judges adjudicating in the common law tradition in different territorial jurisdictions decide individual cases and develop administrative law doctrine.

Accordingly, it is necessary to make another modification to the picture described above:

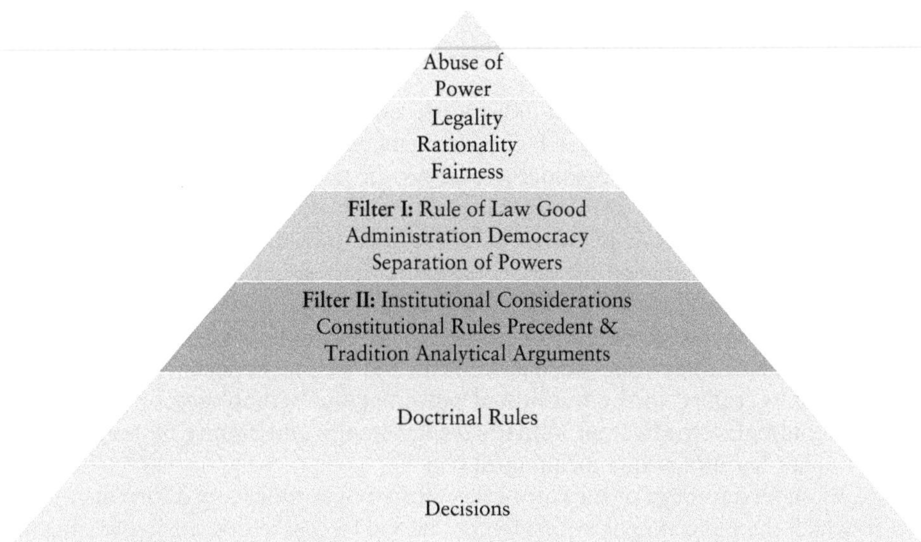

[59] *Huddart, Parker & Co Pty Ltd v Moorhead* (1908) 8 CLR 330; *Shell Co of Australia Ltd v Federal Commissioner of Taxation* [1931] AC 275.

[60] *Reference Re Canada Assistance Plan (BC)* [1991] 2 SCR 525; *Minister for Immigration and Border Protection v WZARH* [2015] HCA 40.

[61] One might also add that even doctrinal rules are not self-applying. Some exercise of judgement will be necessary as Beever and Rickett (n 48) argue: 'The need for judgment arises because there is a gap between the world and our minds. For instance, we must judge whether the facts of a particular case fall under the principles that we have in mind because there is an ineliminable gap between the facts and the principles.' On the role of judgement in judicial decision-making, see R Posner, *How Judges Think* (Cambridge MA, Harvard University Press, 2008).

One might raise the possibility that constitutional considerations and precedent might influence how the administrative law values are understood in a particular jurisdiction. For instance, some judges in the United States of America seem to be influenced by a formal conception of the separation of powers in which discrete tasks of law-making, law-executing and law-interpreting are allocated to the legislative, executive and judicial branches.[62] The American judges who criticise the idea that courts ought to defer to administrative agencies' interpretations of their own regulations rely on a distinction between law executing and law interpreting, with the result that a court should interpret the regulation *de novo* without paying any heed to an agency's preferred interpretation.[63] This would fall under the rubric of 'constitutional rules'. It seems to me, however, that the argument being made by these judges is one that proceeds from constitutional first principles and does not rule out the possibility that separation of powers—in the specific way that it is used by judges in administrative law cases[64]—may co-exist and, indeed, exert greater influence in a wider range of cases than the argument from constitutional first principles.

C. Dynamism

Administrative law doctrine can change over time. Indeed, it has changed rapidly in recent years, increasing both in breadth and depth. This dynamism results from changes in judicial perceptions of the values or changing constellations of the values, or both.

To grasp the idea of a change in judicial perception of administrative law values, consider first two snapshots that highlight changed understandings of the rule of law. In the first half of the twentieth century—in the 'twilight' of administrative law[65]—judicial review was only available of decisions affecting the 'rights' (not privileges) of individuals taken pursuant to a 'judicial' (not administrative) process.[66] The rule of law was satisfied by courts ensuring that bodies acting 'judicially' and affecting 'rights' stayed within the limits imposed by statute and the common law. As the centralised administrative state continued to grow, public bodies began to deliver a range of goods and services—such as housing and welfare benefits—that could not be described as 'rights' in the traditional sense but the withholding or withdrawal of which could greatly affect an individual's autonomy and dignity by reducing her ability to plan her affairs in a meaningful way.[67]

Judicial understandings of the rule of law shifted over time from a formal conception in which the judicial review jurisdiction existed to ensure that a narrow category

[62] Baron de Montesquieu, *The Spirit of the Laws* (1748).

[63] See, eg, *Talk America v Michigan Bell Telephone* 564 US ____ (2011); *Perez v Mortgage Bankers Association* 575 US ____ (2015).

[64] See text to n 45 above.

[65] HWR Wade, 'The Twilight of Natural Justice?' (1951) 67 *LQR* 103; G Le Dain, 'The Twilight of Judicial Control in the Province of Quebec?' (1952) 1 *McGill LJ* 1.

[66] *R v Electricity Commissioners, ex parte London Electricity Joint Committee Co* [1924] 1 KB 171; *R v Legislative Committee of the Church Assembly, ex parte Haynes-Smith* [1928] 1 KB 411.

[67] See, eg, Charles Reich, 'The New Property' (1964) 73 *Yale LJ* 733.

of decision-making bodies respected judicially and legislatively imposed limits to a more substantive conception in which courts could police decisions that have an important effect on an individual's autonomy and dignity interests. For this reason, the twin principles of natural justice—*audi alteram partem* and *nemo iudex in sua causa*—were gradually replaced by a general duty of procedural fairness, inspired by but conceptually distinct from the principles that went before it.[68] An excellent example is the decision in *Barreau du Québec c Khan*,[69] where a student who wished to become a member of the Bar had failed an examination but was prohibited by the Bar's rules from taking notes during her consultation of her flawed exam script. Noting the serious consequences of failing an exam and the importance to the student of being able to learn from her mistakes, the Quebec Court of Appeal held that the restriction on her ability to take notes, with a view to eventually exercising the privilege of practicing law, was a breach of procedural fairness. Yet had fairness not displaced natural justice the student would not have had any enforceable procedural rights whatsoever—the very idea would have seemed ludicrous a century ago.

Furthermore, other doctrinal developments—such as the emergence of a right to reasons and judicial enforcement of substantive legitimate expectations—can also be explained in terms of a shift from a formal to substantive conception of the rule of law; in these cases, recognition that the importance of a decision or a promise to an individual can affect their ability to plan their affairs, interfering thereby with their dignity and autonomy interests, underlies changes in the rules of administrative law.

To be clear, when I describe the importance of changing values, I am not arguing for the sort of clear causal connection that would satisfy the 'but for' test familiar to tort lawyers. My objective is not to demonstrate that, in developing the doctrine of procedural fairness, judges *expressly* relied on a changed conception of the rule of law. As I observed above, the point of an interpretive approach is to demonstrate that the judges have been speaking the language of values all along. When I describe the values as dynamic, I mean only that the values as manifested in the decided cases are capable of evolution over time. While it is not necessarily possible to identify a particular point in time when the values decisively changed it is possible—as with the shift from natural justice to procedural fairness—to say that the values did in fact change during a given time period.

The same is true of changing constellations of the values. The gradual development in English law of review for error of law is an example. Where once it might have been thought that democracy and good administration were best served by giving effect to privative clauses and permitting administrative decision-makers to make errors 'within jurisdiction' (save, of course, where the error appeared on 'the face of the record' such that the violation of the democratic principle was too obvious to ignore),[70] by the time of *Anisminic Ltd v Foreign Compensation Commission*[71] the

[68] D Mullan, 'Fairness: The New Natural Justice' (1975) 25 *University of Toronto LJ* 281.
[69] 2011 QCCA 792.
[70] *R v Northumberland Compensation Appeal Tribunal, ex p Shaw* [1952] 1 KB 338.
[71] [1969] 2 AC 147.

constellation of values had changed. Democracy could be served by ensuring that judges kept administrative decision-makers within the boundaries set down by the legislature (save where pellucid language gave exclusive interpretive jurisdiction—'full and autonomous powers to fix its own area of operation'—to the administrative decision-maker).[72] Good administration was not necessarily compromised, because administrative decision-makers would still be given significant latitude in exercising their discretionary powers. The *Anisminic* approach arguably better respected separation of powers by allocating discrete tasks to different bodies—exercises of discretion about how to distribute resources to administrative decision-makers and questions about law-interpretation to courts.

One might query whether a values-based framework is capable of providing much assistance in developing the law if dynamism is such an important characteristic in administrative law. However, the undoubted importance of dynamism should nonetheless not be overstated. First, the common law, which 'stands as a monument slowly raised',[73] evolves in a 'slow and incremental' fashion,[74] from the bottom up rather than from the top down:[75] 'caution and analogical reasoning are generally valuable accompaniments to judicial activity'.[76] Even *Anisminic*—often seen as a watershed moment in the evolution of administrative law—was not an especially radical break with the past: on the one hand, *Shaw* had already recognised the possibility of correcting errors 'on the face of the record';[77] and on the other hand, *Anisminic* still held out the possibility that some errors of law could occur 'within jurisdiction'.[78] Second, although the understandings of the values might be liable to change, a change in the values will be a gradual process, involving an accretion of decisions and *dicta* over time. Even if the values are liable to be understood differently at different times and in different places, they are nonetheless the same values. When Dicey set out his conception of the rule of law at the turn of the nineteenth century,[79] he was describing the same concept that the Supreme Court of Canada conceived slightly differently at the turn of the following century.[80] Finally, that constellations of the values might change simply reflects the fact that judicial review of administrative action is not static. Clever lawyers will always be able to make arguments in favour of changing the doctrinal rules in one direction or another, but for these arguments to resonate and stand the test of time, they must be faithful to the administrative law values immanent in the decided cases.

[72] ibid, at 207 (Lord Wilberforce). See also *Smith v East Elloe Rural District Council* [1956] AC 736.
[73] Learned Hand, 'Review' (1922) 35 *Harvard LR* 479.
[74] *Watkins v Olafson* [1989] 2 SCR 750 at 760.
[75] *McGinty v Western Australia* (1996) 186 CLR 140 at 231–32 (McHugh J).
[76] *Customs and Excise Commissioners v Barclays Bank plc* [2007] 1 AC 181 at [84] (Lord Mance).
[77] *R v Northumberland Compensation Appeal Tribunal, ex p Shaw* [1952] 1 KB 338.
[78] See, eg, *R v Hull University Visitor, ex parte Page* [1993] AC 682, a situation in which 'the applicable law [was] not the common law of England but a peculiar or domestic law' (700), one of which 'the courts have no cognisance' (702).
[79] AV Dicey, *Introduction to the Study of the Law of the Constitution*, JWF Allison (ed), (Oxford, Oxford University Press, 2013).
[80] *Reference re Secession of Quebec* [1998] 2 SCR 217.

III. LEGITIMACY

A. 'Legitimacy Crisis'

Significant energy has been expended on demonstrations that the expansion of judicial review's breadth and depth is consistent with orthodox understandings of parliamentary sovereignty.[81] Faced, however, with judicial development of increasingly intrusive grounds of review, available against an increasingly broad swathe of statutory and non-statutory bodies—causing a marked shift from a preference for political accountability towards a preference for legal accountability[82]—commentators have been surprisingly quiet.[83]

To the extent there has been serious academic debate about the sweeping changes in judicial review of administrative action, it has focused on whether the judges can claim a statutory warrant for their development of new grounds of review and application of these (as well as older grounds of review) to a wider range of decision-makers, both statutory and non-statutory.[84]

The constraints courts impose on administrative decision-makers can usefully be grouped under the headings of 'legality', 'rationality' and 'procedural fairness'.[85] As discussed briefly in Part I, many of these constraints are not justified by reference to statutory language. Abuse of power, while a useful guide, does not provide the necessary detail to permit courts to perform the task of judicial review—judges must draw on some other resources to determine what sort of action would be an 'abuse' and what sort of 'power' should be subject to judicial oversight. Doctrinal flesh also needs to be put on the bones of 'legality', 'rationality' and 'procedural fairness'. It is true that 'legality' generally means that administrative decision-makers must direct themselves correctly in law and this head of review can thus be said to be tethered to statute: judges can certainly claim simply to be enforcing the express will of the legislature. Yet even here, matters are not always so clear; in England judicial review of factual error comes under the rubric of legality,[86] but one would scour the statute book in vain for legislation that permits judges to intervene because an administrative decision-maker erred badly on factual matters.[87] Rationality and procedural fairness have developed almost entirely autonomously of statute. The idea that a decision can be quashed because it is one that no reasonable decision-maker would have made is one that cannot be traced to statutory language, a point that applies

[81] See the essays collected in Forsyth (n 20).

[82] See, eg, Elliott and Thomas (n 40).

[83] Though see the sources grouped at n 20, bearing in mind, however, that these authors do not purport to provide a descriptive or interpretive theory that would provide a structure for the whole of administrative law doctrine.

[84] See text to nn 15–19.

[85] See, eg, *Council of Civil Service Unions v Minister for Civil Service* [1985] AC 374.

[86] *E v Secretary of State for the Home Department* [2004] QB 1044. Contrast the position in Canada, where review of factual error now falls under the rubric of reasonableness: *Blanchard v Control Data Canada Ltd* [1984] 2 SCR 476; *Quebec (Commission des droits de la personne et des droits de la jeunesse) v Bombardier Inc (Bombardier Aerospace Training Center)* [2015] 2 SCR 789.

[87] Indeed, for a more traditionalist position, see *Richardson v Mahon* [2013] IEHC 118.

a fortiori to the possible introduction of proportionality as a new ground of review of administrative action.[88] As for fairness, it is surely sufficient to recall the famous language from *Cooper v Wandsworth Board of Works* to the effect that where matters of procedure are concerned 'the common law will supply the omission of the legislature'.[89]

Given that the absence of any statutory warrant is obvious enough (the 'legality' grounds of review partly excepted), debate has focused on how best to square this judicial creativity with the orthodox view of parliamentary sovereignty. Two camps emerged, one flying the 'common law' banner which viewed the judges as (largely) autonomous in developing grounds of review,[90] one waving the 'modified ultra vires' banner, whose members insist that Parliament must be taken to intend to legislate consistently with the rule of law, as ultimately enforced by the courts.[91] Remarkably, however, both sides largely agreed that the development of the law of judicial review was, for the judges, permissible as long as some 'reasoned justification' could be provided.[92] They disagreed only about how to accommodate judicial creativity as a matter of constitutional theory.

Curiously, there has been little or no dissent from a third camp that might be thought to have an interest in debating the appropriate limits of judicial power to develop new grounds to review administrative action. So-called 'political constitutionalists' tend to look askance at judicial control of public administration, preferring government to be held to account politically. Political accountability is said to be preferable for normative reasons,[93] and because it coheres better with Westminster-style democracy.[94] Political constitutionalists are particularly sceptical of judicial enforcement of fundamental rights, on the basis that rights questions are best left to the ordinary democratic process.[95] Yet these theorists have left well enough alone as far as judicial review of administrative action is concerned.[96]

In general, the academic commentary on the increased breadth and depth of judicial review has been positive. First, Harlow and Rawlings' treatment of legitimate expectations is a useful example, because these authors are at least sceptical about the displacement of political accountability by legal accountability. Discussing the seminal *Coughlan* case, in which a public body wished to renege upon the promise of a 'home for life' that it had made to residents of a care facility, the authors criticise the more expansive elements of the Court of Appeal's decision but indicate that they would have been content had it treated the promise as merely one factor among

[88] See, eg, *Pham v Secretary of State for the Home Department* [2015] 1 WLR 1591. For a recent collection of useful essays debating this point, see [2010] *New Zealand LR* 265ff.

[89] (1863) 14 CB (NS) 180.

[90] See, eg, P Craig, 'Ultra Vires and the Foundations of Judicial Review' [1998] *CLJ* 63, 89.

[91] See, eg, M Elliott, *The Constitutional Foundations of Judicial Review* (Oxford, Hart Publishing, 2001).

[92] See Craig (n 90) at 89.

[93] See, eg, R Bellamy, *Political Constitutionalism* (Cambridge, Cambridge University Press, 2007).

[94] See, eg, A Tomkins, *Our Republican Constitution* (Oxford, Oxford University Press, 2005).

[95] See, eg, J Waldron, *Law and Disagreement* (Oxford, Clarendon Press, 1999).

[96] J Waldron, 'The Core of the Case against Judicial Review' (2006) 115 *Yale LJ* 1346 at 1353–1354, excepting judicial review of administrative action from his argument against judicial review of legislation.

many others to be considered by the public body in the husbandry of its resources.[97] Even treating a promise unsupported by statute as a relevant factor is to place a constraint on administrative discretion that the legislature did not expressly endorse. Second, in discussing the possibility of judicial review of the reasonableness and proportionality of administrative action, a prominent political constitutionalist could only bring himself to say 'we need a judicial review that is appropriately responsive to, and respectful of ... other constitutional goods and accords them due weight' and that a 'balanced mix' is required.[98] In other words, even those most likely to claim that the invention of judicially enforceable constraints of rationality and fairness are illegitimate power grabs have been—so far—reluctant to do so.[99]

It is nonetheless easy to perceive how the judges might be vulnerable to accusations of overstepping the appropriate bounds of the judicial role.[100] The difficulty for the 'reasoned justification' answer to such charges is that this only seeks to square the legitimacy of judicial development of administrative law with orthodox notions of parliamentary sovereignty, an important exercise but one which does not provide a justification for judicial creativity in general and which does not represent an adequate response to complaints that judicial development of administrative law has, on the whole, gone too far.

B. Legitimacy

Assessing such accusations requires some discussion of legitimacy. Felix Frankfurter once remarked that jurisdiction is 'a verbal coat of too many colors'[101] and the same could surely be said of legitimacy. At the very least, the legitimacy of an activity can be assessed in a number of different ways, sociologically (whether an activity is accepted as a matter of social fact), democratically (whether there is popular input that shapes the activity), procedurally (whether the procedures that generate the activity are appropriate), or morally/normatively (whether the activity is morally or normatively attractive in view of the substantive interests it protects); these assessments may, indeed, be interlinked.[102]

Some can, nonetheless, be discarded quite easily for the purposes of the assessment of the legitimacy of administrative law. In the absence of barricades outside the Royal Courts of Justice it is doubtful that an inquiry into the sociological legitimacy

[97] C Harlow and R Rawlings, *Law and Administration*, 3rd edn (Cambridge, Cambridge University Press, 2009) 232.

[98] A Tomkins, 'What's Left of the Political Constitution?' (2013) 14 *German LJ* 2275 at 2287. Compare the more forthright suggestion in J Griffith, 'The Common Law and the Political Constitution' (2001) 117 *LQR* 42 that judges should confine themselves to ensuring decision-makers stay within the four corners of the relevant empowering statute, but note that Griffith does not provide much in the way of specifics, in particular whether he would have judges eliminate the duty of fairness that is implied into empowering statutes.

[99] See generally P Craig, 'Political Constitutionalism and Judicial Review' in Forsyth (n 15).

[100] See also T Poole, 'Legitimacy, Rights and Judicial Review' (2005) 25 *OJLS* 697.

[101] *United States v LA Tucker Truck Lines* 344 US 33 (1952).

[102] See generally J Balkin, *Living Originalism* (Cambridge MA, Harvard University Press, 2011).

of judicial review of administrative action would be especially fruitful. In addition, given that common law judges develop the law incrementally and only after hearing argument, the procedural legitimacy of administrative law seems secure (at least, that is, in the absence of a more general attack on common law law-making).

Excluding sociological and procedural legitimacy leaves us with democratic and normative legitimacy. Sure enough, it is some combination of these two that makes administrative law vulnerable to accusations of illegitimacy. Here is how Jason Varuhas concludes his critique of the legitimacy of judicial review:

> As the courts increasingly and more readily encroach upon the executive sphere, determining what are substantively good or bad reasons for executive action, the traditional conception of judicial review as a secondary, supervisory jurisdiction begins to break down, as do the dividing lines between the responsibilities of courts and government, and the provinces of law and politics. This is highly problematic because the ideas that judges were only exercising a long-stop, supervisory jurisdiction on review, and that the judicial role is one distinct from the functions of government and removed from ordinary politics have long served to legitimise judicial review. If those struts are removed, judicial review shall be plunged into a legitimacy crisis. Arguably we are already there.[103]

It will immediately be seen that Varuhas is quite measured in his critique (which is appropriate given the focus of his report on a small but important area of administrative law concerning the review of political responses to Ombudsman decisions). Indeed, he stops short of declaring a 'legitimacy crisis'; his view seems to be that judges are in danger of wandering over the dividing line between appropriate and inappropriate judicial intervention. The Rubicon has not yet been crossed—but it is nonetheless fruitful to consider Varuhas's reasons for believing the judges have come too close to doing so, because these reasons form the basis of the claim of an imminent 'legitimacy crisis'.

Implicit in the passage quoted above is an understanding of the appropriate normative role of judges. They are there to provide a sober second look at administrative action, ensuring that administrative decision-makers remain within the boundaries laid down by statute, but never venturing an opinion on the merits of the decision under review. Indeed, the administrative decision-maker has a democratic pedigree, having been assigned by the legislature primary responsibility for making the decision in question. Accordingly, one could characterise Varuhas's critique as an attack on the normative legitimacy of administrative law, underpinned perhaps by a focus on democratic legitimacy, in the sense that judges have not adequately respected the input of the elected representatives who chose to vest decision-making authority in bodies other than courts. But the core of the critique is that judges have moved beyond the judicial domain and are trespassing in the executive and legislative spheres.[104] It is to this core of the critique—and others that may follow, especially from political constitutionalists—that my response is directed.

[103] See Varuhas (n 22) at 50–51.

[104] The converse of this critique has recently been made in the United States: P Hamburger, *Is Administrative Law Unlawful?* (Chicago, University of Chicago Press, 2014). Hamburger argues that the executive branch is illegitimately trespassing in the judicial and legislative spheres.

C. Defending the Legitimacy of Administrative Law

The discussion of legitimacy has to be understood against the backdrop of the characteristics of administrative law described in Part II. Because administrative law *is* open, contestable and dynamic, it is *inevitable* first, that values will influence the structure of doctrinal rules, second, that these values will not always point in the same direction and will thus need to be accommodated in some way in the design of doctrinal rules and third, that these values—or the way they are accommodated—will change over time.[105]

A robust defence of the legitimacy of administrative law would best begin by demonstrating two things. First, the coherence of the increased breadth and depth of judicial review of administrative action. Given the widespread agreement about the purpose of judicial review (at an admittedly elevated level of abstraction), it is sensible to focus, as I have, on judicial review as a whole rather than on its individual component parts; but unless the various doctrinal developments can also be explained by the operation of a coherent general framework, the individual parts risk coming under attack. Without such a framework the great forest of developments in administrative law might go unseen due to a focus on the individual trees, which creates a risk that some group of unhappy scholars or politicians will seek to knock the forest to the ground, one lonely tree at a time. Second, the substantive values that guide the development of the law are legal rather than political in nature. If doctrinal development is simply politics, it can forcefully be argued that judges have taken up a legislative or executive function which they are neither institutionally nor constitutionally capable of fulfilling.

I have developed the argument that administrative law is coherent because its structure is formed by four values—the rule of law, good administration, democracy and separation of powers. These are present in every area of administrative law doctrine, in the rules governing substantive review, procedural review, institutional review and remedies.[106] The individual parts of judicial review of administrative action form a coherent whole, because both the individual parts—everything from the rules governing when elected representatives should recuse themselves from adjudicative functions to the rules requiring applicants for judicial review to exhaust alternative remedies—and the sum of all the parts are shaped by the same four values.

Moreover, this coherence is provided by values that are found *in the decided cases*. They are drawn from what any lawyer or layperson would recognize as sources that judges can legitimately rely upon. They are *legal* values. While they may be congruent with understandings of values found in political theory or discourse, they are not

[105] Just because judicial creativity is inevitable does not make any particular type of judicial creativity legitimate. An ought cannot be derived from an is. Nonetheless, the inevitability of judicial creativity provides an important benchmark against which attempts to justify particular forms of judicial creativity can be measured.

[106] See, eg, Daly (n 2) at 39: 'Administrative law values have been woven into the area of remedies, which forms part of the fabric of administrative law doctrine, cut from the same cloth as the principles of institutional, procedural and substantive review.'

political; they do not represent judges' personal preferences as to how the law ought to evolve.[107] Administrative law values thus provide a structure that is cohesive and legal in nature.

Beyond coherence, these legal values have structured administrative law in a normatively attractive way. First, these values reflect the basic commitments of modern liberal democracy to the protection of individual dignity and autonomy, the existence of an effective regulatory state, the importance of paying due regard to the outcomes of the legislative process and the desirability of ensuring that no one governmental organ has a monopoly on decision-making authority. For instance, the importance accorded to separation of powers maintains distinct roles for courts and administrative decision-makers. While administrators remain responsible for the merits of the decisions they render, courts provide oversight to ensure that primary decision-makers respect legal values in their decision-making processes and decisions. Similarly, the value of democracy is respected because administrative law gives appropriate importance to legislative pronouncements and to the democratic process, by enforcing statutory limits and by honing doctrinal rules to take account of the need to promote open debate in the public sphere.

Second, following a pluralist approach to administrative law ensures that judges strike an appropriate balance when the values seem to come into conflict. As a result, neither individual right nor good administration reigns supreme. For instance, even though the importance of robustly protecting interests that are important for an individual's autonomy and dignity has been recognised by judicial development of a general duty of procedural fairness, this duty is tempered by the need to permit administrative decision-makers to render decisions in an efficient and effective way; the procedures that courts may impose vary based on the context of the regulatory regime under review. Much of modern administrative law's structure is provided by the four values acting in complementary fashion; where they might not act in concert, following the pluralist approach ensures that they will do so.

In short, the values that give judicial review of administrative action its structure are normatively attractive and, taken together, provide a defensible basis for judicial development of administrative law.

IV. CONCLUSION

Having put the descriptive, interpretive, prescriptive and evaluative components of the theoretical spine of my argument in place, it is now possible to make a broader claim about the conceptual unity of administrative law.

The unity of administrative law is supplied by a values-based interpretive framework that brings together in a cohesive structure the doctrinal rules developed in the areas of institutional review, procedural review, substantive review and remedies. Four values immanent in the decided cases provide this structure: the rule of law,

[107] See generally R Dworkin, *Taking Rights Seriously* (Cambridge MA, Harvard University Press, 1977).

good administration, democracy and separation of powers, understood against the backdrop of legal and political theory but used in a very specific way in administrative law cases. In so using the values, judges will act within the traditional constraints of the common law and will have to respect the particularities of the territorial jurisdiction in which they adjudicate. No one value has precedence over the others; indeed, different constellations of the values are possible. Judges ought to reconcile the values in situations in which they seem to come into conflict. Hovering above all this—providing very high-level guidance—is abuse of power, which provides a general sense of purpose; jurists who do not have a sense of the purpose of the activity of judicial review of administrative action will struggle to do more than assemble 'a vast rubbish heap of miscellaneous facts'.[108] More generally, the need for some sort of values-based framework follows from the openness of judicial review of administrative action; and two other characteristics of administrative law—its contestability and dynamism—require the development of a framework that can accommodate multiple values and change over time.

Finally, it may be helpful by way of conclusion to attempt to situate this paper on a larger theoretical plane. Lawyers can be arrayed, in terms of their philosophical commitments, from one pole—positivism—to another pole—anti-positivism.[109] Crudely, positivists believe that judges in developing the law act as legislators, though motivated of course by a concern for good policy; whereas anti-positivists believe that judges inevitably shape the law towards defined ends.[110] Fitting my approach on the spectrum between positivism and anti-positivism is difficult. On the one hand, it is anti-positivist in the sense that it rejects the idea that judges developing administrative law doctrine are legislating around the edges. My perspective is an internal legal perspective, but one which is plainly motivated by an overriding purpose. The development of administrative law takes place in service of combating abuse of power (understood in a broad sense). Judges are not simply going from case to case, legislating new grounds of review as they go along—and administrative law scholars are not blundering from article to article, egging the judges on or warning their Lordships to slow down. On the other hand, this perspective depends on values drawn from the decided cases, an unimpeachable source of positive law. As a result, I hope that those who typically congregate at one of the two poles will find that they can accept the approach that I have laid out.

However, this approach should be described as a matter of theory, its implications are clear. The openness, contestability and dynamism of administrative law accommodates the development of a values-based interpretive framework and a prescriptive pluralist account of how judges ought to reconcile competing values which, taken together, provide a legitimate basis for the judicial creativity that has given us modern administrative law.

108 J Finnis, *Natural Law and Natural Rights*, revised edn (Oxford, Clarendon Press, 2011) 17.

109 See, eg, D Dyzenhaus, 'Form and Substance in the Rule of Law: A Democratic Justification for Judicial Review?' in Forsyth (n 20).

110 For a recent discussion of the positivist and antipositivist traditions in administrative law, see M Lewans, *Administrative Law and Judicial Deference* (Oxford, Hart Publishing, 2016).

6

Unity, Disunity and Vacuity: Constitutional Adjudication and the Common Law

ROGER MASTERMAN AND SE-SHAUNA WHEATLE*

I. INTRODUCTION

THE COMMON LAW is often seen as a unifying and stabilising factor across and within jurisdictions; in the United Kingdom, for instance, the common law is appealed to as a familiar and certain alternative to the unpredictable and overweening impacts of European human rights law.[1] This is in spite of the common law's propensity for reinvention, *and* the internal divisions and tensions within both the substance and methodologies of the common law. These ructions are particularly evident in the *constitutional* common law and its approach to the resolution of fundamental constitutional conflict.

Though primarily regarded as the vehicle for the realisation of the private law of obligations, the last 20 years have seen the English common law assume a distinctly constitutional character.[2] The articulation of fundamental rights, though lacking the coherence and definitive character of a legislatively endorsed bill of rights, had begun to form—prior to the sanction by statute of legislative review in the United Kingdom[3]—the backbone of a constitutional jurisdiction which aspired to partially regulate primary legislation for consistency with individual freedoms. Following the adoption of the Human Rights Act 1998, this nascent jurisdiction appeared to have

* Our thanks are due to Mark Elliott and William Lucy for their comments on a previous draft.

[1] Conservative Party, *Protecting Rights in the UK: The Conservatives' Proposals for Changing Britain's Human Rights Laws* (October 2014) 2.

[2] We acknowledge that the common law has long been considered to be an element of the broad constitutional fabric (eg AV Dicey, *The Law of the Constitution*, 10th edn (London, Macmillan, 1967) 196 ('Our constitution, in short, is a judge-made constitution, and it bears on its face all the features, good and bad, of judge-made law.') or as a component of the 'ancient constitution' (on which see JGA Pocock, *The Ancient Constitution and the Feudal Law: A Study of English Historical Thought in the Seventeenth Century* (Cambridge, Cambridge University Press, 1957)). In this chapter, our focus is less on the place the common law within the constitution, more on the development and deployment by the courts of specific and substantive constitutional rights and principles.

[3] See Human Rights Act 1998, ss 3 and 4; Scotland Act 1998; Government of Wales Act 1998; Northern Ireland Act 1998.

reached its natural zenith, in the form of the principle of legality.[4] But renewed judicial recourse to rights protected by the common law,[5] alongside persistent claims as to the capacity of the common law as a control on legislative action,[6] prompt consideration of the extent to which the common law can operate as a tool of proto-constitutional review.[7]

The development of a constitutional dimension to the common law has seen it proclaimed as undertaking functions akin to those performed by a written constitution.[8] Our enquiry is the extent to which the adoption of an explicitly constitutional dimension by the common law has prompted a departure from its accepted characteristics, holding the potential to destabilise its development. Judicial articulation of constitutional rights and statutes recognised at common law undoubtedly poses a challenge to the stability of the domestic constitutional order, but also reveals a series of conflicts which threaten its capacity to unite or stabilise. Taking account of the incremental methods of the common law, its traditional adherence to doctrine and the judicial articulation of overarching constitutional principles, this chapter examines the unity of the common law's constitutional features and its coherence within the prevailing constitutional order.

II. THE CONSTITUTIONAL AND THE ORDINARY

The Diceyan conflation of ordinary and constitutional law, as is well known, hindered the development of a distinct body of public law until the latter years of the twentieth century. *Droit administratif*, to Dicey, was 'foreign to the spirit and traditions of our institutions'[9] and undermined the idea of formal equality before the law. The consequence of this absence of a substantive distinction between the ordinary law and the nascent law applicable to public administration saw some of the most famous decisions in the canon grounded very firmly in private law causes of action.[10] Gradually, administrative law established for itself a distinctive character,[11] and procedural exclusivity saw the prerogative writs and orders reserved to the sphere of judicial review of administrative action.[12]

Emerging from this developing divergence, the common law has come to permit judicial scrutiny of administrative or executive powers, and increasingly can be seen

[4] *R v Secretary of State for the Home Department, ex parte Simms* [2000] 2 AC 115 at 131.

[5] See, eg, *R (Osborn) v Parole Board* [2014] AC 1115; *Kennedy v Information Commissioner* [2015] AC 455; *A v British Broadcasting Corporation* [2015] AC 588.

[6] See, eg, Lord Woolf, 'Droit Public—English Style' [1995] *PL* 57 at 69; *R (Jackson) v Attorney General* [2006] 1 AC 262 at [102] and [159]; *Moohan v Lord Advocate* [2015] AC 901 at [35].

[7] For a thorough-going defence of the constitutional capacity of the common law, see: TRS Allan, *The Sovereignty of Law; Freedom, Constitution and Common Law* (Oxford, Oxford University Press, 2013).

[8] *Thoburn v Sunderland City Council* [2003] QB 151 at [64].

[9] See Dicey (n 2) at 332.

[10] See, eg, *Entick v Carrington* 95 ER 807 (1765).

[11] The foundations of modern administrative law were only secured in the latter half of the twentieth century (see *Ridge v Baldwin* [1964] AC 40; *Padfield v Minister for Agriculture, Fisheries and Food* [1968] AC 997; *Anisminic Ltd v Foreign Compensation Commission* [1969] 2 AC 147; R Stevens, *The English Judges: Their Role in the Changing Constitution* (Oxford, Hart Publishing, 2005) ch 3).

[12] *O'Reilly v Mackman* [1983] 2 AC 237.

to approach the subjection of legislative power to the controlling (or regulatory) influence of the common law. As such, the common law has begun to reveal the capacity to regulate not only executive or administrative discretion but also public power more broadly construed.[13] While a body of 'constitutional' laws can be described as the cumulative consequence of the development of judicial review and other cases dealing with the regulation of public power, such decisions have been bolstered through the ability of judicial review to touch upon the exercise of legislative power, and through the reflection of a distinctly 'constitutional' approach to judicial decision making.

The very idea of distinctly constitutional techniques of judicial reasoning is, of course, anathema to the orthodox Diceyan conceptualisation of constitutional law as the outgrowth of the ordinary law.[14] However, the image of a uniform terrain of laws is no longer—if it ever was—an accurate reflection of the UK's constitutional landscape. Practically, this transition is revealed in the increasingly complex evolution of the doctrine of implied repeal, a rule traditionally seen as the interpretive expression of that most orthodox and (once) sacrosanct constitutional doctrine—parliamentary supremacy. While implied repeal has been described as the doctrinal representation of the continuing supremacy of each successive Parliament,[15] faithful application of the doctrine also assumes—in normative and interpretive terms—equality of status among all legislation, an assumption that has been subject to challenge in recent decades.

The exposition of constitutional statutes by Laws LJ in *Thoburn* is heralded for piercing the myth of a plane constitutional surface.[16] This feat was accomplished by, firstly, differentiating the nature of constitutional statutes from ordinary legislation:[17]

> We should recognise a hierarchy of Acts of Parliament: as it were 'ordinary' statutes and 'constitutional' statutes. [...] a constitutional statute is one which (a) conditions the legal relationship between citizen and state in some general, overarching manner, or (b) enlarges or diminishes the scope of what we would now regard as fundamental constitutional rights.

However, perhaps more constitutionally consequential was the explanation of the interpretive consequences of that distinction—specifically, the insulation of constitutional statutes from implied repeal:

> Ordinary statutes may be impliedly repealed. Constitutional statutes may not. For the repeal of a constitutional Act ... to be effected by statute, the court would apply this test: is it shown that the legislature's *actual*—not imputed, constructive or presumed—intention was to effect the repeal or abrogation? I think the test could only be met by express words in the later statute, or by words so specific that the inference of an actual determination

[13] As Cane observes, the target of administrative law is 'the day-to-day handling of public affairs particularly, but by no means exclusively, by what we call the "executive branch of government"' whereas 'constitutional law is concerned with the public domain in general' (P Cane, *Administrative Law*, 4th edn (Oxford, Clarendon Press, 2004) 1–2.

[14] See Dicey (n 2) at 203.

[15] *Vauxhall Estates v Liverpool Corporation* [1932] 1 KB 733 at 743 (Avory J).

[16] *cf Ellen Street Estates v Minister of Health* [1934] 1 KB 590.

[17] *Thoburn v Sunderland City Council* [2003] QB 151 at [62].

> to effect the result contended for was irresistible. The ordinary rule of implied repeal does not satisfy this test. Accordingly, it has no application to constitutional statutes.[18]

On the basis of this reasoning, Laws LJ's constitutional hierarchy of statutes was not simply a descriptive label, but a categorisation with clear normative implications.

Thoburn has been characterised as evidencing a substantial, and dangerous, shift in the 'constitutional firmament'.[19] However, preceding Laws LJ's identification of constitutional statutes are earlier judicial suggestions of the existence of a hierarchical normative order. The House of Lords in *Nairn v University Court of St Andrews*[20] rejected an argument that the exclusion of women from the franchise in the Representation of the People Act 1868 was impliedly repealed by the Universities' Election Amendment Act 1881 and the Universities Act 1889 which together permitted women's admission to universities and required women college members to be issued with voting papers. Finding that the 1868 Act was not impliedly repealed, and thereby maintaining the discriminatory law, Lord Ashbourne reasoned that '[i]f it was intended to make a vast constitutional change in favour of women graduates, one would expect to find plain language and express statement'.[21] There is demonstrative constitutional reasoning displayed in the judgment, complete with the ordering of norms and identification of fundamental laws—which clearly construed laws regarding the franchise as possessing superior constitutional status—despite that the consequences in rights terms were firmly against the grain of current constitutional thought and practice. *Nairn* stands out as a clear precursor to the constitutional layering subsequently realised—and rendered generally applicable to *all* constitutional statutes[22]—in *Thoburn* and subsequent case law on constitutional norms. With the endorsement of *Thoburn* by the Supreme Court in *H v Lord Advocate*[23] and *HS2*,[24] both the distinction between constitutional and ordinary legislation—and the interpretive consequences of such categorisation—were made concrete.[25] Indeed, the constitutionalisation of the common law was ushered along by the more exacting 'quasi-entrenchment' laid down in *H v Lord Advocate*, through Lord Hope's repeated incantations that *only* express enactment can result in repeal of a constitutional statute, thereby forestalling the possibility of repeal by irresistible inference as envisioned in *Thoburn*.[26]

Alongside the qualification of implied repeal through the discovery of constitutional statutes, the turn towards a constitutional common law has been anchored in and facilitated by the principle of legality. Lord Browne-Wilkinson's speech in

[18] ibid, at [63].

[19] J Young and D Campbell, 'The Metric Martyrs and the Entrenchment Jurisprudence of Lord Justice Laws' [2002] *PL* 399 at 405.

[20] [1909] AC 147.

[21] ibid, at 163.

[22] F Ahmed and A Perry, 'Constitutional Statutes' (2017) 37 *OJLS* 461 at 463.

[23] *H v Lord Advocate* [2013] 1 AC 413.

[24] *R (HS2 Action Alliance Ltd) v Secretary of State for Transport* [2014] 1 WLR 324.

[25] *H v Lord Advocate* (n 23) at [30]; *HS2* (n 24) at [207]–[208].

[26] F Ahmed and A Perry, 'The Quasi-entrenchment of Constitutional Statutes' [2014] *CLJ* 514 at 520–21.

R v Secretary of State for the Home Department, ex parte Pierson, outlined the basic limitations that the principle imposed on government:[27]

> A power conferred by Parliament in general terms is not to be taken to authorise the doing of acts by the donee of the power which adversely affect the legal rights of the citizen or the basic principles on which the law of the United Kingdom is based unless the statute conferring the power makes it clear that such was the intention of Parliament.

Lord Hoffmann's subsequent formulation—in *R v Secretary of State for the Home Department, ex parte Simms*—explained the constitutional impetus for requiring a clear statement from Parliament:[28]

> [T]he principle of legality means that Parliament must squarely confront what it is doing and accept the political cost. Fundamental rights cannot be overridden by general or ambiguous words. This is because there is too great a risk that the full implications of their unqualified meaning may have passed unnoticed in the democratic process. In the absence of express language or necessary implication to the contrary, the courts therefore presume that even the most general words were intended to be subject to the basic rights of the individual.

Conceived of by Lord Hoffmann as primarily a vehicle for the realisation of individual rights, the 'canonical'[29] articulation of the principle of legality also indicates its secondary purpose, as a means by which English courts might enforce powers of review ('principles of constitutionality') not dissimilar to those exercised by explicitly constitutional courts. While the application of such principles would appear to fall short of providing overt support for a power of judicial strike down, they nonetheless appear to consciously position the court as a counter-majoritarian institution, capable of giving substantive effect to individual rights and constitutional principles via the processes of legislative interpretation.[30] To this extent—and to the extent that it permits derogation from the apparent intent underpinning primary legislation—the principle of legality is a bold departure for a constitution traditionally accustomed to a deferential judicial branch.[31] Although *legislative* development has also permitted the judiciary to wield constitutionally significant interpretative powers in defence of human rights,[32] as Philip Sales has recognised, the development of the principle of legality further evinces a tension between the ordinary and the constitutional: 'Section 3 of the [Human Rights Act 1998] and the principle of legality represent both continuity with earlier canons of construction looking to the object and purpose of the statute and various side constraints (such as the

[27] *R v Secretary of State for the Home Department, ex parte Pierson* [1998] AC 539 at 575 (Lord Browne-Wilkinson).

[28] See *Simms* (n 4) at 131.

[29] HWR Wade and CF Forsyth, *Administrative Law*, 10th edn (Oxford, Oxford University Press, 2009) 22.

[30] For a fuller account see R Masterman and JEK Murkens, 'Skirting Supremacy and Subordination: The Constitutional Authority of the United Kingdom Supreme Court' [2013] *PL* 800.

[31] See Masterman and Murkens (n 30) at 802–04.

[32] Human Rights Act 1998, s 3 (on the constitutional implications of which see A Kavanagh, *Constitutional Review under the UK Human Rights Act* (Cambridge, Cambridge University Press, 2009)).

presumption against retrospective effect), and also a departure from them by reason of the greater interpretive discretion which they confer upon the courts.'[33]

While rhetorically powerful, the force of the principle of legality is undermined by two significant practical considerations. The first is its apparent weakness as a constitutional protection for fundamental rights and principles; while Lord Hoffmann was able to proclaim the ability of the common law to restrain the application of unclear or uncertain legislative measures, he simultaneously conceded that (where legislative purpose is clear) Parliament continues to enjoy the ability to legislate absent legal constraints.[34] Second, the principle of legality's potency as a mechanism of constitutional restraint is undermined by difficulties relating to its application. It is axiomatic that the principle is contingent on the recognition and applicability of a right or fundamental principle existent at common law. Yet common law rights are—by their very nature—lacking in the definitional certainty of rights allocated under a Bill of Rights or other legislative instrument. Whatever vagueness persists in the definition of each right guaranteed in a Bill of Rights,[35] courts can be more sure-footed by reliance on both the wording of the rights provision and the context of the overall instrument. As such, and as creatures of the common law, the normative force of legislative endorsement to the catalogue of common law rights is also absent. In any invocation of the principle of legality it is imperative that the court address these issues of imprecision, lest it becomes a vehicle for the development of powerful, yet vague, limitations on legislative power.

Constitutional differentiation therefore gives rise to complex interpretive questions that have yet to be authoritatively answered. According priority to constitutional legislation over ordinary statutes and constitutional norms over ordinary policy is only the beginning, as courts must discover or formulate techniques to definitively identify constitutional rights, principles and statutes,[36] determine the breadth of these constitutional precepts and resolve conflicts between them.[37] These pursuits are central to developing a mature constitutional jurisprudence, supplying the means for settling the substantive requirements of the constitution over time. The first point of departure in confronting these constitutional questions is that rather than constructing hard lines between constitutional and ordinary interpretive techniques, it is more accurate to view constitutional techniques as the evolution of 'ordinary' common law statutory interpretation and to understand both approaches as mutually educative. The difference between the two is more properly regarded as one of degree rather than kind, which is not to elide constitutional and statutory

[33] P Sales, 'Partnership and Challenge: The Courts' Role in Managing the Integration of Rights and Democracy' [2016] *PL* 456 at 457.

[34] See *Simms* (n 4) at 131. See also *R (Jackson) v Attorney General* [2006] 1 AC 262 at [159].

[35] On which see JAG Griffith, 'The Political Constitution' (1979) 42 *MLR* 1, esp 12–16.

[36] While Laws LJ identified a number of 'constitutional statutes' in *Thoburn*, his definition has been simultaneously criticized for being overly broad (G Marshall, 'Metric Measures and Martyrdom by Henry VIII Clause' (2002) 118 *LQR* 493 at 495–96) and unduly narrow (Ahmed and Perry, 'Quasi-entrenchment' (n 26).

[37] While *Thoburn* provides guidance on the reconciliation of conflict between an ordinary and a constitutional statute, the Supreme Court has declined to offer clear guidance on the resolution of conflict between two constitutional instruments (see *HS2* (n 24) at [208]).

interpretation but to better appreciate the nature and extent of the similarities and distinctions between these interpretive approaches. The connection between both sets of interpretive approaches is unsurprising, in part, because the issues which they seek to resolve track across constitutional and ordinary interpretation. Those central interpretive questions include firstly, whether 'the interpretation of a law [should] be governed mainly by its "letter", or by its "spirit"', and secondly, the extent to which the meaning of a written instrument should 'be determined by the original intentions, purposes, or understandings' of its drafters.[38] The interpretive continuity between constitutional and ordinary interpretation can be seen in the assistance constitutional courts interpreting codified constitutions in other common law nations have derived from familiar techniques of ordinary interpretation, for instance through marshalling reading in and reading down techniques as remedies.[39]

This continuity approach can be further buoyed by reference in UK courts to constitutional interpretative techniques adopted in other common law states, techniques which have shown some resonance in the implementation of the Human Rights Act 1998 and devolution legislation.[40] Signs of such incorporation are clearly in evidence in *Robinson v Secretary of State for Northern Ireland*,[41] where—through application of a 'generous and purposive' approach—a majority of the House of Lords was able to uphold the validity of elections to the Northern Ireland Assembly positions of First Minister and Deputy First Minister, notwithstanding that those elections had fallen outside of the timeframe apparently set down by the Northern Ireland Act 1998.[42] The requirement of generous and purposive interpretation has become a mainstay of constitutional and bill of rights interpretation in Commonwealth countries, and has been steadily recognised as applicable to the expanding category of UK constitutional statutes.[43] As *Robinson* itself demonstrates, however, the adoption of interpretative approaches which seek to give effect to legislation in the light of a contextual assessment of legislative purpose may be in apparent tension with statutory language, and therefore with those who would position the courts as responsive and (broadly) deferential to parliamentary language as the substance of primary legislation.[44] As such—and further illustrating continuity with the corpus of the common law—while generous and purposive methods of construction may be emergent features of the constitutional common law, they are by no means routinely embraced even in relation to the interpretation of constitutional legislation.[45]

[38] J Goldsworthy, 'Introduction' in J Goldsworthy (ed), *Interpreting Constitutions* (Oxford, Oxford University Press, 2007) 2.

[39] R Leckey, *Bills of Rights in the Common Law* (Cambridge, Cambridge University Press, 2015) 40.

[40] See *Brown v Stott* [2003] 1 AC 681 at 703 (Lord Bingham, citing *Edwards v Attorney General for Canada* [1930] AC 124 at 136 (Lord Sankey LC)).

[41] *Robinson v Secretary of State for Northern Ireland* [2002] NI 390 at [11]; D Feldman, 'The Nature and Significance of "Constitutional" Legislation' (2013) 129 *LQR* 343 at 355–57.

[42] See Northern Ireland Act 1998, s 16.

[43] See, eg, *R v Director of Public Prosecutions, ex p Kebilene* [2000] 2 AC 326 at 375; R Masterman, 'Taking the Strasbourg Jurisprudence into Account: Developing a "Municipal Law of Human Rights" under the Human Rights Act' (2005) 54 *ICLQ* 907 at 913–15.

[44] See *Robinson* (n 41) at [65] (Lord Hobhouse). Cf Feldman (n 41) at 492–96.

[45] *Imperial Tobacco, Petitioner* 2013 SC (UKSC) 153 at [14].

III. INTERNAL AND EXTERNAL RESTRAINTS

The constitutionalisation of the common law through these methodological advances can be seen to pose challenges to multiple facets of common law unity. Fundamentally, the internal coherence of the common law is central to its utility as a stabilising force, a coherence that is potentially undermined to the extent that judicial reasoning employs constitutional techniques that outstrip current doctrinal progress. Though the common law is inherently evolutionary, its transformative impulses have been held in occasionally uneasy balance with countervailing tendencies towards stability and cohesion. The general tenor of judicial restraint in the development of the common law is tacit recognition that 'the common law is a process of law-making developed in a pre-democratic era, and maintained by a non-democratic form'.[46]

The internal restraint on common law adaptability in the form of the doctrine of precedent seeks to contain the 'evolutionary quandary' occasioned by common law developments.[47] Beyond the dilemma of reconciling the constancy and changeability of the common law, lies the danger that methodological engines of change will outpace doctrinal substance, thereby undermining both the stability and practicality of the common law. The common law's characteristic incrementalism hampers doctrinal and principle development to an extent that is not seen for methodology. The incremental method, in this regard at least, can be seen to tend towards the fragmentary; as Sir Robert Megarry VC noted in *Malone*, '[n]o new right in the law, fully fledged with all the appropriate safeguards, can spring from the head of a judge deciding a particular case'.[48] Though the common law may expand through the occasional development of new causes of action,[49] there has been no judicial attempt to list or compile those existing fundamental rights which are recognised, and may be protected, by virtue of the common law.[50] This may well be further evidence of the common law's incrementalism, but is also a symptom of the definitional uncertainty which attaches to common law rights; even Laws LJ—a full-throated defender of fundamental rights—has remarked that case law does not fully explain the meaning of the label 'constitutional rights'.[51]

The danger of an imbalance between methodology and substance is also demonstrated in judicial use of constitutional principle (which is discussed in further detail

[46] KD Ewing, 'A Theory of Democratic Adjudication: Towards a Representative, Accountable and Independent Judiciary' (2000) 38 *Alberta Law Review* 708 at 711.

[47] AC Hutchinson, *Evolution and the Common Law* (Cambridge, Cambridge University Press, 2005) 125.

[48] *Malone v Metropolitan Police Commissioner* [1979] 1 Ch 344 at 372.

[49] See, eg, *Hosking v Runting* [2004] 1 NZLR 1.

[50] Extra-judicially, Lord Cooke of Thorndon attempted to list those rights which the common law recognised as 'constitutional'; he included: '... the right of access to a court; the right of access to legal advice; and the right to communicate confidentially with a legal adviser under the seal of legal professional privilege ... [the right of] participation in the democratic process, equality of treatment, freedom of expression, religious freedom ... [and] the right to a fair trial' (Lord Cooke of Thorndon, 'The Road Ahead for the Common Law' (2004) 53 *ICLQ* 273 at 276–77).

[51] *R v Lord Chancellor, ex parte Witham* [1998] QB 575 at 585.

below). On the one hand, the common law's incremental development can be seen as a consequence of the (relative) certainty and predictability required of the rule of law, with constitutional principle serving to condition the extent to which legal change may be judicially engineered.[52] The core requirements of the rule of law act as a brake on accelerated development by way of the common law, and serve to ensure that any such development remains 'judicial' rather than 'legislative' in character.[53] On the other hand, the precariousness of this imbalance is on full display in the pages of the *Jackson* judgment, which spoke to the constitutional fundamentality of rule of law as a means of restraining governmental powers but added little definition to the content of the principle, its normative force and the consistency of both with other potentially conflicting constitutional norms.[54]

The external aspect of the common law's unity encompasses, on the one hand, the reconciliation of the methodology with prevailing norms of the polity, including—in the UK and Australia—parliamentary supremacy, and in other common law countries, the underpinning normative imperative of democratic will, as represented in popular sovereignty (as expressed in statutes) and constituent power (as expressed in the Constitution). In a second and increasingly important respect, the external face of the common law's unity speaks to its ability to foster both connections and communication across common law states. Speaking to the second external manifestation, the importance of inter-common law communications has been highlighted by influential judicial figures, including Lord Toulson and Lord Cooke of Thorndon.[55] Lord Toulson has recommended 'the benefit which can be gained from knowledge of the development of the common law elsewhere', in a judgment in which he encouraged the 'citation of decisions of senior courts in other common law jurisdictions'.[56]

The external constraint imposed by parliamentary supremacy is perhaps a more serious indicator of potential inconsistencies between common law constitutionalism's ascendancy and longstanding constitutional pillars. The legislative supremacy of the elected branch must be accounted for in any convincing and durable constitutional development. There is consensus that the constitutional imperative of legislative supremacy rests in its expression of the majority will but to view it as an immutable *grundnorm* is misleading.[57] Parliamentary supremacy rests on the acceptance of both political and legal actors (constituted powers) and maintains its position on the basis of continued normative justification within the legal

[52] Lord Bingham, 'The Rule of Law' [2007] *CLJ* 67 at 71.
[53] On which see A Kavanagh, 'The Elusive Divide between Interpretation and Legislation under the Human Rights Act 1998' (2004) 24 *OJLS* 259 at 270–74; G Phillipson and A Williams, 'Horizontal Effect and the Constitutional Constraint' (2011) 74 *MLR* 878 at 887.
[54] See *Jackson* (n 34) at [107] (Lord Hope) at [159] (Lady Hale). See also *Reference re Manitoba Language Rights* [1985] 1 SCR 721 at [59]; *R v Nova Scotia Pharmaceutical Society* [1992] 2 SCR 606 at [43].
[55] Lord Cooke of Thorndon, 'Master Goff's Common Law Through Commonwealth Eyes' (The Inner Temple, 1996); Lord Toulson, 'International Influence on the Common Law' (London Common Law and Commercial Bar Association, 2014).
[56] *R (Guardian News & Media Ltd) v City of Westminster Magistrates' Court* [2013] QB 618 at [88].
[57] NW Barber, 'Sovereignty Re-examined: The Courts, Parliament, and Statutes' (2000) 20 *OJLS* 131 at 140–49.

and political landscape.[58] Far from being simply 'a political fact', parliamentary supremacy is, and must be, defensible.[59] Consequently, the evolving shape of the doctrine must be—and has been—justified by normative reasoning. Such reasoning is evident in Lord Bridge's approach in *Factortame*,[60] which sought to uphold (and explain) the supremacy of EU law partly through discussion of the voluntary acceptance of limitations on Parliament's power and the necessity of EU law supremacy for the effectiveness of the Union's system of laws and regulations.[61] This approach achieved greater refinement and maturity in *HS2*, in which the UK Supreme Court developed a more assertive vision of both British constitutionalism and the courts' role in articulating the features of that constitutional landscape.[62] In explaining that the supremacy of EU law is insufficient to settle a conflict between EU law and a domestic constitutional norm, the Court was clear that such a conflict could only be resolved by the application of *UK* constitutional law in *UK* courts. The common law undoubtedly plays a role in allowing the courts to give voice to parliamentary supremacy, a role which has become all the more crucial in the years of constitutional renovation since the enactment of the European Communities Act 1972. This much is evident in *Miller*, where the necessity of parliamentary approval for the delivery of a formal notice of withdrawal from the EU was settled through the 'application of basic concepts of constitutional law'.[63] It is partly through common law reasoning—applying both principles of statutory interpretation and analogical historical argument—that innovations such as the supremacy of EU law and the interpretive and declaratory powers under the Human Rights Act 1998 have been integrated into the constitutional landscape and reconciled with its existing features.

Fundamentally, common law constitutional techniques quite consciously seek to thread the needle between defence of distinctly constitutional norms and respect for legislative will. As such, the principle of legality provides an interpretive mechanism through which courts can enforce both common law rights and constitutional principles, while simultaneously acknowledging that a clear, unambiguous statement from Parliament would settle the matter. In this way the interpretive presumption serves to reconcile parliamentary supremacy and the rule of law and maintains effective inter-institutional interaction in the development of the constitution.[64] In sum, while at first glance the external unity of the common law appears under threat by the march of its constitutionalism, closer inspection reveals a greater complexity in the external aspect of common law unity, which—at the very least—indicates conceptual connections between prevailing constitutional norms and the common law as well as a reinforcement of the bonds between common law jurisdictions through common law constitutional dialogue.

[58] TRS Allan, 'Parliamentary Sovereignty: Law, Politics and Revolution' (1997) 113 *LQR* 443.

[59] P Craig, 'Public Law, Political Theory and Legal Theory' [2000] *PL* 211 at 211.

[60] *R v Secretary of State for Transport, ex parte Factortame (No 2)* [1991] 1 AC 603.

[61] P Craig, 'Britain in the European Union' in J Jowell, D Oliver and C O'Cinneide (eds), *The Changing Constitution* (Oxford, Oxford University Press, 2015) 123.

[62] See *HS2* (n 24).

[63] *R (Miller) v Secretary of State for Exiting the European Union* [2017] 2 WLR 583 at [82].

[64] A Young, '*R (Evans) v Attorney General*—the *Anisminic* of the 21st Century?' (*UK Constitutional Law Association Blog*, 31 March 2015).

IV. THE DEPLOYMENT OF CONSTITUTIONAL RIGHTS

The common law's doctrinal recognition of constitutional rights pre-dated the enactment of the Human Rights Act 1998 and sought to give a degree of legal recognition to the rights of the individual in a constitutional system that had hitherto focused on wrongs and remedies. The means by which such rights could be asserted as against legislative action was relatively clear. To take the finding of the High Court in *Witham* as an example: the court found that the right of access to a court was a 'fundamental constitutional right'[65] recognised by the common law, and that it could not be limited other than by express wording in primary legislation or by secondary legislation whose parent statute provided for the power to make such restriction; 'general words,' Laws J indicated, 'will not suffice' for this purpose.[66] The stipulation was therefore that a right recognised by the common law as fundamental 'can only be denied by the government if it persuades Parliament to pass legislation which specifically—in effect by express provision—permits the executive to place a limitation on that right.[67]

Yet in spite of the fact that, as a tool of proto-constitutional review, the recognition of freestanding common law rights amounted to a considerable advance for the common law, the traditional terrain of judicial review of administrative action did not demonstrate the same capacity to reinvent itself to provide better judicial protection for individuals.[68] Even in those cases in which common law rights could be said to be engaged, '... the courts' capacity to protect the relevant rights was limited by broad adherence to the conventional machinery of domestic administrative law'.[69] Additionally, this burgeoning jurisprudence of common law rights was undoubtedly stifled by the implementation of the Human Rights Act 1998. The Act—by contrast with the common law—provided a defined and expanded catalogue of rights,[70] specified how those rights might be asserted against both legislation[71] and public bodies[72] and made remedies available in the event that one of the protected rights had been unjustifiably infringed.[73] Problems of the definition and scope of the protected rights, issues which the common law had yet to confront in any meaningful way, were also to be partially determined by reference to the extensive jurisprudence of the European Court of Human Rights.[74]

Following the enactment of the Human Rights Act, it was occasionally suggested that further expansion of fundamental common law rights jurisprudence might be

[65] See *Witham* (n 51) at 586.
[66] ibid, at 581.
[67] ibid, at 586.
[68] *R v Ministry of Defence, ex parte Smith* [1996] QB 517. Even post-HRA, the UK Supreme Court has declined to find that proportionality provides a free-standing head of judicial review at common law (*Pham v Secretary of State for the Home Department* [2015] 1 WLR 1591).
[69] M Elliott, 'Beyond the European Convention: Human Rights and the Common Law' (2015) 68 *Current Legal Problems* 85 at 89.
[70] Human Rights Act 1998, s 1.
[71] ibid, at ss 3 and 4.
[72] ibid, at s 6.
[73] ibid, at s 8.
[74] ibid, at s 2(1).

a possibility,[75] but the view from the highest court appeared to suggest that constitutional common law rights were destined to remain a semi-formed quirk of the pre-Human Rights Act era.[76] The tide has, however, turned with recent decisions emphasising the common law's continuing 'dynamic'[77] force in the arena of individual rights. Given broader socio-political concerns surrounding the 'Europeanisation' of the domestic laws of human rights, the assertion of a domestic alternative, or complement, to the 'incoming tide'[78] of Convention jurisprudence can be easily appreciated. There is also force in the arguments—made powerfully by Lord Reed in *Osborn*—that the Convention and its associated case law is generally phrased at such a level of abstraction as to demand implementation at the 'national level *through a substantial body of much more specific domestic law*'.[79]

Though the common law framework of rights continues to evolve—with recent decisions acknowledging the existence of common law rights to liberty,[80] open justice,[81] and against self-incrimination[82]—its potential to independently act as a meaningful constraint on governmental power should not be overstated. First, and even acknowledging the sequential preference for consideration of common law authorities in domestic human rights adjudication,[83] the Supreme Court has acknowledged that application of the Convention rights—and the proportionality standard that the common law has hitherto declined to fully embrace[84]—will often require a more exacting standard of review.[85] Second, imprecision in the realm of common law rights has been compounded by a tendency towards restraint and deference to legislative will. In *Moohan* for instance, Lord Hodge—with whom four of the remaining six Justices agreed—was prepared to acknowledge that the right to vote could be viewed as a 'basic or constitutional right'[86] but declined to find that the common law required that any derogations be 'provided for by law and … proportionate' as a result.[87] This was as a result of the fact that the common law's role had essentially been displaced by statute. In Lord Hodge's words:[88]

> … for centuries the right to vote has been derived from statute. The UK Parliament through its legislation has controlled and controls the modalities of the expression of democracy. It is not appropriate for the courts to develop the common law in order to supplement or override the statutory rules which determine our democratic franchise.

[75] *International Transport Roth GmbH v Secretary of State for the Home Department* [2003] QB 728 at [71].
[76] *Watkins v Secretary of State for the Home Department* [2006] 2 AC 395 at [62].
[77] S Stephenson, 'The Supreme Court's Renewed Interest in Autochthonous Constitutionalism' [2015] *PL* 394 at 399.
[78] *Bulmer Ltd v Bollinger SA* [1974] Ch 401 at 418 (Lord Denning).
[79] See *Osborn* (n 5) at [55].
[80] *R (Lee-Hirons) v Secretary of State for Justice* [2017] AC 52.
[81] See *Guardian* (n 56).
[82] *Beghal v Director of Public Prosecutions* [2016] AC 88.
[83] R Masterman and S Wheatle, 'A Common Law Resurgence in Rights Protection?' [2015] *EHRLR* 57 at 64.
[84] *Pham v Secretary of State for the Home Department* [2015] 1 WLR 1591.
[85] See *A* v *British Broadcasting Corporation* (n 5) at [57].
[86] See *Moohan* (n 6) at [31]. See also *Watkins* (n 80) at [21] (Lord Bingham), [61] (Lord Rodger).
[87] See *Moohan* (n 6) at [34].
[88] ibid.

This finding is entirely consistent with the notion that the courts will be 'slow to develop the common law by entering, or re-entering, a field regulated by legislation'.[89] It is, of course, simultaneously inconsistent with an imperative to prioritise rights and require justification for interferences and confirms the current development of common law rights as lacking both the rigour and normative reach of their Convention-based counterparts.[90] Both characteristics combine to reduce the potential for the doctrinal application of common law rights to upset the orthodox hierarchy of norms stemming from the supremacy of the legislature. The same cannot necessarily be said for the judicial application of countervailing constitutional principles—a matter to which we now turn.

V. 'PRINCIPLES OF CONSTITUTIONALITY'?

The doctrinal unity of the common law's approach to judicial review is potentially challenged by its adoption of a more constitutionalised approach to adjudication. The adoption of an overtly constitutional approach sees a further bifurcation in the common law, as a result of which the relative *terra firma* of administrative law is abandoned in the application of more abstract, and principle-based, reasoning. The move away from administrative law doctrine forces recourse to principles of supposed general applicability which may lack the substance to effectively underpin legitimate judicial decision-making and which expose the limits of *principle unity* within common law constitutional adjudication.

Classical understandings of the common law and the British constitution view both as essentially pragmatic systems that develop and evolve by finding practical solutions to problems. The drift towards reliance on constitutional principles raises questions to which Loughlin has given voice, chief among those being the ability 'to identify principles (the relatively easy bit) but also to unpack them and set them to work to resolve particular social disputes concerning the appropriate exercise of public power'.[91] Lord Hoffmann's speech in *Simms* saw an explicit linkage drawn between the meta-regulatory potential of the common law and the formal powers of constitutional review exercised by supreme or constitutional courts in comparator systems. Similarly, in *Thoburn*, Laws LJ indicated that the common law's recognition of constitutional statutes 'gives us most of the benefits of a written constitution, in which fundamental rights are accorded special respect'.[92] On this reading the principle of legality is positioned explicitly as a constitutionalist restraint—rather than a merely interpretative tool—hinting at its development as a means by which a relatively abstract common law constitution might be enforced. In parallel, emphasising the constitutional credentials of the principle serves to enhance the normative standing of the common law and implicitly rejects the traditional

[89] *In re McKerr* [2004] 1 WLR 807 at [30].
[90] See Elliott (n 69).
[91] M Loughlin, 'Whither the Constitution?' in CF Forsyth (ed) *Judicial Review and the Constitution* (Oxford, Hart Publishing, 2000) 426.
[92] See *Thoburn* (n 17) at [64].

account of the 'negative' mandate in favour of judicial law making, which regarded 'parliamentary interference [in the common law sphere] as unobjectionable'.[93] That such interference may no longer be seen as entirely unproblematic—and that this constitutional common law may enjoy a degree of resilience—has been indicated by the UK Supreme Court. In the *HS2* decision, the Supreme Court confirmed that constitutional law might be considered as apart from other law, *and* that constitutional principles might be resistant to even the superiority of EU law:[94]

> The United Kingdom has no written constitution, but we have a number of constitutional instruments. ... The common law also recognises certain principles as fundamental to the rule of law. It is, putting the point at its lowest, certainly arguable (and it is for United Kingdom law and courts to determine) that there may be fundamental principles, whether contained in other constitutional instruments or recognised at common law, of which Parliament when it enacted the European Communities Act 1972 did not either contemplate or authorise the abrogation.

As with common law rights, the articulation of constitutional principles poses particular difficulties when those principles are deployed as determinative, or partially determinative, tools of adjudicative reasoning. First, there may be disagreement as to the underpinnings or centrality of the claimed principle. A salient example—and one that has already been alluded to—is provided by the principle of parliamentary sovereignty. In the notable decision of *Jackson*, Lord Steyn said the following:[95]

> The classic account given by Dicey of the doctrine of the supremacy of Parliament, pure and absolute as it was, can now be seen to be out of place in the modern United Kingdom. Nevertheless, the supremacy of Parliament is still the *general* principle of our constitution. *It is a construct of the common law. The judges created this principle.*

The consequence of this, as Lord Steyn went on to make plain, was that parliamentary sovereignty itself is a principle that might be moulded or amended by the judges.

Far then from being a *grundnorm*, sovereignty is—on this view at least—both a product of the common law and potentially subject to its limiting force.[96] On this account, the supremacy of the legislature may be the 'dominant' characteristic of the constitution,[97] but it does not necessarily have *overriding* force. It is the nominal first amongst otherwise equal, but nonetheless potentially yielding, principles inhering within the system. The consequence of this for Lord Steyn was that—faced with legislative abrogation of another fundamental feature of the constitution—the courts would have to consider whether that characteristic was one that 'even a sovereign Parliament acting at the behest of a complaisant House of Commons cannot abolish'.[98] It fell to Lord Hope to confirm that while sovereignty may empower and legitimise the legislature, its necessary parallel is legal accountability to the courts; '[t]he rule of law enforced by the courts is the ultimate controlling factor

[93] Lord Devlin, 'Judges and Law-Makers' (1976) 39 *MLR* 1 at 9.
[94] See *HS2* (n 24) at [207].
[95] See *Jackson* (n 34) at [102] (emphasis added).
[96] ibid, at [126].
[97] ibid, at [104].
[98] ibid.

on which our constitution is based'.[99] The extent to which the rule of law might exert a restraining influence upon legislative powers was touched upon by Baroness Hale and Lord Steyn who postulated that the severe legislative restriction of judicial review, or insulation of executive activity from judicial scrutiny, may fall foul of the rule of law.

Though it is the obiter comments of Lord Steyn and Baroness Hale that were the most eye catching, their suggestion that legislative sovereignty should yield in the face of pernicious legislation which infringed the rule of law was not shared by the other judges. The then Senior Law Lord, Lord Bingham, in particular did not so readily agree that Parliament legislated subject to external controls:[100]

> The bedrock of the British constitution is, and in 1911 was, the supremacy of the Crown in Parliament ... Then, as now, the Crown in Parliament was unconstrained by any entrenched or codified constitution. It could make or unmake any law it wished. Statutes, formally enacted as Acts of Parliament, properly interpreted, enjoyed the highest legal authority.

Lord Bingham's use of the present tense is telling. While a number of his judicial colleagues clearly countenanced a shift in the constitutional landscape, he was less willing to concede that Parliament legislates subject to external constraints and made no reference to the common law heritage of the sovereignty principle. Two points can be illustrated through this judicial divergence. First, it is clear (perhaps trite) that significant disagreement exists as to the nature and scope of the potentially applicable constitutional principles. It is uncontroversial to say that even the foremost of those—parliamentary sovereignty—is a contested concept.[101] Such disagreement is also evident in those cases in which other constitutional principles are judicially advanced.[102] But the assertion that recognition of the legislative supremacy of parliament is a purely judicial creation comes close to placing constitutional weight on the common law that its non-democratic structures cannot fully bear.

Second, the parallel appeal to the controlling influence of countervailing constitutional principles requires equal care in its unpacking. Judicial resort to broad constitutional principles is a less compelling mode of judicial argumentation than recourse to rather more precise sub-principles, or rules.[103] While the articulation of constitutional principles in the abstract is a common feature of judicial decision making, those broad principles are best applied when distilled down into rather more precise, applicable, rules. This latter point is displayed in stark relief when the broad principle in question is being used in an attempt to qualify an exercise of Parliament's legislative power. In this regard, the contestability of legislative sovereignty is rather less problematic—due, perhaps, to the democratic imprimatur that adheres to

[99] ibid, at [107].

[100] ibid, at [9].

[101] *AXA General Insurance Ltd v HM Advocate* [2012] 1 AC 868 at [50] (Lord Hope); compare, for instance, TRS Allan, *The Sovereignty of Law* (n 7) with J Goldsworthy, *Parliamentary Sovereignty: Contemporary Debates* (Cambridge, Cambridge University Press, 2010).

[102] In relation to separation of powers, compare, for instance, *R v Secretary of State for the Home Department, ex parte Fire Brigades Union* [1995] 2 AC 513 at 555–68 (Lord Mustill) with *R v* Secretary of State for the *Home Department, ex parte Venables* [1998] AC 407 at 518–27 (Lord Steyn).

[103] *Davidson v Scottish Ministers (No 2)* 2005 1 SC 7 at [53].

primary legislation—than the clarity and scope of whichever constitutional principle is invoked in order to limit legislative power.

VI. PRINCIPLE-BASED REASONING IN *R (EVANS) v ATTORNEY GENERAL*

The Supreme Court decision in *R (Evans) v Attorney General*[104] provides an illustration of the potential difficulties of reliance on constitutional principle in preference to doctrinal administrative law. The facts of the case revolved around the Attorney General's issue of a certificate—pursuant to section 53 of the Freedom of Information Act 2000[105]—which had the effect of preventing disclosure of correspondence between the Prince of Wales and various government departments.[106] Evans, a journalist for the *Guardian*, pursued judicial review proceedings, seeking to quash the Attorney General's certificate. The Divisional Court had dismissed his claim, while the Court of Appeal allowed his subsequent appeal (and granted the Attorney General permission to appeal to the Supreme Court). The pertinent issue before the Supreme Court concerned the validity of the Attorney General's certificate, with Evans arguing that section 53 'did not permit a certificate to be issued simply because, on the same facts and arguments, the accountable person took a different view of the public interest ... when it came to the issue of disclosure'.[107]

A. A Question of Constitutional or Administrative Law?

The multiple judgments delivered by the seven-Justice bench in *Evans* were differentiated not only by their conflicting conclusions on the central question before the court. The judges were also fundamentally divided on the appropriate framing of the issue regarding the validity of the Attorney General's certificate. Two critical approaches are evident, with Lord Neuberger (joined by Lord Kerr and Lord Reed) characterising the question as a constitutional issue and Lord Mance (who was joined by Lady Hale) treating the matter as a question of administrative law.

[104] [2015] AC 1787. For commentary and critical analysis see M Elliott, 'A Tangled Constitutional Web: The Black Spider Memos and the British Constitution's Relational Architecture' [2015] *PL* 539; TRS Allan, 'Law, Democracy and Constitutionalism: Reflections on *Evans v Attorney General*' [2016] *CLJ* 38; R Craig, 'Black Spiders Weaving Webs: The Constitutional Implications of Executive Veto of Tribunal Determinations' (2016) 79 *MLR* 147.

[105] Section 53(2) confers a power on an 'accountable person' (in this case, the Attorney General) to override a notice ordering disclosure by issuing a 'certificate signed by him stating that he has on reasonable grounds formed the opinion that, in respect of the request or requests concerned, there was no failure to comply' with the relevant provisions of the Act.

[106] Prior to the issue of the s 53 certificate, release of the correspondence, referred to as the 'black spider memos', had been resisted by the various government departments (a decision upheld by the Information Commissioner), but ordered by the Upper Tribunal ([2012] UKUT 313 (AAC)). Communications with the Royal Family are now the subject of an absolute exemption from the provisions of the Act (Constitutional Reform and Governance Act 2010, s 46 and sch 7)).

[107] See *Evans* (n 104) at [46]. A secondary issue before the Supreme Court was the consistency of the Attorney General's Certificate with EU Directive 2003/4/EC to the extent that the Certificate applied to communications about environmental matters (see [21]–[29], [98]–[113], [147]–[149], [167], [184]–189]).

In summary, the core focus of the administrative law enquiry was the legitimacy and/or reasonableness of the reasons underpinning the Attorney General's certification. Lord Neuberger's constitutional law enquiry was more clearly focused on the compatibility of a power to issue such a certificate with the rule of law. The main dissent from Lord Wilson sought to deliver a response to both approaches, and can be characterised as conservatively constitutionalist as the more forceful elements of his speech were squarely directed at disputing Lord Neuberger's rule of law-driven 'constitutional' reasoning. The remaining Justice, Lord Hughes, also framed the issue as one of administrative law, though he departed from the findings of Lord Mance and Baroness Hale on the sufficiency of the reasons advanced in support of the Attorney General's decision.

It is the path chosen by Lord Neuberger that most clearly evidences the potential of the constitutional common law, and most clearly illustrates some of its potential pitfalls. Lord Neuberger's judgment focuses on the notion that executive override of a judicial decision 'cut[s] across two constitutional principles which are also fundamental components of the rule of law'.[108] The two fundamentals were identified as first, 'the basic principle that a decision of a court is binding ... and cannot be ignored or set aside by anyone, including (indeed it may fairly be said, least of all) the executive' and second, that 'decisions and actions of the executive are, subject to necessary well-established exceptions ... reviewable by the court at the suit of an interested citizen'.[109]

While Lord Mance, Lady Hale and Lord Hughes (the latter dissenting in part) saw the crux of the decision as lying in the adequacy of the reasons advanced by the Attorney General for issuing the certificate under section 53 (with Lord Mance and Lady Hale finding those reasons inadequate for the purposes of issuing the certificate), the constitutional approach served to lift the issue from the minutiae of the Attorney General's decision. Due to what Lord Neuberger described as the 'constitutional aspect'[110] of the case, both the issue of the certificate's validity and the consequences of the court's determination of that issue, became more general and broader in scope. This generalising of the issue occurred in two ways. First, far from viewing the matter as a concern discretely related to British constitutional law and principles, Lord Neuberger appealed to 'global' legal values, stating that an interpretation of section 53(2) of the Freedom of Information Act 'which entitles a member of the executive ... to overrule a decision of the judiciary merely because he does not agree with it would not merely be unique in the laws of the United Kingdom'.[111] Using this framing, the implications of the interpretation of section 53(2) would therefore extend beyond the provincial by undermining universal values which attach to the rule of law. Second, beyond a geographical expansion of the scope of the issue, elevating it from the detail of administrative law and situating it within the constitutional components of the rule of law suggests that the applicable principles are so

[108] See *Evans* (n 104) at [52].
[109] ibid.
[110] ibid, at [51].
[111] ibid.

fundamental that they not only contain independently applicable norms, but are also impervious to differing views on controversial questions. Lord Neuberger was overt on this score, as after describing the two principles, he explained their normative import in the following terms:[112]

> … the fact that the member of the executive can put forward cogent and/or strongly held reasons for disagreeing with the court is, in this context, nothing to the point: many court decisions are on points of controversy where opinions (even individual judicial opinions) may reasonably differ, but that does not affect the applicability of these principles.

This account of the rule of law approaches the understanding of constitutional norms that obtains in nations with entrenched constitutions, but is, of course, tempered by the acknowledgement that the principles apply domestically 'subject to parliamentary supremacy'.[113]

B. Enforcing the Rule of Law

Evans reinforces a trend in British constitutionalism—specifically the common law variety—for a prioritisation of the relationship between individual and state while being less attentive and more tepid in addressing the relationship between organs of state. Mention of the most dominant of organisational constitutional principles—separation of powers—only appears in Lord Wilson's dissent.[114] While Lord Neuberger's judgment supplies some content to the often elusive rule of law by indicating two 'constitutional principles' that are said to be components of the rule of law, it avoids engagement with the more complex institutional dilemmas engaged by both principles. In a larger sense, his judgment proves that the relative ease of identification of a constitutional principle is balanced—if not outweighed—by the difficulty of extracting and applying its component parts. While identifying the two relevant components as the principle that the decision of a court is binding (the finality principle) and the requirement that executive decisions be reviewable by the court (the reviewability principle), he failed to confront the complexities of both principles and the authorities that support their characterisation as *enforceable* 'fundamental components' of the rule of law.

Regarding the first of these, Lord Neuberger arguably overstates the certainty with which the finality principle finds support in the common law. He sought to support the finality principle using dicta from *M v Home Office*,[115] to the effect that the executive obeys the law as a matter of necessity rather than grace. In light of section 53, the circumstances in *Evans* are qualitatively different from that particular judicial review case. An executive override in reliance on the primary legislative authority

112 ibid, at [52].
113 ibid.
114 ibid, at [171].
115 [1994] 1 AC 377 at 395: 'the proposition that the executive obey the law as a matter of grace and not as a matter of necessity is a proposition which would reverse the result of the Civil War' (Lord Templeman).

of section 53 of the Freedom of Information Act—as in *Evans*—is distinct from the bare refusal of the Home Office Minister to comply with a court order on the basis of advice that the court acted outside its jurisdiction. Lord Neuberger does concede that the finality principle is subject to the contrary views of a higher court or to statute,[116] but goes on to say—even in the light of an available judicial review of the executive override—that 'it can be said with some force that the *rule of law* would require a judge, almost as a matter of course, to quash the executive decision'.[117] In portraying the finality principle as an effectively immovable object—even in the face of his apparent concession to parliamentary supremacy—Lord Neuberger offers only a partial account of the inter-institutional dynamics at play in *Evans*.

The latter point is also evident in Lord Neuberger's treatment of the reviewability principle. While this has achieved broad support and application from at least *GCHQ*[118] onwards, we are all too aware—particularly from cases involving the review of prerogative powers[119]—that given the right amount of deference, a deferential review might differ little in practice from non-justiciability. Reviewability is therefore a concept of varying colours and shades.[120] As such, it is unsurprising perhaps that the Justices unanimously recognised the reviewability principle but differed on the question whether that principle had been breached. While the focus of the minority was on the reasons provided in support of the ministerial override, Lord Neuberger's deployment of the reviewability principle was subtly different. He was particularly exercised by the potential for a certificate under section 53 to be issued on the basis of mere disagreement with a judicial finding in favour of disclosure,[121] finding that section 53 did not permit the issue of a certificate where, 'on the basis of the same facts and issues as were before a judicial tribunal',[122] the accountable person merely comes to a different assessment of where the public interest should lie. For Lord Neuberger the breadth of the statutory power—rather than the specific circumstances of its use in the instant case—was inherently problematic. It is questionable whether Lord Neuberger needed to stress the potential for a certification decision to be taken absent convincing reasons, with a certificate issued simply on the basis of disagreement likely to lack the 'reasonable grounds' required. Neuberger's vision of reviewability—consistently with the broad tenor of his expansionary reasoning and reliance on overarching principle—is less focused on the reasons actually provided, and more driven by the bare compliance of the purported breadth of the statutory allocation of power with the overriding imperative of the rule of law. As such, deployment of the reviewability principle in Neuberger's judgment is tantamount to an abstracted review of the statutory terms employed by Parliament in enacting section 53.

[116] See *Evans* (n 104) at [52].

[117] ibid, at [53] (emphasis added).

[118] *Council of Civil Service Unions v Minister for the Civil Service* [1985] AC 374.

[119] *R (On the application of Bancoult) v Secretary of State for Foreign and Commonwealth Affairs* [2009] 1 AC 453.

[120] On which see M Taggart, 'Proportionality, Deference, *Wednesbury*' [2008] *New Zealand Law Review* 423, esp 451–54.

[121] See *Evans* (n 104) at [46], [50], [51], [52], [58], [59], [88], [89].

[122] ibid, at [50].

The vehicle through which the twin requirements of the rule of law are vindicated in *Evans* is the principle of legality. While *Evans* does not seek to resolve outstanding issues relating to the extent to which the principle will adhere to common law rights, it provides confirmation that constitutional principles—at the very least the rule of law—will not be taken to yield in the face of 'general or ambiguous' statutory language. As such, it focuses attention on the normative aspirations of the principle of legality. In the first instance, it appears to demonstrate that at the general level—as the conduit for the potentially wide-reaching requirements of the rule of law—the principle of legality can operate as a substantive, external, limitation on legislative power. At the more specific level, *Evans* also provides (conflicting) indicators as to the precision with which legislation may have to be formulated to limit rights and/or constitutional principles. Thus, it remains unclear what form of wording is required for the courts to adjudge that the statutory language is clear enough to demonstrate that Parliament has 'squarely confront[ed] what it is doing and accept[ed] the political cost'.[123] Certainly, the plurality and the partial dissent penned by Lord Hughes revealed starkly different views on the clarity of the terms of section 53(2). Lord Hughes had no hesitation in concluding that the section 'can mean nothing other than that the accountable person … is given the statutory power to override the decision of the Information Commissioner, and/or of a court after appeal from the Commissioner, if he disagrees with it on reasonable grounds'.[124] By contrast, in Lord Neuberger's view, the section failed to satisfy the requirements of the principle of legality as it 'falls far short of being crystal clear'.[125] The level of clarity required in Parliament's expression requires resolution to stave off charges of judicial disobedience, but more fundamentally, some settlement must be reached whether the principle of legality has developed to accommodate potential disobedience to parliamentary expression/intent in the face of a countervailing and fundamental constitutional principle.

The cumulative impact of Lord Neuberger's principles of finality and of reviewability—as given effect in *Evans*—is considerable, in practice leaving section 53 an empty shell capable of application only in the narrowest of circumstances.[126] By contrast, the two principles of constitutionality combine to give considerable depth and reach to the common law's capacity to give voice to the rule of law. Lord Neuberger's iteration of the principle of legality additionally sets a high bar for the extent of statutory clarity required in order to legitimately restrict fundamental rights or the rule of law. The sum of this is the delivery of something akin to a stronger form of judicial review than has traditionally been evident in UK constitutional practice. In consequence, Elliott has assessed *Evans* as having performed 'radical constitutional surgery pursuant to the principle of legality'.[127] Others have

[123] See *Simms* (n 4) at 131 (Lord Hoffmann).

[124] ibid, at [153].

[125] See *Evans* (n 104) at [58].

[126] On Lord Neuberger's reading, s 53 would, following a judicial finding in favour of disclosure, appear to be limited to those circumstances where there had been 'a material change in circumstances since the tribunal decision' or if that decision was 'demonstrably flawed in fact or in law' (*Evans* (n 104) at [71]–[85]).

[127] Elliott, 'A Tangled Constitutional Web' (n 104) at 546.

been less charitable, accusing Lord Neuberger of effectively excising section 53 from the statute book.[128] While *Evans* most certainly contributes to debates around the incremental constitutionalisation of the common law—both through adding breadth to the principle of legality and through the overt judicial application of free-standing constitutional principle—it also serves to emphasise that in departing from the *terra firma* of administrative law (and perhaps also from the security of the sovereignty doctrine) both caution and clarity are required. If the unity and stability of the common law is to be maintained then it is beholden on the court to—through the application of fully reasoned and supported decision-making—provide shape *and* substance to its constitutional dimension.

VII. TOWARDS A COHERENT CONSTITUTIONAL COMMON LAW

The importance of method should be underscored in a context in which the resurgence of common law rights and principles can be discounted and minimised by claims that parliamentary supremacy will thwart attempts at strong judicial enforcement of common law norms. The methodological advances of the doctrine of constitutional statutes and the principle of legality lay a path for articulating and applying constitutional doctrine in interpreting legislation. Nonetheless, the continued adoption of new and innovative methodological techniques risks outstripping, and thereby undermining, both the doctrinal content of the constitutional common law and prevailing (and potentially countervailing) constitutional norms. If it is to be a credible and durable force, the emergent constitutional common law must achieve reconciliation with existent common law *and* constitutional tradition.

Similarly, if what we have referred to above as the meta-regulatory potential of common law constitutional principles is to be legitimately realised, then this cannot come at the expense of those characteristics that have in part secured the common law's distinctive position within the polity. If the constitutional function of the courts is to uphold the rule of law,[129] then the common law must, in both its substance *and* methodology, be reflective of such a commitment. Our concern is that seeking to substantiate—and enforce—principle-based constitutionalist reasoning holds the potential to undermine the stability of the common law, and therefore its legitimacy. This is not to suggest that the constitutional capacity of the common law is incapable of orderly development. We tentatively suggest that the common law's constitutionalist turn can be coherently and stably supported through observance of a studied approach that seeks to secure the constitutionalisation of the common law through its full reconciliation with internal and external restraints and completion (filling the gaps) of the doctrinal and principle foundations and requirements of common law constitutionalism. In this light, the following approaches are recommended to usher along the balanced maturation of the nascent common law constitution.

[128] R Ekins and CF Forsyth, *Judging the Public Interest: The Rule of Law vs the Rule of Courts* (London, Policy Exchange, 2015) 11.

[129] See *Miller* (n 63) at [42], [151].

A. Sustained Incrementalism

It is in 'the gradual construction of principle case by case'[130] that judicial power is kept in check, in recognition of the restrictions that principle and expertise place upon judicial activity. Maintaining an incremental approach would serve the twin objectives of respect for prevailing constitutional doctrines of parliamentary supremacy, the rule of law and separation of powers, and acknowledge limitations on the competence of the judicial organ. Such an approach does not bar fundamental changes or judicially driven constitutional moments. Rather, it seeks to ensure that judges 'develop the law in a *judicial* rather than a legislative fashion; that is, on a piecemeal and principled basis that takes due account of pre-existing legal frameworks established by Parliament and previous judicial decisions'.[131] As a methodological or procedural restraint, incrementalism permits reasoned maturation of common law constitutionalism while respecting the constraints demanded by the nature of the common law and the British constitution.

The difficulty in articulating principles with any effective degree of specificity is, paradoxically, a result of the common law's pragmatic, evolutionary pace. However, in the light of this the UK's highest courts have generally been cautious in their application of arguments based solely on abstracted constitutional principles,[132] this caution does not prevent the application and development of precedent by reliance on broader principles or judicial reasoning on *both* precise and general justificatory grounds. Lord Neuberger's judgment in *Evans*—while clearly supportive of the values of the rule of law—was arguably lacking the reinforcement of those specific authorities that would have substantiated his broader vision of the concept. If the principle of legality is to support a species of partially-abstracted legislative review, it must do so consistently with the common law's focus on the instant case in order to remain credible. In short, the courts may persist in giving substantive content to the rule of law, and thereby incrementally chart the contours of the common law's understanding of a 'rights-based democracy',[133] but should not lose sight of those methodological characteristics of the principle—relative certainty, stability, predictability—that maintain its integrity and legitimacy.

B. Completing the Constitutional Circle

The common law's acceptance of a jurisprudence of fundamental rights—activated by a principle of legality capable of offering support where rights (and potentially constitutional principles) are undermined by inadvertent legislative action—undoubtedly provides a narrow basis for a fully-fledged constitutional jurisprudence. Recourse to the apex court in order to resolve, or partially resolve,

130 Sir John Laws, 'Judicial Activism' (*Judicial Power Project Blog*, 12 December 2016).

131 See Phillipson and Williams (n 53) at 887.

132 See *Davidson v Scottish Ministers* (n 103) at 7.

133 On which see J Jowell, 'Judicial Deference: Servility, Civility or Institutional Capacity?' [2003] *PL* 592, 597 and J Jowell, 'Beyond the Rule of Law: Towards Constitutional Judicial Review' [2000] *PL* 671.

constitutional problems—questions often at the intersection of law and political controversy[134]—has arguably already resulted in the extension of the principle of legality, which might bite upon infringements of individual, specified rights,[135] bundles of rights,[136] and (potentially unspecified)[137] constitutional principles.[138] In the field of rights protection, the principle of legality is described as having become equal in force to the interpretative direction contained in section 3(1) of the Human Rights Act,[139] and even some who see the principle as mandating a less robust protection of individual liberty nonetheless portray it as a vehicle for the broader management of judicio-legislative relations.[140] For the principle of legality to fulfil these expanding ambitions, the content and institutional implications of the constitutional principles it is claimed to protect must—alongside fundamental rights—be further developed.

The adverse consequence of the incremental development of the common law—for the development of a *constitutional* common law—has been to view precedents in isolation, rather than as components of a potentially cohering body of constitutional rules and principles. Hence, we clearly envisage *Entick v Carrington* as confirming the principle of government under the law, but have a less defined sense of how that particular requirement links to, and coheres with, other, broader, requirements of the rule of law.[141] The result of this is the tendency to narrowly regard precedents as judicially-applicable, and to be sceptical of principle-based reasoning of the type seen in *Evans*. If principle-based reasoning is to result in the vindication of constitutional principle, then it is beholden on the court to clearly bridge the gap between the applicable precedent(s) and the constitutional maxim to be vindicated.

If a constitutional common law is to flourish, and to range beyond the potentially inhibiting rights-focus of the principle of legality and common law rights jurisprudence, there is also a need for clearer articulation of constitutional principle *and* of the organisational/structural requirements of the constitution. Though *Evans* was in one sense very clearly about the interrelationship between Parliament, executive and courts, the virtual absence of explicit discussion of separation of powers[142] is illustrative of a decision that—while principle-based in its reliance on the rule of law—is otherwise lacking in its detailed consideration of a (perhaps *the*) key concept through which constitutional organisation and division can be articulated. Superficial engagement with separation of powers—also evident in other decisions of comparable constitutional standing[143]—is perhaps unsurprising in a system which has tended to be reflective of only a partial separation of governmental institutions.[144]

[134] See, eg, *Jackson* (n 34); *Miller* (n 63).
[135] See *Simms* (n 4).
[136] See *Miller* (n 63) at [87].
[137] See *HS2* (n 24).
[138] See *Evans* (n 104).
[139] E Bjorge, 'Common Law Rights: Balancing Domestic and International Exigencies' [2016] *CLJ* 220 at 233.
[140] See Sales (n 33).
[141] Again, the scholarship of TRS Allan provides a notable exception (in particular see TRS Allan, *Constitutional Justice: A Liberal Theory of the Rule of Law* (Oxford: Oxford University Press, 2001)).
[142] See *Evans* (n 104) at [171].
[143] See, eg, *Jackson* (n 34); *Miller* (n 63).
[144] On which see E Barendt, *An Introduction to Constitutional Law* (Oxford, Clarendon Press, 1998).

Yet ongoing judicial failure to conceptualise the bases of institutional interactions reflects only an embryonic constitutional jurisprudence.

C. Critical Comparativism

There is longstanding evidence of judicial awareness of the assistance that common law adjudication in any one jurisdiction draws from the experiences and understandings developed in other jurisdictions.[145] References to related cases in other states are also justified by, and build on, the centrality of reason to common law method and development. Accepting reason as the basis for continual judicial refinement of the law, common law adjudication therefore resists firm jurisdictional containment. Thus, cross-jurisdictional common law unity is far from a relic of colonial days past.[146] From at least the 1990s, common law appellate bodies have explicitly endorsed developing the common law in one jurisdiction by reference to the law of other common law states. While that effort was more regularly demonstrated in innovations in tort law,[147] constitutionalisation of the common law has been greatly encouraged by reference to other states' experience with constitutional law. Rather than being undermined by strides in common law adjudication, cross-jurisdictional common law unity has been fostered by such developments. Though not speaking directly to common law constitutionalism, Lord Reed's reflection 'that the approach to proportionality adopted in our domestic case law under the Human Rights Act has not generally mirrored that of the Strasbourg court', but has adopted 'a more clearly structured approach … derived from case law under Commonwealth constitutions', is testament to the synthesis occasioned by constitutional techniques in common law courts.[148]

Moreover, inquiry into foreign law would compensate for the United Kingdom's lack of prolonged experience with judicially-enforced constitutionalism. Highly instructive in this respect is the calibration of constitutional application of the rule of law in Canadian jurisprudence, culminating in increasingly specific derivation of principles from the rule of law, with a keen eye to precedents supporting claimed rule of law applications and to the restraining influences of constitutional text and countervailing constitutional principles. Thus the Canadian Supreme Court cautioned in *Imperial Tobacco* that however robust judicial enforcement of the rule of law, such protection must be conditioned by respect for parliament's legislative authority and the terms of the Constitution.[149] The tailored appeals to the rule of law in Canada

[145] See, eg, *White v Jones* [1995] 2 AC 207; *R v (Anderson) v Secretary of State for the Home Department* [2003] 1 AC 837 at [39]; *A v Secretary of State for the Home Department* [2006] 2 AC 221 at [15]–[17].

[146] See C Harlow, 'Export, Import. The Ebb and Flow of English Public Law' [2000] PL 240 at 247.

[147] See *Invercargill City Council v Hamlin* Respondent [1996] AC 624] (New Zealand); J Stapleton, 'Controlling the Future of the Common Law by Restatement' in M Stuart Madden (ed), *Exploring Tort Law* (Cambridge, Cambridge University Press, 2005) 263.

[148] Lord Reed, 'The Common Law and the ECHR' (Inner Temple, 11 November 2013).

[149] *British Columbia v Imperial Tobacco Canada Ltd* [2005] 2 SCR 473 (SC, Canada) [66]–[68] (Major J).

and other common law jurisdictions could have provided meaningful guidance to Lord Neuberger's *Evans* judgment by helping to justify his claim to the globality of the rule of law principle of finality of judicial decisions as well as contributing to the resolution between judicial application of the rule of law and legislative expression. The wisdom of such pedagogical references to foreign law is underscored by the relative youth of assertive constitutional—as opposed to administrative—reliance on rule of law arguments by UK courts. The trials, errors and lessons of courts more experienced in this endeavour ought to inform the forward march of the constitutional common law.

VIII. CONCLUSION

The potential implications of the constitutionalisation of the common law can be seen in Lord Hodge's warning in *Moohan* that if 'a parliamentary majority abusively sought to entrench its power by a curtailment of the franchise or similar device, the common law, informed by principles of democracy and the rule of law and international norms, would be able to declare such legislation unlawful'.[150] While often cast as judicial supremacy, the requirement that Parliament act consistently with constitutional principle can alternatively be seen as a natural consequence of the advance of constitutionalism in the UK. Rather than automatically resulting in the dominance of the judicial branch, the result would be more appropriately cast as a form of discursive constitutionalist model along the lines of the 'new Commonwealth model of constitutionalism'.[151] In fact, cross-institutional discourse is precisely what is at the heart of the principle of legality: it places a manner and form requirement on legislative activity, the results of which are scrutinised by the court, with room for Parliament to (re)assert its legislative intention.

Beyond tensions with parliamentary supremacy, if a constitutional common law is to flourish, and avoid the charge that its attendant rights and principles are essentially empty vessels, it must acquire the doctrinal underpinning and rigour that has accompanied the growth of administrative law in the post-war period. Furtive steps are being taken in this direction, most evidently in the resurgence of constitutional common law rights in the *Osborn* line of cases and in the concretisation of the doctrine of constitutional statutes in *HS2*. Simultaneously, however, failure—or reluctance—to reinforce the principled underpinnings of this constitutional common law will not only fuel accusations of an over-mighty judicial branch and subjectivity in judicial decision making, but will also undermine the broader unity and stability of the common law.

[150] See *Moohan* (n 6) at [35].

[151] S Gardbaum, *The New Commonwealth Model of Constitutionalism* (Cambridge, Cambridge University Press, 2013). See also Masterman and Murkens (n 30).

7

A Matter of Feel? Public Powers and Functions in South Africa

CORA HOEXTER*

I. INTRODUCTION

THE CONCEPTS 'PUBLIC powers' and 'public functions' unite many common-law jurisdictions, as the amenability of a decision to judicial review often depends on whether it entails the use of such power or the performance of such a function. South Africa is a prime example of this approach. Under its democratic constitution the function matters more than the functionary; even distinctively private actors are capable of exercising public powers or performing public functions. On those occasions their conduct becomes subject to administrative-law review in one form or another and they may also find themselves bound vertically by the extensive Bill of Rights contained in the Constitution.[1] Conversely, exercises of private power are not generally amenable to judicial review even when the actor is patently public in nature.

Given its implications, the question of public powers and functions is clearly pivotal to the application of public law in South Africa. However, despite its importance, the question is not susceptible of an easy or predictable answer. Rather, determining the nature of a power or function is acknowledged to be 'a notoriously difficult exercise'.[2] As in English law and most common-law jurisdictions, there is no litmus test for determining whether a power or function is public. Instead, diagnosis takes place on a case-by-case basis and the courts make use of factors or indicia such as the

* This chapter is based on a paper presented at the Public Law Conference on 'The Unity of Public Law?' at the Faculty of Law, University of Cambridge on 12–14 September 2016. I am grateful to the participants at that conference, to the editors of this book and to the experts who reviewed this chapter anonymously for their helpful comments and suggestions. The research was supported in part by the National Research Foundation of South Africa (Grant No 96285). Any opinion, finding and conclusion or recommendation expressed in the material is that of the author, and the Foundation does not accept any liability in this regard.

[1] Constitution of the Republic of South Africa, 1996, which replaced the transitional or interim Constitution of 1993 (Constitution of the Republic of South Africa, Act 200 of 1993).

[2] *Chirwa v Transnet Ltd* 2008 (4) SA 367 at [186] (Langa CJ).

source of the power, the presence or absence of autonomy, public funding, impact on the public and coercive or monopoly power.[3] Unsurprisingly, this approach leads to problems of indeterminacy and inconsistency similar to those experienced in English law and elsewhere.

The essential difficulty, increasingly acknowledged today, is that few or no activities are inherently public or private. In Harlow's words, 'no activity is typically governmental in character, nor wholly without parallels in private law'.[4] Nor is the concept of public power static: rather, it changes over time.[5] Accordingly, in the diagnosis a great deal depends on the 'prevailing political philosophy concerning the proper role of government'[6]—if there *is* a prevailing philosophy; for one would expect this to be highly contested political terrain.[7] All too often one may be left with judicial intuition:[8] a haphazard affair, as some judges seem more ready to discern public powers or functions while others appear to start from the assumption that the conduct of an apparently private body is private until proved otherwise. To add to the potential for arbitrariness, the factors tend not to be applied uniformly or evenly to the cases, so that features emphasised in one instance might not even be mentioned by the court in another. Neither is there clarity as to how the various factors are or ought to be weighed, whether some count more than others or how many are needed to tip the balance. In the South African context, there is a further variation worth mentioning: the influence of the English jurisprudence on judicial review, whether at common law or under the Human Rights Act 1998. Though generally quite strong in this area, this influence is not consistent but tends to fluctuate from case to case. All of this results in considerable uncertainty and a degree of incoherence. In the end, the boundary between public and private often seems to be a matter of 'feel', as Scott Baker LJ once described it.[9]

This chapter illustrates these problems by exploring some of the most significant South African cases relating to the diagnosis of public powers and functions, though without purporting to be exhaustive of this vast territory. Most of the cases dealt with here concern the amenability of a decision to judicial review in administrative law. Part II explains the more important constitutional and legislative implications of the finding that an actor has exercised public power or performed a public function. The jurisprudence relating to the exercise of public power by private or apparently

[3] For a catalogue of some of the factors, see J Klaaren and G Penfold, 'Just Administrative Action' in S Woolman et al (eds), *Constitutional Law of South Africa* (Cape Town, Juta & Co Ltd, 2008) 63, 63–56.

[4] C Harlow, '"Public" and "Private" Law: Definition Without Distinction' (1980) 43 *Modern Law Review* 241 at 257.

[5] *Mobile Telephone Networks (Pty) Ltd v SMI Trading* CC 2012 (6) SA 638 at [30] (Plasket AJA), citing P Craig, 'What is Public Power?' in H Corder and T Maluwa (eds), *Administrative Justice in Southern Africa* (Cape Town, University of Cape Town, 1997) 25.

[6] M Elliott, '"Public" and "Private": Defining the Scope of the Human Rights Act' [2007] *CLJ* 485 at 487.

[7] See CD Campbell, 'The Nature of Power as Public in English Judicial Review' [2009] *CLJ* 90 and the works cited there.

[8] ibid, at 93–4.

[9] *R (Tucker) v Director General of the National Crime Squad* [2003] ICR 599 at [13]. Interestingly, in *AMCU v Chamber of Mines of South Africa* 2017 (3) SA 242 ('*AMCU*'), [74] the Constitutional Court alluded to the 'look and feel' of a power.

private entities is discussed in Part III. Here, the conduct of sports regulatory bodies is given special attention, as this is an area in which the South African courts are becoming notably more adventurous than their English counterparts. Part IV outlines the legal position where public actors purport to exercise power that is of a contractual nature, and thus wholly private: another ambivalent and uncertain area of South African law. A conclusion follows in Part V.

II. THE IMPLICATIONS OF EXERCISING PUBLIC POWER OR PERFORMING A PUBLIC FUNCTION

A. Qualifying as an 'Organ of State'

An 'organ of state' is a term of considerable significance under the Constitution. The concept is defined broadly in section 239 to include not only 'any department of state or administration', but also any functionary or institution, other than a court or judicial officer, exercising public powers or performing public functions in terms of the Constitution, a provincial Constitution *or any legislation.*[10]

The most far-reaching consequence of the classification is contained in section 8(1) of the Constitution, which makes the Bill of Rights binding on all organs of state. To be more precise, organs of state are bound by this justiciable charter of rights in a direct and vertical manner. 'Direct' implies that any action of an organ of state may be challenged for inconsistency with the Bill of Rights,[11] while 'vertical' reflects the traditional relationship between individual and state. Section 8(2) of the Constitution, in turn, envisages that private actors may be bound directly and *horizontally* by the Bill of Rights, thus apparently allowing for private actors to be duty-bearers just as the state is a duty-bearer.[12] However, the Constitutional Court has made very little use of this mechanism and seems to conceive of horizontal obligations primarily as negative ones (ie as imposing a mere duty not to interfere with a right).[13] Actors bound both directly and vertically, by contrast, are expected to 'respect, protect, promote and fulfil' constitutional rights in a positive manner.[14]

[10] In this context 'legislation' refers most obviously to statutes or Acts, but has been held to include subordinate legislation such as an exemption notice issued by a Minister in terms of an Act: see *AAA Investments (Pty) Ltd v Micro Finance Regulatory Council* 2007 (1) SA 343 ('*AAA Investments* (CC)') at [42] in the majority judgment of Yacoob J, and see further [150] in the minority opinion of O'Regan J. As noted by the Constitutional Court in that case, s 239 expressly defines the concept 'national legislation' to include 'subordinate legislation made in terms of an Act of Parliament'.

[11] 'Indirect' application, by contrast, refers to the process of judicial interpretation whereby ordinary law is harmonised with the Bill of Rights or infused with its values.

[12] Section 8(2) provides: 'A provision of the Bill of Rights binds a natural or juristic person if, and to the extent that, it is applicable, taking into account the nature of the right and the nature of any duty imposed by the right.'

[13] This is suggested particularly by the court's statement on the topic in *Governing Body of the Juma Musjid Primary School v Essay NO* 2011 (8) BCLR 761 at [58]. See M Finn, 'Organs of State: An Anatomy' (2015) 31 *South African Journal on Human Rights* 631 at 650–51.

[14] Constitution, s 7.

The effects of section 239 found vivid illustration in the *Allpay* case a few years ago.[15] Here, the Constitutional Court held that a commercial entity was an organ of state, at least for some purposes, because it had successfully tendered for a massive contract for the distribution of social welfare grants on behalf of the South African Social Security Agency (SASSA). That agency was empowered by section 4(2)(a) of the South African Social Security Agency Act 9 of 2004 to enter into an agreement with any person 'to ensure effective payments to beneficiaries'. Writing for a unanimous court, Froneman J had no hesitation in characterising the administration of such grants as an exercise of public power and the performance of a public function in terms of legislation that had been enacted to give effect to the constitutional right to social security.[16] He went on to describe the role of the company, Cash Paymaster Services (Pty) Ltd, as follows:[17]

> It plays a unique and central role as the gatekeeper of the right to social security and effectively controls beneficiaries' rights to social assistance. For all practical purposes it is not only the face, but also the operational arm, of the 'administration in the national sphere of government', insofar as the payment of social grants is concerned.

The effects of this characterisation were dramatic. The company became 'accountable to the people of South Africa in relation to the public power it acquired and the public functions it performs'.[18] It became subject to public scrutiny to some extent, including scrutiny of its finances under the contract.[19] It acquired some constitutional duties. In particular, it could not simply 'walk away' on dissolution of the contract; it was now under a constitutional obligation to ensure that a workable payment system remained in place until a new one became operational.[20]

Various other consequences of qualifying as an organ of state are noted by Finn.[21] For instance, organs of state are subject to the Public Service Act 103 of 1994 and its associated conditions of employment; and the taxation regime applicable to an

[15] *Allpay Consolidated Investment Holdings (Pty) Ltd v Chief Executive Officer of the South African Social Security Agency (No 2)* 2014 (4) SA 179 ('*Allpay*'). In an earlier judgment, *Allpay Consolidated Investment Holdings (Pty) Ltd v Chief Executive Officer of the South African Social Security Agency (No 1)* 2014 (1) SA 604, the Constitutional Court had found the award of the tender invalid on the basis of various irregularities, but had suspended the declaration of invalidity pending the determination of a just and equitable remedy. For another example in the context of electricity supply, see *City Power (Pty) Ltd v Grinpal Energy Management Services (Pty) Ltd* (2015) 36 *ILJ* 1423 at [23]–[24], where the respondent company was held to be an organ of state.

[16] See *Allpay* (n 15) at [54]. Section 27(1)(c) of the Constitution confers on 'everyone' the right 'to have access to ... social security', while s 27(2) places the state under a duty to take 'reasonable legislative and other measures, within its available resources, to achieve the progressive realisation' of this and other rights.

[17] See *Allpay* (n 15) at [55]. *cf City of Cape Town v Khaya Projects (Pty) Ltd* 2016 (5) SA 579, where it was argued unsuccessfully that a private construction company became an organ of state when it contracted to build state-funded housing in furtherance of s 26, the right of access to housing. The Supreme Court of Appeal resisted the analogy with *Allpay* largely because of the relatively minor role played by the construction company in this instance.

[18] See *Allpay* (n 15) at [59].

[19] ibid, at [78], where the court ordered Cash Paymaster to file an audited statement of expenses incurred, income received and net profit earned under the completed contract.

[20] ibid, at [66].

[21] See Finn (n 13) at 647–49.

organ of state will differ substantially from that of a private entity, and thus from the regime applicable when the entity in question is operating as a private actor.[22] One does not envy the revenue service the task of unscrambling that egg.

A number of South African statutes have borrowed the definition of 'organ of state' found in section 239 of the Constitution for various purposes. An entity that exercises public power or performs a public function counts as a 'public body' under the Promotion of Access to Information Act 2 of 2000, and is subject to a more onerous access regime than a private body (meaning that its records are easier to access). Likewise, as Finn records,[23] such an entity is subject to special obligations and processes under the Prevention and Combating of Corrupt Activities Act 12 of 2004 and the Protection of Personal Information Act 4 of 2013.

B. Performing 'Administrative Action'

Importantly, the exercise of a public power or performance of a public function is also a necessary condition for the application of administrative-law review in terms of South Africa's constitutional rights to just administrative action. The rights in section 33 of the Constitution apply only to 'administrative action', which is predicated on the use of public rather than private power.

Those rights have been given more detailed legislative effect by a statute, the Promotion of Administrative Justice Act 3 of 2000 (PAJA), which ordinarily governs the judicial review of administrative action. In section 1 of the PAJA, administrative action is defined to include a 'decision' of an organ of state exercising any power in terms of the Constitution or a provincial constitution, or exercising a public power or performing a public function *in terms of any legislation*.[24]

The overlap with section 239 is evident; but the PAJA is broader still, for the definition of administrative action goes on to encompass the decisions of natural or juristic persons exercising public powers or performing public functions *in terms of an empowering provision*. An 'empowering provision' is not confined to legislation[25] but is defined to include the common law, customary law and 'an agreement, instrument or other document in terms of which an administrative action was purportedly taken'. But this breadth is immediately followed by narrowness in the PAJA's

22 ibid, at 649.

23 ibid, at 648–49.

24 This requirement is easily satisfied in most instances, but there are exceptions such as *Chirwa* (n 2, and see further n 123 below). The case concerned a dismissal in the public sector. As the statute governing such dismissals had been repealed and not replaced, Langa CJ held for a minority of the court that the decision to dismiss had not been taken 'in terms of any legislation'. Strangely, the majority chose to focus not on the PAJA requirement but rather on the pre-PAJA jurisprudence of the Constitutional Court concerning the s 33 meaning of 'administrative action'. It found that various hallmarks of administrative action were missing—one of these being that there was no 'implementation of legislation' [142]. See text to n 103 below.

25 This is a deviation from the Australian model that inspired the PAJA's requirement of a 'decision' as well as the definition of that term. The Australian statute, the Administrative Decisions (Judicial Review) Act 1977 (Cth), uses the narrower phrase 'under an enactment'. See further I Currie, *The Promotion of Administrative Justice Act: A Commentary*, 2nd edn (Cape Town, Siber Ink, 2007) 59.

definition of administrative action, for a decision will qualify as such only if it also 'adversely affects the rights of any person';[26] has 'a direct, external legal effect';[27] and if it is not hit by one of the nine express exclusions from the definition.[28]

C. Attracting the Constitutional Principle of Legality

More generally, any entity exercising public power in any manner or form is inevitably subject to the rule of law and one particular aspect: the constitutional principle of legality. The stakes here are lower than those of the PAJA, at least in theory, as the principle of legality is supposed to be a mere safety net for non-administrative action (ie exercises of public power that do not meet all the requirements of the detailed definition in the PAJA); judicial scrutiny under this principle is supposed to be considerably less far-reaching than under the PAJA. In reality, however, the principle of legality has increasingly been made to mimic 'regular' administrative law as embodied in that statute. The result today is that any actor exercising public power is required to act both lawfully and rationally and may be taken on review for failure to do so. Furthermore, in appropriate cases the requirement of rationality may demand procedural fairness and the giving of reasons as well.[29]

In part, this development of the legality principle has compensated for the narrowness and complexity of the PAJA's definition of administrative action, as those qualities have virtually guaranteed the existence of a large category of non-administrative action to which the statute cannot apply. To some extent it has also been driven by general resistance to the PAJA, for the statute has other unpopular provisions too—particularly its outer limit of six months for bringing a review application (section 7(1)) and its strict duty to exhaust internal remedies before resorting to judicial review (section 7(2)).

III. PRIVATE ACTORS EXERCISING PUBLIC POWERS OR PERFORMING PUBLIC FUNCTIONS

The outline above shows that in South African law, the implications of exercising public power or performing a public function range widely. I now turn to some of the most important cases on the diagnosis of such powers and functions on the part

[26] As Nugent JA observed in *Grey's Marine Hout Bay (Pty) Ltd v Minister of Public Works* 2005 (6) SA 313 at [23], it seems 'paradoxical' for administrative action to be characterised by its effect in particular cases.

[27] This phrase was borrowed from German law, § 35 of the Federal Law of Administrative Procedure of 1976. As to its meaning, see C Hoexter, *Administrative Law in South Africa*, 2nd edn (Cape Town, Juta & Co Ltd, 2012) 227–34.

[28] The main exclusions are executive powers and functions at the national, provincial and local levels of government, legislative functions and judicial functions: see further Hoexter (n 27) 234–45.

[29] See, further, C Hoexter, 'A Rainbow of One Colour? Judicial Review on Substantive Grounds in South African Law' in H Wilberg and M Elliott (eds), *The Scope and Intensity of Substantive Review: Traversing Taggart's Rainbow* (Oxford, Hart Publishing, 2015) 163, 176–84.

of private or apparently private actors. As will be seen, the importance of the 'public' question is not matched by the clarity of the answers offered by the courts.

Even before the advent of democracy in 1994, South African law acknowledged that a non-statutory and apparently private entity was capable of performing a public function. The leading case in this regard dates from 1983 and is sometimes characterised as South Africa's *Datafin*.[30] In *Dawnlaan Beleggings*,[31] the court found that a decision of the respondent stock exchange, a non-statutory body, was susceptible to judicial review in administrative law.

The judgment was not as radical as that in *Datafin*, for as noted by Plasket, the Johannesburg Stock Exchange (JSE) *did* have 'visible means of legal support' in the form of a statutory framework.[32] Indeed, an important factor in the court's reasoning was that the relevant legislation expressly placed the JSE under a duty to act in the public interest.[33] But the court also recognised the public nature of the function performed by the institution. Goldstone J reasoned that unlike commercial banks, decisions of the JSE affect the public and indeed the whole economy, and that to regard it as a private institution would be to 'ignore commercial reality'.[34] Another factor operating in favour of administrative-law review was the absence of a contractual relationship between the applicant and the JSE,[35] for a decade earlier the same court had declined to apply principles of public law to what it saw as a 'purely contractual' relationship between an applicant and the stock exchange.[36]

A. The Post-1994 Jurisprudence

In the constitutional era there is no doubt that even the most unequivocally private bodies are capable of exercising public powers or performing public functions—or, to put it another way, that what matters is the function rather than the functionary. While that important proposition was originally stated by the Constitutional Court in the context of its test for administrative action,[37] it applies equally to the antecedent question of public power.

The leading case illustrating the use of public power by a private body is *AAA Investments*.[38] The case is remarkable for the sharply contrasting views of the matter taken by the High Court and the Constitutional Court on the one hand, and the

30 *R v Panel on Takeovers and Mergers, ex parte Datafin plc* [1987] QB 815 ('*Datafin*').

31 *Dawnlaan Beleggings (Edms) Bpk v Johannesburg Stock Exchange* 1983 (3) SA 344 ('*Dawnlaan Beleggings*').

32 C Plasket, 'The Fundamental Principles of Justice and Legal Vacuums: The Regulatory Powers of National Sporting Bodies' (2016) 133 *South African Law Journal* 569 at 580, with reference to the well-known phrase used by Donaldson MR in *Datafin* (n 30) at 834G–H.

33 Stock Exchanges Control Act 7 of 1947, ss 4(1) and 8(1).

34 *Dawnlaan Beleggings* (n 31) at 364H–365A.

35 ibid, at 360E.

36 *Herbert Porter & Co Ltd v Johannesburg Stock Exchange* 1974 (4) SA 781, 791E–G.

37 *President of the Republic of South Africa v South African Rugby Football Union* 2000 (1) SA 1, [141] ('the *SARFU* case'). This test predated the detailed statutory definition of administrative action in s 1 of the PAJA and is still used to inform that definition.

38 See *AAA Investments* (CC) (n 10).

Supreme Court of Appeal on the other[39]—a contrast suggesting that the philosophy or starting assumptions of the bench can be crucial.

The case concerned an exemption under the Usury Act 73 of 1968. In terms of the exemption notice issued by the relevant Minister, micro-lenders who wished to qualify for the exemption had to comply with a set of rules made by the Minister and register with a regulatory institution approved by him. The Micro Finance Regulatory Council, which included representatives of the government as well as a range of NGOs, was then identified as the approved institution, and it proceeded to make a more extensive set of rules to govern the exemption. The primary question was the nature of the power wielded by the council when it made its rules, for the applicant argued that in making them, the council—a private body—had exercised legislative power not properly delegated to it.

Drawing on cases such as *Datafin*[40] and *Dawnlaan Beleggings*,[41] the court held that the power exercised was of a public nature.[42] The council's rules, it reasoned, were coercive and would apply to all who wished to conduct business under the exemption. The rules were, in fact, an integral part of the governmental regulation of micro-loans.[43] When the matter came to it on appeal, however, the Supreme Court of Appeal seemed to be more interested in the appearance and form of the body itself than in the nature of its rules.[44] The council was incorporated as a not-for-profit company in terms of section 21 of the Companies Act 61 of 1973. Relying on its articles and memorandum of association (which empowered the council to make rules), the court held that the power exercised by the body was *private* in nature, being sourced in the consent of those wanting to participate in its regime. The council was a 'private regulator of lenders' who chose to submit to its authority by agreement.[45]

On further appeal, this characterisation was rejected by the Constitutional Court.[46] Although it divided on another issue,[47] the court was unanimous in holding that making rules to govern money-lending transactions was a public function.

[39] The superior courts consist of various provincial and local divisions of the High Court (formerly divisions of the Supreme Court of South Africa); the Supreme Court of Appeal (formerly the Appellate Division); and the Constitutional Court, a new court created for the democratic era. Until August 2013 the Constitutional Court was the highest court in constitutional matters and the Supreme Court of Appeal was the highest court in other matters, but today the Constitutional Court is the apex court in all matters while the Supreme Court of Appeal (in spite of its name) has become an intermediate court of appeal.

[40] See *Datafin* (n 30).

[41] See *Dawnlaan Beleggings* (n 31).

[42] *AAA Investments (Pty) Ltd v Micro Finance Regulatory Council* 2004 (6) SA 557 (T) 565H.

[43] ibid, at 564–65.

[44] *Micro Finance Regulatory Council v AAA Investments (Pty) Ltd* 2006 (1) SA 27 ('*AAA Investments* (SCA)').

[45] ibid, at [24].

[46] See *AAA Investments* (CC) (n 10).

[47] On the question whether the rulemaking power had been properly delegated to the council, O'Regan J held that it had been and Langa CJ held that it had not been; whereas the majority reasoned that, absent an attack on the exemption notice itself, the validity of any delegation effected by means of the notice had to be assumed. See further C Hoexter, 'The Importance of Dissent: Two Judgments in Administrative Law' 2015 *Acta Juridica* 120 at 136ff. The court declined to decide a third issue, whether the right to privacy had been infringed by the council's rules.

Not only was this a regulatory duty passed on by the Minister, but it was evident that the Minister controlled the council by determining its constitution and its functions. Yacoob J held that the Supreme Court of Appeal had put form above substance by disregarding the almost absolute control wielded by the Minister and the council's concomitant lack of autonomy.[48] Unlike a private enterprise, the council was not free to decide on its objectives and functions and how to fulfil them.

Since *AAA Investments* the question of public powers has arisen a few times in the context of the PAJA's definition of administrative action. The most interesting as well as the most important of the PAJA cases is *Calibre Clinical Consultants*,[49] for this unanimous judgment of the Supreme Court of Appeal is somewhat in tension with *AAA Investments* in terms of the appropriate inquiry or test to be applied. Indeed, one suspects that the Constitutional Court might have arrived at an altogether different diagnosis.

As to the appropriate test, in *AAA Investments* the Constitutional Court contrasted the position in Canada and the United States with that in South Africa. In the first two countries, Yacoob J concluded, the essential question for determination is whether the entity or function is 'governmental', whereas in South Africa this narrower inquiry is not necessary: it is enough if the power or function is public.[50] He went on to emphasise, too, that in this country, an entity 'does not have to be part of government' to be bound by the Constitution.[51] But in *Calibre Clinical Consultants*, while acknowledging that there is no single or universal test, Nugent JA clearly favoured a narrower 'governmental' inquiry. As he saw it, the performance of a governmental function was also what the English courts had focused on in *Datafin*,[52] *Aga Khan*,[53] *Aston Cantlow*[54] and *YL*[55] and was ultimately what the Constitutional Court had relied on in *AAA Investments*. Indeed, Nugent JA thought that the South African courts had 'almost always sought out features that are governmental in kind' when determining whether conduct is reviewable.[56] His opinion was reinforced by the ordinary dictionary meaning of 'public' powers: pertaining to the people as a whole, or performed on behalf of the community or part of it, which Nugent JA saw as 'pre-eminently the terrain of government'.[57] Furthermore, a 'governmental' inquiry resonated with the notion of accountability to the public, which was what judicial review had always been about.[58]

[48] See *AAA Investments* (CC) (n 10) at [45].

[49] *Calibre Clinical Consultants (Pty) Ltd v National Bargaining Council for the Road Freight Industry* 2010 (5) SA 457.

[50] *AAA Investments* (CC) (n 10) at [39], with reference to cases including *Lebron v National Railroad Passenger Corporation* 513 US 374 (1995) and *Eldridge v British Columbia (Attorney General)* [1997] 3 SCR 624.

[51] *AAA Investments* (CC) (n 10) at [41].

[52] See *Datafin* (n 30).

[53] *R v Disciplinary Committee of the Jockey Club, ex parte Aga Khan* [1993] 1 WLR 909.

[54] *Aston Cantlow and Wilmcote and Billesley Parochial Church Council v Wallbank* [2004] 1 AC 546.

[55] *YL v Birmingham City Council* [2008] 1 AC 95.

[56] See *Calibre Clinical Consultants* (n 49) at [39].

[57] ibid, with reference to the *Shorter Oxford Dictionary*.

[58] See *Calibre Clinical Consultants* (n 49) at [40].

Calibre Clinical Consultants involved a procurement decision of the bargaining council for the road freight industry, established under section 27 of the Labour Relations Act 66 of 1995. The bargaining council had established an AIDS programme and 'wellness fund' for the industry and wished to procure a service provider to manage these. The applicant, an unsuccessful bidder for the contract, sought PAJA review of the council's decision to award the tender to a competitor. Its challenge failed, however, as Nugent JA concluded that this was the performance of a quintessentially domestic function rather than a function that called for public accountability.[59] This conclusion was fortified by other factors, including the council's voluntary nature and that it was not spending public money, and by a possibly fatal concession that the council would not have been under a statutory duty to invite tenders at all. In short, Nugent JA saw none of the elements he had quoted from the English cases. The programme was not 'integrated into a system of statutory regulation' or 'woven into a system of governmental control', and ultimately it was not one for which the public had assumed responsibility.[60]

The court's analysis in *Calibre Clinical Consultants* was detailed and it reads compellingly. Nevertheless, it seems clear that another court could easily have seen the case differently.[61] To begin with, bargaining councils are a key component of the statutory regime for collective bargaining, and they are empowered by section 28(1) of the Labour Relations Act to engage in beneficial activities such as the AIDS programme in this case. In a country blighted by an AIDS epidemic, there is undoubtedly a strong public (and surely even governmental) interest in programmes to combat the disease. And on the approach in *AAA Investments*, the voluntary nature or appearance of the council itself is really irrelevant. As Nugent JA himself recognised, it does not imply that the entity is incapable of exercising public power. Indeed, a High Court has acknowledged that a bargaining council is quite capable of performing administrative action.[62] After referring to *Calibre Clinical Consultants,* Murphy J observed for a full bench:

> There can be little doubt that when a bargaining council requests the Minister to extend a collective agreement to non-parties that it does so either as an organ of state or as a juristic person exercising a public power or performing a public function ...[63]

The High Court seemed to think that the resolution of the bargaining council preceding such a request to the Minister was also an exercise of public power, and possibly one amounting to administrative action.[64]

Notably, in *Calibre Clinical Consultants* the collective agreement embodying the AIDS programme had indeed been extended to the entire industry in terms of section 32 of the Act, meaning that non-parties to the agreement and stakeholders

[59] ibid, at [46]. See also, eg, *Eden Security Services CC v Cape Peninsula University of Technology* [2014] ZAWCHC 148 at [48], where the same conclusion was arrived at in relation to the procurement decision of a 'university of technology', a public institution offering higher education.

[60] See *Calibre Clinical Consultants* (n 49) at [42].

[61] See Hoexter (n 27) at 209–10.

[62] *Free Market Foundation v Minister of Labour* 2016 (4) SA 496.

[63] ibid, at [73], Matojane and Basson JJ concurring.

[64] ibid, at [81].

who did not necessarily support the programme would nevertheless be bound by it. That surely introduced an element of coercion reminiscent of that in *AAA Investments*. Furthermore, the money used to fund the programme had been collected by way of compulsory rather than voluntary contributions from employers and employees in the industry. Would that not count as public money? The court's diagnosis seems ultimately to have depended on the search for 'governmental' features rather than merely 'public' ones, and that approach may well have been too narrow—'public' and 'governmental' are surely not co-extensive. Or it may simply be that the deck was stacked against a 'public' diagnosis. Nugent JA, who also wrote the judgment of the Supreme Court of Appeal in *AAA Investments*,[65] may be one of those judges with distinctly 'private' starting assumptions.

Subsequent judgments have wondered whether the 'governmental' approach is too restrictive[66] and in 2017, in *AMCU v Chamber of Mines*, the Constitutional Court actually pointed out that 'public powers and public functions are wider than governmental powers and governmental functions'.[67] Unfortunately, it did so without engaging with or even mentioning *Calibre Clinical Consultants*, so the tension has not been fully resolved. Significantly, however, in *AMCU* a decision by non-governmental actors (employers and unions) to conclude and extend a collective agreement under section 23(1)(d) of the Labour Relations Act was held to be distinctly public in nature, though not administrative action.[68] In the 'public' diagnosis the unanimous judgment of Cameron J relied on features such as the legislative context, the mandatory and coercive effects of the decision and the rationale for extension, which was the 'plainly public goal' of improving workers' conditions through collectively agreed bargains.[69]

B. Sports Regulatory Bodies

The conduct of sports regulatory bodies has been dealt with in several cases decided both before and since *AAA Investments*. Some of the cases from the constitutional era illustrate a traditional, private-law view that is in line with the attitude of the English courts to such bodies[70] (and the 'governmental' slant of *Calibre Clinical Consultants*). Other cases, particularly the more recent ones, strongly suggest that the South African courts are becoming more inclined to diagnose public power in such bodies.

[65] *AAA Investments* (SCA) (n 44) (with Navsa JA).

[66] See, eg, *Airports Company South Africa Ltd v ISO Leisure OR Tambo (Pty) Ltd* 2011 (4) SA 642, [55]–[56]; *Mobile Telephone Networks v SMI Trading* (n 5) at [34].

[67] *AMCU* (n 9) at [69], with reference to C Plasket, *The Fundamental Right to Just Administrative Action: Judicial Review of Administrative Action in the Democratic South Africa* (PhD thesis, Rhodes University, 2002) 195.

[68] See *AMCU* (n 9) at [83]. In this regard Cameron J distinguished *Free Market Foundation v Minister of Labour* (n 62), which concerned the extension of a collective agreement under s 32 of the Labour Relations Act.

[69] *AMCU* (n 9) at [81].

[70] See generally J Anderson, 'An Accident of History: Why the Decisions of Sports Governing Bodies are not Amenable to Judicial Review' (2006) 35 *Common Law World Review* 173.

A prime example of the first approach is *Cronje v United Cricket Board of South Africa*, decided in 2001.[71] The applicant was a former captain of the national team who was found by a commission of inquiry to have engaged in match fixing. The United Cricket Board (UCB) had resolved to ban him from all UCB activities for life, thus effectively excluding him from the game of cricket. The UCB had given him seven days in which to make subsequent representations about the resolution, but it had not offered him a prior hearing, which the applicant argued was procedurally unfair. Since all contractual relations between the parties had been severed by then, the applicant could not benefit from the principle of South African common law that imports natural justice into contracts of this kind, typically in a disciplinary setting.[72] Besides, the court found that the body had not taken disciplinary action against the applicant (over whom it no longer had jurisdiction), but had merely exercised its freedom of association, a fundamental right protected by section 18 of the Constitution.

Thus, the question became whether the UCB had exercised public power so as to attract the principles of administrative law. With reference to two well-known English cases, *R v Football Association, ex parte Football League*[73] and *Aga Khan*,[74] Kirk-Cohen J held that it had not. The UCB was a voluntary association unconnected with the state; it had its origin in contract rather than statute; its powers were contractual rather than statutory; it was privately funded; and it had no statutory recognition or any official responsibility for the game of cricket in South Africa.[75] Furthermore, unlike the JSE in *Dawnlaan Beleggings*, the UCB was not under a statutory duty to exercise its powers in the public interest.[76]

That is an impressive catalogue of features pointing away from an exercise of public power. However, in that same year, another provincial division took a very different view of the National Soccer League (NSL) when setting aside some of its transfer rules as unconstitutional in the *Coetzee* case.[77] Here different features were emphasised—and, tellingly, no reference was made to *Aga Khan* or any other English case. Instead the court took full account of the monopolistic control exercised by the NSL over professional football. The organisation ran all the professional leagues in South Africa and was the only body recognised by the South African Football Association, which in turn was affiliated to CAF[78] and FIFA,[79] the world body of professional football. Traverso DJP went on to dismiss the argument that the applicant had voluntarily submitted himself to the NSL's contractual regime. It was no answer to say that 'there is no obligation on any footballer to play

[71] *Cronje v United Cricket Board of South Africa* 2001 (4) SA 1361.

[72] The leading case is *Turner v Jockey Club of SA* 1974 (3) SA 633, but the principle is at least as old as *Long v Bishop of Cape Town* (1863) 4 Searle 162 and *Kotze v Murray* (1864) 5 Searle 39.

[73] *R v Football Association Ltd, ex parte Football League Ltd* [1993] 2 All ER 833.

[74] See *Aga Khan* (n 53).

[75] See *Cronje* (n 71) at 1375D–E.

[76] ibid, at 1375H–1376C.

[77] *Coetzee v Comitis* 2001 (1) SA 1254.

[78] Confédération Africaine de Football, or the African Football Association.

[79] Fédération Internationale de Football Association, or the International Federation of Association Football.

professional football'.[80] She rejected this as a frivolous contention, and moreover one that disregarded the constitutional right freely to choose one's profession.[81]

A few years later the same division took a similarly broad view—or perhaps an even more expansive one—in *Tirfu Raiders Rugby Club v SARU*, where again no reference was made to the position in English law.[82] The case concerned decisions by the South African Rugby Union (SARU) that affected the log positions of rugby teams for the purposes of play-offs leading to a championship, which did not relate purely to SARU's internal affairs. These decisions were held to be sufficiently public in nature to attract the application of the PAJA. The main factors relied on seem to have been SARU's control over the sport coupled with the significant public interest in the game of rugby and its organising bodies. Yekiso J noted that SARU occupied a position of authority over provincial unions and their affiliate clubs and remarked on the interest in these organisations on the part of various stakeholders, including sponsors, members of clubs and the 'rugby-loving public'.[83] Though Yekiso J was mindful of the warning in *Marais*,[84] an earlier judgment of his own division, that 'mere public interest in a decision does not make it an exercise of public power or the performance of a public function', he preferred the dictionary definition of public power relied on in *Van Zyl*:[85] 'an ability to act in a manner that affects or concerns the public'.

It is worth mentioning that both of these last two cases concerned decisions of political parties, and reflect tensions in the jurisprudence in that context too.[86] A discussion of the types of power exercised by these hybrid bodies is beyond the scope of this chapter, however. Political parties play such a central role in South Africa's electoral system (party-list proportional representation) and in our constitutional democracy more generally[87] that they are probably sui generis and deserving of a separate study.

In any event, the proposition that interest on the part of the public on its own is sufficient to give a power or function a public character was strongly doubted by the Supreme Court of Appeal in *Calibre Clinical Consultants*,[88] with specific reference to *Tirfu Raiders*. Nugent JA held:

> I have considerable doubt whether a body can be said to exercise 'public powers' or perform a 'public function' only because the public has an interest in the manner in which its powers are exercised or its functions are performed, and I find no support for that approach in other cases in this country or abroad.[89]

[80] See *Coetzee* (n 77) at [27].

[81] ibid.

[82] *Tirfu Raiders Rugby Club v South African Rugby Union* [2006] 2 All SA 549.

[83] ibid, at [27], [28].

[84] *Marais v Democratic Alliance* 2002 (2) BCLR 171, [28].

[85] *Van Zyl v New National Party* 2003 (10) BCLR 1167 at [75], distinguishing *Marais* (n 84).

[86] To mention just one of these, in *Marais* (n 84) disciplinary action by a party against a mayor was found not to be public for purposes of the PAJA even though it would be of great interest to the public; but in *Max v Independent Democrats* 2006 (3) SA 112 the court appeared to regard disciplinary action by a party as reviewable under the PAJA as well as under the common law (which has always governed exercises of *private* power of a disciplinary nature).

[87] For a description, see the important case of *Ramakatsa v Magashule* 2013 (2) BCLR 202.

[88] See *Calibre Clinical Consultants* (n 49).

[89] ibid, at [36]. *cf*, eg, the dictum of Kerr J to similar effect in *Re McBride's Application* [1999] NI 299 at 230.

This dictum prevents 'public interest' in the sense of 'engaging the interest of the public' from playing a decisive role in future, but does not necessarily prevent it from operating together with other factors.

A final case worth noting is *National Horseracing Authority v Naidoo*,[90] which concerned a disciplinary decision of the appellant horseracing authority (NHA). Naidoo was a trainer who had been convicted by an NHA board of inquiry of certain offences and who had by way of review successfully challenged the sanction of warning off. On appeal by the NHA to a full bench, only one of the three judges saw the conduct in question as an exercise of public power and would have been willing to review it as administrative action under the PAJA. That being so, the case was ultimately resolved with reference to the traditional common-law principle mentioned earlier.[91] But the eloquent and thoroughly reasoned judgment of Wallis J (who has since been elevated to the Supreme Court of Appeal) has already been applied by the Western Cape High Court[92] and it would be surprising if its influence ended there.

Wallis J pointed out that sport raises important public issues, as suggested by the fact that the President had appointed commissions of inquiry into both rugby and cricket. The government, too, had a substantial interest in sport, evidenced by the existence of a national department of Sport and Recreation, the National Sport and Recreation Act 110 of 1998 and its Sports Commission.[93] Indeed, Wallis J found it difficult to see what distinguished a national sports body such as the NHA from the Take-over Panel in *Datafin*, particularly in view of the substantial sums of money generated by the sport and by way of taxes on betting.[94] He contrasted the position of relatively minor sports with the major ones—horseracing, football, cricket and rugby—that inspire 'massive public interest' and whose national bodies exercise a virtually monopolistic control;[95] and the restricted availability of judicial review in English law with our own more liberal system.[96] All in all there was much to be said for the proposition that the disciplinary functions of the NHA 'are public functions, or involve the exercise of public powers, albeit by a private body, at least insofar as they impinge upon the right of individuals to participate in horseracing and to earn their living from it'.[97]

In accordance with that view, Plasket suggests that the time has come to recognise unequivocally that in the governance of major sports in South Africa, national controlling bodies exercise public rather than private power.[98] This, he says, would produce a better fit with the 'enhanced idea of accountability for the exercise of power' that is envisaged by the Constitution, and especially section 8(2).[99] He argues

90 *National Horseracing Authority v Naidoo* 2010 (3) SA 182.
91 See the text to n 72 above.
92 By Davis J in *Daniels v WP Rugby* [2011] ZAWCHC 481.
93 See *Naidoo* (n 90) at [22].
94 ibid, at [23].
95 ibid, at [23].
96 ibid, at [26].
97 ibid, at [27].
98 See Plasket (n 32).
99 ibid, at 598, and for the wording of s 8(2) see n 12.

compellingly that it is unrealistic to treat national sports bodies as nothing more than private clubs, for in truth they are custodians of their respective sports—and custodians in the public interest, as suggested by the preamble to the National Sport and Recreation Amendment Act 18 of 2007. Notably, this preamble asserts that the government is under a constitutional obligation to ensure the good and responsible administration of sport, and that 'sport and recreation belong to the nation over which government and its elected representatives have an overall responsibility'. It goes on to record that government intervention is required to eradicate malpractice and bad governance in sport, and speaks of redressing social inequalities by optimising the involvement of previously disadvantaged communities in sport.

The National Sport and Recreation Act thus provides some weighty constitutional reasons for regarding the powers of sports regulatory bodies as public. Indeed, one might think this preamble enough on its own to infuse the actions of all national sports bodies in South Africa with a public and even a 'governmental' character.

IV. PUBLIC ACTORS EXERCISING PRIVATE POWERS IN A CONTRACTUAL SETTING

If it is clear that public functions may be performed by bodies that are or appear to be private, South African law allows public bodies to escape administrative-law review when taking *private* action (other than of a disciplinary nature). As in English law, the issue arises most commonly in a contractual setting. Unlike their English counterparts, the South African courts do not engage in a search for a 'public law element' as such,[100] but tend to rely on a number of factors including the nature and source of the power. Again, the case law reveals vacillation between approaches, even within the jurisprudence of the same court. Some judgments depict the relationship between the parties as a matter of 'pure contract' or see a rigid division between the public and private aspects of the case, while others are more inclined to perceive an interplay between public and private concerns and acknowledge a need to integrate the two.[101]

One of the leading post-1994 cases on contractual action taken by a public body is *Cape Metropolitan Council v MIS,* better known as *Cape Metro.*[102] This administrative-law matter arose under the interim Constitution, some years before the PAJA came into operation, which explains why it was decided without reference to that statute. The case concerned an outsourcing contract entered into between a local council and a private firm regarding certain levies that the council was statutorily required to collect. The agreement was that the firm, MIS, would collect the levies on behalf of the council and claim commission on the amounts collected. All went well until it emerged that MIS had been inflating its claims for commission,

[100] See, eg, SH Bailey, 'Judicial Review of Contracting Decisions' [2007] *PL* 444.

[101] See further C Hoexter, 'Contracts in Administrative Law: Life after Formalism?' (2004) 121 *South African Law Journal* 595; G Quinot, *State Commercial Activity: A Legal Framework* (Cape Town, Juta & Co Ltd, 2009).

[102] *Cape Metropolitan Council v Metro Inspection Services (Western Cape)* CC 2001 (3) SA 1013.

whereupon the council decided to cancel the contract summarily on grounds of fraud. MIS then sought review of that decision on the grounds of procedural unfairness—which would be required only if the decision amounted to administrative action. The court a quo found that it did; but the Supreme Court of Appeal held that it did not, on the basis that the cancellation had entailed the exercise of private rather than public power.

This diagnosis was informed by the test for administrative action laid down by the Constitutional Court:[103] the nature, source and subject-matter of the power; whether it involves the exercise of a public duty (a sign of administrative action); and how closely it relates to the implementation of legislation (another such sign) or the formulation of policy (a marker of executive action). As to source, the Supreme Court of Appeal reasoned that while the council had derived its power to enter into the contract from statute, its power to cancel came from the terms of the contract itself, and from the common law. Furthermore, the terms of the contract had not been prescribed by statute and could not be dictated by the council by virtue of its position as a public authority; rather, they had been agreed to by MIS, a 'very substantial commercial undertaking'.[104] Accordingly, the council had not been in a dominant position in terms of bargaining power when it entered into the contract; and when it cancelled the contract, the council had not been performing a public duty or implementing legislation, but exercising a contractual right founded on consensus in a commercial contract.

In all these circumstances, concluded the court, it could not be said that the council was exercising a public power; for the constitutional rights to just administrative action were not aimed at the public administration 'acting as a contracting party from a position no different from what it would have been in had it been a private individual or institution'.[105] The court went on to distinguish cases involving procurement and employment, where contractual conduct *had* been regarded as administrative action. Finally, in response to the argument that the collection of levies was obviously administrative action, the court drew a distinction between such collection, a matter regulated by statute, and the relationship between the council and MIS, which was regulated by their agreement and the law of contract.[106]

The court's reasoning in *Cape Metro* was not particularly convincing, however, and one suspects that it used the concept of administrative action (and more specifically the element of public power) defensively, so as to avoid the conclusion that procedural fairness had to be observed in this instance.[107] The factors relied on actually seemed to point in the opposite direction, for the council was under a statutory duty to collect the levies, and the governing regulations made specific provision for outsourcing the task of collection—and even for cancelling the contract on the basis of fraud, bad faith or other unsatisfactory conduct by the other party. This last feature was especially inconvenient to the court's characterisation of the case. It not only

[103] The *SARFU* case (n 37) [143].
[104] See *Cape Metro* (n 102) [18].
[105] ibid.
[106] ibid, at [21].
[107] See further C Hoexter, '"Administrative Action" in the Courts' 2006 *Acta Juridica* 303, 312–13.

blurred the line the court sought to draw between statute and contract but made its diagnosis seem arbitrary and formalistic, for the court admitted that if the council had purported to cancel in terms of the regulation, it *would* have been exercising a public power which would have constituted administrative action—which in turn would have brought in the need for procedural fairness.[108]

The chicken of formalism came home to roost in a subsequent case in which reliance was placed on the bright line between statute and contract drawn in *Cape Metro* and also in an unfortunate apartheid-era judgment, *Mustapha v Receiver of Revenue, Lichtenburg*.[109] In the important case of *Logbro v Bedderson*[110] it was argued that once bidders had agreed to the conditions of a public tender process, the tender committee was entitled to exercise its contractual rights at will, 'without having to pass the scrutiny of lawful administrative action'.[111] In particular, as stipulated in one of the tender conditions, the committee would be free to withdraw the property from the tender—and to do so without bothering about the demands of procedural fairness. It was argued that this area of contractual freedom, untouched by the rules of administrative law, had been established in *Cape Metro* and long before that in *Mustapha*.

In *Mustapha* the appellants had by way of contract been granted statutory permission to occupy state-owned land but had later been evicted by the relevant Minister. It was common cause that the eviction had been based partly or solely on the appellants' race. However, a majority of the Appellate Division dismissed a challenge based on ulterior motive and discrimination, holding that the Minister's motives in evicting the appellants were irrelevant. The court reasoned that while the permits were certainly governed by legislation, the relationship between the parties became a contractual one as soon as a permit was granted and accepted in relation to a piece of land.[112] Thus the Minister was merely exercising a *contractual* right when he evicted the appellants, and could do so untrammelled by public-law duties. Schreiner JA famously dissented, pointing out the fundamental differences between a private landowner and a state official, who receives his powers 'directly or indirectly from the statute alone and can only act within its limitations, express or implied'.[113]

The court in *Logbro* resisted the argument made to it partly on the basis that procurement cases had been distinguished in *Cape Metro*, but also took the opportunity to qualify its judgment in that case. *Cape Metro*, it said, applied only to the cancellation of contracts entered into *on equal terms*, and had not purported to give a general answer to the question whether a public body is required to act procedurally fairly when exercising contractual powers. It was clear that in *Logbro*, the tender committee had acted from a position of superiority when it had dictated the tender conditions; so the reasoning in *Cape Metro* was not applicable, and the principles of

[108] See *Cape Metro* (n 102) at [20].
[109] *Mustapha v Receiver of Revenue, Lichtenburg* 1958 (3) SA 343.
[110] *Logbro Properties CC v Bedderson* NO 2003 (2) SA 460.
[111] ibid, at [5].
[112] See *Mustapha* (n 109) at 356G–H.
[113] ibid, at 347E–G.

administrative justice still 'framed the parties' contractual relationship' and continued to govern the exercise of rights derived from the contract.[114]

The court went on to overrule the majority judgment in *Mustapha* and to affirm the correctness of the dissenting judgment of Schreiner JA. Writing for a unanimous court, Cameron JA (who had concurred in *Cape Metro*) deplored the artificiality of the 'total fissure' achieved between the statute and the contract in *Mustapha* and dismissed it as clearly incompatible with *Cape Metro*.[115] He held that the tender committee's contractual powers had to be exercised with due regard to the principles of administrative justice. Even if the committee had been entitled to withdraw the property from the tender, it could only do so in a lawful and procedurally fair manner.[116]

The position after *Logbro* is that the termination of a contract and the exercise of other contractual rights by the state (or any part of it) will be regarded as an exercise of private power only where equal bargaining power was a feature of the agreement. Given the state's hugely superior economic power and resources, one suspects that bargaining power is not likely to be equal very often in such cases. Indeed, it is doubtful whether such equality can *ever* exist where the state is a party, and one might want to interrogate the rather glib diagnosis of equal bargaining power in *Cape Metro* itself. As Quinot shows, there are cogent economic reasons why the state cannot realistically be equated with a private commercial party, such as the reduced impact of market forces on the state and the absence of a threat of bankruptcy.[117]

Leaving aside the sheer unlikelihood of finding such equality, *Logbro* tells us that, in its absence, contractual conduct on the part of a public body will always be framed by principles of public law. The terms of the contract may 'bear on the exact ambit'[118] of public-law duties such as procedural fairness, but the contractual context can no longer suffice to transform what would have been an exercise of public power into something private. Absent equality of bargaining power, it is no longer acceptable either to attempt 'total fissure' between a contract and the legislation authorising and animating it or to take a 'purely contractual' view by focusing on contractual rights to the exclusion of public-law duties.

That position seemed to be affirmed by the Supreme Court of Appeal in the *Trend Finance* case,[119] which concerned the Revenue Commissioner's seizure of consignments of shoes imported by the respondent. The court a quo had based its reasoning on an agreement between the parties that the shoes would be released if certain conditions were met, but the Appeal Court was clear that any 'contractual element' in the exercise of the Commissioner's powers did not alter the administrative, and

[114] See *Logbro* (n 110) at [8].
[115] ibid, at [13].
[116] ibid, at [14].
[117] See Quinot (n 101) at 155–57.
[118] See *Logbro* (n 110) at [8].
[119] *Commissioner, South African Revenue Service v Trend Finance (Pty) Ltd* 2007 (6) SA 117.

thus public, nature of his conduct.[120] The demise of purely contractual reasoning seems also to have been acknowledged, albeit obliquely, in *Snow Crystal*, where the same court remarked that it may be difficult to reconcile an organ of state's contractual obligations with its 'public duties of fairness'.[121] However, as a Constitutional Court judge has observed, the judgments of the Supreme Court of Appeal are not entirely harmonious on the topic.[122] In another case, the Supreme Court of Appeal seemed to ignore *Logbro* and its import altogether. In *Thabiso Chemicals*, referring to *Cape Metro* and making no mention of *Logbro*, the court held that once a tender contract has been awarded, the relationship between the parties is governed by contract law *to the exclusion* of administrative law.[123] The court also dismissed the idea that reliance on a statutory provision when cancelling a contract would make any difference.[124]

More recently, however, when confronted with a purely contractual argument in a case of public-sector employment, Wallis JA noted that *Mustapha* had been overruled in *Logbro* and stated: 'The correct view is that one cannot divorce a contract arising from the performance of statutory functions and the exercise of statutory powers from its statutory background.'[125]

[120] ibid, at [25], referring to *Logbro* (n 110).

[121] *Transnet Ltd t/a National Ports Authority v Owner of MV Snow Crystal* 2008 (4) SA 111, [21].

[122] Froneman J in a separate concurring judgment in *KwaZulu-Natal Joint Liaison Committee v MEC for Education, KwaZulu-Natal* 2013 (4) SA 262 at [101].

[123] *Government of the Republic of South Africa v Thabiso Chemicals (Pty) Ltd* 2009 (1) SA 163 ('*Thabiso Chemicals*') at [18]. See also, eg, *Transnet Ltd v Chirwa* (2006) 27 *ILJ* 2294, where some members of the Supreme Court of Appeal regarded a public-sector dismissal as an obvious exercise of public power while others saw it as 'based purely on contract' (at [15]), as the legislation governing dismissals in that organ of state had been repealed and not replaced. On appeal in *Chirwa v Transnet Ltd* (n 2) a majority of the Constitutional Court held that the dismissal was not administrative action despite being an exercise of public power. Since then, the Constitutional Court has ruled that, as a matter of policy, employment-related conduct in the public sector will not ordinarily amount to administrative action even if it is an exercise of public power, although the position may be different when the conduct is of great public import—for instance, the dismissal of the Commissioner of Police: see *Gcaba v Minister for Safety and Security* 2010 (1) SA 238, [68] and n 107, and see further C Hoexter, 'From *Chirwa* to *Gcaba*: An Administrative Lawyer's View' in M Kidd and S Hoctor (eds), *Stella Iuris: Celebrating 100 Years of Teaching Law in Pietermaritzburg* (Cape Town, Juta & Co Ltd, 2010) 47. Such public import has been identified in a few cases, such as where the Registrar of Labour Relations was stripped of his designation (*Public Servants' Association of South Africa v Minister of Labour* (2016) 37 *ILJ* 185); but one suspects that it, too, is bound to be a matter of feel.

[124] *Thabiso Chemicals* (n 123) at [18]. As Binns-Ward J observed in *Staffmed CC v MEC for Health (Western Cape)* [2014] ZAWCHC 94 at [20], it is difficult to reconcile that view with what was said in *Cape Metro* (n 102). For a less critical application of *Thabiso Chemicals* see, eg, *Hibiscus Coast Municipality v Margate Amusement Park (Pty) Ltd* [2016] ZAKZPHC 24 at [19].

[125] *President of the Republic of South Africa v Reinecke* 2014 (3) SA 205, [16]. Since then, a further difficulty has developed in relation to *Logbro* in the jurisprudence of the Supreme Court of Appeal; in *Tshwane City v Nambiti Technologies (Pty) Ltd* 2016 (2) SA 494 it held that the cancellation of a tender is *executive* rather than administrative action (though it would still amount to an exercise of public power). In the subsequent case of *SAAB Grintek Defence (Pty) Ltd v South African Police Service* [2016] 3 All SA 669 at [16]–[18], the court denied that *Nambiti* was in conflict with *Logbro* on the administrative action issue. It distinguished *Logbro* on the basis that it had concerned a decision at an advanced stage 'in the tender process' rather than the *termination* of a tender process. *cf Head of Department, Mpumalanga Department of Education v Valozone 268* CC [2017] ZASCA 30, where the same court seems to have assumed that the cancellation of a tender is administrative action.

The Constitutional Court itself has not been entirely consistent. It has generally resisted purely contractual reasoning, and a most notable example is *Joseph v City of Johannesburg*.[126] Here, a local authority had disconnected the supply of electricity to an inner-city building because the landlord was seriously in arrears with his payments for the service. This was his fault and not that of the tenants, who had been paying their rent to the landlord all along; but it was the landlord and not the tenants who were given notice of the proposed termination, so the tenants had no chance to make representations to the City about it. The City's explanation for the lack of notice—that the tenants were not officially its 'customers' in terms of the bylaws—satisfied the High Court, but struck the Constitutional Court as both formalistic and unhelpful. The Court found that the City knew that it was providing electricity to tenants in the building through the conduit of the landlord, so it was artificial to conceive of the contractual relationship between the landlord and the City as being unrelated to the benefits that accrued to the tenants. The court below, it held, had been wrong to view the case 'through an entirely contractual lens'[127] (or more accurately, perhaps, to view the two contracts as unrelated).

However, in a more recent case concerning procurement, the Constitutional Court seemed to take a view more in line with *Cape Metro* or *Thabiso Chemicals* than *Logbro*. In *Trencon Construction*, the issue of contract price adjustment, described as a matter to be negotiated after the procurement process has taken place, was envisaged as falling 'squarely within the domain of private law' rather than as being part of the interplay between public and private law.[128] Unfortunately, all the court added by way of explanation was that this type of issue 'is subject to ordinary contractual negotiations between enterprising parties'.[129]

There is no doubt, then, that work remains to be done at the intersection of public law and contract law in South Africa.[130] In its day *Logbro* may have seemed like a real advance on the formalism of *Cape Metro*,[131] but since then, the courts have barely risen to the challenge of working out what 'framing' by the Constitution means in more detailed terms or of indicating more precisely where the interplay between public and private law begins and ends. When and how do contractual terms bear on public-law duties and when and how do they yield to them? It is disheartening that so little progress seems to have been made in answering such questions in the years since October 2002, when the judgment in *Logbro* was handed down. It may be that a complete change of approach is now required.

[126] *Joseph v City of Johannesburg* 2010 (4) SA 55. See also *Masetlha v President of the Republic of South Africa* 2008 (1) SA 566 at [198]: 'The contractual element in the powers of the President must … not be allowed to obscure the fact that the President's powers are derived from the Constitution and the provisions of the applicable statutes and therefore subject to constitutional constraints in their exercise.'

[127] See *Joseph* (n 126) at [23].

[128] *Trencon Construction (Pty) Ltd v Industrial Development Corporation of South Africa Ltd* 2015 (5) SA 245 at [75].

[129] ibid.

[130] See in this regard Quinot (n 101); C Ferreira, 'The Quest for Clarity: An Examination of the Law Governing Public Contracts' (2011) 128 *South African Law Journal* 172.

[131] See further Hoexter (n 101).

In this regard, Cachalia has recently argued that the South African courts' preoccupation with classification into 'public' and 'private' conduct has led to a failure properly to acknowledge the state's uniqueness as a contracting party and has frustrated the development of a body of substantive legal rules appropriate to the peculiar hybrid that is the government contract.[132] Cachalia draws inspiration from jurisdictions such as France which have frankly acknowledged the reasons for treating government contracts differently. Her suggestion, in essence, is that government contracts in South Africa, too, ought to be treated differently, not just some of the time, but *all* of the time, by reason of the special characteristics pertaining to the state: its limited capacity to contract, its duty to act lawfully, accountably and in the public interest and the superior bargaining power flowing from its economic strength. Cachalia's point is that proper recognition of the state's uniqueness as a contracting party obviates the need to engage in public/private classification—an exercise that is bound to fail at this difficult intersection. In her own words:

> We need not resort to classification if we look to the intrinsic features that make the state different as a contracting party. And once we dispense with classification we can start grappling with the more important question of how we deal with this 'special class of contract'.[133]

V. CONCLUSION

Under South Africa's democratic Constitution, significant implications attach to the exercise of public powers and the performance of public functions. These include amenability to judicial review in administrative law and being accorded the status of an organ of state, with all the constitutional and legislative obligations that status brings. But determining which powers and functions are public is a haphazard business. The discussion above suggests that when diagnosing such powers and functions, the South African courts experience the same problems of indeterminacy and inconsistency as their counterparts in England and Wales and in other parts of the common-law world. The factor-based approach is too contingent to be of much assistance, and in the South African context the inherent unpredictability of the exercise is compounded by the current tension between the search for broadly 'public' features or more narrowly 'governmental' ones. In short, the diagnosis is altogether too much a matter of feel. Similar uncertainty infects the law relating to the exercise of contractual powers by public actors, where the courts have simply not grappled sufficiently with the implications of the judgment in *Logbro*.

While the aim of this chapter has been to expose these problems rather than propose solutions to them, it does seem clear that a new approach is called for. In the case of apparently private actors, the introduction of some general rules or default settings would make a refreshing change. One of these might be the recognition

[132] R Cachalia, 'Government Contracts in South Africa: Constructing the Framework' (2016) 27 *Stellenbosch Law Review* 88.

[133] ibid, at 110.

that national sports bodies ordinarily perform a public function by controlling their respective sports and guarding access to them. As regards the contractual actions of public actors, it may (as Cachalia has suggested) even be time to abandon the attempt to distinguish between public and private exercises of power. For the difficulty of doing so is a constant reminder of what we all know and have known for some time: that public-private classification may have worked well enough in Roman and Roman-Dutch law but is increasingly inapposite and unhelpful in a world in which even the most characteristically public function can be delegated to a private actor,[134] and in which private power no longer implies 'apolitical law between equals'.[135]

[134] See Harlow (n 4) at 257.

[135] Froneman J in *KZN Joint Liaison Committee* (n 122) at [92]; see further, A Cockrell, '"Can You Paradigm?"—Another Perspective on the Public Law/Private Law Divide' (1993) *Acta Juridica* 227.

8

Fault and Accountability in Public Law

ELLEN ROCK*

I. INTRODUCTION

THERE ARE FEW who would deny that accountability is a core value that underpins our public law system. However, there are equally few who have explicitly explored the manner in which public law contributes to government accountability. On closer analysis, it is clear that while public law makes a number of important contributions to government accountability, the remedial limitations of public law prevent us from describing it as a comprehensive accountability regime. In the context of public governance, accountability can be understood as a set of four interrelated objectives. The first is to provide transparency in government decision making. The second is to control the exercise of public power and ensure that it stays within legal bounds. The third is to punish abuse of power, and the fourth is to restore interests that are affected as a result. Public law supports the first two of these objectives, however it fails to provide any meaningful contribution to the latter two; public law remedies do not punish or restore.

This raises somewhat of a predicament. How can accountability be a core public law value, on the one hand, but not be adequately reflected in our public law principles, procedures and remedies, on the other? Is accountability simply a rhetorical aspiration, rather than a concrete objective of public law? Are there fundamental or pragmatic reasons why accountability cannot or does not apply in a comprehensive way in the public law sphere? The purpose of this chapter is to commence a dialogue about whether public law is capable of operating as a comprehensive accountability regime. This is not intended as a proposal for law reform, but rather to stimulate discussion about how and why public law has developed in the way that it has, and what this might say about the place of public law as an accountability mechanism within our system of governance. In the context of this discussion there are a whole host of valuable issues that warrant

* I am grateful to the participants at the 'Unity of Public Law?' conference for their valuable feedback, as well as to Peter Cane for his, as always, insightful comments on earlier drafts. My thanks also to the editors of this collection for their comments and advice. All errors remain my own. This research is supported by an Australian Government Research Training Program (RTP) Scholarship.

consideration, to which the present chapter offers insufficient space to do justice. Instead, it kick-starts the proposed dialogue by focusing on just one issue: are the norms that are enforced via public law consistent with the punitive and restorative objectives of accountability?

In answering this question, the first issue to consider is when the punitive and restorative objectives of accountability might be relevant. Though there might be a number of ways of approaching this issue, one possibility is to take the lead from those who have identified a close connection between the concepts of accountability and responsibility. Based on this close connection, one way of giving shape to these objectives is to adopt a personal responsibility-based approach, in which punishment and restoration are viewed as functions of culpability. The notion of fault would play an important role in a culpability-driven accountability regime; if we wish to hold officials accountable outside cases of intentional wrongdoing, we would need to identify a justification for doing so.

The position adopted in this chapter is that in searching for this justification, we might adopt a different approach for each of accountability's objectives. The control objective arguably supports a *strict liability* approach, wherein regulatory orders are justified irrespective of fault. Control is about policing the boundaries of public power, a goal that could not be achieved if we could only intervene where a boundary was knowingly or negligently transgressed. At the other extreme, punishment would only be justified when an official acts in a *subjectively faulty way* (eg, intentionally causing harm) because the punitive objective of accountability is concerned with condemning reprehensible conduct, a goal that would be undermined if innocent excesses of power attracted punishment. Finally, accountability's restorative objective is concerned with putting wrongs right for the purpose of supporting the legitimacy of government. If legitimacy is threatened, we can justify reparative remedies outside cases of fault. However, at least in relation to the exercise of discretionary powers, the most coherent approach would be to limit the obligation to restore to cases where an official acts in an *objectively faulty way* (eg, falling short of a prescribed standard of reasonableness). To summarise, in a culpability-focused accountability regime, we can likely justify imposing regulatory orders on a strict liability basis. However, when it comes to punishment and restoration, liability in such a regime would depend on whether an official's contravention is accompanied by the relevant degree of fault that engages those remedial responses: subjective fault for punishment and objective fault for restoration.

We tend not to think about public law in terms of fault. Indeed, in many ways we think about public law as being a style of strict liability regime, in which public law norms might be contravened irrespective of an official's actual degree of knowledge or intention. This might lead us to wonder whether our public law principles are capable of working within the accountability regime outlined above. If public law is not a fault-based regime, how could it accommodate a remedial framework that hinges off concepts of fault? This chapter explores the generally uncharted fault-based foundations of public law, concluding that two of our core grounds of judicial review can be understood as 'benchmarks' of fault. Bad faith stands as a benchmark of subjectively faulty behaviour, capturing conduct that rises to an unacceptable level of dishonesty or malice. 'Legal unreasonableness', which has taken the place of the traditional *Wednesbury* unreasonableness test in Australian law,[1] stands as a benchmark of objective fault, capturing conduct that falls short of an objective measure of reasonableness and rationality in government decision making. This analysis demonstrates that, at least insofar as accountability is dependent on notions of fault, our public law norms are consistent with the punitive and restorative objectives of accountability.

The purpose of this analysis is to demonstrate the value in using accountability as a 'lens' through which to analyse the make up of our public law system. We are prompted to think about public law in new ways and to recognise features of our current system that we might previously have taken for granted. As demonstrated in this chapter, one thing that the accountability perspective shows us is that public law is not the strict liability regime that we often treat it as. Rather, there are shades of fault-based liability that are bound up in our public law grounds of review. We can therefore conclude that to the extent that accountability requires a fault-based assessment of government decision making, our public law principles are well adapted to this purpose. This argument does not go so far as to state that we should therefore be comfortable in expanding our public law remedies to serve the neglected punitive and restorative objectives of accountability: that is a much wider question of law reform than is considered here. Rather, it shows us that if there are good reasons for public law's failure to provide punitive and restorative contributions to government accountability, these reasons do not lie in any inconsistency between our grounds of review and the fault-based foundations of accountability.

II. AN ACCOUNTABILITY FRAMEWORK

I have written elsewhere about the concept of accountability, and its place within the public law sphere.[2] A brief summary of that argument is set out here for convenience. In the context of public governance, I have argued that accountability is regarded as a core public law value, tied to our rule of law and separation of powers principles. One of the overriding purposes of accountability is to support the broader legitimacy of government, which it does through the pursuit of four objectives. The first objective of accountability is to provide transparency in government

[1] The label 'legal unreasonableness' was adopted by the High Court of Australia in place of the traditional '*Wednesbury* unreasonableness' label in *Minister for Immigration and Citizenship v Li* (2013) 249 CLR 332. The implications of the *Li* decision are detailed in the text accompanying n 58 below. This case represents a move away from the strictness of the *Wednesbury* formula and towards a variable content standard of reasonableness in Australia. However, doubt still remains as to whether this might open the door to variegated intensity review underpinned by rights-consciousness as has been developed in other jurisdictions: see, eg, L McDonald, 'Rethinking Unreasonableness Review' (2014) 25 *Public Law Review* 117 at 132; M Barker and A Nagel, 'Legal Unreasonableness: Life after *Li*' (2015) 79 *AIAL Forum* 1 at 9; G Weeks, *Soft Law and Public Authorities: Remedies and Reform* (Oxford, Hart Publishing, 2016) 154. Therefore, comments on the legal unreasonableness ground must be read within the context of that Australian limitation, though many of the broader themes explored in this chapter are common to other jurisdictions.

[2] E Rock, 'Accountability: A Core Public Law Value?' (2017) 24(3) *Australian Journal of Administrative Law* 189.

operations, by facilitating public scrutiny. In some cases, the transparency achieved through this process may be an end in and of itself, revealing sound administrative procedures and rigorous adherence to principles of good decision making. However, in cases where transparency exposes a breach of norms of good administration, we must turn to the remaining three results-orientated objectives of accountability: to control public power, to punish abuse of power and to restore interests affected as a result.

The control objective of accountability is best understood by viewing accountability as a principal-agent relationship. The ability to control one's agent is a fundamental feature of an agency relationship, enabling a principal to ensure that the agent acts not out of self-interest, but in pursuit of the best interests of their principal. This control may be manifested in a number of different ways, but the key characteristic is coercion; control is not merely a matter of influence, but instead enables the principal to compel their agent to comply with prescribed norms. The punitive objective of accountability serves a different purpose. It is concerned with condemning reprehensible conduct; a 'tar and feather' response to wrongdoing. This objective of accountability serves an essentially expressive purpose, though some suggest that punishment may also serve as a deterrent against future transgressions.[3] If the punitive objective of accountability is focused on the actions of the wrongdoer, the restorative objective is more concerned with the effects of those actions on others. The obligation to repair harm is an important way in which accountability reinforces the legitimacy of government, providing the assurance that where the government causes harm as a result of its wrongdoing, that harm will not go unremedied.

In a practical sense, each of the four objectives of transparency, control, punishment and restoration are supported through the procedures and mechanisms that make up our system of public governance. For example, when we think about the legal system as a whole, we can see that a range of court procedures contribute to transparency, including various evidentiary procedures, trial procedures and even the open nature of the court forum itself. The remaining three results-orientated objectives are in turn supported through the different types of remedies that might be awarded by the courts: regulatory orders (such as injunctions) to provide control, punitive sanctions (such as fines) to provide punishment, and reparative remedies (such as compensation) to provide restoration. When viewed as a whole, then, the legal system contains a number of mechanisms and procedures that are capable of supporting the four objectives of accountability.

I have argued, however, that public law does not make full use of the arsenal of accountability mechanisms that make up our legal system.[4] When an official's compliance with public law norms is in question, proceedings for judicial review may play a role in securing transparency by compelling the official to justify his or her conduct in an open public forum. However, if it is discovered that the official has, in fact, breached norms of good administration, the available public law remedies are

[3] For an overview of theorists who adopt this stance, along with an opposing view, see N Hanna, 'Facing the Consequences' (2014) 8 *Criminal Law and Philosophy* 589.

[4] See Rock (n 2) at 198–200.

inherently regulatory in nature, supporting only the accountability goal of control. Along with injunctive and declaratory relief, the writs of certiorari, prohibition and mandamus are essentially limited to policing the boundaries within which public power can be exercised. These remedies play no meaningful role in punishing the abuse of power. In some cases, an applicant might derive a restorative advantage from these remedies (eg where the court quashes a decision to revoke a benefit, the effect of that remedy is to restore the benefit). However, such advantages are largely a matter of coincidence rather than design. These advantages do not reflect the true character of the remedy, which is to contain public power within defined limits. This all leads to the conclusion that public law is not a comprehensive accountability regime, as it fails to contribute to two of the core objectives of accountability: punishment and restoration.

III. A VALUABLE THOUGHT EXERCISE

Before launching into the argument addressed in this chapter, it is useful to set out a hypothetical scenario. This not only provides us with a concrete way to explore the arguments presented, but also gives us an idea of what might be at stake. This hypothetical is one that I have used before,[5] though for present purposes we can embellish it with a little colour. Imagine that Odette is an official with the local planning authority and one of her responsibilities is to determine whether applications for proposed new developments should be approved or rejected. Odette has just been handed a new file relating to a particular development. She reviews the file and decides to reject the application on the basis that the applicant has not provided sufficient supporting evidence. As it transpires, the applicant, Alex, phoned the planning authority last week to inform them that he had just put some additional supporting documents in the post.

There are three alternate scenarios that help us to better understand the accountability framework that is considered in this chapter. In the first scenario, assume that the administrative assistant who took Alex's call recorded the filenote on the wrong file, meaning that Odette was unaware that Alex was sending further evidence when she made her decision. In the second scenario, the filenote has been correctly recorded on Alex's file. However, when Odette reads this note, she decides that Alex has had plenty of time to get his evidence in: 'enough is enough!' Accordingly, she decides to reject the application before the additional evidence arrives. In the final scenario, Odette is a little more underhanded. On reviewing the file, she recognises Alex's name as one of her neighbours, with whom she is involved in an ongoing dispute. She accordingly decides to reject the application out of spite.

Under our current public law regime, Alex could bring proceedings for judicial review to challenge the legality of Odette's decision. In all three scenarios, the claim might be based on allegations of denial of procedural fairness or failing to take into account relevant considerations. The decision in the second scenario may also

[5] ibid, at 189–90.

be framed as one that is legally unreasonable: Odette's decision not to wait for the additional evidence may be characterised as arbitrary, as in *Minister for Immigration and Citizenship v Li*.[6] In the third scenario, the decision may also be framed as one made in bad faith. Irrespective of which ground Alex stakes his claim on, the available remedies are limited to the prerogative writs and injunctive and declaratory relief. Public law cannot punish Odette, nor can it repair any harm suffered by Alex as a result of her conduct. While the retaking of the decision might have the effect of remedying losses in some cases, there are limitations as to what this might achieve. Most significantly, if Odette ultimately decides the matter in Alex's favour, this will not repair any of the harm that Alex has suffered in the meantime.

If accountability demands punishment and restoration in appropriate cases and if we assume that this is a case in which those responses might be appropriate, what do these shortcomings in our public law system tell us? Are we simply wrong when we describe accountability as a core public law value? Or are we wrong to assign it punitive and restorative functions? Neither of these explanations for the limitations of public law is particularly compelling. There is much to be said for treating accountability as a core public law value. The concept has close ties to our constitutional principles of rule of law and separation of powers, and there are convincing arguments to the effect that accountability is critical to secure the legitimacy of government.[7] There is also much to be said for treating punishment and restoration as core objectives of accountability. Though some might express doubt about whether both of these features are essential in an accountability regime,[8] there is something very hollow in the idea of an accountability regime which is designed simply to expose wrongdoing or to limit the possibility of future infractions. If we discover that an official has engaged in a flagrant abuse of public power, would we say that they have been held accountable simply because their wrongdoing has been unmasked and they have been told not do it again? In appropriate cases, accountability demands that wrongdoers be punished, and their wrongs put right.

If we accept that accountability is a core public law value and that it demands punishment and restoration in appropriate cases, what then can we make of the lack of punitive and restorative remedies in public law? It is my argument that we have much to gain from exploring whether there are fundamental or pragmatic reasons why public law cannot or does not perform a punitive or restorative role in securing government accountability. By investigating these reasons we may ultimately conclude that there is a valid explanation for why our public law regime does not comprehensively reflect one of its core values. However, whether or not we manage to resolve that question, using accountability as a lens through which to explore our public law principles, procedures and remedies provides us with an opportunity to better understand the makeup of our public law system and why it might have developed in the way that it has.

6 See *Li* (n 1).

7 I have expanded on these ideas in an earlier article: see Rock (n 2) at 190–92.

8 See, eg, C Harlow and R Rawlings, 'Promoting Accountability in Multilevel Governance: A Network Approach' (2007) 13 *European Law Journal* 542 at 545; M Philp, 'Delimiting Democratic Accountability' (2009) 57 *Political Studies* 28 at 30.

Bearing this goal in mind, there are a number of potential explanations for the limitations of public law that we might explore through accountability 'spectacles'. I have briefly canvassed two such possible explanations elsewhere.[9] The first is that Australia's separation of powers framework renders public law an unsuitable vehicle to impose accountability via punitive and restorative remedies. This is an idea that is sometimes implicit in arguments against the adoption of a public law remedy in damages.[10] The separation of powers concerns that underlie this position might stem, for example, from concerns about whether the award of damages moves the courts into the impermissible field of 'merits' review, or perhaps from more general concerns that this involves the courts in decisions about the distribution of public funds that are more appropriately assigned to the elected branches of government.[11] A second possibility is a more pragmatic one: that the remedial limitations of public law are overcome through alternate judicial and non-judicial mechanisms that provide punishment and restoration in cases of government wrongdoing (eg liability in tort, liability under the criminal law, and *ex gratia* compensation schemes, amongst others).

This chapter is concerned with a third possible explanation: that the principles making up our public law system are incompatible with the objectives of punishment and restoration, thereby making it unfeasible to use public law to pursue these objectives. In other words, is public law capable of performing the theoretical acrobatics necessary to allow the courts to perform a robust accountability-enforcing role in public law cases? For instance, is there something in the nature of punitive and restorative remedies (eg awards of punitive and compensatory damages) that is fundamentally inconsistent with the structure and functions of public law? Is public law capable of dealing with questions of causation that must naturally arise in determining whether an official has caused harm so as to be responsible to repair it? Are our public law standing tests sufficiently well adapted to confine the availability of any punitive or restorative public law remedies to those who ought to be entitled to obtain them? Are the procedural aspects of our public law system (eg evidentiary procedures and the burden of proof) compatible with the determination of claims involving punishment and restoration? All of these questions offer interesting opportunities to explore and better understand our public law system. In order to demonstrate the value of this thought exercise, this chapter focusses on just one question: are our public law grounds of review capable of supporting the fault-based analysis that might be required within a comprehensive accountability regime?

IV. FAULT AND ACCOUNTABILITY

Some take the view that accountability is closely tied to the notion of responsibility.[12] This chapter takes the lead from these authors, looking at the potential shape

[9] See Rock (n 2) at 201.

[10] See, eg, Administrative Review Council, Federal Judicial Review in Australia (2012) at 180–81.

[11] In relation to the first of these concerns in Australia, see *Attorney General v Quin* (1990) 170 CLR 1 at 35–36. But the concerns are likely to be of broader interest to those in other jurisdictions.

[12] See text accompanying n 25 below.

of an accountability regime that is framed by reference to notions of personal responsibility. Fault would stand as a starting point in such a regime, requiring us to identify justifications for holding a person accountable for unintentional conduct. Before going on to outline the potential justifications that might be relevant in the context of government accountability, it is necessary to expand on what we mean when we speak about 'fault'.

A. What is Fault?

The concept of fault plays an important role in criminal and civil law. With some exceptions, it plays a far less important role in public law. The notion of fault captures a range of factors relating to an individual's state of mind, including intention, motive, knowledge and belief. Intention refers to the degree of deliberateness attaching to a person's conduct, being intentional, reckless, or negligent. Intentional conduct involves a deliberate choice to act. A person may act deliberately with a view to achieving a particular outcome, or may act deliberately with no awareness of what the results of their conduct might be.[13] Recklessness, while also deliberate in nature,[14] sits one step behind intention, involving 'awareness of a risk that certain consequences will result from conduct, and indifference to that risk'.[15] In this context, it is important to distinguish between 'not caring' whether a risk may eventuate, and the legal notion of recklessness, which is more properly characterised as 'deliberately taking a known risk'.[16] Negligence, though sometimes thought about in terms of 'inadvertence' or 'inattention',[17] is more appropriately described as a failure to adhere to a prescribed standard.[18] In other words, the intentionality of a defendant's conduct is irrelevant to the enquiry, as they can be equally accountable for an oversight as for an intended act.

Motives are also often relevant in the assessment of fault. In simple terms, motivation refers to a person's reason for doing something. While related to the concept of intention, the two terms are not synonymous. For example, a person may drive over the speed limit with a murderous desire to harm others, or out of a desire to experience the thrill of driving fast, or out of a desire to race an ill child to the hospital. In each case the conduct of driving over the speed limit is deliberate (intentional), but the motive for that intentional conduct differs. The consequences of that conduct (eg injuring a pedestrian) may therefore correlate with intention (as with a murderous motive), or may be an unintended side effect. This example also says something about the character of motives that may underlie a person's behaviour. Good motives (such as racing an ill child to seek medical care) may in

[13] P Cane, 'Mens Rea in Tort Law' (2000) 20 *OJLS* 533 at 535–36.
[14] ibid, at 536.
[15] ibid, at 535.
[16] P Cane, *Responsibility in Law and Morality* (Oxford, Hart Publishing, 2002) 80.
[17] ibid, at 79.
[18] See Cane (n 13) at 536.

certain circumstances justify otherwise blameworthy conduct.[19] 'Bad' motives may be further divided into intrinsically malicious and collaterally malicious categories.[20] Intrinsically malicious motives are those which are inherently reprehensible, such as wanting to injure others. Other such motives would include spite or wanting to gain at another's expense. Collaterally malicious motives are those which, while not intrinsically bad, are not authorised in the circumstances. The thrill-seeking desires of our dangerous driver might fall into this category, as would acting for personal gain or some other goal which, while acceptable in some situations, would not be allowed in the circumstances.

A person's knowledge is a further state of mind that contributes to their degree of fault. There are a number of observations that we can make about a person's knowledge. First, the fact that a person turns out to have been wrong about what they *thought* they knew is not determinative of fault. To take an example, a person may set fire to a house believing it to be inhabited. If the house is, in fact, inhabited we can say that the wrongdoer 'knew' of it. If it transpires that the inhabitants were not home, we cannot say that the wrongdoer 'knew' them to be inside, but instead that the wrongdoer 'believed' them to be inside. In either case, we are generally concerned with attributing fault based on the wrongdoer's state of knowledge or belief, rather than the empirical correctness of their state of knowledge or belief.[21] Secondly, there are varying degrees of knowledge that may be relevant in determining fault. For instance, we may define fault by reference to a wrongdoer's actual subjective knowledge or belief. Or we may extend fault to also capture knowledge that has been wilfully disregarded, in the sense that a wrongdoer has 'shut their eyes' to information, in the manner of recklessness as discussed above. We may further extend fault into an objective enquiry, so as to capture information that we say a wrongdoer 'ought to have known' or further, by imputing a wrongdoer with information.[22]

Taking these various ideas as a whole, we can view fault as an amalgam of various enquiries into a wrongdoer's mind. We might pull together these ideas to describe three categories of fault, as follows. The first category, *subjective fault*, would capture conduct that is inherently wrongful. Drawing from the three states of mind, this category might include intentional conduct undertaken out of an inherently wrongful motive, such as spite, the desire to harm or to seek personal gain in circumstances where that would be inappropriate. Irrespective of motive, we might also include intentional or reckless conduct undertaken in the belief that harm would, or was likely to, arise. The second category, *objective fault*, would not be concerned with subjective intention, motives and knowledge. Instead, it would be focused on what a person ought to have done, desired or known. Liability within this category of fault involves an implicit judgment that a person either ought to have acted differently

[19] See, eg, ibid, at 541.

[20] This is the terminology proposed by Cane: ibid, at 539.

[21] Note, however, that this is not always the case. The criminal law sometimes distinguishes between these two states of mind in punishing attempts less severely than completed crimes.

[22] Eg, a minister may be taken to have constructive knowledge of information contained in a relevant departmental file: *Minister for Aboriginal Affairs v Peko-Wallsend* (1986) 162 CLR 24 at 31.

or appreciated that their conduct was likely to have certain consequences. While it uses the label 'fault', what we are really dealing with here is a failure to comply with a standard of conduct.[23] The final category, being *strict liability*, is not a quality of fault, but instead reflects the notion of liability irrespective of fault. In this category, a wrongdoer's degree of intention, motives and knowledge are irrelevant, as is the question of whether the wrongdoer has failed to meet an objective standard. All that matters is whether a wrongdoer has committed a prohibited act or produced a prohibited result. Therefore, this category is capable of attaching liability to innocent as well as malicious breaches. It is important to note that these three categories of fault are not mutually exclusive. For example, a strict liability provision may make it an offence to cause water pollution. If a person deliberately pollutes a river out of a desire to damage a neighbour's property, we may not only conclude that they have contravened the strict liability provision, but also that their actions are intentionally malicious (subjective fault), and that they ought to have acted differently (objective fault).

B. Why is Fault Relevant in the Context of Accountability?

Having identified the different qualities of fault that might attach to conduct, the next important question to ask is why should we be concerned with fault in the context of accountability? This chapter considers the potential shape of an accountability regime if it were informed by notions of personal responsibility.[24] There are close ties between the concepts of responsibility and accountability, to the extent that they are sometimes treated as synonymous.[25] Relevantly for present purposes, there are some who would view the concept of 'responsibility' as referring to the normative aspects of 'accountability'.[26] On this view, responsibility involves being a responsible person,[27] while accountability involves the external process of being held to account. A failure to act responsibly is what exposes a person to an accountability process; being held accountable can be seen to reinforce the underlying norms of responsibility going forward. Though accountability and responsibility are best not reduced to synonyms, there are clear symbiotic elements to the relationship between the two

[23] See, eg, Cane (n 13) at 536.

[24] Note, a responsibility-based approach is not the only possible way to understand accountability. This chapter is concerned with exploring what might follow from adopting this approach; different conclusions would be drawn if a different premise were adopted.

[25] See generally R Mulgan, '"Accountability": An Ever-expanding Concept?' (2000) 78 *Public Administration* 555 at 557–58; J Koppell, 'Pathologies of Accountability: ICANN and the Challenge of the "Multiple Accountabilities Disorder"' (2005) 65 *Public Administration Review* 94 at 98; M Dubnick, 'Accountability and the Promise of Performance: in Search of the Mechanisms' (2005) 28 *Public Performance & Management Review* 376 at 380; M Bovens, T Schillemans and PT Hart, 'Does Public Accountability Work? An Assessment Tool' (2008) 86 *Public Administration* 225 at 227; C Harlow, 'Accountability and Constitutional Law' in M Bovens, R Goodin and T Schillemans (eds), *The Oxford Handbook of Public Accountability* (Oxford, Oxford University Press, 2014) 195, 197–98.

[26] See, eg, Mulgan (n 25) at 558.

[27] These are 'the "internal" functions of personal culpability, morality and professional ethics': ibid, at 558.

concepts. If we take the approach that accountability has its basis in notions of personal responsibility, what might this tell us about when and how it is appropriate to hold government officials accountable?

Fault is a recurring theme in the literature on responsibility. Many explanations of responsibility employ as their starting point the idea that a person should only be held responsible in circumstances where they are culpable, and that a person can only be culpable where they possess a requisite level of mental engagement (usually that their conduct was intentional and the resulting consequences were intended, or at least foreseen).[28] At its core, the idea of restricting responsibility (or accountability) to cases in which a person acted intentionally is bound up in the notion of choice: it is appropriate to hold people accountable for the consequences of the choices that they have made.[29] For this reason, we have little difficulty holding a person responsible (or accountable) if they have acted on the basis of subjective fault, out of a desire to cause harm or foreseeing but not caring that they will cause harm. The rationale becomes more tenuous the further we move away from deliberate choice or subjective fault.[30] On what basis can we impose liability where a person has not actually averted to the possibility of harm in any subjective sense? Three possible justifications are the theories of unexercised capacity, outcome responsibility, and relational responsibility.

The idea of unexercised capacity informs Hart's justification for criminal punishment in the absence of subjective fault. The crux of the theory is that a person might be held responsible not only for their deliberate conduct, but also for failing to exercise 'the capacities and powers of normal persons to think about and control their conduct'.[31] In other words, if a person could have acted differently, we can justify holding that person responsible for their choice not to have done so. This enquiry becomes one part objective and one part subjective: we ask whether a person has failed to meet an objective standard and then ask whether that person was in fact capable of meeting that standard.[32] It is in this respect that the unexercised capacity theory falls short of offering a complete explanation for responsibility in absence of deliberate wrongdoing. Asking what an individual could have done differently is a subjective enquiry into their available alternatives. The objective fault criteria considered in this chapter go further, asking what a reasonable person in the

[28] HLA Hart, *The Concept of Law* (Oxford, Clarendon Press, 1961) 173, cited in Cane (n 16) at 95. Lord Bingham expresses a good example of this view in *R v G* [2004] 1 AC 1034: 'It is clearly blameworthy to take an obvious and significant risk of causing injury to another. But it is not clearly blameworthy to do something involving a risk of injury to another if … one genuinely does not perceive the risk. Such a person may fairly be accused of stupidity or lack of imagination, but neither of those failings should expose him to conviction of serious crime or the risk of punishment' (at [32]).

[29] See Cane (n 16) at 95.

[30] ibid, at 95.

[31] HLA Hart, *Punishment and Responsibility: Essays in the Philosophy of Law*, 2nd edn (Oxford, Oxford University Press, 2008) 140.

[32] Such an approach excuses those who were unable to meet objectively established standards by reason of physical or mental incapacity, for example, and has been described as the 'individualisation of the negligence standard': see eg M Moore and H Hurd, 'Punishing the Awkward, the Stupid, the Weak, and the Selfish: The Culpability of Negligence' (2011) 5 *Criminal Law and Philosophy* 147 at 151.

circumstances (not the individual in question) might have done differently. In this sense, when we say that a person ought to have acted differently, it is not a complete answer to say that factors outside the person's control influenced their ability to meet the relevant standard. Therefore, the idea of unexercised capacity does not take us much further than liability based on subjective fault.

Outcome responsibility, as posited by Honoré, provides a second possible justification for responsibility in absence of subjective fault. For Honoré, the notion of responsibility cannot be explained solely by reference to a person's behaviour, fault or choices.[33] Rather, a person can also take on responsibility voluntarily[34] or it may be imposed through societal norms.[35] Irrespective of its source, responsibility for Honoré 'involves a combination of actual or assumed control and risk'; within that frame it is appropriate that a person who can take the credit arising from their conduct is also subjected to the blame (or 'discredit').[36] Honoré employs this notion of a credit–discredit balancing act to argue that when applied consistently over time, imposing responsibility derives overall benefit for individual members of society.[37] However, he distinguishes between the idea of outcome responsibility and liability: some 'extra element' is needed to superimpose a legal sanction.[38] Beyond cases of fault, Honoré suggests that legal sanctions may be appropriate where the wrongdoer's conduct 'carries with it a special risk of harm'.[39] Again, this theory does not take us much further in our accountability analysis. The attribution of responsibility for outcomes does not, of itself, extend to imposing sanctions and the search for Honoré's 'extra element' leads us into a circular quest for the elusive justification for strict liability.

The third theoretical justification holds more promise. This view, proposed by Cane, relies on the relational nature of responsibility to justify remedial responses outside cases of fault.[40] Unlike the unexercised capacity and outcome-responsibility theories, which are essentially focused on the wrongdoer, Cane's argument is that responsibility is a two-sided affair that should take into account not only the wrongdoer, but also the interests of the victim and society more generally. Through a distributional analysis, a balance is struck between the interests of the parties, in some cases supporting the imposition of obligations to repair in absence of fault.[41] In other words, a person might be held responsible beyond cases of subjective fault by virtue of burdens inherent in the relationship between the parties. These observations take on particular significance in the context of accountability, by definition a relational concept. There is much to be said for the view that an accountability mechanism should strike a balance between the interests of the two parties to that

[33] T Honoré, *Responsibility and Fault* (Oxford, Hart Publishing, 1999) 126.
[34] As may be the case where a political leader assumes responsibility by taking on that role.
[35] Such as the responsibility owed to one's family: see Honoré (n 33) at 126.
[36] ibid, at 130.
[37] ibid, at 26–27.
[38] ibid, at 27.
[39] ibid.
[40] See Cane (n 16) at 108.
[41] ibid, at 108–09.

relationship, which in some cases may justify remedial responses beyond cases of subjective fault.

C. How would a Comprehensive Accountability Regime Approach Fault?

We can adapt the foregoing analysis to ask how fault might determine the availability of remedial responses in a comprehensive public law accountability regime. To reiterate the conclusions drawn earlier in this chapter, once transparency has exposed a breach of obligations, the three results-focused objectives of accountability are to control the exercise of power, punish an excess of power and restore interests affected as a result. The current public law regime serves the accountability objective of control through regulatory orders. Fault presently plays very little part in determining whether or not an official has contravened a public law norm or in selection of the appropriate public law remedy. In essence, liability under the current regime is strict, and the available remedies are regulatory. In a comprehensive accountability regime, it is appropriate that regulatory orders continue to be available irrespective of fault. Accountability's control objective is concerned with policing the boundaries of public power. We could not achieve this goal if only faulty excesses of power were the subject of a remedy, so we would have little concern about maintaining a strict liability approach to the award of regulatory orders. The current regime effectively serves the objective of control, but how might it operate in the context of punishment and restoration?

The accountability objective of punishment, served by way of punitive sanctions, is concerned with public condemnation of inherently wrongful conduct. It is this condemnatory character of punishment that might lead us to confine punishment to cases of subjective fault, in line with the choice theory. Where a person has acted maliciously or knowing they are likely to cause harm, accountability may demand a sanction that signifies the inherent wrongfulness of their conduct. Returning to the earlier hypothetical, Odette's spiteful conduct in the third scenario may be of such a character as to warrant condemnation via punitive sanctions. However, if we were to go further and extend the reach of punishment into objectively faulty and unfaulty conduct (as in the first two scenarios), we risk undermining this primary condemnatory characteristic of the sanction. For this reason, we might conclude that there is merit in restricting the punitive objective of accountability to cases of subjective fault.

Turning to the restorative objective of accountability, served by reparative remedies, different considerations apply. These remedies do not bear the same stigma of condemnation as punitive sanctions, so we might have fewer concerns about moving beyond the limits of subjective fault. Having removed this ideological roadblock, it is necessary to identify what quality of fault best supports the restorative function of accountability. In this respect, Cane's relational justification for responsibility is of assistance.[42] The relational approach, as framed in this chapter, sees accountability

[42] ibid.

as a relationship in which the interests of each party must be balanced against one another, so as to appropriately distribute losses between them. The starting point in any such balancing exercise must be to identify the relevant interests at stake; in this respect it might be tempting to turn to concepts of individual or constitutional rights. However, this would be an unnecessary complication. The relevant standards that are enforced via public law are not determined primarily by the failure to respect or protect individual rights and interests, but relate more generally to proper administration of public power. As Varuhas notes, these norms are concerned with ensuring that 'public powers are exercised properly … and in the public interest' and to the extent that they operate to the benefit of individuals, this is a 'subsidiary' rather than 'primary' function of the law.[43] Bearing this in mind, it is necessary to identify the quality of fault that best balances the interests of the government against those of the individual who has been harmed as a result of the relevant 'public wrong'.[44]

It may be that there are certain public law norms that justify a strict liability approach in respect of the obligation to restore. For instance, accountability might be thought to demand the restoration of taxes to individuals who pay pursuant to an invalid demand, irrespective of the degree of fault accompanying that demand. The nature of the public wrong in such a case (taxation without parliamentary approval) might be thought sufficiently fundamental that to limit restoration only to cases of intentional or negligent wrongdoing might threaten the legitimacy of government. Accordingly, we might reach the view that it is appropriate to expand reparative remedies (here, restitution) to such cases on a strict liability basis, consistently with the approach adopted by the House of Lords in *Woolwich*.[45] There may be other public law norms that would justify a strict liability approach to the obligation to restore, however we can leave the task of identifying these for another day. This chapter is concerned with fault and a fault-based approach to liability is appropriate in at least one key area of government activity: the exercise of discretionary powers.

Where Parliament confers discretionary powers on an official, a more finely tuned approach to the restorative objective is required. In deciding when the obligation to restore might be enlivened in such cases, we must ask: what is the minimum degree of liability necessary to maintain public confidence in our system of government? The blanket adoption of either strict liability or subjective fault represents extreme alternatives, neither of which seems advisable. Limiting reparative remedies to cases of intentional misuse of discretion fails to provide accountability in cases of wrongful (but not intentional) excess of power. For instance, an official might unknowingly exercise their powers in a manner that we might describe as extremely unreasonable and arbitrary. We might be justifiably concerned about the legitimacy of our

[43] JNE Varuhas, 'Against Unification' in H Wilberg and M Elliott (eds), *The Scope and Intensity of Substantive Review: Traversing Taggart's Rainbow* (Oxford, Hart Publishing, 2015) 91, 101.

[44] ibid, at 108.

[45] *Woolwich Equitable Building Society v Inland Revenue Commissioners* [1993] AC 70. A further factor that may support the imposition of an obligation to restore in such cases is that the applicable remedy (restitution) is less intrusive than compensatory remedies: see, eg, P Cane, 'The Constitutional Basis of Judicial Remedies in Public Law' in P Leyland and T Woods (eds), *Administrative Law Facing the Future: Old Constraints and New Horizons* (London, Blackstone Press, 1997) 242, 257.

system of government if individuals who suffer harm as a consequence of such an exercise of power are left to bear their own losses. Accordingly, limiting reparative remedies to the subjectively faulty exercise of discretionary power would not further the important objectives of accountability. But does accountability demand that we make reparative remedies available for all reasoning errors that may arise in an official's exercise of discretion (strict liability)? Or only those which fall short of an acceptable standard of reasonableness (objective fault)? While a valid case might be made for the former argument, the position adopted in this chapter is that, in the context of discretionary powers, the more cohesive approach is to adopt objective fault as the relevant criterion for the availability of reparative remedies. This approach represents a 'middle ground', drawing a distinction between those public law contraventions that demand restoration and those that do not, while taking into account the interests of *both* parties in the accountability relationship. This approach also conforms to the modern Australian understanding of unreasonableness, as is drawn out in the following section.

To summarise, then, in an accountability regime that is informed by notions of personal responsibility, the concept of fault might be used to define the circumstances in which it is appropriate to engage each of the three results-focused objectives of accountability. Control via regulatory orders would be appropriate on a strict liability basis, punishment via punitive sanctions would be appropriate in cases of subjective fault and, at least in connection with the exercise of discretionary powers, restoration via reparative remedies would be appropriate in cases of objective fault. Keeping this framework in mind, we now consider whether our public law system is compatible with this approach.

V. FAULT IN PUBLIC LAW

Judicial review grounds are not traditionally thought about in terms of fault; indeed, they are often treated as forming a largely strict liability regime.[46] While it is correct that fault is not determinative of contravention of the majority of the grounds of judicial review, on closer analysis we can see that issues of intention, motive, knowledge and belief do play an important role in public law. In particular, we can see that the judicial review grounds establish benchmarks of subjective fault (in the form of bad faith) and objective fault (in the form of legal unreasonableness). The argument drawn out in this chapter is that there is therefore no inconsistency between public law and the punitive and restorative objectives of accountability, at least insofar as the concept of fault is concerned.

A. Fault in Judicial Review Grounds

When we look at the grounds of judicial review, we can see that two of the grounds of review entail a finding of fault: bad faith and legal unreasonableness. Other

[46] See, eg, Cane (n 16) at 270.

grounds also invite an assessment of an official's knowledge, intention and motives, though not necessarily leading to a conclusion of fault.

(i) Bad Faith: Subjective Fault

The ground of bad faith invites a direct fault-based assessment of an official's conduct. 'There is no such thing as … constructive bad faith'[47] and so determining contravention of this standard is an inherently subjective enquiry. An official will contravene this ground if they act 'in a way that [they] actually knew was wrong'[48] or if they are 'reckless as to whether [the exercise of power] was in a manner required by law'.[49] Though there are many types of behaviour which might amount to bad faith, dishonesty and acting for an improper purpose are most typical.[50] Returning to the language of fault adopted above, bad faith will invariably amount to subjective fault on the part of an official, capturing intentional or reckless conduct engaged in for malicious or prohibited ends. Accordingly, we can conclude that the bad faith ground entails a finding of subjective fault.

(ii) Legal Unreasonableness: Objective Fault

Another ground of review that might be thought to entail fault is that of unreasonableness. Until recently in Australia, this ground was identified by the well-known (and often pilloried)[51] verbal formula derived from the *Wednesbury* decision, which provides a basis to challenge an exercise of power that is so unreasonable that no reasonable official might have adopted that same course.[52]

Taken at face value, the wording of the *Wednesbury* formulation reflects the notion of objective fault, in the sense that it requires evaluation of an official's failure to adhere to a prescribed standard of conduct.[53] However, this raises two related difficulties. The first is whether it is possible for the *Wednesbury* formula

[47] *Minister for Immigration & Multicultural & Indigenous Affairs v SBAN* [2002] FCAFC 431 at [8].

[48] *SCAZ v Minister for Immigration & Multicultural & Indigenous Affairs* [2002] FCA 1377 at [33].

[49] ibid. Cited with approval in *SBBS v Minister for Immigration & Multicultural & Indigenous Affairs* [2002] FCAFC 361 at [48].

[50] *SBAP v Refugee Review Tribunal* [2002] FCA 590 at [49].

[51] Usually on the basis that it is tautological and vague: See, eg, McDonald (n 1) at 124.

[52] The original formulation was set out in *Associated Provincial Picture Houses Ltd v Wednesbury Corporation* [1948] 1 KB 223 at 230: 'so unreasonable that no reasonable [official] could ever have come to it'. Note also that the Australian courts have drawn a distinction between the application of the ground to reasoning processes (irrationality review) and to the exercise of discretion (unreasonableness review): see, eg, M Aronson and M Groves, *Judicial Review of Administrative Action*, 5th edn (Pyrmont, Thomson Reuters, 2013) 284. There remain reasons to maintain the distinction between the two ideas: see, eg, G Airo-Farulla, 'Reasonableness, Rationality and Proportionality' in M Groves and HP Lee (eds), *Australian Administrative Law: Fundamentals, Principles and Doctrines* (Cambridge, Cambridge University Press, 2007) 212, 215. Nothing much turns on this distinction for the purpose of this chapter.

[53] See, eg, P Cane, 'Fault and Strict Liability for Harm in Tort Law' in W Swadling and G Jones (eds), *The Search for Principle: Essays in Honour of Lord Goff of Chieveley* (New York, Oxford University Press, 1999) 171, 178–79; see Cane (n 16) at 271. Harlow wonders whether it might be described as an 'objective bad faith standard': C Harlow, *State Liability: Tort Law and Beyond* (Oxford, Oxford University Press, 2004) 130.

to simultaneously operate as a test of invalidity and fault. For instance, we might wonder whether this touches on the well-canvassed debate around the interaction between public and private law concepts of reasonableness.[54] The supposed movement towards 'convergence' of public and private law standards of reasonableness has many detractors.[55] However, it is unnecessary to enter into the merits of this debate here. The present question is not whether public law unreasonableness can be equated with private law understandings of fault, but whether public law unreasonableness is, in its own right, indicative of fault. This chapter has framed the concept of objective fault in terms of failure to adhere to a prescribed standard of conduct, involving a judgment that a person ought not to have acted as they did. It is difficult to see how the *Wednesbury* test of unreasonableness is not an objective standard of this nature. The task undertaken by the court is to evaluate an official's conduct by reference to an external standard.[56] If the official's conduct falls short of this standard, it is beyond power. In this respect, it is neither here nor there that public law unreasonableness is not solely concerned with individual interests (as is the focus for private law unreasonableness).[57] Rather, the public law norm represents an objective standard of reasonable decision making, breach of which is objectively faulty, irrespective of whether it relates to a failure to respect or protect individual interests.

The second difficulty is whether it is still possible to equate *Wednesbury* unreasonableness with objective fault following recent moves to define it as a dynamic, rather than fixed, standard in Australian law.[58] In *Li*,[59] the Australian High Court adopted a new formulation of 'legal unreasonableness', indicating that *Wednesbury* should not be treated as either the 'starting point' or the 'end point' in determining the relevant standard.[60] Instead, it was to 'be the standard indicated by the true construction of the statute'.[61] The implication to be drawn from these statements is that unreasonableness may mean different things in different contexts, a move which has been described as having robbed the standard of 'any meaningful content'.[62]

[54] See, eg, P Craig and D Fairgrieve, '*Barrett*, Negligence and Discretionary Powers' [1999] *Public Law* 626 at 648; TR Hickman, 'The Reasonableness Principle: Reassessing its Place in the Public Sphere' (2004) 63 *CLJ* 166; R Bagshaw, 'Monetary Remedies in Public Law—Misdiagnosis and Misprescription' (2006) 26 *Legal Studies* 4 at 15–23.

[55] See, eg, Bagshaw (n 54) at 15–23.

[56] See Airo-Farulla (n 52) at 226.

[57] This was one of the criticisms of the convergence theory raised by Bagshaw: see Bagshaw (n 54), 17–18. Varuhas makes a similar point in reference to the suggested convergence of administrative law and human rights law: Varuhas (n 43) at 105–08.

[58] As noted at n 1, there remain doubts as to whether this movement towards a dynamic standard of reasonableness in Australia potentially represents a broader movement towards variegated intensity review or perhaps 'anxious scrutiny' in cases where rights are at stake, an approach which has been developed in other jurisdictions: see, eg, M Taggart, 'Proportionality, Deference, *Wednesbury*' [2008] *New Zealand Law Review* 423 at 433–35. At the very least, there would be serious questions as to how such an approach might be realised in Australia, which lacks the 'normative hierarchy established by rights' against which the approach in other jurisdictions is anchored: see McDonald (n 1) at 132.

[59] See *Li* (n 1).

[60] ibid, at [68]. Further implications of the *Li* decision are discussed below. Note, however, that Gageler J applied *Wednesbury* in the traditional sense of a generic, externally defined standard of reasonableness (at [124]).

[61] ibid, at [67].

[62] See McDonald (n 1) at 130.

For the purpose of this chapter, what is critical to note is that (whatever its content) the *Li* unreasonableness test remains an *objective standard.*

The effect of the *Li* decision was to alter the source or content of the standard, not its nature as a yardstick by which government conduct can be measured. So much is evident in the Full Federal Court's subsequent description of the test as a 'standard of legal unreasonableness [to] apply across a range of statutory powers', with its 'indicia to be found in the scope, subject and purpose of the particular statutory provisions'.[63] In a more recent Australian Federal Court decision, Manousaridis J emphasised that legal unreasonableness remains an external standard.[64] For Manousaridis J, to say that an official must act reasonably 'presupposes the formulation of a rule of conduct that [an official] must have been obliged to follow',[65] meaning that there can be no conclusion on reasonableness until after determining the content of the relevant standard.[66] In Manousaridis J's view, to conflate the two enquiries (being determination of the relevant standard and evaluation of unreasonableness) increases the risk that the courts will simply adopt their own view of reasonableness, rather than measuring the conduct against an objective standard.[67] This must be correct. In reaching a view that a decision is 'arbitrary', 'capricious', 'lacking in evident or intelligible justification' or any of the various other verbal formulae used to describe unreasonableness,[68] the court must determine and apply an objective standard to avoid encroaching on the merits of the decision.

Therefore, even if the source of the reasonableness standard has shifted in Australian law, the underlying task remains the same; the role of the courts is to determine whether an official has failed to adhere to an objective standard of conduct, failing which the official will have exceeded the scope of their powers. In this sense, the *Wednesbury* formula provides a basis to conclude that an official's exercise of discretion is objectively faulty.

(iii) Other Grounds of Review

A number of the remaining grounds of review invite assessment of an official's subjective intention, motives, knowledge and belief, though not necessarily for the purpose of determining fault. The first such ground is that of improper purpose, which involves a direct enquiry into an official's motives in exercising a power. However, unlike the ground of bad faith, conduct that contravenes the improper purpose ground will not necessarily amount to subjective fault. For instance, an official might refuse an import licence out of a desire to harm the applicant or with seemingly good intentions, such as desiring to promote the interests of local goods over imported goods. While both purposes might be improper in light of the terms of the statute,

63 *Minister for Immigration and Border Protection v Singh* (2014) 231 FCR 437 at [48].
64 *SZVMG v Minister for Immigration and Border Protection* [2016] FCCA 631 at [18].
65 ibid.
66 ibid.
67 ibid, at [19]. See also Airo-Farulla (n 52) at 226.
68 A catalogue of descriptions was referred to in *Minister for Immigration and Border Protection v Eden* (2016) 240 FCR 158 at [65].

only the former would amount to subjective fault. In this way, the improper purpose ground involves analysis of an official's intention and motives, without signifying a particular type of fault. Failure to exercise discretion involves a similar analysis,[69] as while the court enquires into whether an official was motivated by the desire to simply rubber stamp a policy or to exercise independent judgment, a finding of contravention does not necessarily equate to a particular degree of fault.

Actual bias is another ground of review that falls into this category. At first glance, this ground may appear to be tied to the notion of subjective fault. An official will contravene this ground if they make a decision in circumstances where they have an interest in the outcome, bear personal ill-will or have already reached a decision before hearing the evidence. Actual biases are clearly a subjective matter, in the sense that we are enquiring into an official's actual mindset in determining whether the standard has been contravened. However, it is doubtful that this ground will always involve subjective fault. Many biases may be subversive in nature, with the effect that an official may not even be aware of their predisposition (eg, a racist official may treat one visa applicant's application more favourably than another). If the official is aware of their bias and acts on it knowingly, this would be a clear case of subjective fault. On the other hand, if the official is unaware of their bias, can we say that they have acted in a subjectively faulty way? Answering this question would draw us into theoretical disputes as to the blameworthiness of particular character attributes[70] that are beyond the scope of this chapter. What we can say, however, is that actual bias may rise to the level of subjective fault in some cases, while constituting a lesser degree of fault in others.

Issues of intention, motives and knowledge are irrelevant in relation to the remaining grounds of review. For instance, it is no defence to an allegation of taking into account irrelevant considerations to say that the official did not appreciate the irrelevance of the information. Similar observations might be made with respect to the grounds of procedural fairness, no evidence, uncertainty, and reasonable apprehension of bias.[71]

(iv) Summary

The above analysis demonstrates that at least two of the judicial review grounds are directly tied to concepts of fault: bad faith equates to subjective fault and legal unreasonableness equates to objective fault. The remaining grounds, some of which invite assessment of an official's intention and motives, may be contravened deliberately, negligently or innocently with the result that we cannot describe conduct contravening these grounds as necessarily entailing fault of a particular quality. This tells us that public law can certainly be understood as involving some assessment

[69] Incorporating the grounds of acting under dictation or the inflexible application of policy.

[70] See, eg, Moore and Hurd (n 32).

[71] Unlike actual bias, apprehended bias may be made out irrespective of whether the official was actually biased or entirely innocent. All that is relevant for the purpose of determining breach of this ground is external appearances.

of an official's degree of fault. But can we go further so as to link these fault-based assessments to the accountability framework set out above?

B. Benchmarks of Subjective and Objective Fault

As framed in this chapter, a comprehensive accountability regime would provide for control by issuing regulatory orders irrespective of fault, punishment by issuing punitive sanctions in cases of subjective fault and (at least in relation to the exercise of discretionary powers) restoration by issuing reparative remedies in cases of objective fault. The following discussion shows that our public law grounds of review are in fact compatible with this framework, as we can view bad faith as a benchmark of subjective fault, and legal unreasonableness as a benchmark of objective fault.

Contravention of the judicial review ground of bad faith will invariably involve subjectively faulty conduct, as it is tied up in the concepts of intentional or reckless pursuit of malicious or prohibited motives. This is not to say that other grounds of review may not also be contravened accompanied by a subjectively faulty mindset. For example, it would be a subjectively faulty contravention of the improper purpose ground for an official to act out of a desire for personal gain. It is difficult to see, though, how such subjectively faulty behaviour would not also contravene the ground of bad faith. In this way, we can view bad faith as a benchmark of subjective fault in public law. The accountability framework set out in this chapter is directed at punishing precisely the type of conduct that is encompassed by this benchmark, and accordingly we might take the view that it would be consistent with the objectives of accountability to allow the courts to impose punitive sanctions where an official's conduct rises to the level of bad faith.

Turning to accountability's restorative objective, it was suggested above that in the exercise of discretionary powers, reparative remedies might be engaged where conduct exceeds a minimum threshold of objective fault. In the public law context, subjectively faulty conduct (that is, conduct rising to the level of bad faith) will naturally go beyond these limits. However, the critical question for present purposes is where to set the *minimum* threshold of objective fault in public law. It was concluded above[72] that legal unreasonableness can be viewed as equating to objective fault, being an external yardstick against which an official's exercise of discretion can be measured, and found wanting. It is possible to think about this ground as setting a benchmark of objective fault in public law, as other types of errors can be made in a way which rises to the level of unreasonableness or irrationality reflected in the standard. This is perhaps implicit in the Australian High Court's description of unreasonableness in *Li*. The plurality indicated that unreasonableness may either be a conclusory label applied to other errors in reasoning[73] or a conclusion to be drawn where, despite no identifiable error, the decision 'lacks an evident and intelligible

[72] See section V.A.ii above.

[73] eg 'having ... given disproportionate weight to some factor or reasoned illogically or irrationally': Li (n 1) at [72] (Hayne, Kiefel and Bell JJ).

justification'.[74] If 'legal unreasonableness' is an umbrella-style concept that reflects the minimum requirements of reasonableness and rationality in the exercise of public power, it can be employed as a benchmark against which particular errors in reasoning can be measured. In this way, it is possible to think about legal unreasonableness as a benchmark of objective fault in public law.

Drawing these ideas together, we can start to see that public law is indeed compatible with a fault-based assessment of liability for punitive and restorative remedial responses. Though we ordinarily think about public law standards of conduct (and accompanying exposure to regulatory orders) as strict liability in nature, our grounds of review are well-adapted to the fault-based analysis contemplated in this chapter. Restoration might be relevant where an official exercises their discretionary powers in an objectively faulty way, by exceeding the generous limits of rationality and reasonableness offered by the legal unreasonableness standard, while officials who act in a subjectively faulty way, as typified by the bad faith ground, might be liable for punishment. The use of 'might' in each of these instances is deliberate, as any discussions around, in particular, restoration, must go on to address questions of causation and loss.

VI. CONCLUDING REMARKS

If we return to the hypothetical set out at the beginning of this chapter, we can start to see that the public law grounds of review are in fact quite cohesive with the fault-based accountability framework set out above. Odette's conduct in each scenario could be characterised as a breach of a range of different public law norms. In all three scenarios, she has failed to accord procedural fairness or perhaps to take into account relevant considerations. However, both the second and third scenarios go beyond procedural breaches, expanding into faulty conduct. In the second scenario, Odette has exercised her discretion in an arbitrary way that might characterise her decision as legally unreasonable, while in the third scenario her decision was motivated by spite, and was therefore made in bad faith.

If we were concerned with approaching these breaches of public law norms from the perspective of enhancing government accountability, the type of breach would be indicative of the accountability objective that might be relevant in each scenario and the character of the remedies that might be thought appropriate to serve those objectives. The control objective of accountability would be engaged in all three scenarios and would be supported by the raft of regulatory orders that are already available in public law cases. The restorative objective of accountability, as understood in this chapter, is engaged in cases where an official's exercise of discretion is objectively faulty, as measured against the standard of legal unreasonableness. Odette's conduct in both the second and third scenarios falls short of this standard, and so restoration (via reparative remedies) might potentially be relevant in both of those scenarios.[75]

[74] ibid, at [76] (Hayne, Kiefel and Bell JJ).

[75] As noted above, the use of 'might' here is deliberate; any discussion around reparative remedies must address important issues of causation and loss which are not considered in this chapter.

The punitive objective of accountability is engaged where an official acts in a subjectively faulty way, rising to the level of bad faith. Only Odette's conduct in the third scenario satisfies this criterion, so punishment (via punitive sanctions) could only be relevant in that context.

Of course, reparative remedies and punitive sanctions do not presently form part of the court's public law arsenal, so Alex cannot rely simply on breaches of public law (however faulty) to avail himself of remedies that serve these functions. The purpose of this chapter is not to suggest that this shortfall in public law reflects an 'accountability gap' that ought immediately to be filled through the creation of public law remedies that perform punitive and restorative roles.[76] There are a whole host of important matters that would need to be considered in the context of such discussions, including valid concerns regarding how the courts might go about determining causation in public law cases and the impact that this might have on the separation of powers. This is particularly so in Australia, which maintains a strict distinction between legality and merits review. Further, it might validly be argued that there are other mechanisms outside public law that are well-adapted to performing these roles, perhaps to better effect than the courts.

As was noted at the outset, the purpose of this chapter is not to suggest any immediate campaign for law reform centred around increasing government accountability. Rather, its primary purpose is to demonstrate that focusing on government accountability can allow us to better understand the principles that make up our system of public law. In this chapter the 'lens' of accountability has shown us that if the punitive and restorative objectives of accountability require an assessment of an official's degree of fault, there is nothing in our public law principles that is necessarily inconsistent with such an approach. On the contrary, our public law grounds of review already embody the types of enquiries that such an approach might demand. This all tells us that if there are good reasons for public law's failure to hold the government accountable through restorative and punitive mechanisms, these reasons do not lie in the public law's inability to embrace a fault-based analysis of the exercise of public power.

[76] One remedy that may be viewed as performing a dual role in this context is an award of damages, which is able to take compensatory or punitive form.

9

Interpretive Presumptions Assessed against Legislators' Understanding

HANNA WILBERG*

I. INTRODUCTION

COURTS HAVE LONG used a range of presumptions in interpreting statutes, as a means of giving some effect to fundamental rights and principles[1] and to international law obligations:[2] they have presumed that, absent indications to the contrary, Parliament must have intended to legislate consistently with these. The presumption of consistency with fundamental common law rights has recently acquired the misleading label[3] 'principle of legality'.[4] Dating back to before the advent of the modern focus on purposive interpretation, a similar idea is still in some contexts expressed, and similar results are achieved, by the simpler device of 'rules of strict construction' of legislation affecting certain fundamental rights and principles.[5] In New Zealand, there is also a presumption of consistency with the Treaty of Waitangi.[6] Most recently, statutory bills of rights have introduced express

* Thank you to Ross Carter, Richard Ekins, Andrew Geddis, Chye-Ching Huang and Danielle Kelly for comments on earlier drafts or for helpful discussions; and to Bree Huntley, Danielle Kelly, Bronwyn Inkster and Komal Kumar for research assistance. Early versions of this paper were presented at the Australian Society for Legal Philosophy Annual Conference (2008), a Victoria University Centre for Public Law public lecture (2008), and the Public Law in Three Nations Symposium (Auckland, 2010). I thank the audience at the Second Biennial Public Law conference as well as at those earlier events. All opinions expressed and any errors or omissions, as always, remain mine.

1 See R Carter, *Burrows and Carter: Statute Law in New Zealand*, 5th edn (Wellington, LexisNexis, 2015) 335–43.

2 ibid, at 512–19.

3 J Goldsworthy, 'The Principle of Legality and Legislative Intention' in D Meagher and M Groves (eds) *The Principle of Legality in Australia and New Zealand* (Melbourne, Federation Press, 2017) 46, 53 notes that the label is misleading, but also notes that it may imply a certain view as to the principle's rationale and scope.

4 eg *R v Secretary of State for the Home Department, ex parte Simms* [2000] 2 AC 115.

5 eg *Anisminic v Foreign Compensation Commission* [1969] 2 AC 147 at 170 (Lord Reid). See also O Jones and F Bennion, *Bennion on Statutory Interpretation: a Code*, 6th edn (London, LexisNexis, 2013) Part XVII.

6 See H Wilberg, 'Judicial Remedies for the Original Breach?' [2007] *New Zealand Law Review* 713; also P Rishworth 'Writing Things Unwritten: Common Law in New Zealand's Constitution' (2016) 14 *International Journal of Constitutional Law* 137 at 150–51. The presumption has been endorsed in *Ngaronoa v Attorney General* [2017] NZCA 351, [2017] 3 NZLR 643 at [46] (under appeal); *New Zealand Maori Council v Attorney General* [2007] NZCA 269, [2008] 1 NZLR 318 at [72] and [74].

interpretive instructions to prefer rights-consistent meanings.[7] Albeit not expressed as presumptions, these instructions represent yet another avenue for achieving similar results, protecting rights through consistent interpretation. The different devices and terminology used can tend to mask the commonality of purpose and result. In this chapter, I will refer to all of these devices as 'interpretive presumptions'.

The strength of use of such interpretive presumptions has fluctuated over time and has varied according to the subject matter and context. Recent decades have seen stronger uses at least in certain areas. Particularly 'adventurous'[8] or even 'radical'[9] use has been made in the United Kingdom of the express instruction in section 3 of the Human Rights Act 1998 (UK) to interpret legislation consistently with the rights in the European Convention of Human Rights.[10] Similarly assertive use has been made in New Zealand of the common law presumption of consistency with unincorporated international treaties.[11] Australia has seen some fairly strong uses of the principle of legality.[12] There has been much spirited debate on whether such strong uses can be justified.[13]

In this chapter, I ask a prior question: how do we decide what amounts to a strong use that calls for special justification? I examine this question from the perspective of one who considers that democratic principles normally call for interpreters of statutes to respect the intention of the enacting Parliament (or better: legislators' likely understanding). An explanation and defence of this position is a topic for another paper; here I provide only a very brief summary (Part II).

My contribution here is to work through the implications that follow for assessing the strength of uses of interpretive presumptions if we take respect for legislators' likely understanding as our starting point. First, I propose a test for distinguishing between assertive uses that call for special justification and weak or moderate uses that do not, and explore the application of that test (Part III). Secondly, I identify and compare the different tests established in the cases for the three main presumptions, and assess each of them against my criterion of respect for legislators' likely understanding (Part IV). My examination extends to the United Kingdom, Australia, and New Zealand—three common law jurisdictions without constitutional bills of rights.

[7] New Zealand Bill of Rights Act 1990 ('NZ BORA'), s 6; Human Rights Act 1998 (UK) ('HRA (UK)'), s 3; Human Rights Act 2004 (ACT) ('HRA (ACT)'), s 30; Charter of Human Rights and Responsibilities Act 2006 (Vic) ('CHRRA (Vic)'), s 32.

[8] *Hansen v R* [2007] 3 NZLR 1 at [156].

[9] R Ekins, 'A Critique of Radical Approaches to Rights Consistent Statutory Interpretation' (2003) 6 *European Human Rights Law Review* 631; J Beatson, 'Interpretative Obligations as Constitutional Tools' in L Pearson, C Harlow and M Taggart (eds), *Administrative Law in a Changing State: Essays in Honour of Mark Aronson* (Oxford, Hart Publishing, 2008) 112.

[10] See, eg, *R v A (No 2)* [2002] 1 AC 45.

[11] See, eg, *Sellers v Maritime Safety Authority* [1999] 2 NZLR 44; also *Zaoui v Attorney General (No 2)* [2006] 1 NZLR 289 and *Ye v Minister of Immigration* [2010] 1 NZLR 104.

[12] See, eg, *Lacey v Attorney General (Queensland)* (2011) 242 CLR 573. Goldsworthy (n 3) at 50 comments it is as if the presumptions 'have been injected with steroids'.

[13] For some examples, see Ekins (n 9); Beatson (n 9); A Kavanagh, *Constitutional Review under the UK Human Rights Act* (Cambridge, Cambridge University Press, 2009); D Dyzenhaus, M Hunt and M Taggart, 'The Principle of Legality in Administrative Law: Internationalisation as Constitutionalisation' (2001) 1 *Oxford University Commonwealth Law Journal* 5.

II. WHAT DOES LEGISLATIVE INTENTION MEAN AND WHY SHOULD WE CARE?

In our Westminster constitutional and political system, legislation acquires the force of law by virtue of being passed by a majority vote in both Houses of Parliament.[14] This reflects the constitutional doctrine of Parliamentary sovereignty. More substantively, it reflects the constitutional value of representative democracy: the most democratically representative institution is the supreme law-making body.[15] It follows in my view that where Parliament has legislated, courts should give preference to legislative policy choices over their own.[16] Statutory interpretation respects the authority of the enacting Parliament if it takes what can be ascertained about the intention of that Parliament as its primary guide, supplemented by other considerations only where this guide is silent or where the other considerations are consistent with this guide.

This presupposes that there is such a thing as ascertainable legislative intention; a question on which there is a large and protracted academic and judicial debate.[17] In my view, there is such a thing, but the most helpful way of thinking about it is subtly different from common accounts and assumptions.

My version turns on legislators' likely understanding.[18] Interpreters should seek to put themselves in the shoes of legislators at the time of the final vote. Going by the words of the statute and by all practically and legitimately available evidence of relevant context of which those legislators would likely have been aware, how would those legislators likely have understood the Bill on which they were asked to vote?[19] It is that understanding that was rendered authoritative by the majority vote in favour of the Bill. Note that this is an objective test, but not a purely constructive one in the sense that intention or understanding becomes a pure fiction: it involves drawing inferences from evidence of the relevant context at the time.

[14] Royal Assent is also required, but by constitutional convention is essentially a formality: A Le Sueur, 'Fundamental Principles' in D Feldman (ed), *English Public Law*, 2nd edn (Oxford, Oxford University Press, 2009) [1.95]. In New Zealand, there is only a single House of Parliament.

[15] See M Gordon, *Parliamentary Sovereignty in the UK Constitution: Process, Politics and Democracy* (Hart, Oxford, 2015) 32–55 for a detailed defence of the proposition that the virtue of Parliamentary sovereignty lies in ensuring the primacy of democracy.

[16] See also VF Nourse, 'A Decision Theory of Statutory Interpretation: Legislative History by the Rules' (2012) 122 *Yale Law Journal* 70 at 76, 85; J Goldsworthy, 'Legislative Intentions, Legislative Supremacy, and Legal Positivism' in J Goldsworthy and T Campbell (eds), *Legal Interpretation in Democratic States* (Aldershot, Ashgate, 2002).

[17] Against legislative intention, see eg D Feldman, 'Statutory Interpretation and Constitutional Legislation' (2014) 130 *LQR* 473; M Radin, 'Statutory Interpretation' (1930) 43 *Harvard Law Review* 863. In favour of legislative intention, see, eg, R Ekins, *The Nature of Legislative Intent* (Oxford, Oxford University Press, 2012); R Ekins and J Goldsworthy, 'The Reality and Indispensability of Legislative Intentions' (2014) 36 *Sydney Law Review* 39.

[18] This approach is set out in detail and defended in another paper I am currently working on: H Wilberg, 'Sidelining Intention to Save Intentionalist Statutory Interpretation', presented at the Society of Legal Scholars conference at the University of Oxford, September 2016. In practice, the approach is broadly consistent with the theoretically distinct account of legislative intention in Ekins (n 17) and Ekins and Goldsworthy (n 17). See also Nourse (n 16).

[19] In bicameral systems, different information may be available to the two Houses, potentially resulting in different understanding. One possible solution is to privilege the understanding of the usually more democratically representative lower house over that of the upper house (on the same logic as that which underpins the Parliament Acts 1911 and 1949).

The earlier statement about the role of legislative intention can be restated in these terms. Statutory interpretation respects the authority of the enacting Parliament if it takes what can be ascertained about legislators' understanding of the final Bill as its primary guide, supplemented by other considerations only where this guide is silent or where the other considerations are consistent with this guide.

Importantly, the test cannot be framed in terms more demanding than consistency with what can be ascertained of legislators' likely understanding. Interpretation by reference to legislators' understanding (or any other version of interpretation by reference to legislative intention) can never fully determine the meaning and application of all statutory provisions. There will probably be questions on which there was no clear understanding either way; there will certainly be questions on which the available *evidence* of likely understanding is inconclusive. As a result, while respect for legislators' understanding does serve to exclude some interpretations, it often leaves more than one interpretive option open. This qualification is crucial for assessing the uses of interpretive presumptions.

III. ASSESSING USES OF PRESUMPTIONS AS WEAK, MODERATE AND ASSERTIVE

A. Strength of Use: A Test for Distinguishing Three Categories

The interpretive presumptions discussed in this chapter are used when the provisions of a statute might otherwise apply to the case before the court in such a way as to conflict with the rights, obligations or principles that are protected by those presumptions: they are used to avoid such conflicting applications. This is clearly a desirable endeavour for courts; few would disagree with that. The question here is where to draw the line beyond which this use of presumptions no longer respects legislators' likely understanding of the Bill, and therefore calls for some special justification for departing from that normal approach to interpretation. The best test for drawing this line is whether legislators likely appreciated the conflict between the final Bill and the right, obligation or principle.

This test, however, requires a qualification, in order to address an important objection. At least where fundamental rights are concerned, should courts not be extremely slow to conclude that legislators must have appreciated that a Bill would operate in conflict with such a right and decided to pass it on that basis? In answer to that objection, remember that the vast majority of rights are not absolute: limits on them may be justified if they are proportionate means of serving legitimate competing objectives.[20] Courts use the presumption to avoid the conflict only if they have

[20] See NZ BORA, s 5 and its interpretation in *Hansen* (n 8); the qualifying clauses included in most of the articles of the European Convention on Human Rights as incorporated by the HRA (UK); HRA (ACT), s 28; CHRRA (Vic), s 7; Canadian Charter of Rights and Freedoms, s 1. The point is uncertain and contested in relation to common law fundamental rights, but I have argued that it does apply there too: H Wilberg, 'Common Law Rights Have Justified Limits: Refining the "Principle of Legality"' in Meagher and Groves (n 3) at 139.

concluded that the particular limit in question is not proportionate and justified.[21] However, the question of proportionality will not often be so clear-cut as to admit of no disagreement: it will more often be plausible to posit that legislators must have taken a view contrary to the court's view, and must have considered the interference to be proportionate.[22] Sometimes, indeed, there will be some positive evidence to support this conclusion, as we will see. Whose view is to prevail where judges and legislators disagree in this way is, of course, a matter of much debate. The answer assumed in this chapter is that ordinarily, absent special justification for departing from this, judges should respect legislators' judgements on the justification of limits. The above test, then, should be restated as whether legislators must have appreciated the *prima facie* conflict.[23]

On the basis of this test we can distinguish between three categories: weak, moderate and assertive uses of interpretive presumption.[24] Weak use is where the available evidence of legislators' likely understanding on balance supports the conclusion that legislators must have understood the legislation as avoiding any such conflict. In such cases, the presumption is not used to modify the interpretive conclusion based on legislators' likely understanding: it is used merely to support and confirm that conclusion.

A slightly different scenario may also be counted as weak use. This is where an interpretive presumption takes the form of a factual presumption. The protected right, obligation or principle is in fact so widely known and universally accepted as a default limit on legislation that we can draw a factual inference, in the absence of evidence to the contrary, that legislators must have understood the legislation as not abrogating that right, obligation or principle. An obvious example is the presumption that legislation will not operate extra-territorially.[25] In such cases, the use of the presumption is weak, because it does not modify the interpretation arrived at by reference to legislators' likely understanding. However, this test is satisfied only if the application to the particular legislation is so obvious that legislators must have appreciated it: since our touchstone is respect for legislators' understanding of this legislation, it is not sufficient that there is reason to believe legislators to be

[21] See also H Wilberg, 'Resisting the Siren Song of the *Hansen* Sequence: The State of Supreme Court Authority on the Sections 5 and 6 Conundrum' (2015) 26 *Public Law Review* 39.

[22] Though note that reservations have been expressed as to Parliament's commitment to carrying out that enquiry: eg C Geiringer, 'Inaugural Lecture: Mr Bulwark and the Protection of Human Rights' (2014) 45 *Victoria University of Wellington Law Review* 367; A Geddis, 'The Comparative Irrelevance of the New Zealand Bill of Rights Act to Legislative Practice' (2009) 23 *New Zealand Universities Law Review* 465. But *cf* P Rishworth, 'The Bill of Rights and 'Rights Dialogue' in New Zealand: after 20 years, What Counts as Success?' (Paper presented at University of Sydney Workshop on 'Judicial Supremacy or Inter-Institutional Dialogue? Political Responses to Judicial Review', May 2010).

[23] If so, that then raises the question whether legislators must have considered the prima facie conflict to be a proportional and justified limit. It is open to argument what the position should be if there is either no evidence on this or the evidence suggests that they considered it unjustified but still passed the Bill.

[24] I proposed somewhat different definitions of these categories (based on an earlier understanding of legislative intention) in Wilberg (n 6) at 721.

[25] *Poynter v Commerce Commission* [2010] 3 NZLR 300 at [15], [36], [38], [78].

generally aware of and supportive of the protected right, obligation or principle.[26] For instance, freedom of expression is a widely known right that most legislators will support, but legislators will often fail to appreciate a Bill's potential to conflict with this right.

Use of a presumption is moderate where the evidence simply does not permit any firm conclusions to be drawn: we cannot say with any confidence whether legislators must have appreciated the prima facie conflict. This may be either because there is no persuasive evidence available either way, or because the available evidence is evenly balanced. In such cases, the presumption does modify the conclusion based on legislators' understanding, but only to the extent of filling gaps in the guidance provided by that source, and only so far as is consistent with that guidance.

Finally, use of an interpretive presumption is assertive if the available evidence on balance supports the conclusion that the prima facie conflict with the protected right, obligation or principle must have been appreciated. Here the presumption modifies the interpretive conclusion reached by reference to legislators' understanding to the extent of contradicting that conclusion. Only assertive uses call for special justification because they fail to respect legislators' understanding; weak and moderate uses maintain that respect.

In addition to the above main test, a further (and more controversial) question to ask is whether legislators specifically expected the particular meaning or application, even if they did not appreciate that it was in conflict with a protected right, obligation or principle. This can again be used to distinguish between weak, moderate and assertive uses of presumptions. I will explore the application of these two tests or questions in turn, and will have more to say on why and to what extent the second question is a valid and relevant question. First, however, let me say something more about the moderate category.

B. The Significance of the Moderate Category

The existence of the moderate category is significant for our argument. Proponents of what amounts to assertive use have argued that section 3 of the UK HRA would have no role at all if it could not be used to support an interpretation contrary to parliamentary intention: after all, it comes into operation only where there is a conflict between Parliamentary intention and a right.[27] If accepted, this would apply to all other interpretive presumptions as well: assertive use would be the only meaningful use. That argument, however, ignores the possibility of moderate uses of interpretive presumptions, which flows from the fact that the available evidence of legislators' understanding often does not fully determine the meaning of a provision.

[26] For discussion of whether interpretive presumptions are limited along these lines, see, eg, Goldsworthy (n 3); B Lim, 'The Normativity of the Principle of Legality' (2013) 37 *Melbourne University Law Review* 372; P Sales, 'A Comparison of the Principle of Legality and Section 3 of the Human Rights Act' (2009) 125 *LQR* 598.

[27] For example, Kavanagh (n 13) at 81, 331.

Where the available evidence on balance does not establish whether the conflict was appreciated, then use of a presumption to avoid the conflict is moderate. It merely determines the choice between two or more interpretations that are consistent with what can be ascertained about legislators' understanding.[28] Such moderate use can make a real difference without calling for any special justification.[29]

C. Exploring the Application of these Tests

(i) What Counts as Evidence that the Conflict was Likely Appreciated?

What, then, counts as evidence that legislators must have appreciated the prima facie conflict? We should start by noting that there will often be evidence pointing in different directions. The various items of evidence then always have to be weighed against each other: no single piece of evidence is conclusive.

The evidence of legislators' likely understanding includes, of course, first and foremost the words of the provision in question. An express provision for abrogation of the protected right, obligation or principle would provide very strong evidence that the conflict must have been appreciated, but this is virtually unheard of. Even short of express abrogation, however, sometimes the irresistible inference from the nature and terms of the provision is that legislators must have appreciated the conflict. For instance in *R v A*,[30] the House of Lords read down a 'rape shield' provision so as to protect the fair trial rights of accused. Yet it seems inconceivable, given the nature of the provision, that legislators would not have appreciated the prima facie conflict with fair trial rights.

Along with the words, the relevant evidence includes the statutory context and the background of the pre-existing law and of the 'mischief' which the new law addressed.[31] These may give rise to a strong inference that the conflict must have been appreciated. In *R v A*, legislators must have understood from the structure of the legislation as well as from the background that fair trial rights were being compromised to a greater extent than under previous legislation, in order to give greater priority to the competing objective of protecting complainants.[32]

What further evidence is available depends in part on the view we take on the use of *Hansard* and similar traditionally inadmissible extrinsic materials on legislative history.[33] Approaches such as mine that seek to respect the intention of the enacting

[28] For dicta according to which this is the proper scope and use of the presumption, see *Nicholls v Registrar of the Court of Appeal* [1998] 2 NZLR 385 at 399, 439.

[29] This may be what P Rishworth, 'Human Rights' [2012] *New Zealand Law Review* 321 at 330–31 means in saying that s 6 of NZ BORA may 'generate interpretive possibilities'.

[30] See *R v A* (n 10).

[31] *Heydon's case* (1584) 3 Co Rep 7a, 7b; 76 ER 637 at 638.

[32] See *R v A* (n 10) at 76 (Lord Hope).

[33] For the debate on this, see, eg, *Pepper v Hart* [1993] AC 593; *R v Secretary of State for the Environment, Transport and the Regions, ex p Spath Holme Ltd* [2001] 2 AC 349; J Steyn, '*Pepper v Hart*; A Re-examination' (2001) 21 *OJLS* 59.

Parliament do obviously render legislative history relevant, but this relevance may still be outweighed by competing considerations such as the rule of law value of certainty.[34] To the extent that such evidence may be considered inadmissible, there would be correspondingly fewer cases in which use of presumptions will be assessed as assertive and requiring justification.

Assuming the admissibility of extrinsic evidence, the strongest and most direct evidence that legislators must have appreciated the prima facie conflict would be legislative history evidence showing that legislators were alerted to that conflict. This might take the form of a statement in Parliament or advice available to Parliament to the effect that a Bill is prima facie incompatible with a right,[35] especially if this was not contradicted during the debates.[36]

For example, *Hansen*[37] concerned a reverse onus provision that was in conflict with the presumption of innocence if it was given its natural meaning as a legal onus of proof. Unlike the House of Lords in *Lambert*,[38] the New Zealand Supreme Court refused to use the interpretive presumption in section 6 of NZ BORA to read this down so as to impose only an evidential burden. That refusal could have been supported, among other evidence, by the fact that advice available to Parliament at the time had pointed out the prima facie conflict.[39]

Such statements or advice available to Parliament also represent the most obvious source of evidence that legislators must have considered the prima facie conflict to be a proportionate and justified limit. Where the statement or advice is to that effect, and where it was not contradicted in the debates, it may readily be inferred that the Bill was passed on that basis. *Hansen* is again an example of a case where this type of evidence could have been used: the advice available to Parliament concluded that the reverse onus was a justified limit on the right.[40] The converse is not necessarily true, however: where the report concludes that the limitation is *not* justified and Parliament nevertheless goes ahead to pass the Bill,[41] then it is not clear from that evidence whether legislators decided to legislate in substantive breach of rights, or whether instead they disagreed with the report on the justification point.

[34] For discussion, see Nourse (n 16); Ekins (n 17); Wilberg (n 18); S Gageler, 'Legislative Intention' (2015) 41 *Monash Law Review* 1; S Glazebrook, 'Do They Say What They Mean and Mean What They Say? Some Issues in Statutory Interpretation in the 21st Century' (2015) 14 *Otago Law Review* 61. Other concerns include Parliamentary privilege: see below, n 66.

[35] In the UK, a minister's statement as to a Bill's compatibility under s 19 of the HRA (UK) includes no details of the reasoning (eg whether the Convention is not engaged at all, or whether any infringement is considered justified). However, details of the main rights issues thought to arise are included in the Explanatory Notes: see Cabinet Office, *Guide to Making Legislation* [11.63]. Available at: www.cabinetoffice.gov.uk. In New Zealand, the Attorney General makes a formal report under s 7 of the NZ BORA only where the limitation is considered *not* justified. However, in practice, advice received by the Attorney General concluding that the limit *is* justified is published online on the Ministry of Justice website. While not presented to Parliament, that advice is certainly available to it.

[36] On the relevance of the statement not being contradicted, see Nourse (n 16), for the similar point that in using legislative history it is crucial to distinguish between winners and losers.

[37] See *R v Hansen* (n 8).

[38] *R v Lambert* [2002] 2 AC 545; also *Attorney General's Reference (No 4 of 2002)* reported as *Sheldrake v Director of Public Prosecutions* [2005] 1 AC 264.

[39] See *Hansen* (n 8) at [55], [99]. The Court did not quite rely on this as evidence that legislators were alerted to the prima facie conflict (see further below, text at nn 58–59).

[40] *Hansen* (n 8) at [63], [99].

[41] This is a relatively common occurrence in New Zealand: see, eg, Rishworth (n 22); Geddis (n 22).

All such evidence tends to show that legislators appreciated the conflict (or, further, that they considered it proportionate) which, in turn, would make use of a presumption to avoid the conflict assertive. However, such evidence often has to be weighed against competing evidence. Moreover, this evidence may also be found to have limits.

(ii) Possible Limits of the Evidence that Conflict was Appreciated

Let me now turn to consider possible limits to the above evidence that legislators appreciated the conflict. Even where legislators clearly must have appreciated the prima facie conflict, the evidence relied on might fall short of showing that legislators were aware of the *degree* of conflict.

What is in issue may be an application at the extreme disproportionate end of the spectrum of situations apparently covered by the provision, and there may be no evidence that legislators appreciated that the provision would extend to such disproportionate applications. For instance, in *Al-Kateb*,[42] *Offen*[43] and *Harrison*,[44] legislators faced with Bills providing for immigration detention, mandatory life sentences and whole-of-life sentences respectively must have appreciated that these represented prima facie conflicts with liberty, for the sake of important competing interests—just as in *R v A* it is inconceivable that they would not have appreciated the relevant conflict. However, there was no evidence indicating awareness that immigration detention might become indefinite if deportation proved unavailable; or that the mandatory sentences might apply in cases lacking anything approaching the level of culpability that could justify them. The conflict involved in those extreme cases, therefore, may not have been appreciated.[45]

Further examples include an aspect of *R v A*. The 'rape shield' provision clearly excluded evidence of prior sexual conduct between the accused and the complainant. However, it was unclear whether it extended to evidence showing the existence and nature of any existing *relationship* between them, such as that they were living together, or had gone out on dates together. If it did, that would be a very extreme limit on the fair trial right: it would result in the jury being presented with an entirely misleading picture of the background. In the absence of clear and express provision to this effect, there was no evidence that legislators must have understood the provision as conflicting with the fair trial right to that extreme extent. That could have supported a more limited use of the presumption to avoid only that extreme conflict.

More generally, it may arguably be moderate to read clearly rights-infringing provisions subject to a proportionality test, whenever there is no evidence that legislators understood the provision to extend to disproportionate applications.[46]

[42] *Al-Kateb v Godwin* (2004) 78 ALJR 1099.

[43] *R v Offen* [2001] 1 WLR 253.

[44] *R v Harrison* [2016] NZLR 602.

[45] In *Harrison*, there was some evidence directly supporting this conclusion: legislators had been led to believe that the mandatory sentence would apply in a much smaller proportion of cases than in fact eventuated: see [90].

[46] See, eg, *R v Waya* [2013] 1 AC 294 and *R (GC) v Commissioner of Police of the Metropolis* [2011] 1 WLR 1230.

The arguments discussed in this section can support a conclusion that an appropriately limited reading down amounts to moderate rather than assertive use of a presumption. This also illustrates that on the facts of the same case, courts may have a choice between different readings down that respectively represent moderate and assertive use of the presumption. Once again, however, this may need to be weighed against evidence to the contrary.

(iii) What Counts as Evidence that Legislators Understood the Provision to have a Particular Meaning or Application?

I turn now to the further (more controversial) enquiry that may be used in classifying uses of presumptions. It may be relevant to ask whether legislators specifically understood the provision as having a particular meaning or application, even if they did not appreciate that this was in conflict with a protected right, obligation or principle. Use of a presumption to contradict such a specific understanding may be considered assertive, unless it is supported by sufficient other evidence contradicting the specific understanding. Under this heading, I explore what counts as evidence of such specific understandings. I will then consider objections to reliance on this under the next heading.

Once again, the evidence of specific meanings or applications that likely formed part of legislators' understanding includes first and foremost the words of the provision in question (the provision may spell out a particular application fairly explicitly), along with the statutory context and the background. An example of both explicit words and relevant background can be found in *Hansen*, where the Court declined to read down a reverse onus provision.[47] First, the provision in question was difficult to interpret as anything other than a legal onus.[48] Secondly, Blanchard J relied on the background: case law on the virtually identical predecessor provision clearly established that it established a full legal burden.[49] That was strong evidence that legislators must have understood the new provision to operate in the same fashion. The case would have been stronger still if there had been evidence that the relevant case law had been drawn to Parliament's attention, but the evidence was fairly strong even without that.

An example of statutory context supporting a particular meaning or application can be found in *Attorney General's Reference (No 4 of 2002)*,[50] where a reverse onus provision was read down to impose only an evidential burden despite that evidence. The Act included an express provision that some defences involved only an evidential onus, but the reverse onus provision was not one of those listed there.[51]

Assuming that extrinsic evidence is admissible, strong evidence of a specific understanding would be a statement in Parliament or a report tabled in or available to Parliament, that pointed out a particular application (without pointing out its conflict

[47] See *R v Hansen* (n 8).
[48] ibid at [39], [54], [159]–[166], [255]–[257], [290].
[49] ibid at [53]; see also Tipping J at [99].
[50] Reported as *Sheldrake* (n 38).
[51] ibid, at [50].

with a protected right, principle or obligation), and that was not contradicted. For instance in *R v Poumako*,[52] the provision in issue made a new penalty retrospective. The fact that the new penalty would thereby apply to persons already before the courts at the time of enactment had been specifically pointed out during the Parliamentary debate.[53]

Similarly, in *Lacey*, the High Court of Australia read down a provision that eroded protection against double jeopardy: the provision gave an appellate court in a criminal matter 'absolute discretion' to vary the sentence, which included increasing it, but the Court held this was available only where there had been error on the part of the sentencing judge.[54] However, the Minister had specifically pointed out that the provision was intended to override the courts' similar narrow and rights-protective construction of the predecessor provision.[55] Moreover, the Minister's statement merely confirmed the inference that would otherwise have been drawn from the background. The fact that the predecessor provision was in more general terms and had been given a narrow construction would by itself have led legislators to understand that the new stronger wording was intended to reduce the protection against double jeopardy.

In both cases, the courts dismissed the statement in Parliament as irrelevant[56]—erroneously, I would argue:[57] while not determinative (being a speech by just one Member of Parliament), it was a relevant piece of evidence as to how legislators likely understood the Bill. Given that this evidence was consistent with other strong evidence including the express words of the section, its background and its evident purpose, the use of the presumption in both cases is best classified as assertive.

In contrast, evidence of this kind was accepted in *Hansen*,[58] where a reverse onus provision was interpreted as imposing a legal onus, conflicting with the presumption of consistency. In determining what Parliament intended, Blanchard J relied on the fact that advice on the Bill, available to Parliament at the time, stated several times that the clause in question imposed a legal onus.[59]

(iv) Objections to Reliance on this Type of Evidence

I turn now to objections to reliance on specific meanings or applications that formed part of legislators' understanding. First, many commentators on statutory interpretation object to considering legislative intention in terms of 'application intentions'

[52] *R v Poumako* [2000] 2 NZLR 695. What was not specifically pointed out was that this conflicted with the right against retrospective increases in penalties: see further text at n 62.

[53] ibid, at [36].

[54] See *Lacey* (n 12) at [62].

[55] ibid, at [30].

[56] See *Poumako* (n 52) at [37]; *Lacey* (n 12) at [61].

[57] That is unless extrinsic evidence is considered inadmissible altogether; but that is different from being irrelevant.

[58] See *R v Hansen* (n 8).

[59] ibid, at [55]. Recall that the advice in question also spelt out the conflict, but that further aspect was not relied on by the Court: see above, text at n 39.

(specific intentions as to how or when the provision should apply).[60] I suggest this need not be fatal to my proposed second enquiry. The objection is twofold. The first is that there is often no evidence of specific application intentions. This objection is irrelevant where there *is* evidence that legislators understood the legislation to have a particular application. The second objection is that, in any event, the interpretive search is properly for intended meaning; this may or may not coincide with intended applications (Parliament may have failed to achieve its particular application intentions by the words it used). This can be met on the basis that the evidence of specific understanding is merely one relevant piece of evidence: it may be outweighed by other conflicting evidence. It does not follow that it should not be given some weight. Where a particular application forms part of legislators' understanding and is consistent with all other available evidence of legislators' understanding, then use of the presumption to avoid this application quite arguably is assertive.

Secondly, it may be objected that courts should not give effect to conflicts with protected rights, obligations or principles unless at least there is evidence that the conflict must have been appreciated by legislators: legislators should not be allowed to override important rights, obligations and principles unawares.[61] That, however, is better understood as one of the possible arguments for *justifying* assertive uses of interpretive presumptions: it is still important for the court to acknowledge if the interpretation it is proposing to adopt, based on this argument, goes against all available evidence of legislators' likely understanding and is therefore assertive.

Thirdly, in the face of evidence of specific understandings that conflict with protected rights, obligations or principles, it may still be argued that legislators would not have voted for the measure if they had appreciated the conflict. That was one of the arguments relied on in *R v Pora*[62] (concerning the same provision as *Poumako*).[63] The provision in issue there provided that a new mandatory non-parole period was to apply retrospectively. The minority judgments queried whether legislators appreciated that non-parole periods amounted to penalties and thus engaged the right against retrospective increases in penalty.[64] A similar argument might be made in the reverse onus cases: perhaps legislators did not appreciate that the presumption of innocence was engaged. There is some doubt about the legitimacy of this type of objection, as it might fall foul of arguments against counterfactual reasoning in statutory interpretation,[65] and also of Parliamentary privilege.[66] In any event, such an argument must also be weighed against all other available evidence.

[60] A Marmor, *Interpretation and Legal Theory*, 2nd rev edn (Oxford, Hart Publishing, 2005) 129–31; J Evans, 'Controlling the Use of Parliamentary History' (1998) 18 *New Zealand Universities Law Review* 1 at 14.

[61] That is part of the argument in *Simms* (n 4) at 132 (Lord Hoffmann).

[62] *R v Pora* [2001] 2 NZLR 37.

[63] *Poumako* (n 52).

[64] ibid, at [15], [45]–[48].

[65] See Marmor (n 60) at 130.

[66] According to *British Railways Board v Pickin* [1974] AC 765, an Act cannot be rendered invalid by Parliament having enacted it under a mistake. However, here the mistake is used not to invalidate the Act but to ascertain legislators' understanding for the purposes of interpretation. On whether use of *Hansard* generally violates Parliamentary privilege, see CJ Iorns-Magallanes, 'The "Just Do It" Approach to Using Parliamentary History Materials in Statutory Interpretation' (2009) 15 *Canterbury Law Review* 205 at 211.

(v) The Outer Limits of Moderate Reading Down

Finally, whenever the available evidence on balance leaves room for moderate use of a presumption, it is still necessary to consider the impact of the proposed re-interpretation on the provision's scope of operation, both in terms of quality and quantity. The outer limits to any moderate use of the presumption must be set by the need for the provision in issue to retain some meaningful scope of operation, to address the 'mischief' that gave rise to it, and to serve its purpose.[67] Whatever particular understanding legislators may have had, they will have understood the Bill as having these features. Legislative purpose is a particularly significant aspect of legislators' understanding:[68] legislators' understanding of the purpose will shape their understanding of the detail of the legislation, as well as centrally influence their decision whether to support the legislation.

For example, a further reason to consider *R v A* assertive is because of the terms of the reading down adopted, which was to give trial judges discretion to admit any evidence of prior sexual conduct that was so relevant that its admission was necessary for a fair trial. For one thing, this very significantly reduced the protection for complainants. Moreover, it re-introduced the 'mischief' that had given rise to the legislation. The discretion solution had been tried in the predecessor legislation,[69] and had been abandoned because it had been found to provide very limited protection for rape complainants. Trial judges had tended to resolve any doubt in favour of admitting the evidence.[70] In *Waya*, the Supreme Court at least purported to avoid this type of problem. In deciding to read a confiscation provision subject to a proportionality test, it emphasised that this was not the same as the judicial discretion in earlier legislation that had been discarded.[71]

Another example is found in *Sellers*.[72] The court relied on the presumption of consistency with international law to effectively exclude foreign vessels from the reach of a statutory power to set minimum safety requirements for vessels departing New Zealand ports. This interpretation excised a very significant proportion of the provision's apparent scope.[73] Moreover it had a major effect on the provision's capacity

[67] See P Rishworth, 'The New Zealand Bill of Rights Act 1990: The First Fifteen Months' in Legal Research Foundation (ed), *Essays on the New Zealand Bill of Rights Act 1990* (Auckland, Legal Research Foundation, 1992) 7, 28. Indeed, the development of purposive interpretation was, at least in part, an attempt to contain excessive use of an interpretive presumption protective of the common law: see New Zealand Law Commission, *A New Interpretation Act to Avoid 'Prolixity and Tautology'* (NZLC R17, 1990) at [36], [40].

[68] See Goldsworthy (n 3) at 61–62.

[69] A Kavanagh, 'Unlocking the Human Rights Act: The "Radical" Approach to Section 3(1) Revisited' [2005] *European Human Rights Law Review* 259 at 267–69 objects to this claim, pointing out that the discretion introduced in *R v A* was more limited than that in the earlier legislation. However, this was at best a difference in degree. The experience showing trial judges' tendency to favour procedural rights for defendants would still render even a more limited discretion a doubtful means for protecting complainants.

[70] See *R v A* (n 10) at [107] (Lord Hope).

[71] See *Waya* (n 46) at [40].

[72] See *Sellers* (n 11).

[73] P Myburgh, 'Shipping Law' [1999] *New Zealand Law Review* 387 at 398.

to serve its most likely purpose, which was to avoid unnecessary waste of resources in marine search and rescue.[74]

In contrast, in *Drew*,[75] neither the scope nor the purpose of a power to make regulations governing the procedure at disciplinary hearings was significantly affected by requiring regulations to be consistent with the right to natural justice.[76] The same is also true of the reading down in *Witham*,[77] despite very assertive rhetoric in that decision.[78] The scope of the Lord Chancellor's power to set court fees was only marginally diminished and any likely purpose was not centrally affected, by reading down that power so as to exclude fees that would take away access to the courts for the impecunious.

The last two examples should not, however, be taken as meaning that use of interpretive presumptions will always be weak or moderate when applied to discretionary powers. It will be assertive if there is any evidence that legislators must have understood the discretion to extend to exercises in prima facie conflict with the protected right, obligation or principle; or if the particular reading down frustrates the purpose or nullifies the operation of the provision. For instance, in *Lacey* the provision in question expressly conferred an 'absolute discretion'.[79] The use of the presumption to place significant constraints on that discretion was arguably assertive because it re-introduced the mischief that gave rise to the legislation.[80]

The more narrowly tailored a re-interpretation is, the less likely it is to be assertive. Uses of presumptions such as those in *Harrison*, *Offen* and the dissent in *Al-Kateb* that avoid only extreme and disproportionate applications of rights-limiting provisions[81] are thus less likely to be assertive.

However, the purpose test leaves significant room for judicial manoeuvre. Where a purpose has to be implied, there is often a choice between broader and narrower options. In *Al-Kateb*,[82] for instance, the majority considered the proposed reading down of the immigration detention provision to be unavailable. That was because for the majority the purpose of detaining immigrants awaiting deportation was to keep dangerous persons out of the community; in contrast, the dissenters considered the purpose to be limited to facilitating deportation. The majority's broader purpose would have been frustrated by even the dissenters' narrow reading down that allowed release where there was no prospect of deportation.[83]

[74] That was certainly how the Director of Maritime Safety understood the purpose of the provision: *Sellers* (n 11) at 48–49.

[75] *Drew v Attorney General* [2002] 2 NZLR 58.

[76] Indeed, there was express provision for a right to be heard at disciplinary hearings elsewhere in the statute; this was relied on as evidence that the regulation-making power in issue was not intended to be used in conflict with natural justice: ibid [12], [56], [58]. In light of this, the use of the presumption in this case was weak: the same conclusion would have been reached without it.

[77] *R v Lord Chancellor ex p Witham* [1998] QB 575. And see now R (UNISON) v Lord Chancellor [2017] 3 WLR 409.

[78] See Part IV.A.(2).

[79] See *Lacey* (n 12).

[80] See discussion at nn 54–56.

[81] See text above at nn 42–45.

[82] *Al-Kateb* (n 42).

[83] See R Thwaites, *The Liberty of Non-Citizens: Indefinite Detention in Commonwealth Countries* (Oxford, Hart Publishing, 2014) 77. For disagreement on purpose affecting the scope for reading down, see also *R (GC) v Commissioner of Police of the Metropolis* (n 46).

IV. THE TESTS AND APPROACHES USED IN THE CASES

The examples used in Part III tend to confirm the view that different interpretive presumptions have been used assertively in different jurisdictions. *R v A* is an example of the UK courts' assertive use of the interpretive direction in section 3 of the HRA. In New Zealand, in contrast, *Hansen* avoided assertive use of the corresponding interpretive direction in section 6 of the Bill of Rights. What has been used assertively in New Zealand is the presumption of consistency with international law, as seen for example in *Sellers*. That presumption has not been used assertively in the UK or Australia. The assertive use in the New Zealand *Poumako* case involved all three presumptions. In Australia, *Lacey* is an example of assertive use of the principle of legality. That presumption has only occasionally been used assertively in the UK; despite assertive rhetoric in *Witham*, the use of the presumption in that case was moderate.

In this part, I turn to examine the tests that have become established in case law for the availability of interpretive presumptions. These differ between the various interpretive presumptions and between the three Commonwealth jurisdictions considered in this chapter. I first compare these tests and then assess them against my criterion of consistency with what can be ascertained as to legislators' likely understanding of the final Bill.

A. Identifying and Comparing the Different Tests

(i) Consistency with Unincorporated International Treaties

For the presumption of consistency with unincorporated international treaty obligations, UK case law still maintains an ambiguity requirement: the preference for a consistent interpretation is triggered only where there is an ambiguity on the face of the statute.[84] It should also be noted, however, that the common law rights protected by the principle of legality (where a different test applies) have often been enhanced in reliance on international human rights instruments.[85] In Australia, two recent decisions of the Supreme Court of Victoria have abandoned the ambiguity requirement,[86] but the High Court has, so far, by and large maintained it.[87]

[84] *R v Secretary of State for the Home Department, ex p Brind* [1991] 1 AC 696 at 747–48; *R (SG) v Secretary of State for Work and Pensions* [2015] 1 WLR 1449 at [115], [137], [239] (but *cf* Lord Kerr's dissent at [254] and [257], proposing an exception for human rights treaties). For international obligations as implied mandatory considerations, see *E v Chief Constable of the Royal Ulster Constabulary* [2009] 1 AC 536 at [60]; but *cf R (Yam) v Central Criminal Court* [2016] AC 771 at [35].

[85] This was noted in Dyzenhaus, Hunt and Taggart (n 13) at 18.

[86] *Director of Public Prosecutions v Kaba* [2014] VSC 52 at [145]; *Royal Women's Hospital v Medical Practitioners Board of Victoria* (2006) 15 VR 22 at [75].

[87] *Plaintiff S157/2002 v Commonwealth* (2003) 211 CLR 476 at [29]; *Kartinyeri v Commonwealth* (1998) 195 CLR 337 at 386. Even where the Act refers to a treaty being implemented, the express provision in s 15AB of the Acts Interpretation Act 1901 (Cwth) for taking that treaty into account is limited to resolving ambiguity, confirming the ordinary meaning or avoiding a manifestly absurd meaning.

Crucially, this requirement means that general words or discretionary powers will not be read subject to international law obligations.[88]

This requirement has been abandoned in New Zealand, where the presumption has been readily applied to general words or discretionary powers.[89] However, the courts have not gone so far as to say that only express words can override international obligations,[90] as has at times been suggested for the principle of legality.[91] There is authority that discretionary powers can be read down only so far as this is consistent with the scheme of the legislation and does not frustrate the purpose.[92] A purposive limit has, however, certainly not been uniformly observed.[93]

(ii) Principle of Legality

For the principle of legality—the presumption of consistency with fundamental common law rights—the test that has been adopted in all three jurisdictions considered in this chapter is that such rights can be abrogated only by express words or necessary implication. General or ambiguous words will be read as not authorising infringements of such rights.[94]

In relation to general words or discretionary powers, this involves the opposite starting point to that adopted in relation to international law in the UK: rather than being automatically incapable of a rights-consistent interpretation, general words or discretionary powers will always be read subject to rights unless there is a good argument to the contrary. Ambiguity on the face of the provision is not a precondition. The established test in this area concerns not whether use of the presumption of consistency is permitted, but whether the presumption is rebutted: only express words or necessary implication will rebut the presumption of consistency.

Much depends, however, on the details of this test. Two points may be noted. First, Laws J in *Witham* insisted that only express words will be accepted as abrogating fundamental common law rights—the class of cases where necessary implication will suffice is 'a class with no members'.[95] However, there is overwhelming authority in favour of necessary implication being sufficient.[96]

[88] See *Brind* (n 84) at 723, 734. See also *Ashby v Minister of Immigration* [1981] 1 NZLR 222.

[89] See *Sellers* (n 11) at 57, 59; *Zaoui* (n 11) at [63]; *Ye* (n 11) at [21], [24]–[25], [31]–[32]. The development is noted, eg, in T Dunworth, 'Public International Law' [2000] *New Zealand Law Review* 217.

[90] Though, where the most important international obligations are at stake, that may be the implication of the severe reading down in *Zaoui* (n 11): see C Geiringer, 'International Law Through the Lens of Zaoui: Where is New Zealand At?' (2006) 17 *Public Law Review* 300 at 317.

[91] On which, see below at n 95.

[92] *New Zealand Airline Pilots' Association Inc v Attorney General* [1997] 3 NZLR 269 at 189–92. This may also be implicit in the reasoning in *Ye* (n 11) at [19]–[21] and [31]–[36]: see H Wilberg, 'Administrative Law' [2010] *New Zealand Law Review* 177 at 201–02.

[93] For instance, see *Sellers* (n 11) and the discussion at n 74.

[94] *Simms* (n 4) 131; *Coco v The Queen* (1994) 179 CLR 427 at 437; *Cropp v Judicial Committee* [2008] 3 NZLR 774 at [27].

[95] See *Witham* (n 77) at 586. Some support for this may also be found in the dissenting judgment of Elias CJ in *R v Pora* (n 62).

[96] Aside from the authoritative statement in *Simms* (n 4), Laws J's view on this point was expressly doubted in *R v Secretary of State for the Home Department, ex parte Pierson* [1998] AC 539 at 575 and rejected in *R v Lord Chancellor, ex parte Lightfoot* [2000] QB 597 at 627–28. See also *Bank Mellatt v Her Majesty's Treasury (No 2)* [2014] AC 700 at [55]–[56]; *Coco* (n 94) at 436; *Cropp* (n 94) at [26]; and the further authorities cited below in nn 101, 104 and 106 on the meaning of necessary implication.

An express words requirement may perhaps apply when seeking to amend constitutional statutes[97]—a related issue. I suggest, however, that this is open to debate.[98] Even if there is good authority for this, it does not follow at all necessarily that the same requirement must be met for rebutting the principle of legality. The line of authority directly relating to the principle of legality and contemplating abrogation by necessary implication is clearly the more relevant on this point.

Despite that rejection of the express words requirement for rebutting the principle of legality, however, a related approach appears to linger on. It is sometimes assumed that general words or discretionary powers are automatically capable of a rights-consistent narrow reading.[99] That amounts to assuming that only express words can abrogate common law rights, although it is not put in those terms. It must be erroneous: once it is accepted that rights can be abrogated by necessary implication, then that test has to be applied to general words or discretionary powers at least as much as to ambiguous words.[100]

Secondly, we need to know what counts as a necessary implication. The most commonly quoted formulation comes from the concurring judgment of Lord Hobhouse in *Morgan Grenfell*:[101]

> A necessary implication is not the same as a reasonable implication ... A necessary implication is one which necessarily follows from the express provisions of the statute construed in their context. It distinguishes between what it would have been sensible or reasonable for

[97] *H v Lord Advocate* [2013] 1 AC 413 at [30]. This paragraph as a whole may be read as endorsing the recognition of a category of constitutional statutes in *Thoburn v Sutherland City Council* [2003] 1 QB 151. If so, then it is authority for an express words requirement for amending such constitutional statutes.

[98] The doubt concerns whether paragraph [30] does endorse *Thoburn*'s category of constitutional statutes. *Thoburn* was cited in argument but is not mentioned in the judgments—a rather pointed omission one might think. The only general principle invoked in this paragraph is the presumption against implied repeal. The first and main argument against amendment is specific to the particular legislation in issue here: the Scottish Ministers derive their very existence from the Scotland Act 1998. That is why the Ministers cannot have any powers to act other than consistently with the provisions of that Act, and other legislation would need to use express words to give them such broader powers. This argument has echoes of the reasoning in support of upholding manner and form restrictions on the powers of colonial Parliaments where those restrictions appear in the instrument that creates the Parliament (*Bribery Commissioner v Ranasinghe* [1965] AC 172 (PC) 197–98). Thus, if paragraph [30] does amount to recognising a category of constitutional statutes, then this category seems a lot more limited than that put forward in *Thoburn*: the statute has to be constitutional in the sense of constitutive of the relevant institution of government. The reference to the 'fundamental constitutional nature of the settlement that was achieved by the Scotland Act' must be read in that light. On that basis, the analogy with the principle of legality is even more distant than it would have been in the case of the *Thoburn* version.

[99] This seems to be implied whenever courts find that a discretionary power can be read subject to a common law right without engaging in any statutory interpretation: see, eg, *Simms* (n 4) 130; *R (Osborn) v Parole Board* [2014] AC 1115 (the legislative framework is outlined at [3]–[11], but this goes no further than establishing that a right to an oral hearing in earlier legislation had been abolished: there is no explicit consideration whether anything in the current legislation might exclude or limit application of the common law right). However, it may also be that courts in these cases work on the assumption that the purpose test will never require disproportionate limits to be upheld: for discussion of this link (which is, in fact, only partial), see Wilberg (n 20) at 163–65.

[100] Some of the cases cited in nn 105 and 106 involved general words or discretionary powers.

[101] *R (Morgan Grenfell & Co Ltd) v Special Commissioner of Income Tax* [2003] 1 AC 563 at [45]. This has been adopted for New Zealand by the Privy Council in *B v Auckland District Law Society* [2004] 1 NZLR 326 at [58] (it was also quoted in *Cropp* (n 94) at [26], but only as part of a statement of counsel's argument).

> Parliament to have included or what Parliament would, if it had thought about it, probably have included and what it is clear that the express language of the statute shows that the statute must have included. A necessary implication is a matter of express language and logic not interpretation.

In analysing Australian case law, Jeffrey Goldsworthy has identified two slightly different versions of the test.[102] *Coco* adopted a practical necessity test: where the implication 'is necessary to prevent the statutory provisions from becoming inoperative or meaningless'.[103] The alternative is an obviousness test, which was stated in *Lee* as applying where the implication 'is compelled by the reading of the statute'.[104]

There is also authority for limiting use of the principle of legality by a purpose test.[105] Some cases recognise this as a version of the necessary implication test:[106] if the purpose of a provision would be defeated by avoiding infringement of the right, then infringement of the right is authorised by necessary implication. However, more often the necessary implication test is stated without express reference to purpose.

How stringent, then, really is the necessary implication test used for the principle of legality? There is no clearly established answer to this. On the one hand, the *Morgan Grenfell* formulation sounds very stringent and not very far removed from the discarded *Witham* approach: rights-infringing meanings will be very difficult to defend except where they are spelt out by express words.[107] On the other hand, if the fact that a consistent interpretation would frustrate the purpose gives rise to a necessary implication, then the test is less stringent than it appeared: rights-infringing meanings will be available wherever they are demanded by a purposive interpretation.

The application of the test has also not been entirely consistent. In some cases, the effect has indeed been rather stringent. For instance, the majority in *Evans*[108] read down a fairly explicit provision in section 53 of the Freedom of Information Act 2000 that allowed the Attorney General to override a Tribunal order for disclosure under that Act by issuing a 'certificate … that he has on reasonable grounds formed the opinion' that non-disclosure would not be unlawful. These words did not give rise to a necessary implication that the relevant rule of law principles were abrogated to the extent of allowing the Attorney General's opinion on reasonable grounds to

[102] See Goldsworthy (n 3) at 60–61.

[103] See *Coco* (n 94) at 436.

[104] *Lee v NSW Crime Commission* (2013) 251 CLR 196 at [173].

[105] Some of the authority pre-dates the modern principle of legality and involves the predecessor presumptions of consistency with particular common law rights: eg *R v Hartz* [1967] 1 AC 760 at 816–17; *Pyneboard Pty Ltd v Trade Practices Commission* (1983) 45 ALR 609 at 617–19; *Taylor v NZ Poultry Board* [1984] 1 NZLR 394 at 402, 405 (privilege against self-incrimination); *Daganayasi v Minster of Immigration* [1980] 2 NZLR 130 at 141 (right to natural justice). Note also the cases on the statutory interpretive directions: below n 116.

[106] *B v ADLS* (n 101) [59]; *X7 v Australian Crime Commission* (2013) 248 CLR 92 at [142]; see also *Lee* (n 104) at [30]. See also, in the context of a different presumption, *Poynter v Commerce Commission* (n 25) at [46].

[107] That must be what P Craig *Administrative Law*, 7th edn (Sweet & Maxwell, London, 2012) 579 has in mind in saying that the approach in *Simms* is 'very similar to' that in *Witham* because it leaves open the possibility of abrogation by necessary implication only in 'extreme cases'.

[108] *R (Evans) v Information Commissioner* [2015] AC 1787 (the 'Black Spider Memos' case).

override the Tribunal. Construed in light of the principle of legality, the power was available only where there had been a 'material change in circumstances' or where the Tribunal's decision was demonstrably flawed.[109]

Even more stringent, of course, is the test applied to statutory ouster of judicial review: the express terms of such provisions are effectively ignored.[110] While that approach pre-dates the modern principle of legality, it represents one of that principle's precursor presumptions of consistency with fundamental common law rights and principles.

In other cases, though, a necessary implication has seemed rather easier to make out. For instance, in *Bank Mellat*[111] the express provisions for the Court of Appeal to employ a closed materials procedure—severely abrogating the right to natural justice—were held to give rise to a necessary implication that the same procedure must be employed in an appeal to the Supreme Court, despite the absence of any provision to that effect. Otherwise, the latter Court would be left with the choice of either requiring disclosure of classified information or deciding the case on the basis of highly incomplete information.[112] One might have thought that if there is a distinction between reasonable and necessary implication (as was insisted in *Morgan Grenfell*), this case would at most satisfy the former.

(iii) Interpretive Directions in Bills of Rights

I turn finally to the interpretive directions in statutory bills of rights. Since these are essentially statutory versions of the principle of legality,[113] one might have expected the same test to apply. However, the statutory formulation is different from the principle of legality (it requires a search for a rights-consistent interpretation) and a new approach is formulated in the cases largely in isolation from the pre-existing case law. It is only occasionally that the express words or necessary implication test is invoked in this context.[114]

The three jurisdictions again diverge on the test. In the United Kingdom, section 3 of the Human Rights Act 1998 has been held to authorise and indeed require a rights-consistent interpretation of other legislation even if that interpretation both

[109] ibid, at [68], [71]–[78], [86]–[89] (Lord Neuberger, with whom Lord Reed and Lord Kerr agreed). For further examples, see the majority in *R v Poumako* (n 52); *Lacey* (n 12).

[110] See *Anisminic* (n 5); *Bulk Gas Users Group v Attorney General* [1983] NZLR 129. See also *Plaintiff S157/2002 v Commonwealth* (2003) 211 CLR 476 where the clause was interpreted by reference to statutory assumptions which led to the same result.

[111] *Bank Mellat* (n 96).

[112] ibid, at [37]–[43], [55]–[59]. For another example, see *Canterbury Regional Council v Independent Fisheries Ltd* [2013] 2 NZLR 57 at [136]–[149] (the part addressing the access to court issue).

[113] *Simpson v Attorney General (Baigent's Case)* [1994] 3 NZLR 667 at 712 (Gault J); *Attorney General v Ngati Apa* [2003] 3 NZLR 643 at [82] (Elias CJ); *Simms* (n 4) at 132 (Lord Hoffmann); *Ghaidan v Godin-Mendoza* [2004] 2 AC 557 at [104] (Lord Rodger); *Momcilovic v The Queen* (2011) 245 CLR 1 at [41]–[51] (French CJ).

[114] See *R v A* (n 10) at [108] (Lord Hope, dissenting); *Lambert* (n 38) at [79] (Lord Hope); *Ghaidan* (n 113) at [117] (Lord Rodger); *Cropp* (n 94) at [26] (reporting counsel's argument without express approval). Also, without noting that this is the test for the principle of legality, *R (Anderson) v Secretary of State for the Home Department* [2003] 1 AC 837 at [59] (Lord Steyn); *R (Rusbridger) v Attorney General* [2003] UKHL 38 at [8] (Lord Steyn); P Rishworth et al, *The New Zealand Bill of Rights* (Auckland,

departs from the intention of the enacting Parliament and is inconsistent with the unambiguous meaning of the words, as long as it is not inconsistent with a fundamental feature of the legislation.[115] While there is a wide variety of statements on what amounts to a fundamental feature, several cases suggest that the 'overall' or 'essential' purpose of the legislation represents a fundamental feature.[116] Even if the overall legislative purpose has to be respected, however, other cases expressly adopt section 3 interpretations directly contrary to the meaning that must have been understood by the enacting Parliament.[117]

In New Zealand, the Supreme Court in *Hansen* insisted that a rights-consistent interpretation adopted pursuant to section 6 of the New Zealand Bill of Rights Act 1990 must be 'genuinely open' in light of the provision's 'text and its purpose'.[118] In clear contrast with the UK position, where there was clear evidence that Parliament's intended meaning corresponded with the natural meaning of the provision, the Court considered that that intention must be respected.[119] This approach, however, has not always been consistently applied.[120]

In Australia, the two state-level bills of rights expressly require rights-consistent interpretations to be consistent with the purpose of the provision being interpreted.[121] The High Court of Australia has interpreted this as entailing an approach along similar lines to *Hansen*.[122]

In comparing these approaches with the approaches to the other two interpretive presumptions, one point is clear. In common with the principle of legality, but unlike with the UK and Australian approach to the presumption of consistency with international law, ambiguity is not required as a pre-condition in any of the three jurisdictions. General words and discretionary powers are amenable to reading down as readily as are ambiguous words.[123] Also as with the principle of legality, it is sometimes assumed that discretionary powers are automatically amenable to

Oxford University Press, 2003) 159; M Amos *Human Rights Law*, 2nd edn (Oxford, Hart Publishing, 2014) 121.

[115] See *Ghaidan* (n 113) at [30]–[33]; *Sheldrake* (n 38) at [28]. In my view, this approach was not necessary to reach the conclusion in the former case; but it was necessary in the latter: see text at n 117.

[116] See *Waya* (n 46) at [21] ('essential purpose'); *Principal Reporter v K* [2011] 1 WLR 18 [69] ('overall purpose'), also [60]; *GC* (n 46) at [23]–[27], [83], [114]–[115], [144]–[145] (Court divided on the application of this test).

[117] See *Attorney General's Reference (No 4 of 2002)*, reported as *Sheldrake* (n 38) at [50], [53].

[118] See *Hansen* (n 8) at [61]; see also [150], [252], [290]. For requiring consistency with purpose, see also *Ministry of Transport v Noort* [1992] 3 NZLR 260; *Zaoui* (n 11) at [36].

[119] See *Hansen* (n 8) at [61] at [156].

[120] See, for instance, *Re Application by AMM and KJO to Adopt a Child* [2010] NZFLR 629 at [31], [50] for interpretation expressly departing from the meaning intended by the enacting Parliament; see also *Poumako* (n 52), *Zaoui* (n 11) and *Hopkinson v Police* [2004] 3 NZLR 704 for distinctly strained interpretations.

[121] CHRRA (Vic), s 32(1); HRA (ACT), s 30.

[122] See *Momcilovic* (n 113) at [46], [62], [146], [170]–[171], [280], [544]–[545], [684].

[123] See *R v A* (n 10) at [44]; *Ghaidan* (n 113) at [29]; *Cropp* (n 94) at [27]. Examples of discretionary powers being read down include *GC* (n 46); *Drew* (n 75). Contrast an early NZ case: *Knight v Commissioner of Inland Revenue* [1991] 2 NZLR 30 at 43 (Hardie Boys J). Under the HRA, a corresponding question arises as to the scope of s 6(2)(b): eg *GC* (n 46); *Doherty v Birmingham City Council* [2009] 1 AC 367.

reading down;[124] but other sources do ask whether such reading would frustrate the purpose.[125]

Beyond that point, it is less certain exactly how the necessary implication approach to the principle of legality compares with the approach to the statutory interpretive directions. The question is relatively rarely addressed; and attempts at comparison are not helped by the fact that that the precise meaning of each approach is uncertain. When the question is addressed, however, the answer appears to vary between jurisdictions. The UK fundamental feature approach is usually considered to be stronger than the approach to the principle of legality.[126] The NZ and Australian purpose and text consistent approach has more often been seen as no different from the approach to the principle of legality.[127]

The directly relevant point of comparison for present purposes is the extent to which each approach is limited to uses that are consistent with legislators' likely understanding. That question is examined under the next heading.

B. Assessing the Established Tests in Light of Proposed Approach

How do these various tests relate to my proposed approach? Recall that my approach seeks to ascertain legislators' likely understanding. It assesses uses of interpretive presumptions as weak, moderate or assertive on the basis of their consistency with that understanding, by asking whether legislators likely appreciated the conflict between the Bill and the right, obligation or principle protected by the presumption.

What is clear is that both the ambiguity requirement and the express words requirement should be rejected on this basis: they simply do not assist in determining the extent to which a proposed use of an interpretive presumption would be consistent with legislators' likely understanding. The remaining tests in the cases can be applied to turn on legislators' likely understanding, but the record on this is uncertain and unsettled. In this section I expand on these three points.

(i) Rejecting the Ambiguity Requirement

Defenders of strong use of presumptions have attacked the ambiguity requirement, casting doubt on whether it ever represented the orthodox position, as well as

[124] See, eg, Rishworth et al (n 114) at 158–59; Rishworth (n 29) at 341, 346. Such an assumption also seems implicit in *GC* (n 46) at [56], [69]; *Television New Zealand Ltd v Attorney General* (2004) 8 HRNZ 45. See also what amounts to an express words requirement in *R v A* (n 10) at [44] (Lord Steyn); but that was expressly rejected in *In Re S (Minors) (Care Order: Implementation of Care Plan)* [2002] 2 AC 291 at [40] (Lord Nicholls).

[125] See, eg, *GC* (n 46) at [23]–[27], [83], [114]–[115], [144]–[145]; A Butler and P Butler, *The New Zealand Bill of Rights Act: A Commentary*, 2nd edn (Wellington, LexisNexis NZ, 2015) [7.13.1], [7.13.14]; M Taggart, 'Tugging on Superman's Cape: Lessons from Experience with the New Zealand Bill of Rights Act 1990' [1998] *PL* 266 at 284; Rishworth et al (n 114) at 140.

[126] *Ahmed v Her Majesty's Treasury* [2010] 2 AC 534 at [117] (Lord Phillips); Sales (n 26) at 610–11.

[127] C Geiringer, 'The Principle of Legality and the Bill of Rights Act: A Critical Examination of *R v Hansen*' (2008) 6 *New Zealand Journal of Public and International Law* 59; Butler and Butler (n 125) [7.16.1]–[7.16.2].

attacking it as lacking in logical justification.[128] On this point, proponents of interpretation according to legislators' likely understanding can agree wholeheartedly. The ambiguity requirement is of no service to this proposed approach to interpretation: neither the presence of ambiguity nor its absence determines whether use of a presumption is inconsistent with legislators' likely understanding and hence assertive. It is always necessary to weigh up all available evidence of legislators' likely understanding, regardless whether or not the words are ambiguous.

On the one hand, even where there is no ambiguity in the statutory text, interpretations supported by interpretive presumptions that depart from the unambiguous meaning may still be consistent with the best available evidence of legislators' likely understanding. This is likely to be rare,[129] since the words are the primary evidence of likely understanding. Still, they are not the only relevant evidence. The balance of the evidence may point to a meaning at variance with the unambiguous literal meaning.[130] Where that is so, the use of an interpretive presumption to support that meaning is only weak or moderate, despite going against unambiguous text.

On the other hand, interpretations supported by interpretive presumptions may be inconsistent with the best available evidence of legislators' likely understanding even where the statutory text is ambiguous and the interpretation supported by the interpretive presumption is one of the available literal meanings. This is likely to be quite common. In such a case, the use of the interpretive presumption would be assertive, despite supporting one of the available literal meanings in the presence of ambiguity. In other words, adherence to the ambiguity requirement would not by itself prevent assertive use of presumptions. In cases where there is ambiguity, the range of possible meanings that could then be chosen based on interpretive presumptions would often include some that would be quite inconsistent with legislators' likely understanding.[131]

I should emphasise that the rejection of the ambiguity requirement and the first point above in particular do not mean that the plain, unambiguous words of a provision will never stand in the way of using an interpretive presumption to depart from the unambiguous meaning: to the contrary, they usually will. Following the approach proposed here, the question is always whether the departure from the plain, unambiguous meaning that is called for by the interpretative presumption is also supported by some strong evidence of legislators' likely understanding that is at variance with the literal meaning. Only then is such departure not assertive.

(ii) Discretionary Powers: Rejecting both the Ambiguity Requirement and the Express Words Requirement

Where discretionary powers are concerned, two of the tests found in the cases clearly fail to serve the purpose of ascertaining consistency with legislators' likely

[128] See, eg, Dyzenhaus, Hunt and Taggart (n 13) at 26.

[129] It is not rare, however, in relation to discretionary powers that are considered 'unambiguous' pursuant to *Brind* (n 84).

[130] This is consistent with Jones and Bennion (n 5) at s 2(1) and s 150: even in the absence of grammatical ambiguity, they say the best meaning (the 'legal meaning' in their terms) of a provision may be one that is a strained meaning of the words.

[131] That would be what Ekins (n 9) has labelled 'semantic opportunism'.

understanding. They are the position in *Brind* that a discretionary power does not represent ambiguity and hence is not open to be read subject to presumptions; and conversely the express words requirement in *Witham*, which lingers on in the occasional assumption that discretionary powers can always be read subject to presumptions. On the approach proposed here, both are wrong.

The position in *Brind* is indeed doubly wrong. First, I have already argued that the ambiguity requirement ought to be abandoned altogether. Secondly, *Brind* is wrong even if ambiguity is to be a precondition to the use of presumptions. On this point too we can agree wholeheartedly with proponents of strong use of presumptions. As they have argued, the legal scope of a discretionary power conferred by statute is assuredly a question for the court to determine by a process of statutory interpretation[132]—indeed that is one central tenets of administrative law.[133] By far the better view, therefore, is that a discretionary power is ambiguous in the relevant sense: the literal words do not determine its scope (once it is accepted that the scope cannot be as unlimited as it may appear to be on the face of the provision).[134] Interpretive presumptions may be relevant to this interpretive choice as much as to any other.

Conversely, the express words requirement and the related assumption that discretionary powers are automatically amenable to reading down are equally wrong. As already noted, determining the scope of a discretionary power requires recourse to all the available evidence of legislators' likely understanding.[135] The fact that a discretionary power may lack any express words authorising its exercise in conflict with the right, obligation or principle cannot be determinative. While interpretive presumptions may be used alongside evidence of legislators' likely understanding in this context as elsewhere, the question is always whether their use contradicts that likely understanding. If it does contradict it—because the available evidence on balance supports the conclusion that legislators likely appreciated and hence accepted the conflict with the protected right, obligation or principle—then the use of the presumption is assertive.

(iii) Assessing the Necessary Implication Test and the Approaches to Statutory Interpretive Directions

The *Hansen* approach to section 6 of the NZ Bill of Rights is consistent with the approach advocated here—except, of course, that it relies on the more usual notion of legislative intention rather than on the likely understanding of legislators in the enacting Parliament.

Whether the necessary implication test for the principle of legality and the fundamental feature test for section 3 of the HRA are consistent with my approach

[132] See Dyzenhaus, Hunt and Taggart (n 13) at 26. See also, albeit in a different context, *Spath Holme* (n 33) at 398 (Lord Nicholls), 400 (Lord Cooke) (both dissenting on this point).

[133] See *Padfield v Minister of Agriculture, Fisheries and Food* [1968] AC 997; more recently affirmed in *Spath Holme* (n 33) at 381, 396, 404.

[134] See Jones and Bennion (n 5): while broad discretions are not *grammatically* ambiguous (s 151(3)), conversely the legal meaning of a provision is not determined solely by its grammatical meaning, even where that grammatical meaning is unambiguous (s 2(1) and s 150).

[135] Part III.C.(v).

depends on the meaning of those tests: they may or may not serve the function of ascertaining consistency with legislators' likely understanding at least to some extent. We saw some support in the cases for treating both of these tests as turning on legislative purpose: a rights-consistent meaning is available and must be adopted unless it would frustrate the purpose of the provision in question.[136] As already noted, legislative purpose is a centrally important aspect of legislators' likely understanding.[137] Accordingly, this version serves to avoid one significant form of inconsistency with legislators' likely understanding, and thus to avoid assertive use to that extent. Similarly, in Australia, the *Coco* version of the necessary implication test avoids use of the principle of legality to render a provision inoperative or meaningless.[138] To that extent, this version also avoids assertive uses.[139]

The fundamental feature approach, however, even in a version that turns on purpose, still calls for disregarding clear evidence of the specific meaning and application expected by legislators.[140] Unless that clear evidence is outweighed by other evidence of legislators' likely understanding, even this version of the approach involves assertive use of the presumption.[141]

The disregard for 'legislative intention' has sometimes been justified on the basis that what matters is the legislative intention behind section 3 of the HRA.[142] That is one of the arguments that might be considered to *justify* assertive use of the section 3 presumption,[143] but it does not render the use moderate: moderate use is consistent with legislators' likely understanding of the legislation being interpreted, not of the HRA.

Finally, recall that it is not clearly established that the necessary implication and fundamental feature approaches do turn on legislative purpose at all. What, then, do we make of them if they do not? It is quite simply difficult to know what they would mean.[144] The main point, however, is this. Rejection of a legislative purpose test would seem to put these tests, like the ambiguity requirement and express words test, into the category of tests that fail to assess proposed uses of interpretive presumptions by the appropriate criterion, namely whether they are consistent with legislators' likely understanding.

V. CONCLUSION

In this chapter, I have taken as my starting point that statutory interpretation should ordinarily respect the likely understanding of legislators in the enacting Parliament.

136 Part IV.A.(ii) and (iii).
137 Part III.C.(v).
138 Part IV.A.(ii).
139 See Part III.C.(v).
140 See Part IV.A.(iii).
141 See Part III.C.(iv).
142 See, eg, *Sheldrake* (n 38) at [53].
143 See, eg, Geiringer (n 127) at 25.
144 For a similar point, see Goldsworthy (n 3) at 59–60 and 69; also J Goldsworthy, "Implications in Language, Law and the Constitution" in G Lindell (ed), *Future Directions in Australian Constitutional Law* (Annandale, Federation Press, 1994) 150, 150–61.

Interpretive presumptions protect important rights, obligations and principles against legislative abrogation. The need for that protection may in some special contexts justify a departure from the normal approach to statutory interpretation (ie a departure from respect for legislators' likely understanding). Legal tests for the availability of interpretive presumptions should function, at least in part, to regulate the extent to which such departures are permissible for that purpose.

Yet an examination and comparison of the various different tests that have been developed in the case law for the availability of the three main presumptions reveals deficits in that regard. Some of the tests are not suited to fulfil this function at all (the ambiguity requirement and the express words requirement); while others are very unhelpfully vague in this regard (the fundamental feature test and the necessary implication test).

In this chapter, I propose one single test for assessing the impact of uses of interpretive presumptions on respect for legislators' likely understanding. The test is whether legislators likely appreciated the conflict with the right, obligation or principle protected by the presumption. This test allows us to classify all uses of presumptions as weak, moderate or assertive. This is important because only assertive uses require special justification for departing from the normal approach to statutory interpretation.

10

'It All Depends on the Circumstances': The Decline of Doctrine on the Grounds and Intensity of Review

DAVID STRATAS[1]

BROADLY SPEAKING, ADMINISTRATIVE law is the body of law governing the activities and decisions of the executive, its agencies and other public decision-makers. From time to time, courts must interfere with their decisions and activities.

But at what threshold is judicial interference warranted?

At one time, nominate grounds of review governed the matter. In Canada, public decision-makers' decisions could be quashed for jurisdictional error for getting a preliminary question wrong.[2] Public decision-makers could lose jurisdiction if they failed to take into account relevant factors or took into account an irrelevant factor. Later, these grounds were seen as easily manipulated, insufficiently deferential to legitimate administrative decision making.[3]

But in replacing the nominate grounds, insufficient heed has been paid to developing sound principles to define when judicial interference with public decision-making is warranted. As a result, sometimes statements are carelessly made and encourage judges to follow their personal sense of right and wrong.[4]

[1] The views herein are my own. This chapter is a reworking and expansion of a speech delivered at the conclusion of the Second Biennial Public Law Conference, Cambridge, 12–14 September 2016, reflecting on the various presentations at the conference. To some extent, it repeats themes explored in a keynote speech entitled 'Reflections on the Decline of Doctrine' delivered at the Canadian Constitution Federation Conference on Law and Liberty, Toronto, Canada, 7 January 2016. (<www.youtube.com/watch?v=UxTqMw5v6rg>). It was given practical application to the Canadian law of judicial review in D Stratas, 'The Canadian Law of Judicial Review: A Plea for Doctrinal Coherence and Consistency' (2016) 42 *Queen's LJ* 27.

[2] See, eg, *Bell v Ontario Human Rights Commission* [1971] SCR 756.

[3] The trend against these grounds began in Canada in *Canadian Union of Public Employees, Local 963 v New Brunswick Liquor Corp* [1979] 2 SCR 227 where (at 233) the Supreme Court warned against 'brand[ing] as jurisdictional, and therefore subject to broader curial review, that which may be doubtfully so'. See also *Smith v Alliance Pipeline Ltd* 2011 SCC 7, [2011] 1 SCR 160 at [36].

[4] *R v Panel on Take-overs and Mergers, ex parte Guinness Plc* [1990] 1 QB 146, 160: 'whether something had gone wrong of a nature and degree which required the intervention of the court and, if so, what form that intervention should take'. See also *Thames Valley Electric Power Board v NZFP Pulp & Paper Ltd* [1994] 2 NZLR 641 at 652.

Increasingly, as I shall point out, the test for judicial interference with public decisions is not really a test at all. Often, we see statements that it all 'depends on all the circumstances', the 'particular context of the case' or the 'colour of the case', without more. Worse, some say nothing and just declare a result. Increasingly, it is not the doctrine that governs. Rather, it is the judges' view of 'the vibe of the thing'.[5]

This seems to be happening more and more in my home jurisdiction of Canada. There, the substantive merits of decisions of public decision-makers can be reviewed for correctness or reasonableness, depending on the circumstances.[6] Reasonableness is the dominant standard and, in the case of public decision-makers' interpretations of legislation, it is presumed.[7] But within the reasonableness standard, what is the intensity of review? The cases show instances where the review is rather fussy; other times, it is rather intense, akin to correctness review.[8] The intensity of review varies.

Yet, as far as explanations and guidance concerning the intensity of review is concerned, the Supreme Court of Canada is silent. It says,[9] and has said again in very recent cases that 'reasonableness takes its colour from the context' and 'must be assessed in the context of the particular type of decision-making involved and all relevant factors'.[10] But, as Professor Audrey Macklin points out in her chapter in this collection, the Supreme Court never says anything about the context.[11]

I would add that while the Supreme Court seems to be suggesting that the colour can vary, it doggedly maintains that there are just two standards of review: complete non-deference or correctness and a single standard of 'deference'—whatever that means.[12]

Worse, a fissure in the Supreme Court is now opening up. It is between those who wish to maintain this undefined reasonableness standard and, in some cases, a presumption in favour of it, and those who want correctness reviewed more frequently.[13] One might condemn both sides: the rationales offered by the bare majority of

[5] *The Castle* (Village Roadshow Pictures, 1997). In this movie, the hapless lawyer, Dennis Denuto supported a constitutional proposition he was advancing by offering that it was 'the vibe of the thing'. Later, the skilled barrister, Lawrence Hammill, having studied the cases, urges an incremental development to the doctrine and succeeds.

[6] *Dunsmuir v New Brunswick* 2008 SCC 9, [2008] 1 SCR 190.

[7] ibid, at [54]; *Alberta (Information and Privacy Commissioner) v Alberta Teachers' Association* 2011 SCC 61, [2011] 3 SCR 654 at [30]–[34].

[8] Compare, eg, cases like *John Doe v Ontario (Finance)* 2014 SCC 36, [2014] 2 SCR 3 with *Nor-Man Regional Health Authority Inc v Manitoba Association of Health Care Professionals* 2011 SCC 59, [2011] 3 SCR 616. Although reasonableness is supposed to be a deferential standard (see *Dunsmuir* (n 6) at [47]), in many cases substantive review under the reasonableness standard is indistinguishable from correctness review: see *Vavilov v Canada (Citizenship and Immigration)* [2017] FCA 132 at [37] and the cases cited therein.

[9] *Canada (Citizenship and Immigration) v Khosa*, 2009 SCC 12, [2009] 1 SCR 339 at [59]; *Catalyst Paper Corp v North Cowichan (District)* 2012 SCC 2, [2012] 1 SCR 5 at [18].

[10] *Wilson v Atomic Energy of Canada Ltd* 2016 SCC 29, [2016] 1 SCR 770 at [22]; *Canada (Attorney General) v Igloo Vikski Inc* 2016 SCC 38, [2016] 2 SCR 80 at [57]; *Communications, Energy and Paperworker's Union of Canada, Local 30 v Irving Pulp & Paper Ltd* 2013 SCC 34, [2013] 2 SCR 458 at [74].

[11] See A Macklin, ch 4 in this volume.

[12] See *Dunsmuir* (n 6); *Khosa* (n 9) at [59].

[13] *Quebec (Attorney General) v Guérin* 2017 SCC 42; *Edmonton (City) v Edmonton East (Capilano) Shopping Centres Ltd* 2016 SCC 47, [2016] 2 SCR 293.

the Court supporting the presumption of reasonableness in all cases of public decision-makers' interpretation of legislation seem made up and without merit,[14] while those supporting the assertion of correctness review offered by the minority of the Court seem to be made on the fly and without regard to previous case law.[15]

Recently, the Chief Justice of the Supreme Court of Canada, Beverley McLachlin, described administrative law as 'a barbed and occluded thicket' where we find 'only confusion'.[16] She is right. In moving away from nominate grounds of review, Canadian administrative law is:

> ... a never-ending construction site where one crew builds structures and then a later crew tears them down to build anew, seemingly without an overall plan. Roughly forty years ago, the Supreme Court told us to categorize decisions as judicial, quasi-judicial or administrative. Then, largely comprised of different members, the Court told us to follow a 'pragmatic and functional" test. Then, with further changes in its composition, it added another category of review, reasonableness, to join patent unreasonableness and correctness. Then, with more turnover of judges, it told us to follow the principles and methodology in *Dunsmuir*. Now it appears that we may be on the brink of another revision: as we shall see, the Supreme Court—mysteriously—is often not deciding cases in accordance with the principles in *Dunsmuir* and other cases decided under it.[17]

The presence of confusion is bad enough. But abandoning the search for doctrine is worse.

Are we now at that point? Perhaps so. In her chapter in this collection, Chief Justice Sian Elias of the New Zealand Supreme Court describes the area of administrative law as 'untidy and tentative'. But she goes further, querying whether 'the search for better doctrine is ultimately doomed'.[18]

[14] The rationales are set out in the majority reasons in *Edmonton East* ibid, at [22], [23], [35]. For a critique, see D Stratas, 'The Canadian Law of Judicial Review: Some Doctrine and Cases', SSRN (5 July 2017) 76–78 <https://ssrn.com/abstract=2924049>. Further criticisms are found in P Daly, 'Which Way Forward for Canadian Administrative Law?' Administrative Law Matters Blog (11 November 2016) <www.administrativelawmatters.com/blog/2016/11/14/which-way-forward-edmonton-city-v-edmonton-east-capilano-shopping-centres-ltd-2016-scc-47/>; L Sirota, 'Law in La-La-Land', Double Aspect Blog (4 December 2016) < www.doubleaspectblog.wordpress.com/2016/12/04/law-in-la-la-land/>.

[15] The minority seems to urge a return to the idea of 'jurisdictional questions' requiring correctness review. But to the minority, a jurisdictional question is a preliminary question setting the bounds of the public decision-maker's power. If adopted, this would return Canada to the state of the law existing decades earlier as exemplified in *Bell* (n 2). *Bell* was only recently overruled in *Halifax (Regional Municipality) v Nova Scotia (Human Rights Commission)* 2012 SCC 10, [2012] 1 SCR 364. 'Jurisdictional question' is nothing more than a label that can be thrown around to justify a result: *Arlington v FCC 569* US 1863 (2013) per Scalia J. It is indistinguishable from an issue of statutory interpretation, a matter that, in many instances, legislatures have empowered public decision-makers to decide, intending a measure of deference, and a matter that, on some occasions, public decision-makers have greater appreciation than the Courts. For example, the granting of power to a securities commission to revoke trading privileges when it is 'in the public interest' or when 'reasonable' may be construed as a delegation of power to the commission to develop its own jurisprudence on the meaning of those terms based on its regulatory appreciation. See *Alberta Teachers' Association* (n 7) at [33]–[34]; Stratas (n 14) at 80–81.

[16] B McLachlin, 'Administrative Law is Not for Sissies: Finding a Path through the Thicket' (2016) 29 *Can J Admin L & Prac* 127.

[17] See Stratas (n 1) at 29.

[18] See S Elias, ch 2 in this volume.

This must not be taken as a statement that the development of doctrine should end. Absent doctrine—and a commitment to develop it—we run the risk of havoc, or worse.

In this area of law, the main concern is the threshold for judicial interference with the decisions of public decision-makers: the grounds and intensity of review. When and just how intensely should courts review the activities and decisions of public decision-makers?

The stakes are high. If the threshold is too low, we run the risk of public decisions regulating us even though they are contrary to law or otherwise unacceptable and indefensible. We end up closer to governance contrary to the rule of law. If the threshold is too high, the executive, its agencies and other public decision-makers are unduly impeded from carrying out the mandates given to them by law. We end up closer to governance by the rule of courts.

Judicial interference with the decisions of public decision-makers can be a controversial thing. The greater the importance of the case, the greater the controversy—and the greater the stakes for public confidence in the judiciary. One need only look to recent events in the United States to find examples where judges have struck down executive orders much to the outrage of their makers and supporters.

The sting of controversy can be reduced when judicial interference is prompted by settled objective doctrine or the responsible, incremental extension of legal doctrine achieved through pathways of objective legal reasoning practised by judges for decades, if not centuries. But not when intervention is based in judges' whims and idle thoughts, their own world views, their own freestanding opinions of the moment about what is just appropriate and right or their own personal sense of what in the circumstances is fair and nice.[19]

Under the constitutional principle of the rule of law, litigants deserve equal application of law and equal treatment under that law.[20] To the extent possible, judges should be giving similar rulings to similarly situated people. The only way that can be done is through reliance on ideas and concepts binding upon them, a body of settled doctrine.

Strong practical reasons also support reliance upon settled doctrine. Imagine a time of significant moment in the future, a time of extreme violence and grave threat. The government reacts by vesting a public decision-maker with broad and draconian powers. The public authority exercises them. Judicial reviews are brought and their outcome has the highest stakes. On the day of the hearing, protesters for and against the public decision-maker and the government violently protest in front of the courthouse. In this situation, what is best? At the end of the day, a judicial decision based on approaches and principles developed years, perhaps even decades, earlier and

[19] See generally, A Hamilton, J Madison and J Jay, *The Federalist*, Modern Library edn (New York, Random House, 1937) 510 (Federalist No 78); *Lochner v New York* 198 US 45 (1905) per Holmes J (dissenting); *AFL v American Sash Co* 335 US 538, 515-516 (1949) per Frankfurter J; O Dixon, 'Concerning Judicial Method' (1956) 29 ALJ 468, 471 (Address delivered at Yale University on 19 September 1955); B Cardozo, *The Nature of the Judicial Process* (New Haven, Yale University Press, 1921) 141.

[20] *British Columbia v Imperial Tobacco Canada Ltd* 2005 SCC 49, [2005] 2 SCR 473.

repeatedly applied since, with every bit of reasoning supported by authority? Or a 'spur-of-the-moment', 'here-is-what-I-think' decision, a decree from on high, with no sourcing, just the say-so of a particular judge?

If decisions are made because of a particular judge's personal sense of fairness or justice, the appearance, if not the reality, is that the decision has sprung from the personal or political beliefs of an unelected person, just like anyone on the street. Such a decision is less worthy of respect. Worse, over time, the outcomes in cases will shift back and forth and all over the place, sometimes radically so, based on the changing composition of a particular court's bench. Over time, respect for the judicial branch will fall.

If, on the other hand, the decision is made from settled doctrine developed over time by many, shaped by the real-life experience of many cases in many different circumstances, the likelihood of respect for the decision is high. The strength of the reputation of and respect for the judicial branch is rooted in the stability of doctrine and time-honoured approaches to the evolution of that doctrine, not the momentary whim of individual lawyers who happen to hold a judicial commission.

Although Chief Justice McLachlin bemoans the 'barbed and occluded thicket' in this area of law, she too recognises the importance of not abandoning the search for doctrine: 'if the rule of law is to prevail, a way [through the thicket] must be found'.[21]

She is so right. We must re-engage with the tough task of reading the cases and discerning the factors that affect the intensity of review.

All cases from jurisdictions with Westminster-style democracies are relevant. They are similar both in their governance and their legal principles. This should be no surprise. The principles that animate the systems we enjoy were won at great cost, with much bloodshed over the centuries. Those principles continue to animate the development of our doctrine. True, as Chief Justice Elias reminds us in her chapter in this collection, we must account for local differences that explain some different approaches.[22] But the foundational principles remain the same.

In all British Commonwealth countries, intensity of review varies. Whether or not explicitly acknowledged in the decisions, we see some administrative decisions being reviewed as intensively as possible, granting the administrator no leeway. In others, review is far less intense. In still others, the review is not intense at all and judicial deference is at its highest.

Prompting this variability is the fact that the cases arise in many different contexts and defy easy categorisation. Decision-makers range from institutional tribunals to lone functionaries. Their decisions range from focused matters similar to those a court might consider to diffuse issues that have quintessentially been the preserve of the executive. The subjects they adjudicate range from pure factual and legal matters to matters of general policy. All of this means that the standard of review not only varies according to the circumstances but *must* vary according to the circumstances.[23]

[21] See McLachlin (n 16).
[22] See Elias (n 18).
[23] See Stratas (n 14) at 77–78.

But it does not follow that the search for a doctrinal basis is hopeless. True, courts seldom explicitly discuss the reasons why review is intense in some cases but not in others. However, the cases decided across the Commonwealth show a reasonable level of consistency and predictability of result. For example, the recent case of *Rotherham*, affording the executive much leeway in the making of certain funding decisions, could have been written by any judge in any Commonwealth court.[24]

A rigorous reading of the cases shows that, despite the different contexts, certain factors leading to certain intensities of review constantly recur in the case law. The factors can be identified and applied and can make the task of judicial review a predictable, one based on doctrine, not a chaotic one based on whim or idiosyncrasy.

Some courts have attempted to do this, to think about the doctrine and to identify in a more explicit way the factors that underlie judicial interference with public decision making.

For example, at this conference, Dr Marcello Rodriguez Ferrere,[25] acquainted us with the New Zealand case of *Wolf v Minister of Immigration*,[26] in which Justice Wild both acknowledged and, to some extent, defined the content of the intensity of review.

Dr Rodriguez Ferrere noted, with disappointment, that appellate New Zealand courts have since largely ignored that judgment and its doctrinal contribution. While the High Court has been working on variable intensities of review—something that lies at the core of administrative law and our understanding of the separation of powers—appellate courts in New Zealand are curiously silent. Yet down that path they must trod.

While Canada could not be further apart from New Zealand in terms of distance and the quality of its national rugby team, it could not be closer in this experience.

Canada's Federal Court of Appeal has been active in trying to work out the factors that affect the intensity of review.[27] Other examples exist.[28] But for the most part, as is the case in New Zealand with *Wolf*, this work has been left unconsidered.

The first and dominant factor is the words the legislator has used in granting the power to the decision-maker. Aside from any constitutional concerns about the validity of the legislation, legislation binds all. Courts are duty-bound to enforce it.

The legislation can shed much light on the mandate of the decision-maker, the breadth of its discretion and the nature of its decision, all factors that can affect the amount of leeway a public decision-maker should have.[29] Cases interpreting

[24] *Rotherham Metropolitan Borough Council v Secretary of State for Business Innovation and Skills* [2015] UKSC 6.

[25] MB Rodriquez Ferrere, '*Wolf v Minister of Immigration*: a New Zealand Administrative Law Moment'. Paper presented at Public Law Conference 2016: 'The Unity of Public Law?' 12–14 September 2016, Cambridge.

[26] [2004] NZAR 414.

[27] Note the list of factors in *Canada (Minister of Transport, Infrastructure and Communities) v Farwaha* 2014 FCA 56, [2015] 2 FCR 1006 and their similarities with those identified in *Wolf*.

[28] See, eg, *Mills v Ontario (Workplace Safety and Insurance Appeals Tribunal)* 2008 ONCA 436.

[29] See, eg, *Re:Sound v Canadian Association of Broadcasters* 2017 FCA 138 at [40]–[43]; *Canada (Attorney General) v Almon Equipment Limited* 2010 FCA 193, [2011] 4 FCR 203 at [53]; *Canada (Attorney General) v Abraham* 2012 FCA 266; 440 NR 201 at [37]–[50]; *Canada (Attorney General) v Boogaard* 2015 FCA 150; 474 NR 121.

the legislation can also constrain the interpretive options available to the public decision-maker.[30] This echoes the words of Palmer J in *AI (Somalia) v The Immigration and Protection Tribunal*, in which he stressed that 'the lawfulness of the exercise of powers by a body that is unusually constituted must be judged against its nature and functions, powers and duties and environment in relation to those of other bodies'.[31]

For example, we know that an administrator which makes a highly discretionary, highly fact-based decision is likely to be granted much leeway.[32] The same is true for an administrator who relies upon policy, that is outside of the ken of the courts, to allocate scarce resources among competing groups or to choose among several potentially worthy options.[33]

But, on the other hand, an administrator who determines a focused dispute, primarily over a question of law, in the presence of a *lis inter partes* or something akin to it, gets much less leeway.[34] Related to this are purely legal determinations where the administrator has no expertise or specialisation that might shed light on the issue. And where fundamental rights are concerned, less leeway is given.[35]

Doctrine must also underlie the remedial discretion of reviewing courts, an important aspect of when and how reviewing courts should interfere with public decisions. Here too, the doctrine has been developing, consistent with the nature of judicial review and administrative law values worked out in the cases.[36]

Alas, the majority of the Supreme Court of Canada has not considered this jurisprudence, instead usually saying nothing more than 'reasonableness takes its colour from the context' and deciding cases on their facts, often on a correctness basis, without explanation.[37] One Justice of that Court has gone further and has said that

[30] *Abraham* ibid; *Canada (Attorney General) v Canadian Human Rights Commission* 2013 FCA 75; 444 NR 120.

[31] [2016] NZHC 2227.

[32] See, eg, *Boogaard* (n 29) at [33]; *Re:Sound* (n 29) at [32]; *Canadian National Railway Company v Emerson Milling Inc* 2017 FCA 79 at [72]–[73].

[33] See, eg, *Re:Sound* ibid at [49]; *Boogaard* ibid; *Canadian National* ibid at [73]; *Gitxaala Nation v Canada* 2016 FCA 187 at [149], citing *Paradis Honey Ltd v Canada* 2015 FCA 89; 382 DLR (4th) 720 at [136]. Courts are 'poorly positioned' to opine on policy issues with 'public interest components' and 'economic aspects' and so 'by legislative design the selection of a policy choice from among a range of options lies with the [administrative decision-maker] empowered and mandated to make that selection': *FortisAlberta Inc v Alberta (Utilities Commission)* 2015 ANCA 295; 389 DLR (4th) 1 at [171]–[172].

[34] See *Farwaha* (n 27) at [92]; *Boogaard* (n 32) at [49]; *Walchuk v Canada (Justice)* 2015 FCA 85 at [33], [56]; *Erasmo v Canada (Attorney General)* 2015 FCA 129.

[35] ibid. See also *Attaran v Canada (Attorney General)* 2015 FCA 37; 467 NR 335 at [49]. Perhaps certain immigration cases decided by the Supreme Court where a correctness review was carried out under the guise of a reasonableness review may be explained in this way: *B010 v Canada (Citizenship and Immigration)* 2015 SCC 58, [2015] 3 SCR 704; *Febles v Canada (Citizenship and Immigration)* 2014 SCC 68, [2014] 3 SCR 431; *Ezokola v Canada (Citizenship and Immigration)* 2013 SCC 40, [2013] 2 SCR 678.

[36] See, eg, *Maple Lodge Farms Ltd v Canadian Food Inspection Agency* 2017 FCA 45; *Stemijon Investments Ltd v Canada (Attorney General)* 2011 FCA 299; 341 DLR (4th) 710; *Robbins v Canada (Attorney General)* 2017 FCA 24; *D'Errico v Canada (Attorney General)* 2014 FCA 95; 459 NR 167; *Canada (Public Safety and Emergency Preparedness) v LeBon* 2013 FCA 55; 444 NR 93.

[37] See text to nn 9–11 above.

the Federal Court of Appeal's approach—exemplified above—is 'not an appropriate development of the standard of review jurisprudence'.[38] But he did not explain why it was not an appropriate approach, instead merely repeating that 'reasonableness takes its colour from the context' without explaining the context.

Silence on the doctrine, repeating bromides like 'reasonableness takes its colour from the context' without elaboration or decrees that such-and-such is so without explanation—in all cases, resiling from the task of developing the doctrine—cannot continue. If it does, we will drown in the rough seas of personal preference and individual ideological and idiosyncratic views about 'whether something had gone wrong of a nature and degree which require[s] the intervention of the court'.[39] Judicial authority and legality will erode.

The consistency and predictability in this area of law and across all jurisdictions suggests an underlying doctrinal explanation. While many courts have avoided trying to explain the doctrine in any comprehensive way, the explanations they give in individual cases can shed light on why the intensity of review varies.

Some good work in the academy is being done in this area and deserves judicial attention and application. Much was on parade at the Public Law Conference, from which this volume derives. More needs to be done.

I was struck by the presentation of Dr Dean Knight.[40] I do not think there has ever been a better exposition of the topic of the grounds and intensity of judicial review. I look forward to his forthcoming book.[41]

To be stable and to be respected, the doctrine in this area needs a conceptual bottom, a substratum of concepts, properly identified and appropriately arranged. In this regard, the paper of Professor Jason Varuhas[42] on mapping public law was exceptional and deserves much study and further thought and development. Legal taxonomy, identification of principles and categorisation in public law is overdue and necessary. Peter Birks' work on this in the private law[43] yielded dividends and the task is surely overdue in administrative law.

And related to this is a greater appreciation of the nature of administrative law and the values that animate it, values that judges in this area of law need to draw upon in exercising their discretions. Here, I applaud the paper of Professor Paul Daly entitled 'Administrative Law: Characteristics, Legitimacy, Unity"[44] and his presentation at

[38] Cromwell J in *Wilson* (n 10) at [73]. He also took issue with the Federal Court of Appeal's use of the idea of 'margins of appreciation'. But this very phrase was used and, thus, was encouraged by the Supreme Court of Canada in *Dunsmuir* ((n 6) at [47]) when it first set out its view of reasonableness review.

[39] See *Guinness* (n 4) at 160.

[40] DR Knight, 'Vigilance and Restraint in the Common Law of Judicial Review: Scope, Grounds, Intensity, Context', Paper presented at Public Law Conference 2016: 'The Unity of Public Law?' 12–14 September 2016, Cambridge. See also DR Knight, 'Modulating the Depth of Scrutiny in Judicial Review: Scope, Grounds, Intensity, Context' [2016] 1 *NZLR* 63.

[41] DR Knight, *Vigilance and Restraint in the Common Law of Judicial Review* (Cambridge, Cambridge University Press, forthcoming).

[42] See JNE Varuhas, ch 3 in this volume.

[43] P Birks, *An Introduction to the Law of Restitution* (Oxford, Clarendon Press, 1985).

[44] P Daly, ch 5 in this collection.

the previous Public Law Conference concerning administrative law values,[45] the latter already put to good work in some Canadian administrative law jurisprudence.[46]

In conclusion, what must our destination be? Conceptual coherence begetting doctrinal coherence, honed by the learning from different jurisdictions unified by their shared Westminster traditions and common law origins.

What destination should we avoid? Doctrinal abdication, where all wallow comfortably, soothed by phrases—like 'viewing things in context" and 'balancing all the relevant circumstances"—perhaps pleasing to the ear, but devoid of any doctrinal content.

[45] P Daly, 'Administrative Law: A Values-Based Approach' in J Bell et al (eds), *Public Law Adjudication in Common Law Systems: Process and Substance* (Oxford, Hart Publishing, 2015).

[46] *Tsleil-Waututh Nation v Canada (Attorney General)* 2017 FCA 128; *Wilson v Atomic Energy of Canada Limited* 2015 FCA 17, [2015] 4 FCR 467 (reversed on another point: see *Wilson* (n 16); *Bernard v Canada (Revenue Agency)* 2015 FCA 263, 479 NR 189; see *Paradis Honey Ltd* (n 33).

Part 2

Comparative Perspectives

11

The Globalisation of Public Law: A Quilting of Legalities

ROBERT FRENCH AC*

I. INTRODUCTION

THE THEME OF this book is the unity of public law. The particular theme on which I was invited to reflect is cross-jurisdictional dialogue or, as I will refer to it, 'inter-jurisdictional dialogue'. Inter-jurisdictional dialogue, occasionally verging on the vaguely cross, is something the United Kingdom and Australia have engaged in over many years. In 2015, some members of the Supreme Court of the United Kingdom described a decision of the High Court of Australia, relating to contractual penalties, as 'a radical departure from the previous understanding of the law'.[1] We were not really in a position to complain about the terminology. We have given as good as we got. In 1966, Justice Menzies of the High Court of Australia described the decision of the House of Lords in *Rookes v Barnard*[2] as 'a radical departure from what has been regarded as established law'.[3] In 1980, the Chief Justice, Sir Garfield Barwick, described the decision in *Director of Public Prosecutions v Majewski*[4] as 'a radical departure from those principles of the common law evolved over a period of time, but particularly elucidated in the last fifty or so years.'[5]

Inter-jurisdictional dialogue encompasses that kind of exchange, but also the more positive use of decisions and writings from each other's courts and academies and the personal exchanges between judges, academics and practitioners at conferences such as the one giving rise to this volume. In assessing the benefits of dialogue, however, it is necessary to acknowledge with harsh modesty that there are limits to the effects it can have on participating jurisdictions. Unity is a mirage, and harmonisation is

* I acknowledge the assistance of my former Associate, Minh-Quan Nguyen, in revising this chapter for publication.

[1] *Cavendish Square Holding BV v Makdessi* [2015] 3 WLR 1373 at 1396, citing *Andrews v Australia and New Zealand Banking Group Ltd* (2012) 247 CLR 205.

[2] [1964] AC 1129.

[3] *Uren v John Fairfax & Sons Pty Ltd* (1966) 117 CLR 118 at 145.

[4] [1977] AC 443.

[5] *R v O'Connor* (1980) 146 CLR 64 at 86.

elusive. Convergence offers a spectrum of possibilities. The metaphor of 'a quilt of legalities', to which I have referred in the title of this chapter, is appropriate. In this chapter, I reflect on some of the potentials and limitations of inter-jurisdictional dialogue.

II. DIALOGUE: POTENTIAL AND LIMITS

The term 'dialogue' applied to interactions between jurisdictions has gained some purchase in the study of comparative public law. The metaphor is useful insofar as it embodies not only references in judicial decisions to sources of foreign law, but also a degree of intellectual engagement with those materials. The ways in which the term has been used among scholars in the field are varied. In this chapter the term 'dialogue' is used to refer to a broad range of exchanges with varying purposes and intensities. The primary focus here is on the use of comparative materials by judges in the course of judicial decision-making.[6]

An early application of the 'dialogue' metaphor to judicial decision-making in a comparative law context appeared in a 1998 paper by Justice Claire L'Heureux-Dubé, then a judge of the Supreme Court of Canada, reflecting on the 'international impact' of the Supreme Court of the United States under the leadership of Chief Justice William Rehnquist. The metaphor flagged a challenge to the assumption—implicit in the topic on which Justice L'Heureux-Dubé had been asked to speak—that her focus ought to be on a rather unidirectional inquiry: how had the United States Supreme Court influenced other courts around the world? The more interesting starting point, her Honour thought, was to ask how courts in different jurisdictions interacted dialogically with one another without presupposing that one jurisdiction might predominate over others. Her Honour said:[7]

> Deciding on applicable legal principles and solutions increasingly involves a consideration of the approaches that have been adopted with regard to similar legal problems elsewhere. ... Judges no longer simply *receive* the cases of other jurisdictions and then apply them or modify them for their own jurisdiction. Rather, cross-pollination and dialogue between jurisdictions is increasingly occurring. ... Reception is turning to dialogue.

Inter-jurisdictional dialogue is an exercise in learning by comparison. Its purpose is not simply the growth of uniformity across jurisdictions. It involves the recognition that different judiciaries may differ about the resolution of particular classes of legal problem. Nor does convergence necessarily follow from dialogue. However, a possible and desirable product of inter-jurisdictional dialogue is the identification of areas in which convergence between jurisdictions might be appropriate.

[6] Some comparative law scholars have used the terminology in a specific way to refer to particular methods and modes of juristic engagement with foreign legal sources. See, eg, Choudhry's distinction between 'universalist', 'dialogical' and 'genealogical' modes of comparative constitutional interpretation: S Choudhry, 'Globalization in Search of Justification: Toward a Theory of Comparative Constitutional Interpretation' (1999) 74 *Indiana Law Journal* 819.

[7] C L'Heureux Dubé, 'The Importance of Dialogue: Globalization and the International Impact of the Rehnquist Court' (1998) 34 *Tulsa Law Review* 15 at 17–18 (emphasis in original).

In the field of commercial law, convergence across jurisdictions, common law and civilian, is supported by economic imperatives. It serves efficiency by reducing transaction costs and, from a domestic perspective, may make the convergent jurisdictions more attractive to each other as destinations for investment or sources of collaboration. It is an obvious enough proposition deployed by advocates of greater commonality of laws across jurisdictions. Konrad Zweigert and Hein Kötz observed in their text on comparative law:[8]

> The advantage of unified law is that it makes international legal business easier. In the area they cover, unified laws avoid the hazards of applying private international law and foreign substantive law. Unified law thus reduces the legal risks of international business, and thereby gives relief both to the businessman who plans the venture and to the judge who has to resolve the disputes to which it gives rise. Thus unified law promotes greater legal predictability and security.

The authors' comments were directed to designs for international unification of law but were plainly applicable to the lesser goal of convergence. Convergence in public law may serve similar ends, particularly in its application to national regulatory regimes which affect the conduct of business within and between jurisdictions. Such convergence may be linked to the emergence of a body of international public law affecting domestic jurisdictions which are parties to trade agreements and investment treaties. Under a number of such agreements, non-State actors can seek review of State action, legislative, judicial and executive, through the mechanism of investor-State dispute settlement. Common standards for regulatory regimes affecting trade and commerce within domestic jurisdictions may inform the answers to questions about fair and equitable treatment, non-discrimination and expropriation under investment treaties.

That being said, it is necessary to focus on the reality of legal diversity generally, and in particular, on the area of public law given its intimate connection with domestic constitutional frameworks, statutory regimes and local legal cultures. These underlying factors will almost certainly act as constraints on the degree of unity achievable across jurisdictions.

The significance of legal diversity is conveniently highlighted by a brief survey of the contrasting trajectories of Australia and the United Kingdom in the field of public law. In many respects the two countries have similar legal cultures and methodologies and a common legal heritage. Nevertheless, they differ in important areas of the common law, differences not directly explicable by reference to constitutional arrangements although they sometimes reflect a particular view of the extent to which the court should go in changing the law. A few examples, which are by no means exhaustive, illustrate the point.

The two countries have taken differing approaches to statutory interpretation in the context of human rights statutes. In *Ghaidan v Godin-Mendoza*, a majority in the House of Lords took the view that section 3 of the United Kingdom's Human

[8] K Zweigert and H Kötz, *Introduction to Comparative Law*, 3rd edn (Oxford, Clarendon Press, 1998) 25.

Rights Act 1998 mandated what may be described as a remedial approach to statutory interpretation, authorising a court to 'read in words which change the meaning of the enacted legislation, so as to make it Convention-compliant'.[9] A provision with some textual similarities to section 3, enacted as part of a human rights statute in the State of Victoria, was considered by the High Court of Australia in *Momcilovic v The Queen*.[10] The Australian approach reflects a more constrained view of the judicial function, limited to a selection of constructional choices which the language of the relevant statutory provision permits.[11] Something akin to that approach had in fact been suggested in the UK in the judgment of Lord Hoffmann in *R (Wilkinson) v Inland Revenue Commissioners*,[12] decided shortly after *Ghaidan*, but it seems that it is *Ghaidan* which has continued to be treated as authoritative.[13]

There have been differences in the two countries' approaches to unreasonableness and irrationality in judicial review of administrative decisions.[14] Proportionality reasoning in the way in which it has been used in rights adjudication in the UK[15] has not loomed large in Australian public law. There is, however, in Australia a long-standing use of a general proportionality formula to determine whether a legislative or administrative act falls within the scope of the relevant constitutional and legislative grant of power,[16] which in turn has provided a basis for the limited application of a more structured approach to proportionality reasoning in recent times.[17] Australian courts have not accepted that the concept of legitimate expectation can underpin substantive entitlements as distinct from informing the content of procedural fairness. The High Court of Australia has come to describe the terminology of 'legitimate expectation' as 'unhelpful' and apt in many cases to distract from the task of examining the underlying legal framework to determine whether a procedure was carried out fairly.[18] That distancing may be contrasted with the gradual acceptance of procedural and substantive legitimate expectations as touchstones of validity in the UK.[19] Of course, jurisdictional error—the heart of a distinction which

[9] *Ghaidan v Godin-Mendoza* [2004] 2 AC 557 at [32] (Lord Nicholls); see also *Sheldrake v Director of Public Prosecutions* [2005] 1 AC 264 at [28] (Lord Bingham), in which it was suggested that s 3 'may require the court to depart from the legislative intention of Parliament'.

[10] (2011) 245 CLR 1.

[11] *Momcilovic v The Queen* (2011) 245 CLR 1 at 48–50 [47]–[51].

[12] [2005] 1 WLR 1718 at [17].

[13] J Beatson et al, *Human Rights: Judicial Protection in the United Kingdom* (London, Sweet & Maxwell, 2008) 459.

[14] M Aronson and M Groves, *Judicial Review of Administrative Action*, 5th edn (Pyrmont, Thomson Reuters Australia, 2013) 361–2.

[15] The development of proportionality review in the UK, including its role independently of European law, was discussed in the judgments of the Supreme Court in *Pham v Secretary of State for the Home Department* [2015] 1 WLR 1591. For an earlier account of the role of proportionality in administrative law in the UK, see S de Smith, H Woolf and J Jowell, *Judicial Review of Administrative Action*, 5th edn (London, Sweet & Maxwell, 1995) 593–607.

[16] *Murphy v Electoral Commissioner* (2016) 90 ALJR 1027 at [32] and the authorities there cited.

[17] *McCloy v New South Wales* (2015) 89 ALJR 857.

[18] *Re Minister for Immigration and Multicultural and Indigenous Affairs, ex parte Lam* (2003) 214 CLR 1 at [34] (Gleeson CJ), [111], [121] (Hayne J); *Plaintiff S10/2011 v Minister for Immigration and Citizenship* (2012) 246 CLR 636 at [65] (Gummow, Hayne, Crennan and Bell JJ).

[19] See *R v North and East Devon Health Authority, ex parte Coughlan* [2001] QB 213.

long ago receded in importance in the UK[20]—continues to occupy a central role in Australian judicial review jurisprudence partly for reasons linked to the character of the entrenched jurisdiction of the High Court.[21]

As I remarked in a sequel to the previously mentioned penalties case in which we and the UK courts differed, the differences between the UK and Australia do not herald the coming of a winter of mutual exceptionalism.[22] Terms such as 'legal exceptionalism' and its grim accompaniment 'judicial isolation' are frequently deployed by the critic of the Antipodean direction to describe it as pointing away from a jurisprudential vector in the critic's frame of reference. Mutual exceptionalism is a useful term because it accommodates multiple frames of reference in which everybody can regard everybody else as headed in the wrong direction. I do not wish to highlight differences unduly. However, they point to the truth that the extent to which inter-jurisdictional dialogue, through use of comparative law materials and engagement between judges, academics and practitioners, can play a part in the development of common approaches in public law, will be constrained. It will be constrained within each jurisdiction by its constitutional arrangements, the presence or absence of Bills of Rights, the general legal system, and the political and legal cultures of the day.

Of course, an important benefit of inter-jurisdictional dialogue is that legal principles, modes of reasoning and solutions to particular classes of problem applicable in one country may inform the development of principles, modes of reasoning and solutions in another. However, the extent of the benefit may be limited by factors similar to those affecting other inter-jurisdictional processes such as the migration or transplantation of laws from one country to another. Change in the laws of any country can be a complex function of history, culture, economy, social conditions and the nature and distribution of public and private power within the society. The adoption by one jurisdiction of apparently similar laws or common law principles from another may be followed by significant differences in their interpretation and application.[23] Factors of this kind have been foregrounded in the writings of 'culturalist' scholars such as Professor Pierre Legrand, who has argued that 'rules cannot travel' and 'legal transplants are impossible'.[24] Such a thesis is not, of course, novel in its origins: it was reflected centuries ago in the following contention advanced by Montesquieu in *The Spirit of Laws*: 'Laws should be so appropriate to the people for whom they are made that it is very unlikely that the laws of one nation can suit another.'[25]

[20] See *Anisminic* ibid, although the effective abolition of the distinction between jurisdictional and non-jurisdictional errors of law is more precisely attributed to its elaboration in subsequent cases, in particular *R v Hull University Visitor, ex parte Page* [1993] AC 682.

[21] *Plaintiff S157/2002 v Commonwealth* (2003) 211 CLR 476.

[22] *Paciocco v Australia and New Zealand Banking Group Ltd* (2016) 90 ALJR 835 at [10].

[23] K Pistor, 'The Standardization of Law and Its Effect on Developing Economies' (2002) 50 *American Journal of Comparative Law* 97 at 99; PK Yu, 'Clusters and Links in Asian Intellectual Property Law' in C Antons (ed), *Routledge Handbook of Asian Law* (London, Routledge, 2017) 147.

[24] P Legrand, 'The Impossibility of "Legal Transplants"' (1997) 4 *Maastrict Journal of European and Comparative Law* 111 at 114.

[25] Montesquieu, *The Spirit of Laws* (Cambridge, Cambridge University Press, 1989) 8–9.

It is not necessary or useful for present purposes to traverse the full spectrum of debate between 'transferist' and 'culturalist' theories of rule-making,[26] a controversy which pervaded earlier comparative law literature but which has probably run its course.[27] It is enough to say that the factors to which I have referred undoubtedly bear on the extent to which different jurisdictions are plausibly able, or at least empirically likely, to draw constructively from bodies of law developed elsewhere. Bearing that in mind in relation to the use of comparative law materials, it may be prudent and useful to apply a kind of common law methodology to encourage case-by-case convergence in solutions to particular legal problems. Such solutions may be more portable across jurisdictional boundaries than large principles. Over time there may be a build-up, in the common law way, of an underlying body of common modes of reasoning of general application and even substantive principles.

Let me offer, by way of illustration, one example from personal experience. On 17 April 2003, in an interregnum between the uprising of 2000 and the military coup of 2006, the Supreme Court of Fiji delivered judgment in a case entitled *Matalulu v Director of Public Prosecutions*.[28] The case was the by-product of a long-running dispute over an election for the office of a paramount chief. Two protagonists on one side of the dispute filed private criminal complaints against an opposing party alleging that in the course of judicial review proceedings arising out of the election, he had sworn a false affidavit. The Director of Public Prosecutions, exercising a constitutional power, took over the proceedings and filed a *nolle prosequi*. The Court of Appeal of Fiji dismissed an application for judicial review of the DPP's decision. The Supreme Court dismissed an appeal from the decision of the Court of Appeal. I was then a sessional member of the Supreme Court which decided that appeal along with Sir Kenneth Keith of the Court of Appeal of New Zealand, later appointed to the Supreme Court of New Zealand and then to the International Court of Justice, and John von Doussa, who was one of my colleagues on the Federal Court of Australia.

Counsel for the DPP, Gerard McCoy QC, referred us to cases concerning the reviewability of prosecutorial discretions from a large number of jurisdictions including New Zealand, Australia, the United Kingdom, Canada, North Ireland, the United States, Hong Kong, Samoa, Guyana, Barbados and the European Court of Human Rights. In the event, we set out a list of grounds upon which such a discretion could be reviewable.

The factual circumstances from which the question arose, and the constitutional and statutory backdrop against which the question was decided, were on their face peculiar to Fiji. Accordingly, I expected that the judgment would disappear into

[26] The 'transferist' school was most notably represented by Alan Watson, who argued that it was 'socially easy' for legal rules to be accepted into any given system, whatever their origin: A Watson, *Legal Transplants* (Edinburgh, Scottish Academic Press, 1974) 95–96.

[27] M Cohn, 'Legal Transplant Chronicles: The Evolution of Unreasonableness and Proportionality Review of the Administration of the United Kingdom' (2010) 58 *American Journal of Comparative Law* 583 at 587–88.

[28] [2003] 4 LRC 712.

the recesses of Fijian legal history which has been punctuated by many more dramatic events than contested decisions by its DPP. It was something of a surprise, therefore, to see the decision referred to, extensively quoted and approved by Lord Bingham in three Privy Council appeals from Mauritius,[29] Trinidad and Tobago,[30] and Jamaica[31] in 2006 and 2007. It was cited and applied in the High Court of Justice in Northern Ireland in 2008[32] and in 2008 and 2014 in decisions of the House of Lords in *R (Cornerhouse Research) v Director of the Serious Fraud Office*[33] and *R (Lord Carlile) v Secretary of State for the Home Department*.[34] It was also cited and applied by the Hong Kong Court of First Instance in 2008[35] and by the High Court of New Zealand in 2015.[36] In that way, the case of *Matalulu* provides a paradigmatic illustration of the operation of inter-jurisdictional dialogue in judicial decision making. Consideration of comparative materials informed the development of legal reasoning which has itself fed back into juristic decision making in other countries. What brought about its portability? Perhaps it was the relatively narrow focus of the problem and its common features across different jurisdictions which enabled the principles explained in the case to be abstracted from their immediate factual and legal milieu.

In Australia, there is nothing novel about the use of comparative materials in judicial decision making in public law and generally. Australian courts may, and do, in interpreting statutes refer to foreign domestic and international judgments which have logical or analogical relevance. When interpreting statutes which give effect to international conventions, it is quite routine for Australian courts to have regard to the decisions of courts of other jurisdictions in which the conventions are applied, the writings of jurists and the opinions of authoritative international organisations. Courts, and in particular the High Court, are frequently invited by parties to develop the common law by reference to judicial decisions and other materials from overseas; naturally, the success of those efforts varies.

In the public law field the constitutional and legal systems of the 'recipient' jurisdiction will affect the extent to which inter-jurisdictional dialogue has a role to play in its decision making. It is a point of difference between Australia, on the one hand and the UK and New Zealand on the other, that Australia has a written federal Constitution allocating enumerated legislative powers to the Commonwealth Parliament and providing for distinct legislative, executive and judicial branches of the Commonwealth government. Much of the Constitution was based upon that of the United States, with responsible government imported from the UK. It provides the framework for Australian public law. Because the High Court exercises final appellate jurisdiction under section 73 of the Constitution, it is the final determiner

29 *Mohit v Director of Public Prosecutions of Mauritius* [2006] 1 WLR 3343.
30 *Sharma v Brown-Antoine* [2007] 1 WLR 780.
31 *Marshall v Director of Public Prosecutions* [2007] UKPC 4.
32 *Re Hamill* [2008] NIQB 73.
33 [2009] 1 AC 756.
34 [2015] AC 945.
35 *RV v Director of Immigration* [2008] 4 HKLRD 529.
36 *Osborne v Worksafe New Zealand* [2016] 2 NZLR 485.

of the common law of Australia[37] which informs administrative law and administrative justice at State and federal levels subject to particular and generally similar State and federal statutory regimes for judicial and administrative review.[38]

For most of the common law world the use of comparative law materials generally raises questions of a practical nature, rather than questions of fundamental principle such as whether it is legitimate to refer to the materials in the first place. Practical questions include relevance to the case at hand, the reputation of the source of the materials to be relied upon, and the extent to which merely ornamental resort to such materials can unduly affect costs and delay in litigation.

Lord Reed wrote, in an article in the *Law Quarterly Review* in 2008,[39] that foreign law and decisions of foreign courts can be a source of ideas and experience. Where new or persistent legal problems arise to which other systems have devised solutions, those solutions will enable the identification of options and possibly even an evaluation of their workability. I respectfully agree. The judge of the court considering foreign law materials can take them or leave them in the same way as he or she might take or leave academic writings or prior case law which is not binding on that court. The ideas or experiences may be used in various ways and to varying degrees. As Lord Reed noted, they may readily be used for purposes that go no further than 'information, stimulation, and reflection'.[40] In some cases, arguments propounded in the materials might be regarded as plausible or convincing and a guide to the resolution of the legal problem before the court. Conversely, ideas advanced or accepted overseas might be used as an argumentative aid to test or challenge a contrary position which the court has adopted or is proposing to adopt, thereby assisting in creating a more rigorous justification for that contrary position. Whatever the ultimate use—if any—to which foreign law materials are put, the selection of such materials does raise methodological questions not unlike those which fall for consideration under theories of the transplantation or migration of laws from one jurisdiction to another. It requires discriminating selection and the avoidance of acontextual readings.

The field of public law, perhaps more than other areas of the law, must be understood, in each country in which the term is used, in its local context. In the first place, whether a jurisdiction has a clearly identified body of administrative law in the way that an Australian or English jurist understands that concept may itself be a point of differentiation. Even in those places where such a body of law has developed, there is considerable heterogeneity of principle and practice. That in turn reflects differences in the underlying political systems, constitutional frameworks and legal cultures.[41] At the level of constitutional law, even though all written constitutions in the world

[37] *Lange v Australian Broadcasting Corporation* (1997) 189 CLR 520 at 563.

[38] Administrative Decisions (Judicial Review) Act 1977 (Cth); Administrative Decisions (Judicial Review) Act 1989 (ACT); Judicial Review Act 1991 (Qld); Judicial Review Act 2000 (Tas); *cf* Administrative Law Act 1978 (Vic).

[39] R Reed, 'Foreign Precedents and Judicial Reasoning: The American Debate and British Practice' (2008) 124 *Law Quarterly Review* 253.

[40] ibid, at 270.

[41] C Harlow, 'Global Administrative Law: The Quest for Principles and Values' (2006) 17 *The European Journal of International Law* 187 at 208.

today reflect at least some (and often quite a substantial) degree of inspiration, learning and borrowing from the constituent documents or uncodified principles of other countries, they are inevitably moulded to suit local conditions—both in their initial design and in their interpretation and practical operation once adopted. If there be such a thing as public law lying across national boundaries, then it probably finds its place within Professor Boaventura de Sousa Santos' metaphor as a 'quilt of legalities'. It was a figure of speech he applied to legal pluralism in Brazil, reflected in the intersection of national law and locally generated rules.[42] The metaphor has been carried beyond national boundaries by others including Professor Thomas Poole who used it to describe the likely outcome of aspirations for the development of a 'common law of judicial review' grounded in human rights. His discussion appeared in an interesting essay, published in 2008, entitled 'Between the Devil and the Deep Blue Sea'.[43] Australia, in that essay, is described as 'the Devil' and the High Court as engaged in a self-referential and arcane Glass Bead Game. I will not hold that against Professor Poole because, as it happens, he said something with which I agree. He drew attention in his essay to the characteristic entanglement of administrative law, constitutional law and local conditions including the structure of politics and public administration and said:[44]

> Normative heterogeneity within a shared but relatively loose judicial framework in part produced by transnational dialogues is a more plausible scenario than homogeneity of administrative law principle. If this is the case, then we should reject 'the common law of administrative law thesis', at least in its stronger formulations, and start thinking instead of the genesis of a 'quilt of legalities' in which functionally independent common law jurisdictions interact within a partly-shared language and normative framework.

III. LOCAL CONTEXT: AN AUSTRALIAN PERSPECTIVE

The point about the persistence of heterogeneity, even where systems seem on their face to have much in common, is illustrated sufficiently for present purposes by pointing to the examples from Australia and the UK which I have already mentioned, including their contrasting approaches to statutory interpretation, the use of proportionality reasoning, the concept of reasonableness in judicial review and the place of the legitimate expectation. The differences to which I refer can be linked, in the Australian context, to its written Constitution and the absence of a general Bill of Rights. There is no national legislation along the lines of the UK's Human Rights Act 1998. There are a number of express guarantees under the Constitution.[45] There is no guarantee of freedom of speech, but the High Court

[42] B de Sousa Santos, *Toward a New Legal Common Sense: Law, Globalization, and Emancipation* 2nd edn (Cambridge University Press, 2002) 163. See also Gavin W Anderson, *Constitutional Rights after Globalization* (Oxford, Hart Publishing, 2005) 54.

[43] T Poole, 'Between the Devil and the Deep Blue Sea: Administrative Law in an Age of Rights' in L Pearson, C Harlow and M Taggart (eds), *Administrative Law in a Changing State: Essays in Honour of Mark Aronson* (Oxford, Hart Publishing, 2008) 15, 22.

[44] ibid (footnote omitted).

[45] Commonwealth of Australia Constitution Act, ss 51(xxiiiA), 51(xxxi), 80, 92, 116 and 117.

has held that the Constitution—through the system of representative and responsible government that it establishes—provides for an implied freedom of political communication. The implied freedom limits legislative power at Commonwealth and State levels and affects the common law particularly in relation to defamation.[46]

The structural and textual features of the Constitution have been interpreted as supporting a separation of the judicial power of the Commonwealth from the legislative and executive powers.[47] In addition, section 75(v) of the Constitution entrenches the jurisdiction of the High Court to review decisions of Commonwealth officers for jurisdictional error.[48]

Chapter III of the Constitution provides for federal judicial power to be exercised not only by the High Court and federal courts created by the Parliament, but also by State courts invested with federal jurisdiction.[49] Implications drawn from that scheme by the High Court have led to a number of propositions affecting State law, which are of fundamental importance to public law in Australia:

— State legislatures cannot abolish State Supreme Courts[50] nor impose upon them functions incompatible with their essential characteristics as courts nor subject them in their judicial decision-making to direction by the executive.[51]
— A State legislature cannot enact a law conferring upon a judge of a State court a non-judicial function which is substantially incompatible with the functions of the court of which the judge is a member.[52]
— State legislatures cannot immunise decision-makers under State law from judicial review by the Supreme Court of the State for jurisdictional error.[53]

The last proposition entrenches for State Supreme Courts their traditional supervisory function with respect to official decision-making in a way loosely analogous to that in which section 75(v) of the Constitution entrenches the judicial review jurisdiction of the High Court.

The constitutional entrenchment of judicial review appears to be a point of distinction between Australia on the one hand and the UK and New Zealand on the other. It follows that, unlike the UK and New Zealand, there has been very little reference in Australia to the concept of common law constitutionalism insofar as it might embrace a residual ability on the part of the courts to resist attempts to abolish judicial review.[54]

[46] *Lange v Australian Broadcasting Corporation* (1997) 189 CLR 520.

[47] *R v Kirby, ex parte Boilermakers' Society of Australia* (1956) 94 CLR 254.

[48] *Plaintiff S157/2002 v Commonwealth* (2003) 211 CLR 476.

[49] Commonwealth of Australia Constitution Act, ss 71 and 77(iii). This arrangement allowing for federal jurisdiction to be conferred on State courts was described in the *Boilermakers' Case* as an 'autochthonous expedient': (1956) 94 CLR 254, 268. As was later pointed out, it is not strictly autochthonous, as the United States Congress had, from its early existence, invested State courts with federal jurisdiction: *Felton v Mulligan* (1971) 124 CLR 367, 393 (Windeyer J).

[50] *Kable v Director of Public Prosecutions (NSW)* (1996) 189 CLR 51; *K-Generation Pty Ltd v Liquor Licensing Court* (2009) 237 CLR 501.

[51] *International Finance Trust Co Ltd v New South Wales Crime Commission* (2009) 240 CLR 319.

[52] *Wainohu v New South Wales* (2011) 243 CLR 181.

[53] *Kirk v Industrial Court (NSW)* (2010) 239 CLR 531.

[54] R French, 'Common Law Constitutionalism' (Robin Cooke Lecture, Victoria University of Wellington, 27 November 2014) <www.hcourt.gov.au/assets/publications/speeches/current-justices/frenchcj/frenchcj27nov2014.pdf>.

The approach of Australian courts to judicial review of administrative action has been constrained in a way spelt out by Justice Brennan in *Attorney General (NSW) v Quin* in a frequently quoted passage:

> The duty and jurisdiction of the court to review administrative action do not go beyond the declaration and enforcing of the law which determines the limits and governs the exercise of the repository's power.[55]

In that context it is possible to understand how, absent a Bill of Rights in the Constitution or a national Charter of Rights, there has been little impetus for the development of proportionality reasoning as that term is understood in Europe and the UK and other jurisdictions.

Australia's closest approach to a general notion of proportionality traditionally has been reflected in the term 'reasonably appropriate and adapted', a formulation of long standing in Australian law. It can, as it happens, be traced back to the United States—namely to Chief Justice Marshall's explanation in *McCulloch v Maryland* of the constitutional limits of the powers of Congress.[56] It is a criterion which has been applied to determine the validity of exercises of purposive powers, including constitutional legislative powers authorising the making of laws to serve a specified purpose;[57] incidental powers, which must serve the purposes of the substantive powers to which they are incidental;[58] and powers conferred by the Constitution or a statute the exercise of which may limit or restrict the enjoyment of a constitutional guarantee, immunity or freedom, including the implied freedom of political communication.[59] Thus, if a law was said to burden the implied freedom of political communication and to do so for a legitimate purpose, the question asked would be whether it was reasonably appropriate and adapted to advance that legitimate purpose.[60] That language is used to mark the limits of legislative power and the borderlands of judicial power. Recently a more structured approach to its application to a law said to burden the implied freedom of political communication was set out in the joint judgment of four Justices of the High Court in *McCloy v New South Wales*.[61] The structured approach referred to three considerations drawn from European and, in particular, German courts:

1 Suitability—whether the law had a rational connection to the purpose of the provision.
2 Necessity—whether there was an obvious and compelling alternative, reasonably practicable means of achieving the same purpose with a less restrictive effect on the freedom.

55 (1990) 170 CLR 1 at 35–36.
56 4 Wheat 316 at 421 (1819), cited in *Mulholland v Australian Electoral Commission* (2004) 220 CLR 181 at 199–200 [39].
57 *Commonwealth v Tasmania* (*The Tasmanian Dam Case*) (1983) 158 CLR 1; *Richardson v Forestry Commission* (1988) 164 CLR 261.
58 *Davis v Commonwealth* (1988) 166 CLR 79; *Nationwide News Pty Ltd v Wills* (1992) 177 CLR 1.
59 *Castlemaine Tooheys Ltd v South Australia* (1990) 169 CLR 436; *Lange v Australian Broadcasting Corporation* (1997) 189 CLR 520; *Betfair Pty Ltd v Western Australia* (2008) 234 CLR 418.
60 *Lange v Australian Broadcasting Corporation* (1997) 189 CLR 520 at 567.
61 (2015) 89 ALJR 857.

3 Adequacy of balance—whether the extent of the restriction imposed by the impugned law was outweighed by the importance of the purpose it served.

The approach thus adopted is treated as a mode of analysis applicable to some cases involving the general proportionality criterion, but not necessarily all. That reflects, among other things, differences between, on the one hand, the development of structured proportionality testing in the context of rights adjudication in Europe and, on the other hand, the origins and applications of the general proportionality criterion in Australia.

The role of proportionality in judicial review has become a lively field of inquiry in the UK, aided by dicta of members of the Supreme Court in a succession of decisions including *Pham v Secretary of State for the Home Department*,[62] *Keyu v Secretary of State for Foreign and Commonwealth Affairs*[63] and *Youssef v Secretary of State for Foreign and Commonwealth Affairs*.[64] Whether proportionality reasoning finds a place in Australia as an aspect of judicial review relating to the reasonableness and rationality of administrative decisions remains to be seen.[65] Undoubtedly, inter-jurisdictional dialogue will feed into any such development.

IV. CONCLUSION

Inter-jurisdictional dialogue is of great value generally and in the field of public law. Its practical effects are constrained by global legal pluralism. I return to the metaphor of a 'quilt of legalities'. It took me, through a Google search, to an international movement called 'Modern Quilting' and an international organisation called 'The Modern Quilt Guild'[66] which has about 170 member bodies. With an eerie relevance to our present topic, it sets out the objectives of modern quilting which include that it be:

1 Functional rather than decorative;
2 Interactive rather than repetitious; and
3 Embracing simplicity and minimalism and most importantly focusing on finishing quilts on a home sewing machine.

Good quilting and good public law have a good deal in common.

62 [2015] 1 WLR 1591.
63 [2016] AC 1355.
64 [2016] AC 1457.
65 See *Minister for Immigration and Citizenship v Li* (2013) 249 CLR 332 at [30].
66 The Modern Quilt Guild, 'About Us'. Available at: http://themodernquiltguild.wordpress.com/about-2.

12

Comparative Public Law in the UK Supreme Court

ROBERT REED*

THERE IS NOTHING new about learning from the laws of other jurisdictions. The earliest example in the literature that I know of is the story, told by the Roman historian Livy, of the embassy sent from Rome to Athens in the fifth century BC to learn about the laws of Solon, for the purpose of preparing the Twelve Tables. Scholars nowadays agree that the story is a legend, but what is significant is that it was thought, even in ancient times, to be just the sort of thing that would happen.

Slightly more recently, the new government established in France after the revolution of 1830 began thinking about changes which might be made to the French legal system. So they sent officials to various countries to investigate their laws. One of those sent was a trainee judge at the law courts in Versailles, who went to the United States to study prisons and penitentiaries. The judge was Alexis de Tocqueville, and the result, in addition to his report on the prison system, was his classic work on *Democracy in America*.[1] It was another French judge, from the court at Bordeaux, who a century earlier, after visiting England shortly after retiring from the bench and meeting some of the prominent British politicians of the day, wrote another classic of political philosophy. That judge was Montesquieu.[2]

It was in the nineteenth century that comparative law really took off. That era's passion for law reform led to the establishment of numerous societies, in the UK and elsewhere, with the aim of improving social and legal conditions, whose annual meetings became occasions attracting large numbers of lawyers from throughout the UK and overseas. The development of the railway network during the same period greatly facilitated travel and made possible the development of legal conferences and similar gatherings. The nineteenth century legal societies were interested in recommending improvements to domestic legislation, and so they wanted to look at other legal systems so as to find out which solution worked best.

* This is a revised version of a keynote address given on 12 September 2016 at the conference on 'The Unity of Public Law?' held at the Centre for Public Law at the University of Cambridge. I am grateful to my judicial assistant, Eleni Dinenis, for her assistance.

1 A de Tocqueville, *De la Démocratie en Amérique* (Paris, Librairie de Charles Gosselin, 1840).

2 C Montesquieu, *De l'Espirt des Lois* (Geneva, Barrillot et Fils, 1748).

It is no accident that many legal societies and bodies, including those concerned with comparative law, were established during this period. The *Deutscher Juristentag*, a law reform society, was founded in Berlin in 1860. In France, the Société de Législation Comparée was founded in 1869. The International Law Association was founded in Brussels in 1873. Other societies for international and comparative law soon followed. In Britain, the Society for Comparative Legislation was founded in 1894 and the Grotius Society in 1915. They subsequently merged to form the British Institute for International and Comparative Law. In the United States, the American Bar Association (ABA) was founded in 1878, and the American Society of International Law in 1906. All these organisations held conferences and congresses, with international participation, and with much the same format as one finds today: the welcoming reception, the lectures, the lunches, the closing banquets. The popularity of these events was reflected in the establishment of the first professional conference organisers, in 1892 in Detroit.

The First World War provided a further impetus, with the Academy of International Law being founded at The Hague in 1923 and the International Academy of Comparative Law founded there the following year. By that time, technology had developed, and ocean liners made it possible for British and North American lawyers to attend each other's conferences. So, for example, in 1924 the ABA and the Canadian Bar Association came to London and Edinburgh for meetings with their English and Scottish counterparts, and all the usual lectures and festivities were held, the UK being happily beyond the bounds of Prohibition. Then as now, judges were invited to address these conferences and congresses. So, for example, Lord Macmillan travelled to Chicago in 1938 to address the ABA conference, and also to attend a dinner held in his honour by the Chicago Bar Association.

The advent of long-distance air travel after the Second World War finally made it possible to attend conferences around the world without too much difficulty. And so we find, for example, the first Commonwealth and Empire Law Conference, as it was then known, being held in London in 1955. In more recent times, there has been a further development. Until the Second World War, it seems to have been usual for delegates to travel to conferences without their spouses. So the only women involved, for the most part, were the wives of the hosts and of any visiting dignitaries, such as Lady Macmillan, who accompanied her husband to Chicago. That has all changed. Most conferences and judicial exchanges now have a programme for the '*personnes accompagnantes*': programmes which are sometimes more enticing than those devised for the delegates.

So nowadays, it is taken for granted that judges travel around the world to attend conferences, to give lectures and to hold discussions with foreign colleagues. The avowed purpose of all this travelling is to acquire legal knowledge. But some, not least those who are haunted by the idea that someone, somewhere, may be enjoying himself, may suspect that the acquisition of knowledge is merely an excuse. It is certainly true that contact between British and foreign judges can result in the formation of professional relationships, and sometimes friendships, which endure long after everyone has returned home. That is one of the most valuable results of much judicial travelling. It achieves the important aim of enabling the participants to get to know and understand their counterparts elsewhere. In my experience, the relationships that are formed can also be of real practical value in facilitating the exchange of information and in generating goodwill.

As to the usefulness of the legal knowledge acquired, there are voices that are critical of the citation by judges of foreign law. In Scottish law schools, one sometimes comes across the view that the distinctive character of the Scottish legal system is liable to be lost if reference is made to English law and the other common law systems which have developed from it around the world. This viewpoint is reflected in the publication of textbooks which adopt a policy of avoiding the citation of non-Scottish precedents. It is also reflected in a form of originalism which seeks answers to modern legal problems in the writings of the founding fathers of the modern Scottish legal system, in the seventeenth and eighteenth centuries. As in the United States, this approach has its origin in the idea that a country's law is uniquely adapted to its people, and expresses their national identity. Like so much else, this idea goes back to Montesquieu: '[T]he political and civil laws of each nation', he wrote, 'should be adapted in such a manner to the people for whom they are made, as to render it very unlikely for those of one nation to be proper for another'.[3]

There is nothing new about objections to the citation of foreign law. Lord Mansfield, for example, was lambasted for his use of foreign material. The *Letters of Junius* asserted in 1770 that:

> In contempt or ignorance of the common law of England, you have made it your study to introduce into the court where you preside, maxims of jurisprudence unknown to Englishmen. The Roman code, the law of nations, and the opinions of foreign civilians, are your perpetual theme; but whoever heard you mention magna charta [sic] or the bill of rights with approbation or respect? By such treacherous arts, the noble simplicity and spirit of our Saxon laws were first corrupted.[4]

The charge that Mansfield cited foreign legal writings was well-founded. As that indicates, the idea that English law developed independently of foreign influences, although it remains widely held, is far from accurate. In reality, the classic case law of the eighteenth and nineteenth centuries, particularly in fields such as contract and commercial law, contains many references to civilian and other foreign law.

More recently, when I was a law student at the University of Edinburgh, we were told about, and I think expected to take to heart, Lord Cockburn's admonition in 1851 of a senior counsel who cited English authorities:

> I really wish we could imitate the example set us by the counsel and the judges of that kingdom, who decide their causes by their own rules and customs, without exposing themselves by referring to foreign systems, the very language of which they do not comprehend.[5]

What we were not told, as far as I recall, was that the recipient of this rocket was the future Lord President Inglis, one of the most admired of Scottish judges and one

[3] C Montesquieu (trans T Nugent, ed DW Carrithers), *The Spirit of Laws: A Compendium of the First English Edition* (Berkley, University of California Press, 1977) 104–05.

[4] 'Junius', *Letters of Junius*, vol II (London, Henry Sampson Woodfall, 1772) Letter XLI, To the Right Honourable Lord Mansfield, 14 November 1770, 50.

[5] *Napier's Trustees v Morrison* (1851) 13 D 1404 at 1409.

who continued, notwithstanding his telling-off, to take account of legal thinking outside Scotland.

In our own time, similar sentiments to those in the *Letters of Junius* have been expressed in the United States, most prominently by the late Justice Scalia in several judgments criticising his colleagues.[6] His remarks provoked a strong reaction in politics and the press, and there were even calls for the impeachment of judges who cited foreign authorities in their judgments. The view sometimes seems to be that the less a judge knows about legal thinking elsewhere, the better; or, at least, the more he knows, the better he should conceal it. No doubt recognising that matters had gone further than he had intended, Justice Scalia later gave a speech in which he said that he was not a xenophobe, that he used to teach comparative law and that he believed that comparative law might well be made a mandatory subject in United States' law schools.[7] He accepted that courts should cite foreign law in the interpretation of treaties, that foreign law was sometimes relevant to the application of American statutes (eg where the statute required a *renvoi* to foreign law) and that it could usefully be considered in response to predictions of disaster if a court ruled a certain way. He remained, however, of the view that foreign legal materials could never be relevant to the interpretation of the US Constitution, with the exception of English law up to the date of the Constitution.

Whatever view one takes of that question, there is, as I have explained, an increasing tendency for judges to exchange ideas, and information about their laws, at bilateral meetings and international conferences. The UK Supreme Court, for example, has regular exchanges with the United States Supreme Court, the Canadian Supreme Court, the German Federal Constitutional Court, the French Conseil d'Etat and the Italian Consiglio di Stato, as well as less regular meetings with other courts and individual foreign judges. At these various meetings, we discuss current problems, particularly in the field of public law. Issues that have come up in recent discussions include freedom of speech, privacy, surveillance, terrorism, migration, and federalism: inter-connected issues which are important in most developed countries.

To give an idea why exchanges like this are useful, it may be helpful to say something about the cases I hear. Recent UK Supreme Court cases have included a case concerned with the question whether a British court could make an order against a person who wanted to bring a complaint against the UK before an international court, preventing him from placing before the international court material which might be harmful to our national security;[8] a case concerned with the jurisdiction of the English courts to decide a dispute concerning a child living in England whose mother had left her husband in Morocco, where proceedings concerning the child had already begun;[9] a case concerned with whether an order prohibiting the

[6] See, eg, *Thompson v Oklahoma* 487 US 815 at 868 n 4 (1988); *Printz v United States* 521 US 898 at 921 n 11 (1997); *Atkins v Virginia* 536 US 304 at 347–48 (2002); *Lawrence v Texas* 539 US 558 (2003); and *Roper v Simmons* 543 US 551 (2005).

[7] A Scalia, Keynote Address at the American Enterprise Institute Conference: Outsourcing of American Law (21 February 2006). Available at: www.aei.org/events/outsourcing-of-american-law-2/.

[8] *R (Wang Yam) v Central Criminal Court* [2016] AC 771.

[9] *In Re J (A Child)* [2016] AC 1291.

publication of information about a person's sexual life, pending a trial of proceedings to prevent publication as a breach of privacy and confidentiality, should be upheld after the story was published on websites outside the UK;[10] a case about the limitation period which governs claims brought against the British Army for alleged brutality against Iraqi civilians in Iraq;[11] cases concerned with the power of British forces in Iraq and Afghanistan to intern insurgents;[12] a case concerned with the implications of exchange rate fluctuations for the recovery of international debts;[13] numerous cases concerned with different aspects of immigration and the rights of immigrants and their families;[14] and equally numerous cases concerned with EU law and with international human rights treaties.[15]

All these cases concern foreign persons or foreign activities, or obligations undertaken by the UK at the international level. I would estimate that cases of that nature form about half of the cases in our highest court. Much the same appears to be true of the highest courts of most other developed countries. That state of affairs reflects the legal challenges arising from a highly inter-connected and inter-dependent world: a world in which a country such as the UK has become a community of people from many different countries, with many different religions and different cultural practices, posing new types of problems, and giving rise to new types of law guaranteeing new types of rights; a country in which ordinary people are engaged every day in international trade, for example when booking hotel rooms online, or when ordering books online from Amazon under contracts which, if you read the small print, are governed by the law of Luxembourg; a country in which we are all subject to unprecedented levels of surveillance, security checks and searches to protect us against globalised terrorism; a country in which we are all at risk of diseases spread globally by international travel; a country in which we are all affected by environmental and other problems which no country can address effectively on its own; and a country whose major companies operate on a globalised basis, undermining the ability of individual states to regulate their behaviour as employers, taxpayers or polluters, unless the countries operate in cooperation, or at least with an understanding of what other states are doing.

This not only affects national governments. Judges, too, have to be aware of the legal world beyond their country's borders. They have to be conscious that, in an increasing range of situations, they face problems which transcend national boundaries, and in which it is important that courts should, where possible, arrive

[10] *PJS v News Group Newspapers Ltd* [2016] AC 1081.

[11] *Iraqi Civilian Litigation v Ministry of Defence* [2016] 1 WLR 2001.

[12] *Mohammed v Secretary of State for Defence* [2017] 2 WLR 327.

[13] *Re Lehman Brothers International (Europe) Ltd (In Administration)* [2017] 2 WLR 1497.

[14] See, eg, *Ali v Secretary of State for the Home Department* [2016] 1 WLR 4799; *R (MM (Lebanon)) v Secretary of State for the Home Department* [2017] UKSC 10; *R (Agyarko) v Secretary of State for the Home Department* [2017] UKSC 11.

[15] On EU law see, eg, *R (Miller) v Secretary of State for Exiting the European Union* [2017] 2 WLR 583; *R (Buckinghamshire County Council) v Secretary of State for Transport* [2014] 1 WLR 324. On the ECHR see, eg, *R (Nicklinson) v Ministry of Justice* [2015] AC 657; *R (Chester) v Secretary of State for Justice* [2014] AC 271; *R (Animal Defenders International) v Secretary of State for Culture, Media and Sport* [2008] 1 AC 1312.

at solutions which can work in harmony with those arrived at by the courts of other countries.

We cannot, for example, sensibly decide whether to make orders against Internet corporations based in California without having some idea whether those orders are likely to be enforced by the American courts, which in turn requires us to know something about the relevant American law, for example on the First Amendment. US courts, dealing with the constitutionality of the National Security Agency sharing intelligence material relating to US citizens with UK intelligence agencies, need to understand the protections to which that material will be subject under UK law, if it is shared. The same applies if our court is called on to consider the sharing of material relating to UK citizens with agencies in the US.

To give some other examples, we cannot decide whether cloud computing, with data stored in servers all over the globe, is legal under EU law or whether it is necessary for businesses to have independent data centres in the EU to serve customers within that bloc, unless we understand the privacy safeguards that exist under the law of the states where servers are located. A British family judge wondering whether to exercise jurisdiction over a dispute which is already before a court in, say, North Africa, will want to know about the relevant law and practice in that country: for example, what rights a mother has under Shari'a-based law, and whether legal representation will be available to her. In the field of commercial law, where cross-border transactions are normal and are assisted by standard forms of documents, the convergence of law and practice across jurisdictions is economically efficient, since it reduces transaction costs. This tends to make jurisdictions sharing a common approach more attractive to each other as destinations for investment or as sources of collaboration. Of course, when interpreting legislation intended to give effect to international treaties, the need for a consistent approach (eg to the rights of air passengers under the Montreal Convention) provides a strong justification for judges considering the decisions of foreign courts.

So, in a globalised world, there are practical advantages in the common law jurisdictions achieving a degree of coherence and consistency in their case law. Even when there may be no apparent practical advantages of that kind, we can learn from the thinking of others. We have already discovered the value of finding out how courts in broadly comparable societies, such as Canada and the United States, have dealt with problems to which we also must find solutions (eg in relation to the detention of insurgents overseas,[16] and counter-terrorism measures).[17] As we have recently said in two of our Supreme Court judgments, although it is 'inevitable that inconsistencies in the common law will develop between different jurisdictions … it seems to us highly desirable for all those jurisdictions to learn from each other, and at least to lean in favour of harmonising the development of the common law round the world'.[18]

[16] See *Mohammed* (n 12).

[17] *R v Gul* [2014] AC 1260.

[18] *FHR European Ventures LLP v Cedar Capital Partners LLP* [2015] AC 250 at [45]; *AIB Group (UK) Ltd v Mark Redler & Co* [2015] AC 1503 at [121].

But the value of comparative law is wider than that might suggest. The judgments of other common law courts can give us a clearer insight into the state of our own law, and see our own thinking, and its possible deficiencies, more clearly. They can make us question received wisdom, and can give us ideas about how our law might be developed.

The use of comparative material, particularly from other common law jurisdictions, is generally taken for granted in the UK Supreme Court. When we are dealing with a novel or difficult problem in equity or trusts, in contract or in tort, we expect to be referred to the judgments of the highest courts of other common law jurisdictions, including in particular Canada, Australia, New Zealand and Hong Kong. It may also be important to have regard to judgments from the United States, depending to some extent on the subject-matter. We consult Australian and Canadian textbooks (and, sometimes, the American Restatement) on these subjects, and expect to be provided with the relevant academic articles from universities there as well as our own. Sometimes we may receive an unwelcome surprise, when reading the comments of scholars who are less concerned than our own to maintain amicable relations with the British judiciary. One can only imagine what Lord Diplock's reaction would have been if he had read, in the second edition of Meagher, Gummow and Lehane, that his speech in *United Scientific Holdings*[19] was 'the low water-mark of modern English jurisprudence'.[20] Lord Diplock's own approach to academic work, domestic or foreign, was encapsulated in his remark to Lord Brandon, 'Books? You don't need books. All you need is a set of Appeal Cases and your own intelligence'. Those were the days.

One can see in our judgments how legal principles, methods of reasoning, and solutions to particular problems in other jurisdictions can influence the development of principles, reasoning or solutions in our own. A recent example was the decision of the Supreme Court in the case of *Montgomery v Lanarkshire Health Board*,[21] in which we considered authorities from the US, Canada and Australia to identify respects in which the then leading British authority on informed consent to medical treatment was unconvincingly reasoned—and had in any event become out of date—and used those overseas authorities to assist us in identifying a principled and practical approach for the UK to adopt. Our judgments, in turn, can influence the thinking of judges in these other countries.

The impact of this sort of dialogue is a complex matter, varying from one area of the law to another. As with other changes in a country's laws, whether comparative law leads to changes in legal thinking, and to changes in the law, depends upon a multitude of factors. The adoption by one jurisdiction of apparently similar laws or common law principles to those of another jurisdiction may be followed by differences in their interpretation and application.

[19] *United Scientific Holdings Ltd v Burnley Borough Council* [1978] AC 904.

[20] RP Meagher, WMC Gummow and JRF Lehane, *Equity: Doctrines and Remedies*, 2nd edn (Sydney, Butterworths, 1984) xi. An attack which Meagher continued in his judicial capacity, describing Lord Diplock's analysis as 'so obviously erroneous as to be risible': *GR Mailman & Associates Pty Ltd v Wormald (Australia) Pty Limited* (1991) 24 NSWLR 80 at 99.

[21] *Montgomery v Lanarkshire Health Board* [2015] AC 1430.

We are, of course, conscious of differences between our legal system and those of other common law jurisdictions, of differences in the constitutional framework and culture, and of differences between our societies. A point which is sometimes emphasised by Australian judges and academics is that our law has in recent times been subject to European influences. But that is nothing new in the common law, if one thinks for example of Lord Mansfield's borrowings from civilian systems, and it is not, in my view, a reason why our judgments should not be of interest to common law courts overseas, or vice versa. We may in recent times have been more inclined to flexible reasoning based on perceptions of fairness than, say, Australian judges, and we may also in recent times have taken a less conservative view of the judicial role in developing the law—although one can also think of counter-examples. We have tended to be less influenced by policy considerations in recent times than the Canadian Supreme Court. These differences do not necessarily diminish the value of considering the reasoning of other judges working in the same tradition. On the contrary, the Australian High Court's refusal to follow our approach to unjust enrichment, for example, or the Canadian Supreme Court's rejection of the unjust factors approach, is all the more reason for us to be aware of, and to question, our own orthodoxies, particularly in an area where domestic thinking may be heavily influenced by a relatively small group of academics.

There is, however, notably less dialogue between us and most other common law jurisdictions in public law cases. Unless we are dealing with international law—as we often are, for example in cases concerned with refugees, or military operations overseas, or immigration—the only comparative common law material regularly referred to in the Supreme Court in public law cases comes from Canada. The jurisdiction whose public law judgments have been most influential upon us in recent years, apart from Canada, is arguably Germany. The only common law textbook I often consult on public law, from outside the UK, is Peter Hogg's *Constitutional Law of Canada*.[22] But I also have books on French and German administrative law on my shelves. And, as I have explained, we have close relationships with the German Federal Constitutional Court and the French Conseil d'Etat, as well as with common law courts such as the Canadian and US Supreme Courts.

Why do we make less use of comparative common law material in public than in private law? Part of the explanation is the degree of embeddedness of public law in a particular historical and political context, a particular constitutional framework, and a particular legal culture. So, for example, one cannot readily extrapolate from the experience of federalism in the United States, Canada or Australia—all of which are different—to devolution in the United Kingdom. So there are reasons inherent in the nature of public law why cross-jurisdictional dialogue in that field is likely to be at the level of the lowest common denominator: a shared general framework of ideas, within which jurisdictions develop independently.

Another part of the explanation for the limited use of comparative common law material in this context is that our public law has become increasingly influenced over the past 45 years by European law. When we joined the European Communities,

[22] P Hogg, *Constitutional Law of Canada*, 5th edn (Toronto, Carswell, 2007).

as they then were, in 1973, English administrative law had only recently awoken from its long sleep. It was applied in a comparatively restrained manner, particularly in relation to questions of social or economic policy. By comparison, European Community law was a system in which the courts played a much more important role in supervising legislative and administrative institutions, and in which a more sophisticated system of public law existed, derived primarily from French and German administrative law.

Our entry into the European Communities led to judicial review of legislation, judicial review of matters of social and economic policy which would previously have been regarded as effectively non-justiciable, and the introduction of new concepts of public law, such as proportionality, equality, fundamental rights, legal certainty and the protection of legitimate expectations. And as the European Communities evolved into the European Union, the ambit of EU law widened so as to cover very extensive areas of public law: not only matters relating to trade, but also such matters as immigration and citizenship, counter-terrorism and the environment. The consequence has been that questions of public law have increasingly become questions of EU law. Since EU law is authoritatively interpreted by the Court of Justice of the European Union, and the UK Supreme Court, like the apex courts of the other member states, is obliged to refer any arguable questions as to the interpretation of EU law to it for decision, our public law is to that extent determined by the Court of Justice.

Furthermore, because EU law asserts primacy over domestic common law and legislation—a primacy which is in principle accorded to it by the European Communities Act 1972—and because the Court of Justice asserts its primacy over domestic courts, this has given rise to constitutional issues which affect us in common with other member states, and in relation to which the German and Italian courts, in particular, began to develop a jurisprudence long before us.[23] That is one reason why their case law is of interest to us. And the public law concepts I have mentioned not only have their origins in Germany and France, but continue to be applied and developed by courts there in relation to similar problems to those which face us. That is another reason why we value our discussions with them.

The other crucial development in this jurisdiction has been the passing of the Human Rights Act in 1998. The peculiarity of that Act is that it does not establish

[23] Italy: see, eg, Case 6/64 *Costa v ENEL* [1964] ECR 585. Germany: see, eg, Case 11/70 *Internationale Handelsgesellschaft mbH v Einfuhr- und Vorratsstelle für Getreide und Futtermittel* [1970] ECR 1125, in which the ECJ held that directly applicable EU law could not be challenged even by a fundamental principle of a nation's constitution. Subsequently, in *Re Wünsche Handelsgesellschaft* [1987] 3 CMLR 225, the *Bundesverfassungsgericht* held that as long as EU law provided protection for fundamental rights substantially in line with the German Constitution, it would not scrutinise EU law by the standard of the German Constitution. The primacy of EU law in the legal order of the United Kingdom was grappled with in the following cases: *R (Buckinghamshire County Council)* (n 15) in which the Supreme Court held that the status of EU law in our legal system is derived from the European Communities Act 1972; *Thoburn v Sunderland City Council* [2003] QB 151 for the principle that the constitutional relationship between EU law and our domestic law was determined by the common law, and that the European Communities Act 1972 fell within a category of constitutional statutes recognised by the common law as protected from implied repeal; *R v Secretary of State for Transport ex p Factortame Ltd (No 2)* [1991] 1 AC 603 in which the House of Lords held that courts could 'disapply' Acts of Parliament in conflict with EU law.

a domestic Bill of Rights, comparable to the German Basic Law, the US Constitution or the Canadian Charter of Fundamental Rights and Freedoms, but instead gives effect in domestic law to guarantees which the UK has given in an international treaty: a treaty of which an international court is the authoritative interpreter. Since its rulings on the interpretation of the European Convention on Human Rights (ECHR) have mostly been given in cases concerned with issues arising in countries with cultures and legal systems very different from our own, there have been uncertainties as to how the ECHR should be applied in the context of a country with a different type of legal system and a significantly different history and culture. That is the principal reason why the court in the common law world whose judgments are most frequently cited to us in public law cases is the Canadian Supreme Court: its Charter jurisprudence applies similarly worded guarantees to those of the ECHR in the context of a broadly similar system of law and government to our own. In theory, we might also be referred to judgments from other jurisdictions with comparable charters, such as New Zealand and the Australian State of Victoria, but in practice their case law has been less abundant than in Canada. And because the ECHR is an international treaty, a host of other international treaties are also cited as aids to its interpretation, turning even more of our public law hearings into discussions of public international law.

These two developments—the increasing influence and ambit of EU law, and the influence of the ECHR—have had major consequences for our public law as compared with that of many other common law jurisdictions. First, and perhaps most importantly, the approach of UK courts has been influenced to a great extent by the general principles of European law. These have been absorbed by British judges, through their constant application, so as to become a familiar and accepted way of approaching issues in public law.[24]

Secondly, there has been a development in the nature of the judicial role in public law cases, and in how it is perceived. We are required, in applying EU law and, more particularly, the Human Rights Act, to make evaluative judgments, sometimes relating to legislation on controversial issues of social or economic policy, which would strike our predecessors as entering more deeply into the merits of decisions in those fields than the *Wednesbury* approach as traditionally understood. The courts have had no alternative but to adopt this approach: a more restrained and legalistic approach cannot supply the answers to the questions which we are required to address.

The Supreme Court is trying in its case law to develop a structured approach to the application of the Human Rights Act, having regard to the courts' constitutional role and their institutional capacities, but it is not straightforward: different judges plainly view the matter in different ways.[25] It seems to me to be important for the

[24] See A Carter, 'Constitutional Convergence? Some Lessons from Proportionality', ch 18 in this volume.

[25] See, eg, such cases as *R (Nicklinson) and another v Ministry of Justice and others (CNK Alliance Ltd and others intervening)* [2015] AC 657; *R (Lord Carlile of Berriew and others) v Secretary of State for the Home Department* [2015] AC 945 and *R (Tigere) v Secretary of State for Business, Innovation and Skills (Just for Kids Law Intervening)* [2015] 1 WLR 3820.

judiciary to be careful in their response to the growing tendency for campaigners on social issues to rely on the courts to pursue their objectives: a tendency which the Human Rights Act has in practice facilitated.[26] If the judiciary allow the courts to become arenas for debates on social policy, they risk forfeiting their only significant asset: public confidence in their independence. In that regard, lessons can be drawn from experience in the United States. When applying a proportionality test, it can be debateable at what point the line should be drawn; but, as it seems to me, judges who see themselves as agents (or opponents) of social reform are on the wrong side of that line.

In approaching this difficult task, however, we have again been assisted by comparative law: above all, by the Charter jurisprudence of the Canadian Supreme Court. We and our European colleagues also try to learn from discussing these issues together. At a recent conference organised by the French Conseil d'Etat, for example, French judges raised their concerns about the difficulty of deciding on a principled basis how much leeway the courts should allow the government when applying the ECHR, and were interested in the way in which we have been developing an approach to that problem.

Thirdly, it has become relatively uncommon for appeals to be brought to the Supreme Court on the basis of English constitutional and administrative law. To the extent that matters are governed by EU law, that is inevitable. But to the extent that matters fall within the ambit of the Human Rights Act, it is not. We have repeatedly emphasised in recent years that the guarantees in that Act are normally fulfilled by applying our domestic law, developed if need be to meet its requirements,[27] but counsel can sometimes be resistant to that lesson. Because of the width of the guarantees in the ECHR, and the description of them in the Human Rights Act as Convention rights, the reaction of some lawyers practising before the courts has been to attempt to turn all questions of public law, and indeed many questions of private law, into questions of human rights, to be decided by applying the case law of the European Court of Human Rights rather than our domestically-created law. To give two examples from the Trinity term of 2016, the Supreme Court heard an appeal concerned with the Inland Revenue's disclosure of a taxpayer's affairs to journalists, in which the ECHR was relied on, but no reference was made to the common law of confidentiality,[28] and another appeal in which damages were sought for an allegedly wrongful prosecution, which was argued entirely on the basis of the ECHR, without any reference to the tort of malicious prosecution or to the law of negligence.[29] Cases concerned with procedural fairness are almost always argued on the basis of the ECHR, while centuries of English law on the subject are ignored.[30] We continue

[26] See, eg, *Nicklinson* (n 25); *Steinfeld and Keidan v Secretary of State for Education* [2017] EWCA Civ 81.

[27] See, eg, *R (Osborn) v Parole Board* [2014] AC 1115 and *Kennedy v Charity Commission (Secretary of State for Justice and others intervening)* [2015] AC 455.

[28] *R (Ingenious Media Holdings plc and another) v Revenue and Customs Commissioners* [2016] 1 WLR 4164. The case was decided on the basis of the law of confidentiality.

[29] *SXH v Crown Prosecution Service* [2014] 1 WLR 3238.

[30] See, eg, *Osborn* (n 27).

to produce an appreciable number of judgments in which the reasoning is based on English constitutional and administrative law, but these points are usually raised and developed by the bench, without much assistance from counsel in researching comparative material.[31]

How and to what extent should comparative material be used? In an article in the *Law Quarterly Review* in 2008,[32] I wrote that foreign law and decisions of foreign courts can be a source of ideas and experience. Where new legal problems arise to which other systems have devised solutions, those solutions will enable the identification of options and possibly even an evaluation of their workability. I remain of that view. I am cautious about using foreign materials as a source of empirical evidence as to how a given legal solution is likely to work in practice in this country. That use of foreign law requires discriminating selection and a very good understanding of the legal system and society where it originates. That said, I felt in the *Montgomery* case that one could view with scepticism the warning that the need for doctors to explain to their patients what the available treatment options were, and their attendant risks and advantages, would throw the NHS into chaos, given that informed consent had been an established part of medical practice for many years in Canada and Australia as well as the United States: countries with some diversity in their approach to the provision of medical services.[33]

Generally, however, I prefer to use foreign law as a source of ideas, and of different approaches to legal problems from our own. I can then use my own judgment to assess whether the ideas in question might provide a good basis for considering our law or thinking about its development. Approaching the matter in that way, I do not need to be excessively anxious about being selective, any more than I worry about being selective in looking at domestic precedents or in deciding which articles I might read. Sir Konrad Schiemann, a now-retired Lord Justice of Appeal and judge of the European Court of Justice, was once asked if X was a bad judge. He replied that there are no bad judges: there are judges who are good, and judges who are very good, and X, he said, is a good judge.[34] In those terms, if I know that Judge A is a good judge, and that Judge B is a very good judge, then I am going to be more inclined to read Judge B than Judge A, whether they are foreign judges or domestic.

Looking to the future, until it becomes clear what our future relationship with the EU and the rest of the world is to be, it is impossible to predict what changes to our law may result and when they may occur. Equally, although the government has spoken of replacing the Human Rights Act with a domestic Bill of Rights, the nature of any Bill of Rights, its timing, and whether the UK will remain a party to

[31] For example, in *Buckinghamshire County Council* (n 15), the question arising under Article 9 of the Bill of Rights 1689 was raised from the bench, and the German authorities cited were also produced by the bench. In *R (Bourgass) v Secretary of State for Justice* [2016] AC 384, the question whether the power was exercised by the person on whom it had been conferred, and the consequent question as to the application of the *Carltona* principle, were raised by the bench.

[32] R Reed, 'Foreign Precedents and Judicial Reasoning: The American Debate and British Practice' (2008) 124 *LQR* 253.

[33] See n 21.

[34] In reality, bad judges are often clever judges who are temperamentally ill-suited to listening patiently (and, for the most part, silently) to other people: something which takes up a large part of a judge's time.

the ECHR, remain to be seen. I am not going to speculate about what may happen. But the changes which emerge, not only in the law itself, but in the aspects of society which influence the law, such as our trading relationships with other countries, our cultural links, and the role of London as a global centre for financial, commercial and legal services, will inevitably influence our law's future relationship with that of other common law and European jurisdictions.

Whatever the future may hold, however, comparative law will remain an important tool in the judge's toolbox. As the German writer Thomas Mann wrote in *Joseph and His Brothers*,[35] it is by comparison with others that we discover who we are, and learn what we could be.

[35] T Mann, *Joseph und seine Brüder* (Stockholm, Bermann-Fischer, 1948).

13

Transplants in Public Law

CHERYL SAUNDERS

I. RATIONALE

THE AIM OF this chapter is to examine the phenomenon of transplants in public law, in order to better understand their dynamics in the early twenty-first century from the perspective of the theory and practice of comparative public law.

The topic fits well in a volume on the unity of common law public law. To the extent that there is unity across jurisdictional boundaries in the common law, it is largely attributable to transplants of some kind. Transplants obviously occurred at the point of colonisation.[1] They have continued over time, through the interactions that naturally occur between broadly similar systems. These include the forms and processes of adjudication that characterise the common law and have played a significant role in its development. Within the common law world, transplants are no longer a one-way street; the United Kingdom is a recipient as well. Ironically, transplants can also contribute to disunity of the common law, when they introduce concepts and institutions from elsewhere.

There is already a large literature on transplants.[2] I justify adding to it on three grounds. The first is that much, although by no means all, of the literature deals with transplants in private law. Transplants in public law, which arguably raise some distinctive considerations, have been much less systematically explored. Secondly and in any event, the current tsunami of transplants in both private and public law that is a continuing by-product of globalisation provides new context for the practice, which merits attention in its own right. Thirdly, it may be that both the theory and practice of transplants in public law can be improved, with benefit to the evolution of systems of public law and to the quality of public law scholarship.

[1] M Graziadei, 'Comparative Law as the Study of Transplants and Receptions' in M Reimann and R Zimmermann (eds), *Oxford Handbook of Comparative Law* (Oxford, Oxford University Press, 2006) 441, 451–53.

[2] The classic is A Watson, *Legal Transplants: An Approach to Comparative Law* 2nd edn (University of Georgia Press, 1993). For an analysis of the impact of his work over time, including principal critiques, see JW Cairns, 'Watson, Walton and the History of Legal Transplants' (2013) 41 *Ga J Int'l & Comp L* 637. A recent interesting addition to the literature is G Frankenberg (ed), *Order from Transfer: Comparative Constitutional Design and Legal Culture* (Cheltenham, Edward Elgar, 2013), of which more below.

At least two definitions are needed at this preliminary stage to clarify the scope of the chapter. One concerns the concept of transplant itself. There is much angst in the literature about the terminology of transplant, in case its properties require fidelity to the natural sciences on which the metaphor draws.[3] In a complication of another kind, the legal ideas that cross jurisdictional boundaries often are so amorphous that the process is more accurately described as diffusion, to use William Twining's term.[4] For present purposes, however, I intend to ride out purist objections to the metaphor by sticking with the terminology of transplant, not least because many of the suggested alternatives are open to a similar critique. At the same time, however, I will confine my argument to the deliberate movement of relatively structured legal phenomena across jurisdictional boundaries. In so doing, I do not underestimate the significance of the complex processes of diffusion of legal ideas but, rather, focus attention on a sub-set. These are likely to be more than ideas but otherwise may take any of the forms constitutive of systems of public law, ranging from theories to legal text. This approach excludes some, although by no means all, references by courts to foreign law. There are plenty of instances of transplants, or proposed transplants of the kind with which this chapter is concerned, although I acknowledge that there may be room for argument about particular cases at the margins.

Secondly, it may be useful at this stage to give more content to the notion of transplant failure. Of course, to return briefly to the metaphor, some transplants may be rejected. In a legal context, this may occur where a transplant is not implemented at all, through neglect or formal repeal. Alternatively, however, more often than not, failure might take the form of a transplant that did not work as intended. This is a more complex proposition, to the extent that the effect of a transplant can never be anticipated precisely. Surprise outcomes sometimes work well enough and may prove to be welcome innovations. But where a transplant falls significantly short of expectations in ways that are unwelcome or undesirable, it can be deemed to have failed. The label of failure might also be attached to proposals for transplants, in the course of advocacy or scholarship, which are unpersuasive for reasons that relate to the case for the transplant itself.

The next part of the chapter sets the scene for a study of transplants, generally and in the fields of public law. It explores in particular the implications of globalisation for transplant theory and practice. The three parts that follow deal respectively with three significant phases of any decision about a transplant: the identification of a possible transplant (choice); evaluation of whether the transplant should proceed (reception); and any adaptation to the transplant in its original form that is deemed appropriate for the purpose. To make the argument less abstract I draw on three examples in particular. One is the proposal to establish a Constitutional Court for the United Kingdom, which emerged in connection with the political struggle over the relationship between the United Kingdom and the rest of Europe, but which is only one of many examples of burgeoning interest in the potential of Constitutional

[3] M Seckelmann, 'Clotted History and Chemical Reactions: On the Possibility of Constitutional Transfer' in G Frankenberg (ed), *Order from Transfer* (Cheltenham, Edward Elgar, 2013) 36, 37–38.

[4] W Twining, 'Diffusion of Law: A Global Perspective' (2004) 49 *J Legal Pluralism and Unofficial Law* 1.

Courts around in the world.[5] The second is the introduction of statutory bills of rights into Australian jurisdictions, drawing on prototypes in New Zealand and the United Kingdom.[6] The third is the now-historic adoption of a referendum process for constitutional change in Australia, which might stand also as a proxy for the adoption of direct democracy in otherwise representative democratic systems.[7] A conclusion will reflect briefly on the implications of transplants for the unity of public law.

II. SETTING THE SCENE

Historically, the debate on legal transplants has divided scholars over the degree to which law was socially embedded so as to hinder its movement from place to place. In his seminal original work on the subject, Alan Watson argued that transplant was such a common feature of the development of law that the study of the relationship between legal systems deserved recognition as a branch of comparative law. Not only did borrowing occur on a 'massive scale', but it was 'socially easy', even where the transplanted matter derived from a 'very different kind of system'.[8] He accepted that a recipient might misunderstand foreign law but that, in any event, a transplant would 'grow in its new body'.[9] His views on the ways in which legal culture shaped the process of selection through legal elites necessarily imposed some practical limits on the most likely sources in terms of form, language and availability.[10] Subsequent writings suggested that he also had in mind that the actual subject of a transplant might be an idea, rather than anything more tangible.[11] Nevertheless, on the basis of these essentially empirical observations, Watson drew a series of conclusions about the relationship between law and society. One, which he described as of 'practical use ... in a time of conscious law reform' was that 'usually legal rules are not peculiarly devised for the particular society in which they now operate and ... that this is not a matter for great concern'.[12]

Critics of the transplant thesis, by contrast, emphasised the significance of law in its social and political context to argue that, at the very least, legal transplantation was complex and potentially fraught.[13] A more extreme position denied the

[5] The proposal is described by M Elliott, 'A Constitutional Court for the UK? My Letter to The Times' *Public Law for Everyone* (5 February 2016) <www.publiclawforeveryone.com/2016/02/05/a-constitutional-court-for-the-uk-my-letter-to-the-times/> last accessed 30 May 2017 (hereafter 'Elliott 'A Constitutional Court'). See also J King, 'On the Proposal for a UK Constitutional Court' UK Const L Blog (8 Feb 2016) <https://ukconstitutionallaw.org/> last accessed 14 August 2017.

[6] In chronological order, these instruments are: New Zealand Bill of Rights Act 1990 (NZ); Human Rights Act 1998 (UK); Human Rights Act 2004 (ACT); Charter of Human Rights and Responsibilities Act 2006 (Vic).

[7] Commonwealth Constitution, s 128.

[8] See Watson, *Legal Transplants* (n 2) 95–96.

[9] ibid, at 27, 116.

[10] ibid, at 112–13.

[11] See Cairns, 'Watson, Walton and the History of Legal Transplants' (n 2) at 646.

[12] See Watson, *Legal Transplants* (n 2) at 96.

[13] O Kahn-Freund, 'On Uses and Misuses of Comparative Law' (1974) 37 *Modern Law Review* 1.

possibility of legal transplants at all, on the basis of an understanding of law that derives its meaning from the 'interpretative community'.[14] Different views about the significance of context, including culture, persist, channelled through what has been usefully, if inelegantly, characterised as 'culturalist' or 'transferist' positions.[15] Over time, however, a mainstream modus vivendi seems to have been reached. Legal transplants are indeed common, although the processes of dissemination may be richer and more complex than Watson assumed.[16] Context always is likely to be relevant to the outcome of a transplant. There are many different dimensions of context, however. One of the most elusive is culture: a multi-faceted phenomenon, often contested within a jurisdiction; susceptible to evolution over time; and existing in a symbiotic relationship with law, in which each shapes the other.[17]

The earlier writings on transplants did not purport to apply to public law. The protagonists did not work in the field and in any event were wary about extending the thesis to what Kahn-Freund described as the 'organic' end of the legal spectrum, where Constitutions lie.[18] For present purposes, it is necessary to try to take stock of the bases for caution about transplants in public law, confining the meaning of the term for present purposes to the closely related sub-branches of constitutional and administrative law. Traditionally they included—and arguably still include—the following. By its very nature, as the law that binds the organs of state, public law is closely tied to the politics and political culture of the state in which it is embedded. Public law claims to derive its legitimacy from the people of a state, at least as a matter of theory and rhetoric. In practice, public law undeniably depends in some degree on acceptance by political elites. Public law may have deep roots in historical experience from which theories develop explaining and entrenching contemporary practice. The principle of parliamentary sovereignty is an example. Over time, the components of a system of public law tend to become integrated, forming an organic, interdependent whole. Australian dependence on administrative law and institutional integrity, in the absence of formal rights protection, illustrates the point. Public law is multilayered, comprising theories, values, principles, practices, rules, institutions, doctrines, interpretations and text. Any one of these may be subject to transplant in public law. Transplantation of one layer without others, which may be the norm, raises some interesting but typically unexplored questions. The fashionable doctrine of unconstitutional constitutional amendment offers an example. In its admittedly complicated origins, it was underpinned by a particular theory of constituent power, which offered some constraint on the circumstances in which it was invoked and the procedures that were followed.[19] Transplantation of the doctrine

[14] P Legrand, 'The Impossibility of "Legal Transplants"' (1997) 4 *Maastricht J Eur & Comp L* 111 at 116.

[15] R G Small, 'Towards a Theory of Contextual Transplants' (2005) 19 *Emory Int'l L Rev* 1431 at 1433.

[16] See Twining, 'Diffusion of Law' (n 4).

[17] R Cotterrell, 'Comparative Law and Legal Culture' in Mathias Reimann and Reinhard Zimmermann (eds), *Oxford Handbook of Comparative Law* (Oxford, Oxford University Press, 2006) 709.

[18] Kahn-Freund, 'On the Uses and Misuses of Comparative Law' (n 13) at 17.

[19] J Colon-Rios, 'Five Conceptions of Constituent Power' (2014) 130 *Law Quarterly Review* 306, analysing five conceptions of constituent power, of which the fifth is relevant here.

without the underlying theory confers extraordinary discretion on public institutions, often the judiciary, unless or until alternative constraints are found, or evolve, to fill the gap.

Notwithstanding these familiar claims about the characteristics of public law, transplants are and historically have been as common in public as in private law. The very concept of a written constitution, as presently understood, is a transplant. The principal generic features of constitutions are transplants: separation of powers; judicial review; federalism; and bills of rights. The legal systems in which they are embedded are transplants, including the core principles and remedies of administrative law. It would be possible, if complex, to construct a branch of comparative constitutional law that traces the relationship between the constitutions of the world, mirroring Watson's claims for comparative private law. In earlier times, transplants sometimes occurred wholesale through processes of colonisation, conquest and other kinds of force. Many now are the consequence of more generalised processes of the diffusion of ideas. But many also are attributable to more deliberate decisions at different points in the life-cycle of systems of public law: when new systems are formed; when pressures for change emerge; during adjudication involving difficult issues; and when the dynamics of public law present multiple paths. Decision-makers may be governments, parliaments, courts and advisers of various kinds. Advocates may be scholars, lawyers and activist groups, including NGOs.

The rapid rise of interest in comparative public law in the decades following the end of the cold war inevitably drew attention to the phenomenon of transplants in public law. Simultaneously, however, the deepening of the contemporary phase of globalisation affected the context in which transplants occur. Globalisation is potentially relevant for present purposes in several ways. Most obviously, norms introduced into systems of public law that derive from or are endorsed by international law are deemed to be held in common and not to be transplants at all, even if they raise challenges for local effectiveness of other kinds.[20] This dimension of globalisation also contributes to the convergence of systems of public law, at least superficially, defusing concerns about horizontal transplants to that extent.[21] These developments in turn encourage arguments that systems of public law now derive a measure of legitimacy from the international sphere, which also offers sanctions for compliance, however patchy and limited.[22] On this view, systems of public law are no longer self-sufficient, if ever they were, but co-exist with each other in an ill-defined network of sorts.[23] If this is right, at least some of the claims for the distinctiveness of public law require qualification. In time, if they continue, these developments may completely change the ways in which we think about public law.

[20] This is the clear inference from UNSG, 'Guidance Note of the Secretary-General: United Nations Assistance to Constitution-Making Processes' (2009) Guiding Principle 2.

[21] C Saunders, 'The Impact of Internationalisation on National Constitutions' in Albert H Y Chen (ed), *Constitutionalism in Asia in the Early 21st Century* (Cambridge, Cambridge University Press, 2014) 391.

[22] N Krisch, *Beyond Constitutionalism: The Pluralist Structure of Postnational Law* (Oxford, Oxford University Press, 2012).

[23] R Michaels, '"One Size Can Fit All": Some Heretical Thoughts on the Mass Production of Legal Transplants', in Frankenberg (n 2) at 56, 76.

For the moment, however, their sticking power remains to be seen. In a still state-centred world, globalisation often involves two-steps forward and at least one step back. The referendum vote in the United Kingdom in favour of leaving the European Union makes the point.[24]

Most particularly for present purposes, the conditions accompanying globalisation in the early twenty-first century have contributed to a proliferation of transplants, as states respond to a myriad of economic, political, security and other challenges, at least some of which are, broadly, shared. The change represented by this development is not only quantitative but also qualitative. The sources of potential transplants are multiplied by information technology, a wilderness of databases and the apparently inexorable spread of English as a shared language for communication. Access to constitutions and other key texts in public law can now readily be secured by the simple task of Googling. The decisions of the courts of many states in which English is not the local language are now available in translation. Networks of public law scholars and jurists further facilitate the spread of ideas about public law. International and supra-national agencies and an army of NGOs are available to provide advice on public law and, sometimes, to insist on acceptance of international norms of various kinds. A concept of best practice is frequently invoked.[25]

Changed conditions challenge old theories and old methods, making way for new ones. In a provocative response to the challenge, Gunther Frankenberg has proposed what he describes as the IKEA theory of constitutional 'transfer'.[26] As the name implies, the metaphor on which he draws is the global dissemination of pre-packaged standardised furniture in a form that requires assembly by a purchaser at home. Frankenberg sketches a multi-stage process of transfer, in which a legal artefact is taken from its source, stripped of contextual complications, placed on a global shelf and taken down by a consumer for use elsewhere, where recontextualisation is inevitable. The result implies superficial convergence although not necessarily universalism. Recontextualisation can be a catalyst for diversity as borrowed legal artefacts are adapted, integrated into different systems, infused by new ideas or otherwise affected by their adoptive environment.[27] As Frankenberg also notes, there are many public law products that do not make it to the global shelves.[28]

The IKEA theory of legal transfer is essentially descriptive. Others have given it a more normative twist, however, arguing that 'one size fits all' may offer adequate, if not perfect, legal regimes across a world in which some states lack capacity and cultures themselves are converging, making a new formalism feasible.[29]

[24] Letter from Prime Minister Theresa May to European Union President Tusk (29 March 2017) <www.gov.uk/government/publications/prime-ministers-letter-to-donald-tusk-triggering-article-50> last accessed 30 May 2017.

[25] R Peerenboom, 'Towards a Methodology for Successful Legal Transplants' (2013) *Chin J Comp Law* 4.

[26] G Frankenberg, 'Constitutions as Commodities: Notes on a Theory of Transfer' in Frankenberg (ed), (n 2) 1.

[27] See Saunders (n 21) at 391.

[28] See Frankenberg (n 26) at 15, 17.

[29] See Michaels (n 23) at 78.

And so the parameters of the challenge are set. The IKEA theory is still something of a caricature, although not to the extent that one might hope. Transplants are commonplace, not least in public law and may be urged, or occur, with scant attention to jurisdictional difference. For pragmatists, whether this matters or not depends on the outcomes. Anecdotally, these are patchy. Opinion nevertheless may differ on where the balance of advantage lies. For the theorist, whether transplant practice is a cause for concern depends also on the accuracy of claims of convergence of systems and cultures, on which the jury is still out. For both, the answer also may depend on whether it is practicable to do better.

In what follows, I argue that context still matters for transplants in public law, threatening both outcomes and the plausibility of advocacy that underplays or ignores it. From this standpoint, while a degree of convergence can be accepted as a reality there are still significant differences, including underlying differences, between national systems of public law, with implications for transplants. This by no means suggests that transplants should not occur, but that attention is needed to what is transplanted and how, drawing on the resources of comparative public law. It may be that, with hindsight, the early twenty-first century will prove to have been a time of transition in public law, from here to somewhere, but that is not the present problem. The remainder of the chapter seeks to substantiate this position, using examples to give the argument substance.

III. CHOICE

The first stage in the story of any public law transplant is the choice of matter to be adopted or adapted. Those who think and write about transplants tend to be ambivalent about the need to understand the context from which it is drawn. In part, this is because, at least in some cases, there are multiple potential sources, the original of which is unknown, in a world in which many of the staples of public law have moved from place to place over a considerable period of time.[30] In part, ambivalence also is attributable to acceptance that transplanted matter in any event will operate differently in a recipient jurisdiction and that if a solution is needed it lies in the manner of reception. A third explanation may lie in the difficulty of understanding the context from which a public law artefact is drawn, at least for an outsider. Depending on the particular transplant in prospect, context for this purpose may extend well beyond formal law, which may be difficult enough to grasp adequately, to history, institutional design, legal culture or political practice, to identify only some of the possibilities.

Each of these arguments has some force in some conditions. As generalisations, however, they offer a siren song which should be treated with due caution. It may readily be accepted that some of the most familiar institutions of public law have multiple sources, as a consequence of being filtered by cascading transplant through

[30] See Frankenberg (n 26) at 9.

multiple, sometimes divergent, channels. This is a large part of the way in which systems of public law have developed in all parts of the world, which must be factored into any methodological account. The point is exemplified by the institution of a specialist Constitutional Court, to which I return below, which was disseminated throughout the world from its Kelsenian origins in Austria, after being given prominence by its adaptation in Germany in the wake of World War II, from whence it spread in various directions around Europe, Asia and Africa.[31]

Usually, when a choice is made of the subject-matter of a transplant the decision-makers have a source in mind. More often than not, a decision-maker has a reason for borrowing that matter from that particular source. Sometimes this may be no more than prestige, or familiarity with the source.[32] Arguably, towards the end of the twentieth century, the emerging democracies in Central and Eastern Europe adopted versions of the German Constitutional Court for either or both of these reasons. In practice, however, it seems likely that expectations of a transplant are somewhat more focussed, not only on the functions that it will fulfil but on the way in which it will do so. To the emerging democracies in Europe, for example, the German court was not only familiar and prestigious but a highly successful example of democratic constitutionalism in action.[33]

Where this is the case, there needs to be some understanding of the proposed transplant in the context from which it is to be drawn, to evaluate it properly. Evaluation might involve decisions about whether a proposed transplant is the right choice for the desired purpose and the adjustments that might be needed to accommodate it in the recipient jurisdiction so as to avoid unwanted consequences, as far as it is possible to do so. Evaluation can also help to identify other factors that support the proposed transplant in its home context. In some cases, these may also be considered for transplant to increase the chances that it will work as expected. In conditions of globalisation, where the constraints that previously limited choice have to some extent been removed, such understanding may be difficult to come by. It may also be accepted that contextual understanding will never be perfect, particularly within reasonable time limits, and that at least some interpretations will be contestable. Prudence suggests, however, that the attempt should be made. Part of the battle is accepting that there is something to know. The conditions of globalisation that complicate transplants also make comparative knowledge more readily accessible.

There is no shortage of examples to illustrate the significance of understanding the context from which a transplant derives. One might use, for example, the principle of proportionality, the robust conception of freedom of speech that prevails in the United States, older monarchical but democratic constitutions that appear to confer

[31] AHY Chen and MP Maduro, 'The Judiciary and Constitutional Review' in M Tushnet, T Fleiner and C Saunders (eds) *Routledge Handbook of Constitutional Law* (Abingdon, Routledge, 2013) 97; L Garlicki, 'Constitutional Courts versus Supreme Courts' (2007) 5 *International Journal of Constitutional Law* 44.

[32] See Michaels (n 23) at 70, suggesting the need to come 'from somewhere' as a rationale, at least for transplants at the IKEA end of the spectrum.

[33] See Garlicki (n 31).

all executive power on the Crown. Horror stories make easy marks: for example, claims that judicial review is unnecessary for constitutionalism because the United Kingdom does without it; federal systems that provide for the administration of national law by sub-national units following Germany or India without considering the relevance of national civil service standards; and the spread of judicial review of the constitutionality of constitutional amendments as a cure for dubious constitutional change.[34]

An example of another kind is the *Chevron* doctrine of deference.[35] Deference on the part of courts in statutory interpretation is often portrayed as an obvious good, although this also depends on context. The *Chevron* label offers an additional cachet, linking deference to a relatively well-established doctrine of a prestigious national court. *Chevron* itself, however, deals with deference towards an agency interpretation through rule-making procedures; a process that takes place in the US to an extent and in a manner that is not replicated elsewhere. As applied, the *Chevron* doctrine extends beyond formal rule-making to other instances where courts determine that Congress has delegated law-making authority to an agency.[36] Even so, the conceptual framework of delegation is determinative. Urging the adaptation of *Chevron* to secure judicial deference to opportunistic agency interpretations, as argued (unsuccessfully) in the Australian case of *Enfield*,[37] without engaging with the potential relevance of the conceptual framework from which it emerged, might be regarded as 'shallow comparativism'.[38]

The difficulty might be overcome by pointing to other United States Supreme Court doctrines supporting deference to agency interpretations on other bases.[39] At this point, however, another potentially more interesting question arises about the relevance of the design and operation of the institutions of government in the United States to evaluation of the suitability of a transplant of the judicial doctrine of deference to agency interpretation of statutes into, say, Westminster-style parliamentary settings. Checks and balances operate differently in these two systems. The lines of political accountability are differently configured. The legislative process differs markedly. These differences inform approaches to statutory interpretation.[40] Transplanting deference to agency interpretation of legislation from the United States to Australia without this contextual background runs the risk of misunderstanding the rationales for the doctrine. In practice, it would almost certainly further consolidate the hegemony of the executive branch in a way that is not possible in the United States.

[34] Y Roznai, *Unconstitutional Constitutional Amendments* (Oxford, Oxford University Press, 2017).

[35] *Chevron USA Inc v Natural Resources Defense Council Inc* 467 US 837 (1984).

[36] *NLRB v Hearst Publications* 322 US 111 (1944). I am grateful to Professor Peter Strauss for his helpful comments on an earlier version of this part of the chapter, which reinforced my views about the difficulties of acquiring accurate contextual understanding of other systems.

[37] *Enfield City Corporation v Development Assessment Commission* (1999) 199 CLR 135 (hereafter *Einfield*).

[38] *N K v Minister of Safety & Security* [2005] 6 SA 419 at [35] (O'Regan J).

[39] *Skidmore v Swift & Co.* 323 US 134 (1944).

[40] The points of contrast are drawn in the reasons of the plurality in *Enfield* (n 37) at 153–56 [44]–[51] (Gleeson CJ, Gummow, Kirby and Hayne JJ).

A more straightforward example of the value of understanding the source from which a transplant is drawn is provided by the institution of a specialist Constitutional Court. A proposal to establish a court of this kind, arguably emulating the Germany Constitutional Court and apparently as a bulwark against European judicial encroachment, received some attention in the United Kingdom in 2016.[41] Constitutional Courts are a useful example for present purposes in any event, however. The concept of a specialist Constitutional Court, in its modern guise, originally evolved in response to the constitutional, legal and political context of the European federations of Austria and the Federal Republic of Germany.[42] In those federations, introduction of review of the constitutionality of legislation was complicated by the absence of a formal doctrine of precedent and the existence of multiple, specialist court hierarchies.[43] The institution of a specialist Constitutional Court built on local assumptions about the role of judges and the limitation of the sources of law to legislation and the Constitution. The legitimacy of review was secured by the express constitutional conferral of jurisdiction on a body that was not an ordinary court; that functioned as a negative legislator whose decisions were binding *erga omnes*; and that was constituted in a 'representative' fashion.[44] The institution has since proliferated around the world. It is still found almost exclusively in civil law legal systems where the conditions to which it originally responded typically prevail, at least to some degree.[45] One lesson now available from experience is that whenever a Constitutional Court is established, a range of difficulties is likely to arise over its relationship with ordinary courts, arising out of the manner in which questions reach the Constitutional Court and the difficulty of drawing a line between constitutional and other questions.[46]

More recently, there has been pressure for the establishment of Constitutional Courts outside the civil law context. One catalyst for the current trend was the successful introduction of a Constitutional Court into the mixed legal system of South Africa. In South Africa, this step can be attributed to the benign purpose of providing a new, competent and diverse set of judges, who were not associated with the previous regime, to preside over the enforcement of the new Constitution during transition from apartheid.[47] A similar motivation exists in other countries in transition, where the judiciary is tainted or lacks competence or both. Equally, however,

[41] See Elliott (n 5).

[42] See Garlicki (n 31).

[43] H Kelsen, 'Judicial Review of Legislation: A Comparative Study of the Austrian and the American Constitution' (1942) 4 *The Journal of Politics* 183.

[44] WC Chang, L Thio, KYL Tan and J Yeh, *Constitutionalism in Asia: Cases and Materials* (Oxford, Hart, 2014) 369–70.

[45] C Saunders, 'Constitutional Review in Asia: A Comparative Perspective' in A Hung-Yee Chen and A Harding (eds), *Constitutional Courts in Asia* (Cambridge, Cambridge University Press, 2017) (forthcoming). The equation between legal system and form of review does not hold good in reverse, however: there has long been constitutional review by ordinary courts in civil law jurisdictions, particularly in Scandinavia and Latin America.

[46] See Garlicki (n 31); V Ferreres Comella, 'The Consequences of Centralizing Constitutional Review in a Specialist Court: Some Thoughts on Judicial Activism' (2003–2004) 82 *Tex L Rev* 1705.

[47] South African History Online, 'Historical Background of the Constitutional Court' (*South African History Online*, 24 March 2016) <www.sahistory.org.za/article/historical-background-constitutional-court> last accessed 30 May 2017.

it might be noted that a Constitutional Court also can be created for less benign purposes, to provide a more compliant judiciary.[48]

Despite the success of the South African initiative, it also underscores the need to understand the context from which a Constitutional Court derives, when transplanting it to a different legal system. Segregating constitutional from other legal questions is even more difficult in common law than in civil law systems, both because of the characteristic common law methods of reasoning and because of the diversity of legal sources that can be brought to bear to resolve a legal dispute. In the United Kingdom and New Zealand, where no written constitutional instrument serves as fundamental law, the distinction between constitutional and other legal questions is more elusive, and contestable, still. Many of the underlying rationales for the establishment of a specialist court are absent as well. There is no systemic reason why ordinary courts in a common law legal system should not apply the constitution together with other sources of law to resolve the questions that come before them. There is less concern in common law states about the legitimacy of judicial review by ordinary courts as a matter of principle, as opposed to the legitimacy of review in practice, when courts are deemed to have overstepped the mark.

These contextual differences were taken into account in designing the Constitutional Court of South Africa, where the process was locally controlled and potential transplants were carefully explored. Even so, it may be that the problem of segregating constitutional from other types of legal questions was underestimated. In any event, the decades after the Constitution came into effect witnessed the progressive expansion of what was considered to fall within the constitutional jurisdiction of the Court. Eventually, the Constitution was formally amended to authorise the Constitutional Court to deal with non-constitutional matters making it, in effect, a final appellate court.[49] Proposals for a Constitutional Court in other common law jurisdictions can learn from South African experience.

This background also assists to put into perspective the proposal for a Constitutional Court for the United Kingdom. It was an easy target for criticism, given the difficulty of defining the British Constitution and the weakness of the case for change. More significantly for present purposes, however, there was no sign that its proponents had taken into account either the distinctive features of the German context that contributed to the results that they admired or the implications for the British legal system of attempting to segregate one category of legal questions in this way.

IV. RECEPTION

Reception of a transplant into a new jurisdiction is another, critical point in the process. On any view, local context is relevant at this stage. It can assist to determine

[48] For critique to this effect in relation to the Constitutional Court of Palestine see ABC News, 'Palestine Establishes Constitutional Court, Tightening Fatah Grip and Deepening Political Divides' (11 April 2016) <www.abc.net.au/news/2016-04-11/palestinian-leader-establishes-constitutional-court/7318148> last accessed 30 May 2017.

[49] Constitution of the Republic of South Africa Act 1996 (South Africa), s 167 (3)(b)(ii), added by the Constitution Seventeenth Amendment Act 2012 (South Africa).

whether a particular transplant is appropriate at all and whether modifications are required. Local context also will affect the operation of the transplant in practice, in the short term and over time. For this purpose, also, the concept of context may be rich, extending beyond the formal legal framework to embrace, for example, legal and political culture and underlying theoretical assumptions. Attention needs also to be paid to the lure of path dependency. Whatever their flaws, existing forms are likely to be familiar and may have deep roots in history and practice. These considerations may need to be weighed in the balance in determining whether change can best be achieved through the adaptation of existing arrangements or the adoption of new ones.

For the most part, the literature on transplants assumes that understanding of the context of the recipient jurisdiction is readily available, because decision-makers are local, with all the knowledge that that implies.[50] There may still be surprises from the operation of the transplant in practice, but these are unavoidable, even with care, attributable to the difficulty of predicting with accuracy the effects of an 'irritant' introduced from outside.[51] On this view, local context is not necessarily a matter for deliberate consideration, but is taken into account as a matter of course.

Local knowledge of the recipient jurisdiction is not an invariable feature of contemporary transplant practice, however. Most obviously, constitution-making processes in developing countries, particularly those emerging from conflict and hoping for democratic transition, typically are assisted by a host of international agencies, NGOs and foreign advisers.[52] Generally, state actors are formally in charge of the process although there are exceptions, as the extreme case of Bosnia-Herzegovina shows.[53] Usually, in consequence, final decisions about change are taken by local political elites, with varying measures of public participation. In some instances, nevertheless, international advice de facto determines the choices that are made.[54] In extreme cases, external advice may come as a package, in the form of a draft Constitution and supporting laws to which little change is made in the final decision-making stages. International advisers working in these conditions have no necessary knowledge of local context which may be entirely remote from their own experiences. To overcome the difficulty, international actors often seek to work with local partners. It is a measure of the challenge of coming to grips with local context that such attempts may fail at the first hurdle of finding local partners who are appropriate for the purposes of collaboration of this kind.[55]

[50] See Watson (n 2) 112–13.

[51] The term is coined for this context by G Teubner, 'Legal Irritants: Good Faith in British Law or How Unifying Law Ends up in New Divergences' (1998) 61 *Modern Law Review* 11.

[52] International IDEA, 'Constitution Building after Conflict: External Support to a Sovereign Process' (2011) Policy Paper <www.idea.int/sites/default/files/publications/constitution-building-after-conflict.pdf> last accessed 30 May 2017.

[53] JC O'Brien, 'The Dayton Constitution of Bosnia and Herzegovina', in Laurel E Miller (ed), *Framing the State in Times of Transition* (Washington DC, United States Institute of Peace, 2010) 332.

[54] See International IDEA (n 52) at 13–14.

[55] Some of these difficulties in relation to international assistance to Nepal are canvassed in IRIN, 'Politicians, Donors Question Donor Neutrality in Nepal' (26 February 2013) <www.irinnews.org/analysis/2013/02/26/politicians-donors-question-donor-neutrality-nepal> last accessed 30 May 2017.

Even without resorting to such difficult cases, the problem of relying on local understanding for the purposes of determining reception of a transplant is more complex than it at first sight appears. In many cases, for example, local understanding is contested, whether for strategic purposes or in the face of genuine disagreement. Current divisions within the High Court of Australia over the reception of the principle of proportionality into Australian constitutional law are a case in point.

Until relatively recently, Australian doctrine has relied on home grown tests to determine the compliance of challenged legislation with some constitutional limitations on legislative power. One familiar formulation involves a decision on the part of the Court about whether legislation is 'appropriate and adapted' to a constitutionally legitimate purpose.[56] In recent years, however, the explicit language of proportionality has entered the reasoning of the court. In *McCloy*, in 2015, a majority of the Justices accepted and applied a proportionality test with a tripartite structure reminiscent of the structure of proportionality reasoning that is familiar elsewhere in the world.[57] On one view this was not a dramatic change that, in any event, paid due attention to context. The 'appropriate and adapted' formulation itself can be argued to involve considerations that are akin to proportionality. The majority justices had made considerable efforts to understand the German context from which proportionality was accepted to derive. The proportionality formulation on which the majority agreed in *McCloy* was presented as a means merely of structuring the 'appropriate and adapted' inquiry in a way that had distinctively Australian characteristics. More recently still, two Justices defended recourse to proportionality in *McCloy* against perception of it as 'some exotic jurisprudential pest destructive of the delicate ecology of Australian public law'.[58]

One member of the Court, however, Justice Gageler, contests the suitability of proportionality in the Australian context.[59] Two other members are uncommitted and their position on this issue remains to be seen.[60] Justice Gageler's critique appears to be driven in part by concern that the *McCloy* constraints on the doctrine will erode over time leaving Australia with a proportionality principle that is 'structured … prescriptive, and … open-ended'.[61] More fundamentally, however, he argues that there are features of the Australian context that make the introduction of proportionality inappropriate. He points in particular to the limited, systemic purposes of constitutional rights protection in the Australian context, where many of the effects of rights protection have been derived by implication from constitutional provision for representative government or the separation of judicial power. Proportionality analysis, on the other hand, more commonly is used to determine compliance with constitutional provisions deliberately designed to protect individual rights.

[56] *Lange v Australian Broadcasting Corporation* (1997) 189 CLR 520 at 562.

[57] *McCloy v New South Wales* (2015) 257 CLR 178 at 195 [3] (French CJ, Kiefel, Bell and Keane JJ).

[58] *Murphy v Electoral Commissioner* (2016) 90 ALJR 1027 at 1038–39 [37] (French CJ and Bell J) (hereafter *Murphy*).

[59] ibid, at 1050 [101] (Gageler J).

[60] ibid, at [299]–[300] (Gordon J). See *McCloy* (n 57) at 269 [255] (Nettle J).

[61] *Murphy*, ibid at 1050 [101]. See also *McCloy* ibid at 234 [140].

There is also a suggestion in his reasoning that Australian conditions call for an approach that allows different standards of scrutiny for different kinds of cases.[62] This may be developing into an argument about whether, in a common law context, 'categorisation' is more suitable for the protection of rights and freedoms that 'structured proportionality'. A pointed suggestion to this effect appears in a paper by Sir Anthony Mason, delivered in the immediate aftermath of *McCloy*.[63] This debate is ongoing. For present purposes, however, it serves to show both the potential for disagreement about what local context requires and the depth at which contextual features may lie.

There is another aspect of the challenge of understanding the context of a recipient jurisdiction that is less familiar and deserves attention for that reason. While local decision-makers can be assumed to have an innate understanding of their own jurisdictional context they may not be sufficiently conscious of relevant contextual difference when decisions about particular transplants are made. This is not as odd as it sounds. Insiders often so take for granted features of their own constitutional arrangements that they overlook them inadvertently in an otherwise authoritative account.

The reception of statutory bills of rights into Australian public law provides an example. Notoriously, Australia has virtually no constitutional rights protection and continues to be resistant to change for reasons that appear to be connected to the constitutional inheritance of Westminster-style parliamentary government. The adoption of statutory bills of rights in New Zealand[64] and the United Kingdom,[65] in forms that preserved the ultimate authority of Parliament but gave the instruments more teeth than most ordinary statutes, consequently attracted considerable attention in Australia. Ultimately, even this mild form of rights protection was rejected at the national level, in favour of a form of parliamentary scrutiny with no judicial review.[66] The idea of a statutory bill of rights was taken up in two sub-national jurisdictions: the Australian Capital Territory (ACT) and Victoria.[67] The former is a territory but the latter is a state with some constitutional autonomy of its own. The discussion that follows focuses on Victoria alone, as the more interesting case for present purposes, although broadly similar points might be made in relation to the ACT as well.

The Victorian Charter undoubtedly is a transplant, in the sense in which I have used the term. The Human Rights Act 1998 (UK) was the primary model, although New Zealand's experience was taken into account as well. Further, while the principal features of the Human Rights Act were retained, it was adapted to local political

[62] *McCloy* ibid at 238–39 [152].

[63] Sir Anthony Mason, 'The Use of Proportionality in Australian Constitutional Law' (2016) 27 *PLR* 109.

[64] New Zealand Bill of Rights Act 1990 (NZ).

[65] Human Rights Act 1998 (UK).

[66] Rejection followed a National Human Rights Consultation. A framework for parliamentary scrutiny is provided in Human Rights (Parliamentary Scrutiny) Act 2011 (Cth).

[67] Human Rights Act 2004 (ACT); Charter of Human Rights and Responsibilities Act 2006 (Vic).

preferences in some critical respects including, oddly, by adding a Canadian override clause.[68]

The Victorian Charter was locally designed, drafted and enacted. Nevertheless, at the time, political attention and advocacy was overwhelmingly focused on the potential of a statutory Charter to preserve the authority of governments and parliaments while enhancing rights protection. In consequence, those driving the change may not have fully anticipated the implications of one obvious contextual difference between Victoria and the donor jurisdictions: the entrenched constitutional environment within which Victorian law applies. The overarching Constitution is that of the Commonwealth of Australia, which is deeply entrenched and interpreted and applied by the High Court, as the apex court for Australia as a whole. In addition, Victoria has a State Constitution of its own, parts of which are entrenched, albeit more lightly, which is interpreted and applied by the Supreme Court of Victoria from which appeals also lie to the High Court. The potential impact of the formal Constitution normally is taken for granted in Australia. Its implications for the Charter were not immediately obvious, however. The immediate political priority was adapting a model that had worked successfully in apparently comparable jurisdictions elsewhere to satisfy political objections to formal rights protection in Australia.

Once the Victorian Charter was adopted, however, the relevance of the formal constitutional context became apparent. With hindsight, it was almost inevitable that this would be so. Questions arose about: the potential implications of the Charter for the single Australian common law that is said to follow as a corollary of the appellate jurisdiction of the High Court; whether either the interpretive provision of the Charter or the provision authorising a court to make a 'declaration of inconsistent interpretation' were compatible with the role of a State Supreme Court in an integrated Australian judiciary; whether it mattered if this question fell to be answered in the exercise of federal jurisdiction, which would be attracted if a resident of another State was in Victoria and affected by an ation to which the Charter arguably applies.[69] Not all these issues came before the courts, at least in a direct form. The still-leading High Court decision on the meaning of the Charter, however, cast sufficient doubt on its meaning and operation in the face of constitutional constraints so as to significantly stymie its future development. While the Charter narrowly survived challenges to its validity, the interpretation section was read down, its relationship to the limitations clause was left uncertain and the power to make declarations was shown to have, at best, a patchy operation.[70]

The example of the Victorian Charter could be trawled for further insights into the processes of transplants. By way of example, the pragmatic and robust Australian political culture may affect the ways in which provisions designed to ensure political

[68] See Charter of Human Rights and Responsibilities Act 2006 (Vic), s 31; Canada Act 1982 (UK) c 11, sch B pt I, s 33 ('Canadian Charter of Rights and Freedoms').

[69] See, eg, S Evans and C Evans, 'Legal Redress under the Victorian Charter of Human Rights and Responsibilities' (2006) 17 *PLR* 264.

[70] *Momcilovic v R* (2011) 245 CLR 1.

accountability for rights compatibility work at the law-making stage in Victoria. Political culture almost certainly also helps to explain the extent to which political decision-making is protected under the Charter, including through provision of an override clause in section 31, further weakening already weak-form review. For the purposes of considering the methodology of transplants at the point of reception, however, I propose to draw on the Charter to make one final, but different point, about the challenges for transplant reception.

However well-tailored to its local context, the effectiveness of a transplant may depend on attention to the demands of implementation. In this respect, a transplant is no different to any major innovation in public law, although understanding of its operation in the context of the donor jurisdiction may cast light on the issues that are likely to arise. The challenges for implementation may range from whatever is needed by way of technical legal change to accommodate a transplant to the legal system in which it will be embedded, to modifications of the prevailing legal, political and bureaucratic culture, which are much more difficult to achieve.

In the case of the Victorian Charter, implementation was taken seriously. There was considerable training of public servants, with results that may still account for the primary effects of the Charter.[71] Judicial training gave Victorian judges preliminary exposure to the questions likely to arise in human rights adjudication.[72] The parliamentary committee required by the Charter to scrutinise proposed laws was put in place, with capable staff.[73] Human rights NGOs were established, offering support for the Charter, and critique of hitches in its development and information about its operation in practice.[74]

As it transpired, however, there are limits to what can be done in the name of implementation in a sub-national jurisdiction of a larger federal state: another difficulty that had not been foreseen. Change in political culture is difficult in a single jurisdiction. The Charter thus tends to be overridden for intergovernmental schemes to which Victoria is a party in collaboration with other jurisdictions not operating under rights constraints.[75] More significantly still, the educational programmes for Victorian judges, deemed essential for Charter interpretation during the critical implementation phase, did not and could not extend to the Justices of the High Court of Australia, with whom final authority over the meaning of the Charter lay. The High Court, for its part, has other preoccupations, not least the maintenance

[71] See Victorian Government, *Charter of Human Rights and Responsibilities: Guidelines for Legislation and Policy Officers in Victoria* (Victorian Government 2008).

[72] See Judicial College of Victoria, *Charter of Human Rights Bench Book* (Judicial College of Victoria, 2016).

[73] See Parliamentary Committees Act 2003 (Vic), s 17(fa); Subordinate Legislation Act 1994 (Vic) ss 12A, 12D.

[74] See generally MB Young, *From Commitment to Culture: The 2015 Review of the Charter of Human Rights and Responsibilities Act 2006* (Victorian Government 2015) <http://assets.justice.vic.gov.au/justice/resources/3848843f-afd1-47a5-9279-1a1a87ac2aad/report_final_charter_review_2015.pdf> last accessed 30 May 2017.

[75] See, eg, the override statement given in respect of the Legal Professional Uniform Application Bill 2013 (Vic): Victoria, *Parliamentary Debates*, Legislative Assembly, 5 February 2014, 149–50 (Robert Clark, Attorney General).

of the single common law of Australia, which includes the principles of statutory interpretation. It was not to be expected that the court would take an overly sympathetic view of a measure that contributed to fragmentation, lying at the innovative edge of the formal constitutional framework. I do not suggest that the High Court consciously sought to minimise the effect of the Charter so as to maintain national homogeneity. This somewhat idiosyncratic challenge to the effectiveness of a transplant is unlikely to be replicated elsewhere, but demonstrates again both the relevance and complexity of context.

V. ADAPTATION

Adaptation is a possible third step that requires attention in a transplant process, from the standpoint of comparative method. There are several reasons why the proposed subject matter of a transplant may be altered before adoption by a recipient jurisdiction. Alteration may be considered necessary, to meet the new conditions. It may be thought to improve the subject matter of the transplant or to meet the perceived needs of the recipient jurisdiction in other ways. Alteration may even be inadvertent, if the subject matter of the transplant is not fully understood or its parameters are viewed too narrowly.

Adaptation is a regular occurrence, of which many examples may be given. One is the evolution of the clause structuring limitations on rights as it moved from the Canadian to the South African Constitution, where the concept of an 'open and democratic society' was elaborated and the factors relevant to assessing proportionality were explicitly identified. A second is the modification of guarantees of freedom of expression in newer bills of rights to allow affirmative action or to exclude protection of hate speech in the light of United States experience.[76] A third, of a different kind, are the various modifications of the model of the German Bundesrat as a blueprint for the composition of second chambers in federations, to secure greater diversity than drawing on the governments of constituent units allows, at possible cost to the federal effectiveness of the chamber.[77] Adaptation is a natural and, in principle, positive dimension of the process by which systems of public law have evolved across the world.

Like other aspects of the transplant process, however, adaptation benefits from and may require understanding of the context of both the imputed source and recipient jurisdictions. The experience of the former informs a decision about whether and if so how adaptation is necessary or desirable. Equally, however, contextual understanding can help to guard against untoward consequences of adaptation. The Australian process for constitutional change offers an example. In this case, moreover, the transplant occurred well before the current phase of globalisation,

[76] See, eg, Constitution of the Republic of South Africa Act 1996 (South Africa), ss 9(2), 16(2).
[77] See, eg, Constitution of the Republic of South Africa Act 1996 (South Africa), ss 60–62; Constitution of Nepal 2015 (Nepal), s 86.

thus also demonstrating, if demonstration is necessary, that constitutional transplants, even between unlikely jurisdictions, are by no means a recent phenomenon.

In settling the procedure for alteration of the Australian Constitution in the 1890s the Convention delegates turned to the referendum requirement in the Constitution of Switzerland as a model.[78] There are many explanations of this somewhat unusual choice. Switzerland was another federal country, about which they had some information.[79] Their choice may have been affected by recent writings by AV Dicey urging adoption of the referendum in England.[80] A popular vote on future constitutional change was a nice complement to the referendum requirement for adoption of the original Constitution, to which they already were committed, before the draft was sent to the United Kingdom for enactment. In addition, however, Convention delegates sought a mechanism for amendment than was less rigid than that in the US Constitution, on which they had relied heavily for other purposes.[81] The record of use of the referendum in Switzerland was encouraging from this perspective. And so the Swiss procedure was incorporated into section 128 of the Australian Constitution, complete with the requirement that passage at referendum required double majorities: a national majority and a majority in a majority of States.

There are all sorts of contextual differences between Switzerland and Australia that might have suggested greater caution about the effects this transplant would produce.[82] In addition, however, the Australians altered the Swiss procedure in one particular respect, which would prove critical. In Switzerland, the referendum procedure was accompanied by the possibility of a popular initiative.[83] In Australia, however, where the culture and processes of parliamentary representative government were dominant, the new Constitution restricted the initiative to a Bill passed by the Commonwealth Parliament alone. Delegates appear not to have considered this change particularly significant, from the standpoint of the ease of constitutional change. On the contrary, their main concern in relation to section 128 was the possibility of deadlocks between the House and the Senate as a Constitution Alteration bill moved through the Commonwealth Parliament.[84] With hindsight, however, it is possible to see that the change was formative in the evolution of the referendum process in Australia, fatally infusing it with the party partisanship that characterises Westminster-style parliamentary government. Over time, this effect was exacerbated, as arrangements for voter education about proposals for change were shaped around the same partisan dynamics.

[78] See J Quick and R Garran, *The Annotated Constitution of the Australian Commonwealth* Revised edn (London, LexisNexis Butterworths, 2015) 139, 1215.

[79] ibid, at 1215.

[80] A V Dicey, *Lectures Introductory to the Study of the Law of the Constitution* (Basingstoke, Macmillan, 1885) cxiv–cxvii.

[81] C Saunders, 'The Parliament as Partner: A Century of Constitutional Review' in G Lindell and R Bennett (eds), *Parliament: The Vision in Hindsight* (Melbourne, Federation Press, 2001) 454.

[82] The Swiss procedures are well explained in G Lutz, 'The Interaction between Direct and Representative Government in Switzerland' (2006) 42 *Representation* 45.

[83] See Federal Constitution of the Swiss Confederation 1999 (Switzerland), arts 138, 139.

[84] See, eg, Quick and Garran (n 78) 214–15.

The consequences are well-known. More often than not, proposals for constitutional change in Australia reflect the priorities of the government of the day. Historically, they also have favoured the expansion of central power. Voters oppose them for these reasons, in addition to the many others that might influence a negative vote on a proposal for constitutional change. There has been no formal alteration of the Constitution through the referendum procedure since 1977.[85] If the goal of this transplant was to strike a balance between flexibility and continuity, it might be said to have failed.

Adaptation of transplants without adequate understanding of the significance of context may have contributed to the rigidity of the Australian procedure for constitutional change. Equally, however, reflection on context assists to identify further measures that might better adapt use of the referendum to Australian conditions. Party polarisation over referendum questions is a problem in Westminster-style democracies, for example, the need to develop and explain proposals for constitutional change in less partisan ways.

Australian experience with the difficulty of adapting the referendum to the rest of the Australian constitutional context might also be used to throw light more generally on the trend of introducing elements of direct democracy into systems of government that otherwise are quintessentially representative in character. There is no obvious single source from which mechanisms of direct democracy are adopted or adapted, complicating consideration of a home context. The potential sources are proliferating, moreover, as recourse to direct democracy expands; they are likely to continue to do so, in the face of dissatisfaction with representative government and the availability of technology that makes direct voting practicable. Nevertheless, as a generalisation, in the world as we presently know it, there are some states, including Switzerland, in which direct democracy is common and others in which the habits of representative government, almost exclusively, prevail. In the former, not only are voters more accustomed to the demands of direct democracy but this approach to public decision-making is embedded in a framework of law and practice that facilitates its integration with representative government. This is likely to include, for example, procedures to disseminate reliable information about what is proposed; normative parameters that guide the purposes for which and the manner in which direct democracy is used; laws that determine whether and when a proposal is adopted and what are the legal consequences of doing so.[86] In the latter group of countries such a framework is much less developed. Given other contextual differences, it is unlikely that these supporting features could usefully be transplanted, holus bolus, as part of a total referendum package. Their existence in some states nevertheless should suggest to others that an occasional referendum process cannot simply be grafted onto a constitutional system premised on the assumptions

[85] See Australian Electoral Commission, 'Referendum Dates and Results' (*Australian Electoral Commission*, 24 October 2012) <www.aec.gov.au/Elections/referendums/Referendum_Dates_and_Results.htm> last accessed 30 May 2017.

[86] See, generally, J Reich, 'An Interactional Model of Direct Democracy: Lessons from the Swiss Experience' (2008) Working Paper < https://ssrn.com/abstract=1154019> last accessed 30 May 2017; see Lutz (n 82).

of representative government without consideration of other conceptual and procedural changes that are necessary to make direct democracy work.

VI. UNITY OF PUBLIC LAW

The position that I sketch in this chapter revolves around two claims. The first is that public law has distinctive characteristics relevant to a process of transplant from one jurisdiction to another. These derive from the ways in which public law is embedded in the life of a state. They shape the context within which public law operates in both a donor and recipient jurisdiction, which should be taken into account, within reason, if a transplant is to be adequately informed. The second claim, connected to the first is that, while globalisation has had a profound impact on national systems of public law it is not (yet?) sufficient to eliminate the relevance of context for the purposes of transplants.

Others may disagree with either or both of these claims. Undoubtedly there are many states in which public law lies more lightly on the surface of national life; although at least some of these also are states in which public law is in trouble. The dynamics of globalisation also now are sufficiently complex and uncertain to leave room for genuine disagreement about the extent of the changes that have occurred, their relevance and likely future directions. Perspectives on these critical questions differ between disciplinary interests and between regions and states including, sometimes, states within regions. Whatever stage has been reached, it almost certainly is not permanent, marking the present as a period in transition.

My position on these questions should not be taken as opposition to transplants or in favour of national exceptionalism. On the contrary, the story of transplants is a large part of the story of the evolution of systems of public law, contributing to their dynamism and capacity for continuing creative change. Rather, my reaction is against practices and theories that encourage transplants divorced from considerations of relevant context. The examples that I have used are intended to suggest what consideration of context might involve.

The history of common law public law suggests that at least some of these concerns about transplants may be unfounded. The common law spread around the world as a transplant with very little reference to context. The result was considerable unity, at least on the surface. Over the intervening centuries, unity has given way to national systems of common law, partly through the diversification of constitutions and legislation and the removal of a shared appellate structure and partly through the operation of public law in local context. On the whole, the results are positive. On one view, therefore, the common law is evidence that decontextualised transplants work, albeit modified over time by recipient jurisdictions. We no longer have the agency of an imperial power, however, to ensure such initial transplants bed down. Systems of public law in the twenty-first century depend on ownership to a much greater extent. The warning is pertinent, nevertheless. It may be that a functioning system of public law will absorb and transform an ill-fitting transplant in ways that often turn out well enough.

This volume provides some evidence, if evidence is needed, that the diversification of common law systems of public law continues. Further change can be expected, through the impact of international law, which enters common law legal systems in different ways and at different speeds and through transplants from outside the common law world. As other chapters in this volume also show, however, a form of unity also persists, in the shared assumptions, concepts and procedures on which the common law depends. Given diversification, these do not preclude the need for consideration of context in decision-making about transplants, even between common law jurisdictions. They make it significantly easier, however, to understand the foundations on which public law in each jurisdiction is built.

14

Unity and Diversity in the United Kingdom's Territorial Constitution

AILEEN McHARG

I. INTRODUCTION

IN 2006, I co-edited a book of essays considering aspects of public law in Scotland, both institutional and doctrinal, which diverged from those elsewhere in the United Kingdom (UK).[1] Such differences had persisted throughout the entire period since the Union of 1707, but had been extended and amplified by the asymmetric devolution arrangements introduced in 1999. In the introductory essay to that volume,[2] I sought, inter alia, to classify and evaluate the nature and significance of the differences under discussion. I concluded that, although there were plenty of points of *difference*, it was harder to identify *unequivocal* examples of genuine *distinctiveness* (ie, fundamentally different answers to the basic questions of public law concerning the constitution, distribution, and regulation of governmental power, and the relationship between citizen and state).

Had I cast my eye more widely, particularly to encompass Northern Ireland, with its long history of constitutional exceptionalism[3] and a contemporary model of consociational governance underpinned by international agreement, I might have found more significant territorial diversity in the UK's constitutional arrangements. Moreover, territorial diversity has increased since 2006, particularly since the 2014 Scottish independence referendum. Further devolution has taken place in Scotland,[4] Wales,[5] and Northern Ireland,[6] each following its own pattern and independent timetable.[7] The changes in Scotland ushered in by the Scotland Act 2016, and to

[1] A McHarg and T Mullen (eds), *Public Law in Scotland* (Edinburgh, Avizandum Publishing Ltd, 2006).

[2] A McHarg, 'Public Law in Scotland: Difference and Distinction' in McHarg and Mullen, ibid 3.

[3] See, eg, H Calvert, *Constitutional Law in Northern Ireland: A Study in Regional Government* (London and Belfast, Stevens & Sons, 1968); B Hadfield, *The Constitution of Northern Ireland* (Belfast, SLS Legal Publications, 1989).

[4] Scotland Act 2012; Scotland Act 2016.

[5] Government of Wales Act 2006; Wales Act 2014; Wales Act 2017.

[6] Corporation Tax (Northern Ireland) Act 2015; Northern Ireland (Stormont Agreement and Implementation Plan) Act 2016.

[7] On the divergent histories and trajectories of devolution in the UK, see in particular J Mitchell, *Devolution in the UK* (Manchester, Manchester University Press, 2011).

some extent replicated for Wales by the Wales Act 2017, are particularly significant, offering both guarantees of the constitutional status of the devolved institutions and giving them a new constitutional competence over their own composition and structure, as well as extending their policy-making and fiscal autonomy. Indeed, once the 2016 Act is fully implemented, Scotland will be amongst the most autonomous sub-state regions in the world.[8] In England, the introduction of English Votes for English Laws in October 2015 was symbolically important in marking the constitutional recognition of England as a distinct territorial entity, while the 'city devolution' programme authorised by the Cities and Local Government Devolution Act 2016 introduces greater internal diversity to the governance of England.

Further territorial divergence is also possible in the wake of the 2016 referendum on membership of the European Union (EU). Withdrawal from the EU (subject to whatever new arrangements may replace it) will remove an important centripetal force from the UK's current constitutional architecture, which has constrained both devolved and UK institutions. It has also created demand for further devolution, not only through the 'repatriation' of powers currently exercised at EU level, but which would otherwise fall within devolved competence, but also for substantial additional powers to enable the devolved governments to mitigate the effects of Brexit.[9] Moreover, the differing territorial results in that referendum are themselves indicative of important territorial cleavages on fundamental constitutional questions, and have served to reopen debates in Scotland and Northern Ireland (which both produced majorities to remain in the EU) about the constitutional future of these territories. This may yet produce some kind of 'differential Brexit' for Scotland and Northern Ireland,[10] although there are severe practical and political obstacles to such proposals. Similar territorial divergence can be found in attitudes to fundamental rights protection. Accordingly, if plans to reform the Human Rights Act ever come to fruition, it seems likely that this will also result in greater diversity of provision in different parts of the UK.

In short, the recent history of the UK's territorial constitution is one of increasing divergence, and one which, given the failure of the 2014 referendum to settle the question of Scottish independence,[11] and the revival of the border question in

[8] See N McEwen, 'A Constitution in Flux: The Dynamics of Constitutional Change after the Referendum' in A McHarg et al (eds), *The Scottish Independence Referendum: Constitutional and Political Implications* (Oxford, Oxford University Press, 2016) 225, 236–37.

[9] See Scottish Government, *Scotland's Place in Europe* (2016) ch 4; Welsh Government, *Securing Wales' Future: Transition from the European Union to a New Relationship with Europe* (2017) ch 7.

[10] See B O'Leary, 'The Dalriada Document: Towards a Multi-National Compromise that Respects Diversity in the United Kingdom' (2016) <www.centreonconstitutionalchange.ac.uk/publications/reports/dalriada-document>; N Skoutaris, 'From Britain and Ireland to Cyprus: Accommodating "Divided Islands" in the EU Political and Legal Order' (2016) <www.skoutaris.eu/working-papers>; Scottish Government (n 9) ch 3; B Doherty et al, 'Northern Ireland and "Brexit": The European Economic Area Option' (2017) <www.papers.ssrn.com/sol3/papers.cfm?abstract_id=2933715>.

[11] Support for independence has remained high since the referendum: the 2016 Scottish Social Attitudes Survey recorded its highest ever level of support for independence (at 46%) and for the first time found that support for independence as the preferred constitutional solution was higher than for devolution: J Curtice, *Scottish Social Attitudes: From Indyref1 to Indyref2? The State of Nationalism in Scotland* (Edinburgh, ScotCen Social Research, 2017). The success of the Scottish National Party in the

Northern Ireland since the EU referendum,[12] appears to be following a disintegrative logic. Accordingly, as territorial diversity has increased, so too has concern about territorial unity. In other words, there is increasing interest in the question of what mechanisms exist to bind the UK state together in the face of territorial divergence.

Early signs of such concerns can be detected in the initial debate over the adoption of a British Bill of Rights—an idea originally promoted by Gordon Brown as a positive means of reinforcing British identity by articulating a common set of 'British values' as a counterweight to devolution,[13] though it has subsequently acquired a more negative, anti-European character. Similar considerations can be found in the debate over the role of the Supreme Court as the guarantor of UK-wide constitutional standards,[14] and in the attempt by the Calman Commission—the progenitor of the Scotland Act 2012—to identify 'principles of Union' which would provide a rational basis upon which to divide powers between the UK and devolved levels.[15]

Again, though, the constitutional shock provided by the relatively narrow 'No' vote in the 2014 independence referendum has served to intensify such concerns, and the EU referendum result has given them additional impetus. A number of organisations and commentators have called for more or less comprehensive constitutional reform to move the UK's territorial constitution in a more explicitly federal direction;[16] one which pays greater attention to the question of 'shared rule', alongside 'self-rule' for the UK's territorial units,[17] a measure by which the UK currently performs poorly compared with other federal or devolved systems.[18] Proposed reforms variously include institutional mechanisms to improve inter-governmental relations, enhance territorial representation in UK-wide decision making, and reduce

2015 Westminster and 2016 Holyrood elections, coupled with the differential EU referendum outcome in Scotland, have ensured that the constitutional question remains high on the Scottish political agenda.

[12] See C Gormley-Heenan and A Aughey, 'Getting Our Country Back or Waking Up in a Different Country: Brexit and Northern Ireland' (2017) 19 *British Journal of Politics and International Relations* 497. Sinn Féin significantly increased its vote share at the March 2017 Northern Ireland Assembly elections and has revived its campaign for a border poll on reunification with the Republic of Ireland.

[13] Ministry of Justice, *The Governance of Britain* (Cm 7170, 2007) ch 4.

[14] See A McHarg, 'Final Appeals in Scots Criminal Cases', *UK Constitutional Law Association Blog*, 4 October 2011.

[15] Commission on Scottish Devolution, *The Future of Scottish Devolution Within the Union: A First Report* (2008).

[16] See, eg, House of Commons Political and Constitutional Reform Committee, *Do We Need a Constitutional Convention for the United Kingdom?* (4th Report 2012–13, HC 371); G Brown, *My Scotland, Our Britain: A Future Worth Sharing* (London, Simon & Schuster, 2014) ch 7; J Gallagher, *The Day After Judgement: Scotland and the UK after the Referendum* (Glasgow, Policy Scotland, 2014); House of Lords Constitution Committee, *Proposals for the Devolution of Further Powers to Scotland* (10th Report 2014–15, HL 145); House of Lords Constitution Committee, *Inter-governmental Relations in the United Kingdom* (11th Report 2014–15, HL 146); Wales Governance Centre, *The UK's Changing Union: Towards a New Union* (Cardiff, 2015); Bingham Centre for the Rule of Law, *A Constitutional Crossroads: Ways Forward for the United Kingdom* (London, British Institute of International and Comparative Law, 2015); R Hazell (ed), *Devolution and the Future of the Union* (London, Constitution Unit, 2015); Constitution Reform Group, *Towards a New Act of Union: A Discussion Paper* (2015); Constitution Reform Group, *Act of Union Bill* (2016); J Gallagher, *Britain After Brexit: Toxic Referendums and Territorial Constitutions*, (Glasgow, Policy Scotland, 2016).

[17] See McEwen (n 8) at 227–33.

[18] ibid, at 237–40.

territorial asymmetry; the articulation of common values and purposes to guide the allocation and exercise of decision-making functions; and/or the establishment of a shared constitutional framework to empower and constrain both UK and devolved governance. To date, however, such proposals have had little or no practical impact.

The aim of this chapter is to assess the need for greater unity in the territorial constitution. However, rather than examining particular reform proposals in detail, its focus is primarily methodological. In other words, how do we decide what degree of territorial divergence is constitutionally acceptable? The chapter explores this question from four different perspectives—empirical, conceptual, normative, and political. Ultimately, I argue that the problem to be addressed—and hence the case for reform—is an essentially political one: a question of discovering how much diversity the state can bear without undermining the conditions necessary for the maintenance of sufficient political solidarity to sustain its common functions. It follows that the solutions are to be found primarily in mechanisms for political accommodation, which may go beyond the strictly constitutional, rather than in the articulation of legal values or the proliferation of legal constraints. Nevertheless, I also argue that there are formidable political barriers to the achievement of a successful balance between unity and diversity in the UK's territorial constitution. The chapter concludes by using Brexit as an illustration both of the failure of political accommodation of territorial difference, and of the severe challenges which this presents.

II. THE EMPIRICAL PERSPECTIVE

Any assessment of the need for greater territorial unity in the UK constitution has to start from a clear understanding of its current diversity. Patently, an empirical approach cannot tell us how much diversity *ought* to be permitted. Nevertheless, since the UK has a long tradition of diverse and asymmetric governance, it can tell us something useful about the nature and degree of diversity that has historically been tolerated, and what has changed—or is perceived to have changed—more recently such as to threaten the integrity of the state. Classifying difference can also help us to understand the various ways in which constitutional diversity might be problematic, and might therefore require different countervailing strategies. However, an empirical perspective is also important in reminding us of the limits of territorial unity. To the extent that differences in territorial governance are the product of differing needs and demands in different parts of the state rather than mere accidents[19]—and perhaps even if they are—they carry their own historical legitimacy which is likely to limit the nature and degree of unity that can be achieved. For instance, an approach which advocated the abolition of the devolved legislatures, or even significant curtailment of their current powers, in the name of constitutional unity is likely to be a non-starter.[20]

[19] See Mitchell (n 7).

[20] Devolution is very popular in both Scotland and Wales: see, eg, A Henderson et al, 'National Identity or National Interest? Scottish, English and Welsh Attitudes to the Constitutional Debate' (2015) 86 *Political Quarterly* 265, Table 2. The situation in Northern Ireland is more complicated, but it is clear

The territorial differences that are to be found within the UK could potentially be classified in a number of different ways.[21] For present purposes, however, it is useful to distinguish between institutional diversity; diversity in constitutional values; and differences in how the state itself is understood. In each of these areas, although the existence of difference is by no means new, there have been important recent changes either in the nature and extent of territorial difference, or in the perception of its significance.

A. Institutional Diversity

The most obvious form of territorial diversity is institutional. Institutional variations in the governance of different parts of the UK are longstanding, and encompass both the extent to which different territories are able to govern themselves, and the models through which they do so.

In the case of Scotland, institutional differences have existed since (and indeed were guaranteed by) the Union of 1707, and have been present to varying degrees in all three branches of state—legislative, executive and judicial—ever since.[22] Whilst the creation of the Scottish Parliament and Scottish Government in 1999[23] involved a significant extension of distinctively Scottish governmental arrangements, legislative devolution clearly built upon—and drew some of its justification from—the high degree of institutional distinctiveness which already existed.

Like Scotland, Northern Ireland also has its own legal system (albeit less distinct from that of England and Wales) and the longest history of legislative devolution. A Northern Ireland Parliament was established in 1921[24] following the partition of Ireland and the secession of the South, which exercised extensive powers over the province until the resumption of direct rule in 1972.[25] When devolution was re-established in Northern Ireland in 1999,[26] this involved further institutional divergence. Not only were the competences of the Northern Ireland Assembly different to those of the Scottish Parliament, but its structure was also materially different—based upon a principle of cross-community consent unique amongst UK representative bodies.

Wales historically enjoyed less institutional recognition, although a Secretary of State for Wales was established in 1964 and there were a number of Wales-specific public bodies.[27] The initial model of devolution established in 1999[28] was much

that the resumption of direct rule would be unacceptable to a significant proportion of Northern Irish opinion: see, eg, A Cowburn, 'British Direct Rule would Place Northern Ireland at "Mercy of Hard Brexit Government", says SDLP', *The Independent*, 11 January 2017.

[21] For a different approach to classification, see McHarg (n 2) at 9–15.

[22] ibid, at 3–4; AC Page, *Constitutional Law of Scotland* (Edinburgh, W Green, 2015) ch 1.

[23] Scotland Act 1998.

[24] Government of Ireland Act 1920.

[25] See references in n 3.

[26] Northern Ireland Act 1998.

[27] See R Rawlings, *Delineating Wales: Constitutional, Legal and Administrative Aspects of National Devolution* (Cardiff, University of Wales Press, 2003) ch 1; Mitchell (n 7) ch 3.

[28] Government of Wales Act 1998.

weaker than its Scottish and Northern Irish counterparts, with no legislative or taxation powers and, until 2006, no formal distinction between the Welsh Government and Welsh Assembly.[29] In 2011, however, the Welsh Assembly gained primary legislative powers[30] and the Wales Act 2014 gave it limited tax-raising powers. Both have been further enhanced by the Wales Act 2017, although some important differences between Scots, Welsh and Northern Irish devolution still remain, regarding not only the scope but also the form of devolved competences.

The governance of England is distinct in having no separate representative structures; the UK Parliament and UK Government departments are by default also English institutions in areas devolved to Scotland, Wales and Northern Ireland—something given a degree of formal recognition by the introduction of English Votes for English Laws.[31] There is limited regional devolution within England. A Greater London Assembly with executive powers was established in 1999,[32] but a planned programme of progressive devolution to other English regions[33] was aborted following an unsuccessful referendum in the North East in 2004. Regional devolution has been revived in the form of the City Devolution programme,[34] again on a rolling basis, but this is more accurately regarded as a form of enhanced local government, which builds upon existing institutions rather than adding a new layer of territorial governance.

The devolution programme of the late 1990s was undoubtedly a constitutional development of major importance. While the earlier experience of devolution in Northern Ireland could be regarded as an exceptional response to the peculiar exigencies of that territory, the creation of new representative structures for Scotland, Wales and Northern Ireland—and the subsequent strengthening, deepening, and widening of the principle of devolution—represents a much clearer commitment to constitutional pluralism. This is apparent not merely from the fact that devolution creates new centres of political power, but also from the willingness to tailor the devolved institutions to the particular circumstances of each nation or region.

Both of these features are significant in understanding the impact of increased institutional diversity. New representative institutions (or in England, the lack of them) appear to have strengthened or at least consolidated sub-state political identities, as expressed in felt national identity, stated constitutional preferences, and electoral behaviour.[35] They have also provided a forum, through the exercise of devolved legislative and executive competences, and the process of electoral competition, for the accentuation and proliferation of political, institutional and policy differences. These effects were muted in the early years of devolution by political

[29] Government of Wales Act 2006.

[30] Following a referendum held under Government of Wales Act 2006, s 103.

[31] Introduced via a change to the House of Commons Standing Orders: see HC Deb, vol 600, col 1159, 22 October 2015.

[32] Greater London Authority Act 1999.

[33] Regional Assemblies (Preparations) Act 2003; Office of Deputy Prime Minister, *Draft Regional Assemblies Bill* (Cm 6285, 2004).

[34] Cities and Local Government Devolution Act 2016.

[35] See, eg, J Curtice et al, 'Devolution', in A Park et al (eds), *British Social Attitudes: The 30th Report* (London, NatCen Social Research, 2013) 139; Henderson et al (n 20).

convergence at UK, Scottish and Welsh levels, and by the preoccupation in Northern Ireland with consolidating the peace process (with the consequent suspension of devolution on several occasions),[36] but have become more pronounced as electoral outcomes have diverged.

As devolution has become better established and territorial divergence has increased, so too the territorial dimension of the UK state has become more pronounced. In particular, demands for territorial differences to be respected have spilled over the boundaries of devolved competencies to include formally reserved matters such as EU withdrawal[37] and human rights reform,[38] as well as more mundane policy issues.[39] In turn, this has made the anomalies arising from asymmetric devolution much more visible[40]—demanding a response which further institutionalises territorial difference and which has an inherent decentralising logic. We see this, for example, in the repeated revisions of the Welsh devolution arrangements, in order to 'catch up' with the stronger arrangements in Scotland and Northern Ireland. It was also made explicit by David Cameron following the Scottish independence referendum, when he insisted that stronger powers for Scotland had to be balanced by territorial recognition for England in the form of English Votes for English Laws.[41]

B. Diversity of Values

In my 2006 essay, I concluded that institutional differences, and the detailed and contextual differences flowing from them, were the most significant marker of constitutional distinctiveness in Scotland.[42] There were some arguable differences in relation to constitutional values, such as the commitment accompanying devolution to a more participatory and consensual style of democracy compared with Westminster, and stronger protection for fundamental rights. However, it was questionable how much difference the former actually made in practice, while the latter seemed to be attributable more to the subordinate status of the Scottish Parliament than to a genuine difference in commitment to rights.

[36] In 2000, 2001 and between 2002 and 2007.

[37] See, eg, the interventions by the Scottish and Welsh Governments in *R (Miller) v Secretary of State for Exiting the European Union* [2017] 2 WLR 583, arguing that their consent to legislation authorising withdrawal from the EU was required under the Sewel Convention because of its impact on devolved competence, as well as their more general arguments for special treatment in the implementation of Brexit: see references in n 9.

[38] Again, the Scottish Government has asserted a right to veto human rights reform via the Sewel Convention: see I Jamieson, 'The Repeal of the Human Rights Act and the Sewel Convention in Scotland', *Scottish Constitutional Futures Forum Blog*, 12 June 2015; M Elliott, 'The Scottish Parliament, the Sewel Convention, and the Repeal of the Human Rights Act: A Postscript', *Scottish Constitutional Futures Forum Blog*, 28 September 2015.

[39] See, eg, T Mullen and S Craig, 'The Immigration Bill, Reserved Matters and the Sewel Convention', *Scottish Constitutional Futures Forum Blog*, 15 April 2016.

[40] See, eg, Henderson et al (n 20) at 271.

[41] D Cameron, 'In Full: Statement on the UK's Future' (19 September 2014) <www.bbc.co.uk/news/uk-politics-29271765>.

[42] See McHarg (n 2) at 9–15, 22.

Since 2006, value differences between Scotland and the rest of the UK seem to have increased. The reduction in the voting age from 18 to 16, first for the 2014 independence referendum[43] and subsequently for Scottish Parliament and local government elections,[44] reinforces the commitment to a more inclusive democracy and creates an important difference in citizenship rights between Scotland and the rest of the UK. Greater differences have also opened up in relation to fundamental rights protection. The current Scottish Government is opposed to any weakening of current human rights protection, and indeed is committed to the extension of protections to include social and economic rights.[45] More generally, constitutional debate in Scotland has not exhibited the same hostility to human rights protection or anti-Europeanism found elsewhere in the UK—something borne out by the clear majority (62 per cent) in Scotland in the EU referendum to remain in the EU.

In Northern Ireland, as already noted, value differences are even more readily apparent. Democratic practices have long been different. During the 27-year period of direct rule from Westminster, democracy in Northern Ireland was deeply impoverished; thanks to their numbers and Northern Ireland's separate party system, Northern Irish MPs had limited opportunity to influence UK level decision making, while local government in Northern Ireland was (and still is) weak compared to other parts of the UK. Following the resumption of devolution in 1999, the adoption of a principle of power-sharing between political parties in the Northern Ireland Executive and Northern Ireland Assembly was a deliberate rejection of the majoritarian style of democracy which had in the past produced (or at least was perceived to have produced) systematic discrimination against the Catholic minority.[46] We also find significant historical and contemporary differences in human rights practice, both in terms of the nature of the rights which are recognised and the extent to which they are respected. Historically, both under devolution and direct rule, there have been extensive departures from human rights norms applied elsewhere in the UK.[47] Since the 1998 Good Friday Agreement,[48] by contrast, rights-consciousness has been much greater.[49] The Agreement includes strong guarantees of respect for the European Convention on Human Rights, along with a commitment to an indigenous human rights process,[50] although due to greater social conservativism in Northern Ireland, rights in areas such as abortion and homosexual equality still lag behind the UK norm.

[43] Scottish Independence Referendum (Franchise) Act 2013.

[44] Scottish Elections (Reduction of Voting Age) Act 2015.

[45] See, eg, Scottish Government, *A Plan for Scotland: The Government's Programme for Scotland 2016–17* (Edinburgh, Scottish Government, 2016) 82.

[46] See, eg, Commission Appointed by the Governor of Northern Ireland, *Disturbances in Northern Ireland* (Cameron Report) (Cmd 532, Belfast, HMSO, 1969); Northern Ireland Office, *The Future of Northern Ireland: A Paper for Discussion* (London, HMSO, 1972).

[47] See, eg, B Dickson, *The European Convention on Human Rights and the Conflict in Northern Ireland* (Oxford, Oxford University Press, 2010).

[48] Northern Ireland Office, *The Belfast Agreement* (1998).

[49] On the significance of human rights to the achievement of peace in Northern Ireland, see C Bell, *Peace Agreements and Human Rights* (Oxford, Oxford University Press, 2000).

[50] See Northern Ireland Human Rights Commission, *A Bill of Rights for Northern Ireland: Advice to the Secretary of State for Northern Ireland* (Belfast, NIHRC, 2008).

However, the extent to which these constitutional differences have been recognised as such has been muted by two factors. One is—again—the perception of Northern Irish exceptionalism (ie, differences tend to be seen as temporary aberrations explained by the Province's troubled political history). The second is the weakly constitutionalised nature of the UK in general, which means that value differences, for instance over matters such as abortion or equality rights, have tended to be regarded as political rather than constitutional. As in Scotland, though, the constitutional significance of value differences has become more difficult to ignore, with issues such as human rights reform and EU withdrawal again exposing important territorial differences between Northern Ireland and the rest of the UK. Both sets of reforms are difficult to reconcile with the terms and spirit of the Good Friday Agreement, and risk upsetting the fragile constitutional equilibrium that has been built since 1998.[51]

Significant value differences are harder to detect in Wales, perhaps reflecting its longer history of close integration with England, and weaker form of devolution, as well as less distinct electoral patterns. The EU referendum result in Wales was very similar to that in England,[52] although here it is English attitudes which are distinct in that Euroscepticism has a correlation with (English) nationalism in England that is not found in other parts of the UK.[53] However, the (Labour-controlled) Welsh Government is also opposed to reform of the Human Rights Act,[54] and the devolution of local government and Welsh Assembly elections by the Wales Act 2017 opens space for further divergence here too.

C. Differing Theories of the State

The final area of territorial constitutional difference concerns how the UK state itself is understood. Formally, it is a unitary state, with a single source of sovereignty located in the UK Parliament. This unitary conception has come under pressure in recent years, particularly as a result of the UK's membership of the EU. EU membership both added another territorial layer of decision-making, and challenged the sovereignty of the UK Parliament. However, the recent vote in favour of Brexit in England and Wales, premised on the need to restore parliamentary sovereignty, along with broader hostility to other features of a more cosmopolitan constitutional order,[55] such as the role of the European Court of Human Rights as an external check on sovereignty, indicates the continued relevance and popular appeal of the unitary state account as a theory of the territorial constitution.[56]

[51] See House of Lords EU Select Committee, *Brexit: UK–Irish Relations* (6th Report 2016–17, HL 76) ch 4.

[52] Wales voted by 52.5% to leave the EU, and England by 53.4%.

[53] See R Wyn Jones et al, *England and its Two Unions: The Anatomy of a Nation and its Discontents* (London, IPPR, 2013).

[54] See D Deans, 'Welsh Government will do "Everything it Can" to Block Repeal of the Human Rights Act', *Wales Online*, 18 May 2015.

[55] See A Somek, *The Cosmopolitan Constitution* (Oxford, Oxford University Press, 2014).

[56] M Loughlin, 'The End of Avoidance', *London Review of Books*, 28 July 2016.

Nevertheless, the unitary state account has long been internally contested. In Scotland, an alternative, 'union state' account, which regards the continued existence of the state as resting upon the consent of its constituent parts, and sovereignty as belonging to the plural peoples of the UK, rather than to the Westminster Parliament, has considerable contemporary resonance, even if its historical credentials as a distinctive Scottish constitutional tradition are a matter of dispute.[57] This account has received some symbolic[58] and practical recognition—most significantly in the willingness of the UK Government to facilitate the holding of a lawful referendum on independence in 2014.[59] Nevertheless, it cannot be seen unequivocally to have displaced the doctrine of parliamentary sovereignty as the fundamental rule of the constitution. For instance, the acknowledgment in the Scotland Act 2016 of the permanence of the Scottish Parliament and Scottish Government (subject to a referendum vote in Scotland) and the statutory confirmation of the Sewel Convention[60] were accompanied by continued assertions that parliamentary sovereignty was unaffected and ambiguous wording both of which undermine their status as legally-binding or justiciable guarantees. Indeed, the Supreme Court held in the recent *Miller* case[61] that the 2016 Act had made no difference to the legal status of the Sewel convention, and had not rendered it in any way justiciable.

The union state account of the territorial constitution also has resonance in Northern Ireland, where the principle that the Province's continued membership of the UK rests on local consent has been recognised by statute since 1949.[62] In addition, the grounding of Northern Ireland's contemporary governance arrangements in the Good Friday Agreement—an international treaty between the UK and the Republic of Ireland—and the sharing of sovereignty across the Irish border on a range of issues is difficult to reconcile with a unitary account of the UK state.[63] Again, though, parliamentary sovereignty has not formally been displaced. For instance, the Supreme Court in the Northern Irish proceedings heard in parallel with *Miller* firmly rejected the attempt to elevate the principle of consent into a general requirement to seek the consent of the people of Northern Ireland for any significant constitutional change.[64]

Even in Wales, where there is no historic legacy of independent statehood, and where devolution did not proceed upon an assertion of a right to national

[57] See C Kidd, 'Sovereignty and the Scottish Constitution Before 1707' (2004) *Juridical Review* 225; S Tierney, 'Scotland and the Union State', in McHarg and Mullen (n 1) at 25; I McLean, *What's Wrong with the British Constitution* (Oxford, Oxford University Press, 2010) ch 3.

[58] See, eg, *MacCormick v Lord Advocate* 1953 SC 396; Claim of Right 1988; Scotland Act 2016, s 1.

[59] See HM Government/Scottish Government, *Agreement between the United Kingdom Government and the Scottish Government on a Referendum on Independence for Scotland* (the 'Edinburgh Agreement') (2012).

[60] The rule that the UK Parliament will not normally legislate with regard to devolved matters except with the consent of the relevant devolved legislature.

[61] *R (Miller) v Secretary of State for Exiting the European Union* [2017] 2 WLR 583.

[62] Ireland Act 1949, s 1; Northern Ireland Constitution Act 1973, s 1; Northern Ireland Act 1998, s 1.

[63] See C Campbell et al, 'The Frontiers of Legal Analysis: Reframing the Transition in Northern Ireland' (2003) 66 *MLR* 317.

[64] *Reference by the Attorney General for Northern Ireland—In the matter of an application by Agnew and others for Judicial Review; Reference by the Court of Appeal (Northern Ireland)—In the matter of an application by Raymond McCord for Judicial Review* [2017] 2 WLR 583 at [134]–[35].

self-determination, the Welsh Government has recently asserted that '[w]hatever its historical origins, the United Kingdom is best seen now as a voluntary association of nations' and that '[t]he allocation of legislative and executive functions between central UK institutions and devolved institutions should be based on the concept of subsidiarity, acknowledging popular sovereignty in each part of the UK'.[65] Thus, the Wales Act 2017 has extended the same constitutional guarantees to Wales as are contained in sections 1 and 2 of the Scotland Act 2016, albeit subject to the same caveats.

As these various qualifications suggest, these alternative understandings of the nature of the territorial constitution have been essentially peripheral. This is true both in a geographic sense—the lived reality for the vast majority of the UK's population resident in England is that of a unitary system of government—and in the sense of being unofficial, 'political' readings of the constitution rather than ones given unambiguous legal expression.

Again, though, in recent years, territorial divergences in how the constitution is theorised have become harder to ignore. On the one hand, the 2014 independence referendum has transformed Scotland's claim to popular sovereignty from a theoretical assertion to a practical reality which threatens to destroy the UK state. Although the right of the Scottish Parliament to call a second independence referendum is not legally secure,[66] the 2014 referendum creates a political precedent which may be difficult to ignore.[67] On the other hand, EU withdrawal and the threat of human rights reform have exposed the fundamental incompatibility between Northern Ireland's transnational constitutional order and the traditional unitary constitution, and the obstacle—albeit again primarily a political one—that its constrained constitution poses to the free exercise of parliamentary sovereignty.

III. THE CONCEPTUAL PERSPECTIVE

Having established the nature and extent of territorial diversity within the UK, the question can now be addressed whether this position is sustainable. One way of approaching this issue is through a conceptual lens; that is, asking how much constitutional diversity can be accommodated within a single state order.

[65] Welsh Government, 'Written Evidence', House of Lords Select Committee on the Constitution, *The Union and Devolution—Evidence* (2016) para 6.

[66] For discussion, see G Anderson et al, 'The Independence Referendum, Legality and the Contested Constitution: Widening the Debate', *UK Constitutional Law Association Blog*, 31 January 2012.

[67] On 28 March 2017, the Scottish Parliament voted in support of a motion requesting the enactment of another Order under section 30 of the Scotland Act 1998 to facilitate the holding of a second independence referendum in Autumn 2019 (Motion S5M-04710 (Nicola Sturgeon) SPOR, 28 March 2017 (Session 5)). Although, at the time of writing, the Prime Minister has indicated that she will reject this request, on the basis that the timing is inappropriate, she has not ruled out the possibility of a second referendum altogether. It remains to be seen whether the Scottish Government will choose to proceed with a referendum Bill without the legal comfort of a section 30 Order, or whether some compromise will be reached over its timing. The degree of popular support for a second referendum is likely to be a determining factor in whether or not the Prime Minister is willing to accede to the Scottish Parliament's request.

Constitutions have classically been associated with states,[68] and this would appear to place limits on the degree to which constitutional arrangements may diverge within a particular state. This 'monist'[69] account of the relationship between state and constitution does not necessarily require a unitary constitution with a single sovereign; on the contrary, federal constitutional systems[70] are intended to accommodate (in varying degrees) a significant measure of internal pluralism. However, the parameters within which sub-state units may diverge in federal systems are typically set by and contained within a single, overarching constitutional framework, which provides mechanisms for resolving conflicts of authority. Federal constitutions, in other words, provide for the division and sharing of constitutional authority within the territory of a particular state, rather than the creation of distinct and parallel constitutional orders.

Monist accounts of the relationship between state and constitution are challenged by pluralist constitutional theories, which argue that constitutional orders can exist without being associated with states, and that multiple constitutional orders can co-exist within the same territorial space without any relationship of hierarchy between them.[71] Although developed to account for the competing supremacy claims of the EU and its member states, the decoupling of constitution from state also suggests that radical constitutional pluralism may exist *within* as well as beyond the state.[72]

Loughlin objects to pluralist constitutional theories on the basis that they fail adequately to account for the link between constitutions and the exercise of governmental *authority*.[73] In a situation of constitutional pluralism, he argues, there is no means of *authoritatively* resolving conflicts between constitutional orders. Interactions between them can be explained only as a matter of pure power politics, or else it is necessary to invoke some set of higher order principles which can be used to determine when one system ought to defer to another (ie, to revert to a form of constitutional monism). He further objects to the decoupling of constitution from state on the ground that this requires constitutional orders to demonstrate their own, independent authority. For a sub-state unit to assert that it forms a distinct constitutional order within the state would therefore constitute a challenge to the authority

[68] See CMG Himsworth, 'In a State No Longer: The End of Constitutionalism?' [1996] *PL* 639.

[69] N Walker, 'The Idea of Constitutional Pluralism' (2002) 65 *MLR* 317 at 337.

[70] These include federations proper, as well as confederations, federacies, models of associated statehood, constitutionally decentralized unions, condominiums, leagues, joint functional authorities and less formal asymmetrical federal arrangements: see, eg, DJ Elazar, *Exploring Federalism* (Tuscaloosa, Alabama, University of Alabama Press, 1987); RL Watts, *Comparing Federal Systems*, 3rd edn (Montreal, McGill-Queen's Press, 2008).

[71] See, eg, N MacCormick, *Questioning Sovereignty* (Oxford, Oxford University Press, 1999); Walker (n 69); M Avbelj and J Komárek (eds), *Constitutional Pluralism in the European Union and Beyond* (Oxford, Hart Publishing, 2012).

[72] See S Tierney, 'Reframing Sovereignty? Sub-State National Societies and Contemporary Challenges to the Nation State' (2005) 54 *ICLQ* 161; S Tierney, *Constitutional Law and National Pluralism* (Oxford, Oxford University Press, 2006).

[73] M Loughlin, 'Constitutional Pluralism: An Oxymoron?' (2014) 3 *Global Constitutionalism* 9.

of the state itself. It follows that, within any system of territorial governance, there must be a degree of constitutional unity to authoritatively explain and regulate the relationship of the parts to the whole. In fact, sub-state national units do typically seek accommodation within or recognition by the host state constitution for their distinct constitutional aspirations, and the absence of such recognition does indeed pose a threat to the survival of the state.[74]

Nevertheless, the need, in the final analysis, to have some means of making sense of the internal diversity of a constitutional order patently does not take us very far in determining *how much* constitutional diversity may be tolerated. Real-world constitutions exhibit widely varying degrees of internal pluralism, differing not only in terms of where the lines are drawn between central and sub-state level decision making and in the amount of variation permitted to sub-state regions in their own constitutional arrangements, but also in the extent of asymmetry they permit.[75] On the face of it, institutional diversity might appear to be less threatening to constitutional unity than value pluralism, which in turn might seem less problematic than divergent theories of the state. But two further conceptual points can be made here. The first is that diversity is not the same as disunity.[76] In practice, it may be possible to maintain a significant diversity of constitutional values without threatening constitutional unity provided that upholding one set of values in one part of the state does not pose any risk, whether actual or symbolic, to the maintenance of a different set of values in another part. What matters, in other words, is not the achievement of homogeneity, but rather the avoidance of conflict. Secondly, it is possible for *interpretive* conflicts to exist, even on matters as fundamental as the theory of the state, without them necessarily having to be authoritatively resolved. All constitutional orders contain gaps and silences, which may have strategic value in the management of what might otherwise be damaging disagreements and tensions.[77] Key aspects of the constitution may thus constitute 'incompletely theorised agreements';[78] that is, they may attract mutual commitment from different groups without agreeing on exactly what it is to which they are committed.

Two conclusions may be drawn from this. One is that, irrespective of whether one adopts a monist or pluralist conception of the relationship between constitutions and states, further criteria are needed to determine the degree of divergence that will or should prevail in any particular context. The other is that institutional arrangements may be just as, if not more, important than constitutional values or theories of the state to the achievement of a successful balance between constitutional unity and diversity, as a key determinant of how effectively territorial conflicts can be avoided or managed.

[74] See Tierney, *Constitutional Law and National Pluralism* (n 72) at 100–01; 125–26.

[75] See references in n 70; G Anderson and S Choudhry, *Constitutional Transitions and Territorial Cleavages* (Stockholm, International Institute for Democracy and Electoral Assistance, 2015).

[76] See Elazar (n 70) at 64.

[77] See M Foley, *The Silence of Constitutions: Gaps, 'Abeyances' and Political Temperament in the Maintenance of Government* (London and New York, Routledge, 1989).

[78] CR Sunstein, 'Incompletely Theorized Agreements' (1995) 108 *Harvard Law Review* 1733.

IV. THE NORMATIVE PERSPECTIVE

A conceptual approach tells us that there needs to be some means of creating order out of diversity in any pluralistic constitutional system. However, a normative perspective may be more helpful in identifying the precise nature and degree of unity that is required. Normative arguments may be directed at identifying common minimum standards that must be respected throughout the state, and/or issues that must be decided in common, and/or common purposes to guide the allocation and regulation of decision-making competences. Such proposals are a prominent feature of the recent literature on reform of the UK's territorial constitution.[79] The difficulty, however, is to identify appropriate normative standards.

One approach is to invoke abstract principles of constitutionalism, such as a shared commitment to democracy, the rule of law and protection of fundamental rights.[80] While the blandness of such values makes them relatively uncontroversial, their very abstraction and universality makes them unhelpful as a unifying force for the UK constitution. Broad statements of principle necessarily permit of a range of different interpretations in practice. If, on the one hand, their purpose is simply to establish a minimum floor below which no part of the state may fall, it is not clear what they would add to existing constitutional protections (particularly at the devolved level) nor that there is any real problem to be addressed. The accusation that there are *systematic* violations of minimum standards of constitutional propriety in any part of the UK is one that (at least under current constitutional arrangements) would be hard to sustain.

If, on the other hand, such principles are to be applied uniformly, then the questions arise as to *who* is to decide how they are to be interpreted and *why* their interpretation is to be preferred. Why, for instance, should the decision of the UK Parliament as to the level of human rights protection prevail over that of the devolved legislatures, especially if the latter are committed to a higher standard, or a broader range of rights? Similarly, why is the view of the United Kingdom Supreme Court on the Convention compatibility of matters within devolved competence to be preferred where the local courts have taken a different view? These are, of course, not merely hypothetical examples, but issues of concrete political controversy,[81] which raise sensitive issues about the asymmetry of the UK's populations, and hence the vulnerability of the minority nations to being overridden by the English majority or carelessly assimilated to an English norm.

The invocation of a set of more authentically 'British' values or purposes would in principle be a more satisfactory form of constitutional 'glue' to hold the UK together. In practice, however, this proves to be even more problematic. Again, any attempt to identify common standards risks simply exposing rather than resolving

[79] See references in n 16.

[80] See, eg, Bingham Centre (n 16) at xiii; Brown (n 16) at 195; Constitution Reform Group (2016) (n 16).

[81] As to the former, the question of whether the consent of the devolved legislatures is required for reform or repeal of the Human Rights Act. As to the latter, *cf* the controversy over the *Cadder* and *Fraser* cases: see McHarg (n 14). See also D Feldman, 'None, One or Several? Perspectives on the UK's Constitution(s)' (2005) 64 *CLJ* 329.

differences. Most obviously, it may expose *territorial* difference. For instance, the idea of a distinctively *British* Bill of Rights quickly ran up against the reality of different legal traditions, as well as different attitudes to rights protection in different parts of the UK.[82] But it also runs the risk of exposing *political* differences more generally. For example, post-independence referendum debates about the appropriateness of devolving welfare and abortion powers to the Scottish Parliament revealed cross-party disagreement about the role of common social rights as a necessary condition of political solidarity across the UK.[83]

A second problem is that the idea of 'principles' or 'purposes' of the Union is profoundly ahistorical. The UK's Constitution has never been a teleological one; on the contrary, its defining feature—the principle of parliamentary sovereignty—is one which explicitly eschews the idea of a fixed ideological purpose. In practice, therefore, attempts to define the purposes of Union tend either towards the tautologous (eg, the Constitution Reform Group's draft Act of Union Bill unhelpfully states that '[t]he purpose of the United Kingdom is to provide a strong and effective union between the peoples of the constituent nations and parts')[84] or else require the imputation of a rationale which is both historically and politically contentious. Gallagher argues, for example, that the Union encompasses principles of political, economic and social integration; hence the development of the territorial constitution must be consistent with the maintenance of the UK's single external face, its fully-integrated economy, and a substantial degree of social solidarity.[85] In reality, though, the rationale for the Union has changed over time; contemporary ideas of a single market or social union would not have made sense at the time the Union was forged. Instead, the initial purpose of the Anglo–Scottish Union was narrowly focused (for the Scots) on ensuring access to markets and (for the English) on securing the Protestant succession to the Crown. These concerns were later superseded by a common commitment to empire, and later still to a high standard of social protection through a common welfare state[86]—a commitment which itself may now be on the wane.[87] In fact, contemporary interpretations of the requirements of economic, social and political union appear to owe as much to the principles of the *European* Union, as they do to any historically authentic British understanding. Moreover, they have a tendency to shift as political circumstances change. Thus, for example, the reforms to the Scottish devolution settlement proposed by the Calman Commission,[88] and implemented by the Scotland Act 2012, were superseded by

[82] Commission on a Bill of Rights, *A UK Bill of Rights? The Choice before Us* (2012) ch 9.

[83] See, eg, HM Government, *The Parties' Published Proposals on Further Devolution for Scotland* (Cm 8946, 2014); T Gordon, 'Revealed: The Devolution Powers Shelved at the Last Minute from the Smith Commission Report', *The Herald*, 30 November 2014.

[84] See Constitutional Reform Group (2016) (n 16) at cl 1.1(1).

[85] See Gallagher (2014) (n 16) at 10–13, 15.

[86] See, eg, L Colley, *Acts of Union and Disunion* (London, Profile Books Ltd, 2014).

[87] T Mullen, 'The Scottish Independence Referendum 2014' (2014) 41 *Journal of Law and Society* 627 at 637.

[88] Commission on Scottish Devolution, *Serving Scotland Better: Scotland and the United Kingdom in the 21st Century: Final Report* (2009).

the post-independence referendum Smith Commission proposals[89] before they had even come fully into effect. Now Brexit has reopened debate about what powers are suitable for devolution[90] before the post-Smith reforms, implemented by the Scotland Act 2016, have themselves come fully into force.

If, as this suggests, the British Union has always been a protean and evolving concept,[91] then any attempt to fix its meaning is arguably misguided, undermining the very flexibility that has ensured its longevity. Paradoxically, therefore, the attempt to identify British values or purposes may itself be regarded as being in an important sense 'unBritish'. This, in fact, points to a final problem with normative projects of this nature, namely the naivety of the assumption that an explicit legal statement of common principles will itself have a cohesive effect. The problem of increasing constitutional divergence is not simply that people have not thought carefully enough about what it means to be British or about the purpose and benefits of the UK state. On the contrary, having to mount an explicit defence of the Union is itself an indication that it is in trouble. As Kidd has argued, the Union was at its strongest when it was simply taken for granted.[92] Thus the demand to (as Gallagher puts it) 'crystallise' the Union seems to ignore the basic truth which underpins the traditional British preference for political rather than legal constitutionalism: if the political conditions for solidarity across the constituent nations of the Union are absent, an abstract statement of constitutional principles cannot fill the void. On the contrary, it may make things worse, if particular territories feel that their political and constitutional aspirations are being curtailed in the name of common 'British' values to which they do not subscribe. Clearly, given the asymmetry of the UK's populations, the minority nations are most vulnerable to being overridden by UK-wide standards, but the reverse situation, in which the English majority is constrained by the values of the minority nations, is equally problematic.

V. THE POLITICAL PERSPECTIVE

As this last point suggests, the problem of increasing diversity in the UK's territorial constitution is, at root, a political, rather than a normative or conceptual, one. The problem is political in at least two senses. First, constitutional divergence is a symptom rather than the cause of political fragmentation across the UK. Certainly, as noted above, devolution has accentuated the pluralisation of political identities and behaviour, and contributed to a weakening sense of common citizenship. But devolution itself must be understood at least in part as a *response to* political fragmentation, and the decline of a compelling sense of common purpose. The reasons

[89] The Smith Commission, *Report of the Smith Commission for Further Devolution of Powers to the Scottish Parliament* (2014).

[90] See references in n 9 and Gallagher (2016) (n 16).

[91] M Keating, 'Can the Union Be Saved from Unionists?', *Centre on Constitutional Change Blog*, 18 September 2015.

[92] C Kidd, *Union and Unionisms: Political Thought in Scotland, 1500–2000* (Cambridge, Cambridge University Press, 2008) ch 1.

for that are complex,[93] and are themselves territorially divergent,[94] but it would be a mistake to assume that it is solely the result of political change in the devolved nations and regions themselves. Behaviour by successive *UK* governments, particularly the hollowing out of the state through the pursuit of a neo-liberal political agenda,[95] and austerity-driven attacks on the welfare state,[96] have also been significant in undermining markers of common UK citizenship, just as it is the UK government which has undermined common constitutional commitments by jeopardising the UK's EU membership and proposing to dilute human rights protections. In the absence of a common purpose, defence of the Union has taken on a transactional quality; something demonstrated vividly during the Scottish independence referendum campaign when the Unionist side struggled to articulate a positive vision of the UK, instead selling it to Scottish voters essentially as an insurance policy against economic and defence-related risk.[97] It is, however, hard to feel a strong sense of solidarity with an insurance provider, especially if some of its functions are potentially capable of replication by other means.

The problem is also political in the sense that territorial conflict has been exacerbated by the lack of a 'federal spirit' or 'federal mindset' at the centre of the constitution.[98] Again, this is not necessarily new,[99] but it is accentuated by the double asymmetry of devolution—ie, the lack of separate representative institutions for England, along with the failure to reform the central constitutional apparatus to take account of devolution.[100] The crude assumption often seems to be that devolution has 'solved' the problem of territorial difference (or if it has not solved the problem, then the answer is more devolution), and hence that matters reserved to the centre can unproblematically be decided according to a simple UK-wide majority. Such an approach often seems insensitive to the intertwined nature of devolved and reserved competences, and hence to the possibility of creating problematic spill-over effects for the devolved institutions. Nor is it sensitive to the contested nature of the territorial constitution, as regards both the appropriate boundaries between UK and devolved competences and the location of sovereign power.

If the problem of constitutional diversity is essentially political, the implication is that it also requires a political solution—that is, one which promotes political

[93] In relation to Scotland, see C Kidd and M Petrie, 'The Independence Referendum in Historical and Political Context' in McHarg et al (n 8) at 29.

[94] See Mitchell (n 7).

[95] See, eg, D Marquand, *Decline of the Public: The Hollowing out of Citizenship* (Cambridge, Polity, 2004).

[96] See, eg, M Simpson, 'The Social Union after the Coalition: Devolution, Divergence and Convergence' (2016) *Journal of Social Policy* 251.

[97] See, in particular, the UK Government's independence analysis papers <www.gov.uk/government/collections/scotland-analysis>; and see J Gallagher, 'Making the Case for Union: Exactly Why Are We Better Together?' in McHarg et al (n 8) at 127.

[98] See McEwen (n 8) at 232–33, 240.

[99] Kidd and Petrie attribute the rising support for devolution in Scotland during the 1980s to Margaret Thatcher's 'unitarist' version of Unionism, and hence her failure to respect Scottish autonomy and difference: (n 93) at 38–43.

[100] See, eg, S Tierney, 'Giving with One Hand: Scottish Devolution within a Unitary State' (2007) 5 *International Journal of Constitutional Law* 730; N McEwen and B Petersohn, 'Between Autonomy and Interdependence: The Challenges of Shared Rule after the Scottish Referendum' (2015) 86 *Political Quarterly* 192.

inclusion and the avoidance of territorial conflict, rather than which attempts to impose or re-impose uniformity. This in turn suggests a focus on institutional rather than substantive constitutional reform. Most obviously, institutional reform would mean addressing the double asymmetries of devolution: on the one hand, creating meaningful self-government for England, as well as addressing those other asymmetries which particularly cause resentment (such as the funding of devolved government);[101] on the other hand, reform of the central state apparatus to give due recognition to territorial diversity, for instance, by strengthening and codifying institutions for inter-governmental relations,[102] or by reconstituting the House of Lords as a territorial chamber.[103] However, other institutional reforms, such as reform of the House of Commons' electoral system, may also be important in promoting territorial inclusion. The first-past-the-post system arguably exacerbates territorial conflict by artificially amplifying geographical differences. For instance, the fact that the SNP won 56 out of 59 seats at the 2015 General Election on only 50 per cent of the popular vote had the unhelpful effect of making normal party competition in the Commons chamber look like conflict between Scotland and the rest of the UK.

In addition, since a 'federal mindset' is about attitudes as well as about institutional structures, a political approach to the problem of territorial diversity suggests a need to pay attention to the broader conditions of political solidarity beyond the formal constitution. Political party organisation, media structures and behaviour, pressure group activity, and so on, may also be important in promoting or undermining territorial inclusion. But a focus on political solidarity also suggests that there may be substantive limits to the degree of territorial diversity that the UK constitution can bear. Since the extent of sub-state autonomy varies widely in different constitutions, it is hard to derive limits to territorial diversity *a priori*; what matters for the maintenance of political solidarity will vary from context to context. Nevertheless, if the state ceases to be a site of meaningful common political identity, then its survival as a state must be in doubt.

It also needs to be recognised that there are significant obstacles to the achievement of the kind of institutional reforms just discussed. The need for devolution to England is easy to state, but remains difficult to achieve. The insight of the Kilbrandon Commission[104] that the UK is too deeply asymmetrical in both its population and history for a symmetrical constitutional model to be feasible still holds true. A federation with England as a single territorial unit would face simultaneous problems of English dominance in central decision-making and a severe democratic deficit to the extent that the minority nations could overrule an English majority.[105] Breaking up England into regional units would solve the geographic problem but

[101] See Henderson et al (n 20) at 271.

[102] See, eg, McEwen and Petersohn (n 100); Calman Commission (n 88); Smith Commission (n 89).

[103] As proposed by the Labour Party prior to the 2015 General Election: see Labour Party Press Release, 'Labour Announces Plans to Give Regions and Nations Greater Power and a Stronger Voice in Westminster' (31 October 2014) <www.press.labour.org.uk/post/101667859054/labour-announces-plans-to-give-regions-and-nations>.

[104] Royal Commission on the Constitution, *Volume 1: Report* (Cmnd 5460, 1973).

[105] See MacCormick (n 71) at 195.

would create its own legitimacy issues, both insofar as there is no obvious demand for strong regional government in England[106] and regional boundaries are contested,[107] and because to treat the smaller UK nations as constitutionally equivalent to English regions would do violence to the former's sense of their historical uniqueness. Other institutional reforms are equally difficult to achieve; reform of the House of Lords and the House of Commons electoral system each raise a whole range of difficult issues going well beyond their implications for territorial relations. As Walker has noted, the more complex and inter-related the constitutional reform agenda becomes, the more it becomes trapped in a 'paradox of initiative'[108]—ie, 'the divisions and centrifugal political forces that make "joined up" constitutional reform so pressing also make it very unlikely to happen'.[109] It is, in any event, difficult to detect much appetite for constitutional reform of this nature[110] and given that dealing with the consequences of Brexit is likely to dominate the political agenda for the foreseeable future, it is hard to imagine that other constitutional reforms will be seen as a high priority any time soon.[111]

VI. CONCLUSION: BREXIT AND THE TERRITORIAL CONSTITUTION

In fact, given the current polarised state of territorial politics, so greatly exacerbated by Brexit, the break-up of the UK seems a more likely prospect than its significant reform. Brexit is, *par excellence*, an illustration of the lack of a federal spirit at the heart of the territorial constitution, and of the dangers of political fragmentation. The decision to hold a referendum on EU membership was driven not by any constitutional imperative, but rather purely by political ones: it was an attempt to resolve long-standing divisions in the Conservative party over the merits of EU membership and to respond to the increasing electoral popularity of the UK Independence Party. Notwithstanding that these were predominantly English concerns,[112] and the clear possibility of a territorially divided result, the Conservative Government's political incentive was to respond to its electoral base in England, even if that led it in a direction which was difficult to reconcile with its avowed stance as a unionist party. Indeed, the decision to press ahead with the EU referendum in the face of

[106] As noted above (n 33 and accompanying text), regional devolution was abandoned in 2004 due to lack of popular support; City Devolution deals have also been rejected in some local authority areas.

[107] See, eg, the dispute over the inclusion of Chesterfield within the Sheffield City Region under the Cities and Local Government Devolution Act 2016: *R (Derbyshire CC) v Barnsley, Doncaster, Rotherham and Sheffield Combined Authority* [2016] EWHC 3355 (Admin).

[108] N Walker, 'Our Constitutional Unsettlement' [2014] *PL* 529 at 542.

[109] N Walker, 'The Territorial Constitution and the Future of Scotland', in McHarg et al (n 8) at 247, 270.

[110] For instance, while the Scottish Labour Party has recently committed to the creation of a federal UK, this is not yet UK Labour policy: see, eg, S Carrell, 'Labour Expected to Consider Possibility of Federal UK', *The Guardian*, 24 February 2017.

[111] The UK Government has already confirmed that human rights reform will be postponed until after Brexit: see D Bond, 'British Bill of Rights Delayed until after Brexit, Liz Truss Reveals', *Politics Home* 23 February 2017.

[112] See Wyn Jones et al (n 53); B Wellings, 'English Nationalism and Euroscepticism Overlap and Support Each Other in Important Ways', *British Politics and Policy Blog*, 29 April 2014.

opposition from the Scottish and Welsh Governments and from most of Northern Ireland's political parties suggests that the UK Government was at best reckless as to its implications for territorial relations.

Both before and after the referendum, a territorially inclusive approach to the Brexit decision was offered but rejected. First, the Scottish National Party attempted unsuccessfully to amend the European Union Referendum Bill to create a requirement of parallel consent to Brexit; in other words, for 'Leave' to win, there would need to be a majority across the UK and in each of its four constituent units. After the vote, the unexpected challenge to the UK Government's right to initiate the process of withdrawing from the EU under Article 50 of the Treaty on European Union (TEU) under the Royal Prerogative created an opportunity to reassert the parallel consent principle in the form of an argument that, if statutory authorisation were required to trigger Article 50, such legislation would also require the consent of the devolved legislatures under the Sewel Convention. Although the Supreme Court in the *Miller* case did not reach a conclusive view on whether or not the Sewel Convention was engaged,[113] its decision that this was a political rather than legal matter enabled the UK Government simply to continue to assert its prior position that devolved consent was not required, on the basis that the decision to withdraw from the EU was a matter reserved to the UK Government with (in its view) no major impact on the devolution arrangements.[114] Similarly, despite initially committing to the 'full engagement' of the devolved governments in establishing the UK's negotiating position on Brexit,[115] this commitment has waned over time in favour of a reassertion of the decisiveness of the UK-wide Brexit vote and of the UK Government's right to determine its meaning.[116] Thus, the Scottish and Welsh Governments' preference for a 'soft Brexit', which would enable the UK to remain part of the EU Single Market,[117] has effectively been dismissed by the UK Government,[118] without any sign of serious engagement with their proposals,[119] and the Prime Minister notified the UK's intention to withdraw from the EU under Article 50 TEU on 29 March 2017 without agreeing a common position with them.

On the one hand, the rejection of a territorially inclusive approach is unsurprising. Given the asymmetry in the UK's populations, it would have been constitutionally problematic—as well as politically difficult for both the Conservative Government and the Labour Opposition—for the minority nations to exercise a territorial veto over Brexit or a decisive influence over the form it takes. On the other hand, it leaves a choice between two equally unpalatable alternatives.

[113] *R (Miller) v Secretary of State for Exiting the European Union* [2017] 2 WLR 583 at [132].

[114] See HM Government, *Supplementary Supreme Court Printed Case of the Secretary of State for Exiting the European Union (Devolution Issues)* (2016); *Explanatory Notes to the European Union (Notification of Withdrawal) Bill* (2017) para 9.

[115] See David Cameron's resignation speech on 24 June 2016.

[116] See, eg, 'Theresa May Urges Scots to Use Local Elections to Reject Independence', *Holyrood Magazine*, 26 February 2017.

[117] See references in n 9.

[118] HM Government, *The United Kingdom's Exit from and New Partnership with the European Union* (Cm 9417, 2017).

[119] See *Holyrood Magazine* (n 116).

The 'constitutionally homogenising' approach that the UK Government currently seems to be favouring leaves little room for territorial influence and would stand both as a dramatic illustration of the democratic vulnerability of the minority nations within the Union, and of a lack of sensitivity to their particular political and constitutional concerns. The suggestion in the UK Government's Brexit White Paper[120] that decisions currently made at EU level will predominantly be repatriated to the UK Government rather than to the devolved governments, even where, prima facie, within devolved competence would also involve a major rebalancing of power within the territorial constitution in favour of the UK level. Predictably, the constitutionally homogenising approach has led to the reopening of the question of Scottish independence,[121] as well as unhelpfully raising the political temperature within Northern Ireland.

Alternatively, what might be termed a 'radically asymmetrical' approach—involving either the negotiation of bespoke relationships with the EU for Northern Ireland and/or Scotland or conceding significant additional devolved powers—would involve such an extensive degree of territorial variation that it is hard to see how any sense of common citizenship could survive. In particular, if Brexit were to lead to differential relationships with the EU, this would introduce fundamental differences not only in institutional relationships, but also in constitutional values and in the nature and location of sovereignty, all of which would have such far-reaching practical consequences that Scotland and Northern Ireland would, to all intents and purposes, become mini-states only loosely connected to the rest of the UK. For this reason alone, quite apart from any technical or political obstacles that such proposals would face, differential Brexit seems like a degree of constitutional diversity too far.

Ultimately, therefore, it is difficult to conceive of *any* satisfactory solution to the territorial difficulties caused by the EU referendum result which does not, sooner or later, put the survival of the UK at risk. In these circumstances, worrying about the need for greater unity in the territorial constitution has the air of shutting the stable door after the horse has bolted.

[120] HM Government (n 118) para 3.4.
[121] See n 67 above.

15

Moving Beyond the Constitutionalism/ Democracy Dilemma: 'Commonwealth Model' Scholarship and the Fixation on Legislative Compliance

CLAUDIA GEIRINGER*

I. INTRODUCTION

THE EMERGENCE OF new forms of codified human rights protection in the Anglo-Commonwealth jurisdictions of Canada,[1] New Zealand,[2] the United Kingdom[3] and (at the sub-national level) Australia,[4] has turned out to be a development of considerable interest to comparative constitutional law. The 'hybrid'[5] nature of these instruments poses a challenge to the apparent hegemony of the American model of constitutionalised human rights protection and has opened up (or at least called attention to) a wide-open hinterland in which elements traditionally associated with fully constitutionalised bills of rights can comingle with other, more politically orientated (and/or more common law-derived) forms of constitutionalism.

These developments have not gone unnoticed; indeed, they have spawned a veritable cottage industry of comparative scholarship.[6] Notably, though, a number of

* Chair in Public Law, Victoria University of Wellington; co-director, NZ Centre for Public Law. For their helpful comments, grateful thanks go to Graeme Austin, Joel Colón-Ríos, Eddie Clark, Catherine Dixon, Aileen Kavanagh, Sir Kenneth Keith, Dean Knight, Nicole Moreham, Geoff McLay, Campbell McLachlan, Sir Geoffrey Palmer, Guy Sinclair and Jana von Stein. Thanks also to two anonymous reviewers for their careful consideration.

1 Canadian Bill of Rights 1960; Canadian Charter of Rights and Freedoms 1982 (Canadian Charter); as well as some (very early) provincial bills of rights.

2 New Zealand Bill of Rights Act 1990 (NZ).

3 Human Rights Act 1998 (UK).

4 Human Rights Act 2004 (ACT); Charter of Human Rights and Responsibilities Act 2006 (Vic) (Victorian Charter).

5 See, eg, J Goldsworthy, 'Homogenizing Constitutions' (2003) 23 *Oxford Journal of Legal Studies* 483; R Weill, 'Hybrid Constitutionalism: The Israeli Case for Judicial Review and Why We Should Care' (2012) 30 *Berkeley Journal of International Law* 349.

6 M Tushnet, 'New Forms of Judicial Review and the Persistence of Rights- and Democracy-based Worries' (2003) 38 *Wake Forest Law Review* 813; M Perry, 'Protecting Human Rights in a Democracy: What Role for the Courts?' (2003) 38 *Wake Forest Law Review* 635; R Dixon, 'Weak-Form Judicial

the key contributions to this body of literature are centrally preoccupied with one question: the ability (or not) of these hybrid bills of rights[7] to resolve the longstanding impasse between constitutionalism and democracy. For writers in this tradition, the starting point for discussion—the interpretive foil, if you like—is the traditional dichotomy between two competing paradigms of constitutionalism: parliamentary sovereignty and judicial supremacy. The point of interest, from this perspective, is the potential of the new 'Commonwealth model'[8] to disrupt this dichotomy and to carve out an intermediate form of constitutionalism.

This genre of scholarship has played a valuable role in stimulating reflection and debate about important questions of constitutional theory and institutional design. But as an explanatory account of the operation of the Commonwealth model scheme of human rights protection (something that scholars in this tradition certainly purport to offer), it is radically incomplete. On the one hand, the preoccupation of this tradition of scholarship with establishing what is distinctive about the Anglo-Commonwealth instruments, as viewed specifically from the perspective of the constitutionalism/democracy dilemma, focuses the inquiry almost entirely on questions of institutional responsibility for the human rights compatibility of legislation. As a result, other possible dimensions of 'distinctiveness' are neglected—for example, the parliamentary character of the respective systems of government, the common law context, and (with respect to all but one of the Commonwealth model instruments) the location of the respective instruments in statute law rather than in a formal constitutional document. On the other hand, the preoccupation with 'distinctiveness' is, in itself, too limited, in that it leads to an abridged account of the factors that drive the respective performance of the model in each jurisdiction.[9]

The most glaring casualty of this double blindfold is any sustained inquiry into the role these instruments play in influencing and constraining the exercise of public functions (whether by the police, the executive or devolved bodies). These questions of public authority constraint are central to any credible evaluation, whether of the distinctiveness of, or of variance within, the Commonwealth model system of human rights protection. Yet the Commonwealth model genre of scholarship, with its dual focus on 'distinctiveness' and legislative compatibility, elides almost completely these important questions.

In expanding on these points below, this chapter joins with other critiques of Commonwealth model scholarship, which have expressed reservations about the

Review and American Exceptionalism' (2012) 32 *Oxford Journal of Legal Studies* 487; S Gardbaum, *The New Commonwealth Model of Constitutionalism: Theory and Practice* (Cambridge, Cambridge University Press, 2013); JL Hiebert and JB Kelly, *Parliamentary Bills of Rights: The Experiences of New Zealand and the United Kingdom* (Cambridge, Cambridge University Press, 2015); S Stephenson, *From Dialogue to Disagreement in Comparative Rights Constitutionalism* (Sydney, Federation Press, 2016).

[7] These instruments are variously self-identified as bills of rights, charters of rights and human rights Acts. I do not regard these terminological differences as significant and, in this chapter, use such terms interchangeably.

[8] For a discussion of terminology, see nn 12–16 and associated text.

[9] In this chapter, I use the term 'jurisdiction' loosely to refer to the national and the sub-national units that have adopted Commonwealth model instruments.

particular 'macro-constitutional'[10] style of comparative inquiry that the Commonwealth model scholarship might be seen to exemplify, and which have contrasted it with a more fine-grained and contextualist style of comparativism.[11] This contextualist critique suggests a need for restraint in the purposes for which Commonwealth model scholarship is deployed. It may well serve an important function in stimulating reflection and debate about the limits and possibilities of constitutional design. But it fails to deliver on its promise to provide a comprehensive comparative account of the efficacy of the Commonwealth model instruments.

II. 'COMMONWEALTH MODEL' SCHOLARSHIP AND ITS CRITICS

I begin with the fraught question of terminology. The best way to describe the collection of human rights instruments with which I am concerned is itself the subject of some considerable debate.[12] In this chapter, I use primarily Stephen Gardbaum's designation: the new Commonwealth model of human rights protection (or Commonwealth model for short) but intersperse it with terminology that I have begun to test drive in my own scholarship: the 'Anglo-Commonwealth' bills of rights.[13] For sure, Gardbaum's label is not without its drawbacks.[14] But it has two advantages. First, thanks to the reputation of Gardbaum's work, its meaning is comparatively well understood. Secondly, unlike some of the other terms on offer, it is neutral as to the particular features of the model we ought to regard as most salient.[15] For my purposes, this is important.[16]

Comparative study of these Anglo-Commonwealth instruments has been dominated by a particular genre of scholarship best exemplified by the work of Gardbaum himself, as well as that of Mark Tushnet and, most recently, Scott Stephenson.[17] This mode of scholarship (which I refer to here as the Commonwealth model genre of

[10] E Carolan, 'Leaving Behind the Commonwealth Model of Rights Review: Ireland as an Example of Collaborative Constitutionalism' in J Bell and M Paris (eds), *Rights-Based Constitutional Review: Constitutional Courts in a Changing Landscape* (Cheltenham, Edward Elgar, 2016) 94, 96.

[11] See nn 37–40 and associated text; nn 118–20 and associated text.

[12] See Gardbaum (n 6) at 13–16; Hiebert and Kelly (n 6) at 410.

[13] S Gardbaum, 'The New Commonwealth Model of Constitutionalism' (2001) 49 *American Journal of Comparative Law* 707; S Gardbaum, 'Reassessing the New Commonwealth Model of Constitutionalism' (2010) 8 *International Journal of Constitutional Law* 167; Gardbaum (n 6).

[14] Most obviously, it is over-inclusive, and it invites confusion with the constitutional forms exported to the 'new Commonwealth' during the decolonisation era. On the latter, see SA de Smith, 'Fundamental Rights in the New Commonwealth (I)' (1961) 10 *International and Comparative Law Quarterly* 83.

[15] Contrast Tushnet's 'weak-form' review (eg Tushnet (n 6)), which focuses solely on the question of judicial enforcement, or Hiebert and Kelly's 'parliamentary bills of rights' (Hiebert and Kelly (n 6) at 410), which makes a deliberate statement about the non-exportability of the model and the importance of the parliamentary context.

[16] Other neutral terms such as 'hybrid' constitutionalism (see n 5) or 'third wave' bills of rights (see F Klug, 'The Human Rights Act—A "Third Way" or "Third Wave" Bill of Rights' [2001] *European Human Rights Law Review* 361) are problematically under-inclusive, at least when applied exclusively to developments in the Commonwealth jurisdictions with which we are concerned. On this point, see Weill (n 5); Carolan (n 10).

[17] See nn 18–30.

scholarship) is centrally preoccupied with what is, undoubtedly, a distinguishing feature of the Commonwealth model instruments: that they confer responsibility for the protection of human rights on all three branches of government without formally allocating the 'final word' on human rights issues to the courts. Scholars in this tradition see in that fact the potential for the Commonwealth model to carve out an intermediate form of constitutionalism—one that, by standing at a halfway point between the traditional models of parliamentary and judicial supremacy, resolves the constitutionalism/democracy dilemma. It is to assessing whether (and how) that potential is realised in practice that these writers address themselves.

Thus, for example, Mark Tushnet, an early contributor to this genre, coined the term 'weak-form judicial review' to describe the forms of non-conclusive review of legislation exercised by the courts within such systems of human rights protection (non-conclusive in the sense that the final word on the content of legislation remains with legislatures). In a series of articles, he poses a range of questions directed at assessing whether weak-form review in fact fulfils the promise it holds out of reconciling constitutionalism and self-governance.[18] Ultimately, he concludes that the model is an 'intriguing' one[19] but doubts that it can provide permanent resolution of the constitutionalism/democracy dilemma. His principal reason for this conclusion is his intuition that weak-form review is inherently 'unstable', that is, prone in practice either to 'degenerate' into parliamentary supremacy or to 'escalate' into strong-form review.[20]

Stephen Gardbaum's analysis is more systematic and comprehensive, but approaches the exercise through much the same lens.[21] For him, too, the key point of interest in the Commonwealth model is its ability to 'transcend the either/or nature of the existing choice' and to offer a 'third institutional form of constitutionalism' that sits in between 'the two traditional and dichotomous ones' (of parliamentary sovereignty and judicial supremacy).[22] His interest, like Tushnet's, is in whether this intermediate form of constitutionalism can be sustained in practice. Following detailed examination of the jurisdictions in which the model operates, he concludes that the model is working in 'at least a minimally distinct way' in all its iterations[23] but that, in practice, the Canadian Charter of Rights and Freedoms (the Canadian Charter) operates too close to the pole of judicial supremacy,[24] and the two sub-national Australian Charters operate too close to the pole of parliamentary

[18] These include whether it provides an answer to the problem of democratic debilitation that is sometimes linked to American-style judicial review (M Tushnet, 'Policy Distortion and Democratic Debilitation: Comparative Illumination of the Countermajoritarian Difficulty' (1995) 94 *Michigan Law Review* 245) and whether legislators are actually able to fulfil the role of constitutional evaluation conferred on them (M Tushnet, 'Weak-Form Judicial Review: Its Implications for Legislatures' (2004) 2 *New Zealand Journal of Public and International Law* 7).

[19] See Tushnet (n 6) at 837.

[20] ibid, at 814, 824. See also Tushnet, 'Weak Form Judicial Review' (n 18).

[21] See Gardbaum, 'The New Commonwealth Model of Constitutionalism' (n 13); Gardbaum, 'Reassessing the New Commonwealth Model of Constitutionalism' (n 13); Gardbaum (n 6).

[22] See Gardbaum (n 6) at 25.

[23] ibid, at 237.

[24] ibid, at 128.

supremacy.[25] On the other hand, both New Zealand and, to a lesser extent, the United Kingdom (while each could benefit from further refinements) have generated distinctively intermediate versions of constitutionalism that succeed in retaining the strengths, while avoiding the major weaknesses, of the traditional alternatives.[26]

Scott Stephenson's 2016 monograph makes an important new contribution to this genre of scholarship.[27] Stephenson, too, is focused on the extent to which the Commonwealth model (or, as he characterises it, 'multi-stage rights review') has succeeded in generating distinct patterns of institutional practice that distinguish it from the traditional poles of judicial and parliamentary supremacy.[28] For him, this model's particular contribution lies in the extent to which it seeks to expand and facilitate direct forms of inter-institutional disagreement about rights (as opposed to the indirect inter-institutional disagreement that, he argues, is common in systems of judicial and parliamentary supremacy).[29] Stephenson's most important contribution, though, lies in the attention he gives to competing constitutional principles or values (including responsible government and the separation of powers) which he sees as being in tension with the model.[30] He suggests that the particular emphasis placed on these competing normative commitments within each of the jurisdictions to have adopted the Commonwealth model helps to explain the different patterns of institutional practice that have emerged.

These works of scholarship have rightly been lauded for the innovative contribution they have made to questions of constitutional theory and institutional design.[31] They engage with what is undoubtedly a central dilemma of Western constitutionalism and, by recasting the debate in new terms, have acted as an important stimulant for reflection and debate—both inside and outside the common law world.

Nevertheless, in recent years, some reservations about this mode of inquiry have begun to emerge. Commentators point, for example, to the questionable utility of the concept of 'final word',[32] to the linearity of the weak-form/strong-form distinction,[33] to an uncomfortable mismatch between the analytical and descriptive

[25] ibid, at 220–21.

[26] ibid, at 235.

[27] See Stephenson (n 6). See C Geiringer, 'Review: Scott Stephenson, From Dialogue to Disagreement in Comparative Rights Constitutionalism' (2017) 15 *International Journal of Constitutional Law* (forthcoming).

[28] Stephenson, ibid at 2–3. Stephenson, though, objects to the characterisation of this distinct form of constitutionalism as 'weak' or 'intermediate': Stephenson, ibid at 112–13.

[29] ibid, at chapters 4 and 5.

[30] ibid, at chapter 7. The other competing principles or values he explores are bureaucratic independence, the rule of law, the hierarchy of laws, and comity.

[31] R Hirschl, 'How Consequential is the Commonwealth Constitutional Model' (2013) 11 *International Journal of Constitutional Law* 1086 at 1086–88; S Choudhry, 'The Commonwealth Constitutional Model or Models?' (2013) 11 *International Journal of Constitutional Law* 1094 at 1094–95; A Kavanagh, 'A Hard Look at the Last Word' (2015) 35 *Oxford Journal of Legal Studies* 825 at 828, 846; A Kavanagh, 'What's so Weak about "Weak-form Review"? A Rejoinder to Stephen Gardbaum' (2015) 13 *International Journal of Constitutional Law* 1049 at 1053; J King, 'Rights and the Rule of Law in Third Way Constitutionalism' (2015) 30 *Constitutional Commentary* 101 at 109–10.

[32] See Kavanagh, 'A Hard Look at the Last Word' (n 31) at 843–46; Carolan (n 10) at 111.

[33] A Kavanagh, 'What's So Weak about "Weak-form Review"? The Case of the UK Human Rights Act 1998' (2015) 13 *International Journal of Constitutional Law* 1008.

claims made within this tradition of scholarship,[34] and to the tendency of writers in this tradition both to obscure commonalities with American-style judicial review,[35] and to downplay the extent to which hybridism is a feature of the comparative constitutional landscape more generally.[36]

Underlying many, if not most, of these critiques is a shared methodological reservation about a particular style of 'macro-constitutional'[37] comparative inquiry which relies on constitutional archetypes (or, less kindly, caricatures)[38] and which focuses on text and formal institutional design rather than culture, context and messy political (and operational) reality.[39] This general concern about the dangers of eschewing 'fine-grained, contextual comparativism'[40] is one which I share, and to which I will return.

What these critiques do not, for the most part, challenge is the almost exclusive focus of the Commonwealth model genre of scholarship on the question of institutional responsibility for the human rights compatibility of legislation.[41] Their point is, rather, that these scholars tend to analyse that question in an overly simplistic way.[42]

The core critique advanced in this chapter is somewhat different. It is that by concentrating singularly on that question of legislative compatibility with human rights, this scholarship presents a flawed and fundamentally incomplete picture of the operation of these new Anglo-Commonwealth bills of rights.

The starting point for the analysis (and arguably the source of the problem) is the overriding preoccupation of this genre of scholarship with the constitutionalism/democracy debate. It is, indeed, something of an irony of Commonwealth model scholarship that, even as it claims to rewrite the terms of that debate, it remains

[34] See Choudhry (n 31) at 1095; Kavanagh 'A Hard Look at the Last Word' (n 31) at 832–36, 839; King (n 31) at 110–13.

[35] G Huscroft, 'Constitutionalism from the Top Down' (2007) 45 *Osgoode Hall Law Journal* 91; Dixon (n 6); Kavanagh 'A Hard Look at the Last Word' (n 31) at 843–46.

[36] See Weill (n 5); Carolan (n 10).

[37] See Carolan (n 10) at 96.

[38] ibid, at 97; Kavanagh, 'A Hard Look at the Last Word' (n 31) at 830.

[39] See especially Dixon (n 6) at 503–06; R Weill, 'The New Commonwealth Model of Constitutionalism Notwithstanding: On Judicial Review and Constitution-Making' (2014) 62 *American Journal of Comparative Law* 127 at 129–30; Kavanagh, 'A Hard Look at the Last Word' (n 31) at 836–37; Kavanagh, 'A Rejoinder to Stephen Gardbaum' (n 31) at 1052–53; Kavanagh (n 33) at 1030–31; Hirschl (n 31) at 1089–91; R Leckey, *Bills of Rights in the Common Law* (Cambridge, Cambridge University Press, 2015); Carolan (n 10) at 96–97, 111–12, 118–19; K Roach, 'Remedies for Laws that Violate Human Rights' in J Bell, M Elliott, JNE Varuhas and P Murray (eds), *Public Law Adjudication in Common Law Systems: Process and Substance* (Oxford, Hart Publishing, 2016) 269, 270.

[40] Kavanagh (n 33) at 1037.

[41] The partial exception is Eoin Carolan's insightful account of 'collaborative constitutionalism' within the Irish tradition, which touches (fairly briefly) on the 'complex, multi-actor and multi-level character of contemporary government' and the 'substantial discretionary powers' of administrative or regulatory bodies: Carolan (n 10) at 111–12.

[42] For example, by over-emphasising the practical significance of formal strike-down powers: Kavanagh, 'A Hard Look at the Last Word' (n 31) at 843–44; Kavanagh (n 33) at 1034–36; Carolan (n 10).

fixated on it and adopts it as the sole or dominant lens through which to view the Anglo-Commonwealth instruments.[43]

This fixation results in an almost exclusive concentration, within this genre of scholarship, on those features of the respective instruments that are thought to promote inter-institutional engagement over the human rights compatibility of legislation. Specifically, these are: the institutional mechanisms for executive or parliamentary engagement with human rights during the legislative process; the powers reposed in the courts to interpret laws consistently and/or to declare laws incompatible with rights (whether with binding or non-binding effect); and the powers and/or obligations placed on the executive and legislature to respond to (or override or ignore) any such judicial determinations. The corollary, as we shall see, is some significant blind spots.

III. COMMONWEALTH MODEL SCHOLARSHIP AND THE AMERICAN ACADEMY

In making sense of this preoccupation with the constitutionalism/democracy debate, it is perhaps helpful to appreciate at the outset that the Commonwealth model genre of scholarship is, at its heart, an external rather than an internal critique of the Commonwealth model instruments. It emerged in the late 1990s and early 2000s from an American academy fixated on the Rehnquist Court's re-assertion of judicial supremacy and intent on generating alternative visions of American constitutionalism.[44] It is no coincidence, I suggest, that the three scholars whose work I discussed above (Tushnet, Gardbaum and Stephenson), though not all American by birth, all produced their insights from within the United States academy.

It is perhaps understandable why, for those looking out at the Anglo-Commonwealth bills of rights from within a particularly muscular tradition of judicial supremacy, the interest in the model might lie in their potential to square constitutional protection of human rights with democratic/majoritarian objections to judicial review. For those of us in Westminster democracies with a strong historical attachment to the doctrine of parliamentary sovereignty (New Zealand, Australia, the United Kingdom), this overriding focus on the potential of the Commonwealth model to solve the constitutionalism/democracy dilemma makes much less sense. From this

[43] See Kavanagh, 'A Hard Look at the Last Word' (n 31) at 843. See also P Brest, 'The Fundamental Rights Controversy: The Essential Contradictions of Normative Constitutional Scholarship' (1981) 90 *Yale Law Journal* 1063 (describing the democracy/constitutionalism dilemma as 'the historic obsession of normative constitutional law scholarship' in the United States); B Friedman, 'The Birth of an Academic Obsession: The History of the Countermajoritarian Difficulty, Part Five' (2002) 112 *Yale Law Journal* 153 at 158, 256 (characterising the United States academy's preoccupation with the countermajoritarian difficulty as a 'fixation').

[44] M Tushnet, *Taking the Constitution Away from the Courts* (Princeton, Princeton University Press, 1999); LD Kramer, 'The Supreme Court 2000 Term—Foreword: We the Court' (2001) 115 *Harvard Law Review* 5; CR Sunstein, *One Case at a Time: Judicial Minimalism on the Supreme Court* (Cambridge MA, Harvard University Press, 2001); RE Barkow, 'More Supreme than Court? The Fall of the Political Question Doctrine and the Rise of Judicial Supremacy' (2002) 102 *Columbia Law Review* 237; Friedman (n 43) at 155; LD Kramer, *The People Themselves: Popular Constitutionalism and Judicial Review* (Oxford, Oxford University Press, 2004).

insiders' perspective, the question of the comparative advantages/disadvantages of the Commonwealth model vis-à-vis judicial supremacy is interesting, yes, but largely hypothetical. After all, the statutory bill of rights model emerged in New Zealand, Australia and the United Kingdom precisely because the prospect of fully fledged constitutional reform was remote. That remains the case to this day.

In these countries, the more realistic debate remains whether to have a bill of rights at all and, if so, what precise iterations of the statutory bill of rights model to adopt. So, for example, the report of the 2012 Commission on a British Bill of Rights (concluding, by majority, that there was a 'strong argument' in favour of enacting such an instrument) made it clear that there was 'no appetite', whether from those consulted by the Commission or from members of the Commission themselves, 'for conferring on our courts a power to hold statutes enacted by Parliament not to be lawful';[45] and, even more recently, the terms of reference for a 2016 Queensland parliamentary inquiry into the desirability of enacting a human rights Act for Queensland specifically excluded consideration of 'a constitutionally entrenched model'.[46]

Let us be clear: in order to support such reform processes, comparative analysis of the Anglo-Commonwealth bills of rights is of enormous utility. But it is a different sort of comparative scholarship that is required: scholarship that addresses, in broad terms, the efficacy of the statutory bill of rights model. How well does it work in practice, what variables impact on its effectiveness, and how ought one to choose between the different variations of the model that are available? As we shall see, this is a far broader set of questions than those that preoccupy scholarship in the Commonwealth model genre.

In making this point, I certainly do not intend to question the value of academic assessments of the relative advantages of supreme law versus non-supreme law protections of human rights. But there is, if nothing else, an irony in the fact that those jurisdictions most likely to derive genuine practical assistance from careful comparative analysis of the relevant instruments are least well served by scholarship in the Commonwealth model tradition.

IV. THE COUNTER-MAJORITARIAN OBSESSION AND THE SEARCH FOR 'DISTINCTIVENESS'

Let us, though, put to one side this internal (and some might say parochial) perspective. The broader point is that the preoccupation with resolution of the constitutionalism/democracy dilemma blinds writers in the Commonwealth model tradition to much of what might, in fact, be 'distinctive' about the scheme of human rights protection found in Commonwealth model jurisdictions. This is, in a sense, the converse of the point about distinctiveness made by Aileen Kavanagh in her insightful critique of Gardbaum's monograph.[47] She suggests that a concern to establish the

[45] Commission on a Bill of Rights, *A UK Bill of Rights? The Choice Before Us* vol 1 (2012) para 96.

[46] Queensland Legal Affairs and Community Safety Committee, *Inquiry into a Possible Human Rights Act for Queensland* (2016).

[47] See Kavanagh, 'A Hard Look at the Last Word' (n 31).

Commonwealth model as distinctive, together with a 'studied focus on who has "the formal last word"', has led authors such as Gardbaum to downplay the messy complexity of legislative-judicial relations and to exaggerate differences in that regard with American-style judicial review.[48] In other words, their preoccupation with resolution of the constitutionalism/democracy dilemma leads scholars of this genre to play up the distinctiveness of the model, specifically as regards the mechanisms of inter-institutional engagement over the human rights compatibility of legislation.

The point that I am making here is that the same factors also result in the converse: the systematic neglect of other areas of potential distinctiveness. Let us consider what some of those might be.

First, might not some of the distinctiveness of the Anglo-Commonwealth bills of rights lie in the parliamentary (and Westminster-derived) character of the systems of government in the relevant jurisdictions? Janet Hiebert and James Kelly certainly think so.[49] Following a sustained empirical analysis of parliamentary rights vetting in New Zealand and the United Kingdom, they conclude that the Westminster context is significant both for external and internal comparisons of the Commonwealth model instruments. On the one hand, Westminster-influenced variables (such as executive domination of Parliament and the centrality of highly disciplined political parties) are so pivotal to understanding the way the model operates in practice that the respective instruments should, in their view, be characterised as 'parliamentary bills of rights' rather than as part of a 'Commonwealth model'.[50] On the other hand, variations in these Westminster institutional factors as *between* the 'Commonwealth model' jurisdictions are, in their view, so substantial that they undermine the utility of grouping the respective instruments into a distinct model at all.[51]

To be fair, the salience of these Westminster factors does receive some attention in Scott Stephenson's recent monograph, which identifies the principle of responsible government as a 'normative trade-off' that sits in tension with operation of the Commonwealth model.[52] However, Hiebert and Kelly's conclusions, if they are correct, present uncomfortable truths for Stephen Gardbaum, whose claim is to be able to abstract out from the experience of these Westminster jurisdictions a distinct, general and transferable constitutional model.[53]

Similar questions present as to how much of the distinctive chemistry of the Commonwealth model system of rights protection arises from the marriage between codified rights protection and common law method. At its most general, this might suggest an inquiry into the exportability (or not) of this model outside the common

[48] ibid, at 843. This is a point to which Scott Stephenson's recent monograph, with its careful attention to the concept of 'indirect' institutional disagreement in systems of judicial and parliamentary supremacy, might be seen to respond: Stephenson (n 6) at 35, 53. See Geiringer (n 27).

[49] See Hiebert and Kelly (n 6).

[50] ibid, at 410. See also Hirschl (n 31) at 1088; Choudhry (n 31) at 1099.

[51] See Hiebert and Kelly (n 6) at 410.

[52] See Stephenson (n 6) at 126–29.

[53] S Gardbaum, 'The Single and General New Commonwealth Model: A Response to Ran Hirschl and Sujit Choudry' (2013) 11 *International Journal of Constitutional Law* 1100 at 1100–01; Gardbaum (n 6) at 11–12.

law world. The more specific (and perhaps more interesting) point relates to the synergies between the Anglo-Commonwealth bills of rights and emerging traditions of common law constitutionalism in the particular jurisdictions at issue. As is well known, during the late twentieth and early twenty-first century, the common law in these jurisdictions (in large part, in response to the absence of codified rights protections) was in a process of fast evolution with respect to the protection of human rights.[54] Observers within the Commonwealth model jurisdictions themselves well understand the close relationship between these common law developments and the relevant statutory human rights protections. The precise contours of that relationship are certainly the subject of ongoing discussion and debate,[55] but few would doubt its symbiotic character.

This common law context, again, raises important questions both for external and internal comparisons of the Commonwealth model. In terms of external comparison, how much does this common law context affect patterns of judicial behaviour with respect to enforcement of the Anglo-Commonwealth bills of rights, and to what extent does that impact on the exportability of the model? In terms of internal comparison, to what extent do differences in the common law context help to account for disparities, as *between* the jurisdictions, in patterns of human rights enforcement?[56] For example, in Australia, the federal nature of Australian common law (as juxtaposed with the sub-national character of the two Australian Charters of Rights) is a structural impediment to the sort of jurisprudential cross-fertilisation that we have been discussing. The salience of this factor in accounting for the comparatively poor performance of the two Australian Charters has not, to date, been well explored, even in the domestic literature. Similar questions might arise as to what importance we should attach, in exploring the significance of the common law context, to the supra-national lineage of the United Kingdom's Human Rights Act 1998, or to the formal constitutional status of the Canadian Charter. With respect to the latter, it is at least questionable whether the location of the Charter in a formal constitutional document (the only one of the Commonwealth model instruments

[54] M Fordham and T de la Mare, 'Anxious Scrutiny, the Principle of Legality and the Human Rights Act' [2000] *Judicial Review* 40; P Rishworth, 'Writing Things Unwritten: Common Law in New Zealand's Constitution' (2016) 14 *International Journal of Constitutional Law* 137 at 144–47, 153.

[55] G Cartier, 'The *Baker* Effect: A New Interface between the Canadian Charter of Rights and Freedoms and Administrative Law—The Case of Discretion' in D Dyzenhaus (ed), *The Unity of Public Law* (Oxford, Hart Publishing, 2004) 61; A Kavanagh, 'The Role of Parliamentary Intention in Adjudication under the Human Rights Act 1998' (2006) 26 *Oxford Journal of Legal Studies* 179 at 188–90, 193; C Geiringer, 'The Principle of Legality and the Bill of Rights Act: A Critical Examination of *R v Hansen*' (2008) 6 *New Zealand Journal of Public and International Law* 59; D Meagher, 'The Principle of Legality and the Judicial Protection of Rights—*Evans v New South Wales*' (2009) 37 *Federal Law Review* 295; P Sales, 'A Comparison of the Principle of Legality and Section 3 of the Human Rights Act 1998' (2009) 125 *Law Quarterly Review* 598; Rishworth (n 54).

[56] See, eg, Geiringer (n 55); C Geiringer, 'Inside and Outside Criminal Process: The Comparative Salience of the New Zealand and Victorian Human Rights Charters' (2017) 28 *Public Law Review* 219 at 229–30; C Geiringer, 'The Constitutional Role of the Courts under the NZ Bill of Rights: Three Narratives from *Attorney General v Taylor*' (2017) 48 *Victoria University of Wellington Law Review* (forthcoming); and C Saunders, ch 13 in this volume.

to be so located) might constitute an (informal if not formal) impediment to cross-fertilisation with the common law.[57]

That point gives rise to a further set of questions as to the salience of the 'ordinary law' status of most of the Anglo-Commonwealth bills of rights. For if one excises the Canadian Charter from the data set, other possible points of 'distinctiveness' present themselves. Might the ordinary law status of the instruments, in itself, impact (whether positively or negatively) on the willingness of the courts and/or other institutions to exert themselves on human rights issues? Does it counteract (or alternatively, augment) the forms of judicial and/or political debilitation associated with supreme law constitutions?[58] Are there any benefits of coordination or integration to be gained from locating a bill of rights within the ordinary law of the state, rather than in the more detached setting of an entrenched constitution? (For example, does it encourage the sort of cross-fertilisation with common law method to which we have just adverted and, if so, to what effect?).

Indeed, how much of the distinctiveness of the statutory bill of rights model lies, not so much in the specification of formal mechanisms for inter-institutional engagement, but in the simple but profound innovation of an enacted list of rights, layered onto a system of parliamentary sovereignty?[59] Might the doctrine of parliamentary sovereignty be functioning, not so much as a point of departure for the Commonwealth model, as a crucial and on-going determinant of the patterns of political and judicial behaviour manifested in Commonwealth model jurisdictions?[60] If so, what does this say for the exportability of the model?

V. BEYOND 'DISTINCTIVENESS': THE COMMONWEALTH MODEL AND THE CONSTRAINT OF PUBLIC FUNCTIONS

The point so far is that a fixation on resolution of the constitutionalism/democracy dilemma, together with the compulsion to present these instruments as a single,

[57] There is, for example, a healthy Canadian administrative law literature bemoaning the estrangement of Canadian Charter jurisprudence from mainstream (common law-derived) administrative law, and advocating a more integrated approach: see JM Evans, 'The Principles of Fundamental Justice: The Constitution and the Common Law (1991) 29 *Osgoode Hall Law Journal* 51; Cartier (n 55). For further discussion, see C Geiringer, 'Process and Outcome in Judicial Review of Public Authority Compatibility with Human Rights: A Comparative Perspective' in H Wilberg and M Elliott (eds), *The Scope and Intensity of Substantive Review: Traversing Taggart's Rainbow* (Oxford, Hart Publishing, 2015) 329, 335–36, 349–51.

[58] For an illustration of both forms of debilitation, see JB Thayer, 'The Origin and Scope of the American Doctrine of Constitutional Law' (1893) 7 *Harvard Law Review* 129. He proposed a 'clear error' rule (a form of judicial debilitation) to address the problem of political debilitation that he saw as an inevitable by-product of more-than-minimal judicial review. See also Tushnet, 'Policy Distortion and Democratic Debilitation' (n 18).

[59] See Hiebert and Kelly (n 6) at 1, noting that it is not all that long since this 'marriage' of Westminster-based systems with codified bills of rights would have seemed 'implausible'.

[60] See Carolan (n 10) at 115, suggesting provocatively that the Commonwealth model might best be seen not as a 'middle ground' but as 'a limited upgrade on a parliamentary model which has now been withdrawn from sale'.

abstractable and transferable model of human rights protection, leads writers in the Commonwealth model genre to neglect a number of possible drivers of distinctiveness within the Commonwealth model jurisdictions. However, we are yet to address the most conspicuous of the blind spots in the Commonwealth model scholarship: the role these instruments play in constraining the exercise of public functions—whether by the police, the executive or devolved bodies. Those administrative law and, indeed, criminal law implications are a major focus of domestic scholarship within the respective jurisdictions, where it is well understood that the constraint of public functions is a major (perhaps one might even argue primary) thrust of the relevant schemes of human rights protection.[61] Within the Commonwealth model genre of scholarship, however, this central thread of rights protection is almost entirely neglected.

So, for example, Gardbaum's book-length evaluation of the Commonwealth model scheme of protection devotes no more than a handful of brief (and conclusory) references, spread thinly across the entire book, to acknowledgement of the role of the respective instruments in constraining the exercise of public functions.[62] To be sure, his account emphasises the claims of the Commonwealth model to distribute responsibility for the protection of human rights across all three branches.[63] But in point of fact, his interest in the executive is limited almost entirely to its role as initiator of legislative proposals. The executive *qua* administrator receives no more than passing acknowledgement.

Stephenson's account appears, initially, to hold out more promise. In his introductory chapters, he stresses repeatedly the significance of the Commonwealth model as 'a concerted effort to bring the executive and legislature into [the] process [of assessing and resolving rights claims] in a deliberate, structured and substantial manner'.[64] The advantage of his focus on 'inter-institutional interaction', he says, is that 'it does not exclude or privilege any specific aspect of the reforms, encompassing the changes made to the powers and responsibilities of *all three* institutions of government'.[65]

But Stephenson does not deliver on this promise. Judicial review of administrative action receives sustained attention from him only as an example of 'indirect institutional disagreement' practiced under the 'traditional' model of parliamentary sovereignty.[66] In contrast, his treatment of the role of the Commonwealth model instruments in constraining public power is even scanter than Gardbaum's—limited

[61] The literature is vast but a small selection might include: Cartier (n 55); J McLean, 'The Impact of the Bill of Rights on Administrative Law Revisited: Rights, Utility, and Administration' [2008] *New Zealand Law Review* 377; T Hickman, *Public Law after the Human Rights Act* (Oxford, Hart Publishing, 2010); C Geiringer, 'Sources of Resistance to Proportionality Review of Administrative Power under the New Zealand Bill of Rights Act' (2013) 11 *New Zealand Journal of Public and International Law* 123; J Boughey, 'The Charter's Effect on Administrative Decision-making' (2016) 27 *Public Law Review* 3. See also nn 80–81 and associated text.

[62] Especially Gardbaum (n 6) at 136, 147, 158, 170–71, 182–83, 208, 235.

[63] ibid, at 68, 77.

[64] See Stephenson (n 6) at 5.

[65] ibid, at 35 (his emphasis). See also ibid, at 6, 48.

[66] ibid, at chapter 4.

to a few fleeting references.[67] Stephenson's real interest in the executive, like Gardbaum's, is solely as a sponsor of legislative proposals.

Most likely, the reason for this systematic neglect of the executive *qua* administrator lies in the perception of both authors that the role the Anglo-Commonwealth bills of rights play in relation to the control of public authorities is not a point of distinctiveness for the model.[68] After all, the invocation of human rights standards in the course of judicial review of administrative action is a feature both of systems of judicial supremacy and of the 'traditional' model of parliamentary supremacy.

We should, though, press harder on this question of distinctiveness. There are a range of questions we might wish to address as to whether the approach to control of public functions generated by the Commonwealth model (or perhaps by the subset of statutory bills of rights) is, indeed, a marker of distinctiveness. What of the simple fact that these instruments place the question of constraint of public authorities front and centre of the respective schemes of human rights protection? In contrast, under fully constitutionalised bills of rights, with their focus on legislative action, there is a tendency (is there not?) for questions of administrative constraint to be somewhat relegated to the shadows. What, too, of the ordinary law status of these instruments? Are there any benefits (or disadvantages) of integration with the administrative law of the state gained by locating human rights protections within a statute rather than a formal constitution? How does the close historical nexus between constitutional law and administrative law in Westminster-derived systems affect the operation of such instruments? And what is the impact of the detailed specification of administrative law duties and remedies found in, for example, the United Kingdom's Human Rights Act 1998 (as compared with the sparser style generally associated with constitutional documents)? In short, the case for non-distinctiveness with respect to constraint of public authorities needs to be substantiated rather than assumed.

Even if it can be so substantiated, the question of how these instruments operate, or fail to operate, with respect to the constraint of public functions is such a key aspect of their comparative success or failure that it is hard to take seriously an explanatory account of these instruments (which the Commonwealth model scholarship certainly purports to offer) that omits these questions from consideration.[69] Primary legislation is, after all, only one possible, and arguably not the most significant, vector by which the state and its institutions have the capacity to trench on (or, indeed, to protect) the rights of individuals. As Janet McLean has put it (in response to repeated criticism of New Zealand by the United Nations Human Rights Committee for omitting from its Bill of Rights a power to invalidate legislation):

> [T]his vision of rights ... is ... an incomplete description of the modern western democratic legal order. More than ever, public power is exercised through the use of discretion and delegated legal instruments, organisations at arms-length from the state, and even contracts, rather than directly through legislation. Given the growth and complexity of the modern

[67] See ibid, at 20, 27–28, 31–32, 152, 186–87, 191.

[68] See Gardbaum (n 6) at 147; Stephenson (n 6) at 187, n 41.

[69] On the tension between the prescriptive and descriptive claims made within Commonwealth model scholarship see, more generally, Choudhry (n 31) at 1095; Kavanagh, 'A Hard Look at the Last Word' (n 31) at 832–36, 839; King (n 31) at 110–13; Geiringer (n 27).

> administrative state, the emphasis the Human Rights Committee places on primary legislation is surprising.[70]

Ironically, a core part of the defence that is sometimes offered of these non-supreme law instruments is that they operate similarly to, and have the potential to be just as effective in relation to, every aspect of human rights protection *other than* the invalidation of legislation.[71] In other words, the case in favour of such instruments is constructed as much on the basis of their *non*-distinctiveness as their distinctiveness. Any comprehensive comparative analysis of the effectiveness of these instruments would surely need to test that claim.

In short, the preoccupation in the Commonwealth model genre of scholarship with 'distinctiveness' leads to a radically abridged account of the factors that drive the respective performance of the model in each jurisdiction. At this point, let me anticipate one possible defence to this charge. 'All you have established', so the defence might go, 'is that the Commonwealth model genre of scholarship does not generate an exhaustive account of the operation of these instruments. But why should it? Our project is narrower—to consider what contribution these instruments make to resolution of the constitutionalism/democracy dilemma. You have established neither that this project is unimportant, nor that we fail to make a significant contribution to it.'

Let me reiterate that I agree both that this is an important project, and that (notwithstanding some validity to the critiques offered by Kavanagh and others)[72] Commonwealth model scholarship has made a significant contribution to it. Nevertheless, there are three (closely related) difficulties with this anticipated defence. The first is that authors in the Commonwealth model genre do not (or do not always) make it sufficiently clear that their project is to evaluate only a subset of the mechanisms of rights protection available under the respective instruments. We can perhaps exempt Mark Tushnet from this charge. He might (reasonably) counter both that his terminology ('weak-form judicial review') signals his preoccupation with the judicial control of legislation; and that his various article-length sallies into evaluating the stability of this weak-form review model make no claims (whether explicit or implicit) to comprehensiveness.[73]

[70] J McLean, 'Legislative Invalidation, Human Rights Protection and s 4 of the New Zealand Bill of Rights Act' [2001] *New Zealand Law Review* 421 at 424. See also Carolan (n 10) at 111–12. Stephenson (n 6) at 43 responds to these sorts of claims by pointing to the (unrealised) capacity of his model to encompass developments in administrative law caused by forces such as deregulation, privatisation and internationalisation. Given that his analysis fails to account for the impact of the Commonwealth model instruments even on more *traditional* manifestations of public power, this feint from Stephenson seems somewhat beside the point.

[71] PT Rishworth, 'The Potential of the New Zealand Bill of Rights' [1990] *New Zealand Law Journal* 68.

[72] See nn 32–42 and associated text; n 48 and associated text.

[73] See, eg, Tushnet, 'Policy Distortion and Democratic Debilitation' (n 18); Tushnet (n 6); Tushnet 'Weak-Form Judicial Review: Its Implications for Legislatures' (n 18). For similar reasons, my critique has less bite in relation to carefully targeted studies of a particular aspect of Commonwealth model protection, such as Hiebert and Kelly's valuable comparative account of political rights vetting in New Zealand and the United Kingdom (although they, too, could be accused of sharing the fixation on the question of legislative compatibility with human rights): Hiebert and Kelly (n 6).

However, one could be forgiven for reading Gardbaum's and Stephenson's book-length accounts of the Commonwealth model as holding out (both explicitly and implicitly) a comprehensive evaluation of the effectiveness of human rights protection under the respective instruments. Stephenson, as we have seen, emphasises repeatedly the benefits of his framework of analysis for its capacity to encompass inter-institutional interactions between all three branches of government under the respective instruments.[74] Gardbaum presents his book as a 'systematic and comprehensive' evaluation of whether the new Commonwealth model is functioning successfully as a 'novel and general model of constitutionalism'.[75] In his concluding chapter, he poses (and answers) broadly framed questions such as 'Is the new model providing greater institutional protection of rights ...?';[76] and 'Is the result [of the institutional reapportionment of responsibilities under the Commonwealth model] a more optimal and proportionate combination of rights protection and political legitimacy?'[77]

The waters are further muddied by the fact that neither author wholly excludes the judicial control of public functions from their analysis. As we have seen, both works contain a smattering of (largely conclusory) references to this aspect of human rights protection. In the result, although both authors do acknowledge at various places their central preoccupation with inter-institutional engagement over the design, interpretation and enforcement of legislation,[78] readers could be forgiven for some confusion as to the scope and comprehensiveness of the overall evaluation.

The second and related point is that this relegation of constraint of public authorities to an 'also ran' makes an implicit claim about what matters, and what doesn't. Readers are left with the sense that what there is of interest to say about control of public functions under the Anglo-Commonwealth bills of rights is capable of being summed up in a few conclusory paragraphs. The impression so created may well contribute to a more general neglect of this dimension in the comparative scholarship. For example, even outside the particular genre of scholarship with which I am concerned, there has been little in the way of comparative investigation of the efficacy of these instruments in controlling police investigative powers; and a comparative literature on the administrative law implications of these instruments has only recently, and tentatively, begun to emerge.[79]

The third point is that it is simply very difficult to provide an overall assessment of the 'strength' of protection offered by the Commonwealth model instruments with

[74] See nn 64 and 65 and accompanying text.
[75] See Gardbaum (n 6) at 16.
[76] ibid, at 235.
[77] ibid, at 223.
[78] ibid, at 25–31; Stephenson (n 6) at 4–5.
[79] See, eg, J Boughey, 'Rights, Review and Reasonableness: The Implications of Canada's New Approach to Administrative Decision-Making and Human Rights for Australia' (2013) 35 *Sydney Law Review* 283; Geiringer (n 57); T Hickman, 'Adjudicating Constitutional Rights in Administrative Law' (2016) 66 *University of Toronto Law Journal* 121. Boughey's monograph (a welcome counter to the fixation with legislative compatibility I have been describing) went to press just as this chapter was being finalised: J Boughey, *Human Rights and Judicial Review in Australia and Canada: The Newest Despotism?* (Oxford, Hart Publishing, 2017).

respect solely to questions of legislative compatibility, and without any reference to their implications for the constraint of public authorities. It is not so easy to prise the two apart. This is both because of the objective importance of that latter dimension to any overall evaluation of the respective instruments, but also because of the heavy reliance that scholars in the Commonwealth model genre place on the secondary literature generated within the various jurisdictions (which, itself, reflects the centrality of questions of constraint of public power).

These factors may explain the uneasy ambivalence with respect to treatment of public authority compliance in both Gardbaum's and Stephenson's accounts. So, for example, despite their purported focus on questions of legislative compatibility, neither author finds it possible to assess the operation of the New Zealand Bill of Rights Act 1990 without making passing referencing to the early, activist approach taken by the New Zealand Court of Appeal to control of police powers.[80] And Gardbaum, at least, feels that he cannot sum up the United Kingdom experience without mentioning, in passing, the view of some domestic commentators that section 6 of the Human Rights Act 1998 (the duty of public authority compliance) is 'the most significant provision' in the Act, and the most frequent basis for litigation.[81] In short, questions of public authority compliance are given an unsatisfactory shadow life—neither properly studied, nor carefully excluded from the scope of the comparative analysis.

This fragmented and cursory approach to evaluating the impact of the Anglo-Commonwealth bills of rights on the exercise of public functions has led to some striking omissions and distortions. So, for example, following a brief analysis of the Australian case law that is largely dominated by the judicial debate over the strength of interpretive presumptions,[82] Gardbaum concludes that the courts in Victoria and the Australian Capital Territory 'appear set on handing back the powers their parliaments bestowed on them'.[83] For him, practice under the two Australian Charters of Rights is almost indistinguishable from the parliamentary supremacy end of the spectrum, except to the extent that the existence of an authoritative text has fostered political rights review.[84]

It is indisputable that the two Australian Charters of Rights have suffered significant setbacks, particularly in relation to judicial enforcement.[85] But there have also been some noteworthy victories. Gardbaum's unequivocal conclusion with respect to judicial enforcement of the Victorian Charter of Human Rights and Responsibilities might, for example, seem puzzling to Kimberley Castles, the Victorian prisoner who

[80] See Gardbaum (n 6) at 136, 147; Stephenson (n 6) at 186, 191.

[81] See Gardbaum (n 6) at 158 citing D Feldman, 'Extending the Role of the Courts: The Human Rights Act 1998' (2011) 30 *Parliamentary History* 65 at 68 and T Bingham, 'The Human Rights Act' (2010) 6 *European Human Rights Law Review* 568 at 571. See also Gardbaum (n 6) at 170–71; Stephenson (n 6) at 152.

[82] See Gardbaum (n 6) at 213–16. Stephenson's account of judicial behaviour under the Australian Charters is similarly devoid of any analysis of public authority compliance: Stephenson (n 6) at 204–09.

[83] See Gardbaum (n 6) at 225.

[84] ibid, at 234.

[85] See, eg, C Geiringer, 'What's the Story? The Instability of the Australasian Bills of Rights' (2016) 14 *International Journal of Constitutional Law* 156, discussing, in particular, the impact of *Momcilovic v The Queen* (2011) 245 CLR 1.

succeeded in overturning a decision by the Department of Justice to deny her the routine visits outside the prison required to facilitate access to in-vitro fertilisation;[86] or to Patrick, a long-term involuntary patient in a psychiatric hospital, who successfully reviewed the appointment of an administrator who could have sold his home against his wishes;[87] or to Nassir Bare, who won the right to a fresh consideration of his claim of police misconduct by the Independent Broad-based Anti-corruption Commission.[88] All of these cases involved landmark victories by Victorian claimants in reliance on the administrative law potential of the Victorian Charter (including the novel requirement in section 38(1) of the Charter that public authorities give 'proper consideration' to human rights in their decision making).[89] Although it is impossible to prove the counter-factual, it is difficult to imagine that all (or perhaps any) of these victories would have been achieved prior to the enactment of the Charter,[90] and at least one of them charts novel territory vis-à-vis other comparator jurisdictions, whether inside or outside the Commonwealth model.[91] Looked at in this light, Gardbaum's conclusion that the Victorian Charter has not moved the state significantly along the spectrum from the pole of 'parliamentary supremacy' is, at best, beside the point.

Putting to one side the question of judicial successes or failures, another fascinating aspect of the Australian experience that falls away from view when the constitutionalism/democracy lens is applied is the overarching preoccupation, both in the conception of these instruments and in subsequent practice, with the development of a human rights culture within government decision-making.[92] In Victoria, for example, the government's terms of reference for the consultation process that gave rise to the Charter expressed an intention 'to address human rights issues through mechanisms that promote dialogue, education, discussion and good practice rather than litigation'.[93] This emphasis on the development of a human rights culture inside

[86] *Castles v Secretary to the Department of Justice* (2010) 28 VR 141.

[87] *PJB v Melbourne Health & Anor (Patrick's case)* (2011) 39 VR 373.

[88] *Bare v Independent Broad-based Anti-corruption Commission* (2015) 326 ALR 198. Bare was unsuccessful at first instance but won his case on appeal. To be fair, this case post-dates Gardbaum's (but not Stephenson's) monograph.

[89] Also found in the Human Rights Act 2004 (ACT), s 40B(1).

[90] That is so even when, as was the case in *Castles*, the judge chose to characterise the result as a straightforward application of the governing statute.

[91] *Castles* (n 86), holding that the Department's refusal to facilitate IVF treatment constituted a breach of Ms Castles' right under s 22 of the Charter, as a person deprived of liberty, to be treated with humanity and with respect for the inherent dignity of the human person. This was despite the fact that the right to found a family had been deliberately excluded from the Victorian Charter and despite the high threshold required to engage the equivalent of s 22 in other jurisdictions.

[92] Stephenson, at least, has demonstrated in other contexts that he is acutely aware of this aspect of the Australian experience: see S Stephenson, 'Constitutional Reengineering: Dialogue's Migration from Canada to Australia' (2013) 11 *International Journal of Constitutional Law* 870, containing insightful analysis of this distinctive Australian preoccupation in the context of an investigation of the transnational migration (and transmutation) of constitutional ideas. Compare Stephenson (n 6) at 52–53, discussing this aspect of the Australian experience only in passing, as part of a critique of dialogue theory.

[93] Department of Justice (Vic), *Human Rights in Victoria: Statement of Intent* (2005), appended to Human Rights Consultation Committee, *Rights, Responsibilities and Respect: The Report of the Human Rights Consultation Committee* (2005) 161, 162.

and outside government was reflected throughout the report that eventuated from the consultation process,[94] in the structure of the instrument itself,[95] and in broader changes made to law and practice in conjunction with its enactment.[96]

This particular focus on public sector self-regulation has continued to feature as a major part of the Charter narrative during the intervening decade. Most recently, in 2015, in a statutorily mandated eight-year review of the Charter (delegated by the government to a senior barrister) it was, again, front and centre.[97] The report made a host of recommendations directed at pushing forward this acculturation process, including the establishment of an inter-departmental committee to provide leadership and coordination for departments and agencies, extended responsibility to the Victorian Equal Opportunity and Human Rights Commission for human rights education across the public sector and in the community, responsibility to the Judicial College of Education for educating judges, and a broader human rights jurisdiction for the Ombudsman and for other public sector oversight bodies such as the Mental Health Complaints Commissioner and the independent broad-based Anti-corruption Commission. Many of these recommendations have been accepted outright, some have been accepted in principle, and others are under consideration.[98]

This is an ambitious vision of public sector self-regulation under the Victorian Charter that, again, raises interesting questions both for external and internal comparison of the Commonwealth model. With respect to the former, as we have seen, even writers in the Commonwealth model genre would agree that part of what is distinctive about the model is the way in which it seeks to distribute constitutional responsibility for compliance with human rights across all three branches of government. To what extent, then, has this generated distinctive patterns of self-regulation within the executive branch, and to what effect? To be clear, this mandates a far broader inquiry than the focus on 'political rights review' advanced in the Commonwealth model scholarship. That discussion only considers the role of the executive in formulating, developing and enacting legislative proposals. In comparison, the focus here is on the executive in all its various capacities.

With respect to the latter (internal comparison), is the extent of public sector self-regulation a point of difference *as between* the Commonwealth model jurisdictions? To what extent, for example, has the seemingly proactive approach in Victoria been replicated in other Commonwealth model jurisdictions? What difference, if any, has the degree of public sector self-regulation made to the extent of human rights protection in the respective jurisdictions?

94 Especially Human Rights Consultation Committee (n 93) chapter 5.

95 Victorian Charter part 4, extending the responsibilities of the Victorian Equal Opportunity and Human Rights Commission.

96 For example, the Charter also added a new 'public sector value' to the Public Administration Act 2004 (Vic) s 7(1)(g), creating non-enforceable requirements for all public sector employees to provide advice and make decisions consistent with human rights and to actively implement and promote human rights.

97 MB Young, *From Commitment to Culture: The 2015 Review of the Charter of Human Rights and Responsibilities Act 2006* (2015).

98 Victoria State Government, *Government Response to the 2015 Review of the Charter of Human Rights and Responsibilities Act* (2016).

To be clear, my point here is not to rehabilitate the Australian Charters, indeed, far from it. I would be the first to admit that their performance has been, in a number of respects, underwhelming.[99] But an analysis of their performance that focuses almost entirely on inter-institutional engagement over the content of legislation fails to present a fully realised picture either of their successes, or of their failures. As to the latter, what, for example, of the simple fact that the Victorian Charter is (and, until 2009, the corresponding Australian Capital Territory legislation was) incredibly stingy in the remedies that it specifies for public authority non-compliance?[100] The flipside of the Victorian Government's focus on the creation of a human rights 'culture' was a strong disinclination to create new judicial remedies for human rights breaches.[101] This was reflected in section 39 of the Victorian Charter. It expressly rules out a damages remedy and provides, more generally, that a remedy for public authority incompatibility is only available if, 'otherwise than because of this Charter, a person may seek any relief or remedy in respect of an act or decision of a public authority on the ground that the act or decision was unlawful'. This provision presents formidable obstacles of interpretation,[102] but is clearly intended to tie the existence of Charter relief, in some way, to the possibility—real or hypothetical—of some other kind of claim being available.[103] In the result, according to the 2015 eight-year review of the Charter, Charter issues are typically 'a second or third string argument' in legal claims and so most proceedings, even when a Charter issue is raised, are decided on other grounds.[104]

The inhibiting effect of section 39 is exacerbated by the fact that Australian administrative law is still organised around the concept of 'jurisdictional error', so the full range of judicial review remedies do not arise from unlawfulness per se.[105] That distinctive administrative law setting is one of a range of contextual factors for which we might need to account in explaining the comparatively disappointing performance of the Australian Charters. Others such factors might include: the impact of federal constitutional doctrines (most prominently, the separation of judicial powers doctrine), the culture of 'legalism' notoriously associated with Australian public law, the vulnerability of human rights arguments in Australian political culture and, as already suggested, the federal character of Australian common law.[106]

[99] See Geiringer (n 85).

[100] See Geiringer 'Inside and Outside Criminal Process' (n 56) at 227–28. This factor is noted, but not analysed, by Gardbaum (n 6) at 208.

[101] See Department of Justice (Vic) (n 93) at 163.

[102] See *Director of Housing v Sudi* (2011) 33 VR 559 at [214], [267], Weinberg J describing s 39 as 'convoluted and extraordinarily difficult to follow'.

[103] See *R v Debono* [2013] VSC 407 at [77]–[82]. For further discussion, see M Moshinsky, 'Bringing Legal Proceedings against Public Authorities for Breach of the Charter of Human Rights and Responsibilities' (2014) 2 *Judicial College of Victoria Online Journal* 91.

[104] See Young (n 97) at 120. The eight-year review recommended that the exclusion of a damages remedy should remain but that the piggy-back character of s 39 should be removed and that both the Victorian Civil and Administrative Tribunal and the courts should have broad powers to provide a remedy for public authority non-compliance with the Charter: see Young (n 97) recommendation 27 and chapter 4. These recommendations are under consideration: see Victoria State Government (n 98).

[105] See *Bare* (n 88).

[106] See, eg, Geiringer (n 85).

VI. DISTINCTIVENESS VERSUS VARIANCE—THE 'PUSH ME PULL YOU' EFFECT

We have seen that their preoccupation with 'distinctiveness' leads scholars in the Commonwealth model genre to offer an account of the respective human rights instruments that is radically incomplete. Some reasons why this is problematic have already been suggested. A further reason lies in the pretensions of this mode of inquiry to be able to explain the drivers of variance, in practice, as between the Commonwealth model jurisdictions.

In expanding on this point, it is helpful to identify an inherent tension at the heart of Commonwealth model scholarship. On the one hand, scholars of this genre seek to establish the model as a discrete form of constitutionalism—distinct from the 'traditional' models of judicial and parliamentary supremacy with which it is contrasted. This project of establishing distinctiveness necessarily mitigates against acknowledgement of the particularities of local circumstance. On the other hand, writers in the tradition also recognise the need to account for variance, in practice, as to how the model is operating as *amongst* the Commonwealth model jurisdictions. This project necessarily requires *acknowledgment* of such particularities.

Scholars in the Commonwealth model genre resolve this contradiction in different ways. Stephen Gardbaum, for example, deals with it by accounting for the variance in local experience almost solely by reference to differences in the formal institutional arrangements relating to the human rights compatibility of legislation, and in the way these formal arrangements are understood or interpreted within the particular jurisdiction. Many of his reform recommendations are proposed on the optimistic assumption that minor tinkering with these formal arrangements (or, in some cases, simply instructing institutional actors to behave differently) can be effective in engineering change.[107] Thus variance, for him, can be explained by reference to the same limited set of factors that drive distinctiveness. With the notable exception of the United Kingdom's supranational commitments,[108] Gardbaum concedes little to the explanatory power of context.

One can perhaps sympathise with Gardbaum's reluctance to throw open his analysis to consideration of multiple points of potential difference as between the Commonwealth model jurisdictions. The problem, however, is that having approached the question of internal variance (within the model) on such a limited basis, he is in a weak position from which either to identify its causes or to propose reforms.

If we wish seriously to confront the question of variance in performance in the Commonwealth model jurisdictions, we need to abandon the focus on 'distinctiveness' and to embrace a far broader search for explanation. A number of potential drivers of variance have already emerged from the preceding discussion. They include, for example, the statutory versus supreme law character of the respective instruments, the precise character of the common law backdrop within the particular jurisdiction, the specific remedies that are provided for public authority

[107] Especially Gardbaum (n 6) at 124–27, 153–55, 197–203, 237–42. See Weill (n 39) at 130, taking issue with this latter assumption.

[108] See, eg, Gardbaum (n 6) at 195.

non-compliance, the political and judicial culture within each jurisdiction, and the sub-national (versus national) status of the respective instruments.

To these, we can doubtless add others. What, for example, of the simple fact that there are substantial differences, as between the jurisdictions, in the substantive content of the rights that are protected?[109] This is such an obvious vector for comparison that one might have thought it would have been canvassed exhaustively. But that is not really so. In fact, writers in the Commonwealth model tradition devote no space at all to considering such differences.

Other under-investigated drivers of variance include operational issues such as the existence (or not) of structural impediments to taking a claim. For example, section 35 of the Victorian Charter requires parties before the Victorian Supreme Court or County Court to notify the Attorney General and the Victorian Equal Opportunity and Human Rights Commission of the intention to raise a Charter issue.[110] Submitters to the eight-year review of the Charter identified this relatively technical provision as one of the 'most significant barriers to Charter litigation in the criminal jurisdictions'.[111] Here, then, might be yet another explanation for the comparative weakness (in practice) of the Victorian Charter.[112]

In short, Gardbaum finds himself in a bind. He recognises the importance, for his project, of accounting for variance in experience, as between the Commonwealth model jurisdictions. But his overriding focus on establishing the Commonwealth model as a single, general and exportable model of human rights protection undermines his ability to account for such variances in any credible way.

Part of the particular value of Scott Stephenson's more recent monograph lies in his attempt both to externalise and to confront this contradiction. As we have seen, he does so through the identification of a set of competing constitutional values or principles (normative trade-offs, as he puts it) that sit in tension with the forms of direct inter-institutional engagement that, for him, characterise the Commonwealth model.[113] This is extremely useful analysis which injects systematic consideration of contextual factors back into the inquiry. But it is, in itself, somewhat reductionist; it condenses salient contextual factors down to a short list of normative constitutional

[109] See Geiringer 'Inside and Outside Criminal Process' (n 56) at 225–27.

[110] Both these agencies have a statutory right to intervene in Charter litigation.

[111] Liberty Victoria, *Submission to the 2015 Review of the Charter of Human Rights and Responsibilities* (Submission 96) 12. See also Victoria Bar Council, *Submission to the 2015 Review of the Charter of Human Rights and Responsibilities* (Submission 54) 19; Victoria Legal Aid, *Submission to the 2015 Review of the Charter of Human Rights and Responsibilities* (Submission 93) 15; Young (n 97) at 167–68; Victorian Equal Opportunity and Human Rights Commission, *Talking Rights: 2010 Report on the Operation of the Charter of Human Rights and Responsibilities* (2011) 51. The eight-year review of the Charter recommended that this requirement be removed in relation to County Court (but not Supreme Court) matters, with judicial officers retaining the discretion to issue notices in appropriate cases: Young (n 97) recommendation 33. The Victorian Government has rejected this recommendation, but proposes to add an explanatory note to the Charter to discourage the notice requirement resulting in delays: Victoria State Government (n 98).

[112] See Geiringer 'Inside and Outside Criminal Process' (n 56) at 230–33. We might learn something here from Robert Leckey's comparative account of judicial remedies for legislative non-compliance with bills of rights in Canada, South Africa and the United Kingdom, with its emphasis on the salience of procedural and technical matters: Leckey (n 39).

[113] See n 30 and accompanying text.

principles and does not leave space for detailed consideration of other contextual (or, indeed, textual) factors that might facilitate or impede effectiveness in the respective jurisdictions. To be fair, Stephenson accepts the relevance and cogence of broader 'environmental factors' of this kind.[114] But he also expresses the concern that focusing on such factors engenders 'a discourse of futility, suggesting that a jurisdiction looking to adopt the Commonwealth's approach can do little to control how it will operate in practice'.[115]

There are two responses to that concern. The first is that lack of manipulability is not a feature of all such environmental factors. Consider, for example, the availability and accessibility of remedies, the availability of accessible fora in which to test one's claims, the existence (or not) of technical impediments to taking a claim, the extent and nature of judicial and intra-governmental training and education that accompanies the introduction of such instruments, and the official and unofficial support structures that sustain a flourishing human rights culture within the jurisdiction. All of these are both amenable to comparative analysis and (at least up to a point) capable of being impacted at the level of institutional design. Yet they are not well accounted for in the Commonwealth model tradition of scholarship.

The second response is that if we are to take the futility critique seriously, then the constitutional principles that Stephenson himself identifies ought to be the first under the gun. To the contrary, what Stephenson's own analysis suggests is that, to the extent non-manipulable contextual factors are present, it is better to be attuned to their existence than otherwise. If nothing else, this knowledge may help us to predict which design options are most likely to thrive within the legal and constitutional culture of a particular jurisdiction.[116] As Stephenson himself suggests: 'The challenge for the comparative constitutional scholar is … to explore why some features have succeeded in generating distinctive patterns of institutional practice while others have not and, importantly, to explain why'.[117]

VII. CONTEXT, COMPARATIVISM AND DIALOGUE

In short, if we wish to account either for the distinctiveness (or not) of the Commonwealth model system of protection, or for variations in the way the model operates in practice, we need to consider a far greater range of factors than those that receive attention from scholars of the Commonwealth model genre. This conclusion is of a piece with a number of existing critiques of this mode of scholarship. These, it will be remembered, express concern about what they see as the failure of this genre to look past the superficial indications of formal institutional design to the messy and contingent reality of how constitutional power is exercised within a particular jurisdiction.[118] Critics see this style of scholarship as exemplifying a genre of

[114] See Stephenson (n 6) at 142.
[115] ibid, at 3.
[116] See, eg, Geiringer (n 61).
[117] See Stephenson (n 6) at 2–3.
[118] See nn 37–40 and associated text.

'macro-constitutional' inquiry which embraces a degree of simplification or reduction in order to formulate constitutional archetypes or typologies.[119] They contrast this form of inquiry with a more contextual (and perhaps more empirically based) assessment, which privileges function over form and which looks to questions of culture, practice, and institutional capacity.[120]

Stephen Gardbaum has offered a rejoinder to this call for 'fine-grained, contextual comparativism' and it is one that we should certainly listen to carefully.[121] In comparative inquiry, he says, typologies or classifications serve a useful function. Yet such typologies or classifications 'necessarily involve generalization; they inevitably and deliberately abstract from the thick level of "the lived life of the law" and do not purport to be accurate in all empirical details'.[122] There is, in other words, 'an inherent tension between classification and fine-grained contextualism'.[123]

Gardbaum has a point. He is, of course, right that archetypes can serve a useful function in comparative inquiry. Further, one can only sympathise with his concern that the 'formidable scholarly bar' set by these calls for fine-grained contextualism might actually come at the expense of the comparativist endeavour.[124] But the contextualist critique of Commonwealth model scholarship pushes us—hard—to think about the purposes and limits of such 'macro-constitutional' inquiry. If comparative analyses of this kind do not purport, as Gardbaum concedes, to be empirically accurate, what exactly is their function?

One answer to that question is to invoke the metaphor of 'dialogue'.[125] The suggestion to which I am referring here is that the risks associated with cross-jurisdictional mistranslation in comparative inquiry are eliminated if recourse to a foreign comparator is used as a stimulus to self-reflection rather than as a model for reflexive adoption. On this account, it does not matter if we have not got all the detail right as the purpose of the comparison is to provoke not imitation, but self-discovery.

I remain to be convinced that a dialogical mind-set counteracts, altogether, the dangers of empirical inaccuracy in comparative inquiry. After all, self-reflection on the basis of an informed appreciation of the counter-factual is surely of more value than self-reflection on the basis of cross-cultural misunderstanding. As Kavanagh suggests, 'however general a constitutional typology may be, its broad contours should map onto constitutional reality to some meaningful degree'.[126]

[119] See Dixon (n 6) at 503; Kavanagh, 'A Rejoinder to Stephen Gardbaum' (n 31) at 1052; Carolan (n 10) at 96–97.

[120] See, eg, Dixon (n 6) at 504; Hirschl (n 31) at 1089; Kavanagh, 'A Hard Look at the Last Word' (n 31) at 836; Kavanagh, 'A Rejoinder to Stephen Gardbaum' (n 31) at 1053; Kavanagh (n 33) at 1031; Leckey (n 39); Roach (n 39) at 270.

[121] The phrase comes from Kavanagh (n 33) at 1037.

[122] S Gardbaum, 'What's So Weak about "Weak-form Review"? A reply to Aileen Kavanagh' (2015) 13 *International Journal of Constitutional Law* 1040 at 1048. See also Dixon (n 6) at 503.

[123] See Gardbaum (n 122) at 1048.

[124] ibid.

[125] See, eg, S Choudhry, 'Globalization in Search of Justification: Toward a Theory of Comparative Constitutional Interpretation' (1999) 74 *Indiana Law Journal* 819; Dixon (n 6) at 503.

[126] See Kavanagh, 'A Rejoinder to Stephen Gardbaum' (n 31) at 1052. Contra Dixon (n 6) at 503.

Nevertheless, where comparative inquiry is intended solely as a stimulus for self-reflection, the call for 'fine-grained contextualism' certainly has much less bite. And there is some real appeal to viewing Commonwealth model scholarship from this perspective—as a form of dialogical or reflective comparativism. As seen through this lens, we might think of this mode of scholarship as an idealised reconstruction of the Anglo-Commonwealth bills of rights, written from within the American academy for the purposes of critiquing dominant traditions of American constitutionalism, and of challenging existing assumptions about the limits and possibilities of constitutional design.[127]

No one can seriously doubt that Commonwealth model scholarship has, indeed, served in this way—as an important stimulus to reflection and debate. The problem is that it seems to promise more. Gardbaum's monograph, in particular, holds itself out as a comprehensive evaluation of human rights protection under the respective instruments that will be of assistance to reformers both inside and outside the Commonwealth model jurisdictions.[128] Indeed, descent into operational detail is part of the particular conceit of his work.[129] He purports to provide not only an evaluation of how well each jurisdiction is performing in practice, but detailed and specific reform prescriptions for how it might do better. Against that background, readers of his monograph might be somewhat surprised to stumble across his casual disclaimer that this kind of comparative inquiry does not 'purport to be accurate in all empirical details'.[130]

When it moves outside its dialogical context, and purports to take itself seriously as a fully realised assessment of the operation and effectiveness of the respective systems of human rights protection, Commonwealth model scholarship is, as we have seen, far from satisfying.

VIII. CONCLUSION: MOVING FORWARD

In short, if we truly wish to account for the distinctiveness (or non-distinctiveness) of the Commonwealth model, its strength (or its weakness), its internal coherence (or its internal variance), a different kind of 'Commonwealth model' scholarship is required. From the preceding discussion, it should already be tolerably clear what shape that might take. At the risk of repetition, let me draw some of the threads together.[131]

[127] Some of Mark Tushnet's work in this field is unashamedly dialogical in this sense: see, eg, Tushnet, 'Policy Distortion and Democratic Debilitation' (n 18).

[128] See also Stephenson (n 6) at 2–4, noting the relevance of his monograph both to scholars of comparative constitutional law and to domestic actors engaged in reform.

[129] See Gardbaum (n 6) at 16.

[130] See Gardbaum (n 122) at 1048.

[131] For an attempt by this author to advance these issues to the next step, and to sketch out an alternative form of comparative Commonwealth model scholarship, see Geiringer 'Inside and Outside Criminal Process' (n 56). See also Geiringer (n 57), tackling an aspect of administrative law compliance in comparative perspective.

First, this chapter is intended as a call for more diversity of approaches to comparative investigation of the Anglo-Commonwealth bills of rights. The biggest problem with the Commonwealth model genre of scholarship is not so much the scholarship itself as the way it has been allowed to dominate the field. To repeat, I do not suggest that the issues that preoccupy scholars in this genre are unimportant; nor even that the additional vectors for comparison that I have identified in this chapter are *more* important. I simply wish to suggest that the picture presented by Commonwealth model scholarship is incomplete in important ways.

Secondly, as part of that call for diversity, we might wish to question the Commonwealth model grouping itself. As we have seen, if we limit the data set instead to statutory bills of rights, a number of additional aspects of distinctiveness present for assessment.[132]

Thirdly, and perhaps most importantly, there is an urgent need for more attention to important questions surrounding how well these instruments succeed in influencing or constraining the exercise of public functions—whether by the executive (in all its capacities), the police or devolved bodies. Recently, and gratifyingly, comparative scholars have finally begun to turn their attention to the impact of these instruments on judicial control of administrative action.[133] But other questions of public authority compliance remain substantially neglected in the comparative literature. These include the intriguing issues that arise from the apparent emphasis, in at least some Commonwealth model regimes, on public sector self-regulation; and the comparative efficacy of these instruments in constraining criminal procedure and police investigative powers.

Fourthly, once this broad question of public authority compliance is brought back into view, a number of neglected vectors for comparison present themselves. These include: the particular rights that have been singled out for protection, the availability and accessibility of remedies, the availability of accessible fora in which to test one's claims, and the existence (or not) of technical impediments to taking a claim. They also include aspects of the broader constitutional context in which these instruments operate, such as the Westminster-derived character of the respective systems of government and the way the respective instruments interact with the common law. Whereas the former has begun to receive some attention in the literature,[134] the significance of the latter remains almost entirely neglected.

Finally, in paying attention to these potential drivers of distinctiveness, and of variance, we should not be afraid to descend into detail. Text and context are both important, and the significance of each can only be brought out through painstaking forensic research. Gardbaum may be right that 'macro-constitutional' inquiry serves an important function in comparative scholarship. But there is a place, too, for the micro-comparativism—scholarship which begins in meticulous context-sensitive forensic investigation, and which casts its gaze far beyond the constitutionalism/democracy dilemma. It is with a plea for more of *this* kind of comparative scholarship that this chapter ends.

[132] See nn 58–60 and associated text and text between nn 68–69.
[133] See n 79.
[134] See Hiebert and Kelly (n 6); Stephenson (n 6).

16

Vindicatory Damages for Violation of Constitutional Rights: A Comparative Approach

JOHANNES CHAN*

WHILE THE RIGHT to remedy lies at the heart of the rule of law (*ubi ius, ibi remedium*)[1] and while damages are probably the most important form of remedy in private law, damages in public law have, until recently, been neglected. Damages, if ever awarded in public law, are normally at a relatively modest, if not nominal, level and little attention has been given to the principles governing the award.[2]

Damages in public law are controversial, not least because an understanding of it is obfuscated by the loose usage of the terms 'damages' and 'vindication'. There are different types of damages.[3] With the exception of exemplary and nominal damages, all other forms of damages are loss-based or gain-based and are awarded primarily upon proof of loss or gain. In this chapter they are categorically regarded as 'compensatory damages' (including restitutionary damages). The focus of this chapter is not on compensatory damages, which are dependent on evidence and are often readily available whatever cause of action is successfully pursued. Rather, the chapter is concerned with whether a claimant would be entitled to a further and additional amount of non-pecuniary damages—known as 'vindicatory' or 'constitutional' damages[4]—for the violation of his constitutional rights. It is argued that vindicatory damages deserve a proper place in public law, and in assessing vindicatory damages in public law, the approach has to be that a violation of constitutional rights is in

* I am grateful to Miss Jennifer Tridgell for her valuable research assistance in preparing this chapter, and to Mr Nick McBride, Miss Cora Chan, Ms Rebecca Lee and Professor Lusina Ho for their valuable comments on an earlier draft and to Professor Mark Elliott for his invaluable editing assistance. Any mistakes remain, of course, my sole responsibility.

1 *Ashby v White* (1703) 2 Ld Raym 938, 953 (Holt CJ).

2 A declaration is conventionally regarded as a sufficient remedy: *Anufrijeva v Southwark LBC* [2004] QB 1124 (Lord Woolf).

3 See, eg, compensatory, restitutionary, performance, disgorgement, general, pecuniary, non-pecuniary, aggravated, exemplary and nominal damages.

4 In this chapter, the terms 'constitutional damages' and 'vindicatory damages' are used interchangeably; likewise 'constitutional law claim', 'public law claim' and 'human rights claim'.

itself an independent wrong. While there are shared objectives between damages in public law and some types of torts, there are also significant differences so that it is preferable to develop the two actions independently. It is further argued that vindicatory damages should be confined to public law and should replace exemplary damages.

I. THE CASE FOR VINDICATORY DAMAGES IN PUBLIC LAW

If there is a right, there is a remedy. When the right to remedies is enshrined as a constitutional right, whether expressly or by implication, the court enjoys a wide discretion, or indeed an obligation to fashion and, if necessary, to create a new remedy to redress a violation of constitutional rights.[5] As De la Bastide CJ observed, in the context of the Constitution of the Republic of Trinidad and Tobago, 'given the breadth of this power, it is not readily apparent to me why in making an order for payment of damages as a consequence of a breach of a constitutional right, the court should be either: (a) limited in providing compensation for the injured party or (b) bound necessarily by the rules which govern the assessment of damages (including exemplary damages) at common law'.[6] Damages, and vindicatory damages in particular, are one form of remedy. There is no inherent reason why they have to be excluded in public law.

The case of vindicatory damages rests on the intrinsic value of constitutional rights. Many such rights have their origin in the common law and have long been protected under it. Yet these rights are recognised to be so fundamental that they are accorded a higher status under the constitution or a Bill of Rights, under which the State has solemnly assumed an obligation to respect and to protect. If their violation attracts no more than the damages that are already available under the common law, this would undermine the constitutional significance of these rights. It would be 'a strange state if relatively innocuous common law breaches were compensated as of right whereas breaches of a constitutionally affirmed human right of an important kind were deemed less worthy of compensatory redress'.[7] The case is even stronger when an alternative common law claim is not available for one reason or another. There is no reason why damages in a constitutional law claim should be affected by or be dependent on the availability of an alternative common law claim.

The purpose of vindicatory damages is to vindicate 'the right itself, for the purpose of securing that right in the public interest'.[8] As Tipping J pointed out, there are two victims in a violation of a constitutional right—the particular victim of the breach and the public (whose confidence in the efficacy of constitutional protection

[5] *Fose v Minister of Safety and Security* (1997) 3 SA 786 at [69] (Ackermann J); *Jorsingh v Attorney General* [1997] 3 LRC 333 at 344 (Sharma JA).

[6] See *Jorsingh* (n 5) at 338.

[7] See *Taunoa v Attorney General* [2008] 1 NZLR 429 at [318] (Tipping J).

[8] J Steele, 'Damages in Tort and under the Human Rights Act: Remedial or Functional Separation?' [2008] *CLJ* 606 at 618.

may be impaired).[9] Public law vindication is not about vindicating the right of the victim as such, but about vindicating the overall right of the public by reaffirming the primacy of constitutional rights. Similarly, as observed by the Canadian Supreme Court, violations of constitutional rights 'impair public confidence and diminish public faith in the efficacy of the protection'.[10] Vindicatory damages recognise 'that Charter rights must be maintained, and cannot be allowed to be whittled away by attrition'.[11] Hence, 'while one may speak of vindication as underlining the seriousness of the harm done to the claimant, vindication as an object of constitutional damages focuses on the harm the Charter breach causes to the state and to society'.[12]

Three consequences follow. First, vindicatory damages in public law are an additional head of damages. Many public law remedies, such as a declaration or an apology, may serve the purpose of vindication. Vindicatory damages, however, come in a tangible form, demonstrating a concrete commitment of the State to the protection of constitutional rights. At the same time, as a public law remedy, vindicatory damages are discretionary and will be awarded only when the remedies taken as a whole are insufficient to vindicate the rights. Secondly, being an additional remedy, vindicatory damages do not preclude compensatory damages. It follows that the mere fact that the claimant has not suffered any personal loss does not preclude the award of vindicatory damages. Thirdly, while the focus of vindication is not on punishment, it does share some similarities with exemplary damages. These shared objectives mean that it is at least inappropriate to grant both vindicatory damages and exemplary damages concurrently.[13]

II. RESPONSES TO VINDICATORY DAMAGES IN DIFFERENT JURISDICTIONS

A. The Starting Point

A convenient starting point is the decision of the Privy Council in *Maharaj v Attorney General of Trinidad and Tobago*.[14] The applicant, a barrister, was imprisoned for seven days for contempt of court without being heard before his committal. He sought redress pursuant to section 6 of the Constitution of Trinidad and Tobago, which provided the High Court with the power to 'make such orders … as [it] may consider appropriate for the purpose of enforcing or securing the enforcement' of the fundamental rights. The Privy Council held that this created a new cause of action in public law against the State directly, and not a private claim in tort for which the State was vicariously liable. Under this new cause of action, the court may grant effective redress, including reparation and monetary compensation.

[9] See *Taunoa* (n 7) at [317] (Tipping J).
[10] *Vancouver v Ward* [2010] 2 SCR 28 at [82] (McLachlin CJ), quoting from *Fose* (n 5) at [82].
[11] ibid, at [25].
[12] ibid, at [29].
[13] *Takitota v Attorney General of the Bahamas* [2009] UKPC 12 at [13].
[14] [1978] 2 All ER 670.

Such damages, as Lord Diplock observed, were a claim in public law for compensation for deprivation of liberty and not a tort claim of false imprisonment. Therefore, the method of assessment of such damages must be distinct from that under the law of tort, and 'would include any loss of earnings consequent on the imprisonment and recompense for the inconvenience and distress suffered by the appellant during incarceration'.[15]

This judgment raised many unanswered questions. If the method of assessment of constitutional damages should be distinct from that under the law of tort, what principles govern the assessment of public law damages? The court referred to loss of earning, inconvenience and distress, but such loss fell within the category of compensatory damages. So for what should constitutional damages be awarded? If there is a concurrent claim in public law and tort law, what would be the justifications for assessing damages in public law differently from that assessed by the tortious principles in private law?

Some of these questions were addressed by the Privy Council in the subsequent case of *Attorney General of Trinidad and Tobago v Ramanoop*,[16] where Lord Nicholls stressed five points. First, vindication in most cases requires more than mere words. Secondly, constitutional claims are independent of common law tort claims. Thirdly, nonetheless, damages in common law tort claims would provide useful guidance. Fourthly, the Privy Council referred to an 'extra dimension' and an 'additional award' to reflect the sense of public outrage, to emphasise the importance of the constitutional right that was violated and the gravity of the breach and to deter future breaches. Finally, this discretionary award is vindicatory, not punitive. Exemplary damages are inappropriate for this purpose. These two decisions form the basis for the development of vindicatory damages in a number of jurisdictions, although unfortunately, the full ambit of *Ramanoop* is not always appreciated.

B. Four Different Approaches

(i) Canada

It is not surprising that different jurisdictions have developed different approaches to the award of vindicatory damages. The Canadian Supreme Court has adopted a composite approach that provides a comprehensive framework to bring together the public law and the private law dimensions in the award of damages for human rights violations. In the leading case of *Vancouver v Ward*,[17] the Court introduced a four-step test. The first step is to establish a breach of the Charter. Step two involves the identification of the purposes of damages. In this regard, damages, which are regarded as a unique public law remedy, are considered to be capable of serving three inter-related functions: *compensation* in respect of both tangible personal loss

[15] ibid, at 680.
[16] [2006] 1 AC 328 at [18]–[19].
[17] [2010] 2 SCR 28.

and harm to intangible interests (eg distress); *vindication* of the right by affirming its constitutional values and importance;[18] and *deterrence*.

Even when damages are functionally justified, the court would have to consider any countervailing factors in determining whether they are appropriate and just. At this third stage, the burden of establishing these countervailing factors falls on the State. Two countervailing factors were identified, namely the existence of alternative remedies and concerns for effective governance.

The final step is the assessment of damages. In general, compensation is the most important objective; vindication and deterrence will play only supporting roles. Tort law may be of assistance in respect of compensation, but is less helpful in respect of vindication and deterrence—matters that engage questions of rationality and proportionality, taking into account the seriousness of the breach, the impact of the breach on the claimant, the seriousness of the State's misconduct, the public interest in good governance, and the need to avoid diverting large sums of funds from public programmes to benefit private interests. The damages have to be just to both the claimant and the State.

The *Ward* approach was recently re-affirmed by the Supreme Court in *Henry v British Columbia (Attorney General)*.[19] The claimant was wrongfully convicted and imprisoned for almost 27 years as a result of the failure of the prosecution to disclose relevant exculpatory evidence. He brought a claim for damages in both tort law (negligence and malicious prosecution) and under the Charter (for breach of the Crown's constitutional disclosure obligations). The tort claims failed on evidence. However, the Court unanimously held that malice, which was rooted in the tort of malicious prosecution, was irrelevant to the constitutional claim. While it then split on the question whether it was necessary for the claimant to establish an intention to withhold exculpatory information and on whether the 'but for' test was appropriate in establishing causation, the *Ward* test has been firmly established in Canada. It provides a comprehensive and balanced framework for the determination of damages in public law. By clearly identifying the functions of damages and separating the function of compensation from vindication, it enables, as well as requires, the court to direct its mind to the different functions of damages.

(ii) New Zealand

In the seminal case of *Simpson v Attorney General (Baigent's Case)*,[20] Hardie-Boys J, after surveying the authorities from India, Ireland, the United States and Canada, concluded that the New Zealand Bill of Rights required a rights-centred approach. This does not necessarily require a remedy in the form of damages or other compensation, but it should be awarded if it is appropriate and proper to do so. The purpose is compensatory and not punitive.[21] The award should therefore be 'moderate' but

[18] The Court drew support from *Fose* (n 5) at [55], [82].
[19] [2015] 2 SCR 214.
[20] [1994] NZLR 667.
[21] ibid, at 703.

should not trivialise the breach.[22] In contrast to the Canadian approach, the majority of the Court distanced itself from tort principles. Casey J observed that there would be problems in adapting traditional common law causes of action to give appropriate redress for the infringement of all of the rights in the Bill.[23] McKay J held that the availability of damages for false imprisonment or trespass should not preclude a separate public law claim; the same damages might be recoverable by either route.[24]

A question arises as to the relationship between damages for infringement of the Bill of Rights and damages in tort. In *Bagient's Case* the Court suggested a pragmatic approach to take account of the damages that would have been awarded under tort law in order to ensure an equitable result and to avoid double recovery. However, instead of distinguishing clearly between vindication and compensation, Cooke P preferred to make a global award without descending into details. The problem of a global award is that it tends to merge the award for compensatory and vindicatory purposes, risking confusion about the meaning of damages in subsequent cases. The subsequent case of *Dunlea v Attorney General*[25] has been considered a marked departure from the autonomous approach to damages in a public law claim. For instance, Butler and Butler have, relying on this case, commented that it would be safe to conclude that at least in areas of concurrent liability, the damages awarded under the NZBOR would typically follow the common law standards.[26] However, this is probably an overstatement, not least because the majority expressly stated that this was not the occasion to consider the question of whether the assessment of damages under the Bill of Rights should be different from that under tort arising from the same facts for essential the same wrong, for the simple reason that this point was not argued or pursued in court.[27] Moreover, their preference for a comparable award in tort was premised on the basis that this was a case of concurrent claim, leaving open the position when there was no concurrent claim.

The relationship between a public law action and a private law claim in tort was further addressed in two important subsequent cases. In *Taunoa v Attorney General*,[28] the claimants were prisoners who were subject to inhuman and degrading treatment. They brought an action under the Bill of Rights only. The Supreme Court pointed out that there were two victims in a Bill of Rights claim: the claimant and society as a whole. The latter consideration required the court to consider what was necessary by way of vindication to protect society's interests in the observance of fundamental rights and freedoms.[29] This led the Court to the view that in assessing Bill of Rights damages it should not attempt to track the quantum of awards in tort

[22] While not disagreeing with this approach, Gault J, in dissent, preferred to develop the remedy in the tort of breach of statutory duty, which was regarded as a familiar and more fruitful route than to chart into the unknown sea of public law remedies: ibid, at 713.

[23] ibid, at 691.

[24] ibid, at 718.

[25] [2000] 3 NZLR 136.

[26] A Butler and P Butler, *The New Zealand Bill of Rights Act: A Commentary* (Wellington, Lexis Nexis, 2005) 991.

[27] See *Dunlea* (n 25) at [37].

[28] [2008] 1 NZLR 429 at [265].

[29] ibid, at [317] (Tipping J). See also [385] (Henry J) and [367] (McGrath J).

law. Blanchard J pointed out that there would be conceptual and practical difficulties in treating the Bill of Rights as a constitutional tort. In developing constitutional damages, tort principles such as causation, remoteness and mitigation might not fit well with cases where fundamental rights have been violated.[30]

The Court was unanimous in holding that declaratory relief was not a sufficient remedy.[31] However, by failing to separate compensatory damages from vindicatory damages, the Court became rather confused on the issue of damages. Blanchard J observed that when a right has been infringed, the court must determine the appropriate non-monetary relief and then ask whether that would be sufficient in the light of the breach and the injury to the plaintiff. The primary task was to 'find an overall remedy or set of remedies which was sufficient to deter any repetition by agents of the State and to vindicate the breach of the right in question'.[32] The overall remedy appears to include damages for compensation, vindication and deterrence.

Elias CJ seemed to adopt a more orthodox view of vindication by distinguishing it from compensatory and deterrent damages. She emphasized that damages are 'to recognize the importance of the right and the gravity of the breach'.[33] They should try *not only* to compensate for the injury suffered through the denial of a right, but also to vindicate the importance of the rights. In referring to an 'additional' award to vindicate the importance of the right,[34] it is obvious that the Chief Justice did not intend to exclude compensatory award, for which assessment the tort principles would still be relevant. Meanwhile, Tipping J stated that the approach should involve considering how much was necessary to achieve respectively the vindicatory purpose and the compensatory purpose, and then awarding the higher of the two sums. This suggests that the two purposes of vindication and compensation were mutually exclusive.

A clearer approach was adopted in *Liston-Lloyd v The Commissioner of Police*, where the court found a violation of section 21 of the Bill of Rights by the police for unlawfully obtaining a buccal (oral) DNA sample.[35] Mallon J held that while it may be appropriate to have regard to common law damages, particularly where the focus of the award is on the compensation function, there is an 'extra dimension' in a public law award of damages because of the constitutional aspect. Hence, common law damages should 'set the floor rather than the ceiling' for public law damages.[36] His treatment of the functions of public law damages—notably his identification of the functions of compensation, vindication and deterrence—bears a remarkable resemblance to the Canadian approach in *Ward*.[37] The court took into account that

[30] ibid, at [307]. He expressly disagreed with the obiter of the majority of the Court of Appeal in *Dunlea* (n 25) on adopting the same approach of common law and public law when both actions are available: *Taunoa* (n 7) at [304].

[31] For example, Elias CJ observed (at [107]) that damages were 'the only practical effective remedy for the denial of the prisoners' rights to be treated with dignity and respect for their inherent humanity'.

[32] See *Taunoa* (n 7) at [253].

[33] ibid, at [111].

[34] ibid, at [109].

[35] [2015] NZHC 2614.

[36] ibid, at [47].

[37] ibid, at [42]–[43] (footnotes omitted).

the breach involved highly personal information, but the distress involved was at the low end and proper precautions had been taken in respect of the use that could be made of the information. An award of NZ$2,500 was made to compensate the claimant for the upset and distress suffered and to recognise her right to be secure from unreasonable search and seizure. Mellon J expressly stated that if this were a common law tort action, an award of NZ$1,500 would have been made. He had adjusted the amount upward to mark the breach of an important right.[38]

A body of precedent in public law damages has gradually emerged in New Zealand.[39] Vindicatory damages are now well established as a discretionary remedy. In assessing damages, New Zealand courts do not seek equivalence with tort law, but ordinary tort principles remain relevant, especially in assessing compensatory damages when there is a concurrent claim in both private and public law. The amount of vindicatory damages should neither be derisory nor excessive; they should adequately reflect the importance of the constitutional rights in the particular society, along with the seriousness and consequences of the breach. Thus, while New Zealand started with a strong autonomous approach to public law damages, there is now considerable convergence with the approach found in Canada.

(iii) The United Kingdom

In the United Kingdom, discussion of public law damages is largely shaped by the judgment of the House of Lords in *R (Greenfield) v Secretary of State for the Home Department* on the relationship between the Human Rights Act ('HRA') and the European Convention of Human Rights ('ECHR').[40] Section 8(4) of the HRA provides that in deciding whether to award damages and the consequent quantum of damages, courts must 'take into account the principles applied by the European Court of Human Rights ('ECtHR') in relation to the award of compensation under Article 41 of the Convention'. The House of Lords held that the award of damages under the HRA was to be closely modelled on awards made by the ECtHR, not on damages awarded under domestic tort law. It also held that the aim of the HRA 'was not to give victims better remedies at home than they could recover in Strasbourg but to give them the same remedies without the delay and expense of resort to Strasbourg'.[41] Lord Bingham gave two reasons for this decision. First, the purpose of the HRA, as revealed in the White Paper that preceded it, was to enable claimants 'to receive compensation from a domestic court equivalent to what they would have received in Strasbourg'.[42] Secondly, as a matter of statutory interpretation, section 8(4) requires the court to take into account the principles applied by the

[38] ibid, at [61].

[39] See further *Van Essex v Attorney General* [2015] NZCA 22, in which the Court of Appeal carried out a survey of awards of public law damages.

[40] [2005] 1 WLR 673.

[41] ibid, at [19].

[42] ibid, quoting from Home Office, *Rights Brought Home: The Human Rights Bill* (Cm 3782, 1997) [2.6].

ECtHR not only when an award would be made but also what the quantum of an award should be. This so-called 'mirror approach' has been universally criticised.[43]

The *Greenfield* decision contravened two major principles of human rights law. First, as a regional treaty, the ECHR is intended to set minimum standards,[44] yet the 'mirror approach' has effectively turned the standards under the Convention into the maximum standards. The HRA, however, does not require this: as the Law Commissions of England and Wales and of Scotland observed in their joint report, the English courts are only required to take ECtHR 'principles' into account, leaving the domestic courts a free hand to determine the quantum of damages.[45] Applied to remedies, the 'mirror approach' is contrary to the general spirit of the Convention to provide a minimum standard of protection when Strasbourg decisions on the quantum of award are taken as the ceiling rather than the base of the award.

Secondly, applying the 'mirror principle' to remedies arguably impedes discharge by the UK of its Article 13 ECHR obligation to provide (including through its courts) effective remedies. The HRA has not incorporated Article 13, but the reason was to afford greater latitude for the British courts to fashion appropriate remedies, rather than to let the Strasbourg court to lead in this area.[46] As Varuhas observed, it was precisely because English courts were 'rich in remedies' that the government considered it unnecessary to incorporate Article 13.[47] Indeed, the primary duty, as set out in section 8(1), is that the courts should grant such relief or remedy as is considered just and appropriate. This broad discretion is limited by section 8(3) so that damages can only be awarded to afford 'just satisfaction'.[48] While this term is borrowed from Article 41, this article is an enabling provision to confer jurisdiction on the ECtHR to award remedies. It is not a provision that imposes obligations on domestic courts to adhere to the remedies granted by the Strasbourg Court. Thus, section 8(3) should be interpreted in light of both section 8(1) and Article 13. The phrase 'just satisfaction' should then be construed as nothing more than the familiar duty to grant 'just and effective remedies'. This is buttressed by the fact that no remedy would be just and appropriate if it failed to take into account the domestic situation and the special circumstances of the case, neither of which are matters that an international court is suitably placed or equipped to assess.[49] This is another reason why the uniformity approach in section 8(4) should apply only to 'principles' and not 'remedies'. It could not have been the intention of the legislature to restrict the discretion of the

[43] JNE Varuhas, 'Damages: Private Law and the HRA—Never the Twain Shall Meet?' in D Hoffmann (ed), *The Impact of the UK Human Rights Act on Private Law* (Cambridge, Cambridge University Press, 2016) 223. See also Steele (n 8); A Burrows, 'Damages and Rights' in D Nolan and A Robertson (eds), *Rights in Private Law* (Oxford, Hart Publishing, 2012) 275.

[44] *Van Colle v Chief Constable of Hertfordshire Police* [2009] 1 AC 225 at [138] (Lord Brown).

[45] Law Commissions of England and Wales and of Scotland, *Damages under the Human Rights Act 1998* (Law Com No 266, 2000) at [4.26].

[46] See Varuhas (n 43) at 227; Steele (n 8).

[47] See Varuhas (n 43) at 227–28.

[48] Section 8(3) of the HRA provides that no award of damages is to be made unless, taking into account all the circumstances of the case, the court is satisfied that it is necessary to afford 'just satisfaction' to the claimant.

[49] This wide discretionary approach was recognised by the Court of Appeal in the earlier case of *Anufrijeva v Southwark London Borough Council* [2004] QB 1124.

court to afford just and effective remedies. Nor does the reference in section 8(4) to Article 41 absolve the State of its treaty obligation to afford and develop effective remedies. The purpose of section 8(4) is to ensure that domestic awards do not fall below those made by the international court, whose awards should provide the floor and not the ceiling.[50]

At the same time, English courts have not been receptive to vindicatory damages. In the leading case of *Lumba (Congo) v Secretary of State for the Home Department,*[51] the House of Lords was split on whether vindicatory damages should be recognised. Pending deportation, the claimants were detained pursuant to an *unpublished* policy. However, it was found that they would inevitably have been detained even if the Secretary of State had applied the *published* policy. The majority held that the State was liable, and three of them (Lords Collins, Dyson and Kerr) held that the claimants were entitled to no more than nominal damages. Lord Dyson drew a distinction between a vindicatory purpose and vindicatory damages. It was one thing to say that an award of compensatory damages was to serve a vindicatory purpose; it was quite another thing to make an additional award simply to reflect the nature of the wrong. As the claimants had suffered no loss or damage as a result of the unlawful exercise of the power to detain, they should receive no more than nominal damages. His Lordship criticised vindicatory damages as arbitrary, unprincipled and unnecessary. As an 'unruly horse', they should be discarded.[52] Besides, if they were available for false imprisonment, there was no reason why they should not be extended to other torts. Lord Collins held that all damages, whether compensatory or vindicatory, served the incidental purpose of vindicating a right; there was no point in making a separate award for vindicatory damages.[53] His Lordship refused to follow *Ward* and *Taunoa*, and noted that exemplary damages under the common law would be adequate to serve the vindicatory purpose where the executive has acted in an oppressive, arbitrary or unconstitutional manner.[54]

The other three judges in the majority (Baroness Hale and Lords Hope and Walker) held that the claimants were entitled to either exemplary or vindicatory damages. They regarded the constitutional rights as so important that their violation should be vindicated by law in some way, irrespective of whether compensatable harm had been suffered or whether the conduct of the authorities had been so egregious as to merit exemplary damages.[55] Of the three dissenting judges on liability, Lord Phillips agreed with Lords Collins and Dyson that only nominal damages would be available if liability were established. Lord Rodger agreed with Lord Brown, who said nothing about vindicatory damages and whose judgment could be read in different ways. An underlying difference between the two groups of judges is the fundamental question of whether the law should only provide damages for the *consequences* of a violation of a constitutional right, so that in the absence of consequences, only nominal

[50] This seems to be the reading of *Greenfield* by Elias CJ in *Taunua* (n 7) at [109].
[51] [2012] 1 AC 245.
[52] ibid, at [101].
[53] ibid, at [236].
[54] ibid, at [221].
[55] ibid, at [217].

damages should be awarded, or whether the law should provide damages for the very act of violation itself, thereby acknowledging that the constitutional right itself has an intrinsic value that deserves protection.

(iv) South Africa

While the Constitutional Court of South Africa is prepared to fashion new remedies, if necessary, to protect and enforce constitutional rights, and has emphasised that an appropriate relief has to be an effective remedy to vindicate the entrenched rights, its approach to constitutional damages is ambivalent. In *Hoffmann v South African Airways*, the Constitutional Court held that a determination of appropriate relief should balance various objectives, including addressing the wrong; deterring future violations; making orders that can be complied with; and being fair to all those who might be affected by the infringement.[56] In the leading case of *Fose v Minister of Safety and Security*,[57] Ackermann J agreed that vindication was the primary object of a constitutional remedy. However, he was sceptical of separating constitutional damages from delictual damages. He rejected the relevance of nominal damages, which were hardly 'effective or appropriate' as they were not compensatory in outlook, purport and effect. They would serve no deterrent or preventive end and a nominal punitive award would only serve to trivialise the rights violated.[58] He further rejected the relevance of exemplary damages, as there should be no place for punitive damages in constitutional law. The Court was content to hold, in light of the facts, that delictual damages under the common law would be sufficient to redress breaches of fundamental rights, and left open the issue whether an action for damages in the nature of constitutional damages existed in law and, if so, whether constitutional damages could be awarded in addition to delictual damages. Likewise, in *Law Society of South Africa v Minister of Transport*, Moseneke DCJ expressed a preference for developing common law remedies to vindicate constitutionally entrenched rights.[59]

The point was taken up in *Member of the Executive Council: Welfare v Kate*, a case concerning a claim for constitutional damages for undue delay in approving applications for social welfare.[60] The Supreme Court of Appeal held that whether monetary damages were appropriate in a particular case must be determined casuistically with due regard to, amongst other things, the nature and relative importance of the rights that in issue, the alternative remedies that might be available to assert and vindicate the rights, and the consequences for the claimant of the breach. The Court found that the delay was endemic in nature and the problem had been in existence for years so a declaration would not serve any useful purpose.[61] It also

[56] 2001 (1) SA 1.
[57] 1997 (3) SA 786.
[58] ibid, at [71].
[59] 2011 (1) SA 400.
[60] [2006] SCA 46.
[61] ibid, at [29].

rejected mandamus as an effective remedy as it would only encourage more litigation without addressing the systemic issues. Having decided that *Fose* posed no obstacle to an award of constitutional damages, the Court held that constitutional remedies should not be regarded as a last resort. Instead, a violation of constitutional rights should be addressed directly via a constitutional remedy and not indirectly by delictual damages. Furthermore, the endemic breach in that case called for a clear recognition of the constitutional right.[62] Constitutional damages were also affirmed and awarded in *Modderfontein Squatters v Modderklip Boerdery (Pty) Ltd*, a case concerning the failure of the State to protect the property right of the claimant against trespassers, resulting in the land being occupied by approximately 40,000 persons.[63]

However, in *The Minister of Police v Mboweni*, the Supreme Court of Appeal distinguished both *Kate* and *Modderklip*, describing them as the only two cases where constitutional damages were awarded.[64] In *Mboweni*, the Court took the view that even if liability could be established (which, on the facts, it doubted), the proper approach was to first consider the adequacy of the relevant common law remedy. If it was inadequate, the Court should consider whether the deficiency could be remedied by a development of the common law. The Court doubted whether constitutional damages would encompass a *solatium* or general damages.[65] These comments on constitutional damages may be *obiter*, as the primary decision was that the claim for loss of the relevant constitutional right had not been established. Nonetheless, it is illustrative of the general position in South Africa. While the appropriateness of constitutional damages has been acknowledged, such damages are regarded as exceptional and secondary—only to be awarded when the common law remedies have been exhausted and found inadequate. The courts clearly prefer to develop the common law remedies rather than to engaging in an award for constitutional damages. However, as noted by Currie and De Waal, there are at least two reasons why development of constitutional damages is necessary. First, there are circumstances that a declaratory relief or other remedies would make no sense and damages may be the only appropriate remedy to vindicate the rights. Secondly, the possibility of a substantial award may encourage victims to litigate, hence deterring further infringements.[66]

C. A Summary

In all four jurisdictions, a breach of constitutional rights is a public law action. Although Professor Forsyth has argued that a breach of the HRA could be perceived

[62] ibid, at [27].
[63] 2004 (6) SA 40.
[64] [2014] ZASCA 107.
[65] ibid, at [24].
[66] I Currie and J De Waal, *Bill of Rights Handbook* (Lansdowne, Juta & Co, 2005) 201, as quoted in JA Robinson and R Prinsloo, 'The Right of the Child to Care and Constitutional Damages for the Loss of Parental Care: Some Thoughts on *M v Minister of Police* and *Minister of Police v Mboweni*' (2015) 18 *Potchefstroom Elec LJ* 1670 at 1676–77.

as a species of breach of statutory duty,[67] no jurisdiction has so far gone down this path and the argument has indeed been rejected in all major common law jurisdictions. While it is also common ground that the court has the discretion to consider what remedy is just and appropriate in each case, only the courts in Canada and New Zealand are prepared to award vindicatory damages. In both jurisdictions, a body of precedent on constitutional damages has gradually emerged. While South Africa is prepared to accept vindicatory damages, they are awarded only in exceptional circumstances. The courts prefer to develop common law principles and have more-or-less confined public law damages to those that are recoverable under common law principles. The position in the UK is awkward. On the one hand, the courts rejected the relevance of tort damages, and were prepared to adhere to Strasbourg jurisprudence. On the other hand, they also rejected vindicatory damages on the ground that such damages do not add anything to common law damages and their recognition would serve no useful purpose.[68] While most commentators advocated for the adoption of tort principles in assessing damages under the HRA, there was little support for the introduction of vindicatory damages.

III. OBJECTIONS TO VINDICATORY DAMAGES

A. Purposes of Vindicatory Damages

(i) The Objections

In *Lumba*, Lord Collins said:[69]

> In my view, the purpose of vindicating a claimant's common law rights is sufficiently met by (i) an award of compensatory damages, including (in the case of strict liability torts) nominal damages where no substantial loss is proved; (ii) where appropriate, a declaration in suitable terms; and (iii) again, where appropriate, an award of exemplary damages. There is no justification for awarding vindicatory damages for false imprisonment to any of the [claimants].

Likewise, Andrew Burrows rejected vindicatory damages as 'entirely arbitrary' serving no valid or useful purpose,[70] whereas Jenny Steele described vindicatory damages as 'unorthodox' and unnecessary.[71] On this view, the existence of exemplary or punitive damages means that nothing useful would be gained by introducing vindicatory damages into English tort law.

[67] HWR Wade and CF Forsyth, *Administrative Law*, 11th edn (Oxford, Oxford University Press, 2014) 637.

[68] *Lumba* was adopted in Hong Kong in *Ghulam Rbani v Secretary for Justice* [2002] 2 HKC 1; the Canadian and New Zealand approach was expressly rejected in *Saeed v Secretary for Justice* [2015] 1 HKLRD 1030 at [332]–[336] although the reason for distinguishing the Canadian and New Zealand cases was hardly convincing.

[69] *Lumba* (n 51) at [101].

[70] Burrows (n 43) at 303–7.

[71] Steele (n 8).

(ii) Different Functions of Public Law and Private Law

These objections raise the question of the distinction between public law and private law and their respective functions. A rigid distinction between private law and public law is untenable. Yet it would be equally artificial to obliterate any distinction between these two spheres.[72] Public law and private law serve fundamentally different purposes. The traditional purposes of damages in private law are to compensate the plaintiff, punish the defendant or achieve restitution, with vindication at best assuming a secondary purpose, save in those torts that protect against interference with a personal right.[73] The emphasis is on what the plaintiff is entitled to receive. The bipolar nature of private law, as succinctly illustrated by Hammond J in *Manga v Attorney General*, means that 'the sort of factors influencing remedial choice in a private law suit (which include plaintiff autonomy; economic efficiency; the relative severity of the remedy; the nature of the right to be supported; difficulties of calculation; the effect of a remedy on third parties; the practicability of enforcement; and the conduct of the parties) are not wide enough for a case involving a violation of a constitutional character'.[74] In contrast, public law serves primarily to address the proper use of public powers. A violation of constitutional rights is a breach by the State of an obligation that is owed to the public. Public law remedies serve an additional purpose of vindicating a public right that the state has solemnly affirmed to respect and to protect. Thus, in addition to considering what the plaintiff is entitled to receive, the court must consider whether the State should be required to pay damages in order to vindicate the breach, denounce the conduct concerned or deter future breaches.[75]

Unlike private law—under which the courts, in awarding damages, typically look back to events that have already taken place in order to determine how to compensate the victim or punish the transgressor—public law damages are concerned not just with the past, but also with the future. As Robinson and Prinsloo pointed out, public law damages should be forward-looking, community oriented and structural,[76] as they have routinely had an impact on governance and public administration that goes far beyond the immediate case before the courts and may affect even third parties.[77] Accordingly, public interest must play an important role in fashioning any appropriate remedy, whereas such considerations may not be apposite in determining private law remedies. It follows that the divergent remedial objectives of public law and private law make the conceptual framework for tort damages ill-suited to providing remedies in respect of breaches by the State of its duties under public law.

[72] Compare JNE Varuhas, 'The Development of the Damages Remedy under the New Zealand Bill of Rights Act 1990: From Torts to Administrative Law' [2016] *New Zealand Law Review* 213.

[73] N Witzieb and R Carroll, 'The Role of Vindication in Torts Damages' (2009) 17 *Tort L Rev* 16 at 42.

[74] [2000] NZLR 65 at [126].

[75] *Liston-Lloyd* (n 35) at [42]–[43].

[76] Robinson and Prinsloo (n 66) at 1676. See also F du Bois, 'Human Rights and the Tort Liability of Public Authorities' (2011) 127 LQR 589 at 599–600.

[77] [2002] 2 NZLR 65 at [126] (Hammond J).

(iii) Distinction Challenged: The Case of Vindicatory Torts

Jason Varuhas challenges those in support of vindicatory damages for taking too narrow a view of vindication in private law. He has argued that different torts serve different functions, and that vindication has long been the primary function of what he calls 'vindicatory torts', such as defamation and those that are actionable *per se*. Damages, he contends, have been awarded to reinforce the inherent value of the particular interests in and of themselves, regardless of any financial loss or injury to feelings.[78] Indeed, one can add that vindication has been recognised even beyond vindicatory torts. In *Rees v Darlington Memorial Hospital NHS Trust*, a case of wrongful birth due to negligent administering of sterilisation by the defendant, the House of Lords awarded substantial damages of £15,000 to recognise the claimant's loss of the opportunity 'to live her life in the way that she wished and planned'.[79] Lord Bingham expressly stated that the damages were neither compensatory, nominal nor derisory, but were intended to 'afford some measure of recognition of the wrong done'.[80] In another context, Pearce and Halson argued that there were occasions where vindicatory damages, which were rights-based, were awarded to provide a measure of recognition of the violation of the claimant's right when other curial measures were inadequate, and the damages were neither compensatory nor restitutionary.[81]

Following this line of argument, Varuhas argued for the adoption of a vindicatory, tort-based approach to human rights damages. The familiar tort principles provided an established and reasonably coherent and principled approach that would promote consistency.[82] Given that current remedies meet the purposes of vindication, and that vindicatory damages perform similar functions to exemplary damages, vindicatory damages are otiose and should be rejected.[83] Interestingly, Varuhas further argued that an administrative law paradigm in public law that focuses on abuse of powers will not be conducive to the development of damages for violation of human rights, which is always the primary focus of tort.[84] This public law paradigm would bring into consideration the balancing of various public interests. As a result, the normative right to conventional damages in tort is reduced to a discretion, and public law considerations are allowed to creep into the process of determination of damages, which considerations would likely result in a lesser amount of damages to be awarded in public law than in tort. Varuhas attributed the failure to extend the vindicatory torts to human rights damages to an outmoded conception of the relationship between public and private law.

78 JNE Varuhas, 'The Concept of "Vindication" in the Law of Torts: Rights, Interests and Damages' (2014) 34 *OJLS* 253 at 291.

79 [2004] 1 AC 309 at [8].

80 ibid.

81 D Pearce and R Halson, 'Damages for Breach of Contract: Compensation, Restitution and Vindication' (2008) 28 *OJLS* 73.

82 Varuhas (n 43) at 223–48.

83 Varuhas (n 78) at 291; Varuhas, *Damages and Human Rights* (Oxford, Hart Publishing, 2016) 125–29.

84 Varuhas (n 72).

(iv) A Rejoinder

This is a thought-provoking thesis. A detailed reply in this chapter is not possible. However, a few observations are offered. According to Varuhas, the core features of vindicatory torts are that damages are as of right and that a wide range of damages are available, including compensatory damages, non-compensatory damages such as nominal damages, gain-based damages and exemplary or punitive damages. In contrast, it was argued that damages in public law are subject to an exceptionally broad and impressionistic judicial discretion, as in *Henry* and *Taunoa,* which he heavily criticised.[85] Amongst other things, it was argued that individual justice was drowned by public concern in these cases and assumed subsidiary importance only. Rather than focusing on what was required to remedy a violation of the claimant's interest, the focus in *Taunoa* was 'nearly exclusively on whether the courts feel they are warranted in imposing liability on government'.[86] Four points can be made in reply.

First, in these cases, the only issue before the court was public law damages. The tort action either failed, as in *Henry*, or was not pursued, as in *Taunoa*, hence no damages could have been awarded in tort. Indeed, in *Henry*, the court extended Charter liability to a situation where the tort of malicious prosecution failed and awarded damages when no tort damages could have been available. Therefore, there is no basis for saying that individual interests were drowned by public concern.

Secondly, a distinction may have to be drawn between compensatory and vindicatory damages. Vindicatory damages are in addition to compensatory damages, so they do not and should not affect whatever compensatory damages the claimant would be entitled to. In *Ward*, MacLachlin CJ referred to the compensatory function of damages. 'Compensation' is used in a general sense and includes both personal loss (physical, psychological and pecuniary) and harm to intangible interests (distress, humiliation, embarrassment and anxiety).[87] Although it is not expressly mentioned in the judgment, there is no reason why gain-based restitutionary loss should be excluded. The court also emphasised in *Ward* that in these areas guidance could be drawn from the common law. While the position in New Zealand is less clear, in *Baigent's Case* and *Taunoa*, the court referred to an amount of damages that was in addition to common law awards. Vindicatory damages are not a substitute for other types of damages. A careful reading suggests that public law considerations were relevant only to vindicatory damages. For compensatory damages, which are loss- or gain-based, it is right that there should not be any room for public interest considerations to reduce the damages recoverable; to this extent, the public/private distinction may be too rigid to allow a wider claim for compensatory damages in public law. Yet when damages are no longer compensatory but are awarded to recognise the State's responsibility for serious miscarriage of justice such as in *Henry* or *Taunoa*, it would be difficult to see that considerations of public policy would not have been relevant even under the tort approach. As McLachlin CJ cautioned, a just and appropriate

[85] ibid, at 247.
[86] ibid, at 240.
[87] *Vancouver v Ward* (n 10) at [29].

remedy in public law has to be just and fair to all parties, including the State, when the purpose of vindication is to mark society's disapproval.[88] With this purpose in mind, it would be difficult to imagine that the conduct of State officials, including any step taken to remedy the wrong or to address systemic issues, would not be relevant in assessing the amount of damages, even under vindicatory torts.

Thirdly, a tort-based approach to damages may be too narrow. Varuhas' argument rests heavily on vindicatory torts, which, apart from defamation, are about deprivation of personal liberty. Not all violations of human rights would constitute an actionable tort. Even when a tort is established, the interest protected by tort may not be the same as the interest that is at stake in public law. For example, trespass to land serves to protect the interest against unlawful interference with possession. If privacy is protected, it is an incidental result. Thus, it is arguable that damages awarded for trespass to land should not be the same as damages awarded for an invasion of one's right to private life under a constitutional claim. Of course, there is a closer convergence with vindicatory tort in terms of the interest to be protected, notably in the area of deprivation of personal liberty, especially when the deprivation is malicious, outrageous or contumelious. In this regard, vindicatory torts may be an exception as their nature is more akin to public law than private law.[89] Yet even in this area, the bilateral corrective justice approach in tort law is less equipped to deal with situations where there is no malice or ill-intentioned conduct, but the violation is a result of mere maladministration or systemic failures.[90]

The requirement of causation in private law may pose another issue for extending tort principles to assessing damages in public law. While it must be right for a claimant for constitutional damages to prove that the loss was caused by the breach, it is questionable whether the private law 'but for' test is appropriate when considering public law damages. Even if that test is adopted, it has limited application for awarding damages for purposes other than compensation. Vindication serves to reassert the primary importance of the constitutional rights and to restore public confidence in the efficacy of the constitutional protection. Thus, it is not easy to apply a 'but for' test, or at least one without substantial modification in the context of vindication.

Apart from ensuring a just outcome for a claimant where no other remedy is available, Pearce and Halson argued that vindicatory damages, in the context of contract, are likely to be relevant 'where the breach causes no loss within the conventional meaning of loss, where an award of compensatory damages would be oppressive as regards the defendant, and where an award of compensatory damages will not be an adequate remedy because all or part of the loss caused by the breach is not loss for which the defendant is liable to the claimant'.[91] Vindicatory damages would also be appropriate to ensure that no undue liability is imposed on the defendant. In *Chester v Afshar*,[92] concerning failure to advise of certain risks in a proposed

[88] ibid, at [53].

[89] Donol Nolan argued forcefully that these vindicatory torts should best be approached as public law remedies rather than from a private law perspective: D Nolan, 'Tort and Public Law: Overlapping Categories' (paper presented at the Second Biennial Public Law Conference, Cambridge, 2016).

[90] See below on exemplary damages.

[91] Pearce and Halson (n 81) at 87.

[92] [2005] 1 AC 134.

operation, the House of Lords held that the claim failed as the defendant's breach had not been the effective cause of the injury and it had not been shown that the breach had increased the risk of the injury. However, the House of Lords also believed that the claimant should receive some damages for the failure to give the warning. Pearce and Halson contended that an outright denial of damages would fail to vindicate the right to be warned, but the imposition of liability to compensate for loss which did not arise from the breach was unduly onerous. Thus, a better solution would have been to award vindicatory damages of a fair and reasonable amount to recognise the wrong.[93]

Finally, it is accepted that there is considerable force in the argument that the amount of damages awarded in tort and public law claims should, as a matter of fairness and equity, be comparable when the violation constitutes a concurrent action in tort and in public law. Otherwise, the value of the right, such as personal liberty, would be regarded as of less worth in one action than the other. Yet it does not follow that vindicatory damages in constitutional claims should be rejected simply because they are available in tort. The reverse is equally true. If damages for vindication under vindicatory torts are recognised and available, it is difficult to see why damages for vindication under constitutional claims for the same wrong should not be recognised or available, as long as there is no double recovery. If they are of the same nature and for the same purpose, the objection to vindicatory damages in constitutional claim is one of form rather than substance. The only serious objections are then double recovery, which can be easily taken care of, or redundancy, which rests on the proposition that the principles for awarding damages for vindicatory purposes in tort law are clear, coherent and apposite for remedying a constitutional wrong. As shown above, even if this were true in vindicatory torts, it is far from clear that this is still the case once we move beyond this category of torts.

B. Vindicatory Damages and Exemplary Damages

A second objection to vindicatory damages is that they overlap with exemplary or punitive damages. As exemplary damages and vindicatory damages cannot be awarded concurrently, this reinforces the argument that the purposes of the latter are already served by the availability of the former.[94] Three points can be made in response to this objection.

First, English courts have traditionally been sceptical about exemplary damages which have thus been available only in restricted circumstances.[95] While the House of Lords in *Kuddus v Chief Constable of Leicestershire Constabulary* was prepared to recognise the role of exemplary damages in buttressing civil liberties, and while Lord Nicholls in that case advocated a more liberal approach to the award of exemplary damages, such damages are still confined to occasions where the wrongdoing

[93] ibid, at 98.
[94] See Burrows (n 43) at 305; Varuhas (n 83) at 126–27.
[95] *Rookes v Barnard* [1964] 1 All ER 367.

of a defendant is 'outrageous' or 'contumelious'; exemplary damages remain the 'last resort'.[96] The purpose of exemplary damages is clearly to punish tortfeasors for their outrageous conduct. Thus, they may not be available when a violation of constitutional rights is serious but it is not malicious or capricious. In contrast, it has been repeatedly stressed that the purpose of vindicatory damages is not to punish the wrongdoer, but to assert the primacy of the claimant's rights in society.[97] This is more than a semantic distinction. The different purposes of vindicatory damages and exemplary damages mean that there are circumstances where vindicatory damages are awarded when exemplary damages are not available.[98]

Secondly, it has already been pointed out that tort law and public law are not coterminous. Not all violations of public law would constitute a tortious wrong, and vice versa. In general, tort law is developed in the context of rights and obligations between private individuals. Save in exceptional circumstances or when there are statutory obligations, tort law in general does not impose liabilities for omissions. When it is extended to public authorities, basically the same principles apply. By contrast, public law is concerned with the powers of the State, and the extensive positive duties imposed in public law means that public law liabilities extend beyond the reach of tort law. In general, there is no duty in tort law to provide benefits, nor any duty of care in the exercise of public functions.[99] The *Malone* case is a classic example where tort law was reluctant to impose liabilities.[100] Even in the area of commission, the extent of liabilities is not the same. Tort law is designed to resolve conflicts between rights-holders, whereas public law is designed to supervise the exercise of public powers. Public law is more ready to impose liabilities on the State because of the power of the State over individuals—hence the possibility of relief for systemic failures or maladministration in circumstances in which there can be no parallel liability in tort.[101]

Thirdly, there is of course the option of expanding the scope and availability of exemplary damages. In *Ashley v Chief Constable of Sussex Police*,[102] Lord Scott suggested that vindicatory damages could be awarded in an action for trespass when the purpose of vindication could not be fulfilled by a compensatory award. Yet he spoke with a lone voice. Lords Bingham and Rodger did not mention any additional award. Lord Carswell (in dissent) expressly rejected vindicatory damages in tort, and

[96] [2002] 2 AC 122 at [63]. While the restriction in *AB v South Water Services* [1993] QB 507 was overruled, the House of Lords left open the question of whether exemplary damages were available under the HRA: [46], [92].

[97] See *Attorney General of Trinidad and Tobago v Ramanoop* [2006] 1 AC 328; *Ward* (n 10); *Baigent's Case* (n 29).

[98] See, eg, *Ward* (n 10) in which the court accepted that the strip search was not ill-intended, malicious, high-handed or oppressive, but a result of insensitivity to Charter rights. Same in *Welfare v Kate* (n 60) and *Dunlea* (n 25)

[99] *Rowling v Takaro Properties Ltd* [1988] 1 AC 473. See also Du Bois (n 76).

[100] *Malone v Commissioner of Police of the Metropolis* [1979] Ch 344, where the absence of prohibition of the police to use surveillance device was taken to mean that it was lawful, contrary to the public law principle that all powers of public authorities should derive from the law.

[101] *Harris v Evans* [1998] 1 WLR 1285; *Neil Martin Ltd v Revenue and Customs Commissioners* [2007] All ER (D) 393; *Rabone v Pennine Care NHS Trust* [2012] 2 AC 72.

[102] [2008] 1 AC 962.

Lord Neuberger joined the dissent on the ground that mere vindication was insufficient to justify the pursuit of a claim for trespass. The Law Commission has also recommended an extension of exemplary damages to any tort or equitable wrong case where the defendant's conduct 'showed a deliberate and outrageous disregard of the plaintiff's rights and [when] other remedies … would be inadequate to punish the defendant for his conduct'.[103] The recommendation was not accepted because there was no clear consensus on whether exemplary damages should be abolished or retained.[104] Had this recommendation been accepted, it would have rendered the objection to vindicatory damages in public law one of form rather than substance. Ironically, an expansion of exemplary damages in tort law in one area would make it more difficult to resist its extension to other areas of private law and hence add to the uncertainty, if this were the concern, whereas development of vindicatory damages could avoid such uncertainty as it is possible to confine vindicatory damages to public law. In any event, given the general judicial scepticism towards an expansion of exemplary damages, there is no cause for optimism that the courts would be prepared to expand the scope of exemplary damages.

C. Uncertainty in the Law

In *Lumba*, Lord Collins argued that:[105]

> The implications of awarding vindicatory damages in the present case would be far reaching. Undesirable uncertainty would result. If they were awarded here, then they could in principle be awarded in any case involving a battery or false imprisonment by an arm of the state. Indeed, why limit it to such torts? And why limit it to torts committed by the state? I see no justification for letting such unruly horse loose on our law.

This objection has been partially addressed above in the context of exemplary damages. The concern was the introduction of uncertainty into private law. Yet this is precisely the reason why it is preferable to develop vindicatory damages in public law independently of tort law; the availability of vindicatory damages in public law does not mean that the same damages would have to be made available to private litigants in private law. In assessing vindicatory damages in public law, the court has to balance a range of countervailing factors, including the adequacy of alternative remedies, concern for effective governance and gravity of the violation.[106] The balancing of these different considerations and the ensuing uncertainty are typical in public law but are not necessarily relevant in private law litigation between individuals; the different nature of the claims points to the inappropriateness of extending a public law approach to a tort claim.[107] Developing vindicatory damages in public

[103] Law Commission, *Aggravated, Exemplary and Restitutionary Damages* (Law Commission No 247, 1997), at 4 (hereinafter referred to as 'Law Commission Report 1997').

[104] ibid, at 78–79.

[105] [2012] 1 AC 245 at [101].

[106] *Macklin v New Brunswick (Minister of Finance)* [2002] 1 SCR 405, [79] (Gonthier J).

[107] See Du Bois (n 76).

law would avoid extending these public law considerations to tort or other areas of private law and hence would minimise the ensuing uncertainty. Conversely, Varuhas argued for an extension of the tortious principles in vindicatory tort to the assessment of public law damages.[108] It is a double-edged argument as principles of public law damages may, in turn, affect the development of private law or even impose undue obligations between private parties. As Hardie-Boys J observed in *Baigent's Case*, it may be inappropriate to extend a duty of care only to those classes of people who are subject to the Bill of Rights, yet it is equally unwarranted to extend it universally or even to violations by private individuals.[109] Hence, ironically, the concern for spreading the uncertainty to other branches of private law is a perfect justification for developing and confining vindicatory damages to public law.

D. Arbitrariness

A fourth objection to vindicatory damages is that the award is likely to be arbitrary. However, the fact that it is difficult to assess vindicatory damages is not a reason to reject them out of hand. Non-pecuniary, aggravated and exemplary damages in private law are equally difficult to assess, but the assessment will become more consistent once the court is able to develop precedents. The exercise is not an exact science; the appropriate amount for vindicatory purposes has to be determined by reference to the social, historical and legal contexts of the particular society. In a tort action, the principle for assessing compensatory damages is *restitutio in integrum*, that is, putting the parties into the position they would have been in if the wrong had not been committed. This concept has also been accepted by the ECtHR and there is no doubt that the approach taken by the common law in similar circumstances will be relevant if not also significant when determining the scope of an appropriate remedy in public law. This, however, is subject to the rider that there is no reason to assume that damages in public law have to be confined or limited by what is available in analogous cases at common law or in equity, given the public dimension of a public law action.[110]

On the amount of vindicatory damages, while there are isolated dicta to the effect that the award could be substantial, the experience of those jurisdictions where vindicatory damages have been awarded shows that concern about excessive awards is unfounded. Indeed, there is an emerging judicial consensus that vindicatory damages must not be extravagant, but must be sufficiently significant so as not to trivialise the breach. In vindicating the constitutional rights, the amount would have to be such that a reasonable claimant would feel that it was worth making the claim, taking into account the stress and perhaps the cost involved, as well as the nature of the infringed right, the nature of the breach, the effect on the victim, the other redress

[108] See the well-known decisions in *Roy v Kensington and Chelsea Family Practitioner Committee* [1992] 1 AC 624; *Wandsworth LBC v Winder* [1985] AC 461 at 480.

[109] [1994] NZLR 667 at 693.

[110] See *Taunoa* (n 7) at [323] (Tipping J).

which has been ordered, and the culture of the relevant society. A nominal award usually benefits neither the society nor the individual. In this regard, the helpful judgment of Blanchard J in *Taunoa* deserves closer attention than it has hitherto received.[111] Some breaches, such as a violation of fair hearing, would not normally require non-pecuniary damages other than quashing the impugned decision. In contrast, some breaches, such as torture and inhuman and degrading treatment or punishment, would normally require an additional amount of damages to reflect social abhorrence of such official conduct, taking into account also the intention behind the impugned conduct and the duration of the breach. The quantum of damages must also 'reflect the ways in which the State has acknowledged the wrongdoing; whether, and with what speed, it has brought to an end the wrongful conduct and put in place measures to prevent reoccurrence; and whether it has publicly apologised to the victim in appropriate terms'.[112]

A further objection to vindicatory damages is that if the purpose is to vindicate a wrong and not to compensate the claimant, why should damages be payable to the claimant who would arguably receive a windfall and how to justify different awards for different claimants in similar circumstances?[113] To some extent the same argument could have been made against exemplary damages. It should not be overlooked that the claimant is both an individual victim and a victim as a member of the public. To the extent that the violation happened to him as a member of the public, he does not receive a windfall if the damages represent public abhorrence of what has happened to him. Public law is not just about what the claimant is to receive, which is taken care of by, inter alia, compensatory damages, but also about what the defendant has to pay for the wrong. As vindicatory damages are to reflect public abhorrence of the violation, the extent of public abhorrence will not be affected by the personal characteristics of individual victims, but will depend on the nature, the manner, the gravity and the impact of the violations.[114] Hence, different awards could be justified.

In summary, the assessment of vindicatory damages is not as arbitrary as has been suggested. Just like any exercise in the assessment of damages, absolute certainty is impossible. However, a number of guiding principles have gradually emerged. First, the remedy has to be just and appropriate; vindicatory damages are not always necessary and are to be awarded only when other remedies are inadequate to satisfy the objectives of damages. Secondly, the purpose of damages is to publicly vindicate the right, and not to punish the State or its officials. Thirdly, the quantum is to be determined by reference to the seriousness of the breach, the impact of the breach on the claimant, and the seriousness of the state misconduct. Large awards are generally inappropriate, but the award has to be sufficiently meaningful to represent

[111] ibid, at [253]–[266].
[112] ibid, at [261].
[113] J Edelman, 'The Meaning of Loss and Enrichment', in R Chambers, C Mitchell and J Penner (eds), *Philosophical Foundations of the Law of Unjust Enrichment* (Oxford, Oxford University Press, 2009), 219; Burrows (n 43) at 280.
[114] See Varuhas (n 78); G McLay, 'Tort and Constitutional Damages: Towards a Framework' [2012] *Public Law* 45 at 60.

a serious response to the breach and the objectives of compensation, to uphold the constitutional values and to deter future breaches. Fourthly, given the shared objectives of vindicatory damages in public law and exemplary damages in private law, the established principles in tort law may still be relevant as a guide.

IV. CONCLUSION

Four different approaches to constitutional damages are discernable: the autonomous public law rights-based approach in New Zealand that rejects the relevance of tort law; the composite approach in Canada that retains the autonomous nature of public law claims but draws upon private law principles whenever possible; a parallel approach in South Africa that gives prominence to private law principles but leaves public law damages available as an exception; and approach adopted in the UK, which mirrors ECtHR jurisprudence and rejects vindicatory damages. Notwithstanding these differences, there is, with the exception of the UK, an emerging trend of converging towards the Canadian composite approach, which is a compromise between a strictly public law approach and a strictly private law tort-based approach.

This is a desirable development. The Canadian approach, with minor modifications, could provide a structured and principled approach to public law damages. A breach of constitutional rights is an independent wrong, for which the court has to provide just and appropriate remedies. The courts have a wide discretion to fashion such remedies. It is undesirable to reduce the discretion by straitjacketing damages into existing categories. The Canadian approach recognises three main functions of damages, namely compensation, vindication and deterrence, and builds in a balancing approach that enables countervailing factors to be addressed. The compensation function ensures that the court does not overlook one of the most important objectives of constitutional claims, namely, to protect individual rights, whereas the vindication and deterrence functions ensure that courts address the public dimension of human rights. While affirming constitutional damages as stand-alone damages, the courts stress that it is desirable to draw guidance from tort principles in assessing damages whenever appropriate.

This approach allows the court to fashion the most appropriate remedies in the circumstances of each case, without disturbing the principles of tort law, which applies not only to the State but also among individuals. Simultaneously, it allows cross-pollination of both private law and public law, by providing the necessary degree of certainty while enabling the court to freely develop both branches of law. This approach addresses the shortcomings of both an entirely separate and autonomous public law approach and a full assimilation of tort law and public law remedies, and goes a long way to address some of the objections to vindicatory damages.

However, if the Canadian approach is to be taken as the best model, it needs to be modified (or at least clarified) in five respects. First, compensatory damages should be recognised as a function of damages in public law and their assessment should not be reduced by public policy considerations. Secondly, vindicatory damages are discretionary and should normally be awarded only when other remedies are insufficient to vindicate the constitutional rights. Vindicatory damages are awarded to reflect public disapproval and are additional to compensatory damages. At the same time, there should be no double recovery. Thirdly, the burden of establishing countervailing factors to reduce the amount of vindicatory damages should rest squarely upon the State; proportionality is relevant only at this stage and not the earlier stage whether vindicatory damages are called for. Fourthly, there is no reason in principle why damages should not be awarded for a violation caused by systemic failure, by the judiciary, or by the legislature, although it would be easier for the State to resist an award if the independence of the judiciary is threatened. Fifthly, given that vindicatory damages would inevitably have some deterrent effect, and given the difficulty of disentangling deterrence from vindication, vindicatory damages should serve both purposes and no further damages need be awarded for the purpose of deterrence.

While vindicatory damages bear some similarity to exemplary damages, they are different. Exemplary damages are punitive; vindicatory damages are affirmative. Exemplary damages focus on the conduct of the offender; vindicatory damages focus on the rights violated. Exemplary damages look to past conduct; vindicatory damages are forward-looking, community-based and structural. Instead of tying the hands of the judiciary to the rather restrictive principles for granting exemplary damages, the judiciary must be given a broad discretion to fashion remedies that are appropriate to the context. Thus, exemplary damages should be excluded from public law damages. Vindicatory damages, which should be confined to public law, may play a similar role to exemplary damages in private law, and would no doubt draw upon, but not hampered by, the principles governing the award of exemplary damages. As time passes, they may develop in different directions.

Constitutions can be thought of as living trees that are capable of growth. It has not been seriously argued that substantive constitutional rights should be developed in the same way as similar rights protected by private law. Why, then, should damages be different? Vindicatory damages have their place in public law, as a primary objective of public law is to uphold and vindicate constitutional rights. Ultimately, a fundamental difference underlying the diverse approaches to damages is whether the function of damages is only to compensate for the consequences of a wrong, or whether the violation itself is the wrong that should be regarded as the compensable injury that deserves vindication. Should vindicatory damages be rejected as an unruly horse that threatens to unseat legal certainty? When the European concept of proportionality was first introduced into the common law, it was greeted with skepticism for being unprincipled, subjective and arbitrary. Likewise, public law damages are still in their early days of development. As we embark on this new journey, it is apposite to recall the advice of Lord Nicholls in *Re Spectrum Plus Ltd* regarding declaratory relief in public law that the best approach is probably 'never say never'.[115]

[115] [2005] 2 AC 680 at 699.

17

Decolonising Jurisprudence: Public Interest Standing in New Constitutional Orders

ELIZABETH A O'LOUGHLIN*

THIS CHAPTER EXAMINES the liberalisation of public interest standing in post-colonial common law settings. The value of public interest standing is well known and its potential instrumental effects are of particular import in countries with extensive socio-economic problems. This piece considers a further justification for instituting public interest standing in developing countries: its role in the proliferation of 'indigenous' constitutional jurisprudence that assists in the maturation and diffusion of a new constitutional order. The argument is in two parts. Part I identifies unifying patterns of relaxation in three East African countries (Kenya, Tanzania and Uganda). It links the liberalisation of standing rules in these countries to earlier developments in India, where widening access to the courts was deemed necessary 'having regard to the peculiar socio-economic conditions prevailing in the country where there is considerable poverty, illiteracy and ignorance obstructing and impeding accessibility to the judicial process'.[1] This part will demonstrate how the three countries under examination have borrowed this sociological motivation for such a trend, indicating that there is a coherence of approach amongst post-colonial common law states that face similar socio-economic challenges.

Part II examines the results of public interest litigation generated by the liberalisation of standing rules by focusing more squarely on the impact of this trajectory in Kenya. Kenya's recent journey to constitutional reform has had several

* This chapter was funded by the European Research Council (Advanced Grant 323656-STC), during the course of the author's PhD. The ideas expressed in this chapter were inspired by many discussions and debates had with the project team. I am particularly grateful to Professor Chris Thornhill, acting both as Principal Investigator and PhD supervisor, for his support and guidance, which nurtured this line of enquiry. I am indebted to Dr Joe Tomlinson and Dr Maria Smirnova for immensely helpful suggestions. Naturally, all mistakes are my own.

[1] *People's Union for Democratic Rights and Others v Union of India and Others* AIR 1982 1473 at 1478.

false starts.[2] The protracted process began under the second president of independent Kenya, Daniel Arap Moi. The 1990s saw the reintroduction of multi-party politics, a resurgence of civil society that had long been dormant and the creation of a legislative roadmap for constitutional reform.[3] Concurrently, both the courts and legislature began incrementally to broaden standing, capturing the interests of under- or unrepresented persons and even in some cases creating new categories of interests, thereby articulating new avenues of rights protection. Therefore, while patterns of liberalisation in certain post-colonial settings have aligned, increasing access to courts gives rise to diverse and jurisdiction-specific results. This argument is further exhibited by a tour of the new constitutional dispensation of Kenya. The 2010 Constitution of Kenya, a document enriched with a new Bill of Rights and permeated with international law standards, constitutionally cements broad rules on standing. The chapter argues that this specifically encourages litigation, providing fertile ground for the development of constitutional rights jurisprudence that is 'robust, indigenous, patriotic and progressive'[4] which, in turn, allows the new constitutional order to be diffused and entrenched. There is, then, observable unity in the liberalisation of standing rules in post-colonial East African countries. This, however, ultimately fosters the development and entrenchment of jurisdiction-specific systems of constitutional law, as evidenced by the distillation of the new Kenyan Constitution.

I. PUBLIC INTEREST STANDING IN THE POST-COLONIAL COMMON LAW WORLD

The focus of this chapter is the expansion of the rule of *locus standi* to include public interest standing. A strict conception of public interest litigation is that which is solely based on standing 'in the public interest', meaning that the litigant bringing the action has no direct connection to the alleged interest that has been infringed. Cases to this effect will be analysed in this chapter. However, to enrich the argument, other cases that are not based exclusively in the public interest will also be analysed, as these add to the corpus of 'public interest law' that is encouraged by relaxed rules on standing. These include third party standing actions and collective actions that are instituted to promote social change and to represent the under-represented and minorities. Such proceedings are often advanced with the aid of public interest lawyers, such as Civil Society Organisations (CSOs), activists, or Non-Governmental

[2] Since gaining independence from Britain in December 1963, the Republic of Kenya has had three draft and three realised constitutions: Constitution of the Republic of Kenya 1963 ('Independence Constitution'); Constitution of the Republic of Kenya (as amended by the Constitution of Kenya Act 1969, No 5 of 1969); Draft Constitution of Kenya 2004 ('Bomas Draft'); Proposed Constitution of Kenya 2005 ('Wako Draft'); Proposed Constitution of Kenya 2010; and Constitution of Kenya 2010.

[3] GR Murunga and SW Nasong'o (eds), *Kenya: The Struggle for Democracy* (London, Zed Books 2007); D Throup and C Hornsby, *Multi-Party Politics in Kenya: The Kenyatta and Moi States and the Triumph of the System in the 1992 Election* (Oxford, James Currey, 1998); The Constitution of Kenya Review Act 1997, No 13 of 1997.

[4] Supreme Court of Kenya, *Judiciary Transformation Framework 2012–2016*, 11 <www.judiciary.go.ke/portal/assets/downloads/reports/Judiciary's%20Tranformation%20Framework-fv.pdf>.

Organisations (NGOs), and the actions are 'directed at altering some aspect of the social, economic, and political status quo'.[5] The Indian Supreme Court has stated the difference between traditional adjudication and public interest litigation as follows:

> In a public interest litigation, unlike traditional dispute resolution mechanisms, there is no determination or adjudication of individual rights. While in the ordinary conventional adjudications the party structure is merely bi-polar ... and the remedy is essentially linked to and limited by the logic of the array of the parties, in a public interest action the proceedings cut across and transcend these traditional forms and inhibitions. The compulsions for the judicial innovation of the technique of a public interest action is the constitutional promise of a social and economic transformation to usher in an egalitarian social order and a welfare State. Effective solutions to the problems peculiar to this transformation are not available in the traditional judicial system. The proceedings in a public interest litigation are, therefore, intended to vindicate and effectuate the public interest by prevention of violation of the rights, constitutional or statutory, of sizeable segments of society, which owing to poverty, ignorance, social and economic disadvantages cannot themselves assert—and quite often are not even aware of—those rights. The technique of public interest litigation serves to provide an effective remedy to enforce these group-rights and interests.[6]

The value of public interest litigation, then, is to protect the rights and interests of many. The non-traditional nature of the dispute affords courts the power to remedy more than a single wrong, advancing broader societal change through their judgments. This expansion of standing to capture the interests of the under- or unrepresented is by no means a new phenomenon. Nor is it particular to post-colonial countries.[7] This part will navigate some of the developments in standing in the common law world, before underlining the notable departure of India from the trend. It underlines the parallels in the development of the rule in three East African states.

A. India and the Judicial Development of Public Interest Standing

Traditionally, standing requires a party to demonstrate sufficient connection to the harm for which they are instituting proceedings. In English law, the requirement that applicants for judicial review must prove 'sufficient interest'[8] in a matter to have standing has been interpreted somewhat inconsistently,[9] though over the decades the

[5] A Sarat and S Scheingold, 'Cause Lawyering and the Reproduction of Professional Authority: An Introduction' in A Sarat and S Scheingold (eds), *Cause Lawyering: Political Commitments and Professional Responsibilities* (Oxford, OUP, 1998) 3, 4. See also Note, 'The New Public Interest Lawyers' (1970) 79 *Yale Law Journal* 1069.

[6] *Sheela Barse v Union of India and Others* 1988 AIR 2211.

[7] K Groenendijk, 'Litigation, Politics and Publicity: Public Interest Law or How to Share the Burden of Change' (1985) 14 *Anglo American Law Review* 337. Groenendijk outlines the relaxation of rules on standing in the Netherlands.

[8] Senior Courts Act 1981, s 31(3).

[9] In *Arsenal Football Club v Ende* [1979] AC 1, the House of Lords held that a ratepayer had 'sufficient interest' to challenge the undervaluation of another property in the same area. See *R v Inland Revenue Commissioners ex parte National Federation of Self-employed Small Businesses Ltd* [1982] AC 617 (the 'Fleet Street Casuals' case).

courts' approach has generally been increasingly liberal.[10] To a limited but growing degree, it seems that the English courts will find standing where matters of public importance are raised, though standing has never expressly been allowed solely in the public interest. Courts will generally endeavour to construe standing by finding some 'sufficient interest', even if that interest is grounded in the expertise of a pressure group, CSO or NGO.[11] In Canada, public interest standing to protect fundamental rights evolved through three cases that pre-date the Canadian Charter of Rights and Freedoms enshrined under the 1982 Canadian Constitution.[12] A post-Charter case summarises a three-part test for public interest standing:

> First, is there a serious issue raised as to the invalidity of legislation in question? Second, has it been established that the plaintiff is directly affected by the legislation or, if not, does the plaintiff have a genuine interest in its validity? Third, is there another reasonable and effective way to bring the issue before the court?[13]

Through the incremental relaxation of the rule in English law, and the creation of public interest standing in Canadian law, the courts still search for some continuity with the traditional strict rules. In English law, finding standing for pressure groups has rested on their relative expertise in a matter or whether a portion of their membership is directly affected, thereby constructing some connection to the substance of the challenge. For example, in *R v Inspectorate of Pollution ex parte Greenpeace*, Greenpeace sought judicial review of a decision to grant applications to British Nuclear Fuels plc to discharge radioactive waste at its premises in Sellafield, Cumbria. Otton J noted that '[t]he fact that there are 400,000 supporters in the United Kingdom carries less weight than the fact that 2,500 of them come from the Cumbria region', thereby interpreting Greenpeace as legitimate representatives of directly affected parties.[14] In both jurisdictions, a broadened approach to standing has crystallised where there was no person sufficiently directly affected to bring the suit.[15] Therefore, the judicial relaxation of public interest standing has been formulated with reference to the original strict application of the rule.

Elsewhere in the common law world, rather than searching to reconcile liberalised *locus standi* with the existing rules, public interest standing has been judicially

[10] In *R v Her Majesty's Treasury ex parte Smedley* [1985] QB 657, the claimant had standing to bring to the attention of the Court of Appeal questions over the legality of payments by the Treasury to the European Community, given the seriousness and urgency of the claim. See also *R v Secretary of State for Foreign Affairs ex parte Rees-Mogg* [1994] QB 552.

[11] *R v Inspectorate of Pollution ex parte Greenpeace (No 2)* [1994] 4 All ER 329. See also: *R v Secretary of State for Social Services, ex parte Child Action Poverty Group* [1990] 2 QB 540; *R v Secretary of State for the Environment ex parte Rose Theatre Trust* [1990] 1 QB 504.

[12] *Thorson v Canada (Attorney General)* [1975] 1 SCR 138; *MacNeil v Nova Scotia (Board of Censors)* [1976] 2 SCR 265; *Canada (Minister of Justice) v Borowski* [1981] 2 SCR 575.

[13] *Canadian Council of Churches v Canada (Minister of Employment and Immigration)* [1992] 1 SCR 236.

[14] *R v Inspectorate of Pollution ex parte Greenpeace* (n 11) at 350.

[15] *Thorson v Canada (Attorney General)* (n 12) (the case concerned the constitutional validity of the Official Languages Act, which was neither regulatory nor penal, but merely declaratory) and *R v Secretary of State for Foreign and Commonwealth Affairs ex parte World Development Movement Ltd* [1995] 1 WLR 386.

developed in a manner that completely departs from the traditional position. As the remaining portion of this part will show, public interest litigation is generally much wider in substance in post-colonial settings. Public interest standing plays a far more vital role than just in instances where there is no identifiable person or group of persons directly aggrieved or harmed. Indeed, the square focus of the trend towards relaxation of rules of standing in the post-colonial world has been to facilitate the defence of the vulnerable in general. It is concerned with furthering socio-economic change, tackling fundamental societal inequalities and giving both a platform and a voice to the marginalised and disadvantaged.

India is the leading and paradigmatic example of judicial jettisoning of standing limitations.[16] Though the Constitution of India does not contain a clause relating to standing, the courts' initial strict approach[17] has been gradually relaxed, and they have found broad standing rights *suo motu*. In *Fertilizer Corporation Kamgar Union v Union of India*,[18] the Supreme Court tentatively set the stage for a new, much broader view of standing, moving beyond habeas corpus or *relator* action petitions.[19] Chandrachud CJ, in the majority, opined that 'in an appropriate case, it may become necessary in the changing awareness of legal rights and social obligations to take a broader view of the question of *locus* to initiate a proceeding'.[20] The concurring opinion of Krishna Iver and Bhagwati JJ noted that Chandrachud CJ's approach 'with its fascinating expansionism, is of strategic significance, viewed in the perspective of Third World jurisprudence'.[21] The Justices recognised the necessity of departing from the Anglo-American legal tradition to meet the demands of development: '*locus standi* must be liberalised to meet the challenges of the times'.[22] In so doing, the Justices specifically underline the sociological motivation behind relaxing the rules on standing. In a country facing such challenges as India, slackening standing rules is a mechanism that enables the courts to monitor and ensure public accountability, while also affording effective access to justice—an important requirement in a country with such rampant socio-economic inequality and poverty.

[16] See, eg, U Baxi, 'Taking Suffering Seriously: Social Action Litigation in the Supreme Court of India' (1985) 4 *Third World Legal Studies* 107; PP Craig and SL Deshpande, 'Rights, Autonomy and Process: Public Interest Litigation in India' (1989) 9 *OJLS* 356; and J Cassels, 'Judicial Activism and Public Interest Litigation in India: Attempting the Impossible?' (1989) 37 *American Journal of Comparative Law* 495.

[17] See *Chiranjit Lal Chowdhuri v Union of India and Others* 1951 AIR 41, where it was held that only one whose rights had been directly affected by a law could approach the Court to question the constitutionality of said law.

[18] *Fertilizer Corporation Kamgar Union, Sindri and Others v Union of India and Others* 1981 AIR 344.

[19] See *Sunil Batra v Delhi Administration and Others* 1978 AIR 1675 and *Hussainara Khatoon and Others v Home Secretary, State of Bihar* 1979 AIR 1369.

[20] See *Fertilizer Corporation Kamgar Union* (n 18).

[21] ibid (concurring opinion of Krishna Iver and Bhagwati JJ).

[22] ibid. This attitude of the Supreme Court had been developing for some time. In *Bar Council of Maharashtra v MV Dabholkar* 1976 AIR 242, Krishna Iyer VR observed that '[t]raditionally ... we search for individual persons aggrieved. But a new class of litigation—public interest litigation— ... emerges ... [i]n a developing country like ours'. See also *Municipal Council, Ratlam v Shri Vardhichand and Others* 1980 AIR 1622.

By 1982 the Supreme Court of India altogether dismissed a traditional approach to the rules on standing, spearheaded by Bhagwati J of the very same concurring opinion discussed above, in *SP Gupta v President of India and Others*.[23] The case concerned the 1975 state of emergency declared in India by Prime Minister Indira Gandhi, which suspended virtually all civil and political rights.[24] Judges who objected were transferred to different locations. In this case, the Court awarded standing to advocates who had filed petitions reviewing those transfers. Bhagwati J found that the advocates had standing, as they were 'vitally interested in the maintenance of a fearless and an independent Judiciary'.[25] Bhagwati J took the opportunity to settle that:

> Where the weaker sections of the community are concerned … who are helpless victims of an exploitative society and who do not have easy access to justice … The Court would … unhesitatingly and without the slightest qualms of conscience cast aside the technical rules of procedure … and treat the letter of the public minded individual as a writ petition and act upon it. Today a vast revolution is taking place in the judicial process; the theatre of the law is fast changing and the problems of the poor are coming to the forefront.[26]

Here Bhagwati J carried further the tone set in *Fertilizer Corporation Kamagar Union v Union of India*, that relaxing *locus standi* and allowing for public interest litigation was paramount to foster social justice and bring about socio-economic change, for individual rights under Part III of the Constitution were meaningless 'unless accompanied by the social rights necessary to make them effective and really accessible to all'.[27]

The creation of public interest litigation by the Indian Supreme Court in the 1980s has since been used to permit bystander standing, securing a court platform for such voiceless groups as migrant labourers,[28] bonded labourers,[29] and children.[30] The model of public interest litigation has birthed a flood of social action jurisprudence that has seen the courts charge the state with positive obligations to effect economic, social and cultural rights (ESC rights).[31] The Indian Supreme Court has specifically invoked a need to create public interest standing that departs from the Anglo-American tradition in order to respond to the distinctive socio-economic

[23] *SP Gupta v President of India and Others* 1982 AIR 149.

[24] Emergency Proclamation of 25 June 1975.

[25] See *SP Gupta* (n 23) (pinpoint citation unavailable).

[26] ibid.

[27] ibid.

[28] See *People's Union for Democratic Rights* (n 1).

[29] *Bandhua Mukti Morcha v Union of India and Others* 1984 AIR 802.

[30] *Lakshmi Kant Pandey v Union of India* 1984 AIR 469.

[31] See *Olga Tellis and Others v Bombay Municipal Corporation and Others* 1986 AIR 180 on the right to livelihood and the right to work; *Vishaka and Others v State of Rajasthan and Others* [1997] INSC 665 on the working rights of women; and *Consumer Education and Research Centre and Others v Union of India and Others* [1995] 1995 AIR 922 on the right to health. It is well recorded that the doctrine of public interest standing in India has been a victim of its own success. The courts have an astronomical backlog of more than 30 million cases, many of which will be litigants seeking to enforce social rights. This has led to the creation of a Social Justice Bench of the Supreme Court to tackle delays on issues of pressing social need. See GN Gill and S Luthra, 'The Social Justice Bench of the Supreme Court of India: A New Development' [2016] *Public Law* 392; and A Khanna, 'Public Interest Litigation: The Interminable Wait for Justice' *Down To Earth* (15 August 1992).

challenges that India faces. Bhagwati J publicly stated that the US model of public interest litigation is 'not a model that can be transplanted to developing countries like India'.[32] Indeed, the US model, not unlike the English and Canadian tradition, limits such actions to allow representation to those seeking to defend interests that do not attach to groups, such as environmentalism.[33] This is not unusual: across the world and particularly for the interests of this chapter, in many African states, protection of environmental interests has predicated trends to broaden standing.[34] Some states have followed the trajectory of India, however, by widening access to the courts to not simply deal in matters where there is no discernable person aggrieved, but also to enable the courts to respond to the most pressing matters of social concern in their jurisdiction, by allowing any litigant with an interest in upholding the constitution standing.

B. India's Legacy: Unifying Approaches to Standing in East Africa

The influence that India's approach to public interest litigation has had on East Africa is palpable, evidenced both by some express citation of Indian jurisprudence and by the invocation of strikingly similar justifications for liberalising standing requirements. In three East African states—Kenya, Tanzania, and Uganda—relaxation of standing followed a very similar trajectory. In each state, the judiciary slackened standing requirements to protect the right to a healthy environment. As noted above, this is not an unusual starting point. What is noteworthy is that in all three countries this has given rise to further judicial slackening to protect fundamental rights and freedoms.

Prior to the promulgation of a new constitutional order in Kenya in 2010, the use of public interest litigation to secure fundamental rights compliance was not widespread. The now-repealed Constitution of Kenya 1969 made no explicit provision for standing in the public interest, granting it only where a contravention related to either a petitioner personally or a detainee.[35] Under the Moi regime in the late 1980s and early 1990s the approach of the courts was to deny *locus standi* to a private individual who sought to sue in the public interest, unless the applicant could prove that they had sustained a personal injury as a result of the public wrong. This has been viewed by some as a tactic used by judges wishing to remain in favour with

[32] PN Bhagwati, 'Judicial Activism and Public Interest Litigation' (1984–85) 23 *Columbia Journal of Transnational Law* 561 at 569.

[33] JP Dwyer, 'Contentiousness and Cooperation in Environmental Regulation' (1987) 35 *American Journal of Comparative Law* 809.

[34] LJ Kotzé and AR Paterson (eds), *The Role of the Judiciary in Environmental Governance: Comparative Perspectives* (Alphen aan den Rijn, Kluwer Law International, 2009); EP Amechi, 'Strengthening Environmental Public Interest Litigation through Citizen Suits in Nigeria: Learning from the South African Environmental Jurisprudential Development' (2015) 23 *African Journal of International and Comparative Law* 383.

[35] Constitution of the Republic of Kenya 1969 (repealed), s 84(1): if 'any of the provisions of Section 70 to 83 (inclusive) has been, is being or is likely to be contravened in relation to him (or in the case of a person who is detained, if another person alleges a contravention in relation to the detained person), then, without prejudice to any other action with respect to the same matter which is lawfully available, that person (or that other person) may apply to the High Court for redress'.

Moi by stifling opposition politics and voices in the wake of the reintroduction of multi-party politics.[36] It is clearly demonstrated through the decision of Dugdale J—infamous for repressing constitutional litigation at the preliminary objection stage—in *Maathai v Kenya Times Media Trust Ltd*.[37] The applicant sought a temporary injunction restraining the defendant from constructing new headquarters for the ruling Kenya African National Union (KANU) party on Uhuru Park in Nairobi. Dugdale J mechanistically applied the narrow English common law position found in *Gouriet v Union of Post Office Workers*, that 'private rights can be asserted by individuals, but, ... public rights can only be asserted by the Attorney General as representing the public'[38] and dismissed the application.[39] This automatous application of the rule that only the Attorney General could bring an action in the public interest was commonplace.[40] The continued adherence to older principles of English law was the norm long after independence was achieved in many African states, given the continued dominance of foreign or indigenous judges who had completed their training in the United Kingdom or India.[41] Further, the independence Constitutions of East African states entrenched the English common law approach.[42] There were, however, notable deviations from this position. In *Kamanda and Another v Nairobi City Council and Another*,[43] Akiwumi J found that Nairobi residents, as ratepayers, had sufficient interest to challenge a public body in court where they contribute to their expenses, relying upon *R v Greater London Council ex parte Blackburn*.[44] The judgment then went one step further, by explicitly endorsing the approach of Lord Diplock in *R v Inland Revenue Commissioners ex parte National Federation of Self-employed and Small Businesses Ltd*,[45] that '[i]t would ... be a grave lacuna in our system of public law if a pressure group ... or even a single public-spirited taxpayer, were prevented by outdated technical rules of *locus standi* from bringing the matter to the attention of the court to vindicate the rule of law and get the unlawful conduct stopped'.[46]

[36] M Mutua, 'Justice under Siege: The Rule of Law and Judicial Subservience in Kenya' (2001) 23 *Human Rights Quarterly* 96; P Kameri-Mbote and M Akech, 'Kenya: Justice Sector and the Rule of Law, A Review by AfriMAP and the Open Society Initiative for Eastern Africa' (March 2011) 36. Available at: <www.opensocietyfoundations.org/sites/default/files/kenya-justice-law-20110315.pdf>.

[37] *Maathai v Kenya Times Media Trust Ltd* [1989] eKLR.

[38] *Gouriet v Union of Post Office Workers and Others* [1978] AC 435 at 477.

[39] See *Maathai* (n 37) (pinpoint citation unavailable).

[40] See also *Jaramogi Oginga Odinga and Three Others v Zachariah Richard Chesoni and The Attorney General* [1992] eKLR; *Wangari Maathai and Two Others v City Council of Nairobi and Two Others* (1994) 1 KLR.

[41] A Aguda, 'The Judge in Developing Countries', Nigerian Institute of Advanced Legal Studies, University of Lagos Occasional Paper No 6 (1980) at 6–7.

[42] YP Ghai and JPWB McAuslan, *Public Law and Political Change in Kenya: A Study of the Legal Framework of Government from Colonial Times to the Present* (Oxford, Oxford University Press, 1970) 374–80; see more generally R Ellet, *Pathways to Judicial Power in Transitional States: Perspectives from African Courts* (London, Routledge, 2013).

[43] *Maina Kamanda and Another v Nairobi City Council and Another* (1992) 1 KLR. See also *Niaz Mohamed Jan Mohamed v Commissioner of Lands and Four Others* [1996] eKLR, where Waki J rejected the rule that only the Attorney General can sue in the public interest.

[44] *R v Greater London Council ex parte Blackburn* [1976] 1 WLR 550.

[45] See *R v Inland Revenue Commissioners ex parte National Federation of Self-employed and Small Businesses Ltd* (n 9).

[46] ibid, at 644; see *Maina Kamanda* (n 43) (pinpoint citation unavailable).

A liberal construction of *locus standi* was statutorily conferred on individuals to enforce environmental rights through the Environment Management and Coordination Act (EMCA) 1999.[47] Section 111 reads: '(2) For the avoidance of doubt, it shall not be necessary for a plaintiff under this section to show that he has a right or interest in the property, environment or land alleged to have been or likely to be harmed.' Waki J has since opined that 'the ogre of *locus standi*, which for a long time shackled Courts of Law, must be tamed. Happily, it was expressly tamed by Parliament in the ... Environmental Management and Co-ordination Act'.[48] By the early 2000s there was also some evidence of judicial relaxation of the rule in relation to the Constitution and rights enforcement,[49] though this approach was not commonplace amongst all judges.[50] The law on standing has since been settled by the new Constitution of Kenya, which provides that every person has the right to approach the court where a right or fundamental freedom contained in the Bill of Rights has been violated and that such proceedings may be brought by a person acting in the public interest, thereby enshrining the procedural novelties of the EMCA into the Constitution and extending their application to its protection and enforcement.[51]

Tanzania's Constitution allows a broad standing clause, stipulating that 'every person has the right, in accordance with the procedure provided by law, to take legal action to ensure the protection of this Constitution and the laws of the land',[52] implicitly setting the scene for a relaxed approach to standing, though it does not explicitly expand on the matter of whether such legal action can be instigated in the public interest.

Nonetheless, a mixed approach to public interest standing has developed in the case law, with headway being made in the area of environmental law even earlier than in Kenya. In 1988, despite the fact that at the time there was no provision in Tanzanian law, statutory or otherwise, for the right to a 'clean and healthy environment', the High Court found that the dumping and burning of waste on a refuse site close to residential area where plaintiffs resided, posed a danger to life.[53] In 1991, applying the previous case, the High Court of Tanzania granted standing to

[47] Environment Management and Coordination Act (EMCA) 1999 (Cap 387) (Kenya).

[48] *Insurance Company of East Africa v Attorney General and Three Others* [2001] eKLR (pinpoint citation unavailable).

[49] In *Ruturi and Another v Minister of Finance and Another* [2001] 1 EA 253 at 263, it was held by the High Court sitting as a constitutional court that 'as part of a reasonable, fair and just procedure to uphold the constitutional guarantees, the right of access to justice entails a liberal approach to the question of *locus standi*'.

[50] See *Law Society of Kenya v Commissioner of Lands and Two Others* [2001] eKLR.

[51] Constitution of Kenya 2010, Art 22. This standing provision is mirrored in Art 258, 'Enforcement of this Constitution', which empowers every person to institute court proceedings where the Constitution has allegedly been contravened.

[52] Constitution of the United Republic of Tanzania 1977, Art 26(2).

[53] *Joseph D Kessy and Others v The City Council of Dar es Salaam*, Civil Case No 299 of 1988 (unreported). See also 'The Right to a Clean and Satisfactory Environment' in C Maina Peter, *Human Rights in Tanzania: Selected Cases and Materials* (Cologne, Rüdiger Köppe Verlag, 1997) 149. It is not uncommon for the right to a clean and healthy environment to be connected to the right to life. For example, the Supreme Court of Nepal recognised that 'environmental conservation is indirectly related with life of the human being': *Suray Prasad Sharma Dhungel v Godavari Marble Industries and Others* Writ Petition No 35 of the year 2049 (1992) (pinpoint citation unavailable).

795 plaintiffs who were challenging the respondent's use of a residential area as a refuse dumping site.[54]

The Tanzanian courts also judicially relaxed standing rules where fundamental rights were at stake in the groundbreaking decision of *Christopher Mtikila v Attorney General.*[55] The petitioner, a 'human rights campaigner-cum-political activist', contended that a number of constitutional and legislative amendments curtailed his constitutional rights to participation in national public affairs and to freedom of association. In granting the applicant public interest standing, Lugakingira J carefully studied the swell of public interest litigation in India and Canada in the 1980s. The judgment made important pronouncements on the necessity of public interest litigation in relation to the country's socio-economic conditions, in a manner very reminiscent of the jurisprudence liberalising the rule in India, and explicitly referenced the development of public interest litigation in India and Canada. Declaring a bar on independent candidates for election unconstitutional, it was held that:

> The relevance of public interest litigation in Tanzania cannot be over-emphasized. Having regard to our socio-economic conditions, this development promises more hope to our people than any other strategy currently in place. First of all, illiteracy is still rampant … By reason of this illiteracy a greater part of the population is unaware of their rights, let alone how the same can be realised. Secondly, Tanzanians are massively poor … Public interest litigation is a sophisticated mechanism which requires professional handling. By reason of limited resources the vast majority of our people cannot afford to engage lawyers … Other factors could be listed but perhaps the most painful of all is that over the years since independence Tanzanians have developed a culture of apathy and silence. This, in large measure, is a product of institutionalised mono-party politics which in its repressive dimension, like detention without trial, supped up initiative and guts … Given all these … circumstances, if there should spring up a public-spirited individual … the Court, as guardian and trustee of the Constitution and what it stands for, is under an obligation to rise up to the occasion and grant him standing.[56]

Just as in Kenya, before the matter was settled by a new Constitution, however, the courts continue to oscillate on the matter of public interest standing.[57] The right to a 'clean, safe and healthy environment' was finally legislatively protected in an Environmental Management Act in 2004 although, unlike its Kenyan counterpart, it makes no provision waiving the requirement to show direct harm or interest.[58]

The Ugandan constitutional framework for access to the courts, like the new Kenyan provisions, directly provides for third-party standing, affording that '[a]ny person who claims that a fundamental or other right or freedom guaranteed under this Constitution has been infringed or threatened, is entitled to apply to a

[54] *Festo Balegele and 794 others v Dar es Salaam City Council*, Misc Civil Cause No 90 of 1991 (unreported).

[55] *Christopher Mtikila v Attorney General*, Civil Case No 5 of 1993 (unreported).

[56] ibid (pinpoint citation unavailable).

[57] See *Southern Region Development Authority (SRDA) v Attorney General and Three Others*, 1997 (unreported); but *cf Felix Joseph Mavika et al v The Dar es Salaam City Council*, Civil Case No 316 of 2000 (unreported).

[58] Environmental Management Act 2004, Act No 20 of 2004, Art 4(1).

competent court for redress which may include compensation ... [a]ny person or organisation may bring an action against the violation of another person's or group's human rights'.[59] In the field of environmental protection, the 1995 National Environment Act 'empowers any person to apply for an environmental restoration order even though such person is not suffering any harm and has no interest in the land in issue'.[60] Notably, the 1995 Ugandan Constitution explicitly provides for the right to a 'clean and healthy environment'.[61] In spite of these rather liberal provisions, the courts were initially reluctant to find standing in the public interest.[62] However, in *The Environmental Action Network v Attorney General*, the High Court granted standing to an NGO seeking protection of the rights to a clean and healthy environment and to life (Article 22 of the Constitution of Uganda) in the public interest.[63] The High Court specifically invoked the reasoning of Lugakingira J in the Tanzanian *Mtikila* case to buttress its claim that in the arena of fundamental rights protection, technical procedural rules should not be a barrier to standing. The Ugandan High Court has used environmental cases to follow the Tanzanian precedent in *Mtikila* and to cement a liberal approach to public interest standing, both to protect environmental rights and fundamental rights more generally, for to say that the Ugandan constitution 'does not recognize the existence of needy and oppressed persons and therefore cannot allow actions of public interest groups to be brought on their behalf is to demean the Constitution'.[64]

As in public interest standing developments in the western world, then, there has been a tendency toward a relaxed approach in environmental rights cases in East Africa. It is of particular significance to afford protection to the environment in East Africa, where terrain is endowed with natural resources that are enriched with forests, minerals, lakes, rivers, wildlife and fisheries. In such nations there is a tendency toward policies that promote economic development at all costs; degradation and exploitation of this range of natural resources is a real and present threat that judiciaries and governments are grappling to account for.[65] The trend in the west has been to substantiate similar judicial relaxation by attempting to reconcile it with the traditional restrictions on standing.[66] Rather than search for jurisprudential continuity in the rules on standing, however, the courts of these three East African states have utilised its relaxation in environmental matters as a stepping stone to a general broadening of access to courts, even where liberal environmental standing has been

[59] Constitution of the Republic of Uganda 1995, Arts 50(1) and (2).

[60] National Environment Act, Cap 153, s 71.

[61] Constitution of the Republic of Uganda 1995, Art 39.

[62] See *James Rwanyarare and Another v Attorney General* [1997] UGCC 1, where the court averred that '[w]e cannot accept the argument ... that any spirited person can represent any group of persons without their knowledge or consent'.

[63] *The Environmental Action Network v Attorney General and Another*, Misc Application No 39 of 2001 (unreported).

[64] *British American Tobacco Ltd v The Environmental Action Network*, Misc Application No 27 of 2003 (unreported) (pinpoint citation unavailable).

[65] P Kameri-Mbote and C Odote, 'Courts as Champions of Sustainable Development: Lessons from East Africa' (2009) 10 *Sustainable Development Law and Policy* 31.

[66] See n 15 above.

legislatively arranged. There is an obvious coherence in approach among the three judiciaries and this is clearly underpinned by the very same socio-economic drivers that gave rise to the birth of public interest standing in India. We see, then, that in the case studies advanced here, there are parallels both in development and justification of public interest standing, which is evidenced by a high degree of transnational judicial dialogue between the four jurisdictions.[67] As in India, the East African courts have broken away from a traditional standing framework following the same pattern and by invoking a desire to provide tailored solutions that respond to the socio-economic challenges of each jurisdiction. As such, in India, public interest standing is required to foster social justice in a rampantly unequal society; in Tanzania, to challenge a repressive state; in Uganda, to represent the needy and oppressed.

II. PUBLIC INTEREST STANDING IN KENYA: THE RESULTS

This part will study the impact that the liberalisation of standing has had in Kenya, both prior to and after the promulgation of a new Constitution in 2010. This trend crystallised in conjunction with the acceleration of constitutional reform efforts in Kenya. The narrow approach to standing was maintained in an era of repression provided by both the regimes of Moi and independence President Jomo Kenyatta, under which a multitude of CSOs, academics, intellectuals and human rights activists were incarcerated.[68] Throughout the 1990s, there was strong agitation for constitutional reform, a resurgent civil society and a reluctant reintroduction to multi-party politics under Moi, which to a large extent was influenced by international pressure.[69] In this socio-political environment, broadened rules on standing were legislatively framed for environmental rights. The multi-party general election of 2002 was underscored by active agitation for constitutional reform, something that formed the basis of the victorious ticket for Mwai Kibaki. The courts were alive to the fact that the results of the general election ushered in an era where citizens felt they could actively petition for their rights without fear of reprisal. The High Court of Kenya, sitting as a constitutional court, in *Ruturi v Minister of Finance*, cemented this:

> In ... public interest litigation ... the procedural trappings and restrictions, the pre-conditions of being an aggrieved person and other similar technical objections cannot bar the jurisdiction of the court, or let justice bleed at the altar of technicality ... We state a firm conviction, that as part of a reasonable, fair and just procedure to uphold the constitutional guarantees, the right of access to justice entails a liberal approach to the question of *locus standi*. Accordingly, in constitutional questions, human rights cases, public

[67] A Slaughter, 'Judicial Globalization' (2000) 40 *Virginia Journal of International Law* 1003.

[68] W Mutunga, *Constitution-making from the Middle: Civil Society and Transitional Politics in Kenya, 1992–1997* (Nairobi/Harare, Sareat/Mwengo, 1999); W Mutunga, 'The 2010 Constitution of Kenya: Its Vision of A New Bench-Bar Relationship' in YP Ghai and J Cottrell Ghai (eds), *The Legal Profession and The New Constitutional Order in Kenya* (Nairobi, Strathmore University Press, 2014) 59.

[69] M Akech and P Kameri-Mbote, 'Kenyan Courts and the Politics of the Rule of Law in the Post-Authoritarian State from 1991–2010' (2012) 18(2) *East African Journal of Peace and Human Rights* 357 at 372.

> interest litigation and class actions, the ordinary Anglo-Saxon jurisprudence, that an action can be brought only by a person to whom legal injury is caused, must be departed from … We must … do justice according to the law in the context of our socio-cultural environment.[70]

Just as in the *Mtikila* case of Tanzania, this line of jurisprudential rationale is remarkably resonant of the Indian Supreme Court's approach to the rule. This has resulted in standing requirements in Kenya being jettisoned both by legislation in environmental cases (as advanced above) and by the courts in public interest matters, in particular where questions of constitutional validity or human rights infringements arise. This part will elucidate how under the old constitutional dispensation, the introduction of public interest standing garnered remarkable, though not widespread, results that have seen the courts seize the opportunity to nurture its own approach to rights and constitutional protection. The chapter will then conclude with an overview of the function of public interest standing in the new constitutional order promulgated in 2010. It will be seen that constitutionally entrenching broad access to courts, in conjunction with inserting international law as a valid source of law in the new constitutional order, is acting as a vehicle to promote a transformation of Kenyan law.

A. Judicial Review of Constitutional Reform: Constitutional Litigation in the Public Interest

Following the 1997 general elections, the Kenyan Parliament passed a legislative roadmap for constitutional reform and created the Constitution of Kenya Review Commission.[71] The Commission wrote a draft Constitution—the 'Bomas Draft'—which was approved at a National Constitutional Conference (NCC) in April 2003. In the public interest case of *Timothy Njoya v Attorney General*, the court was tasked with determining the constitutionality of Parliament's power to pass a new Constitution enacted at the NCC on the grounds that to do so circumvented the Kenyan people's right to a referendum on any new constitution.[72] *Njoya* ultimately saw the Constitutional Review Act declared unconstitutional, because the repealed Constitution only provided for Parliament to amend the existing constitution. Further, Ringera J found that the constituent power of the people conferred on them a right to vote in a referendum on any new constitution.[73]

This judicial intervention in the constitutional reform process came at a time when it had reached political deadlock[74] and by compelling the need for a referendum, made a bold step towards adopting a culture of constitutionalism that has at times

[70] See *Ruturi* (n 49) at 262–63; see also *Khelef Khalifa El Busaidy v Commissioner of Lands and Two Others* [2002] eKLR.

[71] Constitution of Kenya Review Act 1997, No 13 of 1997.

[72] *Njoya and Others v Attorney General and Others* (2004) AHRLR 157.

[73] ibid, at [32].

[74] E Kramon and DN Posner, 'Kenya's New Constitution' (2011) 22(2) *Journal of Democracy* 89.

been overwhelmingly lacking in the Kenyan judiciary.[75] The judgment was groundbreaking in approach and coverage, ultimately concluding that a national referendum on any new constitutional document was compulsory for the Kenyan people to exercise their constituent power.[76] Though the court boldly cited international law provisions raised by the applicants,[77] Ringera J reached his conclusions about the people's right to a referendum with no regard paid to the potential protection of this right in international human rights instruments.[78] Instead, the Court considered the particular value that a referendum would have in a 'multi-ethnic society such as [Kenya] which is still struggling towards a sense of common nationality and unity of purpose, [where] it is important that all tribes should participate in the process of constitution-making so that they can all own the Constitution which will be the glue binding them together'.[79] This recalls the distinctive challenges Kenya faces in finding a cohesive national identity: in the most multi-ethnic state in the world, its political history has seen ethnicity politicised with bloody and devastating results, and given the ethnically fuelled post-election violence that occurred in the wake of the 2007 elections, Ringera J's statement here proved almost prophetic. On 4 August 2010, in the wake of bloodshed that resulted in a reported 1,220 civilian deaths and the recounted internal displacement of around 350,000 persons,[80] the Kenyan people ushered in a new Constitution by referendum, as prescribed by this judgment.

By virtue of public interest litigation, the courts were able to subject the exercise of constitution-making to judicial review and, by so doing, found new rights for Kenyans in a way that 'accorded itself *proprio motu* constituent force' as Thornhill puts it.[81] Broadened public interest standing has afforded an environment whereby the Kenyan courts can and have discerned a distinctly Kenyan answer to a Kenyan question: the matter of public participation in the Kenyan constitutional reform process.

[75] The Commission of Enquiry on Post-Election Violence, set up in the wake of the 2007–08 post-election violence, highlighted that the Kenyan judiciary had 'acquired the notoriety of losing the confidence and trust of those it must serve because of the perception that it is not independent as an institution': Report of the Commission of Inquiry on Post-Election Violence, CIPEV Report <www.knchr.org/Portals/0/Reports/Waki_Report.pdf> at 460.

[76] The impact of the judicial intervention was to effectively stall the reform process. As such, the case is a huge source of contestation in Kenyan politics and many civil society actors view the petition as a vexatious attempt to block a draft that had been constructed with many consultations. It is no secret that President Kibaki's party, the National Rainbow Coalition (NARC), opposed the Bomas Draft's provisions on devolution and dilution of executive power: see Kramon and Posner (n 74) at 91–92.

[77] Prior to the enactment of the 2010 Constitution, the courts emphasised the primacy of domestic law over international law, and would not directly apply international legal provisions. See *Okunda v Republic* [1970] EA 453; and *Mary Rono v Jane Rono and Another* [2005] eKLR.

[78] It would not have been a stretch for Ringera J to appeal to rights of participation contained in, for example, the Universal Declaration of Human Rights 1948, Art 21; International Covenant on Civil and Political Rights 1966, Art 25; African Charter on Human and Peoples' Rights 1981, Art 13.

[79] See *Njoya* (n 72) at [43].

[80] International Criminal Court, *Request for Authorisation of an Investigation Pursuant to Article 15: Situation in the Republic of Kenya*, ICC-01/09-3, Office of the Prosecutor, 26 November 2009 at [56].

[81] C Thornhill, 'The Mutation of International Law in Contemporary Constitutions: Thinking Sociologically about Political Constitutionalism' (2016) 79 *MLR* 207 at 236.

B. Public Interest Litigation and Rights Protection

The Kenyan courts' incremental relaxation of the rules on standing mirrors the general trend in African courts towards allowing access to courts where there has been a violation of fundamental rights and freedoms.[82] Rights litigation in Kenya was sparing until such developments, and the courts were likely to be deferential towards state policy, invoking a position of interpretive restraint.[83] However, the frequency of human rights litigation before the Kenyan courts tangibly increased in tandem with the progression of constitutional reform and the widening of standing. Even before the promulgation of a new constitutional order, this was beginning to give rise to the development of tailored and locally sensitive jurisprudence.

In *Rangal Lemeiguran and Others v Attorney General and Others*,[84] the applicants approached the court as representatives of the Il Chamus, a small and distinct community of 25–30,000 people. The applicants sought declarations that their rights to political representation were effectively denied by virtue of the makeup of the constituency boundary, and wished to be considered a 'special interest group' for the purposes of parliamentary representation, as a result of their status as a minority and indigenous group. At a time where the prevailing position in Kenyan law was that international law provisions were not a valid source of law without incorporation,[85] the three-judge constitutional bench invoked the International Labour Organization Convention Concerning Indigenous and Tribal Peoples in Independent Countries, No 169 (1989), amongst other unincorporated international provisions, to find that '[r]epresentation is a clear constitutional recognition of a positive right of the minority—to participate in the State's political process and to influence State policies'.[86] Where previously the courts have remained very reluctant to recognise the indigenous status of communities,[87] this bench found that the community qualified for special interest representation before Parliament as a result of their indigeneity. It challenged the historical inaccuracy that all 42 Kenyan tribes are indigenous,[88] distinguishing between Kenyan communities 'having a strong attachment

[82] See *Attorney General v Dow* 1992 BLR 119; and *Catholic Commission for Justice and Peace in Zimbabwe v Attorney General and Others* 1993 (1) ZLR 242.

[83] JB Ojwang and JA Otieno-Odek, 'The Judiciary in Sensitive Areas of Public Law: Emerging Approaches to Human Rights Litigation in Kenya' (1988) 35 *Netherlands International Law Review* 29.

[84] *Rangal Lemeiguran and Others v Attorney General and Others* [2006] eKLR.

[85] See n 77 above.

[86] See *Rangal Lemeiguran* (n 84) (pinpoint citation unavailable).

[87] See *Kemai and Others v Attorney General and Others* (2006) KLR 1 (E & L) 326.

[88] In pre-independence Kenya, the Colonial administration configured districts by affording positions in the local government structure to the dominant ethnic community in each area. District councils were therefore 'tribal', and many Kenyans constituted themselves as a 'tribe' to secure themselves land within a district. Groups that were not officially attached to land in this way were not recognised. This led to the long-held myth that Kenya is made up of 42 tribes, 41 being those identifiable through districts, and the 42nd including all others who were not. In reality, Kenya is far more ethnically diverse than this. See BA Ogot, *History as Destiny and History as Knowledge: Being Reflections on the Problems of Historicity and Historiography* (Kisumu, Anyange Press Ltd, 2005) 290; and Z Abubakar, 'Memory, Identity and Pluralism in Kenya's Constitution Building Process' in YP Ghai and J Cottrell Ghai (eds), *Ethnicity, Nationhood and Pluralism: Kenyan Perspectives* (Ottawa/Nairobi, Global Centre for Pluralism/Katiba Institute, 2013) 21, 30–31.

to their culture as opposed to the homogenous ones who have adapted to change with very little attachment to the old ways. The other distinguishing trait is that the indigenous ones are generally minorities'.[89] The court, therefore, invoked a definition of indigeneity that was cogent at the local, regional, and international level.[90] Once again, the courts have been able to address potentially divisive social issues in a nuanced manner by virtue of broadened court access. This interventionist and rights-orientated approach of the courts, while certainly gaining traction, was not widespread before the promulgation of the new Constitution.[91]

C. Kenya After 2010

The 2010 Constitution of Kenya ushered in profound changes to the legal and political structure of the country, restoring a Senate as an upper house of Parliament, introducing a two-tier devolution system and initiating an overhaul of the judiciary. A wide-ranging Bill of Rights (Chapter Four), including extensive protection of social and economic rights (Article 43) is twinned with provisions for the direct diffusion of international law into the domestic legal order.[92] The new document settled the position on public interest standing, with Article 22 requiring that every person has the right to approach the court for the enforcement of the Bill of Rights in the public interest, while Article 258 affords every person the right to institute court proceedings in the public interest alleging contraventions or possible future contraventions of the constitution.[93] The Kenyan Court of Appeal has settled that these provisions are the country's standard guide for standing, highlighting that the 'time is now propitious at this stage of our constitutional development where we can state

[89] *Rangal Lemeiguran* (n 84) (pinpoint citation unavailable).

[90] The African Commission has made plain that in the context of Africa, recognition of indigenous status in relation to Aboriginality is no longer appropriate. Characteristics of indigenous peoples in Africa are those with a culture and way of life that differs markedly from the dominant society and suffer from marginalisation. This aligns with the evolution of indigenous status at international level. See African Commission on Human and Peoples' Rights, *Report of the African Commission's Working Group of Experts on Indigenous Populations/Communities*, (Twenty-Eighth Ordinary Session, 2003), DOC/OS (XXXIV)/345, 58–64.

[91] See *Paul Mungai Kimani and Others v Attorney General and Others* [2010] eKLR.

[92] Art 2(5) ensures that '[t]he general rules of international law shall form part of the law of Kenya', while Art 2(6) stipulates that '[a]ny treaty or convention ratified by Kenya shall form part of the law of Kenya': Constitution of Kenya 2010.

[93] Art 22: '(1) Every person has the right to institute court proceedings claiming that a right or fundamental freedom in the Bill of Rights has been denied, violated or infringed, or is threatened. (2) In addition to a person acting in their own interest, court proceedings under clause (1) may be instituted by—A person acting on behalf of another person who cannot act in their own name; a person acting as a member of, or in the interest of, a group or class of persons; a person acting in the public interest; or an association acting in the interest of one or more of its members'. Art 258: '(1) Every person has the right to institute court proceedings, claiming that this Constitution has been contravened, or is threatened with contravention. (2) In addition to a person acting in their own interest, court proceedings under clause (1) may be instituted by—a person acting on behalf of another person who cannot act in their own name; a person acting as a member of, or in the interest of, a group or class of persons; a person acting in the public interest; or an association acting in the interest of one or more of its members'.

as was stated by the Supreme Court of India in the case of *SP Gupta* ... "It is only by liberalizing the rule of *locus standi* that it is possible to effectively police the corridors of power and prevent violations of law"'.[94] New legal orders constitutionally protecting broad court access in this manner is not a new or unusual phenomenon. The *locus classicus* is the 1991 Constitution of Colombia, which explicitly states that anyone with a 'collective right' can sue to protect it, and a 1998 piece of legislation authorised categories of person, including individuals and NGOs, who could approach to the court in the public interest.[95] The Botswana Constitution allows any person who alleges a violation of fundamental rights and freedoms protected by the constitution to apply to the High Court for redress.[96] The Constitution of Nepal goes further, affording both the Supreme Court and the High Court power to issue orders to protect fundamental and legal rights in actions of 'public interest or concern'.[97] The provision for the enforcement of rights in the Kenyan constitution is remarkably similar to its counterpart in the 1996 South African Constitution.[98] In Kenya, these provisions have precipitated a flurry of social rights cases. The Constitution has opened the gates for public interest and representative litigants to approach the courts on behalf of those who are left wanting of socio-economic means to do so themselves. In so doing, the Kenyan courts regularly invoke the reasoning and jurisprudence of the courts of South Africa and India, while also capitalising on the new place of international law in the Kenyan constitutional order, and the advanced Bill of Rights provisions in the new Constitution.

A flood of cases since 2010 have invoked the new constitutional provisions on economic and social rights, along with international law standards of protection to uphold rights. A number of state-sponsored forcible eviction cases follow the same pattern: the petitioners, appearing in a class action or public interest suit, represent residents of informal settlements that have been ordered to vacate the premises with little or no notice; if they do not respond quickly enough, they are forcibly removed by the state, using inhumane tactics. For instance, in *Susan Waithera Kariuki v Town Clerk of Nairobi City Council*, the petitioners were served notice to vacate within 24 hours; upon expiry of this period, the respondents employed administration police officers to destroy the structures, leaving the petitioners no choice but to put

[94] *Mumo Matemu v Trusted Society of Human Rights Alliance and Others* [2013] eKLR at [31].

[95] Constitution of Colombia 1991; Law 472 (1998), Art 88.

[96] Constitution of Botswana 1966 (rev 2005), Art 18(1), applied in *Dow* (n 82) which held that an injured person can also 'protect the rights of the public' (at 155).

[97] Constitution of Nepal 2015, Arts 133(2) and 144(1). This replicates earlier provisions in the Constitution of the Kingdom of Nepal, 1990, Art 88(2).

[98] Constitution of the Republic of South Africa 1996, Art 38 holds that '[t]he persons who may approach the court are—(a) anyone acting in their own interest; (b) anyone acting on behalf of another person who cannot act in their own name; (c) anyone acting as a member of, or in the interest of, a group or class of persons; (d) anyone acting in the public interest; and (e) an association acting in the interest of its members'. This is perhaps no surprise, given that much of the work of the Constitution of Kenya Review Commission went to great strides to comparatively review other jurisdictions, and the Committee of Experts on Constitutional Review contained a South African scholar, Professor Christina Murray. See *The Final Report of the Constitution of Kenya Review Commission* (2005) <www.katibainstitute.org/Archives/images/CKRC%20Final%20Report.pdf>.

up temporary structures on the same, now uninhabitable, land.[99] In *Ibrahim Sangor Osman v Minister of State for Provincial Administration and Internal Security*, the petitioners were violently evicted from their homes, which they had occupied since the 1940s, on Christmas Eve. Officers resorted to tear gas and other violent methods to clear the land, with no written notice.[100] Regularly, the courts find violations of the right to fair administrative action (Article 47), rights to water and sanitation, to accessible and adequate housing, and to health (Article 43), to information (Article 35) and to life (Article 26) under the Kenyan Constitution.[101] Invoking international standards of protection, the courts award damages and order structural remedies, compelling state respondents to engage with petitioners and to create state policies towards evictions that correspond with the United Nations Basic Principles and Guidelines on Development-Based Eviction and Displacement (2007).[102] The Kenyan High Court has even gone as far as to hand down structural remedies, creating court-administered monitoring mechanisms for its judgments.[103] This approach is directly influenced by similar mechanisms that the courts have employed in South Africa and Colombia. The Judiciary Training Institute has designed training exercises and visits for judges that study the approaches of the South African and Colombian courts to structural remedies for the enforcement of socio-economic rights.[104] Public interest litigation, then, grounded in rights provisions laden with international law standards, has allowed the Kenyan courts the platform to deliver social justice, while also, as this next part will show, to nurture and cultivate its own jurisprudence, in the wake of an overhauled judiciary.[105]

[99] *Susan Waithera Kariuki and Others v Town Clerk of Nairobi City Council and Others* [2011] eKLR.

[100] *Ibrahim Sangor Osman and Others v Minister of State for Provincial Administration and Internal Security and Others* [2011] eKLR.

[101] By recognising that forcible evictions violate petitioners' 'right to dignity, life and security': *Satrose Ayuma and Others v Registered Trustees of the Kenya Railways Staff Retirement Benefits Scheme and Others* [2011] eKLR, the Kenyan jurisprudence falls in line with South African protectionist court attitudes in eviction cases: *Olivia Road v City of Johannesburg and Others* 2008 (3) SA 208.

[102] The former UN Special Rapporteur on the Rights to Housing, Miloon Kothari, has even filed submissions in a public interest case of this kind: *Satrose Ayuma* (n 101). See also *June Seventeenth Enterprises Ltd v Kenya Airport Authority and Others* [2014] eKLR; *Micro and Small Businesses Association of Kenya—Mombasa Branch v Mombasa County Government and Others* [2014] eKLR.

[103] *Mitu-Bell Welfare Society v Attorney General and Two Others* [2013] eKLR: this leading case has regrettably been overturned by the Court of Appeal, awaiting Supreme Court ruling: *Kenya Airports Authority v Mitu-Bell Welfare Society and Two Others* [2016] eKLR.

[104] 'Socio-Economic and Health Rights: East Africa Judicial Training' (training manual, hard copy on file with author). See also 'Closing Remarks by the Deputy Chief Justice Hon Kalpana Rawal, SC, Deputy President of the Supreme Court of Kenya at the Seminar on Socio-Economic and Cultural Rights Jurisprudence for Judicial Officers in East Africa' (Judiciary Training Institute, Nairobi, 21 November 2013) <www.judiciary.go.ke/portal/assets/files/DCJ%20speeches/DCJ%20SPEECH%20SOCIO-ECONOMIC%20AND%20CULTURAL%20RIGHTS%20JURISPRUDENCE%20FOR%20JUDICIAL%20OFFICERS%20IN%20EAST%20AFRICA.pdf>.

[105] It should be noted that lack of compliance in these cases is endemic. For example, in many cases the state respondents do not bother to acknowledge the cases against them, by not filing responses to the petitions or taking part in the legal proceedings. See *Susan Waithera Kariuki* (n 99), and *Ibrahim Sangor Osman* (n 100).

D. Decolonising Jurisprudence: Transforming Kenyan Law

The new 2010 Constitution ushered in an era of judicial reform that ensured its independence and accountability in several ways.[106] The colonial legacy left the judiciary a weak institution and a conservative or restrained approach to judicial interpretation dominated the post-independence era. The courts were highly unwilling to hold the executive or the legislature to account.[107] In the constitutional reform process and in response to the dearth of public confidence in the institution, the bench was subject to an extensive vetting procedure.[108] This overhaul of the judiciary was twinned with a greater readiness on the part of judges to hold public institutions to account. The Judiciary Training Institute published a Judiciary Transformation Framework that trains Kenyan judges to produce jurisprudence that is 'robust, indigenous, patriotic and progressive'.[109] This is a vision that has been repeatedly espoused both judicially and extra-judicially by the out-going Chief Justice Willy Mutunga.[110]

The courts, having directly invoked the transformative power of broadening the rule on standing,[111] have also connected how social justice cases can give rise to 'decolonizing jurisprudence'.[112] In extra-judicial comment and in the wake of the introduction of international law into the Kenyan legal order, the Chief Justice has cautioned against the mechanistic application of foreign or international law.[113] There was already burgeoning evidence of the Kenyan courts' ability to use public interest litigation to proliferate 'indigenous' solutions to Kenyan problems prior to the realisation of a new constitutional order, as this chapter has shown. There are also indicators that this continues with the fortification of broad standing, and reinforcement of international law, in the new legal order. For instance, in the case of *Joseph Letuya v Attorney General*, the Court followed the remarkable pre-2010 judgment of *Rangal Lemeiguran and Others v Attorney General and Others* discussed above.[114] Where previously the courts have declined to recognise the special status of the Ogiek forest-dwelling community,[115] here the allocation of public land

[106] Constitution of Kenya 2010, Arts 160–65.

[107] *Gibson Kamau Kuria v Attorney General*, Misc App No 279 of 1985; *Joseph Maina Mbacha v Attorney General*, Misc App No 356 of 1989; *Republic v Judicial Commission of Inquiry into the Goldenberg Affair ex parte George Saitoti* [2006] eKLR.

[108] Judges and Magistrates Vetting Board, 'Vetting of Judges and Magistrates in Kenya: Final Report' (2016).

[109] See Supreme Court of Kenya, *Judiciary Transformation Framework 2012–2016* (n 4) at 11.

[110] For example, Mutunga CJ has labelled the Judiciary Training Institute 'the nerve centre of a robust, indigenous and patriotic jurisprudence', speaking at the launch of the publication of ICJ Kenya's Judicial Watch Report Series Vol 10 at Serena Hotel, Nairobi, Kenya, 22 March 2012.

[111] See *Mumo Matemu* (n 94).

[112] *Jasbir Singh Rai and Others v Tarlochan Singh Rai and Others* [2013] eKLR at [91] (Mutunga CJ).

[113] Chief Justice Willy Mutunga, speaking at Ending Impunity Symposium, Riara University, Nairobi, 28/29 April 2015. I am grateful to the Kenya Section of the International Commission of Jurists, with whom I interned in April to June 2015, for making my attendance at this symposium possible. See also W Mutunga, 'Kenya: A New Constitution' *Socialist Lawyer: Magazine of the Haldane Society* (October 2013) at 20.

[114] *Joseph Letuya and Others v Attorney General and others* [2014] eKLR; see *Rangal Lemeiguran* (n 84).

[115] See *Kemai* (n 87).

parcels was held to violate the group's right to life, dignity and attendant economic and social rights by virtue of their special status as an indigenous and minority group. The courts, giving square attention to the potentially incendiary issue of allocation of land for enjoyment by indigenous populations in Kenya, have maintained a distinctly Kenyan approach to the highly complex and jurisdiction-specific issue. They have even managed to tease out and dismiss cases where an indigenous claim is used as a ruse to grab land.[116]

The transformative potential of a constitutional document through realisation of socio-economic rights has long been championed in South Africa.[117] The textual design of the 2010 Kenyan Constitution, in particular the Bill of Rights and the inclusion of socio-economic rights, emulates international law and provisions of the 1996 Constitution of South Africa, and international and foreign law had a huge influence on the drafting of the Kenyan Constitution.[118] The desire to achieve social justice that alleviates the conditions of the poor and the marginalised, by increasing access to courts and providing that socio-economic rights are justiciable, has strong roots in India, South Africa and Colombia. Kenya is replicating this method by allowing public interest litigation to flourish and by utilising its internationally derived constitutional rights provisions. The many international and foreign influences on Kenya's constitutional design and interpretation, however, do not give rise to formulaic citation of foreign legal precedent, for 'the process of international influence has changed from *reception* to *dialogue*'.[119] Public interest litigation, then, can be viewed as a mechanism for cultivating both 'transformative' and 'decolonising' jurisprudence. In Kenya, it is beginning to provide a platform for the judiciary to create 'indigenous' case law under the new constitutional order, enabling the courts to respond to the particular challenges that the nation faces, just as it has in other jurisdictions. Both the judicial and extra-judicial pronouncements calling for the proliferation of such jurisprudence, coupled with constitutionally-entrenched provisions for broad standing, shows that the emerging policy of the first post-2010 judiciary has been to actively encourage people to approach the court, in a bid to revitalise the legitimacy of the judiciary. An upsurge in litigation is required in order for a new constitutional order to be both propagated and given life, embedding the new constitution in society.[120] It is, however, early days for Kenya. Since 2010, the judiciary has instituted a progressive programme, both in training and practice, but is a long way from achieving the kind of institutionalised approach to social action

[116] *Simion Swakey Ole Kaapei and Others v Commissioner of Lands and Others* [2014] eKLR.

[117] KE Klare, 'Legal Culture and Transformative Constitutionalism' (1998) 14 *South African Journal on Human Rights* 146.

[118] NW Orago, 'Socio-Economic Rights and the Potential for Structural Reforms: A Comparative Perspective on the Interpretation of the Socio-Economic Rights in the Constitution of Kenya, 2010' in M Mbondenyi, E Asaala, T Kabau and A Waris (eds), *Human Rights and Democratic Governance in Kenya: A Post-2007 Appraisal* (Pretoria, Pretoria University Law Press, 2015) 39.

[119] C L'Heureux-Dubé, 'The Importance of Dialogue: Globalization and the International Impact of the Rehnquist Court' (1998) 34 *Tulsa Law Journal* 15 at 17.

[120] W Mutunga, 'Human Rights States and Societies: A Reflection From Kenya' (2015) 2 *Transnational Human Rights Review* 63.

public interest litigation that we can see in, for example, Colombia.[121] There still remain instances where the reformed Kenyan institution declines to answer key constitutional questions.[122] With Mutunga CJ having left office in June 2016, it remains to be seen whether his successor, David Maraga, will share his vision.

III. CONCLUSION

This chapter has shown that there is a trend towards liberalised standing rules in post-colonial common law settings. The central explanation for its judicial relaxation is quite clear: it arises in the pursuit of a reformist agenda. As evidenced by the more detailed study of Kenya, it occurs in tandem with popular pressure for change.[123] This explanation extends to the mushrooming of 'cause lawyering' that we have seen across the globe, where litigation becomes the primary technique for political agitation and social reform initiation.[124] This has been made possible largely by the phenomenon of judicial activism that has prised open access to the courts.[125] The case study of Kenya demonstrates how the crystallisation of broad standing in a constitutional order infused with international law and social rights language, does not necessarily result in an unimaginative reproduction of global rights application. Rather, the provisions enable the rights in question to go through a process of localisation, responding to and being transformed by local socio-political pressures.[126] For the most part, the legal subjects in question attach their claims to internationally derived standards of protection. That does not, however, mean that there is an obvious global case law on such matters, mimicking the same results in each jurisdiction. In fact, the Kenyan case study tentatively demonstrates that national and sub-national actors (judges and litigants) use internationally set standards to buttress more nuanced and locally sensitive solutions. Although there is increasing linkage between domestic law and global law, as evidenced by the utilisation of international law, this does not necessarily mean that the domestic legal system has been

[121] C Rodríguez-Garavito, 'Beyond the Courtroom: The Impact of Judicial Activism on Socioeconomic Rights in Latin America' (2010–11) 89 *Texas Law Review* 1669.

[122] See *International Centre for Policy and Conflict and Others v Attorney General and Others* [2013] eKLR; and *In the Matter of the Principle of Gender Representation in the National Assembly and the Senate* [2012] eKLR.

[123] In an ambitious empirical analysis of 204 countries, Ginsburg and Versteeg found that the principal driving factor behind greater judicial review has been as a response to endogenous factors arising from the domestic political environment: T Ginsburg and M Versteeg, 'Why Do Countries Adopt Constitutional Review?' (2014) 30 *Journal of Law, Economics and Organization* 587.

[124] S Ellmann, 'Cause Lawyering in the Third World' in A Sarat and S Scheingold (eds), *Cause Lawyering: Political Commitments and Professional Responsibilities* (Oxford, Oxford University Press, 1998) 349, 361.

[125] C Neal Tate and T Vallinder (eds), *The Global Expansion of Judicial Power* (New York, NY University Press, 1995); R Hirschl, *Towards Juristocracy: The Origins and Consequences of the New Constitutionalism* (Cambridge MA, Harvard University Press, 2004).

[126] DM Brinks, V Gauri and K Shen, 'Social Rights Constitutionalism: Negotiating the Tension between the Universal and the Particular' (2015) 11 *Annual Review of Law and Social Science* 289.

'de-nationalised'. In fact, the use of public interest litigation invoking international norms creates space for domestic legal actors to craft native solutions bolstered by the transformative potential of international law. This, therefore, is not 'an imperialist Trojan Horse ... but a contested terrain'.[127] The internationalisation or transnationalisation of domestic constitutional law in Kenya, which has seen public interest standing mechanisms borrowed from other jurisdictions and the entrenchment of international values, enhances domestic constitutionalism[128] by affording the judiciary the optimum environment to cultivate law that is 'robust, indigenous, patriotic and progressive'.[129]

[127] M Mamdani, 'Social Movements and Constitutionalism in the African Context' CBR working paper, No 2 (1989) at 6.

[128] CM Fombad, 'Internationalization of Constitutional Law and Constitutionalism in Africa' (2012) 60 *American Journal of Comparative Law* 439.

[129] See Supreme Court of Kenya, *Judiciary Transformation Framework 2012–2016* (n 4) at 11.

18

Constitutional Convergence? Some Lessons from Proportionality

ANNE CARTER*

I. INTRODUCTION

ALTHOUGH COURTS AROUND the world are increasingly turning to tests of proportionality, questions remain about the degree to which this trend represents a methodological convergence in public law adjudication. For a start, the use of similarly worded tests does not always signify the adoption of an identical analytical approach; differences in context remain important. Despite such differences, the growing use of proportionality reasoning gives rise to certain common problems of application. In particular, judicial assessments of proportionality often depend upon complex empirical questions that are difficult to determine with any certainty. These common factual underpinnings of proportionality invite consideration of whether similar techniques might be adopted to resolve comparable problems.

This chapter explores these questions in the context of the use of proportionality reasoning in constitutional adjudication in Australia and the United Kingdom. While in many areas of law there have been increasing divergences between the two countries, both have—albeit under quite different circumstances—adopted proportionality reasoning to determine the extent of legitimate restrictions on rights or freedoms. This chapter proceeds in three main parts. It begins by briefly recounting the spread of proportionality from its continental origins to its reception in both the UK and Australia. It then considers the degree to which the current Australian approach to proportionality aligns with the established approach in the UK for assessing limitations of rights under the Human Rights Act 1998 (HRA 1998). In the second part, the chapter turns to look at how proportionality is applied by courts, concentrating on the role of factual inquiry within the proportionality inquiry. It explains that, at least at the conceptual level, proportionality involves empirical as well as normative issues and it examines how these empirical questions have been

* Thank you to Cheryl Saunders, Mark Elliott, Jason Varuhas, Shona Wilson Stark and Florence Seow for their comments on an earlier draft. I am also grateful to the participants at the 2016 Public Law Conference, where this paper was first presented, for helpful comments and discussion.

approached by the courts in practice. Finally, given that proportionality gives rise to common problems of fact-finding, the chapter considers the ways in which a comparative approach might assist courts in seeking to resolve these problems.

II. PROPORTIONALITY AS A METHOD OF REVIEW

Within the burgeoning literature on proportionality, claims of convergence abound. The growing popularity of proportionality as a method of review has led some scholars to argue that it has developed into a 'global'[1] or 'generic'[2] model of adjudicating rights. While it is difficult to dispute that courts around the world are increasingly adopting the language of proportionality,[3] these tests do not always take exactly the same form; similarities in terminology may conceal considerable differences in practice. This section briefly outlines the historical origins and global diffusion of proportionality and its adoption by courts in both the UK and Australia. It argues that, despite some differences of emphasis, the Australian High Court's recent adoption of a structured, three-part test of proportionality has clear parallels with the UK approach. These parallels suggest that a comparative inquiry is instructive, notwithstanding the somewhat precarious footing of proportionality in Australia.

A. The Origins and Global Spread of Proportionality

Proportionality is a specific methodology or tool used by courts to resolve conflicting interests. It is, when used in this sense, a distinct formula[4] that comprises three separate sub-questions[5] of 'suitability', 'necessity', and 'balancing' or 'proportionality *stricto-sensu*'. The history of proportionality is by now well-known, and its origins are usually traced to nineteenth-century Prussia.[6] In the 1950s, after the

[1] K Möller, *The Global Model of Constitutional Rights* (Oxford, Oxford University Press, 2012). See also DM Beatty, *The Ultimate Rule of Law* (Oxford, Oxford University Press, 2004) ch 5.

[2] DS Law, 'Generic Constitutional Law' (2005) 89 *Minnesota Law Review* 652.

[3] The main exception to this trend is the United States, although there is extensive discussion and debate there about the extent to which the tiered model of scrutiny in fact involves proportionality review. See, eg, ET Sullivan and RS Frase, *Proportionality Principles in American Law: Controlling Excessive Government Actions* (New York, Oxford University Press, 2009) ch 3; VC Jackson, 'Constitutional Law in an Age of Proportionality' (2015) 124 *Yale Law Journal* 3094; P Yowell, 'Proportionality in United States Constitutional Law' in L Lazarus, C McCrudden and N Bowles (eds), *Reasoning Rights: Comparative Judicial Engagement* (Oxford, Hart Publishing, 2014) 87; M Cohen-Eliya and I Porat, *Proportionality and Constitutional Culture* (Cambridge, Cambridge University Press, 2013).

[4] In this way it can be distinguished both from a 'culture of justification' and also from more general notions of balancing or reasonableness review: S Gardbaum, 'Positive and Horizontal Rights: Proportionality's Next Frontier or a Bridge Too Far?' in VC Jackson and M Tushnet (eds), *Proportionality: New Frontiers, New Challenges* (Cambridge University Press, 2017). For some discussion of the distinction between proportionality as a 'formula' and proportionality as an overarching 'principle', see M Cohn, 'Proportionality in Israel and Beyond: Four Aspects' in G Sapir, D Barak-Erez and A Barak (eds), *Israeli Constitutional Law in the Making* (Oxford, Hart Publishing, 2013) 189, 191, 194–95.

[5] In the UK, the test is framed in terms of four sub-tests. This is discussed further below.

[6] M Cohen-Eliya and I Porat, 'American Balancing and German Proportionality: The Historical Origins' (2010) 8 *International Journal of Constitutional Law* 263 at 273. However, the idea of two

enactment of the Basic Law in West Germany and the establishment of the Federal Constitutional Court, the concept of proportionality quickly developed as one of the cornerstones of German constitutional law. Since then, it has been widely adopted by courts around the world, and it is now regarded as one of Germany's most successful legal 'transplants' or 'exports'.[7]

B. Proportionality in the Common Law World: The United Kingdom and Australia

From its continental origins,[8] variants of proportionality have since been applied by many common law courts, including in both the UK and Australia.[9] While its use in relation to the judicial review of administrative action remains unsettled,[10] in relation to constitutional review it has been applied—at least to some extent—by both the Supreme Court of the United Kingdom and the High Court of Australia. Yet this adoption of proportionality must be understood against the backdrop of each country's constitutional setting. While the UK lacks a single written constitutional text, its constitutional landscape has been fundamentally altered by, amongst other things, the enactment of the HRA 1998.[11] In particular, the nature of the judicial role now expressly includes making evaluative judgments about the extent to which limitations on rights are justified.[12] Although Australia, as a former British colony,

things being in proportion is of course much older, and can be traced to Plato and Cicero: see T Poole, 'Proportionality in Perspective' [2010] *New Zealand Law Review* 369. For some discussion of the historical lineage of proportionality in the UK, see P Craig, 'Proportionality and Judicial Review: A UK Historical Perspective' in S Vogenauer and S Weatherill (eds), *General Principles of Law: European and Comparative Perspectives* (Oxford, Hart Publishing, 2017).

[7] It has, for instance, been described as Germany's 'export hit': N Marsch and V Tünsmeyer, 'The Principle of Proportionality in German Administrative Law' in S Ranchordás and B de Waard (eds), *The Judge and the Proportionate Use of Discretion: A Comparative Study* (London, Routledge, 2016) 13 (citing R Wahl, 'Der Grundsatz der Verhältnismäßigkeit: Ausgangslage und Gegenwartsproblematik' in D Heckmann, RP Schenke and G Sydow (eds), *Verfassungsstaatlichkeit im Wandel: Festschrift für Thomas Würtenberger zum 70. Geburtstag* (Berlin, Duncker & Humblot, 2013) 823). For a diagrammatic representation of the spread of proportionality to different legal systems, see A Barak, *Proportionality: Constitutional Rights and Their Limitations* (Cambridge, Cambridge University Press, 2012) 182.

[8] As Lady Justice Arden has commented: '[P]roportionality is not a common law concept. (The common law tends to like bright-line rules, whereas proportionality requires evaluation.)': M Arden, *Human Rights and European Law: Building New Legal Orders* (Oxford, Oxford University Press, 2015) 56. *cf* A Mason, 'The Use of Proportionality in Australian Constitutional Law' (2016) 27 *Public Law Review* 109 at 121.

[9] While there are multiple jurisdictions within the UK, one of which (Scotland) has a mixed system of law, the Human Rights Act 1998 applies throughout the UK.

[10] In the UK, see *Pham v Secretary of State for the Home Department* [2015] 1 WLR 1591; *R (Keyu) v Secretary of State for Foreign and Commonwealth Affairs* [2016] AC 1355. For some introduction to the debate in the UK see, eg, P Craig, 'Proportionality, Rationality and Review' [2010] *New Zealand Law Review* 265; ACL Davies and JR Williams, 'Proportionality in English Law' in Ranchordás and de Waard (n 7) at 73. In Australia, see J Boughey, 'The Reasonableness of Proportionality in the Australian Administrative Law Context' (2015) 43 *Federal Law Review* 59.

[11] A Kavanagh, *Constitutional Review under the UK Human Rights Act* (Cambridge, Cambridge University Press, 2009) 2–4.

[12] As Sir Rabinder Singh has recently noted, courts in the UK have become 'well accustomed to adjudicating on these questions': see R Singh, 'Making Judgments on Human Rights Issues' (Human Rights

inherited the traditions and institutions of the common law, there are increasingly signs of a 'deepening divide' between Australia and the UK.[13] The Australian Constitution contains few rights-protective provisions and Australia now stands virtually alone amongst Western democracies in not having an express bill of rights at the federal level.[14] In addition, Australian constitutional law has been characterised by a particularly strict separation of judicial power[15] and a dominant interpretive tradition of 'legalism',[16] both of which sit uncomfortably with the types of judgments required by proportionality review. These differences in context continue to permeate how proportionality is defined and applied and help to explain the Australian High Court's continued caution about adopting a structured proportionality test.

In the UK, while proportionality was not previously unknown,[17] it gained particular prominence following the enactment of the HRA 1998. From that point on, the rights enshrined in the European Convention on Human Rights (ECHR) had effect domestically, meaning that UK courts were required to adjudicate upon their limits. In the early case of *R (Daly) v Secretary of State for the Home Department*,[18] the House of Lords adopted a three-part test of proportionality for use under the HRA.[19]

In *Daly*, Lord Steyn insisted that there was a distinction between the traditional (*Wednesbury*)[20] standard of review and the proportionality test under the HRA 1998. Nevertheless, while the new standard was more intense, as well as 'more precise

Law Centre Annual Lecture, 2016) para 8. See also M Elliott, 'Proportionality and Deference: The Importance of a Structured Approach' in C Forsyth, M Elliott, S Jhaveri, M Ramsden and A Scully-Hill (eds), *Effective Judicial Review: A Cornerstone of Good Governance* (Oxford, Oxford University Press, 2010) 264, 281.

[13] For instance, Adrienne Stone has made this observation in the context of the High Court's interpretation of the Charter of Rights and Responsibilities Act 2006 (Vic) in *Momcilovic v The Queen* (2011) 245 CLR 1: A Stone, 'Constitutional Orthodoxy in the United Kingdom and Australia: The Deepening Divide' (2014) 38 *Melbourne University Law Review* 836.

[14] Australia's 'exceptionalism' in relation to explicit rights-protection has been well-noted: see, eg, B Galligan and FL Morton, 'Australian Exceptionalism: Rights Protection Without a Bill of Rights' in T Campbell, J Goldsworthy and A Stone (eds), *Protecting Rights Without a Bill of Rights: Institutional Performance and Reform in Australia* (Aldershot, Ashgate, 2006) 17. The Australian Constitution contains few express rights and those that are included have generally been interpreted restrictively. More significant have been the 'implied rights', such as the implied freedom of political communication: A Stone, 'Australia's Constitutional Rights and the Problem of Interpretive Disagreement' (2005) 27 *Sydney Law Review* 29.

[15] J Stellios, *Zines's The High Court and the Constitution*, 6th edn (Sydney, Federation Press, 2015) chs 9–10.

[16] J Goldsworthy, 'Australia: Devotion to Legalism' in J Goldsworthy (ed), *Interpreting Constitutions: A Comparative Study* (Oxford, Oxford University Press, 2007) 106.

[17] J Jowell and A Lester, 'Proportionality: Neither Novel nor Dangerous' in J Jowell and D Oliver (eds), *New Directions in Judicial Review* (London, Stevens & Sons, 1988) 51.

[18] *R (Daly) v Secretary of State for the Home Department* [2001] 2 AC 532 at [27]. Although note that in *Daly* there were common law rights in issue as well and the case was largely decided on the basis of those rather than the Convention rights.

[19] This test, which had earlier been applied by the Privy Council in *De Freitas v Permanent Secretary of the Ministry of Agriculture, Fisheries, Lands and Housing* [1999] 1 AC 69 at 80, contained three parts: 'whether: (i) the legislative objective is sufficiently important to justify limiting a fundamental right; (ii) the measures designed to meet the legislative objective are rationally connected to it; and (iii) the means used to impair the right or freedom are no more than is necessary to accomplish the objective.' It was based on Zimbabwean jurisprudence, which itself had looked to South African and Canadian case law.

[20] *Associated Provincial Picture Houses Ltd v Wednesbury Corp* [1948] 1 KB 223.

and more sophisticated', it did not equate to full merits review.[21] The approach in *Daly* was confirmed in *Huang v Secretary of State for the Home Department*, where the House of Lords emphasised that proportionality must also involve the 'striking of a fair balance between the rights of the individual and the interests of the community'.[22] Reflecting this,[23] the proportionality test under the HRA 1998 has since been refashioned into a four-part test:

> (i) whether [a measure's] objective is sufficiently important to justify the limitation of a fundamental right; (ii) whether it is rationally connected to the objective; (iii) whether a less intrusive measure could have been used; and (iv) whether, having regard to these matters and to the severity of the consequences, a fair balance has been struck between the rights of the individual and the interests of the community.[24]

The Supreme Court has recently confirmed that proportionality is not a uniform test and that it will vary according to context. In particular, the Court has distinguished the four-part test applied in respect of ECHR rights from the proportionality test applied under European Union law.[25]

In Australia the introduction of proportionality has been even more gradual and there has been no similar defining moment of constitutional change. The first use of proportionality as a distinct concept in the constitutional sphere is often traced to Deane J in the *Tasmanian Dams Case*[26] and is thought to derive from the jurisprudence of the European Court of Human Rights and the European Court of Justice.[27] It is now reasonably well settled that *some form* of proportionality reasoning applies in respect of the characterisation of purposive constitutional powers and in assessing limitations on constitutional guarantees.[28] Traditionally, however, the High Court has preferred to frame its tests using the language of 'reasonably appropriate and adapted' rather than 'proportionality'. Until recently, these expressions have been treated as being largely synonymous.[29]

What is less clear is the extent to which a structured test containing the three specific sub-questions of proportionality[30] forms part of the Australian approach.

[21] See *Daly* (n 18) at [27].

[22] *Huang v Secretary of State for the Home Department* [2007] 2 AC 167 at [19], quoting *R (Razgar) v Secretary of State for the Home Department* [2004] 2 AC 368 at [20].

[23] See Davies and Williams (n 10) at 78.

[24] *Bank Mellat v Her Majesty's Treasury (No 2)* [2014] AC 700 at [20] (Lord Sumption). The introduction of an explicit 'fair balance' requirement clarified the previous uncertainty: see Elliott (n 12) at 266.

[25] *R (Lumsdon and others) v Legal Services Board* [2016] AC 697 at [26] (Lords Reed and Toulson).

[26] *Commonwealth v Tasmania* (1983) 158 CLR 1 at 259–61.

[27] J Kirk, 'Constitutional Guarantees, Characterisation and the Concept of Proportionality' (1997) 21 *Melbourne University Law Review* 1 at 2.

[28] HP Lee, 'Proportionality in Australian Constitutional Adjudication' in G Lindell (ed), *Future Directions in Australian Constitutional Law* (Sydney, Federation Press, 1994) 126; see Kirk (n 27).

[29] *Lange v Australian Broadcasting Authority* (1997) 189 CLR 520 at 567 n 272 (the Court). In *Mulholland*, Gleeson CJ discussed the two formulations but noted that 'whichever expression is used, what is important is the substance of the idea it is intended to convey': *Mulholland v Australian Electoral Commission* (2004) 220 CLR 181 at [32]. See also Kirk (n 27); A Stone, 'The Limits of Constitutional Text and Structure: Standards of Review and the Freedom of Political Communication' (1999) 23 *Melbourne University Law Review* 668; A Stone, 'The Limits of Constitutional Text and Structure Revisited' (2005) 28 *University of New South Wales Law Journal* 842.

[30] As explained above, in the UK the test is framed in terms of four sub-tests.

In recent years this question has divided the High Court. In late 2015 in the decision of *McCloy v New South Wales*, a bare majority of four Justices supported the introduction of a sequential three-part test of proportionality in the context of the implied freedom of political communication.[31] This test incorporated the familiar three stages of 'suitability', 'necessity' and 'adequate ... balance'.[32] This introduction of a structured test of proportionality clarified considerable uncertainty that had surrounded the role and nature of proportionality in Australian constitutional law.[33] Despite this degree of consensus, in the subsequent case of *Murphy v Electoral Commissioner*, decided less than a year later, six of the seven Justices declined to apply a structured proportionality test along the lines developed in *McCloy*.[34] Although *McCloy* was not overruled, the proportionality analysis developed there was thought to be 'inapposite' in the context of Parliament's power to regulate elections.[35]

In both Australia and the UK the adoption of proportionality has been accompanied by some attempt to carve out a distinctive, or national, approach. In the UK, for instance, scholars have observed that the courts draw most frequently on jurisprudence from other Commonwealth jurisdictions, such as the Supreme Court of Canada, rather than on European sources.[36] The Supreme Court itself has explained that its approach will not simply 'mirror' the approach taken by the European Court of Human Rights in Strasbourg and that different considerations apply at the national level.[37] In contrast to the 'relatively broad-brush' approach adopted by the Strasbourg Court,[38] the Supreme Court has expressed a preference for a 'more clearly structured approach' that reflects the common law's 'analytical approach to legal reasoning'.[39] In Australia, too, there are clear signs that the High Court wishes to distinguish its approach from that adopted elsewhere. In *McCloy*, for instance, although the joint judgment referred somewhat obliquely to the European origins of proportionality,[40] it relied predominantly on cases from other common law countries, including the UK.[41] It also emphasised that the '[a]cceptance of the utility of such criteria ... does not involve acceptance of the application of proportionality

[31] *McCloy v New South Wales* (2015) 257 CLR 178.

[32] ibid, at [3].

[33] For further discussion, see A Carter, 'Political Donations, Political Communication and the Place of Proportionality Analysis' (2015) 26 *Public Law Review* 245.

[34] *Murphy v Electoral Commissioner* (2016) 90 ALJR 1027. Only Kiefel J endorsed a structured proportionality test.

[35] ibid, at [39] (French CJ and Bell J). See also [101] (Gageler J), [202] (Keane J), [244] (Nettle J), [297] (Gordon J).

[36] See, eg, Cohn (n 4) at 199–200; Singh (n 12) at para 21.

[37] *Bank Mellat* (n 24) at [71] (Lord Reed). Note that although Lord Reed dissented in the result, Lord Sumption noted at [20] that he did not disagree with his formulation of the concept of proportionality at [68]–[76].

[38] See *Bank Mellat* (n 24) at [70].

[39] ibid, at [72].

[40] See *McCloy* (n 31) at [3]. The joint judgment acknowledged that '[a]nalogous criteria have been developed in other jurisdictions, particularly in Europe,' but stressed that its approach would be tailored to the Australian constitutional setting.

[41] Note that a number of the judgments in *McCloy* make reference to the Supreme Court's approach to proportionality in *Bank Mellat*: see *McCloy* (n 31) at [78], [89] (French CJ, Kiefel, Bell and Keane JJ), [144] (Gageler J), [253] (Nettle J).

analysis by other courts as methodologically correct'[42] and it explicitly rejected the application of a 'margin of appreciation' in the Australian context.[43] Such comments from the courts in both Australia and the UK raise a further question, which awaits future consideration, of whether there are broader differences emerging between common law and continental notions of proportionality.

C. Constitutional Convergence?

Although the recent decision of *Murphy* in Australia signals some retreat from structured proportionality, the joint judgment's approach in *McCloy* continues—at least for the moment—to be applicable in cases concerning the implied freedom of political communication. To this extent, then, we can see some commonality between the Australian approach and that of the UK courts under the HRA 1998. The three questions of 'suitability', 'necessity' and 'adequate ... balance', albeit within the existing *Lange* framework,[44] are expressed in almost identical terms to the conventional proportionality formula.[45] They require, importantly, a sequential application. Articulating the inquiry in this way has the potential to lead to a more structured and transparent approach to assessing limitations.[46] In addition, the joint judgment's open reliance on some form of balancing, which expressly acknowledges the making of 'value judgments',[47] represents a shift away from the 'legalism' that has dominated Australian constitutional adjudication. In several important respects, therefore, the revised approach in *McCloy* can be seen as an analytical shift towards the methodological approach applied in other jurisdictions, including in adjudicating claims under the HRA 1998.

Despite these similarities, the degree of convergence remains limited. As I have explained elsewhere,[48] there remain differences of emphasis in terms of the level of scrutiny with which the new 'proportionality testing' is to be applied and also the precise nature of the balancing inquiry. Underpinning these differences there may also be a more profound divide in terms of how the judicial role is perceived. In particular, the types of judgments required by proportionality reasoning challenge the traditional understanding of the judicial role that has dominated constitutional interpretation in Australia.[49] In addition, the position of proportionality in Australia remains precarious. In *McCloy* itself three members of the Court rejected any alteration to the traditional *Lange* formulation. For Justice Gageler, in particular, the case

[42] See *McCloy* (n 31) at [4].
[43] ibid, at [92].
[44] See *Lange* (n 29) at 567.
[45] See *McCloy* (n 31) at [3].
[46] Transparency is one of the benefits of proportionality reasoning that is claimed by the joint judgment: see *McCloy* (n 31) at [74].
[47] ibid, at [76].
[48] A Carter, 'Proportionality in Australian Constitutional Law: Towards Transnationalism?' (2016) 76 *Heidelberg Journal of International Law* 951.
[49] In the context of section 7(2) of the Charter of Rights and Responsibilities Act 2006 (Vic), Adrienne Stone suggests that judges are 'uncomfortable' with elements of proportionality analysis: see Stone (n 13) at 855.

did not 'warrant consideration of the benefits and detriments of the wholesale importation into our constitutional jurisprudence, under the rubric of proportionality, of a particular and prescriptive form of proportionality analysis'.[50] These types of concerns were again echoed in *Murphy* where, as indicated above, Justice Kiefel was alone in applying a structured proportionality test.[51]

III. APPLYING PROPORTIONALITY: THE ROLE OF FACTS

Notwithstanding these differences between Australia and the UK, a comparative inquiry remains instructive. The structured approach adopted by the majority in *McCloy* has clear parallels with the established UK position. In addition, as will become apparent in the discussion below, even without firmer support for a structured proportionality test the existing tests of constitutional validity in Australia already incorporate aspects of the three-part proportionality formula. There are thus certain common problems of application that confront courts grappling with proportionality reasoning, even if the form of the tests used is not identical. The remainder of this chapter considers how courts apply proportionality reasoning, focusing specifically on the role of facts.

A. Proportionality as a Fact-dependent Standard

Although the rise of proportionality worldwide has spawned a vast body of literature,[52] surprisingly little attention has been given to the role of facts. As I will explain in this section, the three sub-questions of 'suitability', 'necessity' and 'balancing' are underpinned by empirical questions about the effects or likely effects of governmental action. In other words, proportionality cannot be applied in a factual vacuum. Its application will often depend upon complex questions of fact that are difficult to determine with any certainty.

Questions of fact are most pertinent at the suitability and necessity stages of proportionality analysis. At the suitability stage a court is required to assess the connection between the purpose of the law and the means employed to pursue that purpose. This is often understood as an objective test, as it is not the subjective intention of the legislature or decision-maker that is relevant, but the objective purpose intended to be pursued.[53] The very language of rational connection suggests that

[50] See *McCloy* (n 31) at [140]. Justice Gageler's reservations about proportionality might, as Sir Anthony Mason has recently suggested, pave the way instead for the development of an approach based on categorisation: see Mason (n 8) at 120–23.

[51] See *Murphy* (n 34) at [64]–[65].

[52] The existing literature has tended to focus on the theoretical aspects of proportionality or its application in particular settings.

[53] See, eg, B Selway, 'The Rise and Rise of the Reasonable Proportionality Test in Public Law' (1996) 7 *Public Law Review* 212 at 217; see Kirk (n 27) at 6. For some discussion of whether legislative purpose tests are objective or subjective, see A Simpson, 'Grounding the High Court's Modern Section 92 Jurisprudence: The Case for Improper Purpose as the Touchstone' (2005) 33 *Federal Law Review* 445 at 465–70.

the inquiry concerns whether—as a matter of reason or logic—there is a connection between the law and its purpose. When viewed in this way, the suitability test starts to look like a familiar task of statutory construction. In practice the suitability stage is often interpreted as imposing a relatively low threshold,[54] meaning that it is not necessary for the court to make a finding about whether the law will *actually* advance the purpose. Rather, it simply needs to be *capable of* advancing that purpose. This means that it is likely, as Aharon Barak has suggested, that any relevant background facts can be supplied by 'logic and common sense'.[55]

It is at the second stage of proportionality—necessity—that empirical questions are particularly prominent. Although a court's conclusion as to whether a measure is necessary is likely to be a question of law,[56] it is a conclusion that rests upon propositions of fact.[57] Unlike the suitability test, which asks only whether the measure is capable of achieving an objective, the necessity test involves the court assessing the *likelihood* that a particular objective will be achieved. As Barak has observed:

> In order to properly answer the question of whether the alternative means—which limit the right to a lesser extent—equally advance the purpose as the means chosen by the legislator, an understanding of both the purpose and the probability of its being achieved through the alternative means is necessary. An estimate is insufficient; the understanding should be of the concrete factual data, as well as of the probabilities and risks involved.[58]

The necessity test involves considering whether a given measure, and also any hypothetical alternative, will be likely to actually achieve the purpose. This requires making predictions about how the measure might operate in the real world and will often raise 'complex questions of empirical prognosis'.[59]

The third stage of proportionality analysis—balancing or proportionality in the narrow sense—is often seen as a 'bolder judicial endeavour' than the earlier two stages[60] because it compels the court to make evaluative judgments about the importance of the different interests at stake.[61] It is this 'balancing' of interests that has sparked debate about the extent to which proportionality can provide a principled

[54] J Rivers, 'The Presumption of Proportionality' (2014) 77 *MLR* 409 at 422.

[55] See Barak (n 7) at 310.

[56] This has been pointed out by Barak (n 7) at 328. On the distinction between questions of law and questions of fact, see T Endicott, 'Questions of Law' (1998) 114 *LQR* 292.

[57] This has been recognised in the theoretical literature on proportionality: see, eg, Rivers (n 54) at 415; M Kumm, 'Political Liberalism and the Structure of Rights: on the Place and Limits of the Proportionality Requirement' in G Pavlakos (ed), *Law, Rights and Discourse in the Legal Philosophy of Robert Alexy* (Oxford, Hart Publishing, 2007) 131; B Pirker, *Proportionality Analysis and Models of Judicial Review: A Theoretical and Comparative Study* (Groningen, Europa Law Publishing, 2013) 29; see Elliott (n 12) at 267–72.

[58] See Barak (n 7) at 321.

[59] See Rivers (n 54) at 415. The problem of factual uncertainty at both the suitability and necessity stages has also been identified by Alexy, who observes that these stages 'often throw up difficult problems of prognosis': R Alexy, *A Theory of Constitutional Rights* (J Rivers trans, Oxford, Oxford University Press, 2002) 67, 399, 414–15. See also Jackson (n 3) at 3145–46.

[60] See Elliott (n 12) at 268.

[61] Though even when courts avoid an overt 'balancing' of interests, similar evaluative judgments are performed during the other stages. See, for instance, N Petersen, 'How to Compare the Length of Lines to the Weight of Stones: Balancing and the Resolution of Value Conflicts in Constitutional Law' (2013) 14 *German Law Journal* 1387 at 1395.

or objective way of resolving disputes.[62] In particular, it has led to the charge of incommensurability: that proportionality requires the weighing of two things that cannot be compared.[63] Yet even if we accept that at the third-stage judges are ultimately required to make a choice between two competing interests, this does not necessarily exclude any role for fact finding. The balancing that takes place is not performed in isolation, but in conjunction with the other two stages of proportionality (whether or not the test is applied in discrete steps). The bigger problem, then, might be the types of factual assessments that are thrown up by proportionality. As Endicott acknowledges, proportionality involves 'massively complex social facts' for which the social sciences cannot provide 'accurate and verifiable' answers.[64]

B. The Approach of the Courts

Given these empirical problems underpinning proportionality reasoning, this part of the chapter considers the courts' approach in practice. In other words, how have the courts in Australia and the UK recognised and sought to resolve these dilemmas within the framework of the common law adversarial tradition?

(i) Australia

Although the High Court has traditionally been reluctant to develop standards that depend on findings of fact,[65] at the same time it has recognised that at times it will be obliged to determine 'constitutional facts'. These facts, which are distinguished from ordinary or 'adjudicative' facts, are those that are relevant to the validity of legislation.[66] The Court has consistently held that it is its duty, as part of its constitutional function, to determine such facts[67] and has acknowledged that the

[62] See, eg, Beatty (n 1) at 166–71. For criticism of Beatty's work see, in particular, Jackson (n 3); GCN Webber, 'Proportionality, Balancing, and the Cult of Constitutional Rights Scholarship' (2010) 23 *Canadian Journal of Law and Jurisprudence* 179 at 187–90. GCN Webber, *The Negotiable Constitution: On the Limitation of Rights* (Cambridge, Cambridge University Press, 2009) 107–10.

[63] For some discussion, see T Endicott, 'Proportionality and Incommensurability' in G Huscroft, BW Miller and G Webber (eds), *Proportionality and the Rule of Law: Rights, Justification, Reasoning* (New York, Cambridge University Press, 2014) 311; TA Aleinikoff, 'Constitutional Law in the Age of Balancing' (1987) 96 *Yale Law Journal* 943 at 972–76; S Tsakyrakis, 'Proportionality: An Assault on Human Rights?' (2009) 7 *International Journal of Constitutional Law* 468 at 472–74.

[64] See Endicott (n 63) at 336.

[65] S Kenny, 'Constitutional Fact Ascertainment' (1990) 1 *Public Law Review* 134 at 149; J Lennan, 'How to Find Facts in Constitutional Cases' (2011) 30 *Civil Justice Quarterly* 304.

[66] Susan Kenny defines constitutional facts as 'the facts which either the Court has, or might reasonably have, regarded as relevant to the determination of a constitutional issue': Kenny (n 65) at 135. See also B Selway, 'The Use of History and Other Facts in the Reasoning of the High Court of Australia' (2001) 20 *University of Tasmania Law Review* 129 at 135; Lennan (n 65); C Tran, 'Facts and Evidence in Litigation under the Charter of Human Rights and Responsibilities Act 2006 (VIC) and the Human Rights Act 2004 (ACT)' (2012) 36 *Melbourne University Law Review* 287.

[67] *Australian Communist Party v Commonwealth* (1951) 83 CLR 1 at 190–202 (Dixon J), 206–07 (McTiernan J), 262 (Fullagar J), 222 (Williams J).

usual processes of proof may not be appropriate.[68] Despite a relatively long line of jurisprudence recognising constitutional facts as a distinct species of fact, the approach of the Court remains uncertain. Susan Kenny's observations from 1990 remain pertinent today:

> [T]he High Court has seldom discharged its fact finding responsibility satisfactorily. It has failed not only to develop appropriate measures of review, especially in challenges to legislative validity, but also to agree on evidentiary rules, particularly relating to the burden of proof, to facilitate fact presentation and ascertainment.[69]

In the context of proportionality reasoning, the High Court has not consistently recognised the relevance of facts to its inquiry. In the recent case of *Murphy*, Keane J rejected any general proposition that proportionality reasoning might depend on facts, arguing that constitutional validity could not be dependent on changes to the 'milieu' in which an Act operates.[70] In particular, he sought to distinguish the dispute before the Court (which concerned the power to make laws regulating elections)[71] from both the operation of the defence power and from the guarantee contained in section 92 of the Australian Constitution. As the discussion below will show, while in some contexts the Court has been willing to recognise constitutional facts, in other cases the factual aspects of its decisions have been less explicit.

In the context of section 92, the High Court has expressly acknowledged that facts will be relevant to determining whether the constitutional guarantee has been infringed.[72] In the landmark case of *Cole v Whitfield* in 1988, a unanimous High Court framed the test for section 92 in terms of whether the law imposed a discriminatory burden of a protectionist kind.[73] In defining the test in this way the Court ended decades of uncertainty that had dogged the section[74] and also explicitly confirmed that the test depended on an examination of the 'factual operation' of the law.[75] In that case the agreed facts presented by the parties enabled the Court to conclude that the prohibitions against the sale and possession of imported crayfish was a 'necessary means' of protecting undersized crayfish in Tasmanian waters.[76] In subsequent cases the Court clarified that some restrictions on interstate trade and

[68] For a detailed discussion, see JD Heydon, *Cross on Evidence*, 10th edn (Chatswood, LexisNexis Butterworths, 2014) ch 2.

[69] See Kenny (n 65) at 164. See also Tran (n 66) at 288.

[70] See *Murphy* (n 34) at [194]. One of the arguments advanced by the plaintiffs, which was directed to establishing the lack of a 'substantial reason', was the changing nature of the constitutional facts. According to the plaintiffs, this was an 'inevitable consequence' of applying proportionality reasoning: 'That a law, which disenfranchises, disqualifies or excludes from voting a person who is otherwise entitled to vote, may cease to have a substantial reason due to a change in constitutional facts is an inevitable consequence of proportionality reasoning': See AJ Murphy, 'Plaintiff's Annotated Submissions', Submission in *Murphy v Electoral Commissioner*, M247/2015, 11 April 2016 at [8].

[71] See *Murphy* (n 34) at [199]–[200].

[72] Note that the Court has also explicitly recognised the role of facts in determining whether laws are within the scope of the defence power in section 51 (vi) of the Constitution: *Stenhouse v Coleman* (1944) 69 CLR 457 at 469.

[73] *Cole v Whitfield* (1988) 165 CLR 360 at 399.

[74] See Stellios (n 15) at chs 6–8.

[75] See *Cole* (n 73) at 399.

[76] ibid, at 409.

commerce will be legitimate: in *Castlemaine v Tooheys* this was expressed in terms of the legislative regime being 'appropriate and adapted' to the protection of a legitimate objective (in that case, the protection of the environment);[77] in *Betfair*, this was expressed in terms of a criterion of 'reasonable necessity'.[78] Although it is unclear whether the revised *McCloy* approach to proportionality will extend to section 92,[79] the established test arguably already incorporates at least the suitability and necessity steps of the proportionality formula.[80] Despite the Court's long recognition of the relevance of facts to the section 92 analysis, the procedures by which such facts should be ascertained are less clear. In practice the Court often relies upon agreed statements of fact,[81] but this procedure is not always available or satisfactory.[82] As Sir Anthony Mason noted extra-judicially, the question of how the facts relevant to section 92 should be ascertained is 'a hardy perennial to which no answer has yet been returned'.[83]

In contrast to this express acknowledgement of the role of facts, in cases dealing with the implied freedom of political communication, the empirical dimensions of the Court's inquiry have been less explicit. Although the Court often states that it will take account of a law's practical operation, this is rarely accompanied by any explicit discussion of the role of facts or its established jurisprudence on constitutional facts.[84] Instead, when assessing whether the implied freedom is relevantly burdened and whether any burden can be justified, the Court often does not explicitly acknowledge that these questions involve factual elements. Again, the case of *McCloy* provides an illustration. While it has been suggested that a 'functionalist' approach to constitutional adjudication might lead to an 'increased focus on questions of counter-factual analysis, and context' when assessing proportionality,[85]

[77] *Castlemaine Tooheys Ltd v South Australia* (1990) 169 CLR 436 at 474.

[78] *Betfair Pty Ltd v Western Australia* (2008) 234 CLR 418 at [102] (Gleeson CJ, Gummow, Kirby, Hayne, Crennan and Kiefel JJ).

[79] The joint judgment in *McCloy* noted that the 'necessity' stage of the proportionality inquiry, which involved consideration of whether there were any equally effective alternatives, 'mirror[ed], to an extent, that which has been applied with respect to legislation which restricts the freedom guaranteed by s 92 of the *Constitution*': *McCloy* (n 31) at [57]. The joint judgment also noted (at [87]) that it had been observed (citing Leslie Zines's influential book *The High Court and the Constitution*) that 'notions of balancing may be seen in *Castlemaine Tooheys Ltd v South Australia*, in the context of the s 92 freedom'. There is also some hint at [3] that the new approach might apply to other areas.

[80] A number of scholars have argued that the Court's current approach only involves 'abridged proportionality' rather than 'robust proportionality', as it does not involve any express balancing: see N Oreb, 'Betting Across Borders—*Betfair Pty Limited v Western Australia*' (2009) 31 *Sydney Law Review* 607 at 616–17; see Kirk (n 27) at 20; G Villalta Puig, 'A European Saving Test for Section 92 of the Australian Constitution' (2008) 13 *Deakin Law Review* 99 at 116.

[81] See Stellios (n 15) at 196–97. Note that Michael Coper has suggested that the Inter-State Commission might be revived for the purpose of resolving the complex factual issues that arise in the context of section 92: M Coper, 'The Second Coming of the Fourth Arm: The Role and Functions of the Inter-State Commission' (1989) 63 *Australian Law Journal* 731.

[82] M Coper, 'Section 92 of the Australian Constitution Since *Cole v Whitfield*' in HP Lee and G Winterton (eds), *Australian Constitutional Perspectives* (Sydney, Law Book Co, 1992) 129, 146–47.

[83] A Mason, 'Foreword' in Lee and Winterton (n 82) at v, vii.

[84] *cf Levy v Victoria* (1997) 189 CLR 579 where, in response to a submission by the plaintiff, Brennan J acknowledged that it was possible that constitutional validity might depend on facts, but considered, in this case, evidence was unnecessary.

[85] R Dixon, 'The Functional Constitution: Re-Reading the 2014 High Court Constitutional Term' (2015) 43 *Federal Law Review* 455 at 482.

in *McCloy* itself questions of fact assumed little prominence. As Appleby observed, the Court was 'largely ... uninformed' by facts or evidence.[86] Although the case proceeded by way of a 'special case' procedure,[87] the Court had before it a large volume of reports concerning corruption in New South Wales. It made no reference to constitutional facts nor to its established jurisprudence in the area[88] and used the reports simply to demonstrate that a problem of corruption existed in New South Wales and that the legislation was designed to reduce the risk of corruption.

When assessing the question of necessity, the Court was largely happy to proceed on the basis of assumption. As explained above, the question of necessity—and in particular the consideration of alternatives—most clearly raises empirical claims. Yet in the course of both identifying and rejecting the two alternatives suggested by the plaintiffs, the joint judgment simply noted that these had not been adequately explained.[89] Presumably, by this statement the joint judgment was indicating that the alternative measures had not been shown to be equally effective.[90] When discussing the potential alternatives, the other judges proceeded in a similar fashion, although Justice Gordon did make some reference to the comparative practices of other jurisdictions to bolster her conclusion that the proffered alternatives would not achieve the same purpose.[91]

Of the four separate judgments, it was Justice Nettle, who did not adopt the revised formulation of proportionality, who engaged most fully with the factual questions underpinning the legislative measures. Referring to the reports included in the special case, Justice Nettle acknowledged that there was a 'strong factual basis' for the perception of the risk of corruption.[92] However, he hinted that such evidence would not always be required, noting that it was 'not illogical or unprecedented for the Parliament to enact legislation in response to inferred legislative imperatives' and that often this was the only way that the Parliament could deal with matters 'prophylactically'.[93] Further, in relation to the question of alternatives, it appears Justice Nettle was ultimately happy to proceed on the basis of assumption. In particular, he considered that the question of whether the prohibited donor provisions actually had a significant effect on corruption or undue influence was 'essentially irrelevant'.[94] Following the approach of Justice Hayne in *Tajjour*, Justice Nettle

[86] G Appleby, 'Functionalism in Constitutional Interpretation: Factual and Participatory Challenges: Comment on Dixon' (2015) 43 *Federal Law Review* 493 at 494.

[87] This procedure involves the parties stating questions of law for determination by the Full Court of the High Court. The special case states the facts and identifies the documents necessary for the Court to determine the questions of law: High Court Rules 2004 (Cth), rule 27.08.

[88] *cf* Attorney General (SA), 'Submissions of the Attorney General for South Australia, Intervening', Submission in *McCloy v New South Wales*, S211/2014, 10 March 2015 at [28].

[89] See *McCloy* (n 31) at [61]: 'The plaintiffs do not explain how these provisions might be strengthened in a way which would render the capping provisions unnecessary.'

[90] Appleby suggests that the plaintiffs failed to discharge an 'onus', but the joint judgment did not describe the obligation on the plaintiffs as specifically as this: Appleby (n 86) at 494.

[91] See *McCloy* (n 31) at [330].

[92] ibid, at [233].

[93] ibid.

[94] ibid, at [265].

observed that once it could be seen that an impugned law was rationally connected to a legitimate end, 'it is not for the Court to attempt an assessment of how likely it is to achieve that objective'.[95] In this way, Nettle defined the relevant test in a way that minimised any need for factual inquiry.

This brief discussion of *McCloy*, and the comparison with section 92, indicates that the role of facts within proportionality remains unsettled in Australia. Although there is a reasonably well-recognised doctrine of constitutional facts, it is not consistently applied and its contours remain uncertain. The Court has not articulated when evidentiary material will be required in assessing proportionality or how this material should be adduced.

(ii) United Kingdom

When we shift to look at the situation in the UK, although the proportionality test is comparatively more established, until recently, there has been relatively little attention given to the factual nature of the proportionality inquiry or the need for evidence.[96] In contrast to Australia and several other common law jurisdictions,[97] UK courts have tended to be less 'open' about the role of legislative facts.[98] They have not, on the whole, distinguished between different categories of facts,[99] perhaps reflecting the lack of an entrenched written constitution.[100]

[95] ibid, citing Hayne J in *Tajjour v New South Wales* (2014) 254 CLR 508 at [82].

[96] For some brief discussion of the need for evidence, see M Fordham and T de la Mare, 'Identifying the Principles of Proportionality' in J Jowell and J Cooper (eds), *Understanding Human Rights Principles* (Oxford, Hart Publishing, 2001) 27, 86; see Kavanagh (n 11) at 242, 254; G Facenna, 'Proportionality—The Need for Evidence' (Bar European Group and ALBA Annual Summer Conference 2011, Greece, 29–30 May 2011). Available at: <www.adminlaw.co.uk/library/publications.php>. There has also been some debate about the allocation of the burden of proof: see Rivers (n 54); C Chan, 'Proportionality and Invariable Baseline Intensity of Review' (2013) 33 *Legal Studies* 1; C Chan, 'The Burden of Proof under the Human Rights Act' (2014) 19 *Judicial Review* 46.

[97] For instance, courts in the United States, Canada, New Zealand and South Africa have all recognised the distinction between legislative and adjudicative facts: S Gageler, 'Fact and Law' (2009) 11 *Newcastle Law Review* 1 at 18.

[98] J King, *Judging Social Rights* (Cambridge, Cambridge University Press, 2012) 243. See also A Carter, 'Proof of Legislative Facts under the Human Rights Act 1998' (MPhil thesis, University of Oxford, 2011). Interestingly, in the context of judicial review of administrative action, the English courts have shown a greater willingness to review errors of fact: see M Aronson, 'The Growth of Substantive Review: The Changes, their Causes and their Consequences' in J Bell, M Elliott, JNE Varuhas and P Murray (eds), *Public Law Adjudication in Common Law Systems: Process and Substance* (Oxford, Hart Publishing, 2016) 113.

[99] In the early 1990s, in the context of an employment discrimination dispute, a submission was made to the Court of Appeal that as the issues depended on 'legislative and governmental facts, information, and opinion' the appropriate forum was the Divisional Court rather than an industrial tribunal. This submission was rejected by the Court of Appeal: *R v Secretary of State for Employment; ex parte Equal Opportunities Commission* [1993] 1 WLR 872 at 901–02. This finding was ultimately affirmed by the Judicial Committee of the Privy Council: *R v Secretary of State for Employment; ex parte Equal Opportunities Commission* [1995] 1 AC 1.

[100] Note that in *Commonwealth Freighters v Sneddon* (1959) 102 CLR 280 at 291–92 Dixon CJ noted, 'In courts administering English law according to the principles which developed in a unitary system it must seem anomalous that the question whether a given statute operates or not should depend upon facts proved in evidence'. See also Lennan (n 65) at 304–05.

Since the advent of the HRA 1998, however, there has been a growing recognition of the factual issues underpinning the proportionality inquiry. Soon after the enactment of the HRA 1998, there was some scholarly speculation regarding the need for evidence of justification[101] and the potential use of the Brandeis brief.[102] More recently, a number of judges writing extra-judicially have drawn attention to the problems presented by fact-finding in HRA cases. For instance, as Sir Rabinder Singh recently observed, the application of proportionality 'calls for judgement, which is fact-sensitive'.[103] The UK courts have also shown some awareness of the empirical problems underpinning proportionality. Prior to the enactment of the HRA 1998, in the case of *R v Ministry of Defence; ex parte Smith*,[104] which was later taken to the European Court of Human Rights,[105] the Court of Appeal of England and Wales hinted at the unique procedural issues that might arise under a system of rights-based review. In that case the Court had to consider whether the dismissal of members of the armed forces based on their sexual orientation amounted to a violation of the Convention. Lord Justice Henry observed that if the Convention became part of domestic law, there may be a need for 'more material than the adversarial system normally provides'.[106] In particular, he raised, but did not elaborate upon, the possibility of a Brandeis brief procedure being introduced.[107] In cases decided since the commencement of the HRA 1998 there are signs of some relaxation of the traditionally restrictive judicial review procedures, with courts occasionally adopting a more flexible approach to disclosure[108] and even permitting cross-examination of witnesses.[109]

Despite these signs, the courts have not always been consistent in their treatment of facts. At times the courts have felt content to rely on little or no empirical material when making an assessment of proportionality. In *R v Shayler*, although the Court emphasised the need for '[a] close and penetrating examination of the factual justification for the restriction'[110] in that case the only material before the Court consisted of Parliamentary reports that preceded the Bill's introduction.[111] The safeguarding of national security was assumed to be a well-recognised objective and one that gave rise to a wide margin of appreciation. Similarly, in *Lancashire County Council v Taylor*, Lord Woolf was critical of the large volume of evidence adduced by the

[101] RA Edwards, 'Judicial Deference under the Human Rights Act' (2002) 65 *MLR* 859 at 880–81.

[102] A Henderson, 'Brandeis Briefs and the Proof of Legislative Facts in Proceedings under the Human Rights Act 1998' [1998] *Public Law* 563. See also J Jowell, 'Judicial Deference: Servility, Civility or Institutional Capacity?' [2003] *Public Law* 592.

[103] See Singh (n 12) at para 42. See also Arden (n 8) at 70–73.

[104] *R v Ministry of Defence; ex parte Smith* [1996] QB 517.

[105] *Smith and Grady v UK* (2000) 29 EHRR 493.

[106] *R v Ministry of Defence; ex parte Smith* (n 104) at 564.

[107] ibid, at 564.

[108] See, eg, *Tweed v Parades Commission for Northern Ireland* [2007] 1 AC 650 at [2]–[3] (Lord Bingham), [38]–[39] (Lord Carswell), [56] (Lord Brown).

[109] See, eg, *R (Al-Sweady) v Secretary of State for Defence* [2010] HRLR 2.

[110] *R v Shayler* [2003] 1 AC 247 at [61] (Lord Hope).

[111] ibid, at [9]–[11], [25] (Lord Bingham). See also A Kavanagh, 'Proportionality and Parliamentary Debates: Exploring Some Forbidden Territory' (2014) 34 *OJLS* 443 at 462–63.

Secretary of State[112] and took the view that the underlying social purpose of legislation would often be 'self-evident'.[113]

In contrast, in other cases, the courts have placed a greater emphasis on the potential need for factual justification. In *Wilson v First County Trust (No 2)*, for example, the House of Lords clarified that in assessing proportionality the court may on occasion need to have regard to relevant background material, including statements made in Parliament,[114] and provided some guidance on the factual basis of proportionality. Lord Nicholls emphasised that additional material may be required to enable courts to make the necessary 'value judgment':

> When a court makes this value judgment the facts will often speak for themselves. But sometimes the court may need additional background information tending to show, for instance, the likely practical impact of the statutory measure and why the course adopted by the legislature is or is not appropriate. Moreover, ... the court may need enlightenment on the nature and extent of the social problem (the 'mischief') at which the legislation is aimed.[115]

These comments were endorsed by the Supreme Court in *R (F (A Child)) v Secretary of State for the Home Department*.[116] In that case the Court held that indefinite notification requirements for convicted sex offenders, with no procedure for review, constituted a disproportionate interference with the claimants' Article 8 rights. Although the Court referred to the legislative history of the provisions, there was no material to explain the lack of a review procedure.[117] In addition, counsel for the Secretary of State relied on statistical evidence to support a submission that a reliable review of the risk posed by convicted sex offenders was not practicable. However, this evidence was inconclusive and in this circumstance of empirical uncertainty, the Court held it was not possible to rely on the precautionary principle to render the imposition of notification requirements proportionate.[118] This case demonstrates that at times the courts will have to make assessments of proportionality based on incomplete or imperfect information.[119]

More recently, in the case of *Bank Mellat*, the Supreme Court considered the need for evidence in the context of the proportionality of an Order made by the Treasury

[112] *Lancashire County Council v Taylor* [2005] 1 WLR 2668 at [59].

[113] ibid, at [57], endorsing the comments of Lord Nicholls in *Wilson v First County Trust (No 2)* [2004] 1 AC 816.

[114] *Wilson v First County Trust (No 2)* [2004] 1 AC 816 at [54]–[67], [110]–[118], [141]–[144], [173], [178]. For an analysis of this practice, see Kavanagh (n 111).

[115] *Wilson* (n 114) at [63]. See also [116] (Lord Hope). Note that these comments are *obiter dicta*, and that the Court of Appeal had held that the debates served to 'confuse rather than illuminate': *Wilson v First County Trust Ltd (No 2)* [2002] QB 74 at [36].

[116] *R (F (A Child)) v Secretary of State for the Home Department* [2011] 1 AC 331.

[117] ibid, at [53].

[118] ibid, at [56]. See also *R (Royal College of Nursing) v Secretary of State for the Home Department* [2011] PTSR 1193 at [119] where Wyn Williams J commented on the 'paucity' of evidence before the Court.

[119] For another example, see *R (Aguilar Quila v Secretary of State for Home Department)* [2012] 1 AC 621, where the Supreme Court divided over whether immigration rules that were directed at deterring forced marriages were proportionate. In this case the majority of the Court held the Home Secretary had failed to establish that the measure was proportionate, with Lord Wilson commenting at [58] that '[o]n any view it is a sledge hammer but she has not attempted to identify the size of the nut'.

that prohibited all persons in the financial sector in the UK from engaging in transactions with a major Iranian bank due to the significant risk to the UK's national interests.[120] Lord Sumption, in the majority, endorsed Lord Reed's comments that 'the making of government and legislative policy cannot be turned into a judicial process', but he found that the singling out of Bank Mellat had not been adequately justified.[121] In particular, he considered that the distinction between Bank Mellat and other Iranian banks was 'arbitrary and irrational' and that the Order was disproportionate.[122] Lord Reed, in dissent, ultimately came to a different view of the factual case. In considering the question of rational connection, Lord Reed observed that this posed an objective test that could be determined by reference to 'common sense or logic'.[123] Where legislation was based on complex facts or contestable considerations of policy, 'the court has to allow room for the exercise of judgment by the executive and legislative branches of government'.[124] According to Lord Reed, the evidence surrounding the parliamentary approval of the Order was not relevant to the question of rational connection (although it may be relevant to proportionality).[125] The difference between the minority and majority judgments reflects, in part, different views about the relevance and evaluation of evidence.

This brief review illustrates that in the UK, as in Australia, the place of facts remains unsettled. While at times facts are expressly recognised or established by evidence, at other times they are simply assumed. There remains uncertainty about when evidence will be necessary, what sort of evidence will be required and how courts can and should evaluate such material.

IV. RESOLVING EMPIRICAL QUESTIONS: POSSIBILITIES FOR COMPARATIVE ENGAGEMENT?

Given the common empirical problems presented by proportionality reasoning, the final part of this chapter considers possibilities for cross-jurisdictional exchange. It suggests three potential ways in which a comparative approach might be instructive for courts applying proportionality tests. In short, it seeks to identify areas where comparative law and scholarship might be utilised by courts in grappling with the difficult empirical aspects of proportionality.

A. Understanding of 'Facts'

The first possibility for comparative exchange might be in the way that facts themselves are defined. Although the law of evidence in Australia has, broadly speaking,

120 See *Bank Mellat* (n 24).
121 ibid, at [27].
122 ibid.
123 ibid, at [123].
124 ibid, at [93].
125 ibid, at [123]. See also [65].

been developed from the English tradition, in Australia there has been a fairly long recognition that there are different categories of facts. Since at least the 1940s, both the High Court and commentators have recognised that 'constitutional facts' are different from the ordinary facts that arise between parties in litigation.[126] This distinction mirrors the influential distinction between 'legislative facts' and 'adjudicative facts' that was developed in the United States. Writing in the 1940s and 1950s, US administrative lawyer Kenneth Culp Davis sought to show that courts and agencies rely on two quite different types of facts, and not all of them can be established in the same manner.[127] In particular, the rules of evidence were developed in the context of adjudicative facts, which concern the immediate parties to the dispute, and are not well suited to the broader societal questions that often underpin proportionality reasoning and public law more generally.

As I have explained above, courts in the UK have not distinguished between adjudicative and legislative facts. While there has been some recognition of the empirical dimensions of proportionality,[128] the courts have not sought to identify different sorts of facts. Writing extra-judicially in 2011, Justice Hayne[129] offered an Australian perspective on the use of deference in the UK, arguing that the concept of deference was being used to obscure or 'paper over the fact that the courts are unable or unwilling to identify the relevant facts'.[130] He suggested that courts in the UK might learn from the Australian experience:

> All agree that balances must be struck. All agree that this is to be done by identifying the relevant competing considerations. But tabulations of the features of a democratic society do not tell us what is the factual basis, or what are the factual bases, upon which a court is to strike the balance and give effect to those values.
>
> In Australian terms, the question would be: what are the constitutional facts on which validity turns? In turn that raises further questions: are those 'constitutional facts' to be established by evidence? Are they to be the subject of judicial notice?[131]

The distinction between different sorts of facts might, as I have suggested above, be helpful in identifying that not all facts can be established in the same manner. It also has the advantage of providing a common language for identifying and describing issues of fact, which may lead to a more transparent identification of factual issues, in the manner proposed by Justice Hayne. However, as the Australian experience shows us, the framework is not always consistently applied. There remains considerable uncertainty about the scope of the High Court's constitutional fact-finding

[126] See, eg, *Commonwealth Freighters v Sneddon* (1959) 102 CLR 280 at 292; *Breen v Sneddon* (1961) 106 CLR 406 at 411; *Gerhardy v Brown* (1985) 159 CLR 70 at 141–42; *Richardson v Forestry Commission* (1988) 164 CLR 261 at 294; *Thomas v Mowbray* (2007) 233 CLR 307 at [225]–[28], [523]–[29], [613]–[39].

[127] See, in particular, KC Davis, 'An Approach to Problems of Evidence in the Administrative Process' (1942) 55 *Harvard Law Review* 364; KC Davis, 'Official Notice' (1949) 62 *Harvard Law Review* 537; KC Davis, 'Judicial Notice' (1955) 55 *Columbia Law Review* 945.

[128] See section III.B above.

[129] At the time a Justice of the High Court of Australia.

[130] KM Hayne, 'Deference—an Australian Perspective' [2011] *Public Law* 75 at 88.

[131] ibid, at 86.

doctrine and the appropriate bounds of judicial notice. So, while the dichotomy proposed by Davis is helpful in articulating that there are different sorts of facts, on its own it is insufficient. In the context of proportionality reasoning, more attention needs to be directed to articulating precisely where facts are relevant. In addition, further guidance is needed from the courts as to when evidentiary material is necessary and the procedures by which the relevant facts should be ascertained.

B. Evidence and its Evaluation

In addition to clarifying how various types of facts are understood, there is a need for further consideration of the types of material that might be relied upon by courts in making assessments of proportionality. In both Australia and the UK the courts appear to be relatively comfortable with relying on parliamentary and other official materials, in part because such materials already have a recognised role in the sphere of statutory construction.[132] There are, of course, difficulties surrounding how parliamentary materials can be used and where the appropriate boundaries lie.[133] In addition, further difficulties arise when there is either a paucity of empirical material or where the available empirical material lacks certainty. For instance, at times there may be no relevant evidence available or the particular field of expertise may still be developing and not yet subject to scientific consensus. It is in these situations that a comparative approach might prove instructive.

Where courts in another jurisdiction have been confronted with similar issues[134] there are a number of potential ways in which this experience might be of assistance. First, in cases where the available evidence lacks certainty, it may be that other courts have grappled with similar forms of evidence. This jurisprudence might provide guidance in terms of the admissibility and weight to be accorded to new or emerging areas of expertise.[135] Similarly, in cases where there is a lack of evidence, comparative experience might also provide some insights. For instance, in the UK Cora Chan has suggested that courts need to apply greater scrutiny to the government's evidence of justification, including evaluating both first-order reasons (which relate to the merits of the particular case) and second-order reasons (which relate to the government's expertise, institutional capacity or democratic legitimacy).[136] While issues of context will be important here, particularly where the relevant decision-makers

[132] In Australia, this was given statutory footing in 1984 with the enactment of section 15AB of the Acts Interpretation Act 1901 (Cth). For some discussion, see DC Pearce and RS Geddes, *Statutory Interpretation in Australia*, 8th edn (Sydney, LexisNexis Butterworths, 2014) 89ff; MT Stubbs, 'From Foreign Circumstances to First Instance Considerations: Extrinsic Material and the Law of Statutory Interpretation' (2006) 34 *Federal Law Review* 103. In the UK, see *Pepper v Hart* [1993] AC 593; O Jones, *Bennion on Statutory Interpretation*, 6th edn (London, LexisNexis, 2013) 566ff.

[133] For some discussion of these difficulties, see Kavanagh (n 11) at 13–16.

[134] Of course, account needs to be taken of constitutional differences, such as Australia's unique form of rights protection.

[135] In this regard see King (n 98) at 244.

[136] See Chan, 'Proportionality and Invariable Baseline Intensity of Review' (n 96) at 11–14, 18–21; Chan, 'The Burden of Proof' (n 96).

differ,[137] Chan's work illuminates the possibility of probing the government's justification even where there is a lack of direct evidence. Finally, and most controversially, if a court elsewhere has confronted the same issue, this experience may be used to fill the evidentiary gap. As proportionality often requires predictive judgments to be made, experiences elsewhere may be able to illustrate the effectiveness of a potential solution.

These three potential ways in which comparative experience might assist in applying proportionality reflect a broader debate about judicial engagement with comparative law. In particular, they raise different methodological challenges for courts. In the first two scenarios identified above, courts might turn to comparative experience to identify particular arguments or modes of interpretation. When used in this way, foreign law constitutes a 'source of reasons or ideas'.[138] It may lend support to a court's reasoning, but is not used in an authoritative or precedential sense.[139] Some of the traditional objections to the use of comparative law, which arise most strongly when comparative law is used as a source of authority, are less problematic in this context. In contrast, when used to demonstrate the effectiveness of solutions used elsewhere, foreign law might be said to take the form of an 'empirical fact'.[140] As Lord Reed has commented extra-judicially:

> The court is not undertaking a factual inquiry of a conventional nature, otherwise it would require evidence; but its interest nevertheless lies in information of a factual nature. The court's reasoning may then be that a given solution should or should not be adopted in our legal system because, or at least partly because, it has proved successful or unsuccessful in another jurisdiction.[141]

This raises questions about both the possibility and plausibility of drawing empirical conclusions from foreign sources.[142] In addition, as Lord Reed rightly identifies, this form of comparative inquiry carries its own problems of method, as there is a question of how a court can be 'adequately informed about the nature of the foreign solution'.[143]

[137] Note that the scope of constitutional review is quite different in Australia and the UK, as under the HRA 1998 the courts have jurisdiction to review not only primary and secondary legislation but also the decisions of public authorities. In Australia, by contrast, the exercise of discretion by an administrative body (as opposed to the conferral of power on the administrative body) is largely controlled by judicial review of administrative action. For some discussion of the problem of administrative discretions in constitutional law, see Stellios (n 15) at 162–64, 188, 350–51, 581–84.

[138] A Stone, 'Comparativism in Constitutional Interpretation' [2009] *New Zealand Law Review* 45 at 60.

[139] For a discussion of the different ways in which foreign law is used, see C Saunders, 'Comparative Constitutional Law in the Courts: Is There a Problem?' (2006) 59 *Current Legal Problems* 91 at 98–101; C Saunders, 'Judicial Engagement in the High Court of Australia', Public Lecture, High Court of Australia, 20 June 2012.

[140] C McCrudden, 'Common Law of Human Rights?: Transnational Judicial Conversations on Constitutional Rights' (2000) 20 *OJLS* 499 at 525–26.

[141] R Reed, 'Foreign Precedents and Judicial Reasoning: the American Debate and British Practice' [2008] *LQR* 253 at 265. See also R French, ch 11 in this volume and R Reed, ch 12 in this volume.

[142] See, eg, J Basten, 'International Influences on Domestic Law: Neither Jingoistic Exceptionalism nor Blind Servility' [2010] *New South Wales Judicial Scholarship* 8.

[143] See Reed, 'Foreign Precedents and Judicial Reasoning' (n 141) at 265.

C. The Role of Deference or Restraint

A third potential area of interchange between the UK and Australia is in terms of developing appropriate principles for when courts should exercise restraint. In the UK there is a lively and extended debate about the concept of judicial deference. Deference is broadly understood as according weight or respect to the views and decisions of the other branches of government. Although there remains ongoing debate, the two main grounds of deference are often described as institutional (relating to the capacity of a body) and constitutional (relating to the legitimacy of a body).[144] The empirical questions that underpin the proportionality inquiry, which have been elaborated in section III.A above, raise questions of whether deference on institutional grounds is appropriate as courts are often thought to lack expertise and information-gathering powers.

In contrast to the developed debate on the role of deference in the UK, in Australia the term deference is often viewed with suspicion.[145] In *McCloy* itself, as I have explained above, the joint judgment expressly rejected the notion of deference or a 'margin of appreciation' in the Australian constitutional setting.[146] Rather than being openly acknowledged, considerations of deference are subsumed within the High Court's understanding of judicial power. Yet, at the same time, the comparative experience makes it clear that proportionality is not a unitary standard. Rather, it is a flexible standard that can be applied with varying degrees of intensity.[147] This suggests, as Murray Wesson has pointed out, that questions of deference cannot be avoided and that the adoption of proportionality 'necessitates a principled basis for judicial restraint'.[148] In *McCloy*, the question of the intensity of review was one of the questions left open by the Court, and there are signs that this might be a source of future division. Justice Gageler, for instance, rejected a 'template of standardised proportionality analysis'[149] and instead held that in this case the standard of scrutiny was that of 'compelling justification'.[150] The joint judgment did not resolve the question of scrutiny in *McCloy,* but in the earlier case of *Tajjour*, Justices Crennan, Kiefel and Bell were of the view that the test in *Lange* 'does not involve differing levels of scrutiny'.[151] In *Murphy*, where six of the seven Justices avoided a test of structured proportionality, the question of deference was again unresolved.

The comparative experience, including the extensive debate around deference in the UK, may be useful to the extent that proportionality continues to be developed in Australian constitutional law. In particular, it would be preferable if the role of

[144] See Davies and Williams (n 10) at 99.

[145] As Boughey notes, the term 'deference' is contentious in Australia: Boughey (n 10) at 64. See also Hayne (n 130) at 89.

[146] See *McCloy* (n 31) at [90], [92].

[147] J Rivers, 'Proportionality and Variable Intensity of Review' (2006) 65 *CLJ* 174.

[148] M Wesson, 'Crafting a Concept of Deference for the Implied Freedom of Political Communication' (2016) 27 *Public Law Review* 101 at 101.

[149] See *McCloy* (n 31) at [98].

[150] ibid, at [153].

[151] See *Tajjour* (n 95) at [132] (Crennan, Kiefel and Bell JJ), *cf* [151] (Gageler J).

deference was openly acknowledged, rather than being rejected or avoided. The UK experience might provide guidance as to the meaning of deference, the different grounds on which it might apply, and the types of factors that are relevant to determining its proper scope. Differences in constitutional context will of course remain important, particularly where the courts are called to review decisions made by different branches of government.

V. CONCLUSION: CONVERGENCE OR DIVERGENCE?

Australian public law is often viewed as becoming increasingly isolated from other common law systems, including the UK. Any comparison between the two is often characterised by an emphasis on differences. Yet, despite this apparent divergence, the advent of a structured proportionality test in *McCloy* signals some degree of commonality in terms of the methodology by which public law disputes are resolved. Moreover, proportionality carries with it certain common problems of application. In particular, as I have explained in this chapter, underpinning proportionality are certain empirical questions which require courts to consider questions of fact. In both the UK and Australia the courts have shown some recognition of these problems, but have yet to develop a coherent framework to resolve these issues. In light of this, this chapter has suggested that an increased interchange between Australia and the UK might be fruitful. While this may not, ultimately, lead to a convergence of method, as contextual differences will remain important, it might be valuable in terms of developing and refining understandings of 'facts', the identification and evaluation of relevant evidence, and clarifying the role of judicial restraint. These comparative possibilities, of course, present their own challenges, and suggest that questions of comparative methodology will be of ongoing significance.

19

Jurisdictional Error: Do We Really Need It?

JANINA BOUGHEY AND LISA BURTON CRAWFORD

I. INTRODUCTION

IT IS GENERALLY accepted that courts cannot remedy every legal error made by an administrative decision-maker. As Baroness Hale put it, 'a certain level of error is acceptable in a legal system which has so many demands upon its limited resources'.[1] But courts across the common law world have struggled to identify the proper point at which they should draw the line between those legal errors that they can (or should) remedy and those that they cannot (or should not). Historically, it was accepted that this line was represented by the distinction between jurisdictional and non-jurisdictional errors of law, but this distinction was difficult to draw and seemed open to manipulation.[2] For these and other reasons, the concept of jurisdictional error fell into disfavour. It has now been abandoned in most common law jurisdictions. However, the principles that have replaced it are far from perfect: they continue to raise difficult questions for the academy and the courts.[3]

Australian administrative law is—in this respect, as in others—exceptional.[4] The High Court of Australia insists that it cannot follow the path of its common law counterparts, by either abolishing the concept of jurisdictional error altogether or replacing it with some functional equivalent, as the distinction between jurisdictional and non-jurisdictional errors of law is required by the Australian Constitution. Indeed, jurisdictional error has become the 'central' principle of judicial review in Australian law.[5] The retention of jurisdictional error has typically been explained by reference to specific features of Australia's written Constitution. It might therefore

[1] *R (Cart) v Upper Tribunal* [2012] 1 AC 663 at 684 [41].

[2] See, eg, *Pearlman v Keepers and Governors of Harrow School* [1979] 1 QB 56 at 69–70 (Lord Denning); Harry Woolf et al, *De Smith's Judicial Review* 7th edn (London, Sweet & Maxwell, 2013) 200–01.

[3] See, eg, M Elliott and R Thomas, 'Tribunal Justice and Proportionate Dispute Resolution' (2012) 71 *Cambridge Law Journal* 297; D Mullan, 'Unresolved Issues on the Standard of Review in Canadian Judicial Review of Administrative Action—The Top Fifteen!' (2013) 42 *Advocates' Quarterly* 1; D Feldman, 'Error of Law and Flawed Administrative Acts' (2014) 73 *Cambridge Law Journal* 275.

[4] M Taggart, '"Australian Exceptionalism" in Judicial Review' (2008) 36 *Federal Law Review* 1.

[5] JJ Spigelman, 'The Centrality of Jurisdictional Error' (2010) 21 *Public Law Review* 77.

be tempting for lawyers from other common law jurisdictions to dismiss jurisdictional error as an Australian anomaly, which they are thankfully free to disregard or replace. However, we argue that this is not the case.

Contemporary Australian case law reveals that the distinction between jurisdictional and non-jurisdictional errors of law serves an important constitutional function, albeit not one that is usually relied on to explain its retention. Further, other common law jurisdictions—namely the United Kingdom and Canada—have not abandoned the underlying concept to which the label of jurisdictional error refers: that is, a kind of legal error that Parliament did not authorise and so, will ordinarily lead to invalidity. Thus, Australia's conspicuous retention of the labels of jurisdictional and non-jurisdictional error distracts attention from more important points of unity between Australia, Canada and the UK.

Section II outlines the origins and evolution of the concept of jurisdictional error, in the United Kingdom, Australia and Canada. These topics have been examined extensively elsewhere,[6] but it is necessary to discuss them here, in order to clarify the nature and purpose of jurisdictional error and to properly scrutinise the reasons given by the Australian High Court for retaining it. These reasons are explained—and ultimately, rejected—in Section III. In Section IV, we propose a more persuasive justification for the distinction between jurisdictional and non-jurisdictional errors of law, which we call the 'legislative power rationale'.

Properly understood, the distinction between jurisdictional and non-jurisdictional errors of law is a device for distinguishing between those errors of law that Parliament has authorised a decision-maker to make, and those which Parliament has not so authorised. Thus a distinction between jurisdictional and non-jurisdictional errors is required (whether or not those particular labels are used) because Australian Parliaments can impose legal limits on administrative power, breach of which does not invalidate its exercise. While we refer here to the Australian Parliament, this rationale for jurisdictional error is not unique to Australia. For while it is the subject of (perhaps, increasing) criticism, both the United Kingdom and Canada maintain the principle of parliamentary supremacy upon which the concept ultimately depends. In light of this conclusion, we question whether the distinction between jurisdictional and non-jurisdictional errors of law should truly be abandoned or replaced by a more functional approach.

II. THE ORIGINS AND EVOLUTION OF JURISDICTIONAL ERROR

A. Origins

The 'elusive' concept of jurisdiction, and a distinction between jurisdictional and non-jurisdictional errors of law, emerged gradually during the seventeenth century,

[6] See, eg, EG Henderson, *Foundations of English Administrative Law: Certiorari and Mandamus in the Seventeenth Century* (Cambridge MA, Harvard University Press, 1963); M Aronson, 'Jurisdictional Error and Beyond' in M Groves (ed), *Modern Administrative Law in Australia: Concepts and Context* (Cambridge, Cambridge University Press, 2014) at 248.

and was 'crucial' to the development of the writs of certiorari, mandamus and prohibition during the seventeenth and eighteenth centuries.[7]

Prohibition and certiorari both applied to decisions made by courts and court-like bodies. In that context, it was relatively coherent to distinguish between errors that went to whether a court had authority to hear a case, and errors made in the process of deciding a case. The former are legal matters that are determined (at least in theory) at the outset of a hearing, and do not go to the core of the matter that the court is to decide. Henderson explained that the significance of legal errors of this kind:[8]

> … the logic of a court's position as a decider of cases demands that the court should be able to know at the outset of a case whether it has jurisdiction. All the participants waste their time when a court hears a case and renders a decision which is later held to be void, or when it appears in the middle of a trial that the court has no jurisdiction.

This traditional approach to jurisdictional error is frequently labeled the 'commencement theory'.[9] If a court acted without jurisdiction, then anything it purported to do was said to be void (as the above-quoted passage suggests)[10] and prohibition or certiorari would lie. If a court made an error but stayed within the boundaries of jurisdiction, then prohibition was not available, and certiorari would only lie if the error appeared 'on the face of the record' of the decision.[11]

The commencement theory of jurisdiction had some logical appeal, at least in the context of judicial review of the decisions of inferior courts in which it developed. Yet, it does not seem to have been the primary reason for the development of the distinction between jurisdictional and non-jurisdictional errors during the seventeenth and eighteenth centuries. Rather, the distinction seems largely to have been based on respect or comity for the jurisdiction granted to an inferior court to enforce a body of law, coupled with the limited review jurisdiction of superior courts.[12]

Further, the distinction between jurisdictional and non-jurisdictional errors applied both to courts exercising statutory jurisdiction, and those exercising jurisdiction from non-statutory sources—including commonly, ecclesiastical courts. Thus, the distinction cannot have been applied out of respect to Parliament's intent, at least not in all circumstances. Nor was it based on the separation of powers, because that principle clearly has no bearing on the relationship between superior and inferior courts. We consider the significance of this below.

Unlike prohibition and certiorari, mandamus was never restricted to judicial or quasi-judicial bodies and in fact developed in the context of local government,

[7] See Henderson (n 6) at 6, 117.

[8] ibid, at 118.

[9] P Craig, *UK, EU and Global Administrative Law: Foundations and Challenges* (Cambridge, Cambridge University Press, 2016) 31; *R v Bolton* (1841) 1 QB 66 at 72–74.

[10] Now, we know that the concept of nullity is complex: see M Aronson, 'Nullity' (2004) 40 *Australian Institute of Administrative Law Forum* 19.

[11] See Henderson (n 6) at 157–59. Note, certiorari for non-jurisdictional error later fell into disuse, as we discuss below.

[12] ibid, at 119–20. See, eg, *The Case of Marshalsea* (1612) 10 Co Rep 68b, 76–77; *Roberts v Fortune* (1747) (unreported) discussed in *Gaban v Maingay* (1793) Ir Term Rep 20, 40.

as an order to restore officials to positions from which they had been wrongfully removed.[13] As the writ developed into a more general order to compel courts and non-judicial officials to act according to law during the latter half of the seventeenth century, mandamus began to be viewed as an 'analogy' to prohibition, and so attended by the concept of jurisdiction.[14] Though mandamus applied to a wider range of officials than the other writs, the rationale for restricting its availability to cases of jurisdictional error was ostensibly the same: it was said that superior courts should have authority to keep inferior bodies within their jurisdiction, but that it would be 'bad policy and inconvenient' for courts to interfere in matters within the jurisdiction of other bodies.[15]

During the early nineteenth century, the scale and powers of the bureaucracy started to expand dramatically, as in turn did the scope of the writs. The concept of jurisdiction narrowed, and began to be explained differently: as a means of effecting Parliament's (supreme) power to confer jurisdiction on a tribunal to decide whatever matters the Parliament so chose.[16] Indeed, the entire institution of judicial review came to be explained on the basis that the courts were enforcing the sovereign Parliament's will.[17] This shift seemed somewhat logical, given that it was now Parliament which was creating many of these new public bodies and conferring powers or jurisdiction on them. For instance in *R v Commissioners for Special Purposes of Income Tax*, Lord Esher explained, in relation to jurisdictional facts:[18]

> When an inferior court or tribunal or body, which has to exercise the power of deciding facts, is first established by Act of Parliament, the legislature has to consider what powers it will give that tribunal or body. It may in effect say that, if a certain state of facts exists and is shewn to such tribunal or body before it proceeds to do certain things, it shall have jurisdiction to do such things, but not otherwise. ... But ... [t]he legislature may intrust the tribunal or body with a jurisdiction, which includes the jurisdiction to determine whether the preliminary state of facts exists as well as the jurisdiction, on finding that it does exist, to proceed further or do something more. When the legislature are establishing such a tribunal or body with limited jurisdiction, they also have to consider, whatever jurisdiction they give them, whether there shall be any appeal from their decision, for otherwise there will be none.

Often, the term 'vires' was used instead of 'jurisdiction' when referring to non-judicial bodies.[19]

[13] See Henderson (n 6) at 46–53.
[14] ibid, at 81–82.
[15] ibid, at 135, discussing *Dr Patrick's Case* (1662–8) 1 Lev 65.
[16] See D M Gordon, 'The Relation of Facts to Jurisdiction' (1929) 45 *Law Quarterly Review* 459; L Jaffe, *Judicial Control of Administrative Action* (Boston, Little Brown, 1965) 624–30; P Craig, *Administrative Law* 7th edn (London, Sweet & Maxwell, 2012) 5–7; P Murray, 'Escaping the Wilderness: *R v Bolton* and Judicial Review for Error of Law' (2016) 75 *Cambridge Law Journal* 333 at 355. Note, there are examples to the contrary: see, eg, *R v Shoreditch Assessment Committee, ex parte Morgan* [1910] 2 KB 859, 880, where Lord Farwell refers to parliamentary sovereignty, but also suggests that superior courts have an inherent power or duty to assess the jurisdictional limits of tribunals.
[17] Until Dawn Oliver's seminal article: 'Is Ultra Vires the Basis of Judicial Review?' [1987] *Public Law* 543. See generally Craig, *Administrative Law* (n 16) 5–6, 475–76.
[18] (1888) 21 QBD 313 at 319.
[19] See Woolf et al (n 2) at 205.

There were well-documented inconsistencies in the application of the jurisdictional error and ultra vires concepts, as well as in the explanations for them. But by the start of the twentieth century, when the Australian Constitution was enacted, some principles were tolerably clear. First, the application of the main judicial review remedies was limited by the concept of jurisdictional error (however described). Secondly, in the context of judicial review of administrative decision-makers (as opposed to inferior courts), the distinction between jurisdictional and non-jurisdictional errors was often said to reflect the ability of Parliament to define the jurisdiction of statutory bodies on whom it conferred authority.

B. Jurisdictional Error Today

The dividing line between jurisdictional and non-jurisdictional errors has shifted dramatically since the start of the twentieth century. In *Anisminic v Foreign Compensation Commission*, the House of Lords famously held that a tribunal with jurisdiction to enter an inquiry may do something or fail to do 'something in the course of the inquiry which is of such a nature that its decision is a nullity'.[20] This paved the way for the abolition of the commencement theory of jurisdiction across the common law world and, eventually, the abolition of the distinction between jurisdictional and non-jurisdictional errors of law altogether in the UK (and New Zealand).[21] But while both Canada and Australia have accepted *Anisminic*'s much-expanded approach to jurisdictional error, neither has completely abandoned the distinction between jurisdictional and non-jurisdictional errors of law. This section surveys the current approach to jurisdictional error in the UK, Canada and Australia.

(i) UK

The post-*Anisminic* case law suggests that there is now a strong presumption that all errors of law made by administrative tribunals are jurisdictional and hence reviewable.[22] This presumption has been framed in terms of legislative intent. For instance, in *Re Racal Communications Ltd* Lord Diplock stated that:[23]

> [The law now] proceeds on the presumption that where Parliament confers on an administrative tribunal or authority, as distinct from a court of law, power to decide particular

[20] [1969] 2 AC 147 at 171 (Lord Reid). See also 195 (Lord Pearce), 215 (Lord Pearson).

[21] See *Pearlman v Keepers and Governors of Harrow School* [1979] QB 56 at 69–70 (Lord Denning); *In Re Racal Communications Ltd* [1981] AC 374 at 383 (Lord Diplock); *O'Reilly v Mackman* [1983] 2 AC 237 at 278 (Lord Diplock); *R v Hull University Visitor, ex parte Page* [1993] AC 682 at 701–2 (Lord Browne-Wilkinson) (with whom the majority agreed); *Peters v Davidson* [1999] 2 NZLR 164 at 183 (Richardson P, Henry and Keith JJ).

[22] *R v Hull University Visitor, ex parte Page* [1993] AC 682 at 701–2 (Lord Browne-Wilkinson). See, generally, J Beatson, 'The Scope of Judicial Review for Error of Law' (1984) 4 *Oxford Journal of Legal Studies* 22 at 31–35; see Woolf et al (n 2) at 225. It remains unclear whether the position of inferior courts is the same: see Woolf et al (n 2) at 215–16.

[23] [1981] AC 374 at 382–83.

> questions defined by the Act conferring the power, Parliament intends to confine that power to answering the question as it has been so defined: and if there has been any doubt as to what that question is, this is a matter for courts of law to resolve in fulfillment of their constitutional role as interpreters of the written law and expounders of the common law and rules of equity.

His Lordship made it clear that the presumption so described is rebuttable:[24]

> Parliament can, of course, if it so desires, confer upon administrative tribunals or authorities power to decide questions of law as well as questions of fact or of administrative policy; but this requires clear words …

There have been circumstances in which this has occurred. For instance, where legislation provides that an administrative body can certify the existence of a particular state of affairs, and that certificate constitutes 'conclusive evidence' of the existence of that state of affairs, courts have routinely found that the presumption is rebutted in relation to any errors made in the course of the body's finding.[25]

Furthermore, the fact that all errors of law may theoretically attract judicial relief does not mean that they will in practice.[26] UK courts typically filter out most cases at an early stage by refusing to grant leave to proceed,[27] which Aronson argues, fulfils a similar function to the distinction between jurisdictional and non-jurisdictional errors.[28] The decision of the Supreme Court in *R (Cart) v Upper Tribunal*[29] suggests a willingness to triage errors of law, such that only serious errors or those which raise some principle of public importance will be reviewed by a superior court.[30] However, this decision was largely based on pragmatic concerns, and not the Court's assessment of which errors Parliament intended to be reviewable—and hence is potentially problematic, for reasons which we explain below.

In summary, although the UK has notionally abolished the distinction between jurisdictional and non-jurisdictional errors, it has not yet abandoned the fundamental principle that these labels reflect (though *Cart* may be the start of such a process): that Parliament may authorise administrative decision-makers to err in law. Courts will presume that any error of law[31] made by an administrative decision-maker is beyond the scope of the decision-maker's authority. However, the courts concede that Parliament may rebut this presumption, though this is rarely found to have occurred.

[24] ibid, at 383.

[25] See, eg, *R v Registrar of Companies, ex parte Central Bank of India* [1986] QB 1114. See further Woolf et al (n 2) at 210–11.

[26] See further Feldman (n 3).

[27] V Bondy and M Sunkin, 'Accessing Judicial Review' [2008] *Public Law* 647 at 648–49.

[28] See Aronson, 'Jurisdictional Error and Beyond' (n 6) at 263. See generally Woolf et al (n 2) at 915–17.

[29] [2012] 1 AC 663 ('*Cart*').

[30] See especially ibid, 688–89 (Baroness Hale), with whom other judges agreed on this point. See further J Boughey and LB Crawford, 'Reconsidering *R (on the Application of Cart) v Upper Tribunal* and the Rationale for Jurisdictional Error' [2017] *Public Law* 592.

[31] As well as some errors of fact: *E v Secretary of State for the Home Department* [2004] QB 1044.

(ii) Canada

The Canadian approach is, in some respects, a compromise between the UK position discussed above, and the Australia position discussed below. Canada has, at least in theory, retained the distinction between jurisdictional and non-jurisdictional errors, and uses the distinction to demarcate the boundary of the constitutional guarantee of superior courts' review jurisdiction. However, in practice, the categorisation of legal errors is determined by 'pragmatic' and 'functional' considerations.

Although Canada's written constitutional documents do not expressly provide as such,[32] the Supreme Court of Canada has found that the jurisdiction of superior courts to review for jurisdictional error is constitutionally entrenched. The Court's reasoning begins with section 96 of the Constitution Act 1867, which provides that the federal Governor General 'shall appoint the Judges of the Superior, District and County Courts in each Province …'. It is generally assumed that the provision was intended to ensure judicial independence by 'insulating the judges from local pressures'.[33] Early cases acknowledged that this intention would be subverted if provinces were allowed to establish administrative bodies, appoint officers to them, and transfer the powers of section 96 courts to those new bodies.[34]

One of the challenges for Canadian courts has been to determine which powers can validly be transferred exclusively to administrative tribunals and which are protected by section 96.[35] In *Crevier v Attorney General of Quebec*, the Supreme Court struck down provincial legislation that conferred on an administrative tribunal the exclusive, unreviewable power to review decisions of professional disciplinary committees on the basis that it was an attempt to constitute the tribunal as a section 96 court.[36] Strictly, it was the conferral by the province of unreviewable, judicial power on the tribunal to determine the limits of its own jurisdiction that offended section 96, and not the removal of the court's review jurisdiction.[37] Yet, the case is widely cited as authority for the constitutional entrenchment of provincial superior courts' jurisdiction to conduct judicial review of administrative action.[38] For example, in *MacMillan Bloedel v Simpson*,[39] the Supreme Court of Canada cited *Crevier* as the basis for the broader principle that 'powers which are the hallmarks

[32] There is also ongoing debate as to which documents form part of the 'Constitution of Canada' (see, eg, W J Newman, 'Defining the "Constitution of Canada" since 1982: The Scope of the Legislative Powers of Constitutional Amendment under Sections 44 and 45 of the Constitution Act 1982' (2003) 22 *Supreme Court Law Review* 423).

[33] P Hogg, 'Is Judicial Review Guaranteed by the British North America Act?' (1976) LIV *Canadian Bar Review* 716.

[34] J Willis, 'Administrative Law and the British North America Act' (1939) 53 *Harvard Law Review* 251 at 265.

[35] See *Re Residential Tenancies Act* [1981] 1 SCR 714 at 728–36.

[36] [1981] 2 SCR 220 at 234 ('*Crevier*').

[37] *Crevier* [1981] 2 SCR 220, 235–36, 238; Peter Hogg, *Constitutional Law of Canada, Vol 1*, 5th edn (Scarborough, Thomson/Carswell, 2010) 7–55–7–56.

[38] See, eg, C M Flood and J Dolling, 'An Introduction to Administrative Law: Some History and a Few Signposts for a Twisted Path' in CM Flood and L Sossin (eds), *Administrative Law in Context*, 2nd ed (Toronto, Emond Montgomery, 2012) 1, 22.

[39] [1995] 4 SCR 725 ('*MacMillan Bloedel*').

of superior courts cannot be removed from those courts'[40] and held that the Federal Parliament is not permitted to remove the core powers of provincial supreme courts.

Jurisdictional error review of at least some decisions made under federal legislation is also protected. For most of Canada's history, provincial courts have had jurisdiction to review federal administrative decisions—the Federal Court of Canada was not given this exclusive jurisdiction until 1970, upon its creation.[41] In *Canada Labour Relations Board v Paul L'Anglais Inc*,[42] the Supreme Court held that while it was within the constitutional competence of the Canadian Parliament to confer jurisdiction to review decisions made under federal law on the Federal Court, the jurisdiction of superior provincial courts over challenges involving constitutional matters could not be removed, and so could not be conferred *exclusively* on the Federal Court.

Thus, it seems to be generally accepted in Canada that neither the federal nor provincial legislatures are able to confer unreviewable jurisdiction on administrative tribunals, which is often said to amount to a constitutionally guaranteed right of individuals to seek judicial review on the ground of jurisdictional error.[43] Jurisdictional error, rightly or wrongly, forms the core of the constitutionally entrenched jurisdiction of superior Canadian courts. This somewhat limits the ability of Canadian courts to abolish the concept (though some, including a majority of the Supreme Court in obiter, have suggested that they ought to).[44]

However, the concept of jurisdictional error is rarely, if ever, invoked. In *Canadian Union of Public Employees, Local 963 v New Brunswick Liquor Corporation*,[45] the Supreme Court dispensed with the commencement approach to jurisdictional error (usually called the 'preliminary or collateral questions doctrine' in Canada). Dickson J found for the Court that, as it can be manipulated, the commencement approach was unhelpful in determining whether or not an error was within jurisdiction.[46] He replaced it with what became known as a 'pragmatic and functional' approach to determining whether Parliament intended an error made by an administrative body to be within the matters 'plainly confided to it', or not.[47] Errors within power attract a deferential approach to review, on the standard of 'reasonableness';[48] those outside power, a less deferential standard of 'correctness'. This is now known as the 'standard of review analysis'. The pragmatic and functional factors that courts will weigh up to assess whether Parliament intended a matter to be decided by

[40] ibid, at [35] (Lamer CJ, LaForest, Sopinka, Gonthier and Cory JJ).

[41] Federal Court Act SC 1970, c 1.

[42] [1983] 1 SCR 147.

[43] See, eg, *Dunsmuir v New Brunswick* [2008] 1 SCR 190, 211–12 [27]–[30] (Bastarache and LeBel JJ, McLachlin CJ, Fish and Abella JJ); *Trial Lawyers Association of British Columbia v British Columbia (Attorney General)* [2014] 3 SCR 31, 48–50 [30]–[36] (McLachlin CJ, LeBel, Abella, Moldaver, and Karakatsanis JJ).

[44] See, eg, *Alberta Teachers' Association* [2011] 3 SCR 654, 675 [34] (Rothstein J, McLachlin CJ and LeBel, Fish, Abella and Charron JJ).

[45] [1979] 2 SCR 227 ('*New Brunswick Liquor*').

[46] ibid, at 233.

[47] ibid, at 237.

[48] Note that this standard has undergone several iterations: see *Dunsmuir v New Brunswick* [2008] 1 SCR 190, 214–19.

the decision-maker, include: the presence of a privative clause; the expertise of the decision-maker; the purpose of the Act as a whole; and the 'nature of the problem' (ie whether it is more a question of fact or law).[49]

The 'pragmatic and functional' analysis was designed to replace the formalist, textual method of determining whether an error was jurisdictional or non-jurisdictional. Yet, it was ultimately a means of answering the same question: whether Parliament intended for the question in issue to be decided by the decision-maker, or the courts.[50] However, since the pragmatic and functional test was first introduced, the ultimate question of whether Parliament intended an error of law to be within or beyond a tribunal's jurisdiction has been vastly overshadowed by, and eventually lost within, other legal questions involved in the standard of review analysis and tests, such as how many standards of review there should be. This led a majority of the Supreme Court to recently question whether Canadian law should abandon the concept of jurisdiction entirely;[51] a suggestion which was met with strident dissent as to its effect on the constitutional guarantee of judicial review and its reference point.[52]

(iii) Australia

Jurisdictional error plays a far greater role in Australia than in Canada and, even more so, the UK. Although the High Court of Australia has also abandoned the commencement approach to jurisdictional error for the reasons given in *Anisminic*,[53] it has not abandoned the distinction between jurisdictional and non-jurisdictional errors. The Court insists that the distinction is real and not merely chimerical and, moreover, that it is required by the Australian Constitution.

In Australian law, classifying an error of law as jurisdictional in nature has several important consequences, which reflect the historical development of the concept discussed above.[54] While Australian courts do have some authority to review non-jurisdictional errors of law (depending on which jurisdiction the reviewing court is exercising), a non-jurisdictional error attracts more limited relief. Mandamus and prohibition will only lie if a jurisdictional error has been made,[55] as will, in certain

[49] *Pushpanathan v Canada (Minister for Citizenship and Immigration)* [1998] 1 SCR 982 at 1006–11 (Bastarache J, L'Heureux-Dubé, Gonthier and McLachlin JJ).

[50] This was confirmed in *Dunsmuir v New Brunswick* [2008] 1 SCR 190 at 225 [59].

[51] *Alberta Teachers' Association* [2011] 3 SCR 654 at 675–76 [34] (Rothstein J, McLachlin CJ and LeBel, Fish, Abella and Charron JJ).

[52] ibid, at 701–04 [92]–[97] (Cromwell J). See further J Boughey, *Human Rights and Judicial Review in Australia and Canada: The Newest Despotism?* (Oxford, Hart, 2017).

[53] *Craig v South Australia* (1995) 184 CLR 163 at 178–79 (Brennan, Deane, Toohey, Gaudron and McHugh JJ); *Kirk v Industrial Court (NSW)* (2010) 239 CLR 531 at 572–74 (French CJ, Gummow, Hayne, Crennan, Kiefel and Bell JJ) ('*Kirk*'). See also M Aronson, M Groves and G Weeks, *Judicial Review of Administrative Action*, 6th edn (Sydney, Lawbook Co, 2017) 21–24.

[54] The following refers primarily to review by the High Court under s 75 of the Constitution, the Federal Court under s 39B of the Judiciary Act 1903 (Cth), and state and territory supreme courts under the common law. There is no distinction between jurisdictional and non-jurisdictional errors of law under statutory review regimes including the Administrative Decisions (Judicial Review) Act 1977 (Cth).

[55] As to prohibition, see Aronson, Groves and Weeks (n 53) at 841–48 and cases cited therein; as to mandamus see Aronson, Groves and Weeks (n 53) at 874–76.

circumstances, certiorari.[56] Judicial review for jurisdictional error is constitutionally guaranteed in Australia, at both federal and state levels.[57] At the state level, it seems that this is the full extent of the guarantee;[58] it may extend further at the federal level, for reasons described below. The significance of this is that state and federal Parliaments may be able to preclude judicial review on non-jurisdictional grounds.

In recent cases, the High Court has emphasised the ad hoc nature of jurisdictional error. On this view, there is no definitive list of jurisdictional errors. The jurisdictional limitations of administrative power can only be identified by interpreting the particular statute by which the power is conferred.[59] Hence a reviewing court must ascertain whether Parliament intended an error to result in invalidity, and affix the label of jurisdictional error to those that are.[60] That assessment is made by close reference to the text, context and evident purposes of the statute, read in light of the 'established rules of statutory construction'[61]—especially the principle of legality, a particularly robust presumption in Australian law. Some of the principles associated with judicial review are treated as fundamental common law rights protected by this presumption.

Therefore, the courts do not profess to presume that any errors will be jurisdictional (or not), regardless of the context. Yet, legal errors *tend* to be characterised as jurisdictional in nature—it is quite rare for a non-jurisdictional error to be found.[62] For example, the courts will routinely presume that statutory powers are subject to an implied requirement to afford procedural fairness, and that failure to do so leads to invalidity.[63]

'Functional' considerations—such as the effect of the breach, issues of efficiency, and the consequences of attaching the 'jurisdictional error' label—are taken into account, but through this interpretative lens.[64] For example, if it would be extremely

[56] That is, when it is issued by the High Court exercising the jurisdiction conferred by s 75(v) of the Australian Constitution. In other contexts, certiorari is available for non-jurisdictional error on the face of the record, eg judicial review by the supreme courts of the Australian states: *Kirk* (n 53) at 575–78 (French CJ, Gummow, Hayne, Crennan, Kiefel and Bell JJ).

[57] S Gageler, 'The Constitutional Dimension' in Groves (ed) (n 6) at 165, 173. See *Plaintiff S157/2002 v Commonwealth* (2003) 211 CLR 476 at 513 (Gaudron, McHugh, Gummow, Kirby and Hayne JJ); *Bodruddaza v Minister for Immigration and Multicultural Affairs* (2007) 228 CLR 651 at 668–69 (Gleeson CJ, Gummow, Kirby, Hayne, Heydon and Crennan JJ).

[58] See *Kirk* (n 53) above.

[59] ibid, especially 574 [73]. *cf Craig v South Australia* (1995) 184 CLR 163. This approach was presciently explained and defended in S Gageler, 'The Legitimate Scope of Judicial Review' (2001) 21 *Australian Bar Review* 279. See also M Leeming, 'The Riddle of Jurisdictional Error' (2014) 38 *Australian Bar Review* 139.

[60] See *Kirk* (n 53) at 567–68, 577 (French CJ, Gummow, Hayne, Crennan, Kiefel and Bell JJ). See Aronson, 'Jurisdictional Error and Beyond' (n 6) 267.

[61] *Lacey v A-G (Qld)* (2011) 242 CLR 573 at 591–92 [43] (French CJ, Gummow, Hayne, Crennan, Kiefel and Bell JJ).

[62] See J Boughey, 'The Charter's Effect on Administrative Decision-making' (2016) 27 *Public Law Review* 3 at 7.

[63] *Re Refugee Tribunal, ex parte Aala* (2000) 204 CLR 82 at 100–101 [39]–[41] (Gaudron and Gummow JJ).

[64] See *Kirk* (n 53) at 571–72 (French CJ, Gummow, Hayne, Crennan, Kiefel and Bell JJ); James Stellios, *Zines's High Court and the Constitution* (Federation Press, 2015) 298. See generally Aronson, 'Jurisdictional Error and Beyond' (n 6) 264–67.

inconvenient to invalidate a decision on the basis of a certain error, the court may conclude that Parliament did not intend such a consequence.[65] One may argue that this is mere sophistry—that the courts are simply making a pragmatic assessment of when they think invalidity should ensue—but this is not how the process is explained in case law.

As Craig has argued, it seems something of a fiction to suggest that Parliament has always formed some intention as to whether or not an error of law should be reviewed by courts, or result in a decision being invalid;[66] Parliament rarely provides express guidance on the point. The High Court would not necessarily disagree. In recent years, it has expressly endorsed the view that parliamentary intention is indeed a 'fiction'.[67] While it still insists that the objective of statutory interpretation is to give the statute the meaning that Parliament intended, courts need not strive to ascertain what Parliament actually intended, nor even to make an objectively reasonable assessment of what Parliament might have intended. Rather, Parliament is *deemed* to have intended the meaning produced by the application of the rules of statutory interpretation. As French J explained (in a passage since endorsed by the High Court):

> Where the words expressed by Parliament are interpreted by the Court according to commonly understood rules of interpretation a court is entitled to make the normative statement that it has interpreted them in accordance with the legislative intention.[68]

On this view, there is no need to point to any positive indication that Parliament actually intended an error of law to be jurisdictional in nature: the question is what Parliament has, by statute law, authorised. Though it is relatively rare, statutes will sometimes expressly stipulate that certain errors do not lead to invalidity. For example, section 175 of the Income Tax Assessment Act 1936 (Cth) provides that '[t]he validity of any [taxation] assessment shall not be affected by reason that any of the provisions of this Act have not been complied with'.[69] The clauses of this kind that have been considered by the courts have been found to be largely effective.[70] In the absence of such a clause, courts have tended to conclude that errors of law are jurisdictional unless there are strong reasons for concluding otherwise.

[65] eg, *Bare v Independent Broad-Based Anti-Corruption Commission* (2015) 326 ALR 198, in which their Honours considered the broader implications of finding that a breach of the Charter of Human Rights and Responsibilities Act 2006 (Vic) would have on the validity of other provisions of that Act. See further: Boughey (n 62).

[66] See Craig, *UK, EU and Global Administrative Law* (n 9) 139–41.

[67] *Certain Lloyd's Underwriters Subscribing to Contract No IH00AAQS v Cross* (2012) 87 ALJR 131, at 138 [25] (French CJ and Hayne J); *Zheng v Cai* (2009) 239 CLR 436 at 455–56 [28]; *Lacey v A-G (Qld)* (2011) 242 CLR 573 at 592 [44]; *Momcilovic v The Queen* (2011) 245 CLR 1 at 44–45 [38] (French CJ).

[68] *NAAV v Minister for Immigration and Multicultural and Indigenous Affairs* (2002) 123 FCR 298 at 412 [432].

[69] Considered in *Federal Commissioner of Taxation v Futuris* (2008) 237 CLR 146.

[70] See, eg, ibid; *Re Minister for Immigration and Multicultural and Indigenous Affairs, ex parte Palme* ('*Palme*') (2003) 216 CLR 212; *Deputy Commissioner of Taxation v Richard Walter Pty Ltd* (1995) 183 CLR 168. See further LB Crawford, 'Who Decides the Validity of Executive Action? No-invalidity Clauses and the Separation of Powers' (2017) 24 *Australian Journal of Administrative Law* 81.

III. EXPLAINING THE AUSTRALIAN POSITION

The preceding section outlined the significance of the distinction between jurisdictional and non-jurisdictional errors in Australian law. This section examines the bases on which the retention of the distinction—and its centrality—have been explained. These explanations rest, to varying extents, upon specific features of the Australian Constitution, which can only be altered by a rigorous process that includes a national referendum.[71] If accepted, these explanations might support the conclusion that Australia must retain the distinction between jurisdictional and non-jurisdictional errors of law, while other jurisdictions are free to abandon or replace it. However, we argue that none of these explanations is entirely convincing. We argue that jurisdictional error does serve an important constitutional purpose. However, that purpose is not unique to Australia.

Before explaining why this is, it is interesting to note some (one might think, more obvious) arguments that have *not* been used to justify the Australian position or at least not explicitly so. First, the retention of jurisdictional error is rarely justified as a tool for keeping the 'floodgates' closed (ie preserving judicial resources) a concern central to the UK Supreme Court's reasoning in *Cart*.[72] Secondly, despite the statute-centric nature of jurisdictional error, it has rarely been analysed or explained in light of the doctrine of parliamentary supremacy. We revisit this issue below.

A. The Section 75(v) Rationale

Unlike, for example, the King's Bench of England, or (perhaps) the supreme courts of the Australian states, the High Court is not regarded as a court of inherent jurisdiction.[73] It is a creature of the Australian Constitution, and has no jurisdiction besides that which the Constitution provides[74] or permits to be provided by legislation.[75]

One source of jurisdiction is section 75(v) of the Constitution, which gives the High Court original jurisdiction to hear 'matters: ... in which a writ of Mandamus or prohibition or an injunction is sought against an officer of the Commonwealth'. This is not the High Court's only source of jurisdiction, but it has tended to be the focus of the case law and commentary; it is constitutionally entrenched, as explained above. Pertinently, 'section 75(v) is expressed not in terms of a substantive principle but in terms of a conferral of jurisdiction on the High Court of inviolable

[71] Australian Constitution, s 128.

[72] [2012] 1 AC 663, see nn 29–30 and associated text.

[73] See Aronson, Groves and Weeks (n 53) at 39, 41; *Keramianakis v Regional Publishers* (2009) 237 CLR 268 at 280; *Grassby v The Queen* (1989) 168 CLR 1 at 16; Mark Leeming, *Authority to Decide: The Law of Jurisdiction in Australia* (Sydney, Federation Press, 2012) at 4. As to the counter-examples, see Aronson, Groves and Weeks (n 53) at 29, 30 and further J Crawford and B Opeskin, *Australian Courts of Law* (Oxford University Press, 2004) at 131–33.

[74] PH Lane, 'High Court's Jurisdiction to Issue Writs' (1967–1968) 41 *Australian Law Journal* 130 and cases cited therein; M Leeming, *Authority to Decide: The Law of Jurisdiction in Australia* (Sydney, Federation Press, 2012) at 4.

[75] Australian Constitution, s 76. See, eg, Judiciary Act 1903 (Cth), s 30.

constitutional status to grant specified remedial orders'.[76] Furthermore, the list of remedies specified in section 75(v) is limited. It does not include other remedies that were established at common law at the time the Constitution was drafted, such as certiorari.[77] Finally, it is well accepted in Australian law that two of the remedies which section 75(v) does list—mandamus and prohibition—only lie to correct jurisdictional errors of law.[78]

On this basis, one member of the High Court has suggested that '[t]he omission of any reference to certiorari in section 75(v) can ... only be explained by the desire of the founders to confine the remedies available under it strictly to jurisdictional error'.[79] If this is accepted, and if one further accepts that the intentions of the framers are a relevant guide to constitutional interpretation, then one might conclude that section 75(v) of the Constitution only gives the High Court jurisdiction to review for jurisdictional error: no less, but no more. This would explain why Australia differs from other jurisdictions, which are not governed by a written, rigid Constitution—or not one containing an equivalent to section 75(v).

However, this rationale is quite unconvincing. At the least, it cannot explain the retention of the jurisdictional/non-jurisdictional error divide in all areas of Australian administrative law.

The first reason for this is that, as noted, section 75(v) is but one source of jurisdiction, conferred on but one of the Australian courts that perform judicial review. Section 75(iii) of the Constitution[80] also appears to give the High Court jurisdiction to review the legality of executive action, and that jurisdiction is not delineated by the nature of the relief sought. The supreme courts of the Australian states have inherent jurisdiction, yet they also retain the jurisdictional/non-jurisdictional error divide.

Secondly, there is simply no evidence that certiorari was left out of section 75(v) in order to confine that jurisdiction to jurisdictional error review. Certiorari for patent error of law fell into disuse in the nineteenth century, and was not revived until the decision in *R v Northumberland Compensation Appeal Tribunal Ex parte Shaw*.[81] Therefore, it cannot reasonably be supposed that the framers of the Australian

[76] S Gageler, 'Administrative Law Judicial Remedies' in M Groves and HP Lee (eds), *Australian Administrative Law: Fundamentals, Principles and Doctrines* (Melbourne, Cambridge University Press, 2012) 368, 377.

[77] Many have suggested that this seems strange. See, eg, L Zines, *Cowen and Zines's Federal Jurisdiction in Australia* 3rd edn (Sydney, Federation Press, 2002) 51; Aronson, Groves and Weeks (n 53) at 56; Leeming, *Authority to Decide* (n 74) at 249–50. Though see L Burton, 'Why These Three? The Significance of the Selection of Remedies in Section 75(v) of the *Australian Constitution*' (2014) 42 *Federal Law Review* 253.

[78] See n 55.

[79] *Plaintiff S157/2002 v Commonwealth* (2003) 211 CLR 476, 525 [131] (Callinan J). See also S Gageler, 'Impact of Migration Law on the Development of Australian Administrative Law' (2010) 17 *Australian Journal of Administrative Law* 92, 100; W Gummow, 'The Scope of s 75(v) of the *Constitution:* Why Injunction but no Certiorari?' (2014) 42 *Federal Law Review* 241 at 249.

[80] 'In all matters: ... in which the Commonwealth, or a person suing or being sued on behalf of the Commonwealth, is a party; the High Court shall have original jurisdiction.'

[81] [1951] 1 KB 711. See Craig, *Administrative Law* (n 16) at 497; Amnon Rubinstein, *Jurisdiction and Illegality* (Oxford, Oxford University Press, 1965) 71–73; K Costello, 'The Writ of Certiorari and Review of Summary Criminal Convictions, 1660–1848' (2012) 128 *Law Quarterly Review* 443 at 460–62.

Constitution, working in the interval, excluded certiorari for this reason; there are other more convincing bases on which the choice of remedies in section 75(v) can be explained.[82] Even if it *were* accepted that the framers had left certiorari out of section 75(v) for this reason, that is not necessarily determinative: its relevance would depend on whether one thinks that the intentions of the framers inform the meaning of the Constitution.

Thirdly, section 75(v) expressly gives the High Court jurisdiction to hear matters in which an injunction is sought, and it is frequently said that this equitable remedy is not attended by the concept of jurisdictional error.[83] Of course, those statements could be mistaken, but their ubiquity casts doubt on the remedies rationale.

Finally, the scope of the judicial review remedies is a matter of common law principle. Though the common law must conform to the Constitution,[84] we are yet to identify any constitutional principle that would prevent the Court from expanding the scope of these remedies—including by untethering them from the concept of jurisdictional error. After all, the same judicial review remedies are used in other common law jurisdictions that have abandoned the distinction between jurisdictional and non-jurisdictional errors (such as the UK).

For these reasons, the selection of remedies in section 75(v) of the Constitution would not appear to justify the retention, or centrality, of jurisdictional error in Australian law—especially when the reviewing court is acting outside the section 75(v) jurisdiction.

B. The Separation of Powers Rationale

The separation of powers is a general constitutional value, implemented (in various ways and to various extents) in many legal orders. Broadly put, it represents the view that governmental power should be divided and allocated between different institutions, for its own sake and in light of their particular institutional capacities. Arguably, that view has informed the distinction between jurisdictional and non-jurisdictional errors of law in other jurisdictions, in the past if not today. For example, the UK courts may presume that administrative decision-makers are not empowered to conclusively decide questions of law, that being the role of the courts.[85] But in Australia, the separation of powers operates as a hard constitutional rule.

[82] Note, Callinan J did acknowledge that certiorari for non-jurisdictional error had fallen into disuse (*Plaintiff S157/2002 v Commonwealth* (2003) 211 CLR 467, 521 [121]), but his dismissal of this fact is unconvincing: see Burton (n 77) at 260–63.

[83] See, eg, *Project Blue Sky v Australian Broadcasting Authority* (1998) 194 CLR 355 at 393 [100] (McHugh, Gummow, Kirby and Hayne JJ); *Plaintiff S157 /2002 v Commonwealth* (2003) 211 CLR 476 at 508 [82] (Gaudron, McHugh, Gummow, Kirby and Hayne JJ); *Federal Commissioner of Taxation v Futuris Corporation Ltd* (2008) 237 CLR 146 at 162 [47] (Gummow, Hayne, Heydon and Crennan JJ); M Aronson, 'Commentary on "The Entrenched Minimum Provision of Judicial Review and the Rule of Law"' (2010) 21 *Public Law Review* 35 at 37; Leeming, *Authority to Decide* (n 74) at 250; Aronson, Groves and Weeks (n 53) at 44–45.

[84] This is accepted doctrine in Australia (*Lange v Australian Broadcasting Authority* (1997) 189 CLR 520), though it has been questioned by some—including theorists we discuss below.

[85] See Craig, *Administrative Law* (n 16) at 496.

Chapter III of the Australian Constitution is said to implicitly require a strict separation of the judicial power of the Commonwealth from the other branches of government:[86] the judicial power of the Commonwealth can only be exercised by the courts established by or under Chapter III of the Constitution (and not, for example, the executive); and the federal Parliament cannot vest non-judicial power in those courts.

There is no strict separation of the judicial power expressed or implied by any of the constitutions of the Australian states. However, Chapter III of the Australian Constitution indirectly constrains the powers with which state courts can be conferred.[87] As Chapter III assumes the existence of state courts (including by allowing the judicial power of the Commonwealth to be exercised by such courts),[88] state Parliaments cannot do anything that would cause state courts to lose their character as such: that would deprive them of their 'defining characteristics'.[89]

The separation of powers has had a pronounced effect on Australian administrative law. Pertinently, it has been said that it requires the distinction between jurisdictional and non-jurisdictional errors of law ('the separation of powers rationale').[90]

For example, it has been suggested that non-jurisdictional error review may amount to an exercise of non-judicial power.[91] But this rationale is not convincing. The distinction with which we are concerned is between jurisdictional and non-jurisdictional errors *of law*. This is a different distinction from that between errors of fact and law.[92] It is also a different distinction from that between errors of law and errors going to the *merits*. Merits review may amount to an exercise of non-judicial power, especially insofar as that term is understood in Australian law. In Australia, a merits review body will typically assess whether a decision is the correct and preferable one (a far broader inquiry, than whether it was lawful). The merits review body may then substitute its decisions for that of the original decision-maker, who will typically have been exercising non-judicial power. A Chapter III court cannot do either of these things—but judicial review for non-jurisdictional errors of law would not require it to.

[86] *R v Kirby, ex parte Boilermakers' Society of Australia* (1956) 94 CLR 254. Whereas there is no strict separation of the legislative and executive branches, in Westminster style: Australian Constitution, s 64; *Victorian Stevedoring & General Contracting Co Pty Ltd & Meakes v Dignan* (1931) 46 CLR 73 ('*Dignan's Case*').

[87] *Kable v Director of Public Prosecutions (NSW)* (1996) 189 CLR 51.

[88] See Australian Constitution, ss 71, 73 and 77(iii).

[89] See the discussion of *Kirk* (n 53), below.

[90] See, eg, *Re Minister for Immigration and Multicultural Affairs, ex parte Lam* (2003) 214 CLR 1 at 24–25 [76]–[77] (McHugh and Gummow JJ); *Plaintiff S157/2002 v Cth* (2003) 211 CLR 476 at 484 [9] (Gleeson CJ), 511–12 [98] (Gaudron, McHugh, Gummow, Kirby and Hayne JJ); Bradley Selway, 'The Principle Behind Common Law Judicial Review of Administrative Action—The Search Continues' (2002) 30 *Federal Law Review* 217 at 233–34.

[91] *Re Minister for Immigration and Multicultural Affairs, ex parte Lam* (2003) 214 CLR 1 at 24–25 [76]–[77] (McHugh and Gummow JJ); *Re Minister for Immigration and Multicultural Affairs, ex parte Applicant S20/2002* (2003) 77 ALJR 1165 at 1176 [59] (McHugh and Gummow JJ); see Selway (n 90) 233–34.

[92] *Re Minister for Immigration and Multicultural Affairs, ex parte Applicant S20/2002* (2003) 198 ALR 59 at 71 [54] (McHugh and Gummow JJ). Though, note, it is accepted in Australian law that some facts can be 'jurisdictional'.

Alternatively, it has been said that '[t]he Parliament cannot confer on a non-judicial body the power to conclusively determine the limits of its own jurisdiction'.[93] Hence, judicial review for jurisdictional error is constitutionally required, though not (on this basis) judicial review for non-jurisdictional error of law. On this view, the distinction between jurisdictional and non-jurisdictional errors is constitutionally required, albeit indirectly. But this explanation is also problematic. It does not explain the retention of the distinction in all areas of judicial review, because that distinction also applies to judicial review of *judicial* decision-making, and judicial decision-makers can exercise judicial power. Indeed, superior courts of record (such as the Federal Court) are said to have the authority to decide their own jurisdiction; decisions of these courts are treated as legally valid unless and until set aside, even if they are ultimately found to be vitiated by jurisdictional error.[94]

Secondly, it is not clear why determining jurisdictional limits is an inherently judicial power which cannot be performed by the executive, while determining whether any other, non-jurisdictional, legal limit has been breached is not. It is not clear that the separation of powers would permit (let alone require) the existence of legal errors that the courts *cannot* remedy. If the concern here is to ensure that questions of legality are resolved by the courts, and not the other branches of government, then it would seem that there is little utility in hiving off certain legal errors which the courts cannot remedy. Indeed, following the UK House of Lords' abandonment of the concept of jurisdictional error, Hare argued that the separation of powers could actually be used to justify judicial review of all errors of law, and could therefore replace ultra vires as the central principle of English judicial review.[95]

Thus, the relatively strict separation of judicial power from the powers of the other branches in the Australian Constitution does not seem to require that Australia maintain the distinction between jurisdictional and non-jurisdictional errors of law, while other common law jurisdictions could abandon it. In fact, the UK position, in which all errors of law are prima facie reviewable appears to align better with the separation of powers than an approach which automatically assumes that some legal questions may be finally determined by the executive branch.

There may, however, be a related justification for the retention of the distinction. This justification does not proceed from the premise that non-jurisdictional error

[93] *Plaintiff S157/2002 v Commonwealth* (2003) 211 CLR 476 at 512 [98] (Gaudron, McHugh, Gummow, Kirby and Hayne JJ). Similar comments were made by Gleeson CJ at 484 [9]. See also *Craig v South Australia* (1995) 184 CLR 163 at 179 (Brennan, Deane, Toohey, Gaudron McHugh JJ). This aspect of *Craig v South Australia* was critiqued (but not overturned) in *Kirk* (n 53) at 572–73.

[94] M Aronson, 'Jurisdictional Error Without the Tears' in M Groves and HP Lee (eds), *Australian Administrative Law: Fundamentals, Principles and Doctrines* (Melbourne, Cambridge University Press, 2007) 330 at 334 and cases cited therein. See also *Minister for Immigration and Multicultural Affairs and Bhardwaj* (2002) 209 CLR 597 at 645 [150] (Hayne J); *New South Wales v Kable* (2013) 298 ALR 144 at [33] (French CJ, Hayne, Crennan, Kiefel, Bell and Keane JJ).

[95] I Hare, 'The Separation of Powers and Judicial Review for Error of Law' in I Hare and C Forsyth (eds), *The Golden Metwand and the Crooked Cord: Essays in Honour of Sir William Wade* (Oxford, Clarendon Press, 1988) 124, 136–39. See also *Craig v South Australia* (1995) 184 CLR 163 at 179 (Brennan, Deane, Toohey, Gaudron and McHugh JJ), which suggests that the High Court, like the House of Lords, viewed deciding most, perhaps all, questions of law to be a judicial function.

review transgresses the legality/merits divide, or that executive actors cannot determine the validity of their own actions. It pertains more particularly to the limits of the judicial role, vis-à-vis the Parliament. It was hinted at by Selway, in his influential statement:

> Notwithstanding the difficulty, indeed often apparent artificiality, of the distinction [between jurisdictional and non-jurisdictional errors] it is a distinction between errors that are authorised and errors that are not; *between acts that are unauthorised by law and acts that are authorised.*[96]

We explore this rationale in Section IV.

C. The *Kirk* Rationale

In *Kirk v Industrial Relations Court of New South Wales*,[97] the High Court held that the jurisdiction of state supreme courts to review for jurisdictional error is guaranteed by the Australian Constitution 'because Chapter III [of the Constitution] assumes the existence in each state of a Supreme Court, and because that jurisdiction was one of their "defining characteristics" at federation'.[98] This came as a surprise: it was previously assumed that the judicial review jurisdiction of state supreme courts was not entrenched. However, the Court held, judicial review for *non*-jurisdictional error is *not* a defining characteristic of a state supreme court and so this can be precluded by ordinary legislation.

The basis of the conclusion in *Kirk* was part empirical, part functional. As indicated above, it was said to be 'accepted doctrine at the time of federation' that supreme courts could issue certiorari for jurisdictional error and that they could not be prevented from doing so by statute.[99] This common law doctrine crystallised into constitutional law upon the enactment of the Constitution. It was also said that this was necessary to preserve the integrated judicial system established by the Constitution. If state supreme courts could be prevented from performing jurisdictional error review, then the decisions immune from their supervisory jurisdiction would be likewise removed from the appellate jurisdiction conferred on the High Court by section 73 of the Constitution.[100] As Aronson, Groves and Weeks point out, there are parallels between this aspect of *Kirk* and case law from elsewhere, such as *Cart*, in which the UK Supreme Court said that '[s]erious questions of law' must always be 'channeled into the legal system'.[101]

[96] See Selway (n 90), 234 (emphasis added); as quoted in *Re Minister for Immigration and Multicultural Affairs, ex parte Lam* (2003) 214 CLR 1 at 25 [77] (McHugh and Gummow JJ).

[97] (2010) 239 CLR 531.

[98] See Aronson, Groves and Weeks (n 53) at 28–29. See *Kirk* (n 53) at 580 [96], 581 [99] (French CJ, Gummow, Hayne, Crennan, Kiefel and Bell JJ).

[99] See *Kirk* (n 53) at 580 [97].

[100] ibid, especially at 580–81 [98]–[99].

[101] [2012] 1 AC 663 at 685, as quoted in Aronson, Groves and Weeks (n 53) at 41.

If accepted, this provides a clear rationale for retaining the distinction between jurisdictional and non-jurisdictional errors in Australian law at the state level. As the Court stated in *Kirk,* it:

> point[s] to the continued need for, and utility of, the distinction between jurisdictional and non-jurisdictional error in the Australian constitutional context. The distinction marks the relevant limit on State legislative power. Legislation which would take from a State Supreme Court power to grant relief on account of jurisdictional error is beyond State legislative power. Legislation which denies the availability of relief for non-jurisdictional error of law appearing on the face of the record is not beyond power.[102]

This reasoning is specific to the text and structure of the Australian Constitution, and the state of the common law as it stood at the time that document was drafted: the former is said to entrench the latter. Thus it appears to account for the fact that, while the Australian colonies inherited the common law of England upon settlement, Australian administrative law remains wedded to the distinction between jurisdictional and non-jurisdictional errors of law which the UK has since abandoned—and must remain so.

However, there are significant problems with the *Kirk* rationale. Several commentators have criticised the empirical basis of the decision (which was rather flimsy).[103] The idea that the authority to review for jurisdictional error is an essential and defining characteristic of state supreme courts seems implausible, given that until 2010 it was assumed that the review jurisdiction of state supreme courts could be validly ousted by a private clause. All the more so, given the modern incarnation of jurisdictional error endorsed in *Kirk* bares little resemblance to the understanding of the concept that prevailed at federation. The methodology of constitutional interpretation employed by the Court has also been criticised.[104] For example, while it may be accepted that the references to the 'Supreme Court of a/any/the State/s' in the Australian Constitution forbids the abolition of those institutions, it does not necessarily follow that this sparse phrase requires that state supreme courts have any particular jurisdiction or powers, such as authority to review for jurisdictional errors of law.

Furthermore, the *Kirk* rationale only pertains to state supreme courts. It would not appear to explain (or rather, *require*) the retention of the jurisdictional error/non-jurisdictional error divide at the federal level.[105] Indeed, the decision in *Kirk* was ostensibly motivated by the need to bring the position of state supreme courts

[102] See *Kirk* (n 53) at 581 [100].

[103] O Roos, 'Accepted Doctrine at the Time of Federation and *Kirk v Industrial Court of New South Wales*' (2013) 35(4) *Sydney Law Review* 781; N Gouliaditis, 'Privative Clauses: Epic Fail' (2010) 34 *Melbourne University Law Review* 870, 877–88; Stellios (n 64) at 296.

[104] J Goldsworthy, '*Kable, Kirk* and Judicial Statesmanship' (2014) 40 *Monash University Law Review* 75 at 94; N Perram, '*Project Blue Sky*: Invalidity and the Evolution of Consequences for Unlawful Administrative Action' (2014) 21 *Australian Journal of Administrative Law* 62 at 71; J Basten, 'The Supervisory Jurisdiction of the Supreme Courts' (2011) 85 *Australian Law Journal* 273 at 279–84. There may be other, more sophisticated bases on which the outcome in *Kirk* could be justified, but they were not explored by the High Court.

[105] Though see L Beck, 'What is a "Supreme Court of a State"?' (2012) 34 *Sydney Law Review* 295 at 302–03.

into line with that of the High Court, which is said to derive its authority to review for jurisdictional error from elsewhere.

As Justice Basten has noted, there is a strong similarity between the High Court's reasoning in *Kirk* and the reasons that the Supreme Court of Canada have given for the entrenchment of the jurisdiction of Canadian superior courts to review for jurisdictional error.[106] This might indicate that jurisdictional error review is an essential feature of a superior court, irrespective of express or implied constitutional conferral of such jurisdiction. As discussed above, the Supreme Court of Canada has found that jurisdictional error review is a 'hallmark of a superior court' which cannot be removed from superior courts and vested in administrative bodies.[107] However, the empirical origins of this claim are equally as dubious as those set out in *Kirk*. While Canadian courts, like those in other common law jurisdictions, have long been reluctant to give effect to privative clauses, the weight of Canadian authority in the first half of the twentieth century does not appear to support a finding that it was constitutionally impermissible for Parliaments to oust judicial review.[108] It may be possible to argue that it has since become such a characteristic and Canada's less rigid Constitution has thus come to include it. But that would be quite contrary to the principles of constitutional interpretation accepted in Australian law.

IV. THE LEGISLATIVE POWER RATIONALE

The preceding sections have explored the bases on which Australia's retention of jurisdictional error has typically been explained. Clearly, we do not find these explanations convincing; at best, we think that they can explain the retention of that concept in certain limited contexts and not the centrality of jurisdictional error in Australian public law. In this section, we explain a more convincing rationale.

As explained above, 'the [High Court] had always said that whether an issue is jurisdictional is ultimately a matter of statutory construction'.[109] A jurisdictional error is one that Parliament is taken to have intended to lead to invalidity; a non-jurisdictional error is one that Parliament did not so intend.[110] Simply put, the distinction between jurisdictional and non-jurisdictional errors of law is a device for distinguishing between what Parliament has authorised and what Parliament has not.[111] Though it is rarely stated expressly (and the distinction between jurisdictional and non-jurisdictional errors is more commonly explained on one of the

[106] See Basten (n 104) at 276.

[107] *MacMillan Bloedel* [1995] 4 SCR 725 at 752 [35].

[108] See B Laskin, 'Certiorari to Labour Boards: The Apparent Futility of Privative Clauses' (1952) 30 *Canadian Bar Review* 986 at 989–91; K Norman, 'The Privative Clause: Virile or Futile?' (1969) 34 *Saskatchewan Law Review* 1969; R Carter, 'The Apparent Virility of Privative Clauses' (1967) (Centennial Edition) *University of British Columbia Law Review* 219.

[109] See Aronson, Groves and Weeks (n 53) at 1056.

[110] Chief Justice Robert French, 'Constitutional Review of Executive Decisions: Australia's US Legacy' (2010) 35 *University of Western Australia Law Review* 35 at 40.

[111] See *Kirk* (n 53) at 571 [66]; *Re Refugee Review Tribunal, ex parte Aala* (2000) 204 CLR 82 at 141 [163].

unsatisfactory bases discussed above), this case law reveals the most convincing explanation of the constitutional purpose of the device: to respect the legislative supremacy of Parliament, and its power to define the scope of statutory power as it thinks fit. Though elegant, this explanation is not original. As we explained in section I, this is how jurisdictional error was explained in the UK in the late nineteenth and early twentieth centuries. However, it has been overlooked in recent years.

More specifically, the distinction between jurisdictional and non-jurisdictional errors of law reflects the simple fact that Australian Parliaments *can* impose legal limitations on statutory executive power, compliance with which is not essential to its valid exercise. In other words, not every error of law leads to invalidity. There is nothing illogical about this.[112] Moreover, this position is consistent with more fundamental rules concerning the scope of legislative power.

The legislative powers of all Australian Parliaments, state and federal, are subject to legal limitations found in the Australian Constitution. Although that Constitution constrains legislative power in certain, important ways, it does not impose significant constraints on the ability of state or federal Parliaments to define the scope of executive power as they think fit. All laws of the Commonwealth—including those that confer executive power—must demonstrate the requisite connection to a head of legislative power[113] and otherwise conform to the Constitution, but none of the substantive principles of judicial review that constrain statutory executive power are said to have constitutional force. That is, while it is the subject of ongoing academic debate[114] and there have been hints to the contrary from the bench,[115] the High Court has not yet identified any limitations on statutory executive power that are necessarily essential to validity—or indeed, that federal or state Parliaments cannot remove altogether.

For example, there is no recognised constitutional rule that requires administrative decision-makers to afford procedural fairness. In most circumstances, the courts will presume that such a requirement applies, but Parliaments are free to rebut that presumption and define the scope of executive power in different terms.[116] Similarly, while courts will regularly presume that a discretionary power is conditioned by an implied requirement of reasonableness, Parliament may stipulate to the contrary.[117]

[112] See further Feldman (n 3).

[113] Australian Constitution, ss 51 and 52. The ways in which this requirement shapes statutory executive power is explored in LB Crawford, 'Can Parliament Confer Plenary Executive Power? The Limitations Imposed by ss 51 and 52 of the *Australian Constitution*' (2016) 44 *Federal Law Review* 287.

[114] See, eg, J Kirk, 'The Entrenched Minimum Provision of Judicial Review' (2004) 12 *Australian Journal of Administrative Law* 64; L McDonald, 'The Entrenched Minimum Provision of Judicial Review and the Rule of Law' (2010) 21 *Public Law Review* 14; W Bateman, 'The Constitution and the Substantive Principles of Judicial Review: The Full Scope of the Entrenched Minimum Provision of Judicial Review' (2011) 39 *Federal Law Review* 463.

[115] See Aronson, 'Commentary on "The Entrenched Minimum Provision of Judicial Review"' (n 83) at 37. See also the comments made concerning ss 1, 51 and 52 of the Constitution in the following section.

[116] M Groves, 'Exclusion of the Rules of Natural Justice' (2013) 39 *Monash University Law Review* 285. See, generally, Gageler, 'The Legitimate Scope of Judicial Review' (n 59).

[117] *Minister for Immigration and Citizenship v Li* (2013) 249 CLR 332 at 362 [63], 369 [86] (Hayne, Kiefel and Bell JJ), 371 [92] (Gageler J); *Minister for Immigration and Border Protection v Singh* (2014) 231 FCR 437 at 445 [43].

The courts appear to presume that certain limitations are essential to validity, and hence their breach a jurisdictional error; a denial of procedural fairness is, again, such an example. But there is no recognised rule of constitutional law that prevents either federal or state Parliaments from rebutting that presumption. As Gaudron and Gummow JJ observed in *Bhardwaj*: 'the Parliament may give an administrative decision whatever force it wishes.'[118]

In time, the High Court may discover that the text or structure of the Constitution expressly or implicitly constrains Parliament's ability to define the scope of executive power or, more particularly, impose legal limitations on executive power that are not essential to validity.[119] As yet, no such constraints have clearly been identified.

Of course, the courts do retain a degree of control in this regard: it is the role of the courts to interpret statutes; at the federal level, this is an exclusively judicial role. Some principles of judicial review have acquired the status of common law rights, and thus the courts will presume that they apply unless they have been rebutted with irresistible clearness—but still, Parliament retains the capacity to do so.[120]

This explanation does not rest on any particular theory as to the source of legal constraints on statutory executive power within Australian law. That is, it applies equally to the 'ultra vires' theory of judicial review as it does to the common law theory, and those in between. Even under the common law theory, Parliament remains capable of altering or removing common law constraints on statutory power by using clear language. Thus, Parliament remains ultimately responsible for defining the scope of the powers it grants to the executive—whether expressly or by acquiescing to the application of common law constraints by legislating with presumed knowledge of such constraints—and courts must respect the clearly articulated wishes of the Parliament in this respect. In short, a court would act unconstitutionally, if it were to invalidate an exercise of statutory executive power that Parliament had validly authorised.

As long as we assume that these constitutional parameters are correct, it must be the case that there can be legal errors that do not lead to invalidity. The distinction between jurisdictional and non-jurisdictional errors of law reflects this fact; it is a device for drawing this distinction.

We call this the 'legislative powers' rationale for the retention of jurisdictional error. It is not premised upon the specificities of the Australian constitutional text, but more fundamental rules concerning the scope of legislative and judicial power. Moreover, it is not a rationale that is entirely unique to that Australian Constitution: it also seems to have some application to both Canada and the UK.

[118] *Minister for Immigration and Multicultural Affairs v Bhardwaj* (2002) 209 CLR 597 at 613 [47]. Note, this was said to be subject to the Constitution, but we express this caveat above.

[119] Some possibilities are discussed below. See also the arguments concerning the rule of law, discussed in the following section.

[120] See, eg, the principles of procedural fairness: see Groves, 'Exclusion of the Rules of Natural Justice' (n 116); *Saeed v Minister for Immigration and Citizenship* (2010) 241 CLR 252 at 259 [15] (French CJ, Gummow, Hayne, Crennan and Kiefel JJ). As to the principle of legality more generally, see D Meagher, 'The Common Law Principle of Legality in the Age of Rights' (2011) 35 *Melbourne University Law Review* 449.

A. A Common Rationale?

The comparative analysis presented above shows that, despite marked differences in terminology and approach between the three jurisdictions studied, there are also fundamental points of unity. The distinction between jurisdictional and non-jurisdictional errors of law is a highly visible feature of Australian administrative law, but not that of Canada or the UK. This gives the impression of radical divergence between Australia and the other jurisdictions. Yet, both the UK and Canada retain the concept which the label of jurisdictional error denotes.

The ostensible objective of Canada's standard of review analysis is still to determine whether Parliament intended courts or decision-makers to be the final arbiters of questions of law, which then decides whether a correctness or reasonableness standard of review applies. Thus, Canadian Parliaments can insulate the legal errors of administrative decision-makers from review by the courts, provided they are accompanied by reasoned justification. In the UK, the courts presume that all errors of law are reviewable by the courts. However, that presumption seems to carry different weight in different contexts, and is evidently rebuttable.

In each jurisdiction, the issue is also approached from a different starting point. Australian courts profess to start from a neutral position, whereby an error may be jurisdictional or non-jurisdictional, but is usually found to be the former. UK courts start from the presumption that errors of law are outside the jurisdiction of administrative bodies. Canada approaches the issue from a position of deference, whereby most errors of law now attract a reasonableness standard, with deference given to reasoned justifications that have been, or could be, given by decision-makers. For these reasons, it may be more *likely* that limitations will be classified as essential to validity in one jurisdiction vis-à-vis the other. Nonetheless, courts in Australia, Canada and the UK accept that their respective legislatures have the power to impose legal limits on executive power, breach of which does not invalidate its exercise.

This ought not to be surprising once the constitutional justification for the distinction between jurisdictional and non-jurisdictional errors of law is properly understood—the distinction rests upon the principle of parliamentary supremacy, which is common to all three jurisdictions. Indeed, the fundamental rule of the UK Constitution is that the Parliament in Westminster is sovereign: the Parliament in Westminster can make and unmake any law that it thinks fit.[121] The framers of the Australia and Canada were heavily influenced by this doctrine, but modified it to reflect to the nature of those new constitutional orders.[122] For example, legal limitations were imposed on the federal legislatures in both jurisdictions, so as to preserve some degree of legislative autonomy for the regional Parliaments.[123] But neither the Australian nor Canadian Constitutions enshrine each and every one of the established

[121] J Goldsworthy, *The Sovereignty of Parliament: History and Philosophy* (Oxford, Oxford University Press, 2001).

[122] As to the Australian position, see LB Crawford and J Goldsworthy, 'Constitutionalism' in *Oxford Handbook on the Australian Constitution* (Oxford, Oxford University Press, 2018—forthcoming).

[123] Australian Constitution, ss 51 and 52; Constitution Act 1867 (Imp), 30 & 31 Vict, c 3, ch VI.

principles of judicial review; within the limits imposed by those Constitutions, their respective Parliaments are free to enact whatever laws they think fit. These Parliaments are, therefore, largely free to confer administrative powers of whatever scope and kind they choose. Thus in all three jurisdictions, the concept of a legal error that does not lead to invalidity is both coherent, and constitutionally permissible.

These statements are expressly premised upon an orthodox understanding of the nature of legislative power. Does this orthodoxy hold? Some eminent scholars argue that the doctrine of parliamentary sovereignty must be refined or rejected altogether. Many (though certainly not all) such arguments are premised upon a methodology broadly known as 'common law constitutionalism'. This entails that legislative power is necessarily limited by fundamental common law principles associated with the rule of law—and not merely those rules that may be found in the text of a written constitution (if there is one).[124]

This is important, because the rule of law seems clearly concerned with the scope of executive power. As Wade and Forsyth put it:

> If merely because an Act says that a minister may 'make such order as he thinks fit', or may do something 'if he is satisfied' as to some fact, the courts were to allow him to act as he liked, a wide door would be opened to abuse of power and the rule of law would cease to operate. ... Unfettered discretion cannot exist where the rule of law reigns.[125]

If the rule of law constrains the scope of executive power, then the Westminster Parliament would not have absolute freedom to define the scope of executive power as it thinks fit. If legislative power is subject to limitations besides those found in a written constitution, then there may be far broader constraints on the Australian and Canadian Parliaments' powers to define the scope of statutory executive power.

The idea that legislative power is inherently constrained by the rule of law has received support from some members of the judiciary in the UK and Canada.[126] In 2001, Poole suggested that theories of the common law constitution were on the verge of forming 'a new orthodoxy'.[127] However, these theories are patently controversial, and have been robustly criticised.[128] In Australia, these ideas remain at the fringe of legal discourse. The rule of law is said to 'form an assumption' of the Constitution,[129] but the meaning and significance of that remains unclear. In any

[124] The most influential account of the contrary view is that of TRS Allan: see *Sovereignty of Law: Freedom, Constitution and Common Law* (Oxford, Oxford University Press, 2013); *Constitutional Justice: A Liberal Theory of the Rule of Law* (Oxford, Oxford University Press, 2001).

[125] WW Wade and C Forsyth, *Administrative Law* (Oxford, Oxford University Press, 2004) 35.

[126] eg *Jackson v Her Majesty's Attorney General* [2006] 1 AC 262 at 302–3 [102] (Lord Steyn), 310 [126] (Lord Hope), 323–24 [178] (Baroness Hale); *Reference re Secession of Quebec (Quebec Secession Reference)* [1998] 2 SCR 217 at 247–48 [49]; *Roncarelli v Duplessis* [1959] SCR 121 at 142 (Rand J). Note, recent case law to emerge from the UK supports the traditional view of Parliament's powers: *R (Miller and Dos Santos) v Secretary of State for Exiting the European Union* [2017] UKSC 5, [2017] 1 All ER 158.

[127] T Poole, 'Dogmatic Liberalism? TRS Allan and the Common Law Constitution' (2002) 65 *Modern Law Review* 463 at 463.

[128] See, eg, ibid; Goldsworthy (n 121); J Goldsworthy, *Parliamentary Sovereignty: Contemporary Debates* (Oxford, Oxford University Press, 2010), especially chs 1–4.

[129] *Communist Party Case* (1951) 83 CLR 1 at 193 (Dixon J). This passage is often repeated: see, eg, *Plaintiff S157/2002 v Commonwealth* (2003) 211 CLR 476, 482 [5] (Gleeson CJ); 513 [103] (Gaudron, McHugh, Gummow, Kirby and Hayne JJ).

event, there is little enthusiasm for the view that the rule of law forms an inherent constraint on legislative power. That idea seems contrary to well-established rules of constitutional interpretation.[130]

It is not possible to resolve the controversies alluded above here.[131] The point for present purposes is that jurisdictional error raises far deeper constitutional questions than is sometimes supposed. What *are* the legal limits of legislative power? Where do they come from? Are there certain limitations on executive power that are necessarily essential to the validity of its exercise, regardless of what Parliament may purport to say? The need for a distinction between jurisdictional and non-jurisdictional errors of law cannot be conclusively determined without answering these questions.

In all three jurisdictions studied herein, the position remains—at least, for now—that the legislature enjoys substantial latitude to decide the scope of statutory administrative power and that the courts cannot invalidate that which a Parliament has authorised. While this orthodoxy remains intact, there must be some legal mechanism for distinguishing errors of law that lead to invalidity from those that do not. Courts may alter the labels that they use or the method by which the distinction is drawn—though it is questionable whether the task can be reduced to an entirely functional one, as may be occurring in Canada and the UK. If a Parliament has validly provided that the failure to comply with a legal limit on a power does not invalidate its exercise, then the courts are constitutionally obligated to find accordingly.

V. CONCLUSION

Despite its tortured history, the meaning and function of jurisdictional error is now tolerably clear. A jurisdictional error is one that takes a decision-maker beyond the boundaries of the power conferred by Parliament. A non-jurisdictional error does not. The courts in the UK, Canada and Australia all accept the possibility of legal errors of this broad kind—though they use different terms and labels and they do not all profess to identify the limits of statutory executive power in the same way. Thus, while the emphasis on 'jurisdictional error' in Australian law creates an appearance of disunity, more fundamental points of unity can be found.

There can only be legal errors that do not lead to invalidity if Parliament is capable of making them so. In all three jurisdictions, this seems to remain the case. It is the role of Parliament to design and confer statutory executive power. In all three jurisdictions, there are either no or few limitations on statutory executive power that are constitutionally entrenched. Parliaments can impose *legal* limitations on statutory executive power, breach of which does not invalidate its exercise—and courts must respect that choice, regardless of whether these limitations derive from statute or the common law.

[130] See *Amalgamated Society of Engineers v Adelaide Steamship Co Ltd* (1920) 28 CLR 129; *Lange v Australian Broadcasting Corporation* (1997) 189 CLR 520; *New South Wales v Commonwealth (Work Choices Case)* (2006) 229 CLR 1.

[131] These issues are explored at length in LB Crawford, *The Rule of Law and the Australian Constitution* (Sydney, Federation Press, 2017).

This is premised upon an orthodox understanding of the broad nature of legislative power in each of the jurisdictions studied. The scope of legislative power in each depends on the constitutional rules recognised in that system. Hence, the scope of each Parliament's power to stipulate that certain errors do not lead to invalidity will vary from jurisdiction to jurisdiction. In Australia and Canada, it will depend upon the content of the relevant constitutional documents, properly construed. If the fundamental rule of British constitutional law is that the Parliament in Westminster is sovereign, then there should be *no* limitations on statutory power that it cannot make non-essential to validity—though this orthodoxy has been challenged. The retention of jurisdictional error, sometimes dismissed as an arid technicality of Australian administrative law, ultimately depends upon how that challenge is met.

In conclusion, the Australian Constitution does not require the retention of 'jurisdictional error', per se. There is no magic in that label. Pending quite radical changes in the law, however, Australian courts must continue to recognise the concept that that label denotes. So too, we suggest, must the courts of Canada and the UK.

Index

www.ingramcontent.com/pod-product-compliance
Ingram Content Group UK Ltd.
Pitfield, Milton Keynes, MK11 3LW, UK
UKHW050943290926
15470UKWH00005B/1597